Cambridge Group for the History of
Population and Social Structure
Publication number 2

GENERAL THEORY OF POPULATION

ALFRED SAUVY

With a foreword by E.A.Wrigley
Fellow of Peterhouse, Cambridge

Translated by Christophe Campos

METHUEN & CO LTD
11 New Fetter Lane London EC4

First published as *Théorie Générale de la Population*
by Presses Universitaires de France

© 1966 Presses Universitaires de France

English translation first published in Great Britain 1969
by George Weidenfeld and Nicolson Ltd

© 1969 George Weidenfeld and Nicolson Ltd

First published as a University Paperback 1974
by Methuen & Co Ltd
11 New Fetter Lane London EC4

Printed in Great Britain by
Lowe & Brydone (Printers) Ltd
Thetford, Norfolk

SBN 416 82490 0

CONTENTS

PART TWO
THE LIFE OF POPULATIONS

FOREWORD

Professor Sauvy was the first Director of the *Institut National d'Etudes Démographiques* which can fairly claim to be the world's leading centre for demographic research. There he fostered work not only in 'pure' demography – the measurement and analysis of fertility, mortality and nuptiality – but also in the study of the interconnection between the demographic characteristics of societies and their economic and social circumstances, both in the present and in the past. Professor Sauvy has written many books, but the *General theory of population* is his *magnum opus*. In it both the results of the research work carried out on many topics at INED and the fruits of his own reflections are to be found, welded into a work which possesses a freshness, consistency, and pungency usually found only in the best essays, and very difficult to sustain throughout a long book.

The distinguishing mark of the *General theory of population* is perhaps the felicity with which elegant models covering a wide range of demographic, economic, social and biological variables are married with a wealth of empirical information. In all expositions dealing with a broad stratum of social behaviour there is a necessary tension between clarity and comprehensiveness. Theoretical models may possess a delusive simplicity which restricts their value in interpreting the welter of events as they happen, while, on the other hand, to pile up masses of data without giving them structure impedes rather than promotes understanding. To sail neatly between this Scylla and Charybdis requires both originality of thought and finesse. These qualities Professor Sauvy shows he possesses many times in this book. Much of what he writes is, of course, open to dispute. Much may ultimately be replaced or modified in later attempts at building successful general population models. But a special debt of gratitude is owing to any man who first sketches such a grand design.

E. A. WRIGLEY

Peterhouse,
June 1969.

vii

PREFACE

We only think about our knee when we feel pain in it or when it fails to carry out its function. In the same way, problems of population have long been neglected – and still are – as long as no pain is felt in the body politic, from overpopulation or depression, to attract attention to them. And the adverse effect of this neglect on economic theory has been little recognised, since in any case it is widely assumed that economic analyses are seldom fully satisfactory.

At present, the populations of the West are enjoying a period of near equilibrium, having overcome the failings they experienced between the two world wars, whilst the Third World is alarmingly off balance demographically.

Many illusions still persist, even among the enlightened, particularly about the view that technological progress reduces employment. Though the last few years have proved the theory quite wrong, this age-old myth still appears in discussions about automation.

Demography, long a feckless science, without masters or pupils, is slowly achieving recognition. But the drop of water in a cloud is incapable of conceiving the shape of the cloud, and in the same way population is still tragically ignorant of itself.

Society appears rather scared by the self-discovery that awaits it. Since courage is often a synonym of farsightedness, this act of revelation is strangely laboured. The new approaches devised since the last war are still quite insufficient. Nothing is more difficult to reform than a curriculum, no body is more conservative than a university, and in the academic world no curriculum seems more antiquated than that of political economy.

The first section (*The Economics of Growth*) will deal with population from the purely economic angle. In the second section (*Social Biology*) I shall turn to sociological issues so described usually because they lend themselves less easily to measurement.

The reasonings occasionally took a mathematical turn of their own accord. To spare non-mathematicians the difficult spelling out of a language to which they are unaccustomed, I have confined the algebraic notation to footnotes, leaving only the graphic versions in the text.

I must thank those who have helped towards our research, and especially

Mme Anita Hirsch, and G. Malignac, F. Tabah, Mlle C. Gotchac and Mlle B. Garlot – not only for their contributions, but for the satisfaction given me by the rise of new and promising talents.

And I could not end without paying a different kind of tribute to Adolphe Landry, who has so often inspired me or corrected my thought. As a pupil I am grateful to him as economist and demographer; as a Frenchman for his services to the population of our country; in short, I wish to record my deep admiration.

ALFRED SAUVY

GENERAL THEORY OF POPULATION

PART ONE

THE ECONOMICS OF GROWTH

1

SOME ANIMAL ECOLOGY

'Celui qui met un frein à toute la nature
Sait aussi des oiseaux arrêter les complots,
Aux petits des méchants, il donne la pâture
Et sa bonté s'étend sur la fureur des flots.'
RACINE AND TRISTAN BERNARD'[1]

A living species in an environment

All living species are able to multiply, some very rapidly. Given favourable
conditions, even the least prolific of uniparous animals can easily double
their numbers in twenty years and through geometrical progressions this
leads in a relatively short time to very high figures. However, this expansion
meets the resistance of the environment.

Let us first of all assume that the species is on its own in the environment.
Even then it cannot multiply indefinitely. There will be two upper limits:
1. *Physical ceiling*. The total weight of the various elements making up the
environment cannot be exceeded. 2. *Biochemical ceiling*. Since the process of
life demands progressive chemical changes and the presence of substances
that are not assimilated by the organism, the weight of biological material, or
biomass, of the species considered can never exceed a fraction of the substances entering into or helping towards the cycle. This fraction is sometimes
very small, and the biochemical ceiling is usually far lower than the physical
one.

The second ceiling does not stop increase abruptly. As the species increases
in numbers, the inert environment resists this increase more strongly. The
species then redoubles its efforts, causing the environment to fall back and
give up a greater amount of subsistence. But this resistance will continue
to increase until at length the amount of food actually acquired by the species
is no longer enough for its numbers. The species is in its turn affected by the
fall in subsistence available for each individual: either its mortality increases,

---

[1] Tristan Bernard 'modernised' the following four lines from Racine's *Athalie* (act 1, scene
1), by inverting the words and destroying their moral effect:

'Celui qui met un frein à la fureur des flots
Sait aussi des méchants arrêter les complots,
... Aux petits des oiseaux il donne la pâture
Et sa bonté s'étend sur toute la nature.'

3

or it becomes less prolific, or its starts to emigrate. These reactions are usually, but not always, caused by lack of nourishment.

Initial data

We will begin by ignoring the differences caused by age, and assume for the sake of simplicity that all the individuals of the group are identical in productivity and in needs. We will also assume that the ability to benefit from the environment is constant; in other words that for a given population there is a proportionate quantity of supplies per individual. What happens then can be seen in two ways: 1. From the *economic point of view*: as the population increases, the amount of supplies per individual decreases because the natural resources are limited. 2. From the *biological point of view*: this drop in supplies causes mortality to rise and fertility to fall[1] (we will disregard migration for the moment).

A state of balance

What will happen to the population in these conditions? We will show first that there is a state of perfect balance which does not depend on the initial state of the population.

Lotka demonstrated that where the fertility and mortality of each age group in a population are constant, the population tends towards a limiting state at which its age distribution is constant. If, within the invariable structure of this population, the births and deaths should also happen to balance out we should have a *stationary population* with invariable structure and size, the latter depending on its initial state. This equilibrium in a stationary population is not 'stable' in the mechanical sense of the word. What it means is that if an accidental change should occur in numbers or in the way in which individuals are distributed, the population would tend towards a new state of balance, of identical structure but different in size.

However, in the case we are considering, *there can be complete stability*, thanks to the resilience of fertility and mortality or of only one of the two. Should our population increase artificially (by immigration for instance) the mortality will rise and the fertility will fall. As with Lotka's stationary population, an animal population in a state of balance with its environment will in time renew itself totally, in structure and size; its age structure is identical

---

[1] Let P be the total population, P(a) the population at age a, and S(P) the supply produced per individual; S defines economic conditions.

Let f(a,S) be the fertility and m(a,S) the mortality at age a with supply S per individual; these functions define the biological conditions.

Eliminating the variable S gives functions F(a,P) and M(a,P) representing, respectively, the fertility and mortality at age a in populations of size P.

to its survival table. *And it also tends to return tirelessly to this state of balance.*

In order to define equilibrium without recourse to the algebraic equations confined to footnote,[1] I propose to use throughout this chapter an imaginary 'semi-stationary' population. By this I mean a population resembling a stationary population in that its age structure is the same as its survival table, but where the birth and death rates are not identical. Such a population only changes progressively, starting at the lower age groups.

Consider a given species, semi-stationary to begin with. The total population P imposes on each age group a predictable pattern of fertility and mortality, forming a survival table. Its age structure is identical to this survival table. If the number of births and the number of deaths were equal we should have the stationary population we are seeking. But if there are more births than deaths, the population must be lower than at the state of balance, and conversely.

Indeed let us consider a second semi-stationary population in the same environment, with the same structure as the first, but whose size P_1 is larger than P. Here there are more, or at least as many, deaths at each age (because of the bio-economical law); therefore the general rate of mortality (or the inverse of the average life-span) is higher in the second population than in the first.

---

[1] Let us find this final state for the female part of the population. Using the same definitions as in the previous footnote, together with

B, the number of births in a unit of time,

and D, „ „ „ deaths „ „ „ „ „ „ ,

we observe

$F_p(a,P) < O$, and $M_p(a,P) > O$, since fertility decreases and mortality increases as the population increases.

The final equilibrium is defined by:

$$B = \int_{a_1}^{a_2} P(a)F(a,P)\,da$$ (where a_1 and a_2 are the limits of the fertility period)

$$D = \int_{0}^{w} P(a)M(a,P)\,da$$ (where w is the highest age reached)

$$P(a) = \exp\left\{ -\int_{0}^{a} M(a,P)da \right\}(*)$$ (arising from the definition of mortality and in the absence of any migration)

and $P = \int_{0}^{w} P(a)\,da$

Substituting these formulae in the equation

$$B = D$$

gives $\int_{a_1}^{a_2} F(a,P)\exp\left\{ -\int_{0}^{a} M(a,P)\,da \right\}da$

$$= \int_{0}^{w} M(a,P)\exp\left\{ -\int_{0}^{a} M(a,P)\,da \right\}da$$

When the functions F(a,P) and M(a,P) are known, this equation gives the maximum population P, and the formula (*) the population at each age a.

Now consider the birth rate. The fertility rates for each age group are lower than in the first population. It would seem therefore that, for reasons analogous to those given above, the fertility would be lower and that the surplus of births would thus be smaller than before. If we were to increase the size of the population to P_2, P_3, and so on we would eventually reach a state of balance.

But the matter is not quite so simple; in spite of the decrease in the fertility rate of each age group, the general fertility rate might be higher. This apparent oddity can occur if a fall in mortality has affected mainly the age groups fit to procreate, who therefore increase in proportion.[1] But even in this case calculations show that the death rate increases more than the birth rate, so that the difference between them lessens.[2]

Amongst all the semi-stationary populations, there is thus one whose births and mortality are equal. It is at the state of balance.

---

[1] Here is a numerical example, purely theoretical:

Age	1st population	2nd population
0	60	80
1	50	63
2	28	0
3	0	0
	138	143

The age of procreation is 1 and the fertility rate is 2·1 for the first population but 2 for the second. The birth rate is $\frac{105}{138} = 0.76$ in the first case and $\frac{126}{143} = 0.88$ in the second.

[2] Let us give an example of a population simplified to three ages of which only the intermediate age is fertile. The argument can be extended to the general case.
Consider two populations P_1 and P_2 with $P_1 < P_2$.

Age	Before	After
0	$P_1(0)$	$P_2(0)$
1	$P_1(1)$	$P_2(1)$
2	$P_1(2)$	$P_2(2)$
Total	P_1	P_2

Death rate: $\dfrac{P_1(0)}{P_1}$ and $\dfrac{P_2(0)}{P_2}$

Birth rate: $\dfrac{P_1(1)F_1}{P_1}$ and $\dfrac{P_2(1)F_2}{P_2}$

Increase of death rate $\dfrac{P_2(0)P_1}{P_1(0)P_2}$

Increase of birth rate $\dfrac{P_2(1)F_2P_1}{P_1(1)F_1P_2}$

The ratio of the increase of mortality to the increase of fertility is then $\dfrac{P_2(0)P_1(1)}{P_1(0)P_2(1)} \times \dfrac{F_1}{F_2}$
which is a product of two numbers each greater than unity, the first because mortality is increased, the second because fertility is decreased. The product is therefore greater than 1.

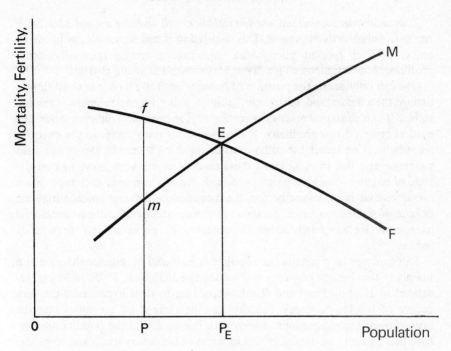

Figure 1. Bio-economic equilibrium (semi-stationary populations).

Figure 1 takes the general case, assuming for the sake of simplicity that the birth rate of the semi-stationary population decreases as long as the total population rises. We have a graph of fertility and mortality against population size in the conditions already defined.

If for a semi-stationary population OP, f is above m, the population is lower than its natural state of balance, represented at E where the two curves intersect.

Progress towards equilibrium

What then becomes of an animal population in a given environment? Its size cannot vary far from the state of balance without, biologically, incurring either strong punishment or strong encouragement. Sooner or later it reaches the requisite size for equilibrium. But its age distribution is unlikely to be such as to preclude fluctuations – there will be either too many young or too many old for births and deaths to balance out. After steadily decreasing oscillations the population may tend toward equilibrium both in structure and size. But a perpetual planetary movement, whether cyclic or not, around the state of balance, is also conceivable. Our main point however is that there must be an equilibrium point, since it exercises a constant attraction.

7

Thus an animal population, when in isolation, will oscillate around a level that can only temporarily be passed. This oscillation is not harmonic, as in mechanics; even if cyclical phenomena introduce a certain regularity, other problematic phenomena cause divergences from harmonic rhythm.

One can only define the position of balance perfectly if certain conditions – mainly the climate and the species' skill in using its environment – remain stable. If the climate worsens for instance, if it becomes colder or drier, the natural ceiling drops gradually. If the species fits itself better to the environment by making better use of its food or reducing its needs, the ceiling rises progressively. But in most cases these tendencies are very slow, so that the state of balance varies very slowly indeed. An environment therefore has a maximum carrying capacity for the population we are considering: *so, in spite of the tendencies of species or environment, and of cyclic or accidental phenomena, we may finally accept the existence of a maximum level imposed by nature.*

This concept of a maximum population is found in various theories and mainly in the 'logistic population' described in 1838 by P. F. Verhulst and re-defined in 1920 by Pearl and Reed. According to their hypothesis, the very nature of the bio-economic function can be defined by assuming that the resistance of the environment varies with the square of the population. The hypothesis cannot be demonstrated in terms of the theory itself, and empirical evidence confirms it only occasionally. The adjustments tried on the various contemporary populations could have been equally successful in their approximations had they been applied to a parabola or any similar curve.

Besides there is no proof that the limit can be reached in infinite time. Nor can any experiment be decisive here, for there is always a moment when the distance between a curve and its asymptote is smaller than the degree of precision of the measuring device. In any case, since the number of animals is finite, the variations cannot be infinitesimal. Achilles catches up with the tortoise.

While not formulating a precise hypothesis on the nature of the laws of fertility and mortality, we may assume that up to a certain population figure, they are more or less constant. Saturation only appears past a certain density. In the first stage the population grows exponentially.

But even if the resistance of the environment were such that the growth of supplies only followed an arithmetical progression, Malthus's hypothesis would only be verified for a short spell, since the geometrical progression would be lessened at the same time as productivity. Let loose a pair of animals in an environment and while multiplying geometrically they will reach Lotka's stable age distribution. Near saturation, progress slows down and stops (usually after a series of oscillations).

The age distribution in the final balance is not the same as in a stable population that has not yet reached saturation. There are more young if the

8

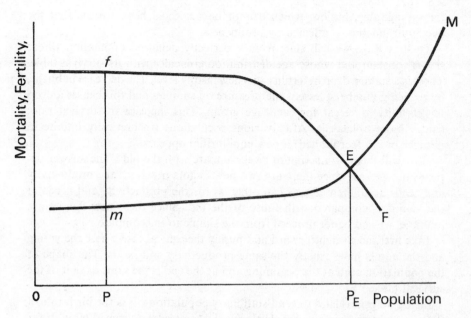

Figure 2. Bio-economic balance. Area of indifference and area of sensitivity.

resistance of the environment acts on the mortality of the old, and more old if the resistance acts on the fertility and mortality of the young.

Effects of a sudden change in bio-economical laws

The reader will remember that we assumed biological variations – and particularly changes in the prolificness or mortality of a species – to be slow and progressive. But we should not overlook the possibility of sudden variations. Though the species may not be able to adapt at great speed, the environment itself can change suddenly. Suppose that the fertility or mortality rate should not remain constant but take on a new stable value. How will this affect the final state of balance?

1. *Change in fertility.* A pair of animals is released into an environment. If their fertility is weaker than before (i.e. if the fertility for each age group is lower, or at best the same as before) they will multiply more slowly and reach their maximum number later, if at all. If they multiply faster they will reach it sooner. But will this state of balance be the same as before?

One may be tempted to say yes, on the grounds that the state of balance imposed by the environment can only be changed by the species itself through a modified ability to benefit from the environment. But if we make allowances

9

for the age distribution, which cannot be neglected here, we see that the maximum number is affected by prolificness.

To show this, we will start from a perfectly balanced population whose size is constant and whose age distribution coincides with its survival table. There is a sudden drop in fertility to a new lasting level. The decrease in births, by reducing numbers, lessens the pressure on supplies and this causes a drop in mortality, different for each age group. This increase in survival rates causes more upheavals. After various oscillations (theoretically infinite in number but in fact limited) a new equilibrium appears.

How will this new maximum level compare with the old? The answer depends on the case since there are two new factors involved: the productivity and needs at different ages, or in other words the productivity and needs of the young as compared with those of the old. Since these new factors are multiple, we had better proceed from the simple to the complex.

Take first the straightforward and purely theoretical case where the young and the adults have exactly the same productivity and needs. The shape of the population both at the beginning and at the end is the same as that of the survival table.

Figure 3 again relates to semi-stationary populations. F is the birth rate of the population whose age distribution is the same as the survival table. If for

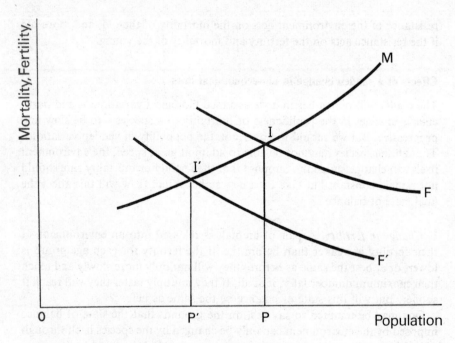

Figure 3. Influence of fertility on the maximum population.

a given population the fertility of each age group is lower than (or at most equal to) the former one, we will get a second population F', lying constantly below the first on the graph, and whose intersection with M (invariable) gives us the new population OP', lower than the old one.

In other words the drop in the birth rate must cause an increase in the survival rates; this depends on better living conditions and therefore on a population lower than the old one.

With a higher fertility, the maximum population would be higher too. We can say in short: *the tendency of a population to multiply faster produces added pressure on its environment, which is led to concede a little to the species.*

We will now introduce the factors of productivity and need according to age.

If, everything else being equal, the productivity of the young rises (or falls), the total output rises (or falls), and so does the maximum population.

If, on the other hand, the needs of the young rise (or fall), these needs are less well (or better) fulfilled, and the maximum population falls (or rises).

But when the young require very little, it is less appropriate to think of the individual animal as the unit and to lay stress on numbers. It is better to use weight as the unit instead, and try to define the conditions in which the ratio of the biomass to the total weight of matter can be as high as possible. The biomass is indeed the measure of the species' victory over its inert environment.

2. *Change in mortality.* In figure 4 we simplify things as we did for fertility,

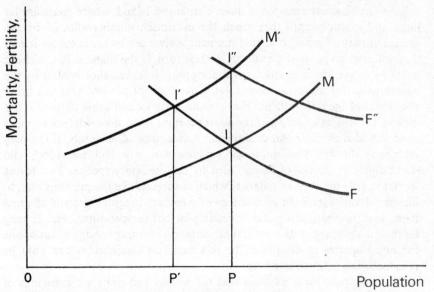

Figure 4. Simultaneous changes in birth rate and mortality.

using the same notation: an increase of mortality from M to M′ causes a drop in the maximum population from OP to OP′ (and conversely).

Thus a permanent increase in mortality (for instance if the animal is being hunted) causes the species to decrease in number. For the species to return to its original size the higher mortality must only be accidental and not a regular feature. A simultaneous increase in fertility (from F to F″) and in mortality (from M to M′) can bring us back to the same maximum population OP, but with a different age composition. Mortality in the very young, incidentally, is the same for the purpose of demographic counts as a decrease in fertility.

3. *Migrations*. In calculations, migrations may be treated as changes in the pattern of mortality. For the species it is the same whether an individual is killed or captured and taken out of the environment. Migrations can therefore be included in the mortality rate, and may lead either to negative 'mortality' or to survival rates larger than unity.

Persistent emigration reduces the maximum even when it leaves the population enough vitality to grow. The new smaller maximum population enjoys a greater amount of supplies.

4. *Case of two rival species*. Two rival species may fight for the same nourishment or they may be food for one another. Sometimes the only stable situation involves the disappearance of one of the species; but it may be on the other hand, that there is a state of balance where the species co-exist.

Take the classical example of Juan Fernandez Island, where goats are let loose and multiply until they reach the maximum number allowed by the annual growth of grass. If at that moment wolves are let loose on the island they will feed on goats and multiply in their turn. If the island is flat, without hills or shelters, the goat species will disappear, followed shortly after by the wolves, who will have no more food. The death of the last goat will bring about that of the last wolf. But if the island is rocky and some parts of it are difficult for wolves to get at, as the goats get rarer the wolves will lack supplies –and will also dwindle. An equilibrium may appear. Conversely, if the prey multiplies through favourable circumstances it will find less food, and stand a greater chance of being killed by the predatory species. Two forces work towards the state of balance, which is subject, like the previous one, to incidental variables such as changes of weather, irregular growth of grass from year to year, epidemics spreading in hot temperatures, etc. It may be that in a given year this accidental variation is strong enough to cause one (or both) species to disappear. In this case, the equilibrium can only be re-established with outside help.

Let us suppose for a moment that the wolves and goats are conscious of their interests and inquire into the best policy to adopt.

First consider the goats: if they possess an enclosure where they are safe from the wolves and another one shared with the wolves, their interest lies in limiting their population to the size allowed by their own enclosure. The wolf species will then become extinct, allowing the victorious goats to multiply again up to the maximum level allowed by supplies, far higher than their number where the two species were coexisting.

Similarly, the wolves would be well advised not to learn to climb into the goats' enclosure. A complete victory would soon bring about their own disappearance. The case may seem far-fetched, but it is worth reflecting on. The moment they begin to 'eat into their capital', not content with the regular dividends brought in by the goat species, which is for them a machine for making animal matter out of vegetable matter, the wolves would be on the road to ruin. Their real interest lies in letting the goats graze over the whole island, to reach their maximum numbers; if the wolves' social organisation were strong enough to stop them from eating goat too greedily, they too would then reach a maximum number which they should be careful not to exceed, even if this meant killing each other. Similarly, if the goats gobbled up too much young tasty grass they might endanger their own livelihood.

Since we have arrived thus far above animal intelligence, we may imagine a particularly bright wolf demographer persuading his fellows to regulate their fertility so as to stay at this maximum number, or even to raise goats in larger herds. An increase in the predatory species may cause its subsequent decrease because it has diminished its capital source of supplies. Its progress will only be a momentary spark of added life unless it brings about some other development, opening up some new source of supply inaccessible or unsuitable until then. Progress is contingent on further progress.

If on the other hand, instead of killing and eating goats, the wolves were to take to a grass diet, while retaining enough strength to oust the goats from their pastures, this would be the end of the goats on the island. In other words *the weak goat species owes its survival to the fact that its individual members are food to the stronger species.*

This is indeed meat for some strange thoughts: in a society under the feudal system, the lower class may have been exploited, but it was better off than if it had not been exploited at all, for it would then have disappeared. Should the owner short-cut his servant, and use natural products directly (by hunting, owning horses; or in the classical case of the princess, by taking a bath in milk), he stopped exploiting his servant and merely deprived him of a living. La Fontaine might have found spicy illustrations to these thoughts. The lion, presiding over the council of animals, would have been provided with an irrefutable reason for eating up the sheep, and the fox instead of remarking 'You did them, sir, a great honour by eating them' could have said 'You did them a good turn.'

13

Several species

These remarks can be generalised to the case of several living species, thus bringing us closer to real conditions. Balance appears between the various species but is continually upset by accidental changes and transformed by slow adaptations. The model can also be transposed to the case of human economy; we shall return to this point when dealing with agricultural societies and technological progress.

The reason why the idea of balance and of 'maximum capacity of habitat' remains the fundamental basis of animal ecology is that changes tend to occur more slowly than the multiplication of species, so that the numbers of each species can be kept for some time close to a relatively well-defined position.

Are animal species undernourished?

Whether or not it is competing with others, a wild species multiplies naturally up to the state of balance where mortality and fertility are equal. Does this state involve drastic undernourishment? This point is interesting because it will be important later with human populations.

There are many examples of the opposite; the hare is energetic and must have well-fed muscles; ants carry considerable loads; birds are always hungry but do not appear weak. Yet the hare often owes its life to its speed, and so cannot multiply so much that this is lost; every animal keeps the energy necessary to ensure survival, and this energy can vary considerably according to the species. Besides, the resistance of the environment does not act only on the mortality of adults. It can slow down physiological fertility or the growth of the young. Some species are provident Malthusians and avoid having to sacrifice themselves to their young, like Vigny's pelican. An improvident and fearless species falls as often as not into the terrible realm of hunger.

Short bibliography

I. P. S. Agrell, *The Collemboles in Nests of Warmblooded Animals, with a Method for Sociological Analysis*, Lunds Universitäts Årsskrift, 1945.

W. C. Alle, O. Park, A. E. Emerson, T. Park, K. P. Schmidt, *Principles of Animal Ecology*, Saunders, Philadelphia, 1949 (with an important bibliography).

D. D. Anderson, *The Point of Population Saturation*, 1929.

A. A. Bitancourt, *Expressao matematica do crescimento de formigueiros*, Arch. Inst. Bio., 1941.

F. S. Bodenheimer, *Problems of Animal Ecology*, OUP London, 1938. *Der Massenwechsel in der Tierwelt*, 1931.

F. Bourlière, 'Structure et dynamique des populations sauvages vertébrés' *Population*, oct.–déc. 1949; *Ecologie*, 1949.

F. E. Clements, *Bio-Ecology*, Wiley, New York, 1939.

Colloques internationaux du Centre national de la Recherche scientifique, XXXIII, Ecologie, 20–25 feb. 1950, Paris, 1952.

A. C. Crombie, *On Competition between Different Species of Graminivorous Insects*, Proc. Roy. Soc., London, 1945. 'Interspecific Competition', *Journal of Animal Ecology*, 1947.

J. Davidson, *On the Growth of the Sheep Population in Tasmania*, Australia, 1938. 'On the Growth of Insect Populations with Successive Generations', *J. Exp. Biol. and Med. Sc.*, Australia, 1944.

E. S. Dewey, 'Life Tables for Natural Population of Animals' *Quart. Rev. Biol.*, 1947.

G. F. Gause, *Vérifications expérimentales de la théorie mathématique de la lutte pour la vie*, Hermann, Paris, 1935.

V. A. Kostitsuin, *Mathematical Biology*, Harrap, London, 1939.

A. Lotka, *Théorie analytique des associations biologiques*, Hermann, Paris, 1935.

D. S. MacLagen, *The Effect of Population Density upon Rate of Reproduction with Reference to Insects*, Proc. Roy. Soc., Edinburgh, 1936.
The Experimental Analysis of the Growth of an Insect population, Proc. Roy. Soc., Edinburgh, 1936.

D. A. MacLulich, *Fluctuations in the Numbers of the Varying Hare*, University of Toronto Press, 1937.

R. Pearl, *The Biology of Population Growth*, Knopf, New York, 1925.

R. Pearl and J. L. Reed, *A further Note on the Mathematical Theory of Population Growth*.

F. Pierre, *Les conditions écologiques et le peuplement des vases d'eau douce*, Le Chevalier, Paris, 1951.

W. R. Thompson, 'Biological Control and the Theories of interactions of Populations', *Parasitology*, No. 31, 1939.

P. F. Verhulst, *Notice sur la loi qui suit la population dans son accroissement*, 1838. *Recherches mathématiques sur la loi d'accroissement de la population*, 1845.

V. Volterra, *Les associations biologiques au point de vue mathématique*, Hermann, 1935. *Fluctuations dans la lutte pour la vie*, Gauthier-Villars, Paris, 1938.

A. D. Voute, *Classification of Factors influencing the Natural Growth of a Population of Insects*, Acta Biotheoretica, Leyden, 1943.

2

THE MAXIMUM POPULATION

'Prenant vigueur de son propre dommage' . . .
RONSARD

A primitive human population (i.e. technologically stationary, incapable of struggling effectively against mortality, and not restricting marriages or births) is more or less in the same position as an animal species: it multiplies until it reaches the maximum level allowed by its surroundings and the use it can make of these surroundings. On approaching this maximum it meets, as the animal species did, the resistance of the environment, in the economic form of a 'drop in efficiency' and the biological form of an 'increase of mortality' (or an involuntary decrease in fertility). We are led back to the laws already defined for animals. Again, as for the animals, it is in men's interest to preserve their natural capital in the form of game, forests, soils, etc.

The concept of a maximum population can still obtain, even where the above definition of a 'primitive' population is no longer quite adequate. Thus men can: 1. Modify the economic factor by making better use of the environment so as to increase supplies and other materials. 2. Modify the first biological factor (mortality) with an unchanged amount of supplies: either by inventing means of reducing competition, or by increasing longevity without a larger food base. 3. Modify the second biological factor (fertility) either by new social habits or by direct physiological action. 4. Organise the distribution of products on a scale larger than that of the family.

The improvements in the first three cases are different from the corresponding changes described in the first chapter in an animal population since they can be due to intellectual action and occur without physiological change. They can therefore be much faster than through evolutionary adaptation, and we will have to adapt the concept of maximum population accordingly.

The upper ceiling, determined by the total weight of supplies contained in the environment, stays the same, but there remains a wide gap between this and the lower ceiling, determined by the resistance of the environment. This may be considerably increased by partial victories over the environment, which gives up an ever-increasing though still very small fraction of its weight. Let us examine in turn the four factors mentioned above, assuming in each case that the other three do not vary, and remembering that these populations are not very advanced.

16

Economic action on the environment

We assume that each man produces the same and that the total output is evenly distributed.

If men make better use of their environment by producing more supplies, the biological factor allows the population and the lower ceiling to rise. This may occur either through some sudden technological development that spreads quickly and becomes permanent, or through a slow improvement.

Sudden improvement: In this case, for a given population, the supplies increase to a new constant level. The immediate effect of this will either be on numbers or on the standard of living. What will the final effect be?

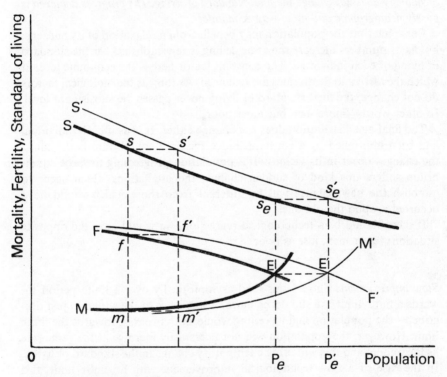

Figure 5. Economic progress and maximum population.

Figure 5, using the same notation as previously, refers again to our supposed 'semi-stationary' population. It is a graph of S the standard of living, determined by economic conditions, and of F and M the birth and death rates, determined by the biological factor against population. The state of balance occurs at E, for a population of OP_e and a standard of living of $P_e s_e$.

17

The thin lines refer to a second situation, where a technological improvement has taken place. The economic factors are changed but not the biological factors. The new curve representing the general comfort or welfare S' is therefore completely above S. To the two points s and s' representing the same standard of living, there are corresponding points on the fertility and mortality curves (f and f'; m and m'). These new points are at the same level as the old.

In particular, since the new equilibrium standard of living s'_e is the same as the old, fertility and mortality are also unchanged at the new demographic equilibrium point E'. The new population equilibrium at OP'_e, is thus larger than the former one but has the same standard of living.

In a primitive population with natural fertility a permanent improvement in technology does not change the final standard of living. The progress achieved is purely demographic and in no way economic.

For some time the population may benefit from a relaxation of its burdens, but as its numbers increase the same ceiling is re-established for the standard of living of each individual. The constant factor here is the economic level at which the birth and death rates are balanced. As long as the biological factors do not change, the final standard of living never passes the subsistence level. In other words, 'more men but more poor'.

The final age distribution does not change either. It is as if each individual had been multiplied by a constant. Since the final equilibrium is the same, the changes occur in its vicinity. If a population progressing towards equilibrium suffers this kind of sudden change, the oscillations which occur to establish the new balance will be different from those which would have occurred around the old one.

If there should be a technological regression, we would have the opposite situation: fewer men, just as poor.

Slow improvement: Should this tend asymptotically over a finite period towards a finite limit, we should be more or less back to the situation just described – the population and its ceiling would both progress towards the finite limit. However, the population will not necessarily increase at the same rate as the ceiling, and this will bring a temporary change in the standard of living. In the case of a slow technological improvement with no finite limit, this temporary time-lag between the population and its ceiling because of different rates of increase, may become a permanent feature.

However in practice when progress begins, we cannot tell how long it will go on. We must therefore study the movements themselves, and for this purpose bring in time as a variable. This amounts to studying the *race between demographic and economic progress*. If a technological development, followed by its economic effects, occurs in a population in constant biological conditions, the population remains below its ceiling as long as technological progress continues at a sufficient rate.[1]

Economic progress thus takes the lead and the population experiences some relief. If this continues there will be a lasting improvement in the standard of living.

It is difficult to find satisfactory experimental conditions in which to check these conclusions, because the factor of economic progress can rarely be isolated. A possible experimental field would be the beginning of European industrial capitalism in the early nineteenth century, but here medical improvements are also involved, and questions of capitalist distribution complicate the issue. Conditions in the Soviet Union are no more suitable, since considerable improvements in medicine were achieved there at the same time as economic growth. Medical progress also complicates the biological issue in the developing countries, as we shall see further on.

On the other hand economic progress may well have unfavourable effects. *A development in technology can give men, to a greater degree than biological improvement can give animals, the ability to eat into the natural capital that provides their income.* At the level of primitive hunting, Man's prey is renewed all the time; if men invent more deadly weapons their species will find increased supplies and multiply more quickly to begin with, but at the expense of the capital. Either game will disappear completely or after a certain point it will resist men and a new balance will appear between the two species which may be less favourable to both than the initial one. This is why certain methods of hunting and fishing are strictly forbidden. Soils too can be disastrously destroyed through erosion due to an exhausting extensive agriculture. Economic progress may also require the consumption of minerals of which only limited amounts are available. Pollution of water supplies is another similar problem.

---

[1] To demonstrate this let us consider the same parameters as before but regard them now as functions of time, t, and ignore their now irrelevant dependence on age.

We start with a population at its ceiling when a continuous technological development occurs.

Let P be the total population, $S(P,t)$ the supplies produced per individual, $f(S,t)$ the fertility and $m(S,t)$ the mortality at time t with supplies per individual S.

Eliminating S gives functions $F(P,t)$ and $M(P,t)$ representing the birth rate and death rate of a population of size P at time t.

Then $F_P(P,t) < 0$, $F_t(P,t) > 0$, $M_P(P,t) > 0$, and $M_t(P,t) < 0$.

The population size P is given by

$\frac{1}{P} \frac{dP}{dt} = F(P,t) - M(P,t) = G(P,t)$ where $G_P < 0$, $G_t > 0$.

and the ceiling Q by

$F(Q,t) - M(Q,t) = 0$, i.e. $G(Q,t) = 0$.

We must show that for each t, $P < Q$.

Since P increases with t, $F(P,t) - M(P,t) > 0$, and so $G(P,t) > 0$

Therefore, as $G_P(P,t) < 0$, we have $P < Q$.

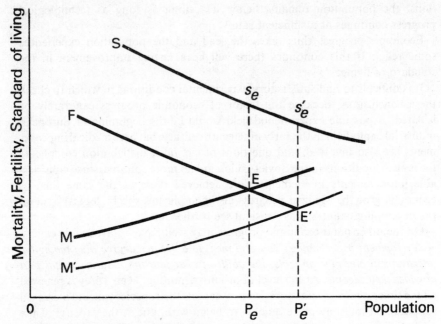

Figure 6. Sanitary improvement with no economic counterpart in a fairly primitive population.

Progress, to deserve its name, must never stop; it must always find new ways of putting to use new sources of wealth. There is no such thing as a stop in progress: only more progress or regression.

Direct action on mortality

We will leave aside for the time being the destruction of a population, and consider the reverse to the situation just described: no economic improvement, but biological progress – a drop in the death rate perhaps, through sanitary improvements – so that the expectation of life is lengthened with the standard of living constant. Since the economic factors remain the same, the graph of standard of living does not change. Neither do the births F. But M moves to M'.

The point of balance E moves to E'. The maximum population rises, but the standard of living drops from s_e to s'_e.[1]

---

[1] Adopting the same definitions as in the previous note, and observing that $F(P,t)$ and $M(P,t)$ change in the same way, we have again: $F_P < O$, $F_t > 0$, $M_P > 0$, and $M_t < 0$.

As no assumptions have been made about these functions, the previous conditions hold, except in relation to the standard of living.

The ceiling Q at time t is defined by

$f[S(Q),t] - m[S(Q),t] = 0$, and as Q increases $S(Q)$, by the very nature of S, decreases.

20

Thus, if a sanitary improvement occurs without economic improvement, the ceiling rises, and will be reached sooner or later. By then there will be fewer births, and mortality will have dropped, but the causes of death will no doubt have changed. *The important thing here is that the standard of living will be lower than before the change occurred. The result is that people will live as long but in less satisfactory economic conditions. Sanitary improvement on its own would thus lower the standard of living of a primitive population.*

Until recently such an improvement rarely occurred without an economic parallel. In a closed society, where progress was brought about by spontaneous internal change, such dissociation would be unthinkable. In a market economy the two kinds of progree would tend automatically to balance each other. In a planned economy the efforts towards economic and sanitary progress would obviously be harmonised. *But when there is outside interference, it is not only conceivable, but in a way logical, that the two forms of progress should be dissociated.*

This is the case in developing countries, where hygiene and medicine have outstripped economic growth. When a population is in physiological distress, medical aid is at once more pressing and cheaper than economic aid.[1] It is easier to produce a vaccine for a million people than to give them consumer goods or equipment together wth the necessary technical education. And yet, without economic support, such medical aid can be a doubtful blessing.

These remarks should not be taken without restrictions, nor should they be too hastily interpreted. It may be that a struggle against mortality, in decreasing the prevalence of morbidity, causes productivity to rise. And saving the life of an eighteen-year-old man is equivalent to preserving a capital that has been invested out of production over eighteen years (see chapter 21). We shall also see, in the second half of this book, that medical progress can be the indirect cause of a voluntary reduction in fertility.

Finally, the introduction of the age factor can have some effect on the bio-economic balance.

In practice there is often a lack of proportion between curative aid and preventative economic aid. But whoever denounces this lack of balance runs the risk of causing the first to be reduced, or even considered harmful or useless. Such was the cruel position of Malthus when he advised against offering help to the poor because it was ineffectual.

We shall return to this problem later when talking of developing countries.

---

[1] This point is already a classical one where individuals are concerned: a tuberculosis patient may be given immediate attention, but the real remedy would be a preventative one on a social scale.

Habits liable to change fertility

These may consist either in carefully controlled sexual relations, particularly in marriage, or in birth control. The first reduces fertility either by putting off intercourse until later in life, or by placing excessive restrictions on its frequency (though on the other hand very early or very frequent intercourse may also reduce fertility).

A drop in fertility usually increases the standard of living of an animal population (see chapter 1) at the same time as it reduces the maximum population. The opposite may however happen if the ratio of output to needs should be higher for the young than for the adults. These principles may be applied to human populations, but only if little or no birth control is practised and they are completely subjected to natural resources.

Greater elasticity of consumption and distribution of goods

Animals seek only their food. Even if they eat more than they need, they cannot, for physiological reasons, absorb more than a certain amount. Men on the other hand can put natural products to various ends. Also, except in the case of mothers protecting their young and the collective life of certain species, each animal usually consumes what it produces. With men, consumption and output are not so closely related: either collective work entails a distribution liable to arbitrary practices, or institutions allow organs of production to be owned.

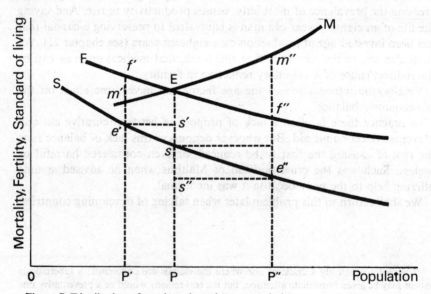

Figure 7. Distribution of goods and maximum population.

Take the most primitive and elementary case, where things are consumed only as food, and leave aside humanitarian or qualitative judgments. How will the method of distribution act on the maximum population?

We start off from an equal distribution: figure 7 plots against population: 1. birth and death rates, F and M; 2. the average output per inhabitant S (standing equally for consumption or average standard of living). This graph is to a different scale. At the point E of maximum population OP, the standard of living is Ps.

Let us now suppose that the distribution is no longer equal. Half the population manages to get to a standard of living of Ps′, higher than Ps, whilst the other half is reduced by the same amount to Ps″.

On curve S, points e′ and e″ correspond to points s′ and s″. A population whose standard of living is Ps″ or P″e″ (but which is not necessarily OP″ since we do not know the relative scales of these graphs) suffers an excess of deaths over births of m″f″, whereas the population whose standard of living is Ps′ or P′e′ has an excess of births over deaths of f′m′. We cannot say which will dominate the other as long as we do not know the precise shape of S,F, and M, or in other words the exact bio-economic factors.

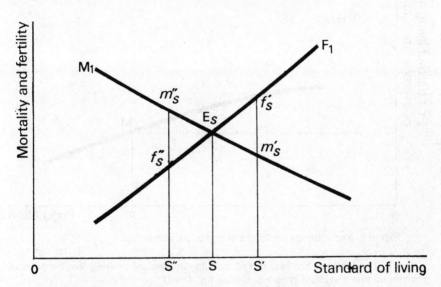

Fig. 8. Distribution of goods and maximum population.

Another graphic representation can be made by plotting the fertility and mortality curves, F_1 and M_1 as a function of the standard of living S. This time, as the population rises, the purely biological curves F_1 and M_1 should be followed from right to left since the standard of living S decreases. E_s the meeting point of graphs F_1 and M_1 represents the maximum population and a standard of living of OS. If we plot on either side of S the symetrical points S′ and S″, it is impossible to determine *a priori* whether f′sm′s is larger or smaller than f″sm″s.[1]

It is thus quite possible that if one half of the population is favoured at the expense of the other, it may gain either through fertility or mortality more than the other loses. In such a case the maximum population rises and inequality allows more people to live. Thus a group of ship-wrecked people on a raft may see their interest in throwing half of their number overboard in order to save the other half.

But this is an extreme case. Let us leave fertility constant whatever the standard of living, and postulate for a moment a precisely defined subsistence level below which people would die off generally and above which the mortality would be independent of the standard of living.

Figure 9 plots average output against population and represents the subsistence level as a horizontal line. M, where the line crosses the graph, is at

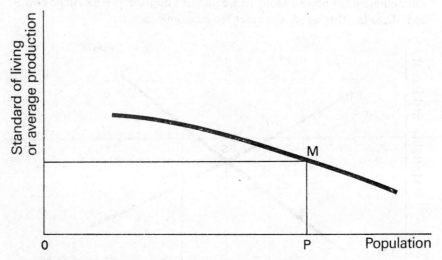

Figure 9. Rigid subsistence level and maximum population.

[1] Let f(S) and m(S) be the fertility and mortality at standard of living S at the point of equilibrium and maximum population; then $f(S) = m(S)$.

Supposing one half of the population has standard of living $s+ds$, the other half $s-ds$, we find on one side an excess f′s − m′s of births over deaths, on the other a surplus m″s − f″s of deaths over births. The sign of the two expressions taken together is indeterminate.

More generally, suppose that the consumption is no longer equally divided, the individual of rank r receiving amount s(r) with $\int_o^r s(r)dr = s$.

The mortality now becomes the probability of death $m[s(r)] = M(r)$, and similarly the fertility F(r). Nothing determines *a priori* the sign of $M(r)dr - F(r)dr$.

24

the maximum population OP. Any inequality in distribution will reduce the population to less than this maximum, as those receiving less than MP will not live and those receiving more will not enjoy any extra vitality.

The more the graph of mortality as a function of the standard of living curves downwards, the further we are from the maximum population because of inequality.

This drop in population is still more likely, and will be greater, if the rich use the natural resources for more than strictly physiological needs. Thus if some use land for pleasure and subtract it from the productive environment, the maximum population is lessened. Cantillon is very discerning on this point, where he makes a distinction between superfluous luxuries and luxurious supplies (see below chapter 8).

There are numerous instances of such occurrences in history, and indeed in the contemporary world. When hunting, the medieval lord rode across his vassals' standard of living, therefore across their very number. Sheep were no less lethal.[1]

But in fact the subsistence level is by no means as rigid as has just been suggested. With 4000 vegetable calories a man lives in comfort but two men can barely survive. With 6000 vegetable calories one man be fed well (2000 absorbed directly from vegetables, and 800 calories from meat), or three men badly.

Suppose that a number of men have to live on a given territory with no hope of improving their technology. If organised as a community they will multiply up to the verge of undernourishment. *The maximum population is undernourished and in indifferent health, but still capable of producing and sharing its output equally.* Its motto could be 'from each according to his ability, to each less than his need'.

If the community is large, this situation cannot be preserved for long. Any inequality in distribution will destroy part of the population. The theoretical maximum is approached when a very small number of well-provided people keep order amongst a very poor population. We will return to this tricky subject in the chapters on the distribution of goods and on agricultural societies.

Old people and children: Social inequality can of course have nobler ends. Thus, whereas with animals the general rule is 'each one for himself', men organise their wealth in other ways and contrive more or less to help the weak and old. Some populations, especially in the far eastern river deltas, are

---

[1] See Thomas More's *Utopia*: 'Your sheep that were wont to be so meek and tame, and so small eaters, now, as I hear say, become so great devourers and so wild that they eat up and swallow down the very men themselves . . . for look in what parts of the realm doth grow the finest, and therefore dearest wool, there noblemen and gentlemen, yea, and certain abbots, . . . leave no ground for tillage, they enclose all into pastures.'

sufficiently developed to practise such distribution while still submitting to the iron rule of maximum population.

The effect of non-producers or small subsidised producers on the maximum population level is similar to that of the young. It can cause the maximum to increase or diminish according to the case. It usually makes it drop (see chapter 7).

Since unequal distributions occur, we should define the difference between marginal output and average output. Marginal output is the output achieved by an extra man, or more precisely the increase in total output resulting from the addition of one man. The average output is obtained by dividing the total output by the number of producers, or if there are non-producers, by the number of inhabitants. We will consider these ideas more carefully in the chapter on the optimum population.

Various factors combined: So far we have studied the effects of each factor separately. If two or more apply together, we may attempt a generalisation by regarding them as acting independently. (Reality does not always prove them to be independent: thus, there is a functional relationship between demographic growth and the rhythm of technological progress. We shall only consider some of these relationships, which are of a sociological kind, in the second half of this book.)

Natural evolution: Consider a population whose technology and social order are stable. Its ceiling is determinate but its numbers are not constant. The variation in crops from year to year, considerable even for a large country, is very large in a small region. It can go as far as doubling or halving itself. Populations such as these can expect only limited help from transport, and have to rely on local resources. Their numbers cannot however follow the mobile ceiling of the supply level exactly: instead, they make lively efforts to absorb its oscillations in time since this cannot be done in space – thus regulating themselves on both the biological and the economic levels.

From the economic point of view this demands efforts in stocking and carrying forward enough supplies. During the good years consumption may be unable to increase with the crops, but a struggle is needed to preserve the goods from the weather, pests and neighbouring peoples; a poor population does not have the elaborate technological and social organisation this requires. In the eighteenth century, the end of the period of maximum population in France (the last great famine was in 1709), many plans were suggested, in vain, to enable crops to be carried forward.

Biological reactions may prove more important: the body's powers of adaptation are generally under-estimated. During the German occupation of France, when very strict rationing was imposed because of the blockade of Europe, there were pessimistic forecasts concerning public health and mortality; but events disproved them completely even though the shortages were more drastic and lasted longer than anyone had reckoned. For some time, therefore, the death rate does not increase markedly and fecundity is maintained. There does however come a stage where the gap between population and supplies is too large. The first bad harvest brings no important change. Occasionally the number of marriages drops, causing a fall in births, but in relation to the total population the change is a minor one. Even if such a population were not to produce a single birth for a year it would only lose 3–4 per cent of its numbers, and since the loss would only be one of very young children, the drop in its needs would be insignificant.

It is through mortality that numbers are tailored to the amount of supplies available; shortages can cause illness and especially epidemics. Consider for instance the number of deaths in Danzig from 1601 to 1630 and in Augsburg from 1501 to 1547[1] ('plague' here refers to any epidemic illness).

Year	Danzig	Year	Augsburg
1601	1 361	1501–03	1 723
1602 (plague)	16 919	1504–05 (plague)	4 164
1603	1 531	1506–10	1 858
1604–11	2 365	1511–12 (plague)	3 925
1612–19	2 721	1513–17	1 789
1620 (plague)	11 936	1518–20	1 841
1621–23	2 508	1521	3 895
1624 (plague)	10 535	1522–31	1 741
1625 (plague)	4 197	1532–34	1 332
1626–28	2 712	1535–36 (plague)	7 246
1629 (plague)	4 185	1537–46	1 375
1630 (plague)	5 039	1547	3 480

The peaks are higher at Danzig, a sea-port – from 1601 to 1602 the deaths increase twelve-fold. For the current population of France, such a jump would mean seven million deaths a year, or seven times as many as during the year of Verdun.

Harvest yields have sometimes had close links with mortality. To stress the bio-economic phenomena involved Meuvret compared deaths to conceptions; during periods of food shortage the first rose and the second dropped. Figure 10 is eloquent on that score.

Certainly the correlation is not complete; for one thing the gauge of shortage and famine used here is only an approximation. But the coincidence is striking with the two sharp peaks in 1693–4 and 1709–10.

Civil or foreign wars may also help to bring populations back to below the economic ceiling. Their link with over-population is much less well established

[1] From Sussmilch: *Die göttliche Ordnung in den Veränderungen des menschlichen Geschlechts*, Berlin, 1765.

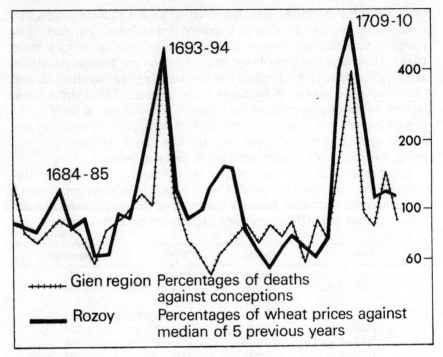

Figure 10. Correlation between famines and mortality.

than in the case of epidemics; famines have even been known to stop or prevent wars.[1]

In any case, whatever the cause-effect relationship, populations vary considerably around their state of balance.

The rigours of the maximum population have affected most populations in history, and still influence more than half of the contemporary world. Each time fertility is not counteracted by social or biological factors, and technology remains stationary or moderately progressive, a limit is imposed on the population which for most of the inhabitants merely amounts to an insufficient standard of living, only to be passed at great risk.

The history of the French-Canadian population shows as eloquently as could be hoped how a population can develop when its environment suddenly expands. If the population of France had multiplied in the same proportions as did the seventeenth- and eighteenth-century settlers, it would now be far greater than the population of the whole earth.

Logistic population: In reviewing, in chapter 1, various authors' works on the logistic population, we have already made reservations on the truth and scope

[1] This point will be taken up in the second half of this book.

of this concept. *It is even more unsound where a human population is concerned.*

For a primitive population there is unquestionably a saturation point, but it may appear in different ways. For a more advanced population there is no longer any reason to apply the principle. The experimental checks made on a period of the past are not conclusive since other functions with negative, or positive and then negative curvatures could be tried out with equal success. One only needs enough parameters. Also, the projection of logistic curves into the future has often been disproved by events.

This objection could of course be used against any demographic forecast. But ordinary provisional reckonings only show where certain factors observed in the present would lead. Sometimes these are intended to make a population realise a danger that threatens it and by this very fact change the trajectory.

Logistic population reckonings introduce an illegitimate determinism and solve too summarily the complex question of a population's maturity.

3

THE MINIMUM POPULATION

'Vae soli!'
Eccles. IV. 10.

It is difficult if not impossible for a population to live isolated or far away from others if it does not exceed a certain figure which one may call 'minimum population'. This problem can be approached and confirmed from three angles: the economic, the social, and the biological.

Biological minimum

The initial population must include at least one couple at a fertile age; but a great deal more are needed to avoid the risks of strong inbreeding. I shall not attempt to describe, or even to summarise, the results of the many works written on the subject by Dahlberg, Haldane, Livi, and Sutter.[1]

Since total isolation never occurs, the minimum size of an 'isolate' depends on the amount of communications it has within its smaller unit. Livio Livi notes that though fertile, certain oases or islands in the Aegean are uninhabited, and believes that demographic stability demands a population larger than five hundred. With five hundred inhabitants there can at least be five marriages and twelve births a year, though obviously there is very little choice of partnerships. Without considering physical decadence through mortality, or involuntary sterility, one can assume that in these small populations the reduced choice lessens the number of marriages and therefore the birth rate. Naturally the number of five hundred can only be a pointer. A smaller population grows fairly quickly to the minimum size, or shrinks, but does not remain stable near its initial state. This minimum of four hundred to five hundred obtains in a case of almost complete isolation. It applies especially to groups where monogamy is a regular practice. It drops with polygamy or free union: thus some eskimo tribes, that of the Thule for example, are stable at three hundred to four hundred, in spite of their isolation, because of seasonal sexual promiscuity.

The genetic factor also helps to determine the minimum figure. The first

[1] See especially Sutter's studies, first published in *Population* and in *L'Eugénique*: 'Problèmes, méthodes, résultats', Institut national d'études démographiques.

30

works on population genetics reasoned mathematically on the hypothesis of complete mixing: matings were assumed to be made at random and each group to duplicate itself from one generation to the next. These assumptions had later to be changed to take into account various factors, such as differential fertility, choice of partner, or mutations. Populations were then considered as combinations of small groups, which Dahlberg in Sweden called 'isolates'. Genetically, an isolate is the range of individuals within which one of them can marry. Dahlberg showed that the size of an isolate can be reckoned from the number of consanguineous marriages which take place in it, and concluded that in Sweden before the industrial era it was probably no more than four hundred to five hundred; this estimate would seem to apply equally well to other western countries and it agrees with the one Livi derived from different data.

Because the isolates were small there must have been strong inbreeding over long periods within these populations. As Haldane showed, this must have kept their mortality high and limited their fertility. The research of Sutter, Tabah, and Goux suggests that this process can still be observed in contemporary France. Though inbreeding is decreasing in Europe, thanks to communications, it is still important in Africa where it explains defects found in some populations.

One might extend these ideas a little and consider sanitary problems as 'biological'. A population can live indefinitely without the help of medicine since natural fecundity can compensate for a very poor sanitary environment, allowing for an average life of only twenty-five years or less. But people may in fact abandon a village voluntarily because there is no doctor there, and this too has to be considered as one of the economic and social factors.

Economic minimum

As technology develops, economic life demands ever larger manpower. At the hunting and gathering stage, one couple, or even an individual, can live alone like an animal. At the industrial stage any restriction on world trade has a painful effect on standards of living.

A careful distinction should however be made between the losses caused by lack of certain raw materials or imported goods and those due to insufficient division of labour. We are dealing with the second kind here. Notice too that the critical change here is not a drop in the standard of living (this will lead us later to the idea of an *optimum* population) so much as the crossing of a threshold below which life is no longer possible. In short we are seeking the *subsistence level*, with all the difficulties that arise from this phrase since it can be taken either objectively or subjectively.

Objectively the 'economic minimum' for a population is probably very small, with a very low standard of living. In certain mild climates and on the most fertile soils, there is nothing to prevent a Robinson Crusoe from living on his own and producing all he needs to live. But, without the benefits of division of labour, his standard of living would be low. And it could not be maintained beyond his span of active life.

In practice, the subjective minimum is more liable to occur, especially if we postulate not total but relative isolation. A family, or even a single man, may easily live on a farm, three or four, or even ten or twenty miles from anyone else, if there are satisfactory means of communication. A group of fifteen or twenty can live much further away, and so on. Introduce a regular postal service and the minimum number drops, but this increases the cost of the service, thus reducing its feasibility.

Thus, populating a large territory (French Guiana, for instance) is always difficult because there are not enough immigrants to begin with. The economic minimum can however be observed most often in mountain villages or small valleys isolated from the rest of the district. This case is worth studying closely.

Case of an almost isolated village or valley: Many formerly prosperous villages empty slowly – sometimes down to a new lower level, sometimes completely. When the locksmith and wheelwright leave for lack of custom, this so impoverishes the other villagers that the baker or shoemaker has to close down in turn. Overheads become heavier, and more and more people leave. Other factors may, however, make for a new equilibrium: more or better land for each, improvements in communications, subsidies to the community, or merely attachment to the native soil.

It is impossible to establish even an approximate figure here, since there is never total isolation. Even a slender life-line may increase the standard of living considerably and reduce the minimum population. But in a given district and in given technological and economic conditions, there is a critical threshold below which life becomes so difficult as to discourage all inhabitants. Authorities are then faced with the alternative of allowing complete depopulation and in the event speeding it up, or of keeping the numbers above the threshold by various protective measures.

Paid workers are the first to leave, as soon as wages outside pass a certain level; after this first stage only owner farmers and craftsmen (bakers, carpenters, etc.) remain. Each craftsman, similar in this to a collective service, represents a sum of overheads to be borne by all the inhabitants. The community pays for the upkeep of the baker as it would for a bus service. We will assume that all these craftsmen have more or less the same standard of living.

The top line of figure 11 plots the marginal standard of living three types of inhabitant against the population size.[1] Some farmers, on fertile lands are

---

[1] Or to be more precise the marginal living 'conditions' (including chores, working hours, etc.) – that is, not only a monetary level.

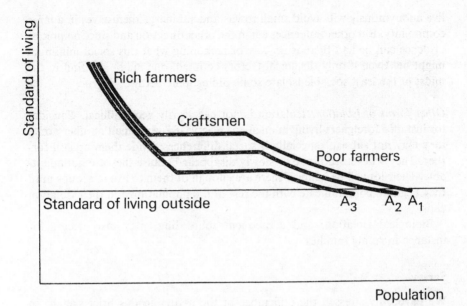

Figure 11. Depopulation of a village, with the critical threshold

richer than the craftsmen, some poorer. The horizontal line represents the standard of living of a worker outside the village. If farmer A_1, whose land is poor, leaves, the craftsmen's standard of living is lowered, and the whole population suffers a similar fall. We then get the second line down. Farmer A_2 will leave in his turn, and so forth. If living standards outside rise, the movement will increase, and living standards inside will drop faster: *as the craftsmen's standard of living approaches that of workers outside, the population drops below a critical threshold and living standards drop rapidly.*

In many ways things are more supple or more static than the diagram suggests, so that many French villages and valleys remain for a long time below this theoretical minimum.

Social minimum

This factor is more difficult to define than the previous two: it could be made to include subdivisions covering everything that is neither biological nor economical, or in other words all that cannot be directly expressed in terms of physical health or material well-being.

Insecurity has often led men to group together, to fortify themselves against single-handed or mass attacks. Then they also wish to have a varied acquaintance or to mix with people of a certain sort. Many a girl or youth has left a village in search of a dance hall or a sports club. Many people who wish to

33

live anonymously will avoid small towns and submerge themselves in a large community. But other influences act in the other direction and since no precise evidence can be had there is no way of reckoning what this social minimum might be. Even if only the social factors counted, one might still find in the midst of the least sociable isolate some philosophic hermit.

Other forms of isolation: Isolation is not necessarily geographical. Consider for instance foreigners living in an alien society. If a very small number arrive they may not subsist, especially if social differences divide them up still further. They will return home or slowly disappear because they are not adaptable. Their lot will be better if there are enough of them to live in groups until they begin to communicate with the rest of the population and their isolation ends.

Biological isolation, and subsequent inbreeding, may also occur, for instance in ruling families.

Survey

We have only stressed the difficulties of the matter in this brief sketch: in practice the various factors are hopelessly intertwined. It is at least useful to differentiate a physical, objective non-viability, from the voluntary dispersal of a population, though even this distinction is precarious.

At any rate, in industrial populations the economic minimum increases constantly as technology develops and division of labour becomes far-reaching. It may exist too in large-scale economics: thus a customs blockade can be a sufficiently isolating feature to relegate a population below the minimum level. Current efforts to obtain European unity may be linked with this view of a minimum population.

Biological difficulties on the other hand decrease. Through communications and the abandoning of over-distant villages the isolates break up one after the other.

In certain primitive civilisations, the biological minimum is an essential feature. Many native African populations should be studied from this angle.

Short bibliography

W. C. Boyd, *Genetics and the Races of Man*, Little, Brown and Co., Boston, 1950.

G. Dahlberg, *Mathematical Methods for Population Genetics*, Interscience Pub., New York, 1948.

Denise Ferembach, 'Quelques facteurs de formation et de développement d'un isolat', *Population*, Jan.–March 1961, pp. 71–88.

J. B. S. Haldane, Various articles in specialised journals such as *Annals of Eugenics* (since 1940).

L. Livi, *Trattato di demografia*, Vol. I: *I Fattori bio-demografici nell'*
ordinamento sociale, Vol. II: *Le leggi naturali della popolazione*, Cedam, Padua,
1940–41.

J. Malaurie, L. Tabah and J. Sutter, 'L'isolat esquimau de Thulé (Groenland)',
Population, Oct.–Dec. 1952, pp. 675–91.

J. Sutter and L. Tabah, 'Les notions d'isolat et de population minimum',
Population, July–Sept. 1951, pp. 481–98.

J. Sutter, 'Génétique de population et connaissance de l'homme', *Impact*, Sept.
1955, VI, No. 3, pp. 138–61.

J. Sutter and J.-M. Goux, 'L'aspect démographique des problèmes de l'isolat',
Population, July–Sept. 1961, pp. 447–62.

L. Thomas, 'Des peuples en voie de disparition: Les Fuegiens', *Les Cahiers*
d'outre-mer, Oct.–Dec. 1953, No. 24, pp. 379–98.

4

THE OPTIMUM POPULATION

'If there is such a thing as over-population and such a thing as under-population, it follows that between the two there must be such a thing as just the right population.'

FAIRCHILD

The phrase 'optimum population' may seem perfectly innocuous, but it can cause violent sentimental reactions because of interpretations of 'optimum' that have become associated with it. P. Vincent and Mrs A. Myrdal, for instance, write: 'this theory of optimum population . . . is a form of Malthus's theory of demographic pressure and supplies'.[1] Let us therefore make a fresh start, and give the words optimum and population their proper meanings.

An innocuous phrase

By 'population' we mean the number of men or inhabitants in a given sphere (district, or occupation, or social class). The word 'optimum' is a very innocent superlative, a synonym of 'best'. When one speaks of 'optimum population' one is seeking for the best possible number of men. The most violent opponents can agree on such a premise, even if they disagree on what they hold to be 'best'.

We all seek for an 'optimum' in everything: in the size of a ship, the length of a film, the age of statesmen, the temperature of a room. And yet it implies limitation, compromise: this is because it is essentially different from mere size alone. A wage-earner may seek not the optimum pay but the highest possible one; yet if he were made to realise that this ambition clashes with another value such as security of employment, he would soon come round to the idea of an optimum. In sport on the other hand there is no identifiable 'optimum' performance, because there is only one aim.

We may therefore soothe some qualms by disregarding for the time being the clash that may occur between optimum and maximum, and use optimum in its most general sense, which can in theory be the same as maximum. *An optimum population is the one that achieves a given aim in the most satisfactory way.* But expressed thus it is a static notion, and we shall see that this is a major flaw if only because it gives rise to misunderstandings.

[1] *Are there too many of us?* (UNESCO, Food and People, 1949).

The idea is very old. Without going back to Plato, we see Thomas More in his *Utopia* setting lower and higher limits for his ideal population.[1] It is also in Botero, Machiavelli, Cantillon, Necker, Rousseau,[2] Voltaire, Quesnay, Auxiron, Genovesi, Adam Smith, Benjamin Franklin, Malthus, Soden, Sismondi, and more generally in the minds of all who have accepted the possibility of overpopulation, however they defined it. But Man's reluctance in every situation to choose, and thus sacrifice, hampered for a long time and still hampers the setting up of a clear, and thereby brutal, doctrine on population. Schmitthenner for instance is content with 'the population arrived at its greatest strength and comfort', without seeing the contradictions in this definition.

Cannan did not invent the word optimum (Wicksell had written, in 1910, *Das optimum der Bevölkerung*), but he it is who is responsible for what is now called the theory of 'optimum population'. Those who maintain this are invariably moved by economic considerations, and assume it to be so eivdently the most important one that they usually fail to mention it. Since Cannan's time the phrase, and the theories that have sprung up around it have only found a very small number of supporters amongst specialists. But the idea seems to appeal to public opinion at its most vulgar and politics at their most base. Such an approach tends to consider welfare more desirable than numbers. The following remarks, therefore, are intended not so much to set up an abstract idea, as to define and name concepts that are generally only grasped confusedly though they lead to quite logical material decisions and collective opinions.

For the time being *the optimum population will be no more than a convenient idea*. The demographer may use it as an intermediate tool, as the mathematician uses imaginary numbers.

Various possible aims

What shall we aim at? Happiness perhaps, as Voltaire put it: 'the point is not to have men to spare, but to lessen as much as possible the misery of those we do have'. But happiness cannot be put into formulae. There are several more precise aims that men may have in mind:

[1] 'To the intent the prescript number of the citizens should neither decrease nor above measure increase, it is ordained that no family . . . shall at once have fewer children of the age of 14 years or thereabout than 10, or more than 16; for of children under this age no number can be prescribed or appointed. This measure or number is easily observed and kept, by putting them that in full families be above the number into families of smaller increase. But if chance be that in the whole city the store increase above the just number, therewith they fill up the lack of other cities.'

[2] 'A political body can be measured either by the area of its territory or by the numbers of its people, and between these measures there is a ratio that gives the State its true greatness' (*Le contrat social*).

1. *Individual welfare*, or a certain number of gratifications that as a whole are the object of a science called economics: this is the economic aim. 2. *Increase of wealth*, or rapidly rising welfare. If happiness depends on the increase of wealth in time rather than on wealth itself, we must ask what is the number, in an increasing (or decreasing) population, which gives the fastest increase of wealth. 3. *Employment*. The optimum population should be able to employ all people of working age who are fit enough; this definition, we shall see, can only be used in a system involving private property. 4. *Power*, or the various means that can be harnessed to a collective aim. This may, but does not have to be, military power. 5. *Long life*, *health*, which, especially in developed societies, is different from wealth. 6. *Culture*, *knowledge*, which may be considered as a form of wealth, but would in practice produce a different optimum. 7. *The sum of welfare*, or more precisely the total income of the population, suitably distributed. 8. *The sum of life*, i.e. population multiplied by the average life of its members. 9. *The number of inhabitants*. Here optimum is the same as maximum. One could imagine other aims such as social harmony (naturally influenced by numbers), stable families, etc. . . . Plato sees the collective optimum in a political light, Dupréel from an aesthetic point of view.

Instead of taking a static figure, one can also aim at an *optimum rhythm of variation of the population*; we shall consider this dynamic idea in chapter 21. Whatever the aim, if we are to study the optimum population we will have to assume that factors other than that of the number of men remain constant. Such an assumption is usually unquestioned, although in practice the numbers rarely vary without changing (or being changed by) some other factor which one can only eliminate in theory. To study a population generally, we must first study the separate effect of each factor. The links between the different factors raise very delicate questions which we must consider later.

Basic hypotheses

We will leave aside for a moment the criticisms that may be levelled at the idea of a static optimum, as well as the uses it may have, and start by listing the main factors assumed to be constant:
1. *Material resources*, including past achievements as well as natural resources. 2. *The level of technology*, which influences welfare to a large extent. (This assumption causes many misunderstandings, for even if it does not conceal latent thoughts, it is suspected of doing so.) 3. *The age structure*, and more generally the variation between the output and consumption of different individuals. We will start off by assuming that all individuals have equal productivity and equal needs, but we shall see that the logic does not change if they are not equal, as long as their distribution into various categories remains constant. 4. *The distribution of goods:* to simplify, we will start by

postulating uniform distribution, though one could merely assume it to be constant. 5. *Internal economic stability:* constant working hours, full employment, no international trade or migration. Our logic can remain valid or be easily adapted if there is a stable unemployment ratio, if migrations balance out, or if external trade does not fluctuate.

This defines an abstract model aimed at isolating clearly the only influence considered here: that of numbers. The reader should keep these assumptions in mind throughout the following chapters where they will continue to apply.

Definition of 'output'

If the materials useful to mankind numbered only one, it would not be too difficult to define output. If we had only to produce wheat the annual figures would be easy to reckon. But the great number of useful goods makes it necessary to use a conversion scale that is necessarily arbitrary. It may for instance be determined by the tastes or choice of aims of individuals (wealth, health, etc.), or again by a compromise between various views.

We need only assume that the population considered *does have* its conversion scales, and we need not enter into their rational foundations. They may depend on the amount of goods of each category produced. The main thing is that it should be possible to assess a given array of goods in 'production units'. We shall see in chapter 9 how this assessment is or can be done effectively.

The economic and social system

We have made precise assumptions in order to isolate the influence of numbers, but we must try for the time being *to formulate general statements, valid as far as possible for any economic or social system.* However, the scale of values or equivalents for measuring output changes with the system, indeed with legislation; so in talking of numbers we shall have to assume that for a population in a given territory the system itself does not vary. In other words the first of the generalisations that follow on this or that optimum will apply to any system; but as they are applied they will become sensitive to changes in the conversion scale.

The optimum population may only be a pointer

One of the latent thoughts, real or suspected, about the optimum population, is that because one reckons the optimum level of population one wishes to attain it. This is not true. When one says that the 500 million inhabitants of India would be more at ease if there were only 300 million, one does not mean that 200 million should be shot. The optimum, like the maximum, can be no more than a useful pointer. Anyone is free to reckon as many optimums as he can conceive of: he will be helping the study of how numbers of men act on various other interesting factors.

The choice of an aim

After this reassuring stricture, which aim shall we choose amongst those mentioned above? We might almost say, with Cantillon, 'that is an ethical matter and I am not concerned with it'. Men may choose this or that aim – the discussion of their choice and their motives is in quite another field. Since our object here is to describe the optimum where a given aim has been chosen and we do not have time to explore every avenue, let us follow the choices men make in practice.

In certain patriarchal or religious societies, there is no rival aim to numbers. Optimum and maximum here are one and the same. Often in authoritarian regimes, the main aim is power – this determines a *power optimum*. In other cases *individual welfare* seems to have the edge over other considerations.

It has been argued, by Sismondi for instance, that 'comfort' or 'welfare' is not a legitimate aim. He was the first to reason on the 'king of England' example: suppose that through extraordinary technological discoveries the king of England were enabled to live alone on his island with an extremely high standard of living. Could this solution be considered an optimum?[1] Without even introducing extra-economic motivations (let us at least allow the poor chap the company of his queen and a few friends) one may find it distasteful from the outset that human lives be sacrificed to improve the lives of others; even if the principle of such selective restriction is admitted, there still remain problems of size and measurement. Notice also that Sismondi's logic rests, as do so many of our own contemporaries, on the assumption that technological progress reduces the economic optimum. We shall see in chapter 15 what to think of that.

This is not the place to defend this or that aim. But it is a fact that amongst western populations welfare does play such an important part that in many minds it becomes the essential aim. Men tend to prefer greater wealth combined with smaller numbers. On the scale of the individual family this ideal almost always predominates. It is therefore useful to see what this wish can and does lead to. And even if the aim is not explicitly pursued, remember that knowledge of the economic optimum can give useful pointers in economic analysis.

One may also take into account the mobility of a population, the fact that it generally grows, and that wealth is essentially relative, and try to determine

---

[1] 'What! is wealth everything and men absolutely nothing? Then there only remains to desire that the king, left on his own on the island, may by turning a handle have the whole work of England accomplished by automates.'

the numbers that will ensure the greatest accumulation of wealth as the population rises.

The other aims are less real in men's minds, or else the problems of methodology they set are the same. Thus by preferring long life to comfort we may change the conversion scales of goods – giving alcohol a lower value for instance – but not the theory. With a few transpositions one could say almost the same of 'culture' as an aim.

We will therefore concentrate on the power optimum and especially on the economic optimum.

5

THE ECONOMIC OPTIMUM[1]

'The criterion of welfare has more supporters than others because it is of all human ambitions the most general, the most constant and the most actively pursued.'

LANDRY

The 'optimum population' is only a convenient phrase. When we say that a country is economically 'overpopulated' we mean that its population is higher than its economic optimum at the present moment.

The assumptions made in the preceding chapter apply here, as does the provisional definition of 'output'. There remains to define 'standard of living', provisionally, as the average output per individual (we will discuss this later when we study the distribution of wealth).

Imagine that fifty to one hundred men have to live in a given territory, England for instance. Even with very advanced technology and culture they will be unable to run railways, steel foundries, etc., and will have to be content to live as craftsmen, or even as shepherds. The standard of living will be very low. If on the contrary 200 to 500 million people were to try to live on the same island they would have to cultivate even the poorest soils, usually by hand, so as to obtain the highest output per acre; the standard of living would be equally low. Between these two extremes there must be more beneficial intermediate positions. *The most beneficial of all is called the optimum.*

Graphic models

In figure 12 the graph plotting the individual standard of living against population gives the bell-shaped curve S. ON_o is the optimum population, N_oM_o is the highest possible standard of living as long as the other factors do not vary.

The question now arises whether there could be two or several optimums. We might perhaps have a camel-shaped curve with two humps. Gini for instance reckoned on two optimum levels, one at the agricultural stage and one at the industrial stage. But we have decided in this chapter not to consider the time factor or the influence of technological progress.

[1] See Giorgio Fua: *La Conception économique de l'optimum de peuplement. Population et bien-être*, Lausanne, 1940.

42

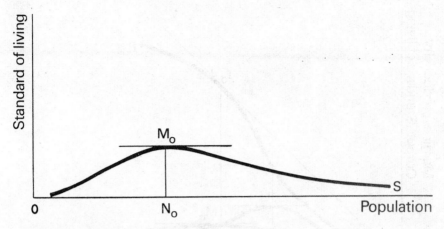

Figure 12. Standard of living as a function of population.

The total output is obtained by multiplying the number of inhabitants ON by their average output M_oN_o.

In figure 13 we now plot against population not only the standard of living or average output (S) but also the total output (P). At any point I the standard of living MN can also be measured by the tangent of the angle ION. Therefore when the standard of living is at its highest (M_oN_o) the tangent at I_o to curve P passes through the origin. On the right of I_o the output does not increase fast enough; the angle ION (not marked) decreases.

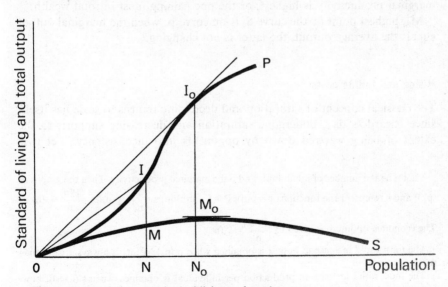

Figure 13. Population, standard of living and total output.

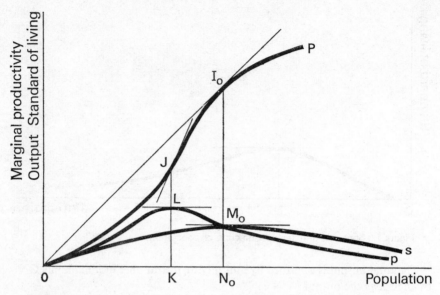

Figure 14. Marginal productivity, total output and standard of living.

We now draw the derivative p of the curve P. It represents the marginal productivity or increase in output by adding one person (see page 38). p is also a bell-shaped curve, but less flattened than S. The maximum L corresponds to the point J where P inflects. OK is the population for which marginal productivity is highest, or the one gaining most in total wealth.

M_o, highest point of the curve S, is on curve p: when the marginal output equals the average output, the latter is not changing.[1]

Rising and falling costs

The classical concept of saturation and decreasing returns to scale has itself, since Ricardo's day, undergone saturation and decreasing support, to the extent of being watered down by opponents into inconsistency. Yet it is

---

[1] Let n be the number of inhabitants and p the marginal productivity. Then the graphs of p, P and s represent the functions $p=p(n)$, $P=\int_o^n p(n)dn$, $s=\frac{1}{n}\int_o^n p(n)dn=\frac{P(n)}{n}=s(n)$

The economic optimum is given by $\frac{P(n_o)}{n_o}=P'(n_o)$

The most rapid increase in output is obtained when $p'(n_e)=0$; n_o is always greater than n_e.

The most rapid increase in production per individual is obtained when $s''(n)=0$; however this equation need not necessarily have any solutions.

44

essential to understanding a society's economic and demographic problems, particularly in the agricultural stage.

The main objection to it is that it is impossible to classify forms of activity according to whether they produce increasing or decreasing returns. Some say that the returns in any activity first increase and then decrease, and end at a state of saturation. In a factory for instance, productivity rises when the number of workers is first increased; then drops when they become too numerous to be properly employed.

The difference reappears however when we consider that the plant itself can be expanded. A mine, a farm, a fishing ground may have decreasing returns because it is difficult to build or find a second similar to the first. But when a factory is fully employed, it is possible to build two or three others without increasing the costs proportionally, and even sometimes to design a larger, more efficient one. The cost of materials going into the building may well rise, but this rise is due to a primary activity, with decreasing returns.

Decreasing returns or increasing costs appear in theory to characterise the exploitation of natural resources, especially in agriculture. Of course, we assume that technology is stationary. The variable quality of land lessens the output of those who have to farm new land, because the best has generally been farmed first. In the same way if one increases the number of men working on a piece of land without varying their technology, output will always increase somewhat, but usually not in proportion to the number of workers.

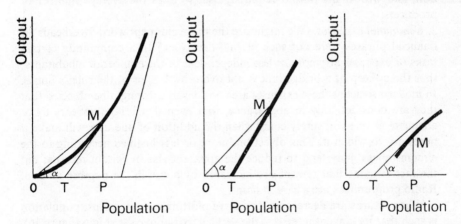

Figure 15. Various types of increasing returns.

When returns are rising, the tangent to the curve plotting total output against population always crosses the vertical axis below the origin. The angle MOP = α represents productivity. On the left-hand graph the function is always convex downwards, on the right-hand one it is concave downwards, and on the middle one the point M follows a straight line. In every case the angle MOP increases as M moves to the right.

The reserves in mines vary; game does not increase proportionally to the number of hunters; fishing grounds have to be moved, and so on. Any exploitation of natural resources (such as hydro-electric dams, forests, agricultural gathering, tidal energy, etc.) has to grapple with habitually decreasing returns.

On the other hand in certain fields two factors make for increasing returns to scale:

1. *Division of labour* allows individuals to specialise and favours productivity and mass production. This is not technological progress so much as making better use of existing means at a given stage of technology. Thanks to division of labour, machines can be used which men may have possessed but could not employ without individuals specialising. For ten readers one uses a typewriter, for one thousand a printing press. Besides even without a machine it does not, for instance, take ten times as long to wash ten plates as to wash one.

Rises in increasing returns usually occur in activities which transform homogeneous materials.

When returns increase with the number of producers, it does not follow that the making of one article should be concentrated into one plant. Differences inevitably arise and set a limit to the concentration. But as the population, and with it the output required, rise, so does the average number of producers.

2. *Communal expenses.* (We might use the more eloquent word 'overheads', if financial phrases were not such eternal deceivers.) In a community certain tasks or expenses are more or less independent of the number of inhabitants: thus the upkeep of a bridge that is not overcrowded, or of the ruler's house. In modern societies these expenses are considerable. It might be objected that they are constant only in appearance, that even if a bridge appears to be adequate a time will surely come when the addition of one user will make it necessary to widen it. This objection, more or less justified according to the circumstances, may tend to reduce the apparent rise in certain returns; but the fact remains that returns are increased by a rise in the number of men. Radio programmes are a case in point.

When returns are decreasing, the curve plotting output against population is such that its tangent intersects the vertical axis above the origin (figure 16). MOP again represents productivity. On the left-hand graph, the curve is constantly convex upwards. On the middle one M moves along a straight line. The right-hand curve is concave upwards, but its asymptote crosses the horizontal axis to the left of the origin.

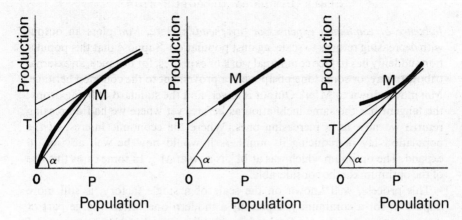

Figure 16. Various types of diminishing returns.

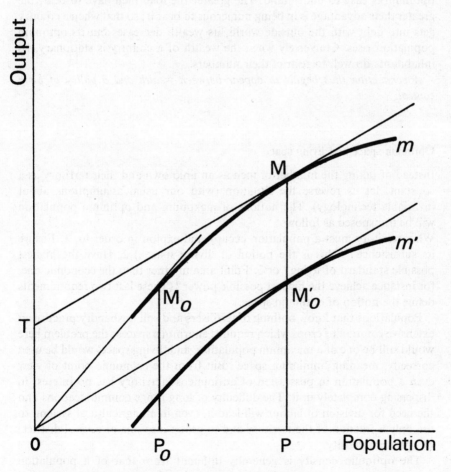

Figure 17. 'Overheads' increase the optimum population.

47

Influence of communal expenses or 'overheads': Here, Mm plots an output with decreasing returns to scale, against population. Suppose that this population suddenly has to face communal work or expenses, for instance, an external tribute to pay, or some long postponed improvement to the common heritage. Mm moves down to M$'m'$. Output is lower, and the standard of living drops; the tangent has the same inclination as before, yet where we had decreasing returns we now have increasing ones. Where the economic interest of the population lay in reducing its numbers it would now be well advised to expand. The optimum which was at M_o, is now at M'_o. In some cases this rise of the optimum can be considerable.

This process, well known on the scale of a single factory, is still more important for a community, especially a modern one where a large part of these communal tasks are financed by 'public expenditure'. The change of optimum is easy to understand. The greater the load men have to bear, the greater their advantage is in being numerous to bear it; so that when a country gets into debt with the outside world, its wealth decreases but its optimum population rises. Conversely when the wealth of a country is stationary, its inhabitants do well to restrict their numbers.

A connection thus begins to appear between wealth and a policy of birth control.

Optimum space and living space

Instead of taking the number of men as an unknown and their territory as a constant, let us reverse the situation (with our usual assumptions about invariable technology). The notions of maximum and optimum population will be transposed as follows:

What territory must a population occupy and exploit in order to: 1. Ensure its subsistence? (This is the notion of 'living space'.) 2. Have the highest possible standard of living? or 3. Fulfil an aim other than the economic one, for instance achieve the highest possible power? (These last two requirements define the notion of optimum space.)

Populations that know nothing of fertilisers and soil husbandry·practise an extensive rotation of crops which requires enormous spaces; the problem here would still be one of a maximum population, and 'living space' would be used correctly, meaning 'minimum space'. But from the economic point of view even a population in possession of an immense territory has no interest in dispersing completely in it. The difficulty of long range communications and the need for division of labour will lead it, even in an agricultural system, to use only a fraction of the territory and to group into one or several districts of optimum density.

The optimum density is generally different from that of a population

48

occupying the whole territory and reaching its optimum numbers.[1] If we were to suppose the space to be completely homogeneous, the two densities would not be very different, but the two problems are made different by the existence of boundaries and limits.

If a huge space is suddenly opened up (take the discovery of the New World for instance) men are driven by individual initiative, a desire for freedom, property or adventure, or by the speculative spirit, beyond the boundaries marking for the time being the most profitable way of settling.

The optimum space for power cannot be found merely by reversing the concepts referring to the optimum population. The population's power optimum is, we shall see, more dense than its economic optimum. But in this case, the number of men being a constant, the possible power varies with output and standard of living. The maximum power occurs where the territory allows the highest output. The power objective is therefore at one with the economic objective.

In the special case of military power, non-economic objectives arise: either to extend the territory by occupying strategic points, or to restrict it in defence against a more powerful enemy.

Take the case of the first Europeans in America; even disregarding the resistance of native populations, the first arrivals would have been ill-advised to spread out too much. They lived as a society and could not manage without each other. Foreign trade was vital and required high densities at certain coastal spots. But too strong a concentration would have reduced the agricultural resources too far; hence the notion of an optimum space which increased constantly with the population.

In the general climate of growth and development during this pioneering age, the problem always lay in building for the future, so that at every period the population used a space larger than the optimum of the time. But in fact attitudes varied a great deal: whereas the English occupied the land methodically and progressively, the Spaniards looked wildly for gold, and the French were often content to seek their fortune in the woods.

Although the Marxist doctrine does not recognise the notion of optimum population, or, therefore, that of overpopulation, the various Communist countries felt it useful to expand westwards into new empty territories in 1945.

There is no known situation where economic reasons have been strong enough to override political ones and bring about permanent restrictions on

---

[1] Let n be the population and E the space it occupies. The total output P is a function of both n and E, $P = P(n,E)$.

If n is fixed the optimum space ensures the maximum output, so $\dfrac{dP}{dE} = 0$

Similarly, where space is fixed, it is possible to calculate optimum population, and thus population density.

the national space. *Thus the idea of optimum space has not the same import as the idea of optimum population.*

On the other hand, the growth of towns is lending an ever greater impact to the idea of *optimum density*. The old wish to live within reach of one's own work and of shops extends today to educational and medical facilities, and leads men to crowd on to a very small part of their national territory.

6

THE POWER OPTIMUM

'For though it be true (as Machiavelli in his absurd subtlety puts
forward) that good soldiers and not money are the nerves of war, yet
those nerves would not move and do great things if the poultice of
money were not applied to them.'

GENTILLET

In history, power has often had the edge over individual welfare as an aim. It
is therefore worthwhile asking which numbers ensure the greatest power in a
given territory (the assumptions made in chapter 4 still apply here). Power
does not necessarily mean military power – it represents a collective aim which
may or may not take the form of armament.

Search for the greatest power

To simplify things for a moment, consider again the 'subsistence level'
described in chapter 3. Above this minimum the output of one man is assumed

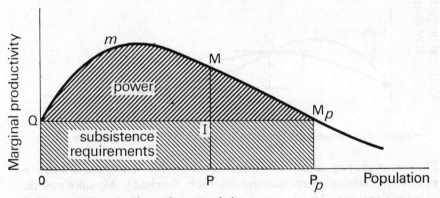

Figure 18. Power optimum for a population.

to be constant; below, it is assumed to be very weak or non-existent, either
because of mortality or a morbid state, or for other reasons.
Here we plot once again the variations in marginal productivity against the
population. This productivity starts at a very low figure, which we will

51

assume for the sake of clarity to be equal to the subsistence level (this assumption does not change our results at all). It rises to a maximum and then falls asymptotically towards zero, or at any rate lower than the subsistence level.

The public authorities acquire material power by levying a certain amount of wealth off each man's output. To get the greatest possible power with a given population, everything above the subsistence level should be levied, leaving each with just enough to live and work, and spending the rest of the resources on the aim pursued (armament for instance).

For a population OP whose marginal output is MP, the total output OQmMPO can be divided into two parts: the rectangle OQIP, ensuring the population's subsistence, and the area QmMIQ, left for the pursuit of the power objective. This area is greatest when M is at Mp and the marginal output of an extra worker is equal to his subsistence level. The optimum population ensuring the highest power is thus OPp. Any extra inhabitant above this figure, not producing enough supplies for himself, would not be useful since he would need part of the output of the others to feed him, thus diminishing the power of the group.

Relative positions of the various optimums

How is this power optimum situated? It is obviously smaller than the maximum population and we can see by how much:

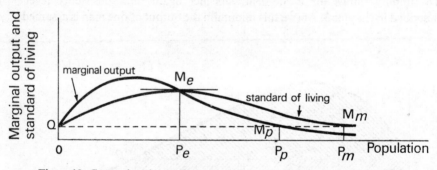

Figure 19. Comparing the maximum population to the power optimum.

The maximum population corresponds to the point Mm whose ordinate is equal to the subsistence requirement. Mm is to the right of Mp since past the economic optimum Mp the curve of average output is above the curve of marginal output. On the other hand, the power optimum is always higher than the economic optimum: except in an extreme situation with no practical equivalent, it is when enjoying the maximum comfort, with the marginal output higher than the subsistence requirements, that a population finds that with increased numbers its power will expand.

Thus when a population rises and the other factors are constant, it goes through successive positions ensuring: 1. *The minimum population*. 2. *Maximum marginal productivity*, or fastest rate of growth in total output – see pages 43–4 and page 44, fn. 1. *Maximum standard of living*, at the 'economic optimum' (see chapter 5). 4. *Maximum power*, at the 'power optimum' – which is also the maximum population attainable in a system without exchange or compensation between producers, each one only receiving the output he had helped towards. This point deserves closer examination (see chapter 10). 5. *Maximum population*, which is also the one ensuring in certain conditions the highest total output.

Military power and an armed population

So far, what we have said applies to any sort of power, or even to any common aim alien to individual comfort – such as exploring outer space – at least in its first stages. Now consider the particular instance of military power.

To have an army it is not sufficient to levy wealth from the output in order to produce weapons; men have to be levied too, and their subsistence taken care of. But why, the reader may ask, differentiate between the men who produce weapons and those who use them? Are they not equally useful to power and useless to the standard of living? Indeed, with certain conventions they could be assimilated to each other. But in practice accounts are kept of the production of weapons while it is difficult to do the same for the 'production' achieved by soldiers. Armament output can easily be included in our marginal productivity graphs, whereas military production is so different in nature that the graph would have to be arbitrarily altered. We will therefore keep to the difference imposed by the facts.

By levying men for military service the factors defining the optimum are altered: non-productive soldiers will be supplied out of the surplus output of active workers, which we have called 'power'. It is therefore exactly as if the soldiers were an addition to the population. *The optimum population is therefore increased by the number of non-productive soldiers.* To take an example, this means that during the last war, each time the Germans requisitioned a civilian in an occupied country and made him take over the job left by a German soldier, it was only in their interest if the immigrant worker produced more than his own subsistence requirements. *The demographic power optimum of Germany was increased by the number of soldiers taken out of production.* But of course any extra supplies diverted to sustain the increased manpower, *were at the expense of the power available for armament.*

Military power thus demands a two-fold increase over the economic optimum: *a first increase from the economic optimum to the power optimum, and a second one to cater for the soldiers using the weapons.* There is a ratio binding these two increases. Military technicians advise on the proportions to be

C 53

maintained, determining the number of soldiers and thus the effective optimum population including the soldiers.[1]

Figure 20 represents this graphically. OP_p is the power optimum where there is no army. The army is represented by P_pP_s, and the new optimum is at

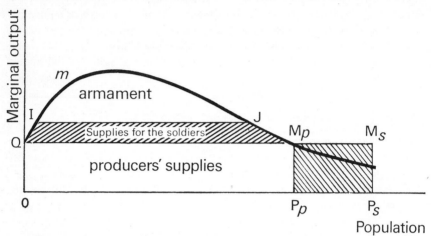

Figure 20. Power optimum, army and armament.

OP_s. The area of the rectangle $P_pM_pM_sP_s$ represents the supplies for the army, and should be deducted from the power QmM_pQ. The area $QIJM_pQ$ is equal to that of the rectangle $P_pM_pM_sP_s$. This leaves the area $ImJI$ for armament. Its ratio to the number of soldiers P_pP_s, or armament per soldier, determines all the elements in the figure.

[1] Let $p=p(n)$ be the marginal productivity.

If there has been no levy of men, the population giving the power maximum is n_p, where $p(n_p)=v$, v being the subsistence requirement.

The power of the population is $P= \int p(n)dn - vn = P(n) - vn$.

Now let s be the number of soldiers, n remaining the number of producers.
The armed strength is $P(n)-(n+s)$ v.

The armament per soldier is $\dfrac{P(n)-(n+s)v}{s}=K$ and K is then the optimal armament

per soldier, which we suppose fixed and known.

Rearranging this expression $s=\dfrac{P(n)-nv}{K+v}$, which is to be maximised since armaments are

in fixed proportion to it. This maximum occurs when $\dfrac{ds}{dn}=0$, i.e. $P'(n)=V$, and thus there is

a value n_p for which $p(n_p)=v$ giving the optimum number of producers.

Now the optimum population is $s+n_p=\dfrac{P(n_p+n_pK)}{K+v}$.

If K is infinite, $s=0$; and if $K=0$, $s+n_p=\dfrac{P(n_p)}{v}$.

It is clear that the power optimum drops as the armament per soldier increases; where it is non-existent (in the extreme case of a primitive population armed with clubs), the optimum rises and approaches the maximum population; where the armament is infinite (the other extreme, where a population builds up a peace-time armoury for an insignificant permanent army) we are back at optimum OP_p. The power optimum thus remains higher than the economic optimum.

However perfect the weapons, and even in the fictitious case of a 'push-button' war, economic overpopulation remains a factor of military power.[1]

If instead of seeking the optimum we start from a factual situation and a given total population, the formulae on page 54, and their elaboration, enable us to divide the population into producers and soldiers, and even into weapon-producers, supply-producers and soldiers.

The subsistence level as a variable

Up to now we have considered the subsistence level as a constant, meaning the supplies necessary to keep production going. This was a convenient assumption to simplify calculations and define clearly the notion of the power optimum. But in practice things work out differently. Even if we think of Man as an animal and consider merely his physiological needs, we have to admit that his output increases with better food and a more clement temperature. This resilience is even greater if we remember that he has acquired needs belonging to the way of life he is used to.

Output can thus decrease even where the drop in welfare does not affect basic bodily needs, and without considering variations in people's 'spirit' or urge to produce. Experienced leaders claim for instance that a worker or a soldier will suffer so much from lack of tobacco, for instance, that his output will fall. A man used to a certain way of life is weakened by a psycho-physiological reaction that it is difficult for him to struggle against immediately. Less well balanced, he will produce less. Thus the subsistence level, even where strictly defined by the output aimed at, varies with countries and circumstances. During the Second World War, for example, it was higher in the United States than in Germany, and higher in Germany than in the USSR.

In the USSR perhaps even the lower limit was crossed: if the life of a nation is at stake, it may be in its interest to encroach into basic subsistence requirements, even if output suffers a little. If a 10 per cent decrease in supplies only leads to a 3 per cent drop in output, power will still be increased. This seems to have happened in the USSR. In such a vast country the conditions cannot be

[1] This claim may however be changed if the armament industry use great quantities of valuable raw materials. But at this stage in our argument we are not considering the influence of shifts in consumption.

rigorously equal for each district and occupation at every moment. If they do not stick as closely as possible to the optimum subsistence level, the authorities run the risk of lacking weapons and losing the war. And if they keep very close to it, the limit will inevitably be crossed here and there. Because the USSR was making such a strenuous war effort and because of the shortages due to the invasion, hitches such as this occurred and there were peaks of mortality. These were kept a very close secret, and yet they do not show that the war was badly conducted or that reckonings were too ambitious. On the contrary the losses may have been required by the national interest. Soldiers are often sacrificed to defend a position; in the same way it may prove necessary to sacrifice part of the civilian population to avoid losses of land and a defeat which would have resulted in the USSR being amputated of even greater numbers. In conditions such as these the importance of the individual obviously shrinks before that of the community.[1]

Maximum power of a given population

At a given stage of technology, power depends on two variables: the number of men and the standard of living they are allowed.

To separate clearly the influence of the standard of living, let us reverse the situation, and assume that the numbers are a constant. This is indeed the problem which faces a country in war-time when it is using the whole of its population fit to work, and cannot call on any foreign labour.

If the standard of living is very low, almost minimal, output will be very low indeed; at the other extreme, above a certain standard of living, output would only increase very little and might even decrease. There is obviously an intermediate standard of living which is equivalent not to a maximum output, but to a maximum available output.

Consider figure 21, which (note the change) plots the standard of living against output P. The supplies required by the population are plotted by the straight line OS (the population is measured by the tangent of angle QOS). P increases quickly at first, then slowly. For a standard of living OJ output is MJ, consisting of supplies IJ and power MI. Power is at its maximum when M is at Mp, the point where the tangent is parallel to OS.

General case: Let us now return to our two variables, since public authorities can usually act both on standard of living and on numbers, by encouraging immigration or making use of inactive people. *What is the best position on the graph to achieve maximum power?*[2]

---

[1] On the losses of population in the USSR during the war, see J-N. Biraben, 'Essai sur l'évolution démographique de l'URSS', *Population*, June 1958, No. 2 *bis*, and October–December 1961, page 894.

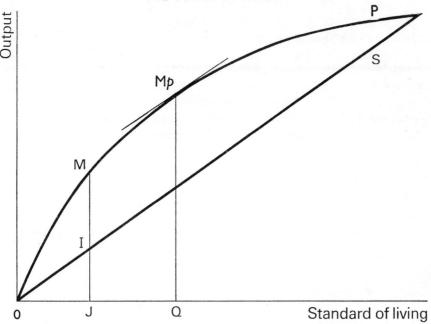

Figure 21. Standard of living ensuring the highest power.

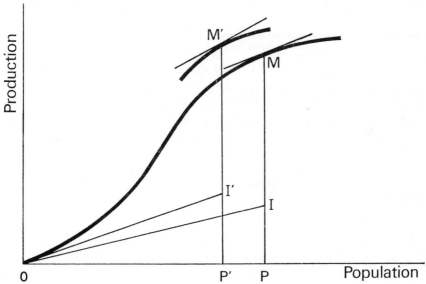

Figure 22

[2] The total output is $P(n,v)$ with $P_v(n,v) > 0$, the consumption is nv and the power $P(n,v) - nv$.

Neglecting s, the number of soldiers, the power is maximum when
$$P_n(n,v) = v, \text{ i.e. } p(n,v) = v,$$
$$\text{and } P_v(n,v) = n.$$
These equations determine n and v.

On figure 22 we see that for a standard of living POI we have a production curve OM with M so placed that the tangent is parallel to OI. OP is therefore the population ensuring the highest power (MI) when the standard of living is POI. For a higher standard of living, P'OI', we have a different graph, with a point M' and a maximum power M'I'. Nothing in the figure can tell us whether M'I' is higher or lower than MI. If, where there is a small variation in the standard of living, the power remains the same, then the optimum has been achieved. The shape of the curve determines it.

Numerical applications: Consider the United States and the USSR, the figures given are not even orders of magnitude, but merely plausible examples, to suggest how sensitive power is to the basic data.

Let us take as our economic unit the output of a Russian in 1963. Assuming the following figures are given for 1963, with a rather arbitrary 'recognised minimum of standard of living', we have this table:

	USA	USSR
Population	190	220
Output per person	2·7	1
Recognised minimum standard of living	1·2	0·3
Total output	513	220
Part used for supplies	228	66
Amount left and available for power	285	154

So in this case the amounts available for power are in the ratio of 1·85 to 1.

These figures need to be made a little less rigid. If an American were prepared to consume 0·6, or only twice what a Russian does, his country's power would increase from 285 to 399 and the ratio of power would be 2·6 to 1. On the other hand, if output per person goes on increasing as it is now, by 1·5 per cent a year in the United States and 5 per cent in the Soviet Union, and the recognised minimum increases with output in the United States and remains stable in the Soviet Union, in ten year's time we will have something like this:

	USA	USSR
Population	220	260
Output per person	3·13	1·67
Recognised minimum standard of living	1·4	0·3
Total output	689	441
Part used for supplies	308	78
Amount left and available for power	381	363

The amounts available for power here would be about equal.

Now take France and the United States. The national output is distributed more or less like this.

	France	United States
Output per person	100	220
Used for civilian purposes	92	194
Used for military purposes	8	26

So as well as having a standard of living more than two and a half times higher, every American can give 3·25 *times more than a Frenchman to his country's power. Since the populations are in a ratio of* 4 *to* 1, *the ratio of military strength is of* 13 *to* 1.

If they were to accept the same standard of living as the French the Americans could have 16 *times more power per inhabitant and* 64 *times more as a nation*. It will be appreciated how sensitive these margins are.

Concept of power extended

As we pointed out, these figures and formulae do not necessarily apply to military power but to a *collective aim* – essentially different from an economic aim, which leads on the contrary to a division of output by the numbers of producers or inhabitants.

Armament is not divided by the number of inhabitants, but it is not alone in this: anything to do with national prestige, for instance cultural dissemination, has the same quality. The monarch who levies as many taxes as he can for his personal wealth does not necessarily seek power, but the result is the same. In building cathedrals collectively, the Middle Ages were seeking the power optimum rather than the economic optimum. The same applies to interplanetary travel.

If however we consider collective aims of another sort – such as internal cultural development, or the progress of medicine – output is no longer independent of numbers. Though a central research laboratory may be a useful investment, from which all will potentially benefit, this cannot be so until vaccine or books can be mass-produced for each individual. This brings us back to the question of 'overheads' or communal expenses. These can be integrated into the economic reckonings defining output as a function of the number of producers, excluding power in the narrower sense. But if the political regime is such that the government wants, at least temporarily, to increase collective satisfaction at the expense of individual comfort, this changes the priorities and hence the output-population graph. The aim will then be to increase the population. For instance, if instead of aiming at making private houses and individual kitchens a country finds gratification in collective housing, its economic optimum will be somewhat increased.

This is one of the reasons for the Soviet 'populationist' policy, as opposed to the tendency of the West towards limitation of numbers.

7

FIRST INTERPRETATION OF THE OPTIMUM POPULATION

'If all men are called by Nature to multiply and to want to preserve their children, and the population has to be limited, then one wants to know beforehand which part of society can order the other to renounce these natural feelings.'

NECKER

The idea itself, though innocent enough as we have seen, has stirred up much criticism. We are now better placed to see the main reasons why.

1. The idea has only been understood in the sense of 'economic optimum', already an unfair restriction. Though even in this work we sometimes abbreviate it by missing out the word 'economic', this does not imply the primacy of the economic point of view.

2. It has often been used in support of Malthusian theory, by people who have implied that the population of the country they were talking of was above the (economic) optimum.

3. The word optimum gives a false impression of scientific precision, whereas in practical applications one can only suggest a rough figure without being precise. The vaguer and less quantitative notion of 'overcrowding' and the even vaguer one of 'underpopulation' are less pretentious.

4. Many people consider the idea of a static optimum to be an abstraction without any bearing on reality. We shall see why such criticism is too dogmatic.

5. The various questions that arise have become confused. It is well worth listing them separately in order to avoid further misunderstandings: a. Is the economic optimum the main aim amongst all the possible ones? *Since a choice is being suggested between the economic field and others, economists are not competent to answer this question.* b. *If the answer to the first is yes,* can the optimum population of a given country at a given time be defined and measured precisely enough? This is a delicate question. Many authors suggest that there is an optimum but gloss over it and do not calculate it. c. If in a given country at a given time reckonings show that the optimum population has been passed, must one try to reduce the gap? d. If so, should one try to change the optimum population or the real population?

Applications of the idea of an optimum

To define the economic optimum we have to assume factors to be constant whereas they are not so: in practice they all vary together. Before studying this variation, let us dwell a little on historical circumstances where the economic optimum has become apparent either because numbers alone have varied or because they have varied so quickly as to put other factors into the background.

After the Black Death of 1348 there was a sudden drop in population, with technology and the other factors remaining constant. According to Y. Renouard[1] this sudden change brought back economic balance to France: 'the sudden scarcity of labour brought an increase in wages and hence in prices; people who lived off investments or owned poorer land, which tenants abandoned . . . were ruined'. Obviously the population had been higher than the economic optimum before the plague, and probably still was even afterwards. In England the same thing is suggested by the improvement in the standard of living, especially amongst labourers.

Now change to the future or the conditional: if part of the population of a country were destroyed by bacteriological warfare, without material equipment being affected, the standard of living of the survivors might, according to the case, rise or fall. One would then say that the population had been above or below its optimum economic level.

The dramatic nature of these examples stresses sufficiently *the unpleasantness of the idea of a static economic optimum*. Practical applications are always linked with some catastrophe – the very idea suggests a harsh sentence passed on the men who could be considered as supernumerary. In the usual analyses of the idea, the air at this point is full of heavy innuendos. Authors usually describe the theory as if the optimum was only there to be exceeded; and since the men judged to be redundant are often of social categories or races already considered inferior, quantitative population control includes a more or less explicit condemnation of the 'undesirables'.

The optimum population is frequently invoked in relation to *unemployment caused by over-population*. Amongst the aims one can have in influencing numbers, we have already mentioned full employment. A lone individual can get food for himself through work, but in a large population an economic or social change may give people, at least those who work, a better chance of work but less opportunity to eat, or the reverse. One could then, perhaps, take as an objective the size of population at which there is work for all. If there are four million permanently unemployed in Egypt, including partially unemployed and underemployed, and eight million if one includes the idlers, we might then say that the population is eight million above its optimum level.

---

[1] *Population* July–September 1948, page 82. Other similar circumstances could be quoted.

Popular opinion

Though the phrase 'optimum population' is not used in everyday conversation, the idea is implied. Take these two popular truisms:

1. *'There is a limited number of jobs available'*. In other words, if the number of workers rises above a certain figure, unemployment will be inevitable. One could translate this widespread idea thus: 'the employable population is higher than a certain figure which could be called an optimum'. In fact popular opinion is not quite so blunt and the limited amount of jobs is not always explicit. But the policies suggested or carried out are based on the accepted idea that 'the number of jobs is a constant in the economic situation'. From it one goes on to think that there are too many workers and that the best use should be made of existing work by containing measures, such as forbidding people to have two jobs, limiting the working hours, lowering the retirement age, keeping women at home, preventing immigration, and so on.

We shall see in chapter 8 that as the number of idle people increases the optimum population rises, being the optimum defined either by the standard of living or by the level of employment. Many remedies suggested for unemployment are in fact directed at preventing certain sections of the population from working, and thus increasing the load borne by the active people. In other words one is increasing the optimum population, which appears too small, but one is also, unfortunately, lowering the standard of living.

2. *'The machines are taking over'*, or 'technological progress reduces the number of jobs'. This very common idea means in short that if productivity rises in a capitalist economy the optimum population falls. This will be dealt with in chapters 14, 15, and 16.

Power optimum or economic optimum?

Various social attitudes can be explained by the fact that the power optimum is higher than the economic optimum – as a general rule whoever holds or seeks power wishes to increase numbers. Consider various examples: The patriarch looks favourably on any birth in his tribe, because it increases his power, which is almost identical with his wealth. The absolute monarch too wants more subjects. His wealth also coincides with his power because it is separate from the rest of the population. Before the nineteenth century this desire for power used to be so predominant that it hampered for a long time the understanding of the economic optimum. At about the time when this was understood, regal authority began to decline.

A dominant class with absolute power is in favour of a large population – the more slaves, labourers, or workers, the more stable its power, since the wealth of the minority can be practically identified with the power of the nation.

The USSR will give priority to power as long as it does not consider that the world revolution has been achieved; here power is not necessarily to be taken in the military sense.

On the family level power contrasts with the standard of living as an aim. As long as children remained under the narrow and direct authority of the father, power was by far the main objective. With the emancipation of children the birth rate has decreased because economic considerations have taken the upper hand. If these were to become the only influence, replacing the need for affection and authority, the optimum would drop to nought and couples would avoid having children altogether.

On the administrative level senior civil servants usually want to increase their staff, since this gives them more power. The contrary occurs in private enterprise, or in a public department which is particularly autonomous and mindful of its efficiency, where the entrepreneur or head will want to reduce the number of people employed on any given task.

Precise calculation of the optimum population

Attempts at this are very rare. Before the last war an American demographer assessed the optimum population of the United States at 120 million. In *Richesse et population* I calculated that if a figure had to be risked for France it would be between 50 and 75 million. A. J. Coale and E. M. Hoover[1] believe that a quarter of the rural population of India is useless because it is undernourished. But these calculations have poor foundations and little meaning. What we really need to know is whether the real population is lower or higher than the optimum: in fact whether the country is under- or overpopulated.

Optimum population and over-population

Let us retain the static point of view for a moment.

Over-population (or a population higher than the optimum: the idea of over-population is easier to grasp) can be defined in different ways, for instance either in terms of supplies or in terms of employment. If marginal productivity drops, society tends not to employ all the men, at least in a system based on private property. In practice overpopulation is evident either in undernourishment or underemployment and both lead to the conclusion that if there were fewer men each would be better nourished and fully employed.

To improve the situation the gap between optimum and real population needs to be closed. With overpopulation, unless emigration is possible, it is better to increase the optimum population than to reduce the real population. This is done by increasing the number of jobs without reducing individual

[1] *Population Growth and Economic Development in Low Income Countries*, Princeton, 1958.

efficiency and welfare. This policy is usually called 'unemployment relief', and it has mixed results. We will see how and in what circumstances the optimum population varies, and will later find clues as to how to decrease chronic underemployment without endangering the standard of living. To do this we must first study the factors that we have so far assumed to be constant.

8

PRODUCERS AND NON-PRODUCERS

'Idleness, yet full of strength . . .'
VALÉRY

The assumption made in chapter 6, that all men are producers and distribute their output evenly, is of course untrue. There are inactive people of various kinds. We will dwell especially on children and elderly people. If we brought in the degree of inactivity this would lead to useless complications. Neither would it be very helpful to consider the sexes here. Their ratio does not vary much and so we could reason as if the total number n consisted of $\frac{n}{2}$ couples, but it is as easy to take the individual as unity. We will assume therefore that a population consists of young and old who do not work at all, and of adults who all work equally.

We will examine how the presence of idle people changes the magnitudes already studied: standard of living, power, maximum population, economic optimum, power optimum. And more generally, how do the idle influence the progress of a population which is seeking the highest possible standard of living or other aims?

Definition of the standard of living

We defined this before as the output per producer, but this definition loses its validity directly inactive people appear; and we will now call standard of living the part distributed to each adult producer, whose needs are not necessarily the same as those of the children and elders. These needs are largely subjective and arbitrary, so we will assume that the society has chosen its aims consciously and that the general standard of living can be measured by the consumption of one adult.

Maximum population and standard of living

If we add a group of non-producers to an active population the standard of living of the whole drops: there are fewer goods available for the same number of producers. This applies even if an idle person consumes less than a producer. If on the contrary a fraction of the producers in an active population becomes idle, the standard of living does not necessarily drop. Also, the presence of idle consumers in a population does not necessarily lessen the maximum population that can live in a given territory in given conditions.

We can see this on figure 23, which plots against population first marginal productivity and secondly the average output per producer when the number of producers varies. This average output would also be their standard of living if there were no non-producers.

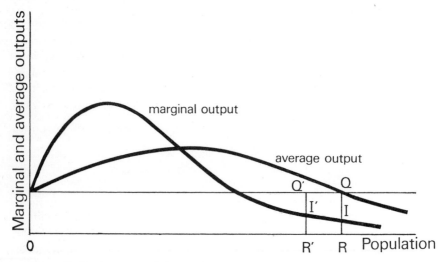

Figure 23. Maximum population including non-producers.

To avoid too tedious a demonstration, we will assume again here that there is a rigid 'subsistence level', QR, below which no life is possible. The number of producers is at its highest where the average output is equal to this level. At this stage the marginal productivity is IR, smaller than QR. Without the help of his comrades the additional producer would be unable to live.

It would therefore seem at first sight impossible to bring an additional inhabitant to the overcrowded territory. An additional producer, not producing his own subsistence, could hardly appeal to the others since they themselves are on the brink of undernourishment. And yet, paradoxical though this may seem, it is possible to bring in an extra inhabitant *as long as he does not work*: possible that is, if the subsistence level for an idle inhabitant is considerably lower than that for a producer. For if we do away with a producer we lose his output IR but gain his consumption QR, which is greater; a quantity QI is left over. If the needs of an idle person are not only lower than QR but also

66

lower than QI, the surplus can feed more than one inhabitant, so that the maximum population rises.[1]

Consider a point R' so placed that Q'I' is equal to the consumption of a non-producer. The number of producers will be OR' and the number of non-producers equal to the area Q'QII' divided by the segment I'Q'. There will be fewer producers, but a higher population. Where the marginal productivity is small, the arrival of one more producer can be more awkward than that of a non-producer. In certain cases it is even in the population's interest to stop some producers from working.

These remarks are not merely theoretical. It is worth remembering Gourou's description of certain deltas in the Far East, where the family only use their buffalo for heavy work, and leave it idling in the marshes the rest of the time. The economic point here is that the yields are low in these over-crowded regions and that an idle animal consumes very little: where his own strength is sufficient, the man prefers to do the work himself and thus gain the extra calories the animal would be burning up at the job. Dumont noticed similar attitudes in the Huerta of Valencia, where men use horses very little because they are afraid of competition from animals.

What applies to the buffalo is also true of men. In a family with insufficient land, cultivated as carefully as a garden, the arrival of an adult is more awkward than that of a child or a non-producer because their needs are smaller.

These ideas can also be applied fruitfully to the differences in ability between individuals. A worker may produce little, not only because he came too late to be given a productive task, but because of lack of ability. A society may find that its economic interest lies in encouraging disabled or inefficient people not to work: it thus saves on various expenses and on the calories that go into muscular work, and also finds various social and financial ways of lowering the standard of living of the idle members.

The worker himself faces a similar problem: a farmer or a fisherman, nearing the stage where his efficiency will drop markedly, may judge that even disregarding the effort involved, extra work would not bring in enough food to make up for the extra energy used. And if he takes his subjective effort into consideration, he will see an even greater advantage in relative idleness.

However, where the needs of a non-producer are equal to or only slightly lower than those of a producer the maximum population and the standard of living are lowered by the arrival of non-producers.

---

[1] Let QR=v and IR=qv, where q is a characteristic of the function p(n) defining the production as a function of the number of workers.

Let r be the ratio of the needs of a non-producer to those of a producer.

Then the maximum population increases when

$IQ = v(1-q) > rv$

Thus $1-q > r$, or $q + r < 1$.

Thus it is difficult to find justification for the suspicion with which most countries greet adult immigrants who produce more than they consume, while objecting far less to those (e.g. children) who consume and do not produce. This is due to their paying heed to misguided Malthusian ideas about optimum population. The same remark applies to the calculations that prescribe the exclusion of so many workers from the labour market for a compensation lower than their salary, or recommend early retirement ages for the same reason. They lead in the end to a drop in the standard of living, and often fail even in their original aim of increasing the number of jobs available.

The economic optimum

Strictly speaking a population seeking to achieve the highest standard of living in the shortest time should only consist of producers. Around the economic optimum it is not beneficial to replace a producer by a non-producer. But this is not a practical aim: this population would have to kill or exclude its older members, not have any children, and only maintain its numbers by immigration. This point can only be illustrated by considering a working unit such as a college or a factory.

We should therefore formulate a hypothesis on the number of non-producers. We will consider two particularly interesting cases (another will be found in chapter 15 on 'Working Hours and Leisure').

1. *The ratio of non-producers to producers is constant.* This tallies with the traditional idea of the family, where each producer carries a load of children and elders, and also with the 'stable' population (after a long period in which fertility and mortality have not varied) or the 'stationary' population. It applies to a long-term situation. There are frequent practical instances to be found, without taking the extreme case of Lotka's 'stable' population. In many western countries the proportion of adults has not varied much in the last century, as we shall see. The old have increased relative to the young; in the case considered, their needs will be considered the same as the young.

2. *The number of non-producers is practically a constant.* This occurs especially where there is emigration or immigration of adults. It may also apply to the situation mentioned above if it is considered that the young consume considerably less than the adults. It applies to a short-term situation.

Non-producers in a constant ratio: the long-term problem

Compare population A, where there are only producers, to population B, in identical conditions but where each producer carries a number of non-producers with him. The number of producers (and hence the population) can be varied as we wish. We want to find, for each case, the optimum

68

population, ensuring the highest possible standard of living. Is the optimum the same for A and B? If not, which is higher?

Figure 24 plots first the average output per producer against population or producers (1), as in the preceding figures. For population A the optimum is OP_1. For population B, output is divided between producers and non-producers. Each producer (or the producers in general) shares his income with non-producers according to a fixed ratio. Therefore, whatever the number the relative fall in the standard of living is the same.

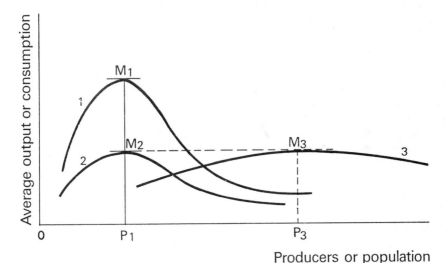

Figure 24. The optimum number of producers does not vary if the ratio of non-producers is a constant.

To plot the standard of living of the whole population as a function of the number of producers (2) all the ordinates of the first graph have to be reduced in the same ratio. *Thus the optimum number of producers is not changed by the presence of a fixed proportion of non-producers.*

The total population however is larger, as we see from graph (3). Here the abscissae of the second graph have been increased in a constant ratio. The optimum population is no longer OP_1, but OP_3. A non-producer does not necessarily consume the same as a producer. The drop in the standard of living thus depends both on the proportion of non-producers and on their consumption.

The rise in the optimum population, on the other hand, depends only on the proportion of non-producers.[1]

[1] Let a be the number of producers, q the (constant) ratio of the number of non-producers to producers and r the ratio of their consumptions.
We then have:

Thus, when the proportion of non-producers is constant: 1. The optimum number of producers does not vary. 2. The optimum population is increased by the number of non-producers. Neither of these factors is affected by the rates of consumption at various ages, which influence only the standard of living.

The long-term problem

Let us leave aside the short-term difficulties, and try to define the situation most favourable to the standard of living in a population where technology is invariable.

We will assume that the population is practically stable, with age structure constant but numbers variable. However many old and young there are, however much they consume, the optimum number of adults is the same. Yet the optimum is a precarious aim, only achieved fleetingly. If the stable population passes it in either direction, it will have to face economic instability – we cannot therefore set up this stable state as an ideal.

However, it is a different matter if fertility and mortality cancel each other out; the population will reach a stationary and invariable state, which may occur at various alternative sizes. One of these ensures the highest standard of living, which will last indefinitely: it is a permanent optimum. *We thus have an ideal population, with numbers, age structure, and standard of living all permanent, the latter being the highest possible.* Any demographic change apart from a periodic massacre of elders would bring about a drop in the standard of living.

But the artificial concept of a stable population is hardly necessary to these principles. Though the proportion of adults is not constant, it only varies in fact over a narrow range on a national scale: the least civilised populations

	Producer	Non–Producer	Total
Number	a	aq	$n=a(1+q)$
Individual consumption	1	r	$(qr+1)/(q+1)$
Total consumption	a	aqr	$a(qr+1)$

The graphs are then defined by the functions

$$(1) \quad \frac{P(a)}{a} = p(a).$$

$$(2) \quad \frac{P(a)}{a(1+qr)} = \frac{p(a)}{1+qr}$$

$$(3) \quad \frac{P(n/1+q)}{1+qr}.$$

The economic optimum, which was specified in the absence of non-producers by $p'(a)=0$, is now given by $p'\left(\dfrac{n}{1+q}\right)=0$.

70

have many young and few old, the more civilised have fewer young and more old; but this structure does not vary quickly.

On page 245 of the admirable *Annuaire Statistique de la France, 1938* (International Section) we find the proportions of men aged 15–60 in the total population for various countries and periods: the highest figure is that of Belgium in 1930: 32·5; the lowest that of Bulgaria in 1890: 25. Of 197 populations studied the ratios in 147 cases are between 26 and 30. If one leaves out the countries that had just experienced a sudden drop in the birth rate, most of the figures are between 27 and 28.

Lengthening of life and of active life[1]

Various factors influence the proportion of non-producers in a population one way or the other.

The lengthening of life has so far helped the proportion of adults to remain constant. But if it were to continue it would act mainly on older age groups. If the average expectation of life were 100 years, with mortality non-existent below, and total mortality at 100, and the birth rate were to drop proportionally so that the population remained stationary, then the proportion of men aged 15–60, previously very stable, would fall from 28 to 22·5. Admittedly in this case the active life would be prolonged too, either because biological senility would appear more slowly or because the heavy burden of non-producers would make it necessary to put back the retirement age. If the proportion of producers over 15 had to be retained, retirement would have to be put off to 71.

Longer schooling also tends to reduce the productive population. One may prefer to consider school children as apprentices, but from the economic point of view they are a temporary burden. However that may be, whereas in the nineteenth century in agriculture and even in industry people used to begin producing at the age of 5, they have since started later and later. The average now is probably about 18.

Consider the typical stationary populations from the United Nations' tables: the proportion of people aged 20–60 is 47·5 per cent for populations with an expectation of life of 20 years, and 51·3 per cent for an expectation of life of 73·9 years, with a maximum of 52·8 per cent for an expectation of 45–50. In short it is as if each producer was counted, together with his non-producers, as *n* inhabitants (2, for instance) instead of 1. Since the number of non-producers does not affect the standard of living curve, we need only consider the producers themselves.

All we have said so far on the stability of populations only applies in practice to the producers and the non-producers as a whole. In all advanced populations the ratios of young and old have in fact see-sawed a great

[1] See chapter 4 in Part 2 for the much debated question of optimum retirement age.

deal around the middle age-groups. Later on we shall have to consider distinguishing between the burden of the young and that of the old.

Non-producers in constant numbers: the short-term problem

In this second case, one wants to vary the number of producers to obtain the highest standard of living. We are almost back at the question of overheads (see pages 48–59).

Figure 25 plots total output against the total number of producers (1), while the other curve (2) parallels the first at a rather lower level. The second

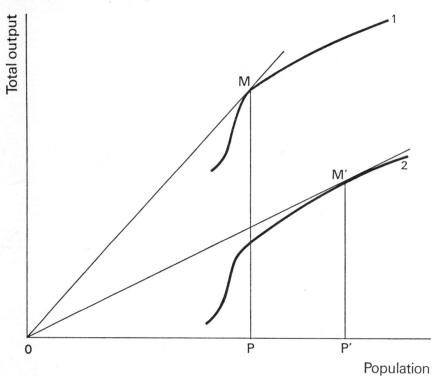

Figure 25. The addition of an idle population increases the optimum number of producers.

curve is derived from the first by a constant shift representing the consumption of the non-producers. The tangent to this curve from the origin determines points M' and P'. OP' is a new optimum number of producers, larger than the old OP.

Thus, with the addition of a constant number of non-producers, the optimum population is doubly increased: 1. By the rise in the optimum number of producers. 2. By the additional non-producers.

The global optimum is achieved when the drop in productivity is so sharp that an extra producer cannot reach the same standard of living as the others, *even if he is given his total output and excused from contributing towards the common burden.*

A population may obviously enjoy a higher but more precarious standard of living by lowering the number of its children and producing an age pyramid in the shape of a hayrick; or it may on the contrary overburden itself with larger numbers of children and elders, with a pyramid shaped like the Eiffel tower, or even like a diabolo. These are transitional periods; the first may encourage emigration, the second immigration. The latter is profitable where the marginal productivity of the immigrant is higher than the average output minus the common burden. If the burden is say 25 per cent, immigration may be profitable even when an immigrant produces 20 per cent less than the average. We shall see later how misinterpretations of this fact lead capitalist countries into misguided immigration or emigration policies, always restricting their population too much.

It is however impossible to limit one's horizon to such a short term as a few years.

If there are a great many old people in a population below its optimum, the aim is obvious: an increase, by the various possible ways. An over-populated country with a high proportion of adults might on the other hand seek salvation by restricting its population, especially through emigration. But it may be that the two basic data, size and structure, point in different directions.

Conflict between structure and size

Consider an obviously overpopulated country. One may be tempted to de-crease its numbers or restrict their growth; this may only be achieved by emigration (loss of adults) or by a drop in the birth rate (loss of young). But in both cases the old people will come to be a relatively heavier burden, so that there will be no improvement after all.

Similarly a population with too many old people may want to spread this burden over a greater number of adult shoulders. But when the adults them-selves grow old they will have to be supported by a further increase in the adults. This may lead to a drop in productivity because of insufficient natural resources. And if the number of adults has been increased by a higher birth rate, rather than by immigration, the young themselves will be a heavier burden.

We are thus led to ask whether the old can be supported indefinitely by a continuous rise in population through a high birth rate ensuring a permanently wide-based pyramid. Obviously not, especially since we are still assuming that technology is invariable.

J. Bourgeois-Pichat showed ingeniously,[1] by comparing a stable population

[1] *Journal de la Société de Statistique de Paris*, March–April 1950.

with a stationary one, that the relative load represented by the young is more or less multiplied by the reproduction rate, whereas the load of the old is divided by it, so that if the two loads are equivalent, which is broadly the case, the total remains roughly constant as long as the reproduction rate does not stray too far from unity.[1]

Though they benefit from technological progress, highly developed populations reach a critical point where it would be in their interest, for purely structural reasons, to try to increase. The lower the retirement age or the higher the relative consumption of an old person, the better it is to expand.[2]

The case is clearer where the population can be increased through immigration, since this does not change the burden of the young. As we have said, this cannot be a permanent solution, but it may be opportune when an accidental lack of adults has to be compensated for. This was the case in France after the First World War when the equivalent of five yearly drafts had been killed. A similar loss was experienced in 1945, partly because of the Second World War, but especially because of the less apparently drastic fact that insufficient births between 1925 and 1945 had given an average rate of reproduction slightly lower than 0·9.

On the whole public opinion is more sensitive to numbers than to ages, and

---

[1] Let Y_o be the proportion of *young* people in the stationary population and let O_o be the proportion of *old* people in the stationary population and, choosing a scale on which the consumption of an adult is 1, y the consumption of a *young* person and o the consumption of a *old* person.

The initial load $L = 1 + yY_o + oO_o$ becomes, with a reproduction rate R, $1 + yY_oR + oO_o/R$.

The most favourable survival table nowadays gives a stationary population divided approximately as follows:

	Percentage	Standardised
0–20 years	26·5	52
20–60 years	51·4	100
over 60 years	22·1	43

thus $T = 1 + 0·52y + 0·43o$

For a reproduction rate not far from unity to lower the load, we need $0·52y < 0·43o$, i.e.

$$\frac{y}{o} < 0·82$$

In this case a wider based population would be more advantageous.

[2] The sight of many old people in hardship may suggest that the average consumption of an old man is small. But in countries that have not been scourged by inflation, wealth tends on the contrary to accumulate in the higher age groups. It is usually passed on to those whose parents have died – the number of such people under 60 drops constantly as mortality recedes. The capital accumulating in higher age groups increases the load they bring to bear on the active population.

However, though the age of the possessors has important social consequences, it has no bearing on the demographic problems, at any rate within our present narrow assumptions. A wealthy idler is as heavy a burden whether he be young or old.

We shall return to the capital burden in chapter 10 (on the distribution of goods) and to the problem of old age in chapter 22 (on social security).

thus prefers a restrictive solution more often than it should. This was obvious in England in 1950: the report of the Royal Commission on Population was not wholly approved of by public opinion because, as so often happens, people were curiously unaware of the increase in their average age.

Influence of non-producers on the power optimum

Non-producers reduce power as well as wealth. Figure 26 again plots against the number of producers the marginal productivity. Where there are only producers the power optimum for the population is OP. Now bring in non-producers.

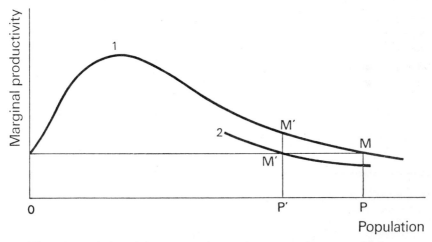

Figure 26. Variation of the power optimum when non-producers are added.

1. *If they are in a constant ratio to the population,* it is again as if each producer has to support a given number of non-producers in the form of a proportional levy on his output (the expense of running a family for instance). This gives us a second graph by reducing the ordinates of the first proportionally. If the last producer is still to produce his subsistence requirement, M will have to move back to M' and P to P'. The optimum number of producers is thus reduced from OP to OP' – it approaches the economic optimum, understandably enough since the upkeep of the non-producers is deducted from the excess output devoted to power. As for the total population, it is equal to OP' multiplied by q, the ratio of total numbers to the number of producers. OP' may be higher or lower than the original optimum OP', depending on q and r and the shape of the graph.[1]

---

[1] Let a be the number of active producers, P(a) the total output, i the number of inactive, v_a the subsistence level of producers, and v_i that of inactive.

If there are many non-producers and they consume little, the optimum population rises; it also rises if the marginal productivity varies sharply. But if marginal productivity is more or less constant, OP' being much lower than OP, the power optimum may well be reduced through the addition of non-producers. In this case, a country seeking power must be more careful in increasing its population than one seeking wealth. The economic optimum remains lower than the power optimum, but the gap between them narrows because the non-producers, in taking a share of the output, are in direct competition with the monarch or the state. We have already seen in the last chapter the particular instance where the non-producers are soldiers.

2. *If they are a constant number* it is another matter. The number of producers must be constantly increased until marginal productivity falls below individual consumption, and then stop. Power will be smaller than if no one were idle, but the optimum number of producers will be the same. As for the optimum population, it naturally rises by the number of non-producers. Thus a country at war and receiving useless refugees would not have to change its policy on the importation of labour, unless this brought about changes in consumption.

Conclusion

This chapter confirms that in a capitalist system, standard of living and employment are often rival factors. Non-producers lower the standard of living but give the producers a greater incentive to multiply: if they seek the highest possible standard of living there must be more of them to share the burden.

Then $P(a) - av_a - iv_i = P(a) - av_a - a(q-1)v_i$ and the optimum number of producers is $P'(a_o) = v_a + (q-1)v_i$. The optimum population is $a_o q$, which can be greater or less than in the case where all are producers, where it is given by $P'(n) = v$.

9

A POPULATION DIVIDED BETWEEN
VARIOUS ACTIVITIES

'And since that time I have loved them all.'
SULLY PRUDHOMME

In order to avoid any confusion arising from the definition of heterogeneous production we have assumed so far that all men were busy making a single product. We will now remove this restriction and admit that different activities produce different goods.

Case of two activities

We will first limit the number of goods to two; we can generalise progressively later. We thus bring in a new unknown quantity: a given population n can

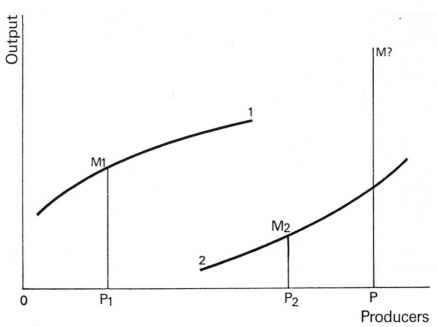

Figure 27. Two activities combined.

split into two in various ways. Let us assume that each worker is wholly devoted to one activity, and that the goods he produces are always the same.[1] Figure 27 shows that, as we have seen, there is for each activity a functional relationship between number of workers and output. The population is OP. But we do not know: 1. How it splits up into two groups OP_1 and OP_2. 2. How the two homogeneous lots of goods M_1P_1 and M_2P_2 will combine to give the total output MP. So in figure 27 we know only the curves 1 and 2 and the position of P. We do not know M.

Definition of composite production

It is often said that heterogeneous outputs cannot be measured quantitatively; and this is often an objection to a theory of optimum population, if not to any economic theory. Let us begin by defining a *composite production A as greater than production B, when A is greater than B in all its parts* – in other words if there is more of each product in A than in B.

If there are two products, 1 and 2, the number of inhabitants, n, can be divided into two groups n_1 and n_2 in $n+1$ different ways. For each group $(n_1 \quad n_2)$ we have an assortment $(q_1 \quad q_2)$ of quantities produced and also $(c_1 \quad c_2)$ of quantities produced per inhabitant. For each product we have $c_1 = \dfrac{q_1}{n}$, $c_2 = \dfrac{q_2}{n}$. Of all these arrangements $(c_1 \quad c_2)$ one is either deemed or considered preferable to the others. This decision will govern the way in which the n inhabitants split up between the two activities.

Now take another population N. It will divide into two groups N_1 and N_2 which will produce assortments $(Q_1 \quad Q_2)$ of quantities and $(C_1 \quad C_2)$ of individual consumptions. We can say that group N is better off than group n when at least one of the distributions of N gives a higher output than the best distribution of n.

If both products have decreasing or increasing returns to scale, the answer is easy: the best individual standard of living will be achieved in the first case by the lowest population, and in the second case by the highest.

Suppose now that the first product has decreasing returns and the second product increasing returns to scale. Of all the distributions open to population N, we will choose the one where C_1 is equal to c_1. If the ensuing C_2 is higher than c_2, the number N is more profitable than the number n, and vice versa. We can achieve the same result by starting off from a C_2 equal to c_2. The workers freed from the making of the second product return to the first and C_1 becomes larger than c_1. Over a whole area both C_1 and C_2 are greater than c_1 and c_2.

---

[1] Alternatively one might easily divide the 'worker' into homogeneous fractions—e.g. working hours.

This will be clearer in a numerical example. We start off with 100 inhabitants. They can split up in ten different ways, four of which give the following outputs and consumptions in litres of corn and kilograms of iron.

Total output		Individual consumption	
Litres of corn	Kilograms of iron	Litres of corn	Kilograms of iron
1100	190	11	1·9
1000	200	10	2
900	210	9	2·1
700	230	7	2·3

We will assume that the population prefers the second arrangement, with 10 litres of corn and 2 kilograms of iron. Now here are some figures for a population of 1000 inhabitants.

Total output		Individual consumption	
Litres of corn	Kilograms of iron	Litres of corn	Kilograms of iron
11,000	2000	11	2
10,000	2500	10	2·5
9000	3000	9	3
8000	3700	8	3·7

For an equal consumption of corn (10 litres) the consumption of iron is higher (2·5 kilograms). If this is reduced to 2, the workers freed from producing it can produce more corn and this figure can go up to 11. It is thus clear in this case that a population of 1000 is preferable to one of 100.

A distribution may even be found that gives the same ratio to the increases in consumptions of corn and iron. But this distribution is not necessarily the best possible one; it may even be that the one considered best includes a decrease in one product compensated for by a large increase in the other. However this may be, N is better off than n because its consumption figures can be higher in both columns.

We can always find out whether one composite output is greater than another, and therefore whether one population is better off than the other. But we do not know by how much. We can decide only that the improvement is between $\frac{C_1}{c_1}$ and $\frac{C_2}{c_2}$. The distribution that allows the two outputs to increase in the same ratio might strictly be taken as a lower limit to the increase in the total output, but we are not bound to accept this. *Since we can compare different sizes of population, we can find the most profitable, or optimum size.*

Figure 28 represents population n as On. Points a_1 and a_2 show the distribution preferred; na_1 is the output of the first product and na_2 that of the second. Since these are material quantities the scales are different for the two products. Angles a_1On and a_2On are no other than the consumptions per head we called q_1 and q_2. Now take the other population N, shown as ON. It can be split up into two groups in N ways. We project points a_1 and a_2 to A_1 and A_2 on the vertical leading from N. For N to be a better figure than n, one of the $N+1$ possible distributions must give 2 points respectively above A_1 and A_2.

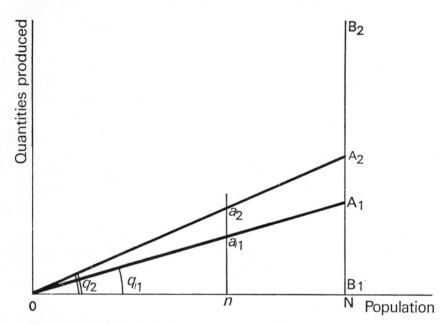

Figure 28. Comparison between outputs achieved by two different sizes of population.

Start from an extreme case where the first group of producers is very small and the second group almost equal to N. This gives us two points B_1 and B_2, very far apart; as we change the distribution of work, B_1 will rise and B_2 will fall. Either B_1 reaches A_1 first, or B_2 reaches A_2. In the first case N is to be preferred to n, in the second n is better than N.

There is no difficulty in generalising this for any number of products.

Introducing the concept of price

So far we have merely said that one output was higher than another if the total figures were higher (for instance 17, 14 and 16, 12). But against what scale can it be measured? In practice all fairly advanced societies use a conventional scale called money: prices are conversion tables for the values of various products (we will not for the time being worry about how they are made up). Prices have two very different functions: to direct consumption and production in a given way, and to help reckonings. A system which achieves the first may not be good for the second.

It is at any rate customary to measure the value of production with prices and to compare its bulk at various stages either by calculating its supposed value had prices remained the same, or by dividing the variation in value by the mean variation in prices. This last practice introduces a distortion that may lead to a complete blunder. An assortment of goods whose every part is higher than that of another assortment may yet be given a lower value.[1] The first method cannot lead to a mistake in the sense of the difference.

1. *In a planned system* the workers can be distributed in the way considered best, without prices having to come into the reckoning. For all purposes the idea of a static optimum population remains valid. It can even be more clearly understood here than in a market system.

2. *In a market economy* prices and wages may serve to direct the workers towards the best distribution; this makes it necessary to reckon them according to the marginal utility of the goods. Where the population is spread in the best possible way, individuals should not see any profit in choosing to produce one thing rather than another. The marginal value of each product should be the same.[2]

Figure 29 plots the two outputs 1 and 2 each to its own scale. It can be

---

[1] Here is a numerical example, taking two successive situations 1 and 2.

	1	2
Output of wheat	10 litres	12 litres
Output of iron	2 kilograms	4 kilograms
Price of wheat	2	3
Price of iron	1	3
Total value of output	22	48

The second assortment is obviously preferable to the first; and yet if the price index is determined by equating 1 litre of wheat to 2 kilograms of iron the price indexes are 4 and 9. By dividing the value by the price index we get 5·5 for the first situation and 5·3 for the second, a result which might suggest that the second situation is less favourable than the first.

[2] Let q_1 be the quantity of product 1 produced by n_1 workers

and q_2 be the quantity of product 2 produced by n_2 workers

Then $q_1 = P_1(n_1)$, $q_2 = P_2(n_2)$, $n = n_1 + n_2$ and

$c_1 = \dfrac{P_1(n_1)}{n}$ is the consumption of product 1 per head,

$c_2 = \dfrac{P_2(n_2)}{n}$ is the consumption of product 2 per head.

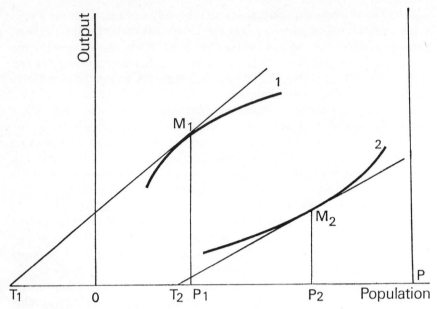

Figure 29. Position of the tangents at the optimum.

shown that the population is at its optimum when the tangents to the two graphs meet the x axis at two points equidistant from the origin.[1] Where the left-hand intersection is nearer to the origin, the population is below its

When n is given we need another equation to calculate q_1, q_2, c_1, c_2, n_1, n_2. This equation is the utility equation, which can be written $G(c_1, c_2, n)=0$, or alternatively $W(n_1, n_2, n)=0$.

We can determine the production P in various ways. For example suppose the constant scale of prices is p_1, p_2; then $P=q_1p_1+q_2p_2$.

If the unit is split as (a_1, a_2), then $P=\dfrac{q_1q'_2+q_2q'_1}{a_1q'_2+a_2q'_1}$(*)

The functions G and W embody not only the desires of the consumer, but also the prices at which products 1 and 2 are offered.

Eliminating n_1, n_2, q_1 and q_2 in the equations above gives P as a function of n.

[1] When the population is optimal the standard of living does not change: thus the two individual consumptions $\dfrac{q_1}{n}$ and $\dfrac{q_2}{n}$ stay the same. The marginal worker produces the same as the others.

Hence $\dfrac{dq_1}{dn}=\dfrac{q_1}{n}$, $\dfrac{dq_2}{dn}=\dfrac{q_2}{n}$, therefore $\dfrac{dq_1 \cdot dn_1}{dn_1\, dn}=\dfrac{q_1}{n}$, $\dfrac{dq_2}{dn_2}\dfrac{dn_2}{dn}=\dfrac{q_2}{n}$, and $q_1/\dfrac{dq_1}{dn_1}=n.\dfrac{dn_1}{dn}$, $q_2\dfrac{dq_2}{dn_2}=n\dfrac{dn_2}{dn}$, so $\dfrac{q_1}{q'_1}+\dfrac{q_2}{q'_2}=n$.

This equation is satisfied when the two tangents meet the x axis at points equidistant from the origin.

optimum, and conversely. If we should want to define output by the ratio of the value index to the price index, the same conclusion applies as long as the graphs do not curve sharply, which they rarely do.[1] *This is a most important feature, most helpful to research and demonstrations: the positions of point T, essential to the determination of the optimum, do not depend on the scale used for the graphs. We may thus eliminate the price factor, which sets so many problems.* Return to figure 27: the position of M is not important – as long as the tangents at M_1 and M_2 intersect the axis at points equidistant from the origin, population OP is at its optimum, whatever the scale used for the two graphs.

Case of several activities

These propositions can easily be generalised. In a market system in particular the sum of OT segments is zero at the optimum position.

Whatever the structure of the economy and the definition of value, the graph of total output is convex upwards at this point, following the shape of the individual curves which make it up and play an appreciable part in determining the optimum. But since everything suggests that the curves are not sharp, its position is not rigorously defined. Population has little influence over a fairly wide zone, so that other factors become preponderant.

It may happen that the occupational structure is very rigid, either because individuals are loath to change their jobs, or because such a change involves them in extra expense, which can be expressed in working hours. In this case a marginal worker will move to another job only if this is really to his advantage. The spread of the population will be a compromise between preferences of consumers and producers. This brings to light a new form of underemployment: the producers in the excess activity will not all find work. We shall come across this distortion again later on.

---

[1] Using the same definitions as in the previous note, the conditions for the optimum are
$$\frac{dP}{dn} = \frac{P}{n}.$$
Taking for P the formula (*) in note 2, page 81 above and expanding, we get
$$\frac{(a_1q_2 - a_2q_1)(q'_2q''_1 dn_1 - q'_1q''_2 dn_2) + q'_1q'_2(a_1q'_2 + a_2q'_1)dn}{(a_1q'_2 + a_2q'_1)d} = \frac{q_1q'_2 + q_2q'_1}{n}.$$
If the terms in Q'' are small, close to the optimum
$$q'_1q'_2 = \frac{q_1q_2' + q_2q_1'}{n}$$
$$\text{i.e.} \frac{q_1}{q'_1} + \frac{q_2}{q'_2} = n.$$
An easy calculation shows that this relation is verified when the tangents meet the x axis at points equidistant from the origin.

The three groups of activities

Various contemporary authors use the phrases 'primary, secondary, and tertiary activities' in slightly different meanings. Here are some of the criteria suggested[1]: 1. The social criterion: manual labour dealing with nature (farmers, miners, etc.), manual labour in conditioned surroundings, and non-manual labour. 2. The hierarchy of needs (food and lodging, manufactured goods, intellectual satisfaction). 3. The rhythm of technological progress (moderate for the primary, fast for the secondary, non-existent for the tertiary) (see Fourastié). 4. The consumption of raw materials. 5. The scale of investment. 6. The rise or fall in returns according to numbers.

I shall use the last criterion

As a rule there are decreasing returns to scale in the exploitation of natural resources, because this is usually done on such a scale that it cannot stand up to a great increase in numbers. Transformation of raw materials on the other hand benefits from mass-production and division of labour. Certain activities have a roughly constant return; these are on the whole the ones that use few materials or tools and a great deal of labour of an intellectual or at least a non-muscular kind. The productivity of barbers or lawyers does not increase much with numbers.

However, the question of tertiary producers in the normal sense of the phrase is more complex: *two heads of state would not do three times as much work as one, but the president of a population of ten million would do for one of twenty million.* This would be all the more true of a novelist or a scientist. *The returns from tertiary producers may not increase with their numbers, but still rise with the total population.* No doubt the number of tertiary workers in a given occupation is never completely independent from the numbers liable to be interested in it as a vocation – but there is no question of a ratio here. Besides if the increase of population demands a rise in the number of tertiary workers, useful specialisations may appear.

The following definitions will apply for the rest of this book:

Primary sector: activities with decreasing returns to scale (usually the exploitation of natural resources).

Secondary sector: activities with increasing returns to scale (usually the transformation of raw materials).

Tertiary sector: activities with constant returns (usually non-manual).

Two centuries ago Cantillon made a first-rate contribution to economics by considering the way individuals consumed their income. *This essential factor has all too often been overlooked since then, though it plays a considerable*

[1] See my article 'Progrès technique et répartition professionnelle de la population' in *Population*, nos 1 and 2, 1949.

part even in developed countries. Cantillon wrote that if an owner used his land as a park or to feed a race-horse he deprived other men of their livelihood. We would say that he consumes primary products and thus diminishes the population of the land or prevents it from reaching the maximum set by the natural resources and the available technology.

Let us apply this theory to the *optimum* population (the maximum population is of no interest in industrial countries). The optimum depends on the way inhabitants direct their consumption and hence on their activities; but a society cannot always exercise full freedom of choice. It must work within limits set by certain imperatives such as the consumption of a certain number of calories.

Societies with a fairly primitive technology must have a large agricultural population (primary producers). Their density, though very low, is often higher than the economic optimum of the time. Observers are often of the opposite opinion: for European populations in the seventeenth and eighteenth centuries and even in materially backward populations nowadays, insufficient numbers are often invoked, where it is obvious that a smaller population would have a higher standard of living. Those concerned with such matters are always tertiary workers and suffer from a power complex, or at least see an advantage in having a large primary and secondary support to justify their own existence.

Changes in consumption

Consider a society based on a market system. We know the various factors giving for each occupation the output as a function of the number of producers; we also know about the variations in utility. The optimum population is therefore well defined. Suppose that for some reason men change their tastes and prefer one product to another. Will this increase or diminish the optimum population? *This much neglected problem dominates the whole of economics.*

Suppose first that there are only two activities, a primary and a secondary one. In an extreme case where the population saw no practical use in the secondary occupation the whole population would be engaged in the primary one, with decreasing returns to scale. The optimum would be at its lowest possible point. If on the contrary the primary occupation were negligible, the optimum would be infinite. It would thus seem that the optimum increases where people switch from primary to secondary activities.

Two illustrations will make things clearer:
1. On a small estate, which includes a cornfield and a coal mine with separate owners, if the owners are very keen on wheat and coal they will exchange their products and the optimum population will be two. But if they take to other things, and want for instance to employ a barber or servants, they will give

work to extra inhabitants, and pay them with part of their coal or wheat. The optimum will rise to three, four, five, or more. It is already clear that unemployment due to overpopulation comes from a closed circuit of producers with decreasing returns to scale.

2. The milk bath. Dramatis personae: a princess and a peasant living on her estate. The princess pays the peasant with the milk from the cows and uses the rest in taking milk baths, because that is what she enjoys. Outside her estate there are barren lands allowing only a mediocre existence. The population consists of two people. One day the princess changes her taste, out of whim or because circumstances provide her with an opportunity. She decides to have a servant and pays her with the excess milk. The population is now balanced at three.

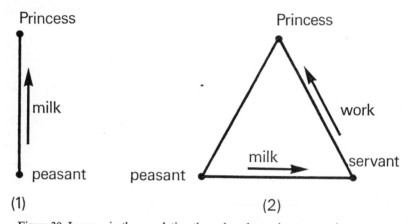

Figure 30. Increase in the population through a change in consumption.

These examples may be made as intricate and realistic as one wishes: the switch towards the consumption of products calling less on natural resources increases the optimum. Thus men, to be more at ease, enlarge as it were their natural environment.

As a rule the optimum rises, and overpopulation diminishes, when tastes switch from primary to secondary or tertiary products.

The general problem, complex and involving production graphs, has only limited practical interest. Without going into the details of research, let it suffice to give the general conclusions.

As a rule the optimum population tends to rise when consumption switches: 1. From the primary to the secondary or tertiary sectors. 2. From a hump-backed production curve to a less humped or a hollow one. 3. From a well-tried product to a newly invented one because of a process of saturation also affecting the shape of the curve. These conditions are not likely to occur together, and they may even act at cross-purposes: a primary product (decreasing returns) may

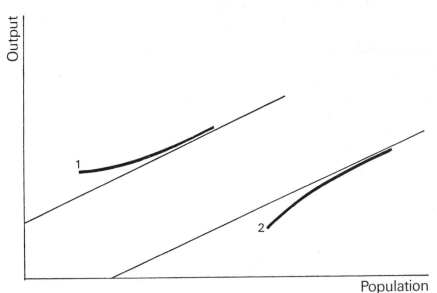

Figure 31. Examples of primary (1) and secondary (2) activities, concave and convex to their upper surfaces respectively.

be concave to its upper surface and a secondary one the reverse (see figure 31), but secondary or new productions are more likely to be concave to the upper surface.

Switch of tastes towards the tertiary sector

Here is a more realistic example than the milk bath model: imagine yourself in a restaurant in Italy consuming primary products. Through not eating at home you are already increasing the optimum population by bringing cooks and waiters into the economic circuit. Two Neapolitan street players stroll by, singing, and pass the hat around. This may not exactly cause a change in your tastes, you may even feel slightly bullied into it, but anyway you give these tertiary producers a tip. You may not go as far as to miss the next course to make up for it, but at the end of the week the result will be the same. These players have forced their way into the economic system. In other words supernumerary men may take up a tertiary activity requiring no raw materials, and by talent or hard work offer the producers pleasures for which they are willing to give up some product. If each is as satisfied as before and the new tertiary workers are equally happy, they will literally have added to the optimum population. An example such as this might even reconcile the physiocrats and the mercantilists.

But why should consumption switch towards the tertiary sector? Either because a new product is offered, or because an old product has reached the saturation level, or particularly when technological progress has lifted people's income to a level where they can aspire to something formerly unobtainable. We shall return to this thorny question in chapters 14 and 15, but this has already shown one way in which technological progress can increase the optimum population.

In the extreme case of a totally tertiary population, there would be no optimum, and no one would worry about it until space or oxygen became scarce. *Thus in a dynamic population real (as opposed to statistical) under-employment drops unless other factors tend to the contrary.*

Some possible cases

Let us illustrate the principle of utility by a distinction between food and raw materials as primary products.

1. The primary population feeds the secondary population. Food answers a need that is not very elastic. Let us go as far as to assume that the number of calories needed is rigorously determined. This means that the primary output must be proportional to the population, which gives us the number of primary workers.[1]

On figure 32 we know the population OP and the food which has to be

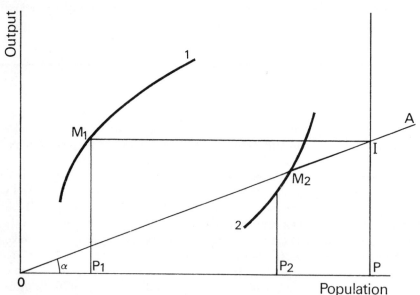

Figure 32. Primary population feeding a secondary population.

[1] The function $W(n_1 n_2)$ then becomes $P_1(n_1) = \alpha n = \alpha(n_1 + n_2)$.

88

consumed, and hence the invariable line OA. OA intersects the perpendicular to OP at I. IP is the food consumption, which can be translated to M_1P_1. We have thus produced the primary population OP_1 which gives us the secondary (or tertiary) population OP_2, and hence the output M_2P_2. The two outputs, M_1P_1 and M_2P_2, may then be combined, as already shown.

2. The primary population gives the secondary population work to do by supplying it with raw materials. If there is no technological progress the secondary output is proportional to the primary output.[1] The graph would be more complicated than the preceding one.

3. These two cases can be combined, since the secondary population needs raw materials as well as food; we can define the agricultural population producing food as in the first case, and then distribute the remaining producers as in the second case.

This model can be complicated in various ways: for instance by introducing a tertiary population, by considering the making of secondary products useful to agriculture, or especially by admitting that needs are less rigid.

Sometimes the primary population is necessarily constant. This was the case in France and abroad during the last war. The great reluctance of secondary and tertiary workers to become primary made the optimum redistribution of jobs impossible. *The effect of food rationing was to create fifty thousand jobs for tertiary distributors, for lack of the five hundred thousand primary producers who would have increased the output of food.* Change in consumption was avoided here by authority. The urban population may have more or less kept its jobs; but had agricultural output fallen too low, this stability might have caused a famine.

Where there is a surplus primary population, people may be equally reluctant to change their status, or rather the land owners may be strong enough to obtain protection ensuring that the distribution of professions is constant (through subsidies, loss exports, distillation of wine, etc.). The problem is then not how to distribute the population but how to seek the best number of people p determined by the constant primary population n, a constant: rigid attitudes such as these helped the United States to carry out the Marshall Aid plan; they led France into a policy of destruction of goods (distillation of beet and wine) which hampered both employment and the general standard of living.

---

[1] The function W is here $P_2(n_2) = KP_2(n_1)$.

10

SOCIAL CLASS AND THE DISTRIBUTION OF GOODS

> 'The first man who enclosed a field and thought of saying "this is mine" and found people naïve enough to believe him, was the real founder of society.'
>
> ROUSSEAU

We have worked up till now on the rather problematic assumption that products were evenly distributed. Inequality of income, and therefore of consumption, has the following effects on the population: 1. The standard of living can no longer be considered as equal to the average output. 2. The structure of consumption and output, and the distribution of population into various categories is altered. 3. Output is either increased through certain individuals having an 'interest' in it, or decreased through dissatisfaction amongst the majority of workers. We will pay as little attention as possible to the influence of this third factor on total output. It is a most vast and interesting field, but it is outside our subject. Again we must avoid any ethical considerations, indeed almost any feeling, in this chapter. The aim is not to criticise or to justify the collective behaviour of men, but rather to observe how distribution occurs in certain circumstances.

Definition of the standard of living

At the outset everyone has the same income. P is the total output, n is the number of people, $C = \dfrac{P}{n}$ the standard of living. Now a small minority m suddenly receives a higher income, the rest still being evenly distributed. This privileged class may be as small as one person.

If S is the part levied by the minority, the standard of living is no longer $\dfrac{P}{n}$ but $\dfrac{P-S}{n-m}$. The way this is achieved (profits, ground rents, taxes) is unimportant.

We will assume for the time being that this change does not affect the structure of consumption (and hence of output). Only S can modify the graph of standard of living against population.

Inequality causes the maximum population to fall

Where a society divides up its output equally, men multiply up to the biological limit at which they get such small rations that births and deaths are balanced (see chapter 2). By exacting food from the majority, the minority causes numbers to drop. We will see later how changes in consumption may influence this result.

Inequality causes the optimum population to rise

a. If the levy is independent both of the number of inhabitants and of their output, the optimum population increases with it, as it did with the 'overheads' studied in chapter 5.

Where the levy varies with numbers, it is often proportional to them: thus for example in the case of a constant profit per worker, or of a capitation tax. Here the standard of living of each individual drops by a given amount, whatever the numbers. In plotting standard of living against numbers, the ordinates must all be varied by the same quantity. The optimum population does not change: therefore in this case output is more important. If the quantity taken does not increase above certain numbers, then we are soon back to the preceding case, where the levy was constant. The optimum population, however, only increases if the people spared do not have too high a rank.

b. Where the levy is proportional to output, it is 'neutral', not affecting the

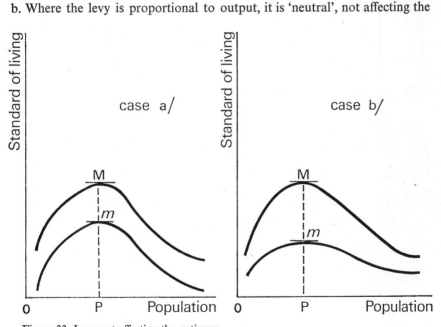

Figure 33. Levy not affecting the optimum.

91

optimum population, since the output per person falls by a constant amount (on figure 33b, by half).

c. Where the levy is progressive (but still not a personal income tax, variable for each individual) and increases faster than the total output, the optimum population drops with the distortion of the curve towards the right.

d. If the levy increases more slowly than output, the optimum population rises.

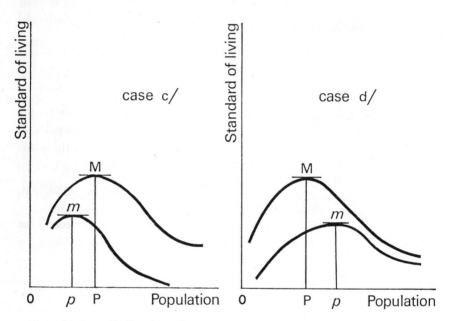

Figure 34. Levy affecting the optimum.

Consider the example of an agricultural holding exploited collectively. How many people should be put there so that with equal distribution of incomes they may have the best possible standard of living?

With no levies or taxes, the optimum population is regulated by the division of labour and the work to be done. Now apply a fixed levy, independent of the number of people on the farm or their output. The community's interest lies in expanding, to *share the burden out over greater numbers*. It may become profitable to cultivate poor, hitherto neglected land. Because of the fixed levy overall returns have dropped.

A numerical example is shown on page 93.

Before the levy, division of labour increases the standard of living up to the fourth inhabitant, but after that its effect is balanced by the fall in productivity or in efforts. The optimum is 4, giving a standard of living of 160. With a levy of 100 (a rent for instance) the optimum is 6, giving a standard of living of

92

Before the levy			After the levy	
Numbers	Output	Output per person	Net output	Output available per person
1	100	100		
2	260	130	160	80
3	450	150	350	116·7
4	640	160	540	135
5	790	158	690	138
6	930	155	830	**138·3**
7	1050	150	950	135
8	1160	145	1060	132·5

138·3. The population will find it profitable to increase by two and increase output, but the standard of living will have to drop slightly.

This stresses a fact seldom realised: in a system based on private property *two different aims, standard of living and employment, can be at cross-purposes.* The existence of the landlord lowers the standard of living but encourages employment. If the two extra inhabitants were on the dole before, *they can be said to have found work thanks to a crippling and no doubt unjust levy.* And the heavier the levy the more people can be absorbed in this way; though naturally there are limits, since above a certain figure the levy would probably cause the workers to leave and take up begging instead.

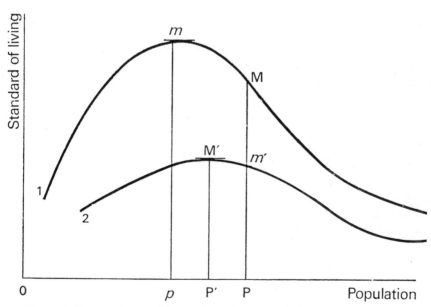

Figure 35. Unequal incomes increase the optimum population.

Figure 35 shows (1) a working population paying a small tribute or tax to the owner. Their standard of living is highest at *m*, giving an optimum population of O*p*; this is however less than the real population OP. The maximum level *mp* can only be achieved if those with the law or the power on their side eliminate a number *p*P of the weak or the unlucky. This may take the form of a new lease of the land, to a farmer for instance. He will not seek the maximum but the optimum, and will thus lower the population.

Now, (2) an 'iniquitous' owner comes along, and raises the rent or taxes. The standard of living drops but the optimum population rises, so that the excess population drops to P'P, and there are fewer people to get rid of – there may even be cause to call some back.

This simple instance shows that the owner and the poorer labourers may have interests in common which oppose them to the farmer. This, we will see later, shows up class interest in an unexpected light. It is already clear, if we think of the state instead of the owner, that taxes increase employment.

If in the same example the tax were to be proportional to output, the optimum would not change. The population would have no interest in increasing its numbers. If the tax were progressive, it would reinforce the factor of diminishing returns, reducing the optimum population. There would be an advantage here in being fewer.

Changes in consumption

We have already suggested that unequal incomes change the structure of consumption. The rich do not buy the same goods as the poor. We must consider how this factor affects the optimum population.

The richer a man the more secondary goods (highly manufactured cars, television sets, etc.) or tertiary services (servants, entertainment, lawyers, restaurants) he consumes. Unequal incomes thus reduce the demand for primary goods and increase it for secondary and tertiary ones. As we saw in the last chapter, *such changes usually increase the optimum population and even the real population.* The next chapter will show how.

Unequal incomes, especially in an agricultural society with private ownership, must raise the optimum population in two ways: through fixed levies on output and through the peculiar structure of consumption. This gives rise to a cruel problem: unequal incomes 'solve everything' except the standard of living of the poor, and yet they may be caused by the very existence of the surplus people.

Rulers and subjects in populations

At this point a double distinction becomes necessary:
  1. *Between classes*. A class system stresses inequality of incomes and stan-

94

dards of living, and gives less relevance to the idea of a global optimum, since there are in fact two populations – the rulers and the ruled. Their numbers should be considered separately, and each can be approached from two points of view. We thus have four optimums: a. The optimum number of subjects in the ruler's interests. b. The optimum number of subjects in their own interests. c. The optimum number of rulers in their own interests. d. The optimum number of rulers in the interests of the subjects.

2. *Between various economic systems.* Though a ruling population generally has the same effect in various systems, a distinction should be made between forms of authority. We will study two types in particular: the feudal agricultural system, with landowners and labourers, and the industrial system, with employers and workers. This will lead us to develop the theory of domination already sketched out on pages 62–3.

11

AGRICULTURAL SOCIETIES

'We need more subjects and more cattle.'
TURMEAU DE LA MORANDIÈRE

We are still considering a static economic system: in this case a population consisting of a ruling class of landowners and a class of farm workers, whether serfs, tenants or labourers. In considering the effect of the numbers of workers, we may simplify things by assuming that there is only one owner, who seeks the number of subjects ensuring the highest possible income for himself.

The landlord's interest

Because of the decreasing returns (either from the soil or from those who cultivate it) there comes a time when it is no longer profitable to increase the numbers of workers. It is only worthwhile developing land when it brings in more than the supplies necessary to those who till it. Any other development would involve subsidising those who carried it out. The marginal districts, returning just enough for the workers to live on, may be developed without bringing any wealth in because they ensure a kind of demographic reserve that may come in useful in a war or an epidemic.

The owner will get his maximum income if he exacts from the workers' output everything above their subsistence requirements. As with the power optimum (see page 55) this may not be a strictly physiological minimum, but may involve psychological factors such as the will to produce; however we assume for the sake of the argument that the minimum (whether physiological or psychological) is strictly defined.

This levy determines the optimum number of primary workers but does not account for the whole subjected population unless the ruler consumes all the primary products directly. In fact he will not find use for them all, however large his appetite or taste for pleasure-gardens or horses, and he will spend his surplus revenue on secondary products such as clothes or jewels, or on tertiary services such as servants, footmen or soldiers, or even invest it into future productivity, for instance by clearing new land for agriculture.

Since the secondary activities in an agricultural society are crafts rather than industries, their returns do not increase with manpower, and are more or less stable. We may therefore consider all those who do not work on the land as tertiary workers.

The landlord thus uses the revenue that he does not consume directly in financing a number of men (see the numerical example on page 98). The situation is comparable to the search for the power optimum (see chapter 6), with the tertiary, or pure workers, equivalent to unarmed soldiers, and the secondary ones, who use raw materials, to armed soldiers.

The situation can be summed up even more simply if we consider that the landlord consumes either primary products (food, and also the wool in his clothes) or work. Primary consumption, whether direct or not, demands a certain number of labourers.

Thus the optimum number of subjects in the ruler's interest, consisting of these labourers plus the secondary and tertiary workers, depends not only on the size of the land but on the landlord's way of life. The figure will not be the same for two different rulers of a given estate. For one who hunts, raises horses and eats a great deal, the optimum is fairly low; another who eats less but likes his food carefully cooked, and appreciates expensive materials and jewels demanding more labour than raw materials, will need more men to get the highest possible satisfaction from his land.

Even in the extreme case where the ruler did not consume any primary products, the number of subjects would remain lower than the maximum for the estate, since the maximum number would include people not producing their own food, and there would be no question of the ruler subsidising development which did not enable workers to meet their subsistence needs.

From the ruler's point of view, all the extra men over the optimum have no right to exist: they are given no food, and disappear in one way or another.

The interest of the subjects

The peasants and serfs in France before the Revolution were not able to en-quire into this, though it was a different matter in the nineteenth century with the awakening of the workers. But we may still try to reckon where their interests lay.

Where the landlord exacts everything above subsistence requirements, the optimum number of subjects is irrelevant since their standard of living will not change. They have no reason either to increase or to decrease their numbers. This alone would be sufficient reason for the usual proliferation of subjects under such rule.

If however the levy is limited so that the subjects get at least some of the products of the soil, then there is an optimum number for them. *Again, private property causes a limitation in numbers.* This optimum is lower than the one wanted by the ruler, and it also varies with the ruler's way of life. The following numerical example will show how.

1. Number of farm workers	100	200	300	**400**	500	600
2. Marginal output (in food)	100	150	170	160	130	100
3. Total output	100	250	420	580	710	810
4. Output per head	1	1·25	1·40	**1·45**	1·44	1·35
5. Landlord's levy (20 per cent)	20	50	84	116	142	162
6. Amount left for the workers	80	200	336	464	568	648
7. Left for each worker (or standard of living)	0·8	1	1·12	**1·16**	1·13	1·08
8. Landlord's food consumption	5	10	20	20	20	20
9. Amount left in food to pay tertiary personnel	15	40	64	96	122	142
10. Number of tertiary workers that can be employed (lines 7 and 9)	18	40	57	82	107	131
11. Total population	118	240	357	**482**	607	731

This chart shows the effect of various numbers of primary producers, assuming that their whole output can be converted into a unit such as wheat. As numbers increase the marginal productivity (line 2) does not drop until the fourth hundred of workers, thanks to division of labour – at this point output per person is at its highest.

Here the landlord comes into the reckoning: to separate the influence of his levy from that of the use he makes of it, we first assume that this levy is proportional to output (line 5), thus taking away any direct influence of his on the optimum. The highest standard of living of the subjects is now lower, but it is again reached for a number of 400 – this time however the figure only includes the primary workers.

If the landlord consumed all the output himself, the optimum would indeed be 400. But, even with the help of his horses and dogs he cannot, and is saturated at 20 units (line 8). If we subtract this figure from his levy (line 5) we get the wages he can offer his servants, musicians and soldiers (line 9), who must have roughly the same standard of living as the land workers. This gives us the number he can employ (line 10), and, by addition, the total population, whose optimum is 482 with a standard of living of 1·16.

Thus by consuming only 20 units of the primary products he levied, *the landlord gives a living to 82 extra people.* In his place another landlord might eat 100 units instead: the optimum would then drop to 413.

With 600 workers the standard of living falls almost to the subsistence level. This is the landlord's optimum. He has no interest in further expansion. The workers will have 600 units. He takes the extra 210, using 20 for himself and feeding 190 men with the rest. There will be 190 tertiary workers and a total population of 790. The second landlord, consuming 100 units, would only employ 110 tertiaries, giving an optimum population of 710: he would cause 80 men to die of hunger.

Having isolated the influence of consumption, we will now see how the fixed levy influences the situation, and then combine the two factors. Take again the previous example, assuming this time that above 116 units the levy increases more slowly than output, for instance because the ruler is satisfied or because of the difficulty of collecting taxes from a population improverished by decreasing returns. We no longer need the first two columns, so the chart reads as follows:

1. Number of farm workers	300	400	500	600
2. Marginal output for extra units of 100 (in food)	170	160	130	100
3. Total output	420	580	710	810
4. Output per head	**1·40**	**1·45**	**1·44**	**1·35**
5. Landlord's levy	84	116	120	122
6. Amount left for the workers	336	**464**	590	**688**
7. Left for each worker (or standard of living)	1·12	1·16	**1·18**	1·15
8. Landlord's food consumption	20	20	20	20
9. Amount left in food to pay tertiary personnel	64	96	100	102
10. Number of tertiaries that can be employed	**57**	**82**	**85**	**89**
11. Total population	357	482	**585**	689

Since the levy is smaller above a certain level, it is in both the landlord's and the labourers' interest that their number should be 500 rather than 400, since this increases the possible number of tertiary workers and the optimum population jumps from 482 to 585. Thus: 1. If there were no landlord to serve, the subjects would have an economic optimum (400 in this example). 2. Since they have to pay this levy, their interest lies in increasing to 482 if the levy is proportional to output and 585 if it is in inverse proportion to output. 3. If the levy were to increase faster than the output, the optimum would be smaller. In this case the landlord's own interest lies in an optimum of 790; but no form of population restriction can be advantageous to the workers since in any case they are only at the subsistence level.

The subjects do not want their ruler to demand too much from them. But if he does, their interest lies in being numerous to share it out. The ruler too prefers to have a great deal of subjects, in order to increase his levy. *Thus the interests of ruler and subjects are at odds from the point of view of standard of living, but more in agreement where the optimum population and employment are concerned.*

How the real situation develops

Not wishing to limit their growth, the subjects multiply naturally past the optimum that would ensure their highest possible standard of living, and only stop when their numbers are such that they are having to develop sub-marginal land. If the ruler is in a position to enforce his will on his subjects, now suffering from excessive numbers, he will exact as much as possible, limited only by the effects of hunger, of excessive mortality, or of their possible escape from the production circuit (into banditry or beggary). These reactions occur either because the ruler's optimum has been passed or because the levy is operating unsatisfactorily. A badly planned levy may prevent the optimum from being passed, but both factors have been known to operate together.

The population can therefore attain neither the maximum the land could support with equal distribution of goods, nor sometimes even the optimum giving the landlord his highest possible income. Numbers are limited by deaths and 'desertions'.

In real life feudal lords do not see the subtle distinction between maximum power and maximum population, even when they rule absolutely and care little for their subjects: they do not therefore seek the economic optimum. This is easily understood: the owner of an estate limits his domesticated animals but allows game and other useful wild animals to multiply freely; a fruit farmer prunes his wall fruit but lets the 'outside' trees develop as they will. In the same way the landlord wishes his 'free' workers to multiply indefinitely into a 'reserve population' which is ill-defined since there are usually no precise limits between worthwhile and sub-marginal lands or activities.

In any case, high mortality amongst the subjects, caused by famine, serious epidemics, etc., encourages the rulers rather to make up for the losses by allowing numbers to rise, than to improve the living conditions of their subjects. If one remembers too that levies are never as well distributed and collected as in theory, it will be seen that a real population never does exceed what would be the ruler's optimum, and the problem rarely occurs of a surplus rural population on sub-marginal lands needing subsidies.

As recently as the eighteenth century there was a widespread belief, shared by Montesquieu, that there had been considerable depopulation since antiquity. This attitude may have been due to the large numbers of men swallowed up by wars, famines, and epidemics. People were more afraid of being below than above the power optimum. Because incomes and taxes were unevenly distributed, there always remained some underdeveloped land, indicating that the maximum had not been reached. Hence the frequent plans to send the numerous tramps and beggars back from the towns to the land: the aim was to set everyone to work and tolerate no parasites. Rulers can never have too many servants.

The theory of domination found a remarkable exponent in the eighteenth century in the person of Turmeau de la Morandière, gentleman demographer, who expounds it in his three works with a cynical ingenuity that makes him more instructive than clearer sighted authors. Not making the distinction between optimum and maximum, he writes naively 'we need more subjects and cattle'.[1] He is a rabid populationist, by inclination rather than by calculation, since he lacks the concept of overpopulation. No one defended this theory more frankly, though many held and expressed the same ideas less clearly.

So for the absolute ruler there are in practice never too many subjects. The most provident rulers are merely those who avoid too much wastage and leave their subjects just enough to survive without any drop in productivity. Boulainvilliers, who was the first to think of what we now call social security, wrote in *Mémoires au duc d'Orléans* 'the common folk are useful, they must therefore be preserved'. Even this precaution was sometimes forgotten: only after wars or terrible famines did one usually see preservative measures. (Colbert protected very large families.)

The number of slaves on the other hand must be limited. One may indeed breed them with a mind to resale, but unless they are supplied by violent capture, the master's interest lies in providing them with food and a minimum of care. This interest may not always have been recognised in practice, but it is mandatory, especially in a stable society. This is why slaves may be less severely treated than a free working class in an overpopulated land. Linguet, who enjoyed paradoxes, stressed this in vain.[2]

As for the subjects, they lead too primitive a life to be conscious of their numbers and their effect on the standard of living. But others, whom we shall meet again, may worry for them, out of charity or for other reasons.

The optimum number of rulers

Obviously their own interest lies in being as few as possible. The lord or the king has no need for a human oligarchy absorbing part of the wealth produced by the work. He may however be interested in social pleasures, or see a need for security, which would demand a certain increase. Rulers may even establish a certain division of labour, or rather of functions, amongst themselves: indeed the domination of their subjects, like any other task, entails optimum numbers.

In the Middle Ages the rulers' numbers were limited by wars, and later, before the Revolution, by celibacy, particularly through the priesthood, which avoided crippling divisions of wealth.

---

[1] *Appel des étrangers dans nos colonies*, 1763. His other works are *Principes politiques sur le rappel des protestants en France*, 1764, and *Police pour les mendiants*, 1764.

[2] 'I have not been forgiven for showing . . . that the lot of the horse, well fed, well groomed, well sheltered and treated against illness, was preferable to that of a free labourer' (*Annales Politiques*, I).

The subjects are equally keen to have as few rulers as possible – indeed they would prefer to have none at all, and to share their output equally, ensuring a higher standard of living and greater numbers. But societies which have not progressed far do not know how to achieve this: their interest lies rather in having as few rulers as possible. Even if in multiplying the rulers were to maintain the same levy, their consumption of primary products would be increased, reducing the optimum and real numbers of subjects.

Ancient Egypt

This particular instance of an agricultural system is well worth dwelling on. At the point where irrigation ends complete desert begins, with no transition through hills or poor soils, and returns fall suddenly to nothing; also, the intensive methods of agriculture were not elastic, so the marginal worker could not produce any significant amount. The Nile fertilised the soil and a determinate number of men cultivated it. This situation was eminently favourable to inequality of wealth. The workers would no doubt have been happy to consume secondary and tertiary goods through a better distribution; but their numbers were rigidly determined by the invariable output of food. The mass of servants and non-agricultural slaves could not have joined them and increased the food output and hence the population. The ruling class certainly ate better, but did not thus diminish the population noticeably. 'In short', the pharaoh might say to some court of final judgement, 'the drastic inequality in incomes which benefited me did not kill many people.' The energy which could not blunt its edges against non-existent marginal soils was in a way condemned to deploy upwards. The master, whose authority was guaranteed by the invariability of the society, was also provided with servants and artists who achieved the fantastic contrasts in this civilisation.

Balance between rulers and subjects

Where there are no middle classes to separate them, the rulers and subjects thus reach a *modus vivendi, by which unequal incomes and overpopulation adjust mutually*. The landlord might say, like the pharaoh, 'By levying a large part of your output I may diminish your standard of living, but by consuming secondary and tertiary products I increase your optimum and real numbers. Without me many of you would be killed in the struggle for higher standards of living that could only be achieved by a fall in numbers. I weigh on you lightly and serve the weakest.'

Such logic is by no means fanciful. People have, at various periods, defended luxury on the grounds that it brings employment. Even today in many overpopulated agricultural countries, the argument may not be used expressedly, but still the economy rests on the *modus vivendi* between demographic pressure and unequal incomes. In a heavily populated town the buildings rise high up, particularly in the centre; incomes tend to act in the same uneven way in a population that is too large.

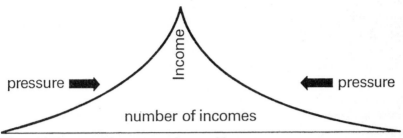

Figure 36. Demographic pressure and unequal incomes.

The subject classes might answer that the secondary and tertiary consumption, the lace, coaches, and theatres the rich indulge in, might come to them instead, and equal incomes be achieved easily. *But they do not attempt spontaneously to maintain the pattern of demand*: their need of primary products is so great that any increase in income is spent on these, reducing the optimum population and causing unrest.

Such societies do not have any middle classes which would disturb the *modus vivendi*: in a fairly primitive country it is difficult to introduce one, since it would compete directly with the poor for primary products with decreasing returns, and the rich would soon set this right. Even if a rich man has an income of 100 units when a poor man earns 1, the rich man cannot consume many more calories in food than the poor – at the most it would amount to 20 units; whereas 20 members of a middle class with an income of 4 each can each consume three times as much as a poor man, or in all as much as 60 poor men.

Middle classes thus fight against overpopulation. In this struggle some one must win and it is sometimes the middle class, sometimes the old system. Middle class societies are in favour of birth control; whereas in overpopulated countries both subjects and rulers want to reduce the intermediate classes to a minimum.

The social function of the owner

We have seen the owner explicitly, or the system implicitly, defending his function: he gives little to each; without him each would have more, but only because there would be fewer people at the share-out. His social function is not only to protect and keep order: *he is also a distributor, a rationing system, allowing a higher population*. His function puts him in a position to pay himself an excessive amount for his troubles, but he makes up for this by not competing directly with his subjects as far as vital supplies are concerned.

This well-paid part as rationer has by no means always been properly played. It demands a well-established organisation, allowing each one his subsistence and a little over. In fact before the Revolution in France taxes were so unevenly distributed that they were often crippling. Also, the land-lords often had recourse to exporting goods, which was fatal. Every time the Russian court sold wheat abroad in order to buy luxury goods, it increased the death rate somewhere in its own territory. Cantillon reckoned, and Con-dillac too pointed out, that in trading Champagne wine for Brussels lace, France was exchanging the output of sixteen thousand acres for something produced by one acre. If the goods in question were foods, the loss would be immediately convertible into human lives. Nowadays one could reckon the lives it costs when some middle-eastern millionaire buys a Cadillac.

But the landlord's social function exists nevertheless. The classical debates over the use of luxury are based on a misunderstanding. Where luxury is harmful, the inequality of possessions and incomes is to blame. Where this is necessary, one should first enquire into how the incomes are used. Cantillon was the first to see this: it is remarkable not only that he should, with amazing foresight, have recognised how important the orientation of demand was, at a time when political economy was in its infancy, but that his lessons should have been forgotten. The real appropriation is not that of the soil or some other possession, but the consumption of goods. It is this that eliminates human beings. Instead of 'property is theft' Proudhon should have said 'consumption is theft'.

Effertz[1] seems not to have known of Cantillon, but he wrote in the same spirit:

'When we consume goods that have cost soil to produce, we are depriving our fellows of the enjoyment of the soil. . . . Charitable old people who build hospitals for elderly dogs are made of the stuff of angels; those who own stables are murderers.'

Quesnay and the French physiocrats held the contrary opinion: that luxury goods increased the consumption of agricultural products, causing an increase in 'land rent' and thus encouraging agricultural investment.

The Cantillon-Quesnay debate is still alive in some countries, and so is worth studying closely. Of these two original minds, Cantillon is right. Instead of consuming a product of the soil directly, a landlord who goes in for decora-tive luxury gets it consumed by others who would be unable to live without it. This has no effect on the price of grain or on the tempo of agriculture.

Even if we were to suppose that direct primary consumption of goods encourages the landowner, we might still ask whether he will want to in-

[1] His main works were: *Arbeit und Boden,* 1888; and *Katechismus der Politischen Economik,* 1893.

vest in the land. Mirabeau says he should: 'A landowner who leaves one of his barns roofless is a murderer of the whole population'.[1] A good landowner, inspired by *physiocrat principles*, will indeed invest the income he cannot consume and create new sources of wealth, but what reasons are going to persuade him to increase his income indefinitely if he cannot even then spend the extra part? Public welfare? A desire to increase the population? It is not property in itself that makes non-proprietors poor, but the consumption of goods. And whoever possesses intends to consume. Mirabeau sees the owner as a paternalist and an untiring benefactor who 'lends' to the soil to enable it to feed more people. A deserving part, but too saintly to be played for long. Everyone is not, as Mirabeau styled himself, the 'Friend of man'; indeed the Friend himself did not carry friendship that far on his own estates.

If it were impossible to consume secondary or tertiary goods, would the only recourse be to invest unceasingly? It is difficult to visualise a monarch considering a rise in his population as an end in itself; the dominant class always has found itself other pleasurable forms of consumption, such as hunting, which was as lethal for men as for the game because of the destruction wrought on the fields and the land it used up. Diminishing returns also begin beyond a certain point to discourage the efforts to force the hand of Nature. It is a fact that in spite of very high land returns in France before the Revolution a great deal of land was fallow, because tastes were directed rather towards clothes, carriages, perfumes, and all that men's already inventive minds thought up to create new needs.

In short, the rulers of an agricultural society may use their surplus income in three ways: 1. Consume supplies produced by nature, which is deadly to the population. 2. Consume human labour, which causes a slight but definitive rise in the population. 3. Invest to create new supplies, which is the only way that makes for an indefinite rise in the population, but its effect decreases slowly as long as technology does not change.

For both Cantillon and the physiocrats, property being at the time an unquestioned dogma, there was no other possible solution. The same cannot be said today of the developing countries which are still at this stage. We shall return to them later, after first following the logical and chronological development of domination.

---

[1] *Les économiques.* 1769,

12

RELATIVE DOMINATION AND PATERNALISM

THE CUE FOR MALTHUS[1]

'A parish priest might, properly enough, not be warranted to join a couple unless they could make it appear that their children were not likely to become a burden to the parish.'

STEUART

The subject in revolt

Do we really need more subjects and cattle? As well as taking care of cattle, feeding them and protecting them against illness, the master prevents them from multiplying naturally, because he realises that there is a certain optimum number above which the ouput of meat, milk, or wool would drop. (This is not so with a wild species, which may multiply as it wishes unless it is deemed a pest.)

The attitude of rulers towards their subjects is similar. We have shown that they do not worry about the workers multiplying too much; but remember that this view demands total submission on the part of the workers. If the subject species escapes, or becomes a pest in any way, the ruler's attitude changes.

When a tax or imposition is too unevenly distributed and is not sufficiently lenient on marginal lands, the subject worker may throw it off and attempt to earn a living in some other less honest way: begging, vagrancy, crime. The surplus population then appears, under various names: free companies, high-waymen, bands of sturdy beggars, etc. In thus leaving its reservation and turning into a consumer, the subject species becomes a pest, like the rabbit. The ruler will try to re-establish his wavering authority, or to cut his losses.

He will first try to thrust the escapers back under the yoke of production. From the Middle Ages until very recently, as long as overpopulation sub-sisted, innumerable laws, orders, and measures against beggary tried to repress the escapers and force work on them. But it was difficult to repress those who had followed the landlords' exodus to the towns, or had served in the army.

[1] When I mention Malthus, as I often do further on, I refer to a doctrine and a frame of mind rather than to the gentleman himself.

Those who had not found places amongst the crowds of servants in the orbit of the rich man preferred to pick up the crumbs from his feast rather than work to supply them to him. In the large towns where the rich live in agricultural countries, the same can be observed to this day.

Where La Morandière (once again) and others drew up plans to send back to the land all lower class parasites, they were still being unrepentant populationists. But the moment it appears that these people are a more or less permanent and irreducible burden, the idea of cutting their numbers is put forward. This is the cue for paternalism and Malthus' theory.

Class paternalism

Humanity, pity, even social solidarity may also appear in the ruling class, but only when they see suffering nearby. When poverty is geographically distant or difficult to discern, it is not such a painful matter.

It is indeed difficult to distinguish between what is deserving and what is not in such charitable actions. But whatever the motives at the back of the human mind, the results are there. The critical point in England was after 1750, when the enforcement of the 'Poor Laws' gave the poor certain rights, however slender. Joseph Townsend and even Steuart expressed worry: 'Nations may for a time increase their numbers beyond the due proportion of their food, but they will in the same proportion destroy the ease and comfort of the affluent.'[1] Townsend criticised the application of the poor laws and suggested, like La Morandière, that those idlers be sent back to their servile status. Hunger would discipline them. Malthus saw things a little differently. He considered the poor laws as a deplorable but established fact, and tried to find ways of reducing the burden. He was as logical as Townsend in his own way. Since the ruling class was no longer all-powerful, it was becoming profitable if not necessary to restrict births.

In France where there were no poor laws, things happened differently. Of all the authors who studied the problem of vagrancy, not one suggested diminishing it merely by the limitation of births.

The same trend in the family

Yet even in France Malthus' moment had arrived within the family. The question of domination reappears here.

As long as the father had absolute power and all his children worked, his main interest lay in having a large family. The economically optimum size of a family is the same as the maximum when the children roam freely, begging or pilfering; the situation is more or less the same as that of an absolute ruler

[1] J. Townsend, *A Dissertation on the Poor Laws.*

and free subjects. There is no idea of an optimum. The children brought up in this way die in large numbers but those who survive earn for their parents as soon as possible: at the age of eight to ten, or even before.

In a more advanced society, a reasonably well-fed child is a burden for a few years, but is still 'productive' from the economic point of view. If the parents have no property they have no reason to limit their offspring unless they have some inkling of a power optimum that would be passed if they multiplied too much.

However, a decrease in parental authority changes the ruler's position. Where infant labour is prohibited or not practised, and education is compulsory, the subject's children can even become a real burden; the optimum is also decreased by any family possessions, and falls to two, one, or even no children as long as reasons of a religious or an emotional kind have no part to play.

The father may invest constantly in his family, like Mirabeau's ideal landowner. But he may also be tempted, like the eighteenth-century landlord, by the new pleasures that are daily offered to him.

Children may become the object of formidable competition; in money as in the time given to them. Many authors mention a tendency around 1760–70 for couples to reduce the number of their children. Luxury was accused of being a great decimator.

But it may not have deserved this reputation. The wealthy were in fact replacing the children by servants, and this created new jobs for people who probably consumed fewer primary products than the children would have done, so that they may have actually increased the population. Cerfvol, one of the critics of luxury, wrote: 'Whoever has twenty servants and no child should have instead ten children and four servants', not realising that it is the first situation that is 'populationist' where the system exposes people to deadly famines.

Colonialism

Originally this was essentially a commercial proposition. The aim was to extract wealth, products or even men from the new territories. Since there was an ample provision of men for the market, at very low purchase prices, it was profitable to treat them more cruelly than animals. The new rulers, both in Asia and in Africa, were thus regardless of the numbers of their subjects.

In conquering Algeria it was planned to push the Arabs southwards where they could 'colonise the desert'. Only in central Africa, especially in the last years of colonialism, did the spread of sleeping sickness and other causes of mortality give rise to the phrase *'faire du nègre'* (to breed blacks).

During the twentieth century, with the help of the two world wars, the pattern of domination has changed, as it had for social classes in the eighteenth century. In French North Africa until the end of the Second World War, the French governors showed no interest in any form of census. Not until 1947 was the problem of population formulated clearly enough for forecasts to be made and plans to be laid down to deal with the probable increase.[1]

Paternalism thus followed the same trend towards restriction in the colonies as in the family or state; *the increase in numbers became a cause of worry the moment the extra subjects became a burden*, and restrictions appeared desirable, if not on numbers, at least on the rate of increase.

But if restrictions are not applied, trouble is unavoidable as long as colonial domination continues, even if it is of a paternalistic kind. Subjects who cannot find a place in the economic framework inevitably rise up in the end. The uprisings of colonised peoples may have appeared to be due to political reasons but were in fact caused by mere pressure of numbers.

On the world-wide scale

This type of paternalism has also operated in a wider field; a feeling of international solidarity has helped to create anxiety about the overpopulation of the world. As the commercial, if not the political domination of the western world, weakened, and various forms of economic aid somewhat similar to the Poor Laws appeared, people were bound to worry over excess numbers. Naturally, this preoccupation developed mainly in the richest country of all, the United States: with the thought of having to feed industrious populations or to open to them the vast tracts of barely exploited land in the United States, a restrictive policy understandably appeared. The western world is behaving rather like the lord of the manor, who looks favourably at the prospering birth rate amongst his own labourers and farmers, but is worried by the increasing numbers of gypsies or irregular workers who wander on the fringes of his land. This attitude has been known to take an unpleasant form; we shall return for instance to Vogt's *Road to Survival*, which spread anxiety amongst the 'Whites' and fury amongst the Reds.

The working classes in the Anglo-Saxon countries have on the other hand become conscious of the privileged place they have in the world. The American worker knows that his purchasing power is far higher than that of an Asian or even a European, so that he would lose more than he would gain by a world-wide share out, even if the Rockfellers were included in it.

The class problem is tending to fade out and is reappearing on an international scale.

Conclusion

To sum up the ruler's position towards the subject population:

[1] See *Le problème démographique nord-africain*, Louis Chevalier, P.U.F.

The absolute ruler wishes, as far as possible, to exterminate the dangerous or useless subjects and multiply the useful ones, though he may occasionally have some notion of an optimum.

The limited ruler wishes to limit numbers, and in an extreme situation he will relinquish power because it has become too costly.

13

TECHNOLOGICAL PROGRESS AND THE MAXIMUM POPULATION

'The peacock makes a wheel of its tail,
Chance does the rest.
Then God takes a seat in the wheel,
and Man pushes him along.'

PRÉVERT

Let us now at last release the very important factor of 'technology' from our restrictive assumptions. Any technological change or physical discovery modifies the living conditions of a population through various phenomena, which may be divided into two categories: 1. The art of producing; 2. The way of consuming.

We will not dwell at this point on the thousand and one definitions of productivity and progress: we defined output in chapter 9 and will take it that technological progress occurs when a greater output can be achieved in the same number of (direct or indirect) working hours. To isolate further the influence of productivity we will assume working hours to be constant. A special section (chapter 18) will deal with the influence of working hours.

Techniques of consumption are usually linked with techniques of production; but tastes and fashion may well change consumers' habits without output having varied. We have already seen that these changes are important for the living conditions of the population.

The maximum population

Technological progress raises the maximum population and the standard of living. If each man produces more it becomes possible, given all the necessary social adjustments, to feed a greater number of people.

Figure 37 first plots output per head against numbers. MP is the subsistence level and OP the maximum population. A development in technology will give a different graph (2) entirely above the first. M moves to M' and the maximum population is now OP'. Where the slope at M is very slight (this means that there are a great deal of sub-marginal lands or occupations) the population may increase considerably. This happens for instance where hunting and gathering gives way to agriculture.

111

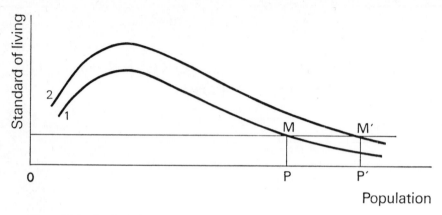

Figure 37. Technological progress increases the maximum population.

There are however possible objections: for instance, does the maximum population not fall when agriculture gives way in its turn to cattle raising? The value of the total output has increased because the pound of meat is more valuable than the five pounds of grain it replaces. But this is only an illusion, since the new value presupposes a smaller number of consumers: if the meat were shared out amongst the former numbers, they would all die of starvation.

The word 'progress' and the phrase 'maximum population' should obviously be properly understood. The maximum population is not the real population resulting from a new technique, *but the highest numbers that could be fed using the available technology fully and with a calculated distribution of goods.* In this case the replacement of crops by cattle causes an unfavourable change in the pattern of consumption of an overpopulated land; where there is acute overpopulation this might lead to the suppression of men, as with Thomas More's lethal sheep (see page 27), whereas we are trying to feed as many as possible.

A normally fertile population, tending to expand as much as it can, may really be reduced by a technological novelty, if this is used to serve other ends than numbers. Cantillon's name reoccurs; he realised that numbers depend on the way of life, which in its turn arises from the state of technology, the efficiency of consumption, and the inequality of incomes; to achieve the maximum population it is necessary to distribute goods equally, produce as much and consume as little as possible.

Even where the economic system is based on the family, the 'discovery' of cattle might cause the total population to drop, either by mortality because the number of food calories is sacrificed to their quality or to certain forms of comfort, or because of a drop in marriages or births.

The 'hungry horse' theory

One could also deny the beneficial effect of technological progress by considering it not as a road to greater consumption but as an improvement in production techniques measured quantitatively: this is the 'hungry horse' or 'greedy machine' theory.

Tom and Dick produce 20 consumption units, or 10 each, from two acres of land. Their output is 20, their standard of living is 10. Now technology steps forward: a horse is trained. Thanks to the horse one of the two men can cope with the two acres, but the horse itself consumes 7 units. Tom will be satisfied, since he will be producing 20 units, and instead of giving 10 to Dick he now only gives 7 to the horse. But how about Dick, who has had to go and live on higher ground where horses are of no help? He only produces 5 units here, so that the two men can only consume 18 between them or an average of 9 each instead of 10. Their global standard of living has dropped, and if they are to share their output they will realise that the horse has impoverished them. This drop may even cause the population to fall: if their subsistence level is 10 and they do not stop to think, Tom and Dick may die, stupidly, to feed the horse; or if Tom is stronger than Dick, he may let him starve on his rocky land. The alternative seems to be to reject such deadly progress.[1]

We meet here, once more, the question of how to define technological progress: should we assume that it is not progress to train the horse if this does not increase the average consumption? This is unsatisfactory, since if Dick did not exist, Tom's standard of living would rise from ten to thirteen and the horse would be an improvement. This model does at any rate show that an invention may or may not constitute progress, depending on the size of the population. Instead of having a new output and consumption curve completely above the first, we have two curves crossing in one way (figure

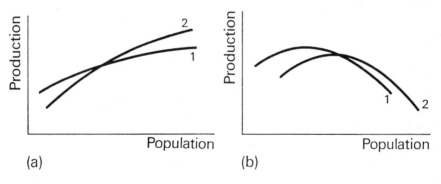

(a)   (b)

Figure 38

<hr />

[1] See also (page 62 above) the case of the idle buffalo described by Gourou.

113

38a) or the other (figure 38b), certain technological developments only being worthwhile if there is a sufficiently large population.

As with the 'hungry horse', so with the *'greedy machine', that relieves men not only of their work, which is fair enough, but also of their food, which is a nuisance.* Of course the competition in terms of consumption is less direct here, and thus the danger less apparent.

We may however avoid this difficulty by assuming from here onwards that in each situation the population is using the techniques giving the highest available output for consumption. The new graph of population against output may thus coincide in part with the first but never be below it. If a technological invention should reduce the population it will not be called 'progress' for this population.

Given these reservations, we may say that technological progress always increases the maximum population and affords a given population an opportunity to increase its standard of living or its numbers. This is of course not the only possibility: progress could in fact bring about social reactions unfavourable to numbers, though this is not generally the case.

An exception should however be made from the long-term point of view. As with animals (see above, chap. 1) technological progress might permit men to bite into their natural resources and thus let themselves in for dark days. The example of soil erosion cannot fail to come to mind.

14

TECHNOLOGICAL PROGRESS AND EMPLOYMENT

THEORIES AND REALITY

'Men have not yet found around them other mankinds to study them and explain where they are heading.'

TEILHARD DE CHARDIN

The influence of technological progress on employment is an emotional question, which it is essential to approach calmly and without presuppositions.

History

The question must have been raised by the invention of the first machine. When an engineer offered to design a machine to raise the columns of a temple, Diocletian refused, saying, 'let me rather feed the common folk'. However progressive Montesquieu was, he criticised water-mills for 'depriving labourers of their work'. In 1739 in his *Treatise on Political Ethics* the Abbé Duguet wrote:

'Tis for the Interest of the Publick, that no Manufactures be allow'd which injure the poor and inferior Tradesmen, by depriving them of their Work, and that no Manufactures be carried on by Machines, which would have employ'd Numbers of the People. . . . He [the prince] may praise and reward those who make new discoveries in Mechanicks; but if they prove a prejudice to the Poor, he ought to reckon it sufficient that he reward the Inventor, but at the same time forbid the use of what would only serve to increase the number of the Poor and Indolent.

At the beginning of industrial mechanisation, there were strong reactions in France and England by workers, supported by public opinion, and even by a great many factory owners. When Jacquard invented his power-loom in 1803 and the *préfet* requested him to go to Paris, he was in some doubt whether it was to be rewarded or arrested. On every occasion since then, machines and increased productivity have been greeted with hostility or fear. In the 1950s rumours involving the rather magic-sounding word 'automation' caused many hopes but as many fears. As recently as 1962 Breton peasants were destroying factory farms.

The better informed technicians often write that employment will drop with increased productivity. And everyday opinion sums this up: 'Technological progress must reduce the available working hours and hence the number of workers employed, unless the individual contribution to work is decreased.'

Theories

Theorists have always been uneasy about the question; the mercantilists do not offer an opinion, the physiocrats do not think beyond reclaiming new land. The classical liberals (Adam Smith, J–B Say, etc.) are optimistic; in their view workers will find other jobs, either in their own factory if progress increases outlets sufficiently, or in the making of the new machines, or even in other fields benefiting indirectly from the progress achieved. Yet their explanations are not clear and their optimism is rather forced and not entirely free from dogmatism. In the first half of the nineteenth century, they could not remain insensitive to the misery of the workers. J. S. Mill tended towards socialism, Sismondi was a firm believer in technological unemployment and even foresaw a 'press-button' system (see above, page 42). Later, liberal and even Keynesian economists tended to shy away from this dangerous topic.

On the other hand, socialist thought, and Marxism in particular, tackles it firmly: in a capitalist system the 'reserve army' of workers created by the machines is a constant drag on wages and condemns the proletariat to poverty or unemployment. Marx does not reason any more convincingly than the liberals, but his answer is unambiguous.

In short, theories here are influenced as usual by deeply held prejudices, and tend on the whole to be pessimistic. Workers, current opinion, informed men, and even many specialists, generally consider that machines reduce employment.

Experience: overall summary

After two centuries of intense mechanisation we should be able to appeal to the all-powerful idol experience.

The fact is that in all industrial countries the active population is much larger now than it was two centuries ago. After intense mechanisation and huge steps forward in productivity, there are more people employed. Here are approximate figures, based on present-day frontiers, comparing the active employed population in certain countries in 1962 with the equivalent, estimated as about half of the total population, just before the French Revolution. Everywhere the number of employed has risen appreciably.

There remains to see whether this change applies equally to working hours. It is often said that working hours have dropped sharply compared with the conditions obtaining in industry around 1830. Yet men so badly fed and so often ill may have been 'at work' for 13–14 hours a day but could hardly work

	Active population around 1789 (in thousands)	Active employed population around 1965
Belgium	1450	3700
France	13000	21000
Germany (West)	8700	27000
Great Britain	5500	24800
Holland	950	4800
Italy	8700	21900
Switzerland	750	2600

efficiently during that time – they could still produce no more than the 2,000–2,300 calories they absorbed. In any case this was a transitional situation only involving a small minority.

Before and at the beginning of the industrial era even active men lacked work. Apart from the long winter unemployment, peasants were far from able to employ themselves as much as they would have liked. Widespread underployment was only counterbalanced by domestic service. In his remarkable *Travels in France*, Arthur Young stressed the overpopulation of most districts. The same was true of the other western European countries. Except perhaps at certain periods such as harvest times, there was no difficulty in finding labour. This applied to tertiary occupations too. L.–S. Mercier wrote, 'Stamp your feet on Paris cobblestones and you can conjure up an army of clerks, runners, secretaries, and public writers. Look for one and a hundred will besiege you.'[1]

It is thus true to say that the total number of working hours undertaken in industrial countries is far greater than the equivalent number before mechanisation. This first contradiction to current opinions may be tested and confirmed by various facts (practical disappearance of begging, sharp drop in domestic employment, etc.) and by the evidence provided by the countries that have remained at the agricultural stage. The Middle East, North Africa, and even southern Italy and Portugal, suffer today from a great deal of underemployment. M. Seklani estimates this at 50 per cent for Egypt.[2]

It is widely believed that underemployment is an industrial phenomenon: this is due first to the strong impression left by the great slump of 1924–36, and secondly to a statistical illusion. In industrial countries underemployed workers are subsidised or at least counted and recorded, whilst in agricultural countries they are not officially registered and constitute 'hidden unemployment', though it is not difficult to recognise.

Even the decrease in child labour amongst the working class needs to be properly interpreted: in 1966 children start producing much later than they

[1] *L'Habitant de la Guadeloupe*, 1782.
[2] *Population*, July–September 1962.

E   117

did in 1780, but this comes after a greater educational effort, without which there would be no high outputs, and which is thus a kind of apprenticeship.

The overall long term situation can thus be clearly summarised: *technological progress in general (and mechanisation in particular) has made for a considerable increase* in the amount of work done. Chronic unemployment, for instance, is a form of overpopulation that has disappeared. In short, technological progress has increased the optimum population.

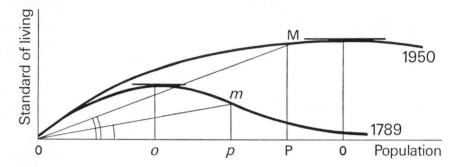

Figure 39. Technological progress increases the optimum population.

It would be wrong to conclude from the overall figures that progress has always made for fuller employment and especially that it has never caused unemployment in certain occupations or districts; observations should therefore be made separately of the time factor and of the particular activities and districts.

Differences at various periods

During the first half of the nineteenth century the working class suffered miserably from poverty and unemployment. Conditions were said to be worsening, but nothing proves this. As early as 1820–25 there was a strong enough drift towards the towns to cause a drop in the rural population here and there. This suggests that there was more poverty in the country than in the town. It did however become more visible and shocking in the towns than it had traditionally been in the country.

At the most it can be said (and without much certainty) that employment did not increase fast enough to absorb the rise in population caused by medical progress.

By 1840–50 the French proletariat felt its burden lightening a little. According to the most reliable research on wages in France[1] here are the yearly figures:

[1] 'Salaires et coût de l'existence à diverses époques jusqu'en 1910', (Statistique Générale). 'Salaires et pouvoir d'achat des ouvriers et des fonctionnaires entre les deux guerres' (A. Sauvy et P. Depoid. 1940). *Journal de la Société de Statistique de Paris* (G. Malignac, second quarter 1951). Also personal research.

Cost of living		Nominal wages		Purchasing power	
1810	100	100		100	
1820	108	105		97·2	
1830	113	110		97·3	
1840	115·5	117		101·3	
1850	115·5	124·5		107·5	
1860	129	146		113	
1870	139	173		124·5	
1880	148·5	200		135	
1890	139	224		161	
1900	135	244		181	
1910	140·5	268		191	
1920	531	965		182	
		Without social security	With social security	Without social security	With social security
1930	840	1820	1983	216	236
1939	1036	2642	2965	255	286
1950	18800	34300	45500	183	242
1965	39600	134000	185400	338	466

These are the workers' annual wages for the full working hours of each period, and without tax deductions. So they do not show the benefit derived from shorter hours or holidays with pay. Neither do they take into account benefits from Works Insurance, introduced in France in 1900. It should also be added that, as Fourastié shows in his remarkable work, cost of living reckonings are mainly based on primary goods, so that if other goods (such as bicycles, railways, nylon stockings) had been taken into account, purchasing power would have appeared to rise even faster. Finally, the above tables do not reckon with the changes in distribution through social promotion, which increase the average wage (see below, page 199).

If the number of jobs available had dropped, wages could hardly have risen, since the labour market was free. The figures for other European countries are even clearer. From the increase in population of working age, it appears that the jobs available increased slowly (too slowly) until about 1850, and then faster. (We need only record these facts at this stage – they will be interpreted later.)

It is worth while adding that emigration to the New World almost stopped in the industrial countries after the First World War (much earlier in France because of the small population) and that it even turned into immigration after the Second World War.

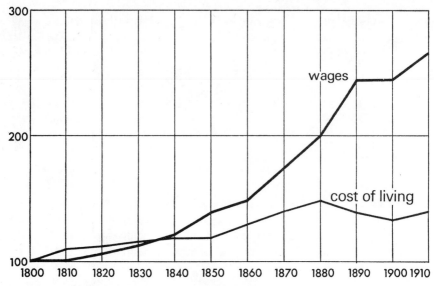

Figure 40. Wages and cost of living in France since 1800.

In the last few years

Before the war, and as early as the recovery from the great slump, public opinion firmly believed that Europe was economically overpopulated. When Hitler blamed unemployment on the Versailles Treaty and the loss of the German colonies, he found democrats in France and England ready to believe him. The idea was still alive just after the war. An account will be found on page 139 of the huge blunder committed by Morgenthau and the Americans in post-war Germany. The better informed people still thought that Europe was on the verge of gigantic unemployment. Malthusian views were so firmly established that when Federal Germany slowly absorbed its millions of refugees the phrase 'German miracle' was used. Yet this 'miracle' was followed by other demonstrations of black magic, in Austria, Italy, Holland, Switzerland, and Japan. Here are approximations of the actual population effectively at work in several countries in 1939 and 1965 (in thousands):

	1939	1965
Germany	19700	27000
Great Britain	19800	24800
Holland	3500	4800
Italy	17500	21900
Japan	33900	47500
Switzerland	1950	2600
United States	46100	74900

120

This marked increase in jobs over less than a generation does not stem from poor productivity. It is linked with a strong rise in individual productivity, and is in a way derived from it. As a rule it is in the countries where the output per person rose quicker that the number of jobs increased faster.

Changes by occupations and districts

Studies of individual occupations and districts point to very varied results: the overall increase in jobs hides local drops.

Since Colin Clark and Fourastié have shown in well-known studies the drift towards tertiary occupations, there is no need to dwell on the depopulation of the countryside. In the secondary occupations there are very different trends. Here are the numbers employed in certain trades in France, reckoned on a basis of 100 for 1906.

Slow progress in technology	1906	1926	1931	1954
Building	100	135	161	250
Fabrics	100	69	65	35
Bookbinding	100	94	99	—
Fast progress in technology				
Engineering	100	182	189	228
Typographic industries	100	137	151	174

The most important technological progress took place in engineering, and in this field employment rose sharply. On the other hand in bookbinding and fabrics, which were less well favoured, employment fell.

But this is by no means the general rule; there was a sharp rise in numbers in the building industry, where there is little technological progress but needs were consistently greater. Numbers also rose in the tertiary field (barbers, tradesmen, civil servants, etc.) where there is no progress and there may even be regressions. Since several factors are at work, this brief survey can only show that the problem is a complex one.

The variation by districts is extremely complex. Rural depopulation is an obvious fact but technological progress only acts through other factors.

As a rule in a given form of activity technological progress increases numbers in a first stage and then reduces them; but it causes new forms of activity to appear.

121

Summary

Experience in this field thus seems to give the lie to the apprehensive and emotional doctrines. The misapprehension is due merely to shortsightedness. But there remains to explain how technological progress generally causes available work to increase, and what exceptions there may be to this rule.

15

TECHNOLOGICAL PROGRESS AND EMPLOYMENT

AN EXPLANATION AND VARIOUS VIEWS

'He who does no work should not eat.'
ST PAUL

Since the problem hardly arises, or at least appears differently in a planned socialist system, we will only consider capitalist societies here. In our terminology, we want to find out whether technological progress reduces or can reduce the optimum population. If there are any grounds for the scare caused by the threat of automation, then the quest for a better standard of living will lead mankind to prune itself of its excessive numbers.

The basic relationship

The productivity of a man or a group of men is expressed by the relation: $p = \dfrac{P}{T}$ where P is the output and T the time spent on it. If p rises, either P increases giving a higher standard of living, or T diminishes, which means more unemployment or leisure.

This simple relationship can be seen in a particular social light: for anyone observing a given development in a given field, P is seen as the constant and T the variable. This view is easily explained in a market system: because output always appears excessive and difficult to dispose of, the mind instinctively concludes that T is going to fall. This would, incidentally, reestablish the balance on a local scale, and so it is a process clearly recognised. On the contrary, where P increases this is not immediately visible, because the whole economy is sharply affected. It does frequently happen, of course, that output fails to increase in the activity considered, but rises in others because purchasing power and employment have switched to some new unrelated activity.

In any case the mind is more ready to accept that T diminishes, changing nothing in the old order as long as the gain in time is distributed amongst all the individuals and changed into leisure.

The most simple model

Marx censured models as 'crusoe-isms' but they are very useful for grasping a phenomenon before making assumptions – they also allow sociological meanings to appear. We will therefore imagine our friends Tom and Dick marooned on a rocky island. They just manage to survive by laying fishing-lines at the best points. They cannot increase their output, because these points are limited in number and keep them fully employed all day.

Technological progress now occurs. Whether P rises or T falls will depend entirely on the *kind* of progress. Take three possible cases:

1. Tom finds a way of doubling the output of fish without using more fishing points. Tom and Dick will both continue to work and henceforth be fully fed. P has risen and T remained stationary. There are still two jobs and there might even be three or more if the formerly poor points, now become worthwhile, were exploited.

2. Tom finds a way of tending all the points himself without increasing their output or the efficiency of the uneconomic ones. Either Tom and Dick will both work part time (and be underemployed – since they are not fully fed one cannot call this leisure), or Tom, who is stronger, will suppress Dick and live on his own and feed himself well: here there will be one job instead of two. In both cases P will not change and T will fall.

3. And yet Dick need not despair. Tom could let him fish on his own and exact half the produce. Dick would still be underfed, but not overworked, whilst Tom would have greater leisure or more time for other activities. Or else Tom could go on fishing and use Dick as a servant or get him to build a house for him. There is once more work for two because Tom's consumption as owner-producer is now removed from raw materials.

This simple model contains in germ the whole theory of progress and employment.

1. Progress may cause employment to rise or fall according to the form it takes. 2. Even if progress causes a temporary fall in employment, a switch in consumption may turn people away from the production of primary goods and bring back full employment or increase the number of jobs.

To return now to the optimum population, we will show that where this rises, an increase in P is preferred; where it falls T tends to drop.

Progress in a given activity

The word 'activity' does not necessarily refer to a specialised occupation. It implies that output is homogeneous; but to produce food off a piece of land a ploughman and a cowherd may have to co-operate. The main condition is that within this communal activity changes should be possible without social disorder or difficulties of adaptation.

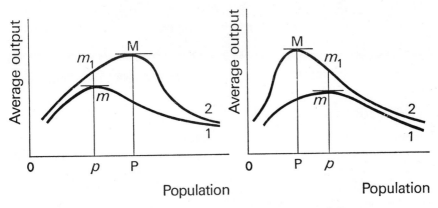

Figure 41. Technological progress can cause the optimum population to rise or to fall.

Let us return to our graph of population and average output.

A second more advanced stage of technology gives a graph entirely above the first in one of two shapes: on the left the optimum has risen, on the right it has dropped. If the rise in productivity did not depend on the numbers of men, the ordinates in the second case would be proportional to those in the first and the optimum would not change.

We want to find out how numbers vary with progress. At point m, now moved to m_1, will the tangent slope up or down?

When the optimum population rises (on the left) men can easily take advantage of progress. Employment and standard of living both rise. In the opposite event, a 'superfluous' population appears which could only find work if its standard of living were to fall, though it would not fall as low as it was originally.

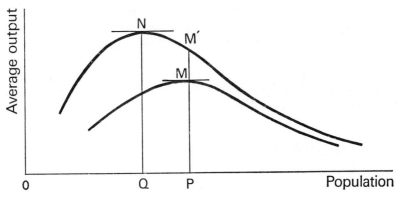

Figure 42. Drop in the optimum population and rise in the standard of living.

In figure 42 the optimum falls from OP to OQ but with an average standard of living PM' still higher than its former level PM. Theoretically a collectivist economy could ensure that all producers have a standard of living at OP higher than before. But in a market economy the tendency to seek always the highest possible standard of living may make some men redundant.

Intensive and extensive progress

Progress can make either Man or his environment more productive, thus respectively decreasing or increasing the optimum. This distinction may appear to fit the difference between extensive and intensive progress.

Take for instance a land to be tilled. Improvements in tools or merely better organisation may allow one man to till a greater area and thus obtain the same output off the same land with fewer men. Here men have increased their power with relation to the land: this 'extensive' progress tends to reduce the optimum. If on the other hand progress increases the area of land that could be put to use, it is as if the environment had been expanded with relation to Man; this 'intensive' progress causes the optimum to rise. Mining would provide another illustration of this.

The same distinction can be made for secondary activities: 'intensive' progress 'enlarges' the environment by achieving a given end with less raw material; or, with the same working hours and raw material, makes better, longer lasting, or more popular goods. A saving in raw materials is equivalent to progress in a primary activity – it is as if the miner or farmer had increased their output. But when the same secondary goods are produced in a shorter time, man has 'increased' with relation to his environment and the optimum falls.

This distinction is however a matter of point of view rather than an objective feature. Often a consequence that occurred in reality is taken as a norm when others could well have been achieved. Developments appearing to be extensive may be put to an intensive use, and conversely. Thus the use of fertilisers and insecticides in agriculture, an intensive advance in appearance, may cause employment on the land to rise, but it may encourage farmers to neglect more difficult but more efficient and productive ways of using the same land. The distinction between intensive and extensive progress only applies to the result: we must push the matter a little further.

Processive and recessive progress

We will use as a point of reference, 'neutral progress', i.e. an advance in technology leaving the rise in productivity constant whatever the number of producers.

Figure 43 represents (a) a neutral development in a primary activity and (b)

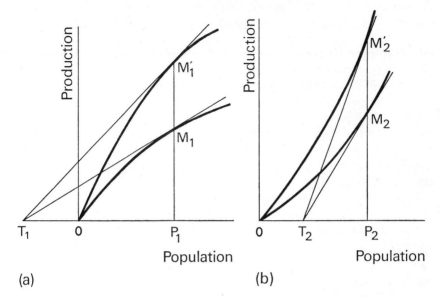

Figure 43. Two kinds of neutral progress.

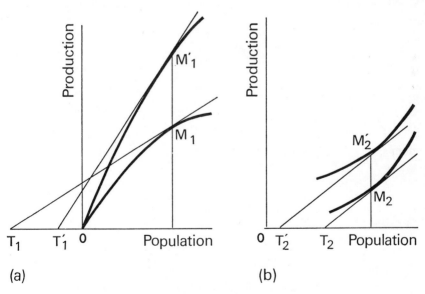

Figure 44. Processive and recessive progress.

the same in a secondary activity. Output moves to $P_1M'_1$ and $P_2M'_2$. The intersection T_1 or T_2 of the tangent with the x axis does not change. (We have already seen that the position of this point determines productivity, which rises as it moves to the right.) Progress in a tertiary activity would have no effect on T either (this was our definition of a tertiary activity).

If the number of workers rises with productivity we will call the development '*processive*'; the opposite will be '*recessive*'.

Figure 44 (a) shows a processive development operating in a primary activity, and 44 (b) a recessive development operating in a secondary activity. A processive development moves T to the right and increases the optimum population. Overpopulation is absorbed and even changed into underpopulation.

'Processivity' is a more meaningful norm for progress than 'intensiveness', but it does not lend itself to illustration. In fact a cut of as much as 50 per cent in the abscissae may well increase the optimum though it appears to be 'extensive'.

Case of several activities

Where several activities are combined, we know that the sum of segments OT_1, OT_2, etc. is zero for the optimum population. If progress were neutral in each one (a situation which never occurs except as a stage in an argument) these points would all be the same and there would be no change in the optimum so long as the distribution of population between the various activities did not change. It would be as if the unity for each activity had changed:

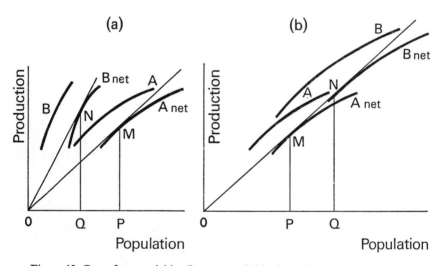

Figure 45. Case of two activities. Increase or fall in the optimum.

consumption and output would rise together to scale. Around this theoretical position one could imagine several changes: several activities combine and give a point T whose position determines the scale of growth in returns. If progress moves T to the right the optimum rises; if to the left it falls.

Take the example of a farm owned and exploited by a family. The work is of two sorts; first everyday work that always has to be done and demands a constant manpower; secondly, extra tasks requiring various specialists. Output is not proportional to the number of these latter 'floating' workers.

Figure 45 plots (A) output as a function of the number of floating workers, and then (A_{net}) as a function of the total number of workers. A_{net} is displaced towards the right of A by a constant amount. OP is the optimum, PM the output. Remember that the tangent of angle MOP is the standard of living.

(a) *An extensive advance occurs*: better machinery permits the same area to give the same output with only one third of the workers. A moves to B, by the two-third reduction in the abscissae and B_{net} is displaced from B as A_{net} was from A. The optimum is now OQ and the output QN. Output has risen but the optimum has dropped. Man has expanded with relation to the environment. The family's interest lies in reducing its numbers.

(b) *An intensive advance occurs*: for example, by deep ploughing, which doubles the overheads, the 'floating' work force may be increased by half with the same output per individual as before. A moves to B by an increase of one half in both abscissae and ordinates, and A_{net} increases to B_{net} to scale as if in an enlargement. The optimum rises by half from OP to OQ. *It is as if the area of land had increased by half and Man had enlarged his environment.* Here the family will expand or engage more farm workers.

In this example there are switches of activity within the farm but they cannot be considered as changes of trade. The case can easily be transposed to a complex system: here however the changes in activity should have social significance. They must therefore be further studied.

Take the simplified model of a society where food supplies are well assured and need not be considered. Primary workers produce raw materials and secondary workers transform and fashion them. Suppose that they are always carrying out the same work: making iron instruments of a regular sort. There will be a constant ratio between the primary and secondary productions.

On figure 46, since the scales are irrelevant (the unities involved are different) we may choose them for the sake of convenience, so that the primary and secondary outputs have the same ordinates. We will also assume that the primary production curve is concave downwards and the secondary production curve concave upwards.

To start with, the optimum is achieved when the tangents at M_1 and M_2

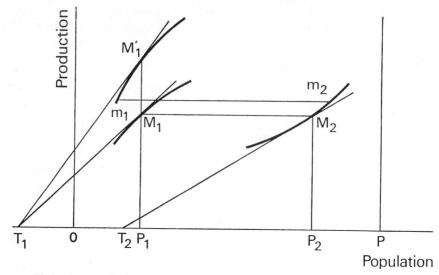

Figure 46. Transfer of activity from primary to secondary sector.

intersect the axis at two points T_1 and T_2 equidistant from the origin. From M_1 and M_2 we can deduce P_1 and P_2 and hence the optimum OP.

Suppose now that neutral advance begins in the primary activity. Population OP_1 will soon be able to produce $P_1M'_1$ instead of P_1M_1 but in doing so will become partly redundant, and will therefore switch towards secondary activities, causing OP_1 to fall and OP_2 to rise, and the outputs to be divided differently. M_2 moves to m_2 and M_1 to m_1. Points T_1 and T_2 move to the right, so that the optimum has risen both for the primary population, now higher than OP_1, and for the secondary population, now higher than OP_2. We assume, of course, here and in the next section, that new activities have not appeared because of the changes in the structure of consumption.

Changes of activity caused by the technological development

Some authors point out that the manufacture of the machine itself demands labour. The extra labour would never be greater than that saved by the progress achieved: a firm would not prefer machines if they were to increase the overall production cost. Yet if this were to remain the same, and the working hours were unchanged, the change-over would still be economically influential in that it would involve *a switch in the type of activity*. An agricultural machine saves on primary labour, but is made by secondary and tertiary workers. This change favours or hinders employment, and modifies the optimum population.

Take an invention causing an apparently 'neutral switch' (i.e. labour saved =labour created). Figure 47 gives the output of the primary activity. M_1 is

130

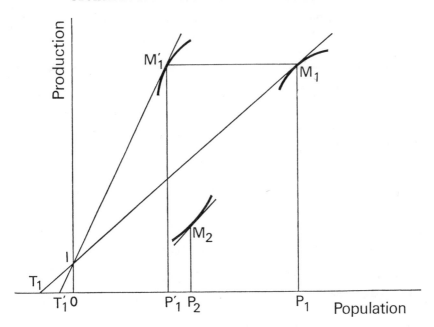

Figure 47. Switch in activity with no increase in production.

the optimum population, taking into account the other activities and overheads. A new invention allows population OP_1 to achieve the same output but in two groups: a small primary group OP'_1 produces the same output thanks to the machines built by the larger secondary group OP_2. This output P_2M_2 has no effect on the standard of living; it is used up each year and its use is already included in the output $P'_1M'_1$.

If OP_1 were larger it could be reduced in the same ratio; the tangent at M'_1 therefore passes through I and point T'_1 is to the right of T_1. The optimum has thus risen. But at this moment part of the secondary population becomes redundant because of the increasing returns from the construction of machinery, which demands fewer and fewer workers while freeing more and more from primary activities. The surplus population may start a new primary production, so that M'_2 will be found to the right of M_2 and the optimum reduced a little. But the overall effect is to increase the optimum. *Though mechanisation does not appear to affect the number of jobs available, it stands a good chance of multiplying them.*

Now take the opposite situation, pushed to absurd extremes: if primary production had infinitely decreasing returns, any technological development in secondary production would free a number of completely useless workers. If there were a strictly limited number of coal mines, it would be useless to save time in steel foundries – though it could be useful to save on materials.

Thus if the new secondary activity consumes primary products with heavily decreasing returns, the switch to the secondary production can be detrimental. In practice so far, such cases of 'greedy machines' have been rare.

Large numbers of technological changes increase tertiary activity. A switch this way is only 'processive' if on the graph the activity losing manpower has negative curvature. This is obvious from the graph. In most cases technological inventions have precisely the effect of decreasing activities with negative curvature that appear completely or temporarily saturated. Should the new situation include overheads needed to pay the tertiary manpower, the optimum population is doubly increased; more producers are needed to support the overheads, and the tertiary population is also added to the optimum.

Changes in consumption

Many inventions, especially in the art of producing, only change consumers' habits: their effect is to introduce more varied needs, thus increasing employment and the optimum, and separating the final product further from the raw material.

If progress brings about a relative drop in the price of a product, consumers benefit from it. If the working hours necessary to produce it are halved and output doubled for the same reason, then all is well. However complex the economic equations, nothing is changed except the unit used: what was *true for pounds becomes true for kilograms*. This has sometimes almost occurred in practice: no one has to change jobs and there is not even temporary unemployment.

Usually, however, consumption varies by more or less than 100 per cent so that either people change to another trade or there is a rush towards this one. At any rate, someone always benefits from this advance; consumer, factory owner, workers, or the state if it steps in and increases its levy. If the beneficiary consumes the same products as the displaced workers, they become redundant, as we have seen. However things do not usually happen this way in an industrial system. Neither the worker nor his boss will go and spend his extra income on bread or potatoes; they go rather for secondary or tertiary goods.

Nothing shows in theory that such changes in consumption create more jobs than before; but experience points to an extremely favourable balance.

The concept of processive progress extended

We have seen that for a given product, progress is 'processive' when the increase absorbs the extra numbers; it is now profitable to extend this idea and distinguish between three different sorts of progress:

1. *Directly processive progress, enlarging the natural environment and thus multiplying employment:* discovery of mines, profitable working of poor seams,

132

intensified agricultural methods, increases in the number of men working on a given area of land, economy in raw materials, new sources of energy. Contemporary examples include: progress in the building of hydroelectric dams, or in the use of atomic energy, cuts in the amount of coke necessary to produce a given amount of steel, cuts in the weight of transporters of a given useful capacity, economy of materials for a product appealing to an elastic market (building, appliances, etc.), increases in the number of phone calls taken by a cable of given dimensions, discoveries of natural oil, progress in teaching techniques, savings in the time needed to plant trees over a given area, cuts in the labour needed to produce export goods which command a wide and responsive market.

2. *Directly recessive progress causing a drop in manpower but becoming processive through the changes brought about in consumers' habits.*

3. *Definitely recessive progress, reducing employment.* Contemporary examples of this include the regrouping of land ownership in France, better distribution in retail trading, saving of labour needed to load ships or to run railways.

The first and second categories are useful but the third is harmful to workers unless combined with the others. Classical theory only considers the first two, whereas Marxist theory only believes in the third.

In a given field, developments in technology can be either processive or recessive: for instance in viticulture an economy in the use of copper sulphate or of sulphur is directly processive, but other improvements which save labour will be recessive.

We obviously need to widen the meaning of the phrase 'natural environment': let us say that progress is processive if it saves an accumulated capital, which has become part of the environment, and generally speaking if it saves anything rare or in limited supply.

When progress is directly recessive it is difficult to say whether it will eventually help or hinder employment. This will depend on who benefits from it and on the uses he puts it to. It is more likely to be processive if it favours someone with a large income. Here the internal contradiction in the capitalist system reappears – even when the beneficiary of the surplus income is known, the outcome is not always very certain, since he himself is not absolutely sure on this point.[1]

When recessive progress is suggested in a firm, especially if it is small, this in fact means that the employees are being asked to jump into a void, with the promise that their parachutes will open. One understands their protests.

---

[1] A great deal of progress has however been achieved through studies of needs and of elasticity of consumption, the first of which was published in *Population*, Oct.–Dec. 1950, by A. Girard.

Workers and employers

Let us study, on a very simple model, the effect of technological progress on wage-earners, and separate, as we did in chapters 10–12, the point of view of the 'rulers' and that of the 'subjects'. For the time being we will not consider the number of rulers, only that of the workers.

On figure 48, the optimum population is OP_o and the real population OP. Wages, equal to marginal productivity, are represented by the slope of the OS parallel to MT. The total of wages paid is PI and the profit is MI. Now a technological development takes place which appears to be recessive. In other

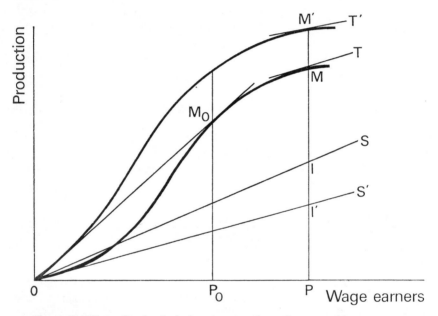

Figure 48. Effects of technological progress on the optimum number of workers.

words it reduces marginal productivity (we do not really care about the optimum here). M'T' slopes less sharply than MT; the wages are now represented by the slope of OS' and the total wages paid out are reduced from PI to PI'. So in this case although output has increased wages have dropped. *The ratio of men to environment has increased, and the owner of the environment is now in a stronger position.*

If the progress were neutral, wages would increase in the same proportion as profits.

In other words *recessive progress reinforces monopoly, whereas processive progress weakens it.*

134

Marxist theory implicity assumes that progress is recessive. There is nothing to prove that this is generally the case, but it seems to have obtained fairly widely at the beginning of the industrial era. Marx was thus no mere oddity. He came at an appointed time, exactly as Malthus before him and Keynes after him.

Progress in an overpopulated and undernourished country

Here progress limited to agriculture may reduce the optimum population. In a system based on private property it makes things difficult for the redundant workers. Their effect on the already crowded labour market makes conditions worse for the employed workers. We have described above the very simple model of Tom and Dick.

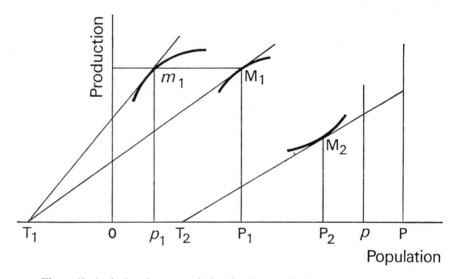

Figure 49. Agricultural progress decimating the population.

Figure 49 represents a rather more complicated model. Initially the real population is at its optimum OP, divided into the primary population OP_1, and the secondary population OP_2, with respective outputs of P_1M_1 and P_2M_2. Points T_1 and T_2 are equidistant from O. Now the primary population achieves technological progress and applies it extensively, thus reducing its numbers to Op_1. *It consumes all the output of food now available*, or exchanges it with population OP_2 for the secondary products that used to be consumed by the now redundant population pP. The new optimum Op has a higher standard of living, since it can share the same output as before amongst smaller numbers. The redundant pP now has either to till poorer lands, or, as

135

is more often the case, act as a drag on the wages of the others; the poverty of the lower classes increases.

Where it allows the owner to be sole master and exploiter of his land, progress feeds him better and eliminates the auxiliary workers.

This situation also exists at the beginning of the industrial age. As long as a certain saturation in foodstuffs is not assured, technological progress may tend to reduce the optimum population through private appropriation.

This situation brings us back once again to the argument between Malthus and Marx. Malthus or his disciples would have been right in saying: 'as long as we retain private property, the working population will see its interest in having fewer children in order not to pass the optimum.' Marx on the other hand was right to a certain extent in blaming the workers' misery on capitalism, since this regime encouraged technological progress to produce even worse misery. The Marxists however have not progressed, and their views are still based on the situation in 1850.

How the situation developed

We are now in a position to reconstitute the way progress has worked. Before the French Revolution, there was extreme poverty, as described by Vauban, Arthur Young, Boisguillebert, or by Fourastié in *The Causes of Wealth*. At the beginning of the Industrial Revolution secondary activities still only increased their returns slowly: tools were so primitive that primary consumption was still important – thus the optimum population was only increased slightly by a change from consumption of food to that of woollen clothing.

As some people's conditions improved, their higher consumption of meat and the rise in the population caused poverty among the weakest. In a population not providing enough for its own consumption, processive progress that could increase the optimum is hampered by the lack of credit facilities.

In Europe, during the first half of the nineteenth century, *the optimum did not increase any more than the real population, so that poverty did not diminish.* Villermé described it effectively. One might say that the middle and lower middle classes developed prematurely, though this does not excuse from moral responsibility people who lived opulently without lifting a finger to improve the atrocious lot of those who were building up their fortunes for them. However, economic progress is more complex than contemporaries, and especially Marx, realised. In 1840, had another plague decreased the population by 45 per cent or even 10 per cent, its effect would have been, as in the Middle Ages, an improvement in the standard of living and even in the part of production earmarked for wages.

Now that the market for foodstuffs is largely saturated, consumption in general is more diverse. In 1969 a rich man eats less than he would have done in 1760 or even in 1860. He can spend so much on other things such as cars or plane journeys that he consumes fewer foodstuffs than his forefathers. On the other hand because of mechanisation and of general overheads, secondary activities have begun to have more steeply increasing returns. The possibility of exchanging manufactured goods for raw materials from other countries has also played a large part, by putting more of 'Nature' within the grasp of Europe.

In a semi-developed society the workers' standard of living is determined by the output of foodstuffs, or, more precisely, by the quantity of food available after the rich have consumed theirs. The market system causes an increase in agricultural production to make for more employment outside agriculture. The development of savings must also be taken into account. Tertiary activity, which has tended more and more to replace primary activities, demands few investments. For these various reasons the optimum has increased sharply and the condition of the workers has improved. Pressure from the trade unions (and also from the tax authorities) has encouraged managements to greater efficiency and has itself had a favourable effect on technological progress without necessarily improving distribution, which was its real object.

Pauperisation

The Marxist phrase 'pauperisation' is most confusing. We must distinguish between three ideas:

1. *The amount of goods consumed:* this may be fairly precisely measured, in spite of technical difficulties, and a clear reply may be given. The worker now consumes a great deal more than before industry began. There only remains to explain the passion with which certain economists refuse to acknowledge this. The only really questionable thing is the extent of the increase.

2. *The distribution of the national output:* here the facts are far less clear and more complex, and cannot be studied at this point.

3. *The variety of needs: this has enriched society but impoverished individuals,* or, to be more precise, caused them financial embarrassment. The new reasons for spending have begun to affect not only primary consumption but also the bringing up of children, whence a fall in the birth rate. As people have preferred opulence to numbers, the increase in the population has slowed down.

The new needs, which have changed the rich man's budget, are also, more cruelly, accessible to the poor. Some have even become essential. The city worker may not gather bits of firewood in forests during his free time, as his great-grandfather used to: he has to use gas and pay for it. Other needs are almost essential: it is difficult to walk to work as did one's ancestors, since train or bus services exist. The less vital temptations are no less pressing: the cinema, radio, compete by their very nature with primary needs. Window dressing and publicity accentuate these new needs. The overall situation of workers' budgets is thus at least as strained as before: progress has created more needs than it has satisfied. The very inequality of conditions creates purely social needs, such as keeping up with fashion. The bright set that constantly discovers new luxuries makes life more difficult for everyone, as Marx pointed out. A collectivist system avoids this tension temporarily by eliminating needs that may not be satisfied by mass production.

Thus it is possible to speak of relative pauperisation, though the phrase is ambiguous; once bodily needs have been satisfied, and even slightly before, new ambitions appear, which multiply at least as fast as output increases, creating a source of discontent as well as new jobs. Pauperisation consists of virtual employment.

A few examples

In many occupations, it seems to be accepted that we have arrived at the critical threshold above which P no longer increases, thus causing T to decrease, together with employment in the area considered

1. It has often been said that progress in *preventive medicine* would considerably reduce the number needing to be cured, thus indirectly reducing medical and para-medical personnel. Vaccines have indeed decreased illness, and the mind, which always tends to imagine developments along the lines it can see, creates the universal vaccine, which could be inoculated in the first few days of life and would considerably decrease the number of doctors and the attention needed.

In fact progress has followed the opposite direction. Not all illnesses are infectious, and even those which are sometimes demand a different sort of treatment: tuberculosis requires staff specialised in prevention and detection, but also elaborate precautions for the survival of those who have been weakened by the illness. Also, many medical techniques have been discovered or developed in unexpected proportions, thanks to general economic progress (radiography, chemical analysis, etc.). Thirdly, the number of doctors has increased considerably, while the number of nurses has become notoriously insufficient everywhere. If we were to adjust it to the numbers asked for, leaving aside financial considerations, they should undoubtedly be doubled.

2. Before the last war many prophets announced that because of the powerfulness of bombing techniques, *war would be a push-button affair*, employing very few men. In fact, one bombing raid on Germany in 1943–4, would require not only 1500–2000 airborne personnel, but 10,000 ground staff, or the equivalent of a division of soldiers, working for several days; not to mention those who merely made the bombs.

3. When calculating machines became widely used after the last war, it was announced that staff would virtually disappear in this field. Yet since then it has in fact multiplied: in France, there are twenty times more people employed

on official statistics than before the war, and even so there are not enough to do the work.

One could take many more examples from various fields. Forecasts of manpower needed are always insufficient. Drops in employment have mostly occurred in fields not affected by technological progress and crippled by their own stagnation.

Technological regression

Another way of thinking, and experimenting, would be to observe the opposite process, technological regression, and ask whether it causes employment to rise or fall.

The pessimistic attitude to progress is strong on this point: it is claimed that less productivity means more employment. Workers' trade unions have long believed this, and suggested remedying unemployment by attempting large-scale jobs with wheelbarrows instead of lorries.

In fact technological regression usually reduces total employment. However, while poor productivity has an unpleasant effect on general welfare, it can, in overloaded professions where the personnel is difficult to convert, contribute temporarily to full employment. During the last war the occupied countries suffered a deep technological regression: fewer fertilisers, less power, badly serviced machines, etc. This caused the optimum population to fall. Admittedly, labour was in acute demand. But this is explained by the financial system used: massive issues of currency and severe price control, combined with rationing. A market economy would have led to a large-scale expulsion of workers from the narrowing circuit, unless they had been prepared to accept very poorly paid jobs.

The temptation of underproductivity is strongest in tertiary activities because its effects there are harder to spot. In any case the resulting employment situation should not only be assessed in the narrow field considered; any lack of productivity causes harm to some other sector. Thus, to pay a useless civil servant the state has to collect taxes which could have created work in a productive section of the economy.

A remarkable example of misunderstanding of the problem of technological progress and employment was given by Morgenthau and the American authorities in 1945 after Potsdam. As the Germans filtered in from the East serious economic difficulties were contemplated. The solution preferred at the time was a 'return to the land': to live without being a burden the Germans would have to return to cattle raising. This was an enormous mistake: this activity demands immense spaces and provides little employment for a given area. On the contrary, industry combined with intensive agriculture provides many men with a satisfactory income. In this case the Americans were misled by Malthusian preconceptions concerning low productivity.

139

Saturation or indefinite progress?

We seem therefore to have a wide and clear experience of mechanisation. Employment in the 'mechanised' countries has surpassed all expectations. No doubt it is far from working as smoothly as it might, and has caused a great deal of suffering. But chronic unemployment is not in the least incompatible with a rise in employment. It only shows that the system is not well oiled.

The question really lies, not in the past or in the present, but in the future. Will mechanisation continue to operate indefinitely, or will it soon reach a saturation stage? What might men come to lack in their search for new and worthwhile activities?

Natural resources, land, raw materials might run out. This view is rather old-fashioned, since technological progress has so far always satisfied the increased consumption it causes. Oil is found at greater and greater depths; products are synthesised. With solar energy we may well produce fertilisers from air and water. And yet if western Europe were deprived of the raw materials from the rest of the world it would have difficulty in providing for its 315 million inhabitants' welfare and finding sufficiently well-paid employment for them. It is also conceivable that a very sharp rise in the number of men might make it impossible for them to consume raw materials on a comparable scale. Here technological progress might well come to demand fewer men, the reverse of the present-day situation.

Public opinion does not seem to be affected by such possibilities. It believes that mankind enjoys the prospect of an unlimited amount of work as long as a saturation of needs does not occur: with men provided with all they need, P would no longer increase because there would be no demand and T would drop, increasing unemployment or leisure. Contrary to what many people think, there is no danger of a secular decline in purchasing power, which is fairly easy to create if needs be. Society may perhaps fail to organise the distribution of available work amongst everyone properly, and divergences may well appear here between Man's need for consumption and the kind of activities he wants to undertake. But his numbers have nothing to do with this kind of unemployment.

We must therefore ask *whether men's needs are really unlimited* or whether they may not fall of their own accord towards a point that might one day interrupt the process of mechanisation that has lasted for thousands of years and has been particularly sharp during the last two centuries. Here again the natural way of seeing the problem points to a solution that reflexion does not confirm. In a market economy, needs constantly appear to be satisfied or about to be satisfied. There is a constant difficulty in disposing of output; this is incorrectly interpreted – the mind has difficulty in imagining new needs, and underestimates for instance the transfer of upper-class needs to the other classes.

140

The forecasts made at different periods are instructive. Around 1840 an imaginative progressive foresaw that the workers might accede to middle-class food, lodgings, and comfort, and even, he added in an audacious moment, to the piano. Afterwards, however, he thought there would be no more needs to satisfy. He was not the last short-sighted prophet. Saturation is said to be at hand in the United States. And yet one has to go a long way up the income ladder there to find satisfied people with no further needs. Many families are still limited by their income: if they were not they would hardly consider hire purchase payments. Central heating had no sooner become generalised than air conditioning was invented, opening up a new market. One generation ago it seemed extravagant to suggest that French workers might progress beyond bicycles; today they own cars and pleasure boats, and travel abroad. There is a great deal to do and to produce before these new needs are satisfied, and by that time others will have appeared. Technological progress creates more needs than it satisfies. After every new development a factory, a hospital or a laboratory becomes obsolete, and new requirements appear: humanity is marching towards an ever-receding horizon.

This explains the Soviet Union's attempts to stop the rising flood of needs. It avoids the spread of the motor car, which would make, within the space of a quinquennial plan, for an unending race to build motorways, motels, city garages, etc. One of the functions of the Iron Curtain is to prevent the virus-like spread of needs from the West: if these were to increase unendingly, distributive communism would recede indefinitely.

There is however one limit to spending: time. Many heads of industry accumulate money because they do not have enough leisure to spend much. But the drop in working hours, so widely advocated, yields leisure and the time and chance to spend more, as well as creating new needs.

If raw materials and food remain plentiful, the optimum will rise, and with it employment, thanks to the spread of tertiary activities. *Once clothed, fed, etc., men will always find excuses to perform small jobs for each other.*

An obstacle

One obstacle however slows down the favourable effects of progress on the optimum population: the fact that tertiary workers are paid more than others. In a capitalist system a certain discrepancy is justifiable, since there must be professional migration from the primary to the tertiary. But if it is too large consumption is in its turn slowed down too much.

Non-manual labour is highly paid mainly for historical reasons. Originally education, even of a modest kind, was confined to a small minority. Nowadays, with a greater number of jobs available, this difference is no longer justified. It is apparently small for the less important jobs, but still appreciable if one considers the visible and invisible advantages of a monthly salary.

141

In many liberal professions salaries are maintained because of pride or feelings of social position. Members of these professions often accept smaller salaries on the condition that no one knows about it. In a situation where partial unemployment is constant, they spend more time looking for work than carrying it out. The manual worker remains a victim, producing a great deal and consuming little.

This difference makes tertiary labour more costly than it should be and thus causes a double distortion: *the professional migration of man* (*accelerated*) *precedes the migration of consumption* (*slowed down*).

Here we have another kind of chronic unemployment, not stemming from technological progress, but due on the contrary to a lack of it. Unemployment in America appears superficially to be caused by automation but it is due in fact to a slowing down of the rise in tertiary productivity.

The tertiary sector is in any case far from homogeneous: it includes highly productive technicians and unqualified people who shun hard work and, not finding jobs easily, swell the crowd of the unemployed.

16

PRODUCTIVITY AND EMPLOYMENT

DIFFICULTIES OF ADAPTATION AND CONCLUSION

'Twelve to fifteen thousand water carriers will no longer be employed; they may be incapable of any other work, for their strap is printed between their shoulders.'

L. S. MERCIER

Man adapting to his new environment

Even if new kinds of employment appear in sufficiently large numbers, the progress from initial to final stage remains a subject for concern. Temporary inactivity, causing suffering and reduced outputs, should be avoided. This adaptation involves a change in the distribution of occupations. Otherwise progress would have to be perfectly adapted in each sector to the elasticity of consumption. Governments may conceivably achieve this (worthy rather than useful) feat by economic planning. But discovery and innovation follow unpredictable paths and always cause some distortion.

If the changes to be made in occupational structure can be moderately slow, the normal process of population renewal may suffice to direct the young towards careers where employment is rising and away from the others. Such change is all the less painful for the workers since it usually involves progress from the primary towards the secondary and tertiary sectors, which is the answer to Man's usual wish to escape from an enslavement to nature.

But in a fairly advanced, stationary population, no more than 2–2·5 per cent of the active population are aged twenty and still unsure of their vocation: progress usually demands more mobility of labour than this. Also inertia slows down the change-over: children take up their father's occupation almost automatically, especially in agriculture or amongst craftsmen. Technological progress thus often demands changes of occupations or 'conversion' during the worker's active life.

The cost of reintegration

Such changes cost society money, even leaving aside the worker's own reluctance to change his position, and the worry this causes him. It is expensive to retrain and reintegrate evicted workers, making up for their drop in skill and therefore in output, abandon existing plant, finance geographical migration. This cost must be deducted, exactly as that of investment into machinery, etc. from the advantages of increased output. In the capitalist system, this situation has not existed for long. Progress used to be defined by entrepreneurial costs, and was therefore often, on a national scale, false progress. It would have been in the general interest for the expense of integration to have been met by the factory which was the first to benefit from the operation.[1]

In other words on the national scale technological change brings: 1. On the positive side, a national saving in working hours or in monetary units. 2. On the negative side, a loss of the investment required and the expense involved in reintegrating and retraining workers.

In principle an annual gain always makes up for an initial loss in the long run; society therefore seems to benefit. Yet the changeover may not be profitable as a whole since amongst the enormous amount of investments that should have been undertaken and were not, some would have been more remunerative.

For this to be most satisfactory economically, the factory should pay not only for the investment but for the retraining of workers. Suppose that this is the case and that progress occurs. Migration of labour may then take place either through the young naturally choosing expanding occupations, or by people changing occupations in the course of their active life. We shall study migration of labour in greater detail in chapter 20, and will merely point out a few difficulties in adaptation at this stage.

Attraction and rejection

A person may change his occupation either because a more pleasant or more profitable one *attracts* him, or because he is *rejected* by one that is diminishing in numbers.

Attraction is the result of progress in an industry characterised by an elastic consumption function. This was the case with the car industry after 1920 and with almost all the main industries at their outset. They attracted new personnel by offering slightly higher salaries. The less favoured occupations, deprived of their usual labour, are in their turn forced to make technological efforts to replace it under penalty of disappearing.

People are *rejected* by industries with an inelastic consumption function, so that they have to dismiss personnel. Pressure may also cause an owner-farmer or a craftsman, no longer able to earn his living, to change his job. If

---

[1] However the process made possible technological improvements, which would not have been so otherwise. It therefore accelerated progress, but the investment or the initial saving were partly borne by the wage earners. One might call this a progressivist injustice, a crushing action which benefited society.

the optimum population is rising or stationary, the rejected workers should be able to find another job. But it takes some time for those who are making money out of the new process to increase their consumption and develop their needs, thus influencing other sectors, and meanwhile the rejected worker is unemployed or retraining himself. Unless he is paid for this by some organisation, it is painful and never voluntary, and he may face a moral crisis.

Both attraction and rejection have often occurred during industrialisation. It is often difficult to separate them properly. The move away from the land for instance is the result of 'voluntary decisions' strongly influenced by the situation.

Even where technological progress increases the optimum, it is more satisfactory when the elastic sectors are well ahead of the others, so that the process at work is the attraction rather than the rejection. Thus in present-day France it would be more profitable to save labour drastically in the building industry than in retail trades.

Small-holding and conversion

The wage earner may find it easier to be mobile if he does not have to migrate geographically and especially when the cost of the new skill is borne either by society or by the firm giving him his cards. Under the age of forty at any rate a man can adapt fairly easily in these conditions.

Lively struggles are however put up by the marginal small-holders (peasants, craftsmen, shopkeepers), who do not wish to 'become proletarianised' and want to continue exploiting as well as owning. This leads to highly individualistic political movements such as *poujadisme* and peasant revolts such as the famous *jacqueries*. The individual's right to have his conversion paid for by society is far more questionable in this case than with wage-earners; it is however in the general interest to make resettlement easier by financial help, rather than to subsidise archaic activities – this would only be justified in the case of elderly people incapable of conversion.

Two kinds of unemployment

Permanent unemployment appears to be more important and more deserving of direct action than transitional unemployment. There are reservations however.

1. Since technological progress is achieved according to a continuous rhythm, temporary unemployment may well exist all the time. There may well be a constant number of occupational migrants, which looks like permanent unemployment. This should however be distinguished from the kind of unemployment due to chronic overpopulation, since the remedies to be applied are not the same.

2. It is more difficult to foresee the variations in the optimum population and in the final number of jobs than the difficulties of a given adaptation.

3. Unemployment due to adaptation difficulties is more vividly feared, and this fear should be prevented from appearing and slowing down any technological progress, as often happens. The first steps towards the bright horizon in the distance are the most important.

4. Whether permanent or temporary, unemployment is always painful; an unemployed worker never knows where or when he will be reemployed.

It is therefore advisable to try to increase the number of jobs as well as helping in the process of conversion. In a sector with a very elastic consumption function both objectives are achieved simultaneously. In this case one could profitably combine progress making workers redundant with progress creating a greater need for workers, so that the difficulties of adaptation drop to a minimum.

A general view of technological progress

It is a question of life and death for capitalism to know how to use technological progress. Generally and on a long term basis, it creates more employment than it suppresses. At the beginning of industrialisation, where there are large food requirements to satisfy, this is not always the case. Here progress may well turn against the workers and aggravate their poverty. Generally speaking there were two main phases in European capitalism: 1. A drop in the optimum population, or at least a rise smaller than the demographic rise. Technology progressed effortlessly, but the workers were poor. 2. Later, progress increased the optimum population, at the same time as the real population multiplied more slowly.

However the fear of unemployment still paralyses European economics, especially because of the bitter memories of the great slump. Though fears about technological unemployment have fewer grounds than a century ago, they are at least justified by three things: 1. Naturally enough the need for security increases as much as other needs. 2. Progress rejecting workers does not always take into account the expense of reintegrating them and is therefore false progress, or progress based on some injustice. 3. The difference between primary and tertiary earnings makes progress more difficult to digest.

Wage-earners in these societies do well to encourage progress expanding the material base of society, or natural environment, and limit the kind of progress which enlarges the needs of man in relation to his environment. The second kind must be harnessed to the first. Indeed, even in a collectivist society, the kind of progress that leads to natural resources being worked out faster is only profitable if there is a sufficient hope that progress will itself lead to the discovery of new resources. Otherwise, men should remember the story of the wolves whose larder disappeared because they got better at catching the goats.

Capitalist systems are paralysed by the fear of unemployment and over-production. The individual accepts progress and seeks it in his own sphere, the state encourages it in its plans, but the occupational group, trade union or corporation, fears changes whose effect often turns against them. This explains why in an age where there are more technological inventions than there ever have been, many of them remain partly unexploited.

The economy of United States is based on a dangerous wastage of raw materials. Entire forests are used to feed newspaper publicity, in other words merely to try to sell off existing goods. This example should not be followed. In Europe, though official speeches delight in calling for productivity, it is in fact a much feared enemy. Suggestions for saving manpower are often disregarded.

Insufficient competition makes transitory unemployment inevitable and longer lasting. It is therefore no longer advisable to leave investment in the hands of private initiative, especially in overpopulated countries.

The plans formulated by capitalist countries are more in the nature of fore-casts. They tend to conclude too easily that better productivity will decrease the need for manpower. Observers find it difficult to avoid this Malthusian point of view, into which the best minds often fall. To avoid such a situation, continual reductions in the value of money have become a kind of system.

During the 1950s there were notable achievements in economic studies of occupational distribution on a national scale, of the kind of progress to be expected, and of the elasticity of consumption functions. The use of Leontief's technique concerning exchanges between sectors, together with a better know-ledge of subjective needs, may provide capitalism with new and powerful tool to study its future path. This kind of analysis shows clearly that in a country with natural resources or able to buy the necessary raw materials, employment has no limits. The only problem lies in adjusting men's activities to their truly limitless needs. If, in spite of this intellectual step forward, the capitalist econ-omy remains paralysed by the fear of productivity, it will be on the road to ruin.

It is essential to learn to change without suffering. If capitalism does not know how to expand men's material environment, lessen the sufferings caused by all sorts of technological change, and find useful employment for the mar-ginal workers unforgettably portrayed by Charlie Chaplin, it will have to give way to a system better adapted to such ends.

17

WORKING HOURS

'If a labourer was offered all the ornaments of wealth as a reward for an assiduous working day of twelve to fourteen hours . . . not one would hesitate to choose less luxury in exchange for more leisure, fewer trinkets in exchange for more freedom.'

SISMONDI

We have already mentioned several times that any increased burden such as a larger number of inactive people, increases the optimum population and lessens the standard of living: this furthers employment but not necessarily wages. More details on the theory of this will be found on pages 174–7.

There are various ways of reducing productive working time: the working life can be cut by an earlier retiring age or a later school leaving age, the working year can be shortened by longer holidays with pay, and the working week or the working day can be reduced. We shall consider mainly the last phenomenon.

Here are some approximate figures relating these various reductions in the total of working hours. In 1962 in France a drop of 2 per cent in the total working hours could be obtained: 1. By making people retire fifteen months earlier. 2. By pushing back the school leaving age by one year. 3. By giving everyone an extra week's holiday a year. 4. By reducing the working week by 0·9 hours.

Basic assumptions

If a drop in working hours were followed *immediately* by a rise in productivity leaving output unchanged, the standard of living and the maximum and optimum populations would also remain the same. Everything would be identical except that there would be more leisure. A case as simple as this does not attract anyone's attention: no one dreams of complaining that his burden has been reduced too much. We will therefore assume that a cut in working time causes initially a provisional drop in output. If working hours are reduced over a certain period such as a year or two, productivity may well make up for this through its normal rate of rise: it is as if the working value of one man were reduced in a given ratio, which is not necessarily the reduction in working hours. For instance a cut of one quarter in working hours may only cause

148

output to drop by one fifth. We will suppose that this ratio is always the same: five men take the place of four. We also assume that all men are producers, that the structure of consumption and of the various activities does not change immediately, and that output is equally distributed amongst all. These factors will be varied later on.

Increase in the optimum population

A cut in working hours causes output, standard of living, and the maximum population to drop. But it increases the optimum population. Figure 50 shows, in an initial situation, output (1) and output per worker (2). The optimum population is OP.

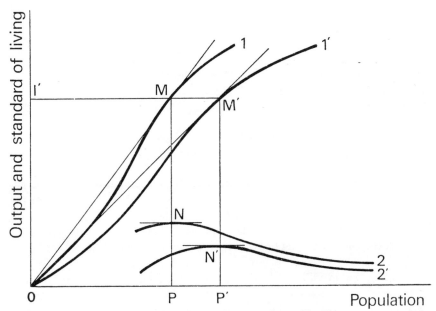

Figure 50. Increase in the optimum caused by a cut in working time.

In the second situation the output graph (1') is obtained by increasing the abscissae of (1) in a constant ratio r: the work done previously by n people is now done by nr. The standard of living graph (2) is replaced by (2'). The standard of living is lower but population OP' is higher than OP.

On the other hand an increase in working hours would act in the same way as recessive technological progress, at least in the vicinity of the optimum.

Employment and wages

We will now suppose that there are two classes: employers and wage earners. A drop in working hours increases the optimum population and improves the distribution of wealth, but decreases the quantity to be distributed. The final

F   149

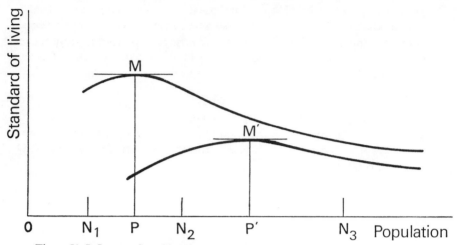

Figure 51. Influence of working time on wages and employment.

effect on the workers will depend on circumstances. Various possibilities can be envisaged:

1. The population (ON_1) was already below the optimum (OP): in spite of the relative improvement in the conditions of the workers, their standard of living will drop, at least in the near future. This is because the cut in working hours can only reduce unemployment due to overpopulation; it has no influence on unemployment caused by other things, such as the failure of the population to adapt its structure to that of demand.

2. The population was above the optimum, and becomes lower at ON_2 through the cut in working hours. Figure 52 uses the same symbols as figure 48. The first curve shows the initial situation, where population OP is higher than the optimum OP_0, and its wages are taken from the marginal output MT; the wages paid out are PI and the profit is MI (the proportions given are necessary for clarity.) As the situation develops as far as the second curve, tangent MT moves to M'T'. There is no way of knowing how the slope of MT has changed. On this figure it has become steeper but the opposite could occur. Wages drop unless productivity decreases sharply.[1] There is thus an optimum working period, making for maximum wages.

---

[1] Let P(n) be the initial output, becoming $P\left(\dfrac{n}{r}\right)$ after a reduction in working hours.

The marginal productivity is P'(s) before, and $\dfrac{1}{r} P'\left(\dfrac{s}{r}\right)$ after the reduction, where s denotes the number of wage earners. For the total wage per person to increase, $\dfrac{1}{r}P'\left(\dfrac{s}{r}\right) > P'(s)$, i.e. the output must increase more slowly than the logarithm of the number of wage earners. Working time is optimal where $\dfrac{1}{r} P'\left(\dfrac{s}{r}\right)$ is maximal, i.e. $sP''\left(\dfrac{s}{r}\right) - rP'\left(\dfrac{s}{r}\right) = 0$.

150

3. The population was and remains above the optimum: in this case the unemployment due to overpopulation is reduced. The total amount paid out in wages may increase through a better distribution of incomes, but it may not. Here again it is a question of making careful empirical calculations.

These rigidly defined situations have to be adapted to take into account various other factors.

One understands why trade unions always include amongst their claims cuts in working hours. It is always in the employers' interests to keep working hours long,[1] but workers want the hours that will give the highest possible wages conciliable with full employment. If the real working hours pass this optimum amount, then claims for a shorter working week are justified. But such claims must always be realistic. No contemporary worker clamours for a twenty-hour week, because in the present state of technology this would cause general impoverishment.

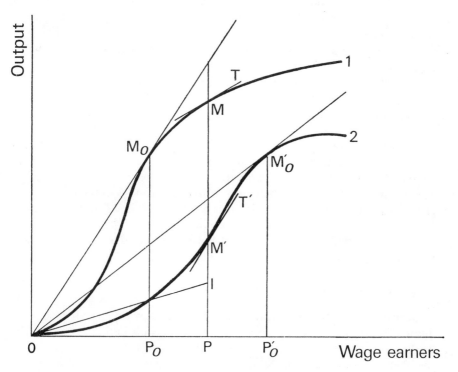

Figure 52. The reduction in working time causes the optimum population to pass the real population.

[1] In 1936 French employers, paralysed by the slump and rumours of over-production, did not object to reductions in working hours as such, but to the increase in wages which, by law, would have had to follow.

Increases in hourly wages

The total wages paid out, and even the output itself, may be maintained if extra manpower is recruited. But since the wages of each worker are thus reduced, the process becomes a mere division of available work between all the workers. This is why they always claim (and very often with the support of the law) that each person's wages should be maintained, or in other words that the hourly pay be increased. Several reactions are then possible.

1. *A cut in the employers' consumption:* financially, a large firm may reduce its dividends, thus increasing the consumption of the workers in general by comparison with that of the employers. This is a simple transfer in consumption though its new structure may have other effects. It is the solution most workers wish for basically, but it only happens in exceptional cases since the employer usually tries to defend his private way of life.

2. *An effort towards higher productivity:* sometimes higher efficiency and better organisation allow a part or the whole of the time lost to be made up. The result is favourable. In an extreme case, if all the time were made up, the workers' added leisure would be a net gain and the firm would not suffer any loss. However this development is usually accompanied by an increasing rhythm of work, causing greater fatigue.

3. *Rise in prices:* in this case the cost of producing one item is transferred to the mass of consumers. This often happens when production costs have increased too sharply. The effort towards higher productivity is too demanding. The spring is broken.

4. *A cut in investment:* the employer, who does not want to decrease his private expenditure, cuts his investments. This solution is in the long run contrary to the interests of the worker.

These various effects show how dangerous sudden and widespread changes can be. If a cut in working hours is made by stages and is staggered over various branches, the normal increase in productivity can 'digest' it. The effects may pass unnoticed by the public, yet they exist nevertheless, as examples will show further on.

Producers and non-producers

The existence of non-producers does not change these reasonings. If each producer supports a constant number of non-producers the optimum number of workers remains the same whatever this number. A cut in working hours has the effect, already considered, of increasing the optimum number of workers. It also increases the total optimum population in the same ratio.

Changes in occupation and in consumption

We have so far assumed that the distribution of occupations remains constant

This is not the case in fact, because of the various switches in consumption considered above. As a rule these are unfavourable at the beginning of an industrial period when the country is still suffering from overpopulation: we have seen how at this stage a strong inequality of incomes may be acceptable.

At a more advanced stage the changes are more favourable and even strongly beneficial. In present-day France for instance the consumption of meat is increasing at the expense of less vital forms of consumption such as foreign travel. If however there is a levelling out of incomes, the revenue from taxation is decreased and national investments may drop. One cannot deny this without attributing to the system a harmony it does not possess. We shall see in chapter 19 that the system is fundamentally detrimental to wage earners. It is therefore not surprising that unfavourable effects should follow for them.

Technological progress combined with a cut in working hours

These two factors are often closely connected, either because the advantages conferred by technological progress are consumed in the form of increased leisure, or because the cut in working hours encourages progress by giving men more difficult aims, which they would not have considered otherwise. We must keep the following influences in mind:

	Technological progress	Working time
1. On the standard of living	increase	decrease
2. On the optimum population:		
(a) directly	probably an increase	increase
(b) through a change in consumption	increase	probably a decrease

So there is usually an increase in the optimum population. Remember that it is always possible to adapt the working time to the needs, so that the standard of living is not reduced. In other words unless there is recessive technological progress it should always be possible to achieve the ideal aim of improving both standard of living and employment.

Public opinion for the most part believes that any cut in working time in the past has had results disproving the pessimism of technicians and employers, and has not cost the country anything. This belief should be qualified.

In the beginnings of industry, the twelve to thirteen working hours a day could not consist of intense work. A cut in working time did not change the worker's output noticeably, and firms were curiously mistaken if they really believed that the twelfth or thirteenth hour was their profit margin.

More recently in France when the eight-hour day was introduced in 1919, the law stressed that weekly wages should be maintained. But this decision was very difficult to enforce and even to control since prices were increasing all the time. The effect on output was equally difficult to observe because of demobilisation and reconstruction. All one can therefore say is that national output probably recovered by 1924–5, technological progress having made up for the cut in working time. But it is impossible to say to what degree this progress was itself helped by the reduced working time. Immigration had to be quite strongly encouraged. It may be that the country would have done better to invest more for five years through longer working hours, though of course 1919, the year of the demobilisation, was a good opportunity for a cut.

The forty-hour week in 1936 in France

This change is better analysed in documents, but it has not been properly interpreted by economists or the public. This is partly because it was introduced in the period December 1936 to May 1937 between two devaluations which gave the economy the classical fillip, as in all countries at this time. Let us study the result of this cut on the three main factors: output, employment, and purchasing power of the workers.

1. *Output*. The index of industrial production dropped from 91 (December 1936) to 85 (July 1937) and 82 (May 1938).

2. *Employment*. The effect of the forty-hour week can be separated here from that of devaluation by studying two countries, Switzerland and Holland, which devalued their money at the same time as the franc but did not cut their working time.

Figure 53 represents the three unemployment graphs.

Between November 1936 and May 1937 unemployment in France was lower than in the other countries but the gap narrowed. The second devaluation (June 1937), helped it a little but by 1938 the French graph was above the other two. The explanation of this little-known result is only too obvious.

3. *Purchasing power* of the workers. Prices rose rapidly in France. The purchasing power of a week's wages dropped by 3·3 per cent between October 1936 and October 1938, whereas normally technological progress should have caused a rise in wages of 4 per cent.

Thus not only did the country lose from this untimely decision, but the workers themselves did not benefit. Civil servants and old-age pensioners suffered greatly. Conversely, in 1938–9, contrary to unanimous liberal, Keynesian and Marxist forecasts, the number of the totally and provisionally un-

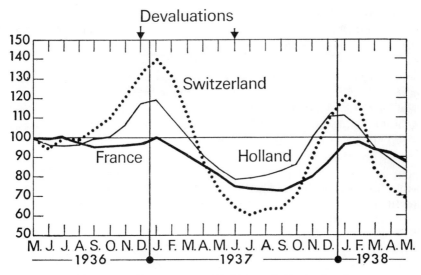

Figure 53. How unemployment dropped in France, Switzerland, and Holland in 1936-8.

employed decreased as the legal working hours increased (see pages 192-3).

This historical example, which is as clear as it is little known,[1] is not given here to criticise the principle of reducing working time, but to show that in a modern economic system, where the rhythm of work is intense, such a change cannot be painless, and is not necessarily beneficial to the working class. But one can of course prefer more leisure and less wealth.

Conversely the lengthening in working time, encouraged by the relaxation of the laws, brought a drop in unemployment and a rise in the purchasing power of the workers.

Progress or Malthusianism?

Trade unions are traditionally strongly attached to cuts in working time. They hope to reduce the working manpower and thus improve the labour market. There is reason in this, as we have seen, but only within certain limits. This form of Malthusianism, creating more leisure, is at least more defensible than the Malthusianism of the employers, which decreases wealth. Individual workers, however, prefer the opposite. Even today, some prefer to carry out arduous overtime work in order to increase their income. The new, constantly rising needs (relative pauperisation) urge them in this direction.

[1] For more details see *Le pouvoir et l'opinion*, Payot, 1949; and *L'opinion publique*, P.U.F. 1961, chapter 8.

We may add that whilst no one would want to return to the long working weeks of old, if in history the precise consequences of every cut in the working week had been estimated, there would always have been good reasons to put it off. For the future it is important to weigh up the various possible applications of technological progress, and choose either more wealth or more leisure in its various forms. It should not be forgotten in such predictions that any new leisure time automatically creates new needs, at least in a modern society. Thus, the third week of holiday with pay opened up new horizons to workers with fairly low wages. The equilibrium thus created is much firmer than is usually believed.

In order to progress surely towards an extension of leisure, whether in the week, the year, or the working life, one would have to limit needs as in the Soviet Union, and this would imply profound changes in society.

18

EXTERNAL TRADE AND THE MERGING OF COUNTRIES[1]

'The living space of each country is the whole world.'

PAUL REYNAUD

So far we have assumed generally, in order to stress internal factors, that the population lived in an enclosed space where exchanges were constant. In fact we should have said that external trade could exist, as long as its influence was neutralised by its being adapted to the variations in output: an adjustment of proportions rather than of absolute quantities.

We will now consider this factor separately, assuming the others, apart from the population, to be constant or at least not strongly influential. Technology for instance does not change, or only changes slowly.

An extension of trade is equivalent to technological progress

Consider a peasant living as it were as a hermit. Either he uses his land for the crops that fit them best, and as a result produces goods bearing little relation to his various needs, or he varies his crops to take his needs into account, and only gets small returns from some of them.

Neither policy is fully satisfactory, and usually we have an intermediate situation with some loss on both scores.

When the peasant can begin to trade he improves his situation either by satisfying his needs better or by increasing the returns from his land, or both. The same applies to a group living in enclosed surroundings or only practising limited trade because of artificial rules such as customs barriers. Because of these barriers the relative values of goods are not the same inside and outside. By suppressing them, goods with a certain internal value will be exchanged for goods of greater value – in other words the value of available goods will increase. The sudden liberation of trade has the same consequences as a technological development.

This is a summary proposition. It cannot be precisely demonstrated in all cases since one would have to foresee some exceptions and take into account for instance the real cost of shocks from without which would characterise the

[1] See M. Gottlieb, 'Optimum population, foreign trade and world economy', *Population Studies*, September 1949.

new system. We can only offer a rigorous demonstration by making our data more precise.

As on figure 41 (see page 125), curve (2) representing the goods newly available is entirely above curve (1), showing the earlier position. A spontaneous increase in external trade therefore causes:

1. *A rise in the maximum population*, or at least no kind of drop. Theoretically there might be a situation analogous to the case of the hungry horse, with new means of communication causing a sharp increase in the consumption of goods with decreasing returns. We can however exclude this problematic case by assuming that only truly beneficial trade appears. A country opening itself to the external world is thus enabled to feed at least as many people as before and probably more.

2. *A rise or a fall in the optimum population*, according to the case. Since the standard of living has risen there is obviously either more or less room for men. This is the important point. The age-old controversy between protectionists and free-traders is effectively illuminated if we look at it from the point of view of the optimum population.

Influence of trade on the optimum population

Foreign trade creates situations of such complexity that one either has to talk of very general cases or of very particular ones. We will try both methods.

In general, the freeing of trade increases output by a certain ratio. If the population is larger, is this increase greater or smaller? At first sight one might think that the relative value of the increase diminishes, because its absolute value tends to remain constant. The new trade now possible with the outside world meets increasing difficulties, since, whatever the population of the land considered, the external environment is always the same and is thus somewhat inert. *Progress is therefore more recessive here than with technological progress over a whole field.* Leaving out of account the changes in consumption that the increased wealth will bring, we will conclude that the optimum population falls more often than it rises.

A particular case, in the form of a simple and 'neutral' model, with no *a priori* processive or recessive characteristics, may serve to check this hypothesis. Consider a country with a stable economy, suddenly deprived of a customs barrier, which makes a certain kind of trade possible. Our reasoning will only be based on two activities, and two goods, numbered 1 and 2 but not necessarily primary and secondary. The country will now be able to buy the first kind of goods in exchange for the second, in a given ratio. But what will the size of the exchange be? We leave aside the number of people employed in the extra trade: in practice it is fairly small, and in any case it can be incorporated into the terms of trade of the two kinds of goods. In order to make a convenient graphic representation, we will choose our scales so that the price ratio is equal to unity: if three pounds of product 1 are exchanged for one pint of product 2, one unit of the ordinates will be the same for one pint of product 2 and three pounds of product 1. To simplify the case even further we will assume that the two activities are represented graphically by straight lines, at least in the region we are considering.

On figure 54, M_1 and M_2 represent the division of a total population which is not represented. The market conditions allow an amount ab of product 2 to be exported and an identical quantity of product 1 to be imported. This exchange is beneficial because the slope of line 2 is greater than that of line 1. The population will find it advantageous to work more in the sector with the greater marginal output.

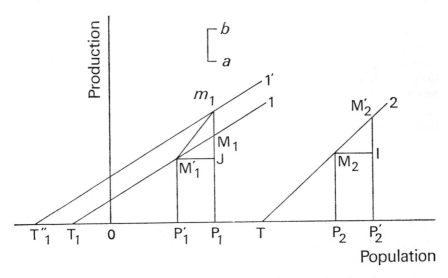

Figure 54. Situation where numbers do not influence external trade.

Part of population 1 will thus be transferred to activity 2, becoming P_2P_2', so placed that its output $M_2'I=ab$. This transfer causes population OP_1 to fall to OP_1'. The output lost is only JM_1 instead of Jm_1 ($Jm_1=IM_2'=ab$). This difference m_1M_1 represents the profit of the operation. It is as if population OP_1 produced P_1m_1 instead of P_1M_1.

All the points M_1 are moved the same distance M_1m_1. Line 1 is replaced by line 1'. Point T_1 moves towards the left and the optimum population drops.

Now let us extend the argument:

1. The improvement might have applied to 2 instead of 1. This would have given a new line 2' (not represented), parallel to and above 2. Point T would also have moved towards the left, showing a decrease in the optimum. Thus in these two extreme cases, where either 1 or 2 benefit from the increase, the

optimum drops. There may be an intermediary position, but in any case the optimum will still drop. The progress is recessive.

2. Why assume that the quantity to be exchanged is a constant? It is this hypothesis that dictated the conclusion.

We assumed that the external surroundings did not change and therefore could not provide or absorb more than this given quantity. However if the returns from activity 2 are increasing, as in the figure, the country may well be able to produce more and more of 2 against a constant quantity of 1, without losing in the process.

This description should therefore be supplemented by a reckoning of elasticity, which might well attenuate our conclusion. If the returns increase sharply, output might increase enough to make the progress processive. This would be the case if two secondary products, for which the respective countries were particularly suited, were being exchanged. We should however take into account the increased difficulties that almost any widening of trade meets, especially in the form of opposition from the other countries, unless it causes their own optimum population to rise: because of this, one may assert that recessive developments are fairly frequent in these circumstances. In other words the number of jobs tends to drop, so long as there are no changes in consumption.

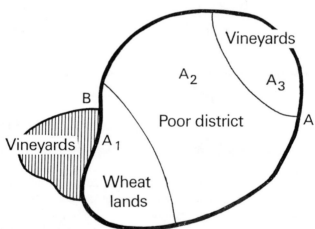

Figure 55. External trade reduces the optimum.

After this quantitative model, let us now look at a geographical model. Country B is rich in vineyards and poor in wheat fields. Country A possesses a wheat-producing area A_1 and a vine-growing area A_3, separated by a large very poor area A_2. With sufficient protection trade is practised within A, with high transport costs.

Should this protection disappear trade will naturally spring up between A_1

and B. Because of the unfaithfulness of A_1, poor A_3 will no longer be able to exploit its vineyards since it has no market for them. It will have to cultivate some of the poorer land of A_2 in order to feed the wine-producers. Its population will therefore have a lower standard of living than that of A_1, where wage levels may tend to fall *and it will appear to be excessive in numbers*. Through the cut in the constant overheads of transport between A_1 and A_3, and the 'short-circuit' with decreasing returns achieved between A_1 and B the optimum population will drop.

All hope is not yet lost: through its increased wealth, population A_1 may avoid a complete 'short-circuit', and use tertiary workers, which would increase the optimum again. But this is a problematic step, which even if it does take place will require painful adaptation.

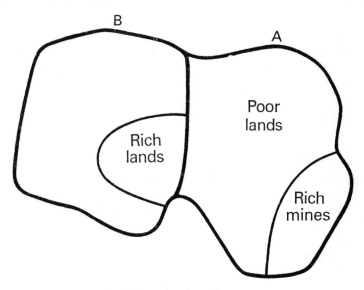

Figure 56. External trade increases the optimum.

On this second geographical model the opposite will occur. Country A, whose leaders are really rather dim, tries to protect the population exploiting its poorer lands, in order not to ruin them. Because of this the rich mines it possesses are scarcely exploited, for lack of fertile land. One day protection disappears. Two factors will now cause the optimum to rise: 1. The combination of fertile land and of mines will favour the creation of industries needing large numbers of workers for their returns to increase: processive progress. 2. The expensive transport between the fertile lands and the mines will consist for a large part of fixed overheads – we know that overheads of this kind increase the optimum. It is worth noticing here that two factors, one preventing poverty and the other wealth, both cause the optimum to rise. If the wealth develops more than the poverty, tertiary needs will also appear, increasing the optimum still further.

Free trade and protectionism

Protectionists are mainly concerned with employment, and free-traders with standards of living. Their doctrine diverge because their aims do likewise.

By a more or less conscious reasoning, protectionists believe that protection will increase the optimum, so that, other conditions being equal, more people will find work. Free-traders are mainly concerned with increasing welfare and protectionists with increasing the work available. Each chooses to concentrate on one of the two fundamental needs experienced by capitalist régimes, when the population is above the optimum, or else (and this comes to the same so far as policy is concerned) is thought to be above the optimum.

These are however no more than doctrinal positions: in fact every form of protection does not increase the optimum, and many protect firms rather than workers. Protection is only justified on a national scale if it is beneficial to workers, even if this contradicts appearances and intentions.

A few examples

Consider the Italian economy in the first half of this century. The population was above the optimum, so that emigration appeared advisable, which is rarely the case, as we shall see. For reasons of prestige and power the Fascist régime discouraged it and guaranteed work to part of the surplus population by meagre salaries and protection, causing poverty. As soon as the country was freed this surplus population appeared clearly. The workers in their turn protected themselves through their unions, and large numbers of men found themselves with nothing to do. From 1950 onwards, and until the Common Market appeared, new employment was created by investment and the training of technicians, and not by developments in foreign trade.

Now take the case of Britain: in the early eighteenth century its population was far higher than its optimum, in a mainly agricultural system. At the time of the industrial revolution the population optimum was increased through possessions abroad. However the real population also increased rapidly and, as in France, technological progress at its beginnings was recessive or only faintly processive. The situation around 1840 was therefore critical and poverty was widespread. In 1846 Peel and the Manchester school managed to reduce tariffs. It is difficult and hardly necessary to say whether Britain was above or below its optimum at that time – even disregarding the special situation in Ireland. The free entry of corn allowed industry, with increasing returns, to develop strongly, and enlarge the optimum. This development was processive. By 1933–6, the conditions had changed: the world had become industrialised

162

so that it was more and more difficult to export manufactured goods. Then, protection of agriculture, combined incidentally with appreciable technological progress, increased the optimum. In both cases the politicians were proved right.

Consider finally Holland in the seventeenth and eighteenth centuries. Contemporaries often quoted it as a model, because either through the pressure of population or the lack of natural resources, or the native industry of its inhabitants, it opened itself to trade. This obviously increased the maximum population; probably the optimum was increased too, by the new tertiary employment, though perhaps other countries suffered from it.

Obviously at a given stage of technology the optimum population does not only depend on natural resources. Towns have populations far higher than the natural optimum. If one is able to attract industry and trade one increases the optimum more than by comparable improvements in agricultural techniques.

Difficulties

In other countries the home and foreign economic policy has not always tried, as in Britain or in Holland, to avoid overpopulation. Also, a situation justified at a certain period may well be left behind by events. Tariffs existing at one time do not therefore guarantee the highest possible optimum for ever.

For the reasons already given above, and also because protectionism is not always ill-inspired, free trade is not processive as often as technological developments: for one thing it cannot be as continuous an event.

On the other hand free trade usually demands a certain degree of reciprocity; but though in terms of total output it always benefits both parties, it only has to be unfavourable to one in terms of the optimum, or to be thought to be, for agreement to be very difficult to achieve. However, in such a situation complete decontrol combined with common protection has often ensured that both parties reaped the double advantage of welfare and full employment. We will now consider how.

Economic unity and the fusion between two territories: the maximum population

We will now suppose that two territories, separate until now, unite politically or at least economically. When this happens the maximum population of the whole will be equal to or larger than the sum of the two maximum populations considered: it cannot be smaller.

Take an extremely unfavourable case: suppose we were to join on to China a fairly poor land, for instance a rocky island only able to provide a few fishermen with a living. The maximum population for the whole would be equal to the sum of the two partial maximums. Poverty may not be improved by being adjoined to poverty, but it will not be worsened either. There is always the possibility that more people than before will be able to live there, and in general, federation is favourable even in unfavourable conditions. The halt and the blind do well to unite their half existences.

Now take two lands A and B. The first one is poor in fertilisers but suitable for growing wheat; the second has the phosphates, potassium and nitrates but is rocky. By joining the two lands it will be possible to produce more food in A and therefore support more inhabitants in the federated A and B. The maximum population will have risen. Here, economic union is the equivalent of technological progress; it provides new tools and increases output for a given number of people.

In the extreme case of two identical countries with the same natural resources and the same kind of inhabitants, economic union may not appear at first sight to be able to change the situation. However, in the three sectors considered separately there may be important progress: 1. In the primary sector, land can become more specialised through economy of transport. 2. In the secondary sector there will be a larger market, allowing production costs to drop or new industries to be created under joint protection. 3. In the tertiary sector certain services (customs, currency exchanges) can be cut, especially if there is political as well as economic union.

There is all the more reason therefore for two countries whose economies are complementary to find new opportunities for production without progress in technology.

Economic union and the optimum population

As usual the optimum is more difficult to deal with: it can rise or drop according to the case.

Suppose the United States were to annex a very poor island: their interest may lie in vacating it completely and transporting its population onto the continent where it will produce more. In this case the island will be useless, and the optimum population of the joint territory, the same as that of the continental United States, will be lower than the sum of the two partial optimums.

However, two territories such as those represented on figure 56 gain from the union both in output and in optimum population. In favourable conditions, the increase may be very large.

Attraction and rejection

The intermediate movements are just as important as the changes of optimum. Exactly as in the case of technological progress, the freeing of trade causes migration of labour which can be painful in the case of rejection, or may equally be welcomed in the case of attraction. However, trade increasing the

164

optimum population should attract more than it rejects but the rejection may well take place before the attraction, and cause a difficult situation, temporary but just as important as the final situation. Migrations from one country to another may also cause special difficulties.

Breakdown of isolation

Economic union or fusion is not necessarily the result of a political decision. Progress in communications has often brought two economic systems into much closer contact: this is notably the case in mountain valleys. A great deal of controversy has arisen over the part played by railways or roads in the depopulation of such areas. The optimum population provides an interesting tool for studying this.

Consider for instance an alpine valley, practically isolated economically: not only producing its own food and building its own houses, but using home-made clothes and tools. Demographically it may be in various situations: there is a minimum population below which life is not possible (see chapter 3), an optimum population benefiting from the division of labour without having to cultivate poor land, and a maximum population. Generally the real population of such valleys was above the optimum, either in order to ensure safety, or through the excess of births over deaths and ignorance of Malthusian ideas. Now suppose isolation is suddenly destroyed by a road or railway. Two things may happen:

1. Communications may encourage fresh enterprise (new mines, development of tourism etc.) which will increase the optimum population, reduce the overpopulation, and perhaps even cause immigration.

2. The new development being insufficient, the population may spill over into the plain, where progress is being achieved, as in the case of the island annexed to the United States. The optimum of the valley will fall to zero and the optimum of the whole country will probably drop.

The first situation often occurs along railway lines or at the crossing of roads, and the second in less developed areas. But even in the second case the new means of communication is not the real cause of depopulation, because isolation was never complete. It merely accelerates the movement, caused by lack of balance, that would otherwise have taken a longer time because of the inertia of a long-established population.

Take the frequent case where the optimum population of newly opened valleys has dropped almost to nothing. What will happen for the country as a whole? Since its size has not changed it may seem that the optimum population of the whole has dropped. The population has become concentrated within a smaller optimum space, and man has grown in relation to nature, abandoning some of its resources. He has thus encouraged overpopulation.

And yet real overpopulation may not have occurred. It is difficult to dissociate the opening up of valleys and technological progress itself, which has caused it and fed off it at the same time. The primary workers who left the valley have become secondary or tertiary workers, which is good for the optimum. They have increased the optimum elsewhere, and contributed more, through taxes or otherwise, towards the general expenses of the country.

In France at any rate the movement has not yet ended: in many regions and valleys the population is still higher than the optimum. Sometimes technological inventions such as winter sports or cable railways, or changes of consumption caused by general prosperity, expressed in the tourist trade and children's camps, may increase the usefulness of these condemned districts and hence the optimum. But when mountainous lands are abandoned, afforestation is possible, which is vital not only for this district but for others. Nature evacuated does not mean Nature lost.

Colonial exploitation

The discovery of the New World had an interesting influence, studied by Gottlieb, on the population of Europe.[1] It allowed Europe, which was over-populated: 1. At the commercial stage, to pour part of its excess population into the new world and get useful goods back from it. 2. Later, at the industrial stage, to exchange manufactured goods for raw materials. 3. Later still, to profit from tourists coming from the more fortunate countries and classes.

Leaving aside for the time being the effect of emigration (see chapter 22) consider first the commercial stage. The imported goods were gold and rare products. The main effect of gold was to raise prices. Colonial goods did not change much except the consumption of the rich classes; this may have led to a certain drop in employment for certain tertiary workers, although employment rose in navigation and trade. But on the other hand primary products such as timber were consumed or exported. On the whole the optimum did not rise much at this stage and the main relief came from the drop in the real population.

At the industrial stage on the other hand, *the exchange of secondary goods for primary goods helped enormously towards the increase of the optimum in Europe*. The agricultural population, with decreasing returns, became secondary or tertiary. England consciously exploited this situation by suppressing agricultural protectionism in about 1850. The population of Europe did not benefit much from new outlets, as is usually thought, but it did acquire *new sources of raw materials*. Outlets for exports are only an accessory phenomenon. though they appear more clearly.

It may be absurd to say as Vogt[2] does that what has happened has not been a matter of technological progress so much as the massive consumption, over

[1] *Population Studies*, September 1949.
[2] W. Vogt, *Road to Survival*, New York, 1948.

three centuries, of the resources of a whole continent (this reasoning would lead to think in terms of the maximum population); but the lack of new geographical discoveries has caused a relative saturation by a slowing down of the increase in the optimum. It might cause an actual drop in the optimum, by the exhaustion of mineral resources, if vigorous efforts were not made to discover new ones or to promote certain materials to better use; hence the interest of atomic research.

Loss of colonies

When a country loses its political supremacy over another, its economy may be affected in various ways. It usually loses an outlet for its manufactured goods, a source, direct or circuitous, of raw materials, and a certain amount of tertiary jobs (in civil service, trade etc.). These losses reduce its optimum population and may therefore affect the conditions of its workers. One of the unfortunate effects on France of the expulsion of the French from North Africa was that it brought home more tradesmen than technicians, who would have been useful to the mother country. In spite of appearances and of general opinion, the ruling class is not alone in suffering from such losses, and it may not even be the main victim.

The direct loss of private property abroad, whether in a country that is dominated politically or not, causes similar misapprehensions. When a magnate or a large concern has rubber plantations or oil wells confiscated somewhere in the world, public opinion does not react strongly, thinking that the dominated class has suffered no loss, since the national income only decreases at the expense of the ruling class. This is one of many illusions due to reckoning in money rather than in men. Consideration of the optimum population is much more relevant. The magnate only consumes a small amount of the rubber that constitutes his income. He brings rubber to his country and levies part of the national output in exchange, but this part is often of a secondary or tertiary kind, so that in losing his external income he reduces the optimum and worsens the conditions of the employed population. These thoughts are little known in France but more familiar to the English Labour Party. They take part of the sting out of the class struggle. The British worker has more to lose in sharing his wealth with the Ceylonese or Rhodesian worker than he has to gain in sharing out the possessions of his former lord.

The Common Market

As any customs union, the Common Market should in theory increase the maximum population. But this is of little importance. The main question is whether the optimum is increased, and whether employment or the income of workers will rise as a result of it.

167

If limited to coal and steel, which are recessive, the union might have been unfavourable to workers – here, however, the changes in consumption brought by increased productivity due to a better distribution of employment, could be expected to correct the recessive effect and it seems that things did turn out this way.

However, many other factors were involved and it would be hasty to thank only the customs union for the progress achieved from 1950–60 in Germany, Italy, Holland, and France. For instance some effects were apparent before frontiers were abolished and even before the treaty was ratified in 1959. In France in particular, industry was slumbering under the cover of severe protectionism in the form of annual quotas. When the customs union was announced the country awoke and made up for the time that had been lost during the slump and the war and which no one had bothered about during protectionism.

It seems, however, that concentration and specialisation are still only timidly attempted. For instance, the film industry, given a large market, increases its returns rapidly: one only needs to build a few extra theatres and to print a few extra copies of the films. Because of the partitioning of Europe, many American films of poor quality are imported into each country, whilst exports are discouraged. Economic union here should have a processive effect and employment should be increased: directly through the growth of the industry, and indirectly through the changes in consumption, and through the purchases of raw materials made possible by exporting films. The diversity of languages is a difficulty, but not an unsurmountable one since American films are projected everywhere.

Many other goods could be made in greater quantities and more cheaply, either through specialisation, or by aiming at an optimum size for the firms whilst maintaining the same degree of competition. For instance, it is difficult for each country to undertake the construction of long-range passenger planes; therefore each country has to choose between producing them at high prices or buying them from the United States. This applies to many other goods that are highly specialised but need to be produced in certain quantities (electronics, etc.).

Consider the example of synthetic rubber. If the optimum size for a factory fits into a nation of the size of France, Germany, or Italy, the national factories will do well to compete. If the optimum size is too large for the national needs a larger market must be opened up. In both cases, by abolishing any barriers to the importation of synthetic rubber from other EEC countries, processive effects follow and the number of jobs rises.

These examples do not mean that any extension is profitable. Economic blocks such as the Common Market probably have an optimum size beyond which disadvantages that are slender now would grow larger than the advantages.

19

INDUSTRIAL SOCIETIES

'There is a great deal of money to earn here, but for those who have some already.'

TALLEYRAND

After studying technological progress and employment, we may now move on to the problems of an industrial society. This is different from an agricultural society in that (amongst other things): 1: it is *further from nature* and affected less by decreasing returns than by increasing returns to scale. 2: it is *mobile*, and is transformed continuously through investment, the training of workers, occupational migration, geographical concentration etc. 3: in terms of incomes *the middle classes* have a larger part to play. 4: *births are restricted* by birth control.

As usual we will study the problem from the point of view of population, disregarding as far as possible political and financial phenomena.

A static model

Suppose, first of all, that technology is constant or only progressing slowly. The accumulated capital can in a sense be equated with the 'natural resources' in our previous models. In a sufficiently liberal system, though property may belong to a few, work belongs to all. Since every new man has on certain conditions the same rights as the others the work available is distributed amongst those who are unable to acquire property (we shall consider the question of the appropriation of work further on).

Without adopting J. B. Clark's theory, we will assume to start with that in a static economy, wages tend towards the level of the marginal productivity.

Figure 57 shows the distribution of output and income amongst owners, management, and workers. It plots output against the population of workers. OP_0 is the optimum number of workers, giving the highest average productivity. The real number of workers, OP, is larger. Marginal productivity is determined by the slope of the tangent MT, and the individual wage is quite close to this value. If we trace OS, parallel to MT, the angle SOP is the individual wage and the segment PI represents the total wages. The profit, or rather the income of the management, is MI.

169

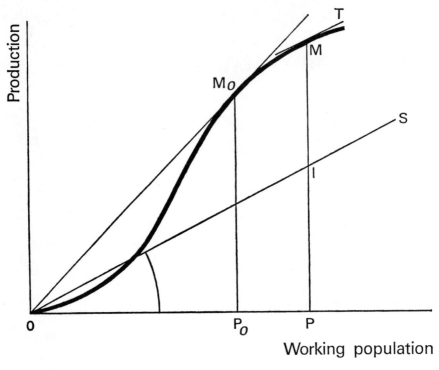

Figure 57. Distribution of output amongst management and workers.

As previously, we may consider the optimum number of workers separately from the owner's point of view and from the workers' point of view.

The ruling owners would like the population to rise until marginal productivity is just equal to the (not strictly physiological) subsistence level. On the other hand it is in the workers' interest to stop exactly at the optimum number OP_0, which would reduce the profits of the owners to nothing, at least in this simplified model.[1]

Thus, in this static model numbers can play an important part. The surplus workers weigh upon the salaries. It is possible to extend this to a dynamic economy: if the number of workers increases too fast and overflows the productive framework, the workers suffer from their numbers and the rulers, to use a Marxist phrase, exploit the state of the production relations.

[1] Various other factors usually prevent this. If the population is below the optimum, this model does not apply either. Various difficulties (inequality of workers, insufficient investment) may occur. The income of the employers is limited but that of the employed can also drop. The workers' initial advantage is more than destroyed by the stagnation of the national income, the consolidation of monopolies, and the crystallisation of work patterns.

Unemployment due to overpopulation

It is tempting to attribute all unemployment to overpopulation. The mind instinctively concludes that if the men without work did not exist there would be no unemployment. This, however, assumes that the imaginary drop in numbers could apply precisely to the men without jobs.

In fact there are various forms of unemployment and various sorts of people on the dole. If we leave aside the socially unfit who belong to no circuit at all, and those unemployed seasonally or accidentally, we are left with two main kinds: 1. Unemployment caused by an occupational structure not adapted to the structure of demand. 2. Unemployment due to overpopulation in absolute numbers, given the natural resources and equipment existing on the land.

We will concentrate first on this second form, which we have already shown to be possible, and see how it or its effects can be avoided.

On figure 58 population OP is above the optimum. Output is PM, profit MI and wages paid IP. It is in the workers' interest to demand higher wages in order to lift OS to OS'. But since this policy might eliminate marginal workers it would not necessarily be in the interest of all. The workers actually

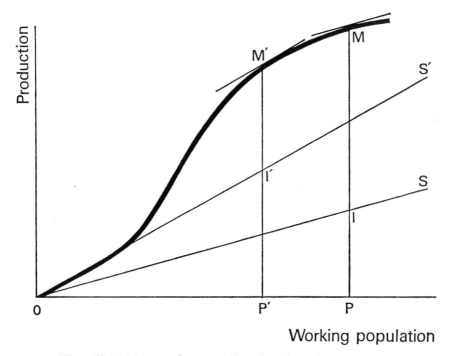

Figure 58. Rise in wages in a population above the optimum.

171

employed would drop from OP to OP', determined by the tangent parallel to OS' at M'.

Society may offer compensation to the workers eliminated and ensure their survival in different ways. A levy on the profit M'I' consolidates the advantage for the workers and usually increases their total gain. The advantage often subsists even if they have to subsidise unemployment themselves. In other words, in some cases it is in the workers' interest to withdraw voluntarily part of their numbers. This can be compared with cutting the length of working hours (see chapter 17), which ensures a better distribution of national output, but since this policy reduces output it cannot be carried far.

Distribution through taxation

In an agricultural economy even the most iniquitous taxation increased the optimum population and sometimes the real population, making for a stable situation under certain conditions. In an industrial system, can any form of taxation increase the optimum and thus allow a better distribution of the national income? Consider a population at or slightly above the optimum, as income is distributed to start with. It is at a state of balance: any extra man would cause the standard of living of the whole group to drop. Can taxation increase the workers' standard of living and the optimum population, and even allow extra workers to be added without the standard of living dropping? The problem is more complex than with an agricultural economy.

Appropriate changes, such as investment or training of men, can increase marginal productivity and raise the whole output curve OM, and thus incorporate more workers without lowering wages. This is the mechanism of technological progress, already considered from other angles. The static model is clearly insufficient here. The situation will have to be studied more directly.

High wages and employment

When J. Rueff stated after the war that there was a correlation between high rates of pay and unemployment, people did not disagree with his observations so much as with the conclusions to be drawn. The liberals and private enterprisers took this as an excuse to oppose rises and even to demand cuts in wages. The defenders of the workers and the interventionists denied such an inhuman law unanimously.

Observations and correlations were far from convincing: in the fraction $\frac{W}{P}$ (ratio of wages to wholesale prices) which was the basis of the demonstration, P played the essential part. There would have been an equally good correlation between unemployment and the ratio $\frac{1}{P}$, since when the economy is expanding prices and employment increase.

There is no instance, in the last forty years, of a voluntary cut in nominal wages suppressing or even reducing unemployment while prices remain the same. But cuts in real rates of pay or increases lower than the increase in productivity have often coincided with a drop in unemployment.

This pessimistic doctrine, connected with that of Ricardo and many other classical economists, was countered by the theory of purchasing power: according to Ford, higher wages would allow more cars to be sold and give industry a fillip. This reasoning was also supported during the slump by workers' trade unions and several economists more or less connected with the Keynesian school. But such debates are sadly insufficient, at least as they are usually posed. Neither of the opposing parties dared to follow its line of argument as far as applying it to reality. Even the most advanced theorists would hardly say that it would be possible suddenly to double or treble wages in any country, without production becoming uneconomical. Neither would anyone in the United States say that they could reintegrate the four million unemployed by general pay cuts.

At any given moment there is an *optimum position* even from the point of view of full employment. The only question worth debating is whether in a given economy at a given moment a pay rise of *n* per cent will act favourably or not on employment. Since this problem is difficult to solve, and might turn out to justify one of the parties, but which one cannot be foreseen, the opponents prefer to remain on doctrinal grounds.

It is not surprising that liberal minds are more easily reconciled to the idea of 'necessary unemployment', of a conflict inherent to the fluctuations of the trade cycle; or that others consider full employment the primary objective. Each one will follow his feelings and choose either authoritarian planning or fluidity. But in a given system at a given moment the facts have to be studied in order to find the best solution it allows.

When a rise in wages might cause a recession and make full employment more remote, which can obviously happen if the population is below the optimum, this opposition between employment and high wages, denied by the trade unions for tactical reasons, is in fact a strong charge against the system. Here, revolutionary trade unions are placed in a contradictory position: they cannot but propose a reformist policy. For what would workers say whose comrades told them that because capitalism cannot adapt itself, it is useless to try to improve it by asking for higher wages? One should at least prove its helplessness daily.

Rueff's law might have found a place in *Capital*. It would not of course be difficult to deduce it from Marxism, with a completely opposed conclusion.

It was not enough to criticise this law; a counter-offensive was necessary, and this was the theory of high wages and purchasing power.

Inequality of incomes

More generally, consider the benefits and disadvantages of unequal incomes, apart from any question of right or justice.

As we have seen, in an agricultural society demographic pressure is relieved by unequal incomes: this may not be the ideal solution but pressure is inevitable within the system.

In an industrial society the situation is much less clear; the lack of primary or natural products is far less obvious, at least if there are facilities for importing them from abroad. Large middle classes thus become possible and it is much less important that the rich give direct employment to many servants. Sometimes even (take the case of France's excessive agricultural output, or that of the manufactured goods demanding mass-production) a rise in low incomes has economic advantages.

The latter situation is by no means the reverse of the former, even from the point of view of pure consumption. Inequality has three effects: on consumption, on taxation, and on investment.

Consumption

Unequal incomes cause a certain pattern of occupations. Wherever there are rich people there are jewellers, furriers, luxury cars, etc. This pattern consolidates in its turn the unequal incomes, all the more strongly since it is rigid. *Any attempt towards a better distribution of incomes starts off by causing unemployment in the trades serving the rich*, as well as an increase in the prices of necessary goods such as food. If the improvement is effective, changes become necessary in the structure of production and therefore in occupations.

But such a transfer appears retrograde. The rich people consume new tertiary and secondary goods; by changing the distribution of incomes one would be ordering artists, ski instructors, precision engineers, to become farmers, textile workers, quarrymen. Such a step backwards meets such lively opposition from the interested parties that social equity has often to be abandoned or modified for a policy tailored to maintain inequality.

Winter sports for instance, practically the monopoly of a well-to-do class, must not be directly hit and may even be encouraged. Indirect taxation of consumer goods, on the other hand, will remain high. Even progressive parties would object to heavy taxation of winter sports to relieve the taxation on bread, meat, or potatoes slightly. They would prefer to tax the rich by some other means and spend the money obtained on sending workers to winter sports: in this way consumption would not be disturbed and there would be less of a tendency to a return to equilibrium. But this levelling policy would have to be accompanied by authoritative regulations on consumption.

This is only one example among many; since high incomes provide a bud-

174

ding industry creating employment with its first outlets, politicians, supported by public opinion, are careful not to discourage superfluous consumption.

In any case the custom of the rich is particularly prized and tertiary occupations are more pleasant and better paid: the distribution of occupations therefore sometimes gets ahead of technological progress so that underemployment or depression soon appear in the industries and trades living off the rich. Firms reduce their payroll and the risk of widespread unemployment causes unequal incomes to be maintained.

This is not all: since new industries are usually directed towards rich customers, *any incentive to progress benefits the rich first.* Fashion designs and unnecessary travel are subsidised or encouraged whilst consumer goods and housing are heavily taxed. Thus industrial society 'feels' without being fully conscious of the fact, that unequal incomes increase the optimum population and employment. The search for full employment maintains inequality of incomes.

Progressive taxation

This is recognised as providing a certain degree of equality. But it may be unfavourable to the lower incomes because strong inequality of income is favourable to the Treasury. If the incomes of the twenty million families in France were suddenly levelled off, taxation would become less profitable and its level would have to be raised sharply. This would be unfortunate not only for those with incomes above the average, but also for those below the average, who thought it would be in their interest to demand a share-out. Thus there are influences at work, besides the rich classes, seeking to avoid equality of incomes as likely to freeze resources.

Investment

The amount of income saved usually rises with the income. This rule is so widely recognised that people often argue as if all the workers' incomes were spent and all the employers' profits invested. This is not true but there is an important difference, shown by the self-financing of companies, common since the war because of the double influence of inflation and of the split between shareholders and directors of large firms. When the employers' incomes drop, investment suffers because their budget begins to lay stress on consumption. It is not easy to cut down on one's way of living.

Since investment creates more employment than it suppresses, it is the most favourable solution for the workers, especially if their numbers are increasing. Investments have a useful effect, no longer on the maximum population as with Mirabeau's agricultural investments, but on the optimum population, which improves the distribution from the worker's point of view or at least prevents it from becoming worse. In agricultural systems investment ensured survival – here it raises the standard of living; but the rulers are in much the same position as in Louis XV's time.

Without needing to define its policy, the middle class only spends its excess income on investment and thus enjoys a favourable position. The profits are low but will increase through the number of workers above the optimum level. This is why the workers' trade unions are not totally opposed to self-financing though it constitutes a genuine Marxist 'plus-value' – a levy on the mass unfavourable to the workers either as producers or as consumers, which is reflected in property or stock market values increasing.

The worker's interest would not lie in sharing-out (this would kill investment) or in self-financing as it is practised, but in the creation of a social organisation representing all the accumulated national capital. This kind of solution has not yet been applied, partly because of the resistance from firms but also because it would bring no immediate advantage to the workers. Their great weakness lies in being mainly attached to consumption.

The social function of a business

The manager's profit can be justified by the better organisation he provides. If national income is increased by a certain amount the firm may seem useful if it only absorbs a fraction of this surplus. Let us leave aside this classical argument for a time and concentrate on the advantage derived from the use made of this income. Given that the system, as we have seen, demands a certain inequality of incomes, the middle class, at its forefront, is in a position to direct the economy in one way or another. Like Mirabeau's landlord it can: 1. Consume natural goods or the fruits of capital. 2. Consume work, in other words employ men. 3. Save and invest.

Could the ruling class, like the pharaoh, justify unequal incomes by arguing that it does not compete directly with the workers for the same goods and that it is thus less of a burden than might appear? This may have been true after the last war, during the food shortage following the abolition of rationing in France. They might have said: 'Why increase your pay, when you won't be able to consume more food than there is on the market; whilst we spend *our* surplus profits on pictures and jewels, which does you no harm at all.' This was not said in so many words, perhaps because it would not have been understood, but it is how things turned out, when rationing was relaxed but the purchasing power of the workers could not be increased until food supplies became more plentiful. The system uses this way of defence implicitly through the stability of inequality and the equilibrium of incomes, which does not necessarily prove it right.

The pharaoh, now the director of a large firm, might also say: 'If I invest indefinitely all the income exceeding what I deserve for my work as director, what harm could I cause to the workers or to the company since I am not consuming any more than the fruits of my work?' Indeed if neither he nor his assistants ever touch this accumulated capital, the result would be the same in terms of incomes and of consumption as in the Soviet Union, where investment is a collective act. But even in the narrow field of the division of national output, privilege still exists. The capitalist may sell part of his 'plus-value' bonus shares every year without biting into his capital. This will be paid for, directly or not, by someone who has saved money to buy the shares; and it could have been used, as we have seen, to nourish a social fund.

One should also remember the power given by this wealth: economic power in the choice of investment, political power by various means, some of which are perfectly legal but nevertheless corrupting.

The system is therefore stable. Since vital investment comes out of the same fund as superfluous consumption, any policy aiming at directly improving the distribution automatically causes opposing forces to appear. *Through their function as investors, the rulers lead the game.* Society in order to develop has to give them sufficient profit to increase their desire to invest. On this point the *Société d'Etudes et de Documentation économiques, industrielles et sociales* wrote on 1 December 1955: '. . . it seems absurd to complain on grounds of national interest that company profits should have increased somewhat more than salaries since 1952. Such increases provide the firms with investing power and make for increased productivity and healthy rises in salaries.'

We should add that it is extremely difficult to distinguish between amortisation and self-financing. The greatest experts are unable, even in political terms, to define amortisation correctly. When in doubt public authorities are usually tempted to decide in favour of the companies for fear that investment might drop and economic development slow down.

The ruler is thus still useful in that he makes a sort of gift of his excess income to society, exactly as the squire finances the local mutual aid fund or the sports club. This state of affairs ensures that he always survives in any crisis. His needs will always be generously provided for since *only his surplus is invested in the general interest.* In spite of this obvious fact the ruled class obstinately refuses to look for its underlying causes. A small minority of politicians and trade unionists are conscious of them, but unable to put their views across to the crowd, which only believes in the results it sees.

The only positive effect of this process is the depreciation of money or at least of its purchasing power, which is a fairly painful real loss for any capitalist, though not for the largest ones.

The two German recoveries

Germany achieved brilliant recoveries twice in twenty years; in 1933–9 under Schacht and in 1950–60 under Erhard. In both cases to begin with wages were low. After the end of the second recovery in about 1955 they increased sharply; after the first this would have been equally possible had the Germans been interested in buying butter rather than making heavy artillery. Both recoveries contradicted the economic theories accepted at the time: the first was carefully planned, which went against accepted liberal views, the second took place in a liberal system despite all Keynesian principles: the purchasing power of workers was low, interest rates high, etc. The results are misguidedly attributed to the 'Sorceror Schacht' or to the 'German miracle'. Yet they can be explained. We shall see later that in both cases a great many sufficiently qualified men were available, which was a necessary condition for such quick progress.

These non-conformist events are too unpleasant to be considered frankly especially since one of their merits is to show how difficult it is for a capitalist system to achieve social justice. They suggest reformist or revolutionary conclusions, and not recognising them is a way of consolidating the régime. Socialists (or social democrats) have long believed that these inherent difficulties could be attenuated by a stagnating or even recessive population, which would reduce the number of wage earners at the same time as the need for investment, and by the same process the domination of the owners. But we shall see how this Malthusian belief is ill-founded.

Expansion through investment

We will now concentrate not on distribution but on the mechanics of growth, which is quite clearly linked with the political system. The simplest model will use three variables:

R, the national income.

I the total investments, or else, $\frac{I}{R}$ the ratio of these investments to the national income.

T the national interest rate of these investments, equal to $\frac{r}{I}$ where r is the resulting increase in the national income over every subsequent year. Its inverse $\frac{I}{r}$ is the capital–output ratio. If for example an investment of 100 increases the national income by 30 a year, T $=30$ per cent. The national interest rate is always higher than the capitalist interest rate on the same investment, since the latter has to take into account not only the profits but also the salaries and other expenses, as well as the multiplying effect that may result.

Usually the national interest rate is between 20 and 50 per cent. If the state makes the investment, its budget receives not only the taxation on the surplus value of the national income, but also the capitalist profit on the operation. For instance if T $=30$ per cent and taxation claims 25 per cent of the national income, the budget receives, each year, the capitalist profit if there is one, plus 7·5 per cent of the initial capital, which would for instance allow it to pay back a compulsory loan. The operation is therefore without peril even if there is no capitalist profit, as happens for instance with scientific research, education, health services, etc.

It may also be profitable to invest in a way that allows unused or ill-used resources to be put to use; thus uneconomic irrigation in a dry country may well be financially profitable to the state, especially if the population is underemployed.

The higher the public expenditure and the resulting taxation, for whatever reason, the greater interest the state has in strong public or private investment. It will wish to encourage saving, and in a system of private property this may lead it to continue to favour high incomes. We are led once again to denounce the contradiction in the capitalist system.

Let us assume for the sake of clarity that the national interest rate of each year's investment is constant: the rate of growth in the national income is IT. If $\dfrac{I}{R}$ is constant every year, there will be a geometic increase in national income at the rate $\dfrac{IT}{R}$. And if the population itself remains the same, the increase of individual income or the average standard of living varies geometrically in the same way.

Population growth

Now introduce into this model an important variable: the increase in population, which adds to the country's burden of costs but provides it with a larger output. What are the additional costs?

Many authors have used for the increase in population the same capital coefficient as for the increase in the national income. In other words if 4 per cent of the national income has to be invested to increase the national income by 1 per cent during the following years, 4 per cent would also be needed to provide for an increase of 1 per cent in the population with constant individual incomes. But this simplification is sometimes very far from the truth. It can never be justified, except by coincidence, or where the additional people are totally unproductive, as could happen, we shall see later, with elderly people.

Demographic investment

This phrase is generally used to refer to any national expenditure aimed at preventing the population growth from causing a drop in the standard of living. The aim is thus either to increase the productivity of the active people so that the available goods increase as much as the population, or to enable the newcomers to produce as much wealth as the old. Thus in a mainly agricultural colony new land has to be cleared and prepared to avoid a drop in the standard of living.

It is not always easy to distinguish (at least from the point of view of their application) between a material *demographic* investment intended to parry the increase in population without cutting the standard of living, and an *economic* investment intended to raise the standard of living: any new building (housing or factories) causes the average of existing equipment to improve.

New housing, for example, is intended on the one hand to renew old housing, and on the other to provide for the additional population. Suppose that a house lasts n years and is used by an average of p people, and that the population increases at the rate of r per cent per year. New houses must be built at a rate given by the equation

$$\frac{P}{pn}+\frac{Pr}{p}=\frac{P}{p}\left(\frac{1}{n}+r\right)$$

where r only refers to the present rate of growth, it being assumed that growth in the past has been negligible. (If the latter were introduced into the equation, it would lead to an even higher requirement for the present.) Given this assumption, the number of houses to build per inhabitant, or the intensity of the building drive, is therefore $\frac{1}{p}\left(\frac{1}{n}+r\right)$. We can consider p as a sociological constant, usually equal to 3 or 4. The housing drive is higher where houses last less and the population is larger where houses last longer. In an extreme case, if houses lasted eternally, it would be the only factor.

Let us take a numerical example: $n=100$, $r=2$ per cent. The number of houses to build with the same purpose in mind, always assuming that the inhabitants are all housed in the same way, is three times as much as with a stationary population. This reckoning can be extended to other sorts of building. The increase in population is all the more expensive, in relative value, if these buildings are long-lasting. This occurs for instance in land development (Dutch polders).

Differences between age groups

We have already seen how unsatisfactory it was to identify the coefficient for demographic investment with that for economic investment. The distinctions are made clearer by studying the three age-groups (young, middle-aged, old) separately. The first will be dealt with separately in chapter 24.

Increase in the numbers of old-aged people

If this happens suddenly, causing the population to rise by $\triangle P$, the available output, still constant, will be shared out amongst a greater number of people, so that welfare decreases. If we assume for the sake of simplification that an aged person consumes the same as an average person (and it would be easy to correct this assumption if necessary), the standard of living is multiplied by $\dfrac{P}{P+\triangle P}$.

To restore the standard of living one may not need extra investment adding up to $\dfrac{\triangle P}{P}\dfrac{R}{I}$. For instance, if the population increases by 1 per cent and $i=$ 25 per cent, then 4 per cent of the national income will have to be invested to maintain the standard of living. This is the only case, except where there is numerical coincidence, in which the two rates considered are the same, although many people assume them to be equal. The equality in this case is not surprising since the economic investment here is intended to increase output enough to make up for the population rise.

This investment will ensure that each inhabitant retains the same public or private consumption. It can be of three sorts: 1. Private investment aimed at increasing everyday consumption (food, clothing). 2. Private or public investment aimed at increasing so-called social consumption (housing, hospitals). 3. Public investment (means of communication, post office, etc.).

These investments, like the economic investments already described, aim at increasing the output and productivity of the active population, and its welfare, but not the number of jobs available.

However, it is only possible to assimilate such demographic investment with economic investment if the plant is fully employed and the population fully active. In fact this cannot be: certain public services, such as roads, railways, and post offices are quite likely to be in surplus; this can also occur in private industries – for instance a drop in the consumption of bread causes flour mills to be underemployed. Here, the growth of the population will allow existing plant to be put to better use, and unemployed people to be employed, without involving any extra expenses in the sector considered. Demographic investment is thus usually slightly lower than the corresponding economic investment. It is already obvious that population growth can repair defects of structure, which makes it less costly.

Another consideration is that the additional old-aged people have a limited expectation of life, which reduces the value of the investment needed for their upkeep. The national rate of interest applied to investment should indeed be reckoned so as to ensure an indefinite rise in output, not that equipment lasts for ever, but because the national income is reckoned on a net basis, after amortisation. Taking into account the expectation of life does not reduce the investment necessary; but since it will be larger than required, though generally still useful, after a few years, it may be considered that it is partly an economic investment.

181

Growth in number of adults

This may happen when fully trained immigrants enter the territory, or where there are bulges in the age distribution, as in France and England from about 1965 in the relevant age-group. Our reasoning applies to this population as a whole, so that we can simplify by assuming that it is all economically productive.

These adults will not only need consumer goods, like the old-aged people, but also working materials, and this will demand extra investment. But they will produce as soon as these tools are available. If the investment gives the newcomers a productivity equal to that of the present population, society will finally have gained through a drop in the ratio of idle people. But it is an initial burden to have to invest in advance.

In fact, if the increase in population is small, investment does not necessarily have to be made in advance: often the newcomers take up not very productive jobs which have been abandoned by the old or left vacant by deaths, in which case no investment is necessary. This often happens in agriculture and building: men would have left in any case and freed serviceable buildings and machinery. The productivity of the newcomers is small but they are not a burden to society. It can also happen that the newcomers are attracted by expanding industries offering highly productive jobs. In this case they can be smoothly introduced into the circuit by arrangements such as double shifts, allowing them to produce immediately and provide, as it were, part of their own investment.

Capital per worker

We must still, however, study the amount of investment necessary to provide work for one man. This has been variously estimated. Not only does it vary a great deal from one industry to another but also from one author to another: from one to five years' work or even more.

This variation is due to the lack of well-defined ideas and insufficient information on a national scale. It is dangerous to take particular examples: a hydro-electric dam may have cost thousands of working years and be operated, after completion, by only a few people; but one has to take into account the workers who use the electricity produced. The same applies to an automated factory. Research on this point would be very fruitful.

The total cost of growth

If the cost of training men (see chapter 24) is added to that of the productive machinery, a total is obtained which may reach ten to twelve working years, or something of that order.

As a result an increase of only 1 per cent in the population would absorb 10–12 per cent of the national income, a much higher figure than those quoted above concerning the capital–output ratio. It would be easy to conclude that any demographic increase is expensive in itself and that from the strictly economic point of view a population should not increase and should even decrease.

This conclusion is, however, too much at odds with various observations to be readily accepted. There are the miraculous recoveries of certain countries, and the examples in chapter 28, to be considered. In any case the cost of growth must always be weighed against its good effects. These can be evaluated in various ways, all unsuccessfully used so far; we will merely try to indicate those that could be profitable.

The individual method

Knowing what a man has cost in equipment and training, this outlay is compared with his net output, or the difference between his output and his consumption (see chapter 25). The difference is due to the many levies on his output, and also to his own expenses in bringing up children, or his investments, for instance into a house, which will be useful to others later. If the fraction consumed is one third of his output, and he produces during forty-two years, society benefits from twenty-eight of these years. One would still have to deduct from this figure his consumption later on after his retirement, and perhaps introduce the interest rate or the rate of growth of the national income; however one can still take it that society gains. Such a reckoning is only an example of the method that could be used, and a great many other factors should, of course, come into account.

The advantages which spring from growth

Growth demands a great deal of investment and may, after a certain stage, come up against the law of decreasing returns or of increasing difficulties; but it has its particular advantages from a static point of view, some of which were dealt with in chapter 5. For instance, the country's 'overheads' are distributed among more individuals. Though where a great deal of equipment is needed growth is costly and demands an impoverishing share-out or reparatory investment; on the other hand any debt or expenses not dependent on the population are worthwhile, since a share-out in this case increases wealth.

Growth is also more desirable where there is an important proportion of old people.

Again, we have already seen that at the industrial stage, returns sometimes increase with output. An industry that is not workable for ten million consumers may be so for twelve to fifteen million: examples include publishing, whether of books, newspapers, or films; the car industry; and machinery of many sorts.

This reasoning may not appear to be confirmed by a comparison between large and small countries: this is because the small countries such as Belgium or Sweden depend largely on collaboration with other countries through international trade. Also they have made special efforts to make up for their handicap: the Swiss have developed their hotels and watch industry, the Norwegians built up a merchant navy. We will return to this important factor in a moment.

Demographic investment necessarily involves new construction. This stimulates the spirit of renewal. But it brings us to the verge of sociology. Let us veer away for the time being and mention what is perhaps the least known and studied of the advantages: the possibility demographic investment gives of repairing flaws in structure or in proportions that would be difficult to correct in a stationary population. This phenomenon is described in the following chapter as far as the structure of occupations is concerned.

How do these advantages of growth influence the much-simplified model $R=IT$? Obviously through T, which is too often evaluated only from the technical angle of investments. It is, in fact, the result of very different factors, including the multiplying effect (due to previously unused elements being put to work), the distribution of overheads over a larger number of heads, the improvement in productivity due to mass production or to the division of labour; there are also unfavourable factors such as the shortage of raw materials, or of space, or special difficulties in the export market.

Optimum growth

The reasoning set down from a static point of view in chapter 5 can be used again here and applied to a more practical use. A stationary or very slowly moving population does not benefit enough from the advantages of growth. There is no historical example of a stationary population having achieved appreciable economic progress. Theoretically it is not impossible, but in practice, in our period especially, it does not happen.

On the other hand, if a population increases very quickly it has to face up to enormous burdens which may exceed its technological and political stamina. Even if the country has large resources and credit facilities, rapid growth comes up against various obstacles, due to inertia in certain sectors. A society, like a vegetable or animal organism, cannot grow faster than its nature permits. We are thus led from the idea of optimum population to that of *optimum rhythm of growth*.

Growth and acceleration

Compared to a static agricultural economy, a dynamic industrial society works as it were on credit, for long-term results. It can afford to wait several years for these since it is richer, more inventive and harder working.

At a normal cruising rate, with no hitches, society has to spend a great deal of its resources on training men and shaping the capital they will have to manage. If this amount remains proportionally constant, development will be continuous, with no extra effort or suffering. The common opinion according to which as capital per head increases growth becomes more costly in modern societies, is therefore wrong. Everything depends on the profits achieved. What is expensive or painful is acceleration, whether demographic or in modernisation of equipment. It may be either that obsolescence or old-fashioned habits have to be fought (as after the last war), or that an agricultural system must be developed into an industrial one. The proportion of the national income to be invested must increase, and this is not easy.

Conversely, a slowing-down is beneficial for a time. A country suddenly deprived of youth or tired of technological progress and refusing to renew its tools, would feel its standard of living improving, in spite of structural trouble resulting from the demobilisation of investments, since every effort could be directed towards consumption.

The proportion of income invested is currently 20–25 per cent, including the price of education. There is no reason why it should not be even higher one day.

The part played by men in economic growth

We have followed the usual approach in showing the influence of investment; on its own, however, this would lead one to neglect essential human phenomena. It is convenient to disregard them as we did in the factor T, but this is in practice difficult to achieve and should not excuse one from analysing and observing these phenomena carefully.

Consider the various western European countries at the beginning of industrialisation, except perhaps for Ireland, Portugal, Spain, and southern Italy. These countries were variably endowed with natural resources: some possessed coal and iron, others not; the lands were more or less fertile; their sizes were different; their demographic growths have been different and bear no relation to the diversity of natural resources. We could therefore expect to find in these countries extremely different individual incomes. Yet the differences are in fact small and attributable to accidental causes: thus Switzerland and Sweden are currently slightly above the others because the relative advantages derived from the last war have still not been levelled out. Before the First World War these countries were practically at the same stage, with Britain, for historical reasons, slightly above the others.

What can the levelling factor be or have been? Only one is possible – cultural unity in the wider sense of the phrase. This allowed small or less well-favoured countries to make up for their handicap by intensifying an occupation or a process that others had neglected. In other words men were of greater value than natural resources, density of population or rate of population growth. We shall return to this idea in part 2, but the distinction between sociology and economics is very difficult to make here, since the latter is restricted in general to measurable phenomena or issues which will conform to precise argument.

Though the importance of the human element in economic progress cannot yet be measured sufficiently well, it is so obvious in so many fields that it is perhaps worth studying through a few examples.

1. *Technical schools and qualifications:* Many firms run technical training schools for their personnel. There is no guarantee that trainees will stay in their service and not go to work for a rival firm. Yet they still go on with the scheme and seem to find it profitable in spite of the losses suffered. A director of Renault estimated that this training was a worthwhile proposition even if half the trainees were lost. Few other occupations or productions are so profitable that the profits would subsist even after half the output had been whisked away.

The importance of qualifications appears clearly in the differences between wages; even this does not do it justice, for in a free labour market there would be even greater differences.

2. *War damage:* After each war observers are surprised by the speed with which countries rebuild, whatever the economic system in force: thus Spain in 1940, France in 1870, 1918, or 1945, the Soviet Union in 1945. The damage is precisely a loss of capital, of the tools of production. If capital were the deciding factor in development, output should progress less fast after wars – yet the opposite happens. Usually in five years or a little more, the pre-war national income is more or less restored. After this, precisely when the productive capital is back to normal, the increase in output slows down to its long-term rate. This appears paradoxical.

There are, of course, sociological explanations: during these periods men are willing to go without, and consumption can be reduced more easily than at other times. But why should production slow down when it reaches the pre-war level? Because this level is that of men's knowledge and capability. Kick an ant hill and you destroy a capital; the ants get to work on this calamity. Sometime later, you will find the ant hill restored to its original state, neither larger nor smaller, neither better equipped nor retarded – it represents the cleverness and the capability of the ants.

When Marx described the accumulation of capital, the situation was very different from nowadays. The accumulation of knowledge has become more important.

3. *From Saint-Simon to modern society:* Now take an imaginary example. Suppose that in an advanced country like England or France all medical

apparatus were suddenly destroyed overnight, from isotope separators to mere thermometers. This would be rather unfortunate, since the best doctor in the world could not do much without instruments. But the disaster would be short-lived: factories would work day and night, and imports would be quickly arranged. Rare machinery would be put to better use, by shifts. Three to six months later the essential damage would be made good. Public health would not have suffered very much.

Now imagine that all the doctors in the country disappeared overnight. This would be a terrible catastrophe. Medical science would need a century or more to recover, for an enormous wealth of knowledge would have been destroyed.

In his famous parable Saint-Simon made a similar comparison: he imagined first that one thousand valuable scientists disappeared, then that one thousand politicians, aristocrats, and bishops, *important personalities lacking scientific knowledge*, were spirited away. According to him the country would only suffer in the first case. Saint-Simon suffered anyway, since the remark earned him a sentence for contempt of court.

Misunderstanding of this phenomenon

It would be possible to start from the opposite point of view, showing how popular opinion and theory necessarily neglect the importance of the human element. This is because since men cannot be sold (with the possible exception of footballers) they do not appear on balance sheets.

If an individual wants to start a business he first tries to find capital, and only then is able to recruit the personnel he needs. But on a national scale this no longer applies: men count most. Yet they are rarely counted: the mind translates onto this level what is true on an individual level, and the result is a blunder. Since full employment is never achieved in any country, the superficial opinion gets around that it is 'money' that is lacking.

Floods and irrigation

Ever since Law, Mirabeau and his assignats, and Schacht's 'labour vouchers', a great deal has been said and written about the risks of inflation, and, conversely, the economic advantages of monetary expansion. This is a controversial question because reasonings and models do not usually consider men's ability to produce wealth.

Water falling on a land may cause either a disastrous flood followed by erosion, or beneficial irrigation. The result depends, of course, on the quantity of water but also on the receptiveness of the soil: if it is loose and well-prepared it absorbs water and the plants benefit. In the same way showers of money on an economy increase production without danger of inflation on two conditions: that there are available men and that they are capable of taking part immediately in the creation of wealth, which acts as a sponge to the paper money put into circulation.

These conditions were fulfilled in Germany in 1933–9 and 1950–60. In both cases there were a great deal of men available and capable of productive work. The result was the same whether the economic system was liberal or regulated. In the second case there was even a lack of capital: factories, machines, tools, had been destroyed or taken away, and the refugees from the East had left their houses and educational facilities back at home. Only a few years were needed for factories, tools, universities, and housing to reappear.

But if a similar policy were applied in Bolivia, Egypt, or Pakistan the result would be a disastrous flood. Even though there are plenty of men available there, they are not capable of producing wealth quickly on demand.

Man without capital

To see the situation as clearly as this, it is necessary to abstract a great deal since the superficial events are such a poor reflection of reality. As soon as one returns to problems as they really occur, the abstraction is liable to break down. It could also be objected that men's ability would be useless if they did not possess capital in the form of productive tools. This, however, is only a partial objection: capable men without tools may be very resourceful; they may obtain the necessary materials and, putting them to able use, pay for them quickly. Capital is always attracted by productive men. And there is always the last resort of constructing one's own tools, as the Germans did between 1950 and 1960, a transitory policy involving initial hardship, but ending in success.

The accumulation of knowledge

Rostow's concept of the 'take-off' is very attractive: each country has indeed a critical threshold to pass before being admitted as it were to the 'industrial club'. What it needs for this is men trained in various fields. The Japanese can sell transistor radios throughout the world because they have electronic engineers; the Swiss, watches and clocks because their personnel is highly qualified.

Because on the average a man is not adult for much longer than fifty years, one may be tempted to think that knowledge does not really accumulate whereas certain kinds of capital last long enough to merge with the natural heritage. But there is a real corpus of knowledge, transmitted not only by schools and books but by the family, the factory, and even by conversations in the street. Youngsters today understand almost spontaneously things that their parents found difficult: a Van Gogh painting, the theories of Einstein or

Freud, the Christiana turn, contained inflation, etc. This is because their environment has changed.

The need to reckon with numbers of men

This essential factor in economic development does not appear on balance sheets, and this is an enormous handicap. There are various forms of inert opposition, on the part of financiers for instance, to any creative project because of the enormous competition between such projects. Whoever can prove the high profitability of what he proposes has a good chance of being preferred to the others.

Yet if the importance of training was correctly stressed and approximately measured, educational expenditure would increase and replace other more spectacular expenses: investment programmes would change in a way that would shock traditionalists but quickly be vindicated in terms of international competition. It is far from impossible to introduce quantitative measures in this field: think of the many phenomena that were supposed to be qualitative and non-measurable only twenty years ago which can be measured today. The national income of tomorrow will depend for each country on the qualifications of its active population, and this can be practically measured already in the school rooms where youth is at work, and from the kind of education that each receives.

The great need of modern societies is not to be overtaken by confusion. Capitalism can only maintain itself in the world if it opens its eyes and stops crudely making out that its particular problems are those of the whole nation. The socialist countries, even before they were able to reckon in men, did not hesitate to place their money on culture, and this was to become a far more effective weapon than economic planning.

20

SOCIAL CATEGORIES IN THE ACTIVE POPULATION

'The greatest sin of the modern world is refusing to acknowledge the invisible.'

JULIAN GREEN

Unemployment due to overpopulation is usually only a sign of underdevelopment; we will now concentrate on the kind of unemployment caused by structural defects, which is the more important and perhaps the lesser known of the two in developed countries.

The requisite numbers

In a country such as Britain, each inhabitant spends or invests his income as he wishes, causing a demand for a certain amount of work of various kinds, in agriculture, mines, industry, public and private services, etc. The total required by the whole of the population, including public services, can be converted into the 'numbers required', divided by given ratios into farmers, miners, shoemakers, caterers, engineers, etc.

We may now vary the supposed income of each Englishman until the employed population required coincides in numbers with the real employed population, at say thirty million. But though the numbers coincide, the structure will not necessarily do so: there may be more tradesmen and fewer teachers and builders than required. The usual result of this kind of situation is unemployment or underemployment in the socially desirable activities. All the necessary ratios for the 'required' population are achieved on the basis of the least popular occupations, but the more popular ones exceed their proper global ratio.

Suppose, for instance, that there are only three occupations, A, B, and C. To satisfy the expressed requirements, the numbers would have to be proportional to a, b, and c. But in fact in the active population they are $a+a'$, $b-b'$ and $c+c'$. The numbers employed will be as shown on the facing page, hinging on the number in B: there will be unemployment (or underemployment, according to the type of occupation) in A and C. Figure 59 shows a more complex situation with the proportions required on the left and on the right

190

Occupation A $\quad\quad (b-b')\,\dfrac{a}{b}.$

Occupation B $\quad\quad (b-b').$

Occupation C $\quad\quad (b-b')\,\dfrac{c}{b}.$

$\overline{}$

Total employed $\quad\quad \dfrac{b-b'}{b}\,(a+b+c).$

Leaving in excess of the numbers required:

Occupation A $\quad\quad a'+a\,\dfrac{b'}{b}.$

Occupation C $\quad\quad c'+c\,\dfrac{b'}{b}.$

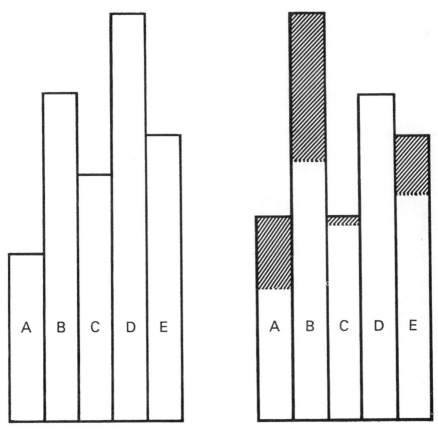

Figure 59. A defect in the structure of occupations causing unemployment.

191

the real population for the five occupations. Since D is most undersubscribed, the others will align themselves on it according to the proportions in the required population, though, as we shall see, these proportions may be slightly distorted by various kinds of resilience. The dotted lines represent the population employed. For the occupations A, B, C, and E the shaded area represents the excess numbers that are unemployed or underemployed.

If demand increases, sector D cannot provide enough, and inflation occurs. There may therefore be 'overemployment' even before full employment. The government will have to resort to deflationary tactics even though most of the sectors are depressed. Public opinion never seems to be able to understand this: it always believes purchasing power to be insufficient, because it is only conscious of the depressed sectors.

Correcting the distortions

This model however is too rigid, since these unfortunate distortions can be avoided by adjusting:

1. *External trade.*

2. *Immigration* to the under-subscribed sectors, or *emigration* from the over-subscribed ones. External trade and migration are obviously limited. But it is already obvious that any immigration into an under-subscribed occupation reestablishes the proportions and thus *gives work to the depressed activities*, thus reducing unemployment and underemployment (see below page 223).

3. *Working time*, through unequal working hours. This can be considered as a kind of unemployment if the workers as a result work at less than the legal rate. This does not however change the fact that by increasing working hours in occupations short of labour, unemployment generally is reduced.

4. *Various adjustments* especially through the channels of prices and salaries. We should perhaps be mindful in talking of an 'inflated' or under-subscribed occupation, of the fact that inflation is not always visible (see Tucker's objections, page 223 below) and is usually only fictive, since the market has reached an equilibrium through the surplus workers being unemployed. It may appear only if demand increases generally. But since this increase is inflationary for these occupations, increases in prices may occur even before the offers of employment are made.

Historical example

The least known of all the possible examples is France's recovery in 1938–9, already mentioned above (page 154). It is the most conclusive over the economic history of the last thirty years, for political circumstances were very unfavourable. No economic theory has yet taken it into account, yet it should be taught to students of political economy as the battles of Austerlitz and Tannenberg are taught at military academies.

The main, or at any rate the most effective decree of November 1938, lengthened working hours by relaxing the regulations governing them. The sages were unanimously against this: such a policy would increase unemployment and cause the standard of living of the workers to drop. From November 1938 to June 1939, the last month before the annual holiday, industrial output increased by 15 per cent, building by 36 per cent, the volume of exports by 17 per cent. There was an exceptional spurt in all occupations. Unemployment dropped: full-time unemployment, rather difficult to reduce, only dropped slightly; but part-time unemployment (i.e. less than forty hours a week) dropped by more than half (from 20·4 to 9·4 per cent of the work force).

Prices, which had been rising fast, slowed down. In ten months the average wholesale prices only increased by 1·5 per cent. The average retail prices, behind as usual, rose by 3·3 per cent in nine months instead of 6·5 per cent during the same period in the previous year. The purchasing power of the working week increased by 7·4 per cent in spite of increased taxation intended to pay for armaments.

Those who never foresaw this recovery were not taking into account structural features. They did not realise that if working hours increased by 9 per cent in metal industries, textile industries would be given an additional outlet because of the higher spending power.

Changes in the structure

If the structure of occupations was invariable, an equilibrium would finally appear between offer and demand in various sectors. This would not necessarily entail full employment, since certain occupations are particularly sought after (artistic and liberal professions, trade, etc.). When it becomes customary for some reason to give an unusually high hourly wage or large fees in one occupation, it develops chronic underemployment, by attracting people who want to live it up and raise their status. When their income remains in fact moderate because of the underemployment, it does not occur to them to change their occupation. Underemployment is then given as the cause for the high wage: cause and effect become entangled in an equilibrium which may even resist an increase in the active population of other sectors and become permanent and traditional.

Apart from this special problem, in an industrial system the required structure of occupations changes all the time, whether through planning or through the liberal mechanism. As well as the famous migration from secondary to tertiary occupations (see Fisher, C. Clark, J. Fourastié), there are also variations inside each sector because of various factors, especially technological progress. Under such conditions the real structure of occupations must follow the movement. If it does not, or it lags behind, economic progress will be slowed down together with the very application of the new technology. It is thus essential that the active population be open to distortion, either by changes in occupation during the active life (retraining) or by a movement of more young people to the expanding occupations.

The first method is the more difficult, since it entails suffering for the worker and loss of capital for the firm. The second is easier to apply, but has limitations, since the active population is only replaced slowly. Since the one is only necessary if the other fails, we shall first consider the second.

Renewal of the active population

First take a stationary population, considering particularly the men, with an expectation of life of seventy (United Nations Table type $e_0 = 70$), and assume that they start work at eighteen and retire at sixty-five.

In such a population 2·27 per cent of the active men die or retire each year, and are replaced by the same proportion of young men. Even if all these are channelled towards the under-subscribed occupations, this renewal could not cover all the needs: indeed in the limiting case, when an occupation must disappear because of technological change, this process would require forty-seven years if it were to be achieved through the mere extinction of the workers in it. This is however fairly rare in practice, only occurring in a limited number of specialised occupations such as the running of horsecabs. Usually, as in agriculture, the population only has to decrease in relative numbers.

For retraining to be necessary, in no sector must the active population drop in absolute numbers. Here, stationary populations appear much less adaptable than growing populations. For if the latter are stable (i.e. if each age-group increases every year in the same ratio), the renewal can be fast. Suppose that the same population, still with an expectation of life of seventy years, now grows by 1 per cent each year. The proportion of young men of eighteen starting work changes from 2·27 to 2·87 per cent, an increase of a quarter, which may not seem very much. However, it must be remembered that in no case are the young totally mobile. This is fortunate in that if, for example, all the sons of farmers were to abandon farming, the agricultural population would become excessively old. The young often stay in depressed occupations through inertia. If this applies to 50 per cent of them, then the ratio of mobile ones rises from 1·13 per cent in the stationary population to 1·73 per cent in the growing population, thus increasing by more than a half.

Thus population growth makes the structure of occupations adaptable and progress more beneficial. The quicker the progress the sharper the demographic growth required.

For example, the ratio of the agricultural to the non-agricultural sector should slowly drop. If the total population is rising, this can take place without too much trouble. If the population is stationary, the agricultural population will have to reduce its absolute numbers, possibly causing serious trouble. Thus in France under the Empire ten to eleven million people lived off the land. Those who remained in the country suffered chronically from poor sales, because the population of consumers was not large enough. To restore the ratio, it was necessary to depopulate some agricultural districts excessively.

In the same way, if there is a relative surplus of tradesmen, they can be, as it were, floated again by the rising tide of consumers.

The general case

What is true of the structure of occupations is true for any distribution of the population. One can change the proportions making up a whole in two ways: by adding or by amputating. Both methods can be used with materials: the painter adds, the sculptor amputates. With a population, amputation always causes suffering and thus encounters difficulties.

Take universities for example. The state of knowledge at a given moment may require eighteen chairs in one faculty and twelve chairs in another. A little later knowledge may develop so that the numbers should become even. If the number of students and the financial resources are constant, the answer should be to create three new chairs in the second faculty and suppress three in the first. But the second action may be very unpleasant and may not be carried out, so that the university will no longer be equal to the needs. However, if the numbers of students and the financial resources are to increase by 20 per cent, they can be directed towards the creation of six chairs in the second faculty, thus establishing the correct balance without having to amputate the first faculty.

This phenomenon is as clear in geography. France, for example, has too small a population for the whole of its land to be occupied. The necessary expansion of towns causes excessive depopulation in certain districts and the population here falls below the optimum level, indeed, sometimes below the minimum level, causing a general decay of transport and public services.

The same is true of age groups. In any society or firm there is an appropriate ratio of young to old. If the old become too numerous, they will have difficulty in finding employment. This is the classical problem of unemployment amongst elderly engineers. It is a complete misapprehension to think that in such a situation fewer young people are needed. The answer is to reestablish the balance of ages with more young, so that they float the surplus of older people and give them better chances of employment. Here we come back up against the Malthusian point of view, which considers any apparent and relative excess as a real and absolute excess and reasons on numbers instead of ratios.

The orientation of rising generations

The young starting work produce more than they consume. As we know, their output has to cover not only their needs but those of the adults, the old, and the children. Good accounts on a national basis can even calculate these needs fairly precisely, and reckon the structure of occupations required amongst the rising generations.

When we talk about professional orientation we usually speak of course from the individual's point of view: it consists in finding out a person's aptitudes and advising him accordingly. But global orientation could be practised too. Here are two possible approaches.

In about 1958 the Italian Minister of Education asked SVIMEZ to study the probable structure of the active population in 1975.[1] The purpose was to determine, from what was known of the technological and economic evolution of the years to come, the numbers of men at the various levels of education. From this probable future population, SVIMEZ reckoned the number of pupils to be trained each year at the various levels in schools and universities, as well as the number of teachers needed. This was obviously an extremely interesting study.

Another way would be to construct an economic plan following Leontief's method of exchanges between sectors, and to translate the classical matrix in terms of employment. Unfortunately, the planners are only moving very slowly in this direction. Yet, however difficult technically, it is the right one, for economics are based on men. Any planning will fail if it does not forestall inflationary shortages of personnel, together with depression in other sectors.

The classical Leontief matrix expresses the value of everything that each sector buys from every other sector. It would be an improvement to the matrix to introduce physical quantities of goods, and take note of the raw materials or intermediary products entering into the composition of any finished product or that will be consumed by any given sector. Another important

men → Finished ↓ products	Engineers	Technicians	Skilled workers	Labourers	Office workers
Car					
Council flat					
Classroom					

[1] See Nino Novacco, 'Prévision pour l'année 1975 sur la population, italienne selon la qualification professionnelle et l'instruction', *Population*, 1961, No. 3.

improvement would consist in considering men instead of goods, and translating the various final products into working hours for men of various qualifications, as suggested in the model table.

With these data the intentions of the population regarding goods could be translated into working hours and required qualifications, and we would know the *required population*. This would be the absolute matrix, determining the plan in function of men's intentions and of the current technology.

Genetics upside down

There is a case where the orientation of the young cannot easily be carried out in function of needs, for these depend on future generations. Thus, when there is an unforeseen increase in births or a development of education in a country, the required number of teachers rises: but these teachers have to be found amongst the generations already trained. This happened in France and in many other countries after the last war. It is, as it were, the situation of genetics turned upside down.

Consider for example a stationary, semi-developed population, with an expectation of life of forty years (see United Nations tables): the group aged twenty to sixty-five (age of teachers) is renewed by 2·9 per cent each year. If the birth rate or educational requirements suddenly increase by 10 per cent, the number of pupils aged six to fourteen increases by 10 per cent in eight years, an average of 1·25 per cent per year. On top of the normal 2·9 per cent of teachers we shall have to recruit an extra 1·25 per cent, a total of 4·15 per cent. The number of teachers to be recruited at the age of twenty will thus suddenly increase by 43 per cent.

In an advanced population (expectation of life seventy years), the renewal by 2·4 per cent a year will have to rise to 3·65 per cent: recruitment will thus have to rise by more than a half, causing considerable difficulty.

Employment of the young

To the question as to whether recruiting the young is helped or not by increases in population, the instinctive reply is 'no', but the problem is more complex than it appears. One must distinguish between a population growing larger and growing younger, between one growing smaller and growing older. If a stationary population suddenly has a larger generation of young people than usual, they may have difficulty in finding places, for society has not suddenly expanded in the same ratio. Conversely, if a younger generation were to be only half as large, it would find employment very easily.

But these are only transitory situations, caused by surprise effects after sudden changes. When growth or shrinkage is regular, the effects are very different. As we have seen, the suppleness given to the structure favours economic expansion and hence employment.

Promotion, mortality, and growth

Let us now consider employment from the qualitative point of view. Consider first an active stationary population. If the death rate is high, the age pyramid becomes very narrow towards the top: promotion is quite fast. Thus, when an army suffers heavy losses a lieutenant stands a better chance of becoming a general, as long as he survives. On the contrary, where the death rate is very low, and the pyramid becomes cylindrical, this probability becomes much smaller. Confused thought on this point leads people to reckon that a high death rate has advantages; yet it is better to be only a colonel or even a captain than to be dead. For the same reason, any lengthening in active life constitutes social progress and not regression, even if it makes promotion slower, since all the intermediary stages of life are thus lengthened.

Now consider a stable, growing population: everything else being equal, will an individual stand more or less chance of reaching the top of the hierarchy, for instance the post of director, than in a stationary population? The question can be simplified by taking the case of an administrative structure with a constant ratio of directors and where promotion is decided on length of service, so that choice only operates between people of the same age. The chances of becoming a director are the same whatever the rate of growth: when the young generation arrives at the appropriate age for directors, the number of posts will have increased in the same ratio, at least in a normal expansion. The young now grown old will be more numerous but they, in their turn, will have more young to direct.

However, in an expanding economy the assumption that promotion goes with length of service is not very plausible. New businesses, new departments appear. This causes a tendency not to choose systematically the oldest employee, but to favour deserving youngsters. Thus in Europe in the nineteenth century it was easier for the young to reach important positions. Their increase in number is therefore not, as might appear, an obstacle to their careers.

But even apart from the problem of an ageing population, various sociological phenomena are tending at the moment to stop promotion of the young: more and more stringent regulations in the Civil Service, industrial and commercial concentration, the appropriation of certain occupations, 'acquired rights', etc.

Social promotion

Leaving aside the problem of social mobility which is a sociological matter, let us concentrate on the direct consequences of a change in structure increas-

198

ing the ratio of the higher jobs. The word 'job' can be taken in the most general sense, but it is more directly applicable to wage-earners. Social promotion thus defined in the general sense causes *the average income of the population, and hence the standard of living, to rise more than the income of each category.*

Take an active population, divide it into four social categories and consider it at two different moments. Here is the initial situation.

Social category	Number of people	Income level	Total income
1	10	8	80
2	25	6	150
3	40	3	120
4	150	1	150
Total	225	2·2	500

A change occurs causing a marked increase, say of 50 per cent, in output, and therefore in the total income to be divided up; this coincides with a change in structure which no doubt was helped by it. We now have the following situation:

Social category	Number of people	Income level	Total income
1	15	9	135
2	40	6·25	250
3	70	3·29	230
4	100	1·35	135
Total	225	3·3	750

The income per person and the average standard of living have increased by half, but this has not happened in any individual category. It may even have dropped in every category while increasing for the total population.

This is by no means an imaginary phenomenon, but seems to be the rule in contemporary societies: 1. Technological progress demands fewer labourers and more skilled workers, organisers, technicians, teachers, etc. 2. Because of the ageing of the population the slowness of promotion tends to be compensated for by the multiplication of higher positions. For instance there are now proportionally more colonels than there were in the past.

Now in no social category does a man compare his lot with his former situation or that of his parents; he rather remembers the situation of people in the same category at a former period. A lawyer whose father was a peasant wishes to live as what he thought a lawyer was, and not as a peasant. As a result there

199

is a feeling of frustration in every social category, whose representatives, statistics in hand, show that the income of this category has clearly increased less than the national income.

This misunderstanding is all the more widespread since the process described has little chance of becoming widely known. It is one of those unpleasant things which no one likes to describe or teach since it may make one's own pay claims appear to be less legitimate.

Since the increase in the national income has been wholly or partly absorbed by promotion, the various social categories quarrel over imaginary wealth that has already been distributed. This can lead to widespread trouble. Thus the French Revolution was not, as is still taught, due to inordinate greed on the part of the leading classes under the old system. The number of claimants, together with the mass of needs, had increased without a parallel increase in output. This lack may be attributed to various causes, and especially to the revocation of the *Edict of Nantes*, which deprived the country of a progressive élite. The average standard of living had increased, whilst the standard of living of each category had barely been maintained and had perhaps even dropped, causing an explosive situation.[1] In England, on the other hand, since economic progress had been sufficient to cover the additional needs arising from social promotion, there was no such explosion. A fairly similar situation occurred in 1848.

In general public opinion is very conscious of the inequality of incomes but not of the number of claimants. We have already seen the importance of this number as regards consumption in agricultural societies; we shall see it again in chapter 23, in shapes as real and present but as little known.

Tertiary occupations

We have already said that the tertiary sector is not homogeneous and can be defined in various ways. If we consider mainly individual occupations we can introduce another kind of distinction, taking into account two different ways in which the general structure changes to the benefit of the tertiary sector:
1. Out of *necessity*; technology demands new forms of employment (more engineers for instance) and so does the multiplication of needs (more hotels and nurses for instance). This goes with the general trend of the economy.
2. Through *individual decisions* dictated by need or by convenience. This may be caused by real overpopulation; but it might also be due to a wish to avoid hard work and choose an attractive profession.

The classical example is that of tradesmen. The surplus of tradesmen is by no means a characteristic of advanced societies, as a glance at middle eastern bazaars will show. In an overpopulated country the lack of land and the diffi-

[1] See Jacqueline Hecht 'Un problème de population active au XVIIIe siècle en France: la querelle de la noblesse commerçante', *Population*, April–May 1964, pp. 257–90.

culties caused by decreasing returns and by the lack of industry, lead men to activities that are marginally unproductive. Past certain numbers they can constitute a surplus population consuming part of the national income without adding anything to it. The surplus is no less serious in advanced societies, though less frequent than is commonly thought. Certain sectors, such as the property market, could very well work with a much smaller number of people and especially of firms.

This is not a case of over-population, as certain doctrinaires may say. It is not that the number of jobs is insufficient, but that these professions are attractive because they free the worker from manual labour. Although professional qualification is very useful, someone without much knowledge can manage more or less to hold the job. A tradesman never needs to know as much about the goods he sells as someone who makes or repairs them. The surplus of tertiary workers thus appears as an unavoidable consequence of poor training: a certain degree of education creates qualified people but also badly qualified people, by turning them away from manual labour without giving them the ability to carry out other jobs well; they turn to trade as a last resort. This state of affairs is further worsened by the readily confirmed fact that selling is better paid than producing: servicing firms are much more interested in providing spare parts or new machines than in carrying out actual repairs.

The trend towards the tertiary sector does not exist only in the capitalist system. Although office workers are badly paid in socialist countries, the authorities there have to struggle continually against the inroads of bureaucracy.

Even when it answers a real need, the expansion of the tertiary sector changes the laws of industrial systems dealt with in this chapter and the one before. The low rate of increase in productivity in these occupations, together with the ambition to improve one's standard of living, causes a slowing down already described in chapter 15 (page 141). The countries where industrial expansion has passed a certain threshold will enter into another economic era, which at present one can only glimpse.

Maturation

Thirty years ago during the slump, which was a crisis of intelligence much more than a crisis of wealth, various theories of maturation were formulated according to which society had reached the end of the road, or at least the end of a long stage. According to some, all needs were satisfied, or almost, and progress was no longer necessary; according to others, even technology was growing tired and the era of inventions had ended. While disproving these pessimistic theories, events suggested other forms of maturation: some now speak of a civilisation of leisure, with technological progress about to provide Man with more leisure than wealth; other directions could equally well be suggested.

201

We wish to discover here the development and life open to a stationary population. As we have seen, no such population has known economic progress up to now, and only where there has been mobility of labour has a certain growth occurred. It is, however, possible that growth may stop in certain countries, either by a spontaneous drop in the birth rate or by improvements in contraceptives or sterilisation, or because the exhaustion of natural resources leads governments to encourage Malthusian policy because growth would be considered too costly. Let us at any rate suppose that this happens. Will such populations find a way of stopping their growth without beginning to suffer from excessive age?

Two vitally different situations may occur, according to whether the expectation of life continues to increase or not. This expectation had been more or less fixed at twenty-five to thirty years for thousands of years and doubtless since prehistoric times; over the last two centuries it has increased considerably and has reached seventy years in developed countries. But this trend is misleading, since it is due mainly to lower mortality in the very young and the middle-aged, which cannot drop very much further: already at the age of sixty, in an advanced society, eighty-three people survive out of 100 born. Mortality above this age, which had never dropped very much, appears to be increasing again in very advanced societies, either because there is less natural selection and men are more fragile or because the way of life (food, occupations) is unfavourable. We may therefore suppose either that mankind has advanced one step by suppressing exogenous illnesses, but will be stopped by the barrier of excessive old age, or that new discoveries will provide the means of countering this excess. In both cases there will be profound changes.

1. In the case of *a stationary population in the demographic sense of the word*, can such a population profit from future technological developments? This is by no means impossible, but there will, as we have said, be difficulties of structure and adaptation. If the population reacts against its own rigidity, it may achieve sufficient mobility of labour. But since the stationary position has a stabilising influence, there would need to be exceptional responsibility here for the population not to fall a victim to laziness. A socialist society would in principle be better suited to solve this internal problem, but even here there would be considerable difficulties.

2. In the case of *an ageing population*, if medical progress manages to prolong human life to eighty or ninety, society will be faced with a dilemma which already exists: *to expand or to age*. It may well age without any expansion, by reducing its birth rate so that generations no longer replace themselves; France has been doing this for the last fifty years. In any case to study the problem of the active population a new distinction will have to be made according to whether medical progress can act on ageing itself or on its effects.

In the first case a man aged sixty would have a physiological age of forty. It would be as if the birth certificates of the inhabitants had been altered. One would of course have to move the retirement age to well above sixty. The main problem in this kind of revolution would be one of adaptation.

The second case sets additional difficulties: if men are as old as they are now at sixty, but have the prospect of thirty years of old age instead of fifteen as at present, pension funds will become totally unbalanced. Either the active life will have to be prolonged to the extreme, or the social system will have to be drastically changed, since the system of private property will make it impossible to operate an enormous transference of income from the active to the inactive sectors. As for the problems of distribution of the active population, and of mobility of labour, they will be the same as in the first case.

The need for research into social biology

This field is still little explored, not only by planners but also by sociologists and historians. It would be profitable to study the growth of populations as a biological phenomenon, jointly with biologists specialising in problems of growth; without necessarily suggesting a return to the old organicist doctrines, it seems that a partnership of this kind would lead to the exploration of one of the most difficult problems of all. A drop of water is not conscious of being part of a cloud; similarly, men experience great difficulty in considering themselves as a whole.

21

THE THIRD WORLD

'The Scriptures should be taught to savages because even if we were
only to teach them enough religion to want to wear clothes this would be
a great help to the English textile industry.'

BAYLE

When I first used the phrase 'Third World' in 1952,[1] it applied better than
today to a specific part of the globe; since then its political and its economic-
demographic definitions have to some extent moved apart. Politically the
Third World includes relatively advanced countries outside the big blocs,
such as Yugoslavia; from the economic and demographic point of view it can
comprise China and Albania, Guinea, and even perhaps Cuba. This second
definition will apply here.

A new type of economy

The countries of the Third World are characterised by: 1. A high birth rate,
above 4 per cent. 2. A rapid growth of population of the order of 2–3·5 per
cent a year. 3. A small national income per inhabitant, of the order of $100–
350 a year. 4. A mainly agricultural economy.

They are different from the classical agricultural systems described in
chapter 11 because of their rapid growth of population through falls in mortality. They differ from industrial societies by their high birth rate and their small
national income. On the one hand, they are changing like industrial societies,
and yet in the preponderance of agriculture and the low level of incomes they
are similar to agricultural societies.

Because of their need for wealth and the paucity of their means these countries are in a difficult situation and call for new policies. They thus constitute
a third type of economy: that of a country with small resources but faced with
the need for vast transformations to cope with a large demographic growth.

---

[1] 'For this Third World, ignored, exploited and despised, exactly as the Third Estate was
before the Revolution, would also like to become something.' *L'Observateur*, 14 August
1952.

204

The split between the economy and the population

The countries of the Third World have suffered biological progress without the corresponding economic progress. It was easier and cheaper to introduce them to medical techniques than to economic techniques; hence a huge, unprecedented, distortion in their structure. The lengthening of life in these countries has not coincided, as it did in Europe in the nineteenth century, with a rise in the standard of living. Taking as a unit the standard of living in western Europe around 1789 we have the following table:

		Standard of living	Length of Life (years)
Western Europe	1789	100	30
	1870	160	40
	1913	280	50
	1938	340	60
	1962	450	70
Latin America (temperate part)		212	64
Latin America (tropical part)		116	54
Asia (less USSR, China and Japan)		49	48
Africa (non-whites)		52	42

Thus with a standard of living smaller than half of that of Europe two centuries ago, Asia and Africa have an expectation of life more than a third larger. With a standard of living equal to a third of that in western Europe in 1913, tropical America has a higher expectation of life. These quantities appear on figure 60, where the countries of the Third World are well above the line representing the progress of Europe. In terms of standard of living the gap between the Third World and advanced countries can be expressed in centuries; in terms of length of life it can be expressed in dozens of years or sometimes even in single years.

The growth of population is over 2 per cent a year in all the Third World, and approaches 4 per cent in certain countries (Philippines, Formosa, Costa Rica). In western Europe it has almost never been greater than 1 per cent a year on the whole, and it is now well below this figure.

These data are thus completely new as far as population is concerned, and they set entirely new economic problems. It is as if in the early Middle Ages France had received from some distant world medical knowledge allowing the population to grow by 2·5–3 per cent a year and double in less than a generation. This intervention would have been welcomed from the sanitary angle, but would have been difficult to cope with.

205

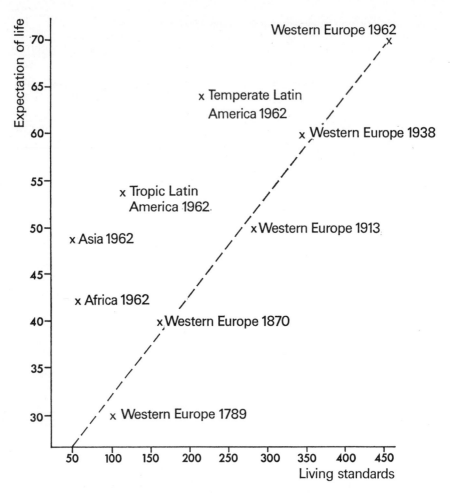

Figure 60. Living standards and expectation of life in various regions at different times.

Population and resources

The two classical tests of over-population are both conclusive: there is a deficiency of food (especially proteins) and underemployment. Yet this is only overpopulation if compared with the present-day resources as they are exploited: such is the characteristic of underdevelopment.

A study of potential resources, or of the output that could be obtained with present-day technology either by exploiting new lands or by putting already cultivated land to better use and developing mineral resources, would lead to conclude, on the contrary, that there are very few overpopulated countries in the world. South and Central America are very sparsely populated, and so is the greater part of Africa; the Middle and Far East and Indonesia also have a great deal of as yet untapped resources. Even India and China could manage to feed a larger population.

Absolute overpopulation exists or threatens specially in islands; Mauritius, Réunion, Formosa and Java, the West Indies, and perhaps Egypt, which has many of the features of an island. Here, resources are limited and it is difficult to introduce large industries: there will have to be emigration some day. Egypt can expect still greater gifts from its age -old benefactor the Nile, though one may hardly go on calling gifts what demands considerable labour.

Even in countries in possession of large virgin spaces, such as Brazil, quick growth demands large-scale investment that a poor population can only achieve with some difficulty. We will dwell more particularly on this problem.

Investment and growth

Chapter 19 showed the relationship between investment, the growth of national income and that of the population. The Third World is faced with the same problem, but coupled with a faster growth. We will first assume that the population is stable, so that its growth applies equally to the young, the adults, and the old.

For 'economic' investment, intended to raise the standard of living, the national rate of interest can be estimated at 20–50 per cent (capital-output ratio between 5 and 2). This rate can be determined approximately by referring to the figures for previous years, or derived from the wealth of resources available nationally. It also depends on men's capacity to produce, and on their political system.

The definitions of national income and, especially, of investment still vary a great deal from one author to the next. We should really include self-investment (the case of the peasant digging a well in his own field), since the output resulting from it will be included. But in practice, non-financial investment is very difficult to account for.

It does not seem advisable to use the same capital-output ratio for demographic as for economic investment; this might be acceptable if we were considering the young and the old who are not producing, but it is not so when adults form the bulk of the population (see pages 180–1). However, the existence of extensive underemployment leads to a fear that the extra adults may really form a surplus, with only a low marginal productivity. The 'multiplier' effect is small.

We will first assume that the capital-output ratio is 4 for economic and 3 for demographic investment; this leads to the following table, giving the increases in national income per head in various circumstances:

National income invested	Growth of population per year			
	2%	2·5%	3%	3·5%
10 per cent	1%	0·6%	0·25%	0·1%
15 per cent	2·25%	1·9%	1·5%	1·1%
20 per cent	3·5%	3·1%	2·75%	2·4%
25 per cent	4·75%	4·4%	4%	3·6%

Thus, given our assumptions, if a population growing by 2 per cent a year wants to increase its standard of living by 1·5 per cent a year it will have to spend 15 per cent of its income on investment. Conversely a population growing by 2·5 per cent a year, which can only invest 10 per cent of its income, will only be able to increase its standard of living by 0·6 per cent a year.

A different capital-output ratio would lead to a different table.

Birth control

A common reflection is that a cut in the birth rate would lessen these difficulties by causing a drop in the investment needed and in consumption demands. Even in the first few years there would be a gain in food, and later the number of teachers and the amount of housing required would drop.

This problem (difficult from the sociological point of view), is only dealt with in the second part of this book. We will merely recall here that such a cut is improbable in very poor and illiterate populations. In any case, even if it did occur, there would still be an important need for investment, since the population would still increase (see Japan for instance) and the rise in employment would need to be maintained for fifteen years or so. We can therefore disregard this objection. If it is proved true we shall have to revise the calculations, but it would be unwise to rely on it.

The need for savings

In the very common case where the national rate of interest for investment is 25 per cent and the demographic growth 2·5 per cent a year, 15 per cent of the national income has to be invested for the standard of living to increase by only 1·9 per cent a year. If such a rhythm were maintained the country would achieve a certain development in time, but it would still be underdeveloped, perhaps even more drastically, since underdevelopment is a comparative concept and developed countries increase their standard of living fast. For its underdevelopment to be 'digested' our country would have to raise its standard of living faster than developed countries.

Leaving aside the two extremes, the USA and the USSR, and considering Europe, which is in an average position, we can estimate its average progress at 4 per cent a year; the table shows us, by interpolation, that to achieve such progress with a population increasing by 2·7 per cent a year, 24 per cent of the national income would have to be invested. This is impossible in a poor country where even 10 per cent is an ambitious figure.

Here is how the national income can be distributed in two cases in a population increasing by 2·5 per cent a year.

	Standard of living maintained	Standard of living increasing by 2 per cent a year
Consumption by the young	22	20
Consumption by the other inactive people (elderly, invalids)	10·5	10
Consumption by active people	60	54·5
Demographic investments	7·5	7·5
Economic investments	—	8·0
	100	100

These figures are naturally only indications; education, with the exception of school building, is included in consumption, according to (mistaken) practice. So in order to increase their standard of living the active people need to consume less than 55 per cent of their own output, a proportion easy to achieve in a developed country but much more difficult in a poor one. If the poor country consists of smallholders or of tribes with communal property, financial saving is very unstable. If it consists of large owners exploiting poor masses, saving is more conceivable but only through a deplorable kind of social system. Let us now study the various ways in which high incomes can be used, since they often occur in the initial situation.

Capitalist investment: Here those with high incomes change their way of life, give up certain luxuries and attempt to increase their output. This can be encouraged by the spread of new techniques or by a desire for power. It is, however, questionable whether such motives are sufficient to cause a deep change in their life. Their class interests could of course lead them to try to reduce the pressure menacing, but history does not provide many encouraging examples of such an intelligent self-appraisal. A feudal landlord will not suddenly change into an ambitious builder for the sake of living up to Mirabeau's ideal.

Division of land: This is fervently encouraged by those wishing to combine conservatism with social progress. In giving the land to those who use it they hope to create a stable and stabilising class. We will disregard the technical question as to whether or not the division of land increases output – this depends on the circumstances. We will assume that the output stays the same for a given number of farmers.

This solution may seem attractive, but if applied carelessly it can be dangerous and end in a deadly famine, through the premature creation of middle classes before the necessary food has become available. The following numerical example is similar to that in chapter 11.

1. Number of farmers	500	525	550	575	600	700
2. Marginal productivity	30	28	26	24	22	10
3. Total output	710	738	764	788	810	820
4. Total output per farmer	1·42	1·41	1·39	1·37	1·35	1·17
5. Proprietor's levy	110	111	112	113	114	115
6. Leaves for the farmers	600	627	652	675	696	705
7. Leaves to each farmer	1·20	1·193	1·185	1·172	1·16	1·01
8. Proprietor's food consumption	20	20	20	20	20	20
9. Leaves in available food	90	91	92	93	94	95
10. Number of non-farmers this can feed	75	76	78	79	81	96
11. Total population	575	601	628	654	681	796

Take for instance the situation in the last column but one: a population of 681 of whom 600 are farmers. If we abolish the levy the 600 farmers will have 810 units, and since they are underfed they will consume mainly primary products, which are thus retained by the agricultural sector. What will become of the eighty-óne non-farmers? They might of course cultivate the poor lands if there are any, but since marginal output is too low to feed them and they are perhaps not suited to such work, they will disappear. This disappearance can spread quite a long way, for overtaxed peasants have extremely elastic food requirements. The consumption of meat leads to a consumption of intermediary calories, and therefore of land, six times larger than the consumption of cereals and twice as large as the consumption of milk. Also, cattle-raising requires fewer men for the same area, so that if freed from the levy, the holder of the land may get rid of some of his labourers.

When a fairly large proportion of people begin to consume meat without the output having increased sufficiently, the optimum population drops. The weak are eliminated. In an overpopulated country he who eats meat eats men.

Thus in spite of appearances, a division of land not backed up by other measures in the public interest is dangerous. In suppressing the rationer it suppresses rationing, and may well starve part of the population in spite of the extra goods freed by the rationer. Besides, the owners tend to reduce their secondary or tertiary consumption rather than their consumption of food. The first famines in Soviet Russia immediately after the Revolution were blamed on peasants voluntarily holding back their products. This was not necessarily sabotage, nor was there mistrust of the currency: the under-nourished peasants were now able to consume more calories than under the old order.

If this risk is avoided and the smallholder encouraged to develop his land in the correct way, the division of land is a very good solution. In certain situations cooperative exploitation may be preferred to straightforward division, but the main care must be to prevent the country from holding back its food output.

Division of incomes: On page 118 of *The Causes of Wealth*, Fourastié considers what would happen if the income of a maharajah were split between the workers, and shows that their standard of living would hardly rise at all. We should go further than he and say that if the share-out is not absolutely equal, if the inequality of incomes is merely spread and not abolished, thus benefiting the middle classes, these will as we have seen consume more primary goods, eat more meat, and leave less food for the others. This seductive but imperfect revolution will lead to dangerous mistakes, if not supplemented by other measures.

Taxation in the public interest: Let us now assume that the levy, instead of being operated by a wicked rich man, is carried out in the community's interest and used, not to equalise the incomes of all, for this would reduce the optimum population, but to pay useful civil servants. Their services are an asset to the population as a whole, and bring the phrase 'average standard of living' back into its own; better still, the number of tertiary civil servants can be higher than the number of servants employed by the landlord, since the landlord's own larder has been abolished. The table on page 210 is thus modified (see overleaf): The 600 farmers can now feed 698 people instead of 681 previously; and to feed 681 people only 584 farmers would be needed. The standard of living has risen from 1·16 to 1·17 as regards food and from 1·16 to 1·33 as regards goods and public services.

There are thus three solutions: a private levy, no levy at all, a public levy; and the third is the most favourable. But it is temporary: it only has

Number of farmers	584	600
Total agricultural output	796	810
Total output per farmer	1·36	1·35
Levy	113	114
Leaves for the farmers	683	696
Leaves to each farmer	1·17	1·16
Number of tertiary workers who can be fed	97	98
Tertiary output	113	114
Total population	681	698
Total output	909	924
Standard of living	1·33	1·32

permanent value if the levy is put to a productive end. This can be used for investment, and the secondary and tertiary workers freed under the new system can begin to exploit fresh natural resources.

In terms of population such a change leads to a transformation of the direct and indirect servants of the rich class into masons, canal diggers, producers of fertilisers etc. This is exactly the policy of popular democracies: to transfer the income of the rich class to investment, without attempting to raise the standard of living of the workers immediately. All these states do not suffer from the famines that occurred in the USSR, partly because of a more favourable starting point in the production of foodstuffs, but also because retention of goods in the country was carefully avoided.

In this case the community takes over the part assigned by Mirabeau to the owner investor.

Summary of the various situations

Leaving aside the social usefulness of the ruler, which is a matter of circumstance, there are various possible uses for income above the subsistence level in an underdeveloped agricultural society: 1. *Direct consumption of the product of nature by the rulers*. This system is the most disastrous for the subjects, since they are eliminated from nature and society. It is never more than relative. 2. *Consumption of men* (tertiary or secondary) *by the rulers.* This ensures a higher population but not much more progress. 3. *Distribution of the ruler's income* to his subjects: a generous improbability which does not even always help the subjects much, because it might reduce their numbers. 4. *Consumption of (tertiary) men to serve the community:* equitable for the immediate future but not afterwards: the men of tomorrow are sacrificed to those of today, either in numbers or in the standard of living. 5. *Large scale investment by the rulers*: this ensures the future life of the subjects but it is only partially and temporarily practised. It is the conservative solution and is usually insufficient. 6. *Investment by and for the community*.

Food accounting

In all countries national accounts have progressed a great deal, but they are still made out in monetary units. This is satisfactory for an approximation in a developed country. But in a system where the subsistence level is still a subject of concern, it can give rise to many mistakes – we have only to recall the division of land and the abolishing of feudal taxes which we have just studied. To count in food it is not sufficient to include agricultural output and imports; one should keep track of the consumption of each social class, and especially the transfer of food from country to town.

Reckoning this way imposes the sixth solution: this maintains almost wholly the strict rationing imposed originally by the landlord, and can very rarely be achieved by consent. Strong authority is necessary, however resigned or enthusiastic the former subjects may be. Their ruler may have disappeared but the rule of nature has not, and a new effort is needed to achieve liberation.

When food output reaches a certain level it becomes easier for everyone to find employment. The country has a surplus and can buy industrial products, encouraging exchange between town and country and ringing the changes for the industrial era.

Marx and Malthus

In this debate the Marxist solution has obvious advantages: used to one rule, the workers support another without much difficulty. Since most of the servants and workers are now being switched to investment, the population growth can be coped with. Here, Malthus does not come into the reckoning.

The rulers' position is a difficult one: they have to reconcile themselves to investing in a way that changes their life or does not result in a capitalist income. As for limiting the growth of the population that may threaten their rule, they do not usually think of this. India and Japan have opted for birth control but the countries of the African and American tropics are very far from it.

There are also rulers and subjects, or at least large-scale inequalities of conditions, amongst the countries of the world. Direct domination had long existed in the shape of colonialism. While this was absolute or almost so, the rulers did not worry much about population growth. But as soon as the native Algerians received rights claimed to be equal to those of the French – though in fact much smaller – it was feared that the number of partial subjects, the costly ones, might rise excessively.

Domination can occur in other shapes: at a time when world consciousness is beginning to appear, the rich countries fear the proliferation of people who are acquiring rights. It may one day be necessary to organise not only regular deliveries of goods to them, which would merely be rather uncomfortable, but also to accept immigrants from them, which would bring about such dramatic changes that the very possibility is never mentioned. F. Notestein writes characteristically: 'By launching a programme of modernisation the now dominant powers would in effect be creating a future world in which their own peoples would become progressively smaller minorities, and possess a progressively smaller porportion of the world's wealth and power.'[1]

In this delicate situation we may see the classical attitudes of ruler and relative subject: the ruler tries to limit the number of his subjects or at least their growth. The Soviets refuse to look at the problem from this angle: they still emphasise, as Marx did for social classes, that there is no overpopulation problem. In this they are ill-informed and old-fashioned.

The following dialogue might sum up the thought of Marxists and Malthusians:

The Malthusian: 'If you follow Malthus, then Marx becomes unnecessary. Limit the population and the inequality of incomes diminishes, strengthening the system.'

The Marxist: 'Apply Marxism first, and see about Malthus later. Through better distribution you can suppress the over-population inherent in the old system. As for absolute overpopulation, we don't know of it. We will see, when we are the masters of the land.'

But behind these expressed thoughts there are others, more real.

The Malthusian: 'It is friendship and concern for the underdeveloped countries that leads me to encourage birth control.' (Meaning: 'Thanks to birth control I shall not have to divide or give away my wealth.')

The Marxist: 'Poverty is only the result of private property and of colonialism.' (Meaning: 'Let poverty spread, avoiding any reforms, and it will destroy capitalism.')

---

[1] 'Demographic Studies of Selected Areas of Rapid Growth', *Milbank Memorial Fund*, New York, 1944, p. 156.

Foreign aid

Savings in underdeveloped countries are likely to be insufficient, and so foreign aid has to be envisaged. This is not the place to describe its mechanism, the errors it leads to, or ways of improving its efficiency. In spite of the serious deficiency of reckonings in monetary units, we shall try to define briefly some general proportions. Dividing the world into five relatively homogeneous districts we have the following table for 1965.

	Population in millions	G.N.P. (in billions of dollars)	National output per head (in dollars)
1. Developed western countries	516	1214	2353
2. USSR and Socialist countries of Europe	353	397	1124
3. Semi-developed countries[1]	186	130	698
4. China and Socialist countries in Asia	793	164	207
5. Less developed countries	1487	314	211
Average total	3335	2219	665

The gross national output given here was reckoned by converting national monetary units into dollars, not using exchange rates, which would have exaggerated the differences, but the purchasing power of the various countries. The same table could be expressed in ratios as follows:

	Population	GNP
1. Developed western countries	15·5	54·7
2. USSR and Socialist countries of Europe	10·6	17·9
3. Semi-developed countries	5·5	5·8
4. China and Socialist countries in Asia	23·8	7·4
5. Less developed countries	44·6	14·2
Average total	100	100

Leaving aside the socialist world and the semi-developed countries, we can assume that group 5 needs, to eke out its national savings, a sum equal to 16 per cent of its income; for instance, it could meet the population growth through its own resources, and achieve with the extra 16 per cent an increase

[1] Spain, Portugal, Greece, Japan, Argentina, Chile, Uruguay.

of 4 per cent a year in the national income per head, which would double its income in eighteen years. To achieve this it would be sufficient to transfer to them 50,200 million dollars a year, or 4·1 per cent of the income of the developed countries, a sum far smaller than their armament expenditure and more or less equal to their annual growth. From this angle the immense surge of poverty or of the numbers of the poor could be prevented without much technical difficulty. Let us consider the practical side, rather than the political difficulties involved in such a policy.

Action on raw materials

Many people have objected that foreign aid in this form can be interpreted as charity or be offered only on conditions harmful to national sovereignty: instead they suggest, for instance, adjusting the prices of exported goods, and add that not only does the ratio of prices put the Third World at a disadvantage but this disadvantage increases constantly.

Indeed, from 1956 to 1962, the Moody's Index of prices of raw materials (New York) dropped by 10 per cent and the Reuter Index (London) by 9 per cent, whereas during the same period the prices of manufactured goods increased by 11 per cent in England and 8 per cent in the US. The scissor effect is obvious. According to many authors it even equalled the total foreign aid, so that the developed countries have simply taken back in an underhand way what they officially gave. This estimation may be a little excessive, and not take into account capitalist income on these same raw materials (oil and cotton for instance), but the phenomenon is serious enough to attract attention and provoke seductive suggestions for remedies.

Various plans for instance estimate that it will suffice to freeze the prices of raw materials at a slightly higher level to improve the conditions in the Third World; some are even being applied. Yet they forget both the most elementary laws of economic hydraulics and the countless experiments on markets in many countries, sometimes bearing on the very same raw materials. A market cannot be controlled if quantities are not controlled: the freezing of prices is only an accessory operation or a result. Yet acting on quantities involves defining quotas for each country, and, even in the best possible case, transferring the apparent surplus and lack of sales to other goods. It is a Malthusian method, attractive, but with innumerable ill effects. It is a kind of symptomatic medicine, that acts on results, and is too easily preferred in such debates to action in depth, less spectacular and more difficult to conceive. Besides, the foreign aid already being given may quite possibly be contributing to the deterioration of the market. Perhaps the very basis of the system will have to be changed.

The prices of raw materials will increase, of course, if they are consumed more, or when the Third World becomes industrialised. Yet to improve the conditions in these countries it is not even necessary to raise the prices. Productivity, and profits, can be strongly increased. Progress would cause prices to drop in relation to wages and incomes.

In spite of these observations, international policy is still fatally attracted towards easy and even spectacular but technically inappropriate measures. This is politically inevitable; it will at least have the advantage of failing eventually and prompting a more serious study of the matter.

The proper exploitation of nature

This unprofitable trade is remarkable in that *paradoxically, the poor countries exchange their natural resources, in other words their capital, against labour.* They then buy back the same materials at a higher price after they have been manufactured and had their value increased by labour. The situation is therefore quite different from that of the capitalist employer and his workers. It is due to the fact that the peoples of the Third World do not yet know how to domesticate nature and its products. As long as they do not learn, the world will be doomed to fight unsuccessfully against poverty through expedients.

Chapter 19 condemned illusions about the importance of capital as a factor of production, and showed the importance of men. That idea can be applied vividly here. If the whole world were cultivated by modern techniques, it could feed about twelve billion inhabitants. This is a reasonable figure, but there are unfortunate optimistic interpretations of it, which suggest that there is some immediate technical answer, whereas even if properly applied, known methods take a great deal of time to be introduced. One first has to educate instructors, foremen, etc. and then they have to instruct others. The key to development lies in the training of men. Though it earns millions of dollars from crude oil, Iraq is tragically underdeveloped; and one may with profit recall the decadence of Spain in the seventeenth century after it had 'exchanged its men against metals'.

The means of development

The working efficiency of men being the key to development, leads us to an important distinction between the younger generations that can be educated and those already educated that have to be used as they are.

One has to train the young generations to apply modern techniques (adapting men to the situation), but at the same time use already trained generations according to their capacities and their knowledge (adapting the situation to men). China seems to have attempted both methods, but they can of course be achieved in several ways. The use of already trained generations is a particularly delicate matter, mainly because it is not spectacular and is difficult to demonstrate convincingly. But, as G. Ardant showed, the main wealth to be

217

exploited consists in the men. Real underemployment (not to mention bad employment) easily reaches 50 per cent in many areas. Two consequences arise from this:

1. Recessive developments are not really useful, indeed are harmful, when they are achieved through the purchase of foreign machinery. Developments are useful if they economise the rarest factor of production: this is sometimes land, sometimes technicians, sometimes machines, but it is never human strength.

2. It is better to apply already trained men to simple tools which they can use immediately and which fit in with the institutions they are used to. R. Dumont is profoundly right when he suggests supplying some African countries with craftsmen rather than industrialists. Uneducated men can learn fairly quickly to use a hammer, a saw, a spade, a plough, and become very proficient with it. This kind of policy is however often misinterpreted: it is accused of keeping men in an inferior condition, a telling criticism in the present-day political and sentimental circumstances. But it is the direction to be followed.

Development is above all a question of adaptation and careful reckonings, aimed at adapting men whenever possible and oneself to them when not.

22

MIGRATIONS

'Tired of dragging their haughty misery . . .'

J.-M. DE HEREDIA

We shall not consider migrations from the social or political point of view (see Part II), nor the economic consequences of social or ideological factors, but only the purely economic factors, and more particularly the causes and immediate effects of migrations.

International migration

This can be considered from several angles: 1. The migrants' interests. 2. The interests of the country they leave. 3. The interests of the country they go to.

Since the individual's interest lies in the highest possible standard of living he will only emigrate from A to B if he is likely to find in B better living conditions than those he left in A. This condition may be fulfilled for certain categories of the population even if the average standard of living is higher in A than in B. A worker will move if the wages in B are higher; if the rates of interest on capital exploited by its owner are higher in B, it is in the capitalist's interest to migrate together with his capital.

The interests of individuals may be opposed to those of one of the countries and sometimes even of both. For the countries, emigration is desirable, if the population is higher than the optimum, and conversely.

In the classical case of emigration from the Old to the New World, the population was higher than the optimum in Europe and lower in America, after the first steps of colonisation. Besides, the standard of living for the lower classes of society was higher in America than in Europe. Everyone's interests were therefore in agreement. The same was true of the immigration of Poles and Italians into France between the two World Wars.

The immigration of subjects is generally profitable to rulers, and their emigration unfavourable; but it is another matter when the rulers have certain duties, such as unemployment relief, towards their subjects. In Italy the fascists were opposed to emigration, but after the war Italian democracy encouraged it.

Since opportunities of employment are rarely denied him, the immigrant becomes assimilated to the workers of the host country and shares with them the collective ownership of the labour market. This is why all trade unions are opposed to immigration in their sector, and demand strict work permits. They are afraid not only of sharing their wealth with the newcomers but of being replaced by them in the favours of the rulers; since they are used to a lower standard of living the foreign workers agree more readily to harder working conditions.

Immigration of workers with low wages can however be beneficial at the same time to employers, wage-earners, and immigrants: the last are content if wages are higher than they were in their home country, which is often very easy to achieve. The global population, including rulers and subjects, should welcome immigrants producing for instance ten dollars worth of goods while they only consume five. It would be possible, at least theoretically, to divide the collective gain, through taxation relief for instance, between employers and native workers. But such a policy is too close to slavery to be adopted or even suggested. Trade unions would reject it not only out of comradeship for the foreign workers, but for fear of the situation turning against them one day. The inequality between home and foreign labour is therefore never apparent in wages.

It is however increasingly so in their prospects of employment. The difficulty is turned by allowing immigration only into the worst-paid and more arduous occupations. This is especially the case in France, where for thirty years and more, deep miners from central Europe were welcomed; immigration from Algeria was equally directed to the more difficult forms of labour.

The home workers thus profit from immigration, when their numbers are below the optimum level, by reserving for themselves, legally or otherwise, the more attractive part of the labour market. The immigrants are in a servile condition, though this may not appear because they have the same wages and the same social status as home workers in the same occupation, and they may one day become fully integrated. They pay as it were an entrance fee in the shape of an unpleasant occupation, similar in this way to the 'indentured servants' who used to pay for their trans-Atlantic fare by several years in domestic or salaried service in the New World. The Swiss trade unions have recognised and encouraged this kind of immigration, which helps their native members to achieve social promotion.

Age and selection

A voluntary migration of an economic kind, the classical case in the modern world, is subject to two selections: 1. The migrants select themselves physically and to a certain extent morally: invalids and madmen do not usually attempt to leave their country; emigrants are generally people with a certain degree of initiative and enterprise. 2. The host country lays down conditions concerning age, health, occupation, morality (legal record), etc.

Their country of origin thus deprives itself of good producers and contributors to social security, and is left with those benefiting from national welfare. Society would benefit if a chronically unemployed person or an old man were to leave, but this rarely happens. This fact is often neglected, causing grave errors: emigration is sometimes encouraged merely because the population is above its optimum. This misapprehension of the value of men is one of the most obvious kinds of Malthusianism. It was widespread in western Europe after the last war.[1]

Migration of skilled workers

Certain workers are a considerable asset to society. A healthy and childless worker pays 25–30 per cent or more of his wages towards national welfare, This amounts to a 'capitation tax', which, as we saw earlier, increases the optimum population if its total output is constant. If a worker is particularly skilled, he may produce even greater outputs, measured not directly, but by the resulting increase in national output: up to ten times greater than the output of others who might fill the same job. If such workers emigrate, the country always suffers a loss.

This problem has not been given the attention it deserves. When a large American firm recruits young technicians by offering them a contract, quite legally, at the door of their training college, it causes a considerable loss to their country. When a young man from Asia or Africa comes to Europe or to the United States for higher education and stays on afterwards, this is an even greater loss to his home country, since it lacks skilled workers. Public opinion is apt to ignore this, partly no doubt because of the principle of individual freedom, but also through the Malthusian misapprehension of the value of men which characterises liberal economists. If a country were to take wheat, copper, or machines from another it would be severely censured; when gold from the national banks trickles away towards other countries, a climate of terror sets in. There should be international conventions setting down compensations for the loss of skilled workers. When a developed country attracts one from an underdeveloped country, it should be made to offer an equivalent amount of technical assistance.

Influence of the nation's overheads

Beneficial immigration may be condemned or may fail through neglect of this marginal phenomenon, because it is not apparent to private interests. On the following very rough model, we introduce only the state and a firm consisting of one employer and his workers.

[1] Ole Just (*Au-delà des mers et des frontières*, Rio de Janeiro, 1948), suggested that forty million Europeans should emigrate, without even mentioning the age distribution.

	Initial state	After the arrival of one immigrant		
		A	B	C
1. Number of workers	25	26		
2. Marginal output	360	340		
3. Total output	12000	12340		
4. Constant public expenditure	2960	2960		
5. Proportional public expenditure	1040	1080		
6. Total	4000	4040		
7. Gross wage per head	360	340	360	360
8. Net wage per head after direct taxation	288	——	288	288·3
9. Total gross wages	9000		9360	9360
10. Gross profit	3000	Trade union refuses	2980	2980
11. Direct taxation on the firm	2000		> 1980	1980
12. Net profit after taxation	1000		< 1000	1000
13. Indirect taxation of the employer	200		——	189
14. Employer's profit after the double taxation	800		Employer refuses	801
15. Indirect taxation of the workers	1800			1862
16. Total net wages	7200			7498
17. Public profits	4000			4040

The wage per head is equal to marginal productivity; direct taxation is estimated at 20 per cent of this. After the arrival of the immigrant three things can occur: 1. The *liberal solution* (sub-column A): the immigrant would cause wages to drop to 340, and the trade union refuses to allow this, and demands that the previous wage of 360 be maintained. 2. *Union's suggestion* (sub-column B): the gross profit would drop from 3000 to 2980 and in spite of the productivity of direct taxation, the net profit would obviously be lower than before. Realising this, the employer steps in and refuses to employ an immigrant producing 340 and being paid 360. *There will be no immigration.* 3. *There is however a solution* (sub-column C): the state would benefit from the arrival of the immigrant since public expenditure would only rise by 40 whereas he would pay 80 or 90 in direct taxation. The state may therefore re-establish the balance by cutting indirect taxation from 20 per cent to 19·9 per cent. This causes the net wage to rise, together with the net profit, with public expenditure still being paid for.

Where the population is increasing through births, such an obstacle is not apparent because the progress is slow and the necessary adaptation takes place under the pressure of needs, which is not the case with immigration. Yet immigration is the more economic solution, since it costs nothing whereas a home-grown man costs several working years to train.

But social attitudes make this solution difficult to apply. Besides, where taxation is high, the number of jobs offered by capitalist enterprise is lower than those the general interest would demand. Submarginal workers do not manage to integrate into society.

Trade union policy

Trade unions almost always adopt a restrictive, Malthusian policy towards immigration, imposed by the appropriation of part of the market. This policy is usually in the interests of each union, exactly as a sector where monopolies occur usually tends to reduce output below the competitive level. Professional unions are even more protective than workers' unions. *This policy, though logical for an individual occupation, may however be detrimental not only to the rulers, and even to the population as a whole, but to the unions themselves.* If there is approximately one doctor for every thousand people, and one doctor arrives in a lot of a thousand immigrants, the medical profession has not been injured, and the 'market' has increased in the same ratio as the doctors.

It may however happen that the trade union movement has interests opposed to those of the rulers and of the population as a whole. This is not due, as is usually thought, to the position of the labour market, but to the general demographic situation, the state of industrial plant and the distribution of occupations. Any small bottleneck in an occupation, even if it is not clearly apparent, is against the general interests of the workers.

Unions and governments are often excessively restrictionist, for fear of unemployment. By admitting that foreigners should only be allowed in when they can prove that they are taking up a vacant position, they in fact prohibit any immigration in the long term. Tucker's objections to their logic retain their strength and their savour:

> If a vacancy had to be noticed in certain occupations, and proved to be permanent before foreigners were to be allowed amongst us, what kind of occupation would they find? And what sort of buyers would wait that long?
> Do not young people become apprentices, bakers, butchers, tailors, etc. every day? Do they only choose a career after noticing a vacancy in trade? And could it be that a man lacking bread, meat, or clothes, waits until the apprentices have finished their training and set up shop for themselves?
> ... If therefore there were only ten thousand inhabitants in this island, would not some of them still lack work?

Obvious vacancies only occur in exceptional circumstances nowadays. There was a shortage of coal miners in France after both world wars, and in other countries such as Great Britain and Belgium after the last war. Yet even where the disproportions in the structure of occupations are much less apparent, immigration may be beneficial.

The existence of unemployment, even widespread, is not sufficient disproof of such vacancies. On the contrary, an economy is too manifold, too dynamic, to lend itself to such rigid interpretation. If immigration is sufficiently filtered, the qualitative improvement causes productivity to rise, together with the optimum population, and unemployment to drop, contrary to the usual opinion amongst workers. In any case, if the same employment policy were applied to home workers as to immigrants, if they were only allowed to work if there was no unemployment, they would themselves remain in permanent surplus.

The installation costs of an immigrant

The preceding chapter gave some figures concerning the capital necessary for the housing, public services, and tools of a marginal adult, whether an immigrant or no. We may add briefly that to install a family of immigrants costs approximately twelve thousand dollars, though this figure can vary considerably. From a strictly economic point of view, it would be in a country's interest to reduce its birth rate and allow already trained men to immigrate. A home-trained worker costs five working years to rear and five more to settle, a total of ten working years. An immigrant only has to be settled, and costs five working years.

The advantage here appears so clearly that it is difficult to see why a country with a poor birth rate cannot easily find room for immigrants to make up for this deficiency. It may happen, although this is uncommon, that a family has saved for a child money that it would have spent otherwise; but the main reason is that the capital needed by an immigrant is more apparent. A normal adult can easily live for a time at home or with friends. An immigrant needs a new home immediately. *Social attitudes are against him.*

In the case of immigration to a country with a growing population and not much capital, it is more and more difficult to pay for the settlement of an immigrant: he is a surplus, marginal operator, and, more important, he stands out clearly as such. On the other hand, for the reasons outlined, the installation of a foreigner arriving to join a colony of people of the same nationality already settled, costs less than that of a home worker. The expense exists, but is not defrayed by the host country, unless the immigration is sponsored by public authorities.

Money sent home by immigrants

This factor makes up for some of the losses caused by emigration. Its importance lies in that an immigrant who saves money to send it back home consumes primary goods (food) and sends abroad what he would have saved or spent on tertiary services, in other words the part of his income which would have been most useful to the country he is living in. The country he has left benefits appreciably: with the money, it can buy the goods it wants, notably raw materials, at least in liberal economic conditions.

General

The cost of immigration is no longer reckoned mainly in human lives. It is no longer conceivable that men should be piled up in the hold of a ship and then emptied out on to a shore, at the price of a high mortality. *Our economy of human lives costs a great deal.* International migration, especially into new countries, is very expensive nowadays. Against it one should set the annual gain in output which will eventually stem from the better use of men. Immigration is thus similar to investment: it costs a great deal to start with but produces annual returns. It may not, however, be the most profitable investment open to the receiving country.

Consider Brazil for example. Its population increases by 3 per cent a year; because of this it is burdened by demographic investment, and massive immigration is no longer economic. Foreigners will be admitted only if they belong to certain particularly skilled categories, able to open up some bottlenecks.

Even where immigration would be the most profitable investment, it may be limited by lack of capital: the new country may have none, and the already developed country may be unwilling to finance such an operation. *Massive migrations thus become increasingly unlikely.* Indeed there is currently a reversal of the age-old movement of Europeans towards tropical countries. In Europe industrial development is constantly increasing the employment offered, whereas the underdeveloped countries have an already rapidly rising population. Migration to Europe and North America has therefore occurred spontaneously wherever it was allowed: Algerians come to France, Puerto Ricans to the United States, Jamaicans and Maltese to England. This trend will accelerate if it does not meet political obstacles set by one of the two countries.[1]

[1] See 'Reversal in the direction of traditional migration', *Migrations*, Jan.–Mar. 1962, and *Population*, Jan.–Mar. 1962.

23

GENERAL IDEAS ON OVERPOPULATION

'If ten million men ever manage to support themselves in these provinces (the United States), it will be a great deal.'

ABBÉ RAYNAL

We have already mentioned overpopulation several times in a rather fragmentary way. Using the concepts already defined, we shall now deal with it directly, since it is one of the most important topics in demography.

Overpopulation exists in general when there are too many men for a given supply. For instance, if forty students have to use a room designed for twenty-five, this room will be said to be overpopulated. Since this is a relative concept, one can usually say either that there are too many men or that there are not enough supplies for them. In the above example one could say that there are too many students or that the room is too small. These two approaches appear similar but point to two very different solutions: reducing the number of men or increasing the insufficient materials.

In the case of a country, the classical and most common tests of overpopulation are unemployment and the lack of food. Here a doubtless summary judgment suggests that if there were fewer men they would all have work and food.

Temporary and permanent overpopulation

Usually, lands where these two things occur are poorly exploited: overpopulation is thus only a sign of underdevelopment. Although this phrase was not used in the early nineteenth century, it was what the socialists of the time had in mind when they criticised Malthus. Owen said that one should not talk of overpopulation until the whole earth was cultivated as carefully as a garden.

It can happen, however, that on a fairly small land there are too many inhabitants not only for the supplies available but for those that might become available, at any rate with the technology of the time. We mentioned (p. 207) islands that seem to be in this situation, and whose only way out is a reduction of population through emigration.

Agricultural technicians could conceivably determine the limit to the food output and judge whether the demands are higher. This can however be very delicate in certain cases: thus a large part of Egypt is a desert, but a great deal of water still flows into the sea through the Nile. When the Assuan Dam is completed, others can be envisaged, but only because of the experience gathered from the first. One might even go as far as to forecast a general improvement in agricultural techniques for the future, thus making the idea of absolute overpopulation more and more hazy. One is led to consider the available space, or the biomass, as the only ceiling, as we did in chapter 1.

However, before this absolute and still distant ceiling is reached, two factors will intervene: the elasticity of needs and the possibility of producing by secondary or tertiary techniques the food that cannot be obtained from the land.

Needs and welfare: Suppose that real and potential resources have been completely surveyed. If a limit is set to men's needs, taking into account various vital factors such as food and heat, a precise number of inhabitants will be able to live in these conditions, above which there will be overpopulation. But if the needs are set at another level, by the addition of various commodities such as clothes, housing, and transport, the possible number of inhabitants will be smaller, and the concept of overpopulation will have to be adjusted. This brings us back, a long time after Cantillon, to the ideas of maximum and optimum population. Thus the Soviets do not believe in overpopulation, mainly because they intend to set limits to individual needs.

Secondary and tertiary activity: If primary resources are lacking, a country may well obtain them through other methods. Though Venice had shown it the way, seventeenth century Holland set an example by feeding more inhabitants than its land could support, by trade; it was often mentioned by the economists of the eighteenth century, and imitated by the western European countries in the nineteenth century: they made up for their lack of raw materials and land through their industry. In the second half of the nineteenth century Britain even sacrificed its agriculture systematically in order to concentrate on industry, which was more profitable. The most striking instance today is that of Switzerland which was overpopulated at the beginning of the nineteenth century, with two million inhabitants, and now employs, as well as a population of 4·8 million, an extra seven hundred thousand foreign workers.

Age-old overpopulation

Nature has given man an apparently small fecundity, but that can lead through geometrical progression to very big increases. A 'natural' population in not unfavourable conditions has a mortality of 3–3·5 per cent and a fertility of

4–4·5 per cent or even more. The species can therefore increase its numbers naturally by about 1 per cent a year if there are no particular obstacles.

Since until very recently technology was far from progressing at the same rate, all populations have tended to overflow their natural surroundings; at least, except for those that had recourse to birth control, if for some reason they did not multiply, they soon had to struggle against more prolific neighbours. This basic increase necessarily met with various obstacles, and was in fact counterbalanced by an excessive death rate due to three kinds of evils: epidemics, famines, and wars. The first were no doubt encouraged by undernourishment and dense population; the second were a direct consequence of overpopulation; but it would be superficial to think that this was also true of the third. The population was thus cut back to numbers more in keeping with its surroundings.[1]

Chronic overpopulation was so to speak a vital necessity; it was at any rate the most reliable way for a population to perpetuate itself, by constant pressure on the environment. There was generally more lack of food than of work. In the face of decreasing returns a population can react in two ways: accept working with very low efficiency or stay idle beyond a certain point. In the extreme situation a man sees no need to work beyond a marginal productivity that would barely return the food calories he has spent on it; but this extreme cannot be measured exactly. Overpopulation can thus exist not only in the carefully cultivated river deltas of the Far East, but also in lands sparsely populated because they are hostile to man.

Social causes of overpopulation

If a vital element such as food is lacking, morality dictates a distribution according to needs. This communal policy was abandoned as soon as tribal civilisation gave way to organised society. Inequality therefore increased overpopulation. But we have shown various times, particularly in chapter 11, that, although economists will not recognise it, this overpopulation is not caused by unequal incomes but by unequal consumptions. A person with a high income who spent it on giving work to the underemployed did not aggravate overpopulation or the conditions of the workers; but the consumer of rare products did.

This is a permanent phenomenon, which recurs in an unexpected shape in

[1] Overpopulation was the general trend but not the absolute rule: Central Africa and part of North America were sparsely populated when the Europeans burst in. In Africa there were various causes: inbreeding, sexual taboos, abnormal mortality, and mainly the weakness of technology and the wastage of natural resources. In the northern part of North America abortion seems to have been an important factor. But this example confirms what we have said: the demographically strong populations, in Asia and tropical America resisted better, whereas the Indians of North America were exterminated.

modern economy, where sectors not usually considered from this angle may be said to be over-populated.

Poverty of the developed countries

There is no longer any danger of overpopulation in the absolute sense in developed countries: there is no lack of vital subsistence. But welfare may well be held in check by numbers: we return to the ideas of optimum population and optimum growth. In spite of appearances the developed countries are not in a state of affluence, but lack goods. Only the classical illusion of the market in search of customers suggests the opposite. If all the goods manufactured under full employment were distributed directly, excepting certain goods such as cereals and potatoes which are only a small part of the needs, they would have to be rationed. This point needs expanding.

The last war taught us that there are three ways of reacting to the lack of goods: 1. Submission to the law of the highest offer, or rationing by money. 2. Authoritative distribution or rationing. 3. No rules at all, leading to literal and metaphoric queueing for goods.

Socialist countries often prefer the second or the third method: the authorities distribute incomes of slightly higher value than the current output, so that everything is sold, and the rarity of goods is apparent.

Capitalist countries apply the first method, which suggests a permanent glut of goods. It may lead to a slight retention of output but this is in fact far lower than the amount of needs unfulfilled. In the United States the saturation of public and private needs is still a long way off. But as soon as the market is hindered, the insufficiency of goods becomes apparent. This is not necessarily due to a surplus of men over resources, but to the fact that in spite of immense progress, technology does not manage to fulfill the new needs it has helped to create.

Consider for instance air travel. In the West, in a market economy, airlines often complain that their services are undersubscribed. In the United States an average of only two-thirds of the seats are used, which suggests that there too many flights. Non-Communist countries for a population of two thousand millions provide 120,000 million passenger-kilometres per annum: this only amounts to sixty kilometres per person per year. Yet if there were sufficient facilities, many men would want to travel at least six thousand kilometres a year, a figure easily exceeded by rich people: this would mean an air traffic one hundred times greater and a corresponding expansion of airports, plane factories, hotels, etc.

A smaller number of men would not necessarily be better served. All the ceilings generally recognised for population have been easily exploded by the events of the last few years. Besides, there is no lack of raw materials, at least given the very low industrialisation of the greater part of the world. Where shortage appears in vital needs (except in periods of war of course) this has nothing to do with disharmony between natural resources and numbers of men, but is due rather to imperfect legislation. This is true for instance with housing (an artificial shortage, in France at least), schools, and hospitals.

In the same way the unemployment that exists in industrial countries (see chapter 20) is not due to overpopulation but to defects in structure, in proportions. Underemployment in certain occupations does not point to an absolute surplus. There is only a comparative surplus in these occupations.

Modern forms of overpopulation

However, some shortages, due to raw materials and not easily remedied by higher outputs, can be ascribed to overpopulation in a wide sense. Take for instance the shortage of space, in its various forms: it is ill-defined since there is as yet no absolute shortage of supplies – the three thousand million men currently possess 160,000 square metres each. Yet oceans are only used fleetingly, and there are deserts, and men prefer to congregate in pleasant or already populated places, that is to say in tourist resorts and towns, a problem which needs closer examination.

Urban overpopulation: Men derive considerable advantages from crowding into towns, but here a market economy is not the optimum system. The marginal individual who moves into a town only produces the average output per inhabitant, whereas he costs the community the marginal cost; when the optimum is exceeded, this marginal cost rises more than the average cost, so that growth continues although it is unfavourable to society.

As a result certain materials such as space, air, and light become objectively rare. But this is more or less apparent according to whether they are subject to the laws of a market. When rents are competitive a certain number of buildings are offered for hire, but this supply is rationed by money. Here housing shortages and overpopulation are obvious in the very existence of slums and shanty towns. (This is not true with goods such as food, because an insufficiency of sales will appear clearly, whereas undernourishment is more difficult to spot. One can walk around and look at slums but not at people's lack of fruit or meat.) On the other hand, where rents are controlled the shortage is only apparent in the larger space occupied by the more favoured families, and the frequent wastage. Neither financial rationing nor taxation, which can provoke a shortage, are sufficient to check population increases, or even to prevent immigration.

More generally in a property system land returns increase constantly through the rise in population and public expenditure. This is not so much a result of speculation (the word implies a certain risk) as a gift from society to the landowners. The market does of course provide a corrective by pushing the prices up and causing a certain amount of decentralisation, but this is not apparent, for various sociological reasons; urban overpopulation is still, in many countries, a tragic sign of oppression by property.

Excessive traffic is another kind of overpopulation. Private cars cause no disruptions in towns as long as they are confined to a small minority. As they spread shortage of space becomes unavoidable as long as no market is established. If every citizen wishes thus to occupy freely a hundred square feet and move these hundred square feet around by travelling to the centre of the town at rush hours and leaving them near a theatre or a football ground on holidays, a great deal of space is taken up. The owner of a car forgets that at home, if he lives in a flat of five hundred square feet in a building five storeys high, he occupies the equivalent of one hundred square feet of land and has to pay rent for it. His hundred mobile square feet of car are free, since taxation of cars and petrol is in fact low. He is therefore an unconscious oppressor, and one who causes more trouble than others who are more obvious. The victim is the man who uses public transport, and only uses five square feet or even less throughout the day. For social and political reasons this fact is often not properly analysed and interpreted: the victims are isolated, unorganised, and unconscious. Yet even the oppressors finally suffer from this form of overpopulation.

Tourist resorts: Here again, as long as only a privileged class had enough leisure and money to use them, there was no overpopulation. Now, with greater welfare and holidays with pay, the middle classes and even the lower classes are flocking there. In some fields the market system has been maintained: land gathers a surplus value with no economic justification, and thus appears a new kind of oppression by property. But this financial rationing does not apply to other spaces such as beaches. Highly organised and densely populated camps spring up nearby. Free access to roads and the sea still exists almost everywhere; there is therefore a strong disproportion, during the holiday seasons, between the free space and the space needed.

This form of seasonal overpopulation is not of course lamented as much as the food shortage in other countries. But it obeys the same laws, particularly the law of decreasing returns and the oppression constituted by the consumption of goods. A millionaire who disliked the sea and acquired a large pleasure estate in a barren countryside would not deprive anyone of space, whereas a small financier would, if he were to buy up five hundred yards of popular coast line.

Communism and overpopulation

To return to more classical considerations, orthodox communists do not conceive of over-population. The Soviet *Encyclopaedia* states that it cannot exist in a socialist system. This is due to the historical reaction against the egoism of the Malthusians as much as to the limitation of needs by authority: such a policy leads to dissimulation rather than real suppression of needs. It only applies in any case to static overpopulation. The accumulation of capital in a strongly increasing population demands large investments that Marx could not foresee because of the mortality that scourged his times. The example of Poland, which has had to limit its births for economic reasons, and that of China, which will soon appear, show how old-fashioned the doctrine is.

Malthusianism

Without the word overpopulation necessarily being used, an apparent surplus of men, if for instance there is unemployment, easily suggests Malthusian solutions, which are to no effect when the structure is at fault. In the same way an apparent excess of goods suggests a downward adjustment and the reduction of output to the apparent level of consumption. This policy may be worthwhile on a local and temporary basis, but it will only aggravate a large scale crisis. Development and continuous adjustment from above are preferable.

The history of the last forty years is full of examples of Malthusianism, involving either voluntary reduction of wealth or reduction of work because of a belief that work was in limited supply. Amongst these, one of the less well known is that of the immigration of Spaniards into France in 1938–9. At this time seventy million Germans were making weapons and preparing to invade Europe. About half a million Spaniards, fleeing Franco's oppression, took refuge in France in two waves. They were men of all ages and all occupations, and eminently adaptable as are all refugees. They might therefore have helped not only to increase national output, which was badly needed, but to decrease unemployment by an adjustment of the structure to the needs. But the Malthusian spirit was so strong that these men were parked in camps, not for political reasons but to prevent them from working. They were merely fed, out of charity, and thus allowed to consume wealth but prevented from producing any. No section of public opinion and no political party was conscious of this extravagant contradiction.

The creative spirit

Malthusianism is a kind of atrophy of the creative spirit. In a population with low mortality a certain amount of control is necessary over births; but economic Malthusianism is always unfavourable to society. It is a widely spread illness, which has not yet been denounced or studied, or indeed given a name.

Overpopulation can always be fought by increasing the available quantities of the product which is lacking, through investment. The problem should always be seen from this dynamic angle.

24

THE COST OF PRODUCING MEN

'It takes twenty years to bring a man from the vegetable life he leads in the womb to the stage where his mature reason begins to bud. It took thirty centuries for him to learn a little about his constitution. It would take him all eternity to learn anything about his soul. It only takes a moment to kill him.'

VOLTAIRE

From Petty to Lotka various authors, including Stalin, have studied the value of one man. Stalin is even quoted as saying, rather non-commitally, 'man is the most precious capital'. The economic value of one man can be approached very differently according to the way one defines it. We could thus choose: 1. The cost of training him, or his 'cost price'. 2. The output to be expected from him, as one calculates the output value of machinery. This can be the output benefiting the family (as with the early German *Wehrgeld*, or the modern compensation for death), or the master (in a system of slavery or of serfdom), or society. 3. The cost of saving him or of prolonging his life.

We leave aside in spite of their interest various questions such as ransoms or the *pretium doloris*. It is the second angle which has attracted most attention usually from a capitalist point of view. After wars, for example, the losses incurred by the nation in men have been studied carefully, and expressed in monetary units.

Historical

The first reckoning of this kind seems to have been that of Petty. More recently there are those of Pareto, Engel, Mortara, Heyman, Dublin and Lotka, Beveridge, Glass and Malignac, Henderson, Rapso, Weisbrod, those of the Royal Commission on Population in Britain,[1] and various studies in the

[1] V. Pareto, 'La mortalità infantile e il costo dell' Uomo Adulto', *Giornale degli Economisti*, 1893.

E. Engel, *Der Werth des Menschen*, Berlin, 1883; 'La consommation comme mesure du bien-être des individus, des familles et des nations', *Bulletin de l'Institut International de Statistique*, Hague, 1887.

G. Mortara *La mortalita secondo l'eta e la durata della vita economicamente produttiva*, Rome, 1908; 'O custo de produçao do homen adulto e sua variaçao em relaçao a mortalidade', *Estudos brasileiros de demografia*, October 1946.

Revue française de recherche opérationnelle (1960–2). There were also documents and research on the cost of slaves.

In 1748 Claude Dupin, after a rather rough reckoning, estimated the value of one man at three thousand *livres* or approximately nine tons of wheat.[1]

In 1910–11 Alfred Barriol[2] estimated the 'social value of man in various countries' or what an individual will pay back to society in spending of various kinds. This was:

United States	23600 francs	Norway/Sweden	14000 francs
Britain	20700 francs	Italy	11000 francs
France	14500 francs	Western Russia	10100 francs

He reckoned that the social value of the active population in France was 0·4 billion francs, though he did not set too much stock by such figures. The value of one Frenchman was equivalent to thirty tons of wheat.

Various economic theories have also included the cost of a man and linked this to workers' wages (see Lassalle, Marx, etc.). But though certain results are useful[3] the general economic value of men has still to be reckoned, and the basic concepts to be better defined. Such studies are always unpleasant. But the growth of the Welfare State leads little by little to reckonings of this kind, as the next chapter will show. We shall first study the cost of training one man, then, in the following chapters, his productive value and the cost of efforts to save him. As a preliminary here are some indications on the cost of slaves.

The cost of slaves

In the countries where slaves were not supplied by violent conquest, the price of a young slave was related to his cost. His master, like the owner of an animal, had to provide him with just enough supplies to subsist, develop, and work, and become marketable. The value of a man is here approached as in our first definition. These conditions obtained in the United States from 1808 onwards, when the importation of negroes was prohibited though the slave trade did continue in secret for some time. In certain plantations Negroes were even bred to be sold.

L. Dublin and A. Lotka, *The money value of a man*, New York, 1930.

Malignac, 'Minimum vital et niveau d'existence suivant le nombre d'enfants', *Population*, No. 2, 1949.

Henderson, 'The cost of children', *Population Studies*, vol. III, No. 2, vol. IV, No. 3.

Royal Commission on Population: Report, London, 1949.

[1] *Œconomiques.*

[2] *Revenue économique internationale*, Brussels, 1910 (p. 552) and 1911 (p. 356).

[3] For instance L. Dublin and A. Lotka, *The money value of a man*, and the series of articles already mentioned in the *Revue française de recherche opérationnelle.*

However, the information on the price of a slave is rather contradictory.[1] Around 1814, the most frequently quoted price is 500 dollars. Sismondi mentions 2000 francs (i.e. 400 dollars). But the price was probably as much as 1000 dollars for a young and healthy man, rising slowly to about 1500 dollars just before the Civil War, under the influence of the cotton market rather than with the breeding costs. Even the latter figure is very far, as one might expect, from the cost of a man of eighteen as we reckon it further on – especially so since prices in general dropped slightly (wholesale prices by about 33 per cent) between 1808 and 1914.

It would also be relevant here to quote figures concerning the sale of children in the nineteenth century, and the sale of women in certain countries for marriage or for prostitution.

Components of the 'cost price' of a man

Whether the social system is based on the patriarch, the family, the community or on mutual aid, the training of a man costs the society he belongs to a certain amount of effort or of wealth: the adult population of producers provides the young with goods and services which can be assessed in various ways. In western societies, and in most modern countries, this cost includes: 1. The financial cost: the one usually found in reckonings as a levy on the national revenue. This is the consumption of goods and traded services (food, industrial products, medical care, education) by the child. 2. The reduced gains, or the drop in national income through motherhood: women with children cannot produce as much material wealth as usual. 3. Unpaid services: some forms of care given by mothers can be costed although they are not paid for. This is partly a duplication of the loss of national income, but may produce a larger figure since mothers may work longer hours for their family than they would at a job.

The cost of training a man can thus vary according to the definition of national income. We shall leave aside the direct suffering and hardship which cannot be evaluated quantitatively, and also the satisfactions involved. But we shall not be tempted to consider only the financial cost, a method suggested by the usual accounts based on money, and appealing to our old capitalist habit. It is unsatisfactory in several ways: for instance it would make the cost of a child brought up in an orphanage appear to be greater than that of one brought up by its family in similar conditions. Expenses undertaken by the state are more obvious than others.

We shall have to include at least the loss of national income caused by the incapacity of the mother to work; otherwise comparisons might be of no value

[1] Sismondi, *Reflexions sur la traite des nègres*; H. A. Texter, *Slavery in Missouri, 1804–65*, 1914; Chambers, *Slavery and Colour*, London, 1857; J. C. Ballogh, *A History of Slavery in Virginia*, 1895; R. M. Taylor, *Slave-Holding in North Carolina*, 1926.

either in time or space when there is a varying degree of community help. Besides, benefits such as those given in France to a family only drawing one wage and where the woman stays at home, make it necessary to include this factor, even in conventional accounts.

We must also distinguish between the absolute 'production cost' of a man from birth to the age of production, and the relative cost at various ages, including that of children who die before reaching productive age. We will begin by this second aspect, since the facts are more certain if not translated into absolute monetary units, working hours, or in terms of the national revenue.

The cost of child mortality

For a given population we need to know: 1. The age at which a child begins work, or at least the age at which accounts are drawn up. 2. The cost of the child at each age. 3. The survival table.

Figure 61 plots the number of survivors from 100,000 conceptions against the cost at various ages or periods of life. These periods are not necessarily

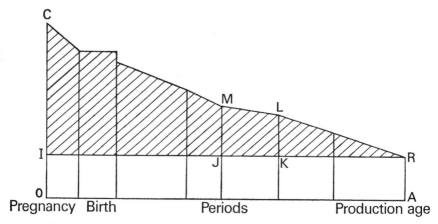

Figure 61. Cost of child mortality.

equal, and must be chosen so that within each, mortality is more or less uniformly distributed in time. The cost of training children is equal to the rectangle OIRA, and the additional cost because of the dead children is equal to the area CIR. In each period this cost is figured by areas such as JKLM, except for the birth period, which is instantaneous and therefore represented by a rectangle. If mortality drops, the point R rises and the area of extra cost drops in absolute value and still more in relative value.

Let us now try some numerical applications. The production age is very different according to climate and degree of civilisation, and is always difficult to determine because the change from idleness to activity is usually progressive: we will simplify the logic and the reckonings by assuming that this happens suddenly. The production age seems to be eighteen years as an average, and we shall choose it, as Lotka does, as representative of developed industrial countries.

The cost at various ages is not easy to determine, even in relative value. The published results usually deal with the financial cost for the family, studied either by real observations of family budgets, or by reckoning their needs. They are reliable as far as spending on food goes. Both these methods neglect public expenses and the loss in national income due to the professional inactivity of mothers.

Here are the relative costs suggested by two of the authors already quoted.

Period (years)	Dublin– Lotka	Mortara	Period (years)	Dublin– Lotka	Mortara
Pre-natal period and birth	87·5	93·5			
1st year	100	100	10th year	124	187
2nd	99	107	11th	124	200
3rd	104	114·5	12th	127	214
4th	105·5	123	13th	131	230
5th	110	132	14th	133	246
6th	110	141·5	15th	135	264
7th	111	152	16th	141	282
8th	116	162·5	17th	142	303
9th	120	174	18th	142	325

Mortara uses a geometrical progression of 7 per cent and Lotka experimental results. The final difference is enormous.

Malignac[1] calculated vital needs. The expenses he gave for various ages are as the following numbers:

5 years	100
8	133
12	176
16	215

The increase between 5 and 15 years is very similar to that of Mortara, but the figures are slightly higher at 8 and 12 years.

Beveridge uses the following relative values, denoting an increase between those of Lotka and Mortara:

Below 5 years	100
5–9	134
10–13	157
14	170

[1] *Population*, 2nd quarter 1949, p. 262.

In the present state of our knowledge it is advisable to be content with a suitable geometrical progression without trying to include secondary variations. The rate of 10 per cent used by the Belgian *Office Central de Statistique*, in reckoning by units of consumption, seems too high,[1] particularly since the loss in professional activity of mothers, which we are considering too, is especially high when their children are very young. This is not compensated by the steep rise in public expenditure for the higher ages.

Our reckonings, based on a progression of 5 per cent, give for the 18th year a cost of 229, which is higher than that of Dublin-Lotka and practically in agreement with the figures of Beveridge. Estimating at 50 the cost of pregnancy and at 80 that of birth, and assuming that the cost is constant throughout the first year, we have as follows:

Period (years)	Cost	Cost of child from conception to end of period	Period (years)	Cost	Cost of child from conception to end of period
Pregnancy	50	50	8th	140·8	1085·2
Birth	80	130	9th	147·9	1233·1
1st	100		10th	155·3	1388·4
1st 2 months	16·7	146·7	11th	163·1	1551·5
following months	83·3	230	12th	171·2	1722·7
2nd	105	335	13th	179·8	1902·5
3rd	110·2	445·2	14th	188·8	2091·3
4th	115·8	561	15th	198·2	2289·5
5th	121·6	682·6	16th	208·1	2497·6
6th	127·7	810·3	17th	218·5	2716·1
7th	134·1	944·4	18th	229·4	2945·5

The classical survival table must be completed by data on stillbirths and miscarriages. These do not enter into reckonings until the fourth or fifth month, since until then the cost of the pregnancy whether in food, care, or loss of activity is low. These reckonings do not include the cost of abortions, whether induced or spontaneous, up to the fourth month. Since the rates of pre-natal mortality and of stillbirths are not well known, they have been estimated approximately.

Figure 62 applies this method to a population with low mortality (New Zealand women in 1934–8, roughly equivalent to United Nations Table $e_0 = 67$) and to a population with high mortality (Indian men, 1921–30, roughly equivalent to United Nations Table $e_0 = 27$). In the first population the cost of a man is hardly affected by mortality, which is of less than 1 per cent, and can therefore hardly be reduced by a further drop: it is not worth reckoning with an even higher survival table. In the second population on the other hand,

[1] *Bulletin de Statistique*, November 1945.

238

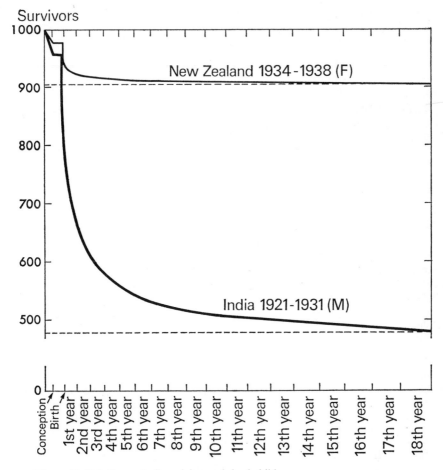

Figure 62. Relative cost of surviving and dead children.

child mortality raises the cost of a man by 15–20 per cent. Of course in such populations work begins earlier: the loss of a man of seventeen still exists but can be accounted for elsewhere.

Here are the figures given for various countries by Mortara, with a similar method but a different scale of costs per age.

United States	1939–41	0·88 per cent	Japan	1926–30	3·87 per cent
New Zealand	1921–22	1·20 per cent	USSR	1926–27	4·84 per cent
England and Wales	1930–32	1·54 per cent	Chile	1929–32	4·64 per cent
France	1928–33	1·75 per cent	Mexico	1929–33	5·91 per cent
Italy	1930–32	2·38 per cent	India	1921–30	10·18 per cent

This assumes that both the relative cost at various ages and the productive age in each country are the same. Little information is available on the first point, but we do know that in countries with low mortality the productive age is higher.

At each age the cost of the surviving children is increased by a percentage due to the children dead before that age. This ratio varies with the age. With a high mortality rate it seems to be maximal after the first or second year, and then to drop to a constant by about the fourteenth year. Here are the results for the Indian (male) mortality table from 1921–30.

Period (years)	Cost during the period	Survivors at end of period (1,000 conceptions)	Cost of survivors at end of period (000s)	Compound cost of dead children to end of period (000s)	Ratio of cost of dead to cost of the living (per cent)
Conception	50	960	48	1·0	2·0
Birth	80	900 72	117	8·8	7·5
1st two months	16·7	785	115	24·7	21·4
2nd–12th month	83·3	675	155	49·9	32·2
2nd	105	614	206	67·1	32·5
3rd	110·2	580	258	80·3	31·1
4th	115·8	556	312	92·4	29·6
5th	121·6	541	369	101·7	27·5
6th	127·7	532	431	108·4	25·0
7th	134·1	525	496	114·5	23·1
8th	140·8	519	563	120·6	21·4
9th	147·9	514	634	126·4	19·9
10th	155·3	509	706	132·9	18·8
11th	163·1	504	782	140·2	17·9
12th	171·2	500	861	146·8	16·9
13th	179·8	496	943	154·0	16·3
14th	188·8	492	1029	162·0	15·7
15th	198·2	487	1115	172·9	15·5
16th	208·1	482	1204	184·9	15·3
17th	218·5	477	1296	198·0	15·3
18th	229·4	472	1390	212·2	15·2

Absolute cost

Let us first settle a controversial point. The cost of a man can be defined: 1. As his subsistence needs, plus the cost of occupational training. This definition considers a man as a mere production machine. It is objective, although it cannot be strictly defined because of factors of climate, race, and efficiency. It is also arbitrary, as the subsistence level always is, and can therefore rarely be applied in practice. In fact the real cost of a child always depends on the income of its parents. 2. As the cost of all the vital and social needs of the child including education. This is a more extensive definition and lends a wider meaning to the word 'needs'. 3. By reckoning the real cost of the child in a family of a given social category, in other words the part of the family expenses devoted to the child's needs. This is the most practical definition and raises few difficulties. 4. As the extra income necessary to the family for its living standards not to drop with the arrival of a child. This is the most important definition from the social and demographic angle, because of its effects on fertility where birth control is practised.

To the third and fourth definitions, which consider the cost for the family, should be added the cost to society (education, public health, etc.). The first definition gives figures lower than the second and higher or lower than the last two according to the case. The fourth gives higher figures than the third. The cost can be expressed in monetary units, or in physical units such as the working hour or year. For the monetary costs conversions have been made from price or cost of living indices on this basis:

$$1 \text{ franc } (1914) = 224 \cdot 7 \text{ francs } (1962)$$
$$\text{and } 1 \text{ dollar } (1914) = 3 \cdot 07 \text{ dollars } (1962).[1]$$

To determine the cost according to one or the other of the definitions suggested, surveys can be conducted or theoretical data on needs can be used. Enquiries into family budgets do not however usually distinguish the section devoted to the children, even for food and clothing. We cannot use the difference in spending between childless couples and families, since spending here varies mainly with income.

Dublin and Lotka[2] reckoned the total cost of a child of eighteen in 1935–6 in two categories of families, according to our third definition. The cost was 7766 dollars (1936), i.e. 17,140 dollars (1962) for average incomes of 2500 dollars; and 16,337 dollars (1936) for higher incomes (5–10,000 dollars). Here are the percentages:

[1] The conversion of dollars into francs and vice versa is difficult since exchange rates do not correspond to the different purchasing powers. Here are some indications on the path followed.

In 1914–30 the surest index is that of the cost of living in the Paris area: 581 (1914=100). In 1938 the index for France is 116·3 (1930=100) or 677 (1914=100). Since 1938, by operating various links, the following indices are the most acceptable.

1938= 100	1949=1740
1944= 432	1950=1914
1945= 593	1955=2480
1946= 826	1960=3370
1947=1123	1961=3481
1948=1558	1962=3625

So that 1 franc (1914)=6·77×36·25=224·7 francs (1962).

Public opinion always overestimates these rises in prices by selecting its memories unfairly. In fact if at the right moment we were to introduce into reckonings goods with a high rate of technological progress (bicycles, cars, nylons, plastics etc.) the indices would be lower than those given.

[2] The Money Value of a Man, p. 44 onwards.

	Average incomes	High incomes
Birth	3·9	4·6
Food	29·3	22·2
Clothing	9·1	10·4
Medical expenses	3·8	5·2
Living accommodation	34·1	35·3
Education	1·1	1·7
Transport and amusement	14·5	17·1
Various	4·2	3·5
	100	100

The 'education' entry may appear small, but it only includes expenditure on books and stationery. Lotka gives details on what it costs society: in state schools the average yearly cost is 196 dollars (1962), i.e. 2350 dollars for twelve years' schooling. Lotka adds to this the interest on these sums (this could be very controversial, and we will leave it aside) and also the loss due to child mortality, estimated at 1·3 per cent. The total for families with lower incomes is 17,370 dollars (1962), i.e. more than three years of the family income, or 16 per cent of this income in any one year.

Including state education the cost of a child is thus 19,750 dollars (1962), not including maternity expenses, loss of income of the mother, or public expenditure other than on education (hospitals, national assistance).

At the time of these calculations the yearly generations in the United States did not vary much: making allowances for concealed births, there were about 2·4 million births a year, with a drop in fertility making up for the rise in population. This permits a rough reckoning of the total expenditure on youth: by multiplying the cost of a child over eighteen years by the number of children in one generation, we get about 21,600 million dollars (1935–6) or more than a third of the national income. This proportion seems too large, because 32 per cent of the total population was under eighteen, so that the annual expenditure on a child would be higher than that on an adult. This seems to show that the average expenditure must be smaller than that suggested by Lotka. Besides, an annual income of 2500 dollars for 1935–6 is a fairly high figure, since the national income only amounted to 435 dollars per person and 700 dollars per adult person.

In Britain the Royal Commission on Population estimated the weekly cost of two children at 30 shillings (1945) or £1 (pre-war). This means 15 shillings (1945) per child per week, or £39 (1945) per year, or, for a life of eighteen years, i.e. approximately £742 taking mortality into account. This figure is lower than that for France, and is too low, as are those suggested by Beveridge. It records customs rather than requirements, and families with children were customarily in difficulty.

242

For France we may use G. Malignac's figures, already quoted, which correspond to our fourth definition. After adjustment to the various ages we find for Paris, from conception to eighteen years of age, a cost of 1·6–2 million francs (1950). These figures should be corrected by a reduction of 8·5 per cent to apply to the whole of the country, and by an increase of 1·5 per cent to take into account the mortality below eighteen. This gives 1·53–1·86 million francs (1950), or 28,970–35,210 new francs (1962). Though the definition leading to this price was wider, the price is far smaller than that of Lotka which was excessive.

The difference between the United States on the one hand and France and England on the other can be attributed to a difference in the way of life; but the difference between France and England is due to a variation in definition.

Cost in working years

The cost of training a man is more significant if expressed in working years. This may be done for a given occupation, by comparing what a child costs its family to the salary of the father or both parents; or else on a national scale, by operating on averages. Here are a few indications on the method.

On the family scale: In 1950 the *Commission du minimum vital* (subsistence level) estimated the monthly requirements of a French working class family as follows (in francs and compared with Malignac's figures).

	Commission on the subsistence level (1950)	Malignac (1949) Lower limit	Higher limit
Adult	15200	12300	16350
Child (average age)	7000	9180	11450
Ratio child: adult	46 per cent	74·7 per cent	69·9 per cent

The child-adult ratio is smaller in the results of the Commission, and many observers will consider it more realistic. But it records customs rather than objective requirements: a fifteen-year old adolescent should get more food than an adult, and because he is growing he also needs clothing of a higher objective value. But, in spite of family allowances in France, family incomes are far from their requirements, even in the poorest classes. P. Paillat reckoned that in 1961 a navvy with four children had living standards 12 per cent lower than a childless couple. Since the latter usually has a second wage the difference is probably as much as 50 per cent. But because families usually adapt their expenditure to their income it is easy to accept that even in small budgets the needs of a child are not greater than 50 per cent of those of an adult.

We will however keep to the figures given by the Commission. An unskilled worker in metal industries in the Paris area was earning roughly 14,000 francs a month; if, as we are assuming, a child was costing half of this income, he had by the age of eighteen cost nine working years. (Without family allowances three children would therefore have cost twenty-seven working years and left no food for the father. This stark reckoning shows how necessary the allowances are to families).

To convert these data into present-day currency and keep them as 'requirements', costs must be reckoned according to the price index rather than the salary index. This gives a monthly cost of 13·23 francs in 1962, a yearly cost of 1587 francs and a total cost for eighteen years of 28,470 francs. Since the wage of an unskilled worker in the Paris area has risen faster than prices during this period, the cost of the child is now 5·7 years instead of 9. Allowances reduce this figure even further than they did the first, in a variable ratio according to the number of children.

Such calculations underline the vagueness of the idea of 'subsistence requirements' as soon as one is no longer considering a theoretical economy of subsistence. It is perhaps better to consider the national situation and calculate from average figures.

On the national scale: Take the working year as unity. In France in 1963 national output was forecast at 298,000 million francs for 20 million active people, i.e. 14,900 francs per active person = one working year. If we assess the cost to the country of training a man we can convert it into this unity. This cost is borne partly by the community and partly by the family.

1. *Public expenditure*: (not including family allowances, because they reappear in family accounts.) The main sources of expense are health and education. In 1962 France spent 11,442 million francs on education (public and private) of which 2,082 was capital expenditure. If the generations to educate were all of comparable numbers to the youngest (6–16 years), or approximately 800,000 this figure would be approximately 12,000 million francs. The average cost of educating a child is thus on an average 15,000 francs, or roughly 1·1 working years.

A different approach is possible: The INSEE[1] published the total cost of school life in 1955 for various categories of people. The working year in 1955 was 710,000 francs, giving us the result shown in the table on the facing page.

The average cost found (1·1) is between that of the skilled worker (1) and that of the eighteen-year old school leaver (1·45). Taking into account investment into buildings and material equipment, we may increase it to 1·3.

Public expenditure on health for children is much smaller than on education: it will increase the figure to 1·5 approximately.

[1] *Coût et developpement de l'enseignement en France*, 1958.

	In 000s of francs (1955)	In working years
Basic elementary education	315	0·44
To school leaving certificate	1031	1·45
To university degree	1455	2·05
Skilled worker	708	1·00
Technical ecucation (secondary)	2405	3·38
Technical education (higher)	3132	4·41
School teacher	2180	3·07

2. *Other expenditure:* All the above figures are normally included in accounts. The lost income of mothers, and their maternal and domestic expenses are not. How much does this cost the nation? In other words how much more would the nation earn if women could work all the time? We may leave aside the domestic work of a childless woman, which is often carried out as well as a job.

The surveys of the *Institut national d'études démographiques*[1] suggested the following domestic working hours per week.

	Country	Town
No child	48·1	42·5
1 child	63·1	65·7
2 children	71·7	77·7
3 and more	79·8	83·2

The first child thus makes for 13·3 to 15 hours of domestic work, and the second 8·6 to 11·9. For more children the decrease is less large but substantial: it only expresses the limit to the time or energy mothers have. We may take an average of 10 hours a week per child, of which 8·5 are provided by the mother and therefore not paid for. Over eighteen years this gives a total of 9370 working hours, or 3·9 years if there are 2400 working hours in a year; of these 3·3 years are carried out by the mother or someone in the family.

The national output does not lose the whole of this work, for if she had no child the mother would work less. But on the other hand this extra work, this marginal burden, often leads her to give up her job altogether, since part-time work is not satisfactorily organised.

There are no reliable statistics on the activity of women according to the number of their children. The French *Securité Sociale* reckons that more than 90 per cent of women with an occupation and two children have given it up; and up to 70 per cent of women with one child. These ratios appear too large, even taking into account the tendency not to take on part-time work because of family allowances.

We were really interested not so much in the total percentage of inactivity

[1] *Population*, April–June, 1959, p. 280.

as in the fraction of it caused by the children. Since there are no reliable statistics, we will be content with the previous estimate and consider it as a higher limit.

Summary

The cost of training a man is thus, in working years:

Cost to the family	3·9
Public expenditure (education, health)	1·5
Unpaid work	3·3
Total	8·7

These are only approximations. Many other factors should of course be considered and many corrections made. The total in any case is roughly nine working years, and tends to increase with the progress of education. The general increase in standards of living, on the other hand, does not act proportionally on the cost of children.

Influence of the standard of living

The cost reckoned is an average for the whole country; in fact it varies with the standard of living in lower classes or less developed countries. In a developed country, the relative family expenditure on children decreases with the income. This drop, however, is not felt below a certain income, since it is contingent on the importance of non-domestic expenses.

These facts are difficult to check statistically; even if one managed to distinguish between requirements and customs, there would have to be delicate differential measurements, difficult to carry out with the usual imperfect methods of observation. One should also take into account the differences in the ages at which a child begins to be economically active, which differ with social classes: but here the prospective social class of the child and not that of the parents should be considered. In a fully democratic system the sons of workers, as well as those of doctors or businessmen, should be able to study up to the age of thirty to become doctors. In fact this does not occur, so that the relative cost of the child is higher in the classes aiming from very early on at a higher education for their children: this cost is highest with relation to income amongst urban workers and the middle classes. Such differences in cost play a part in voluntary limitation of fertility; fertility in the country is partly due to the work children can carry out at a fairly early age.

In a less developed agricultural country the relative cost of the child is smaller because of this. His absolute cost at a given age drops at the same rate as the economic level of his parents, and perhaps even a little more if the child begs or obtains food from outside. We may, for a start, retain the same scale. But on the other hand the productive age is much lower. If the child begins to earn as much as he costs from the age of ten or eleven, our calculations must stop here: and a child of ten and a half costs only half as much as a child of eighteen, so that even if we add 18 per cent to the cost for child mortality (instead of 1–2 per cent in a developed country) the child costs over 40 per cent less in retarded countries. *Through lack of wealth society spoils men.*

The countries where men cost most are those with the requirements of industrial civilisation but which have not developed to the appropriate level economically. They have the signs of wealth, including a high proportion of tertiary workers, but not the wealth itself, and are in a difficult period; in these cases it is only too frequent to see only the higher classes having access to secondary and higher education.

Variations in time

These geographical differences are paralleled by historical variations. At the beginning of the nineteenth century training still cost very little, because in the country and even in the factories children worked very young. With the length of education this cost has increased constantly, without being compensated by the drop in child mortality. The trend still continues. If it persists in economies which are stationary or sluggish, the cost of a man increases in relative as well as in absolute value.

Conclusion

In primitive and underdeveloped populations, where there are more men than riches, objects are repaired and taken care of, but men are not. It is much more economical to create new ones. In developed populations the value of men increases, and it is the objects that are thrown away as soon as they are slightly worn, because they are easy to replace. Technological development and the increasing complexity of society therefore lead to more highly-trained men, and the trend is far from ending.

But because of the importance of the care lavished by mothers, society is unable to bring up its children in communities. By a well known rule of economics a service which becomes too expensive turns into a do-it-yourself service: witness the disappearance of servants and chauffeurs, and even of certain categories of manual workers. Children must needs be brought up by their mother at the moment because this method is free: whatever moral, biological, and pedagogical reasons could be invoked, this economic necessity is law. This explains why family life has become popular again in the last twenty years, however old-fashioned the trend may have seemed to some people, who were themselves not quite up to date.

25

THE COST AND VALUE OF A MAN TO SOCIETY: SOCIAL SECURITY

'It seems that to keep one of two Children to manhood or working age as much land must be employed as for the subsistence of an adult Slave, whether the Proprietor raises them himself in his house or has the children raised there or that the Father brings them up in a House or Hamlet apart. Thus I conclude that the daily labour of the meanest Slave corresponds in value to double the produce of the land required to maintain him.'

CANTILLON

Whether in a family, a tribal, a capitalist (with or without social security) or a collectivist system, a man in the course of his life: 1. First consumes without producing or consumes more than he produces. 2. Then, if he lives long enough, produces more than he consumes. 3. Then, if he lives long enough, again consumes more than he produces. Let us disregard completely the legal or social aspects of the transfer of output from one group to another.

A simple model

The economic and demographic accounts of a society present intricate problems. Let us first of all take the simplest model, by assuming that the population is stationary, that consumption and output at each age are constant, and that at its death, each generation has given back to society exactly what it has cost. The reasoning is based not on an individual, but on a generation, for instance one hundred thousand people all born in the same year.[1]

In these conditions we may follow a generation from birth to death, which

[1] Let $S(a)$ be the number of living people of age a.
Let $R(a)$ be the excess of consumption over output at age a.
The value or cost of a man at age a is

$$V(a) = \frac{1}{S(a)} \int_o^a R(a)\, S(a)\, da$$

$$\text{with} \int_o^w R(a)\, S(a)\, da = 0.$$

$R(a)$ changes its sign at two ages a_1 and a_2. At an age between a_1 and a_2 the value of a man is zero.

amounts to following the population from age zero to its limiting age. Since the final accounts are balanced, the value of the generation at every moment is equal to its cost up to then. This gives us a graph shaped as follows.

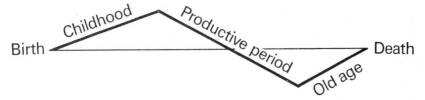

Figure 63. Changes in the economic value of a man during his life.

The value of a man rises during his childhood, drops during his productive age past zero and becomes negative. During his old age it rises up to zero again. It is because we must take into account mortality before the limiting age that we consider a generation and not an individual.

Consumption and output of an individual

Before going on to numerical examples, let us define the excess consumption or output. On a national scale, the financial arrangements are unimportant: it does not matter whether the children's subsistence is provided by state, family of a form of national insurance, or in what kind of economic system. The same applies to the excess output of the adult, and to the consumption of the pensioner. We disregard the question of how heterogeneous outputs can be measured and compared and assume that a suitable unity has been defined. A person consumes a certain amount of wealth (food, clothing), and produces another: we are concerned here with the difference in value between the two however this difference is made up.

A numerical example

The example shown overleaf could apply roughly to a stationary population defined above. It is based on the French survival table of 1946–8. The excess output at each age has been roughly estimated in round figures. The beginning of the active age is placed at 15–20 years, the point at which the value becomes negative at 40–45 years, and the point of lowest value between 60 and 65.

Figure 64 represents this graphically. The vertical scale has not been drawn in, so as not to suggest that fairly arbitrarily absolute values are concrete ones. But we may assume that at the top of the curve the value is roughly five working years.

1	2	3	4	5	6	7
Age or period	Survivors at the beginning of the period (in 000s)	Average survivors during the period (in 000s)	Excess in consumption (+) or output (−) for 1 man during the period (in unities of value)	Excess consumption of the survivors during the period (col 3 × col 4) (in 000s)	Excess consumption of the generation to the end of period (col 5 added up)	Excess consumption per survivor at the end of the period (col 6 / col 2 displaced by one line down)
Conception	1050	1020	+ 65	+ 66	+ 66	+ 66
0–1	1000	962	+ 50	+ 48	+ 114	+ 121
1–5	943	935	+225	+210	+ 325	+ 351
5–10	926	923	+332	+306	+ 631	+ 686
10–15	920	918	+450	+413	+1044	+1143
15–20	914	913	+350	+319	+1364	+1498
20–25	910	904	−260	−235	+1129	+1256
25–30	898	892	−300	−268	+ 861	+ 973
30–35	885	877	−350	−307	+ 553	+ 634
35–40	870	861	−350	−302	+ 252	+ 296
40–45	852	840	−320	−269	− 17	− 21
45–50	828	812	−290	−236	− 253	− 318
50–55	795	771	−260	−201	− 454	− 608
55–60	747	715	−215	−154	− 608	− 889
60–65	684	642	− 85	− 55	− 662	−1103
65–70	599	545	+350	+191	− 471	− 959
70–75	491	426	+400	+170	− 301	− 834
75–80	361	290	+500	+145	− 156	− 716
80–85	218	158	+650	+103	− 53	− 535
85–90	99	65	+650	+ 42	− 11·2	− 361
90–95	31	14	+700	+ 10	− 1·4	− 233
95–100	6	2	+700	+ 1·4	0	0

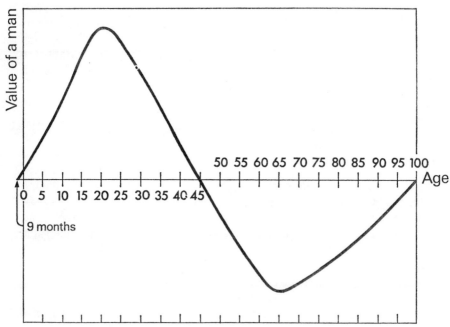

Figure 64. Example of the economic value of a man at various ages.

250

This is relevant to the problem of immigration. Countries usually only accept young immigrants well below 40. But if there is no overpopulation or need of capital, an immigrant is only a burden over the age we have reckoned at 40–45 years.

From the critical age when a man's value is zero the economic interest of society lies in mortality: if mortality rises by mistake it cuts society's debit. These are brutal reckonings and might lead to the most savage conclusions. But one can also stress that having to provide for the weak so heightens society that without this burden it would fall into decay, even in economic terms.

B. A. Weisbrod[1] based similar reckonings on the income of men at various ages instead of their output. On this very questionable basis the value of a man would pass a maximum around the age of 35 and only reach zero at 70 years.

Generalisation

Our model gives an idea of the value of a man during his life, but is very different from the real mechanism. Several other factors should be taken into account:

The permanent achievements of a generation: A generation leaves no heritage only if technology is stationary. In Europe this heritage has increased constantly over the last few centuries:[2] in developing societies each generation produces on average more than it consumes. This factor would have to be taken into account by costing consumer goods and capital goods separately. There would certainly be a surplus of the latter, whilst the former might theoretically be balanced – in fact it never is, as we are about to see.

Variation of the functions of production and consumption at each age: This may occur in different ways of which the following are important. 1. *Change in active ages*, especially in the case of the young, who become active later because of longer schooling. This may cause the difference between consumption and production to change from negative to positive. 2. *Increase of output and of consumption in time.*

Investment, which we have already mentioned, causes the output not only of consumer goods but also of capital goods to increase. No country is heroic enough to invest all its efforts in the future; in any case these capital goods are themselves consumed more and more. This in fact benefits not only the adult producers but the young and the old, either through family or social allowances or through capitalist investments. In such conditions the welfare of a

[1] 'The valuation of human capital', *The Journal of Political Economy*, October 1961.

[2] Mathematically one could imagine models including a continuous rise or fall in the heritage although the final accounts for the generation were balanced. But these cases have no practical applications.

generation rises with its age. A child born in 1900 consumes more in 1962 than the sixty-two-year old did in 1900.

Consumptions are balanced each year (stocking apart), but a balance of consumptions over a generation is not necessary, though there is a certain compensation due to the productive period being included between two non-productive periods.[1]

Variations of populations: Starting from a stationary population, change may be caused by immigration or by variations in fertility or mortality. As we have already said, the arrival of young trained men is most advantageous to a country which is not overpopulated. This is not usually what the country thinks, but only because it has Malthusian views and does not consider a new-comer as an acquisition but as a competitor (see page 232). An increase in population through a change in fertility is more complex since it involves an initial burden. This raises the whole question of the optimum and the optimum growth.

Drop in mortality

This factor is worthwhile studying separately, assuming that all the others remain constant.

Let us compare two generations both providing their own supplies while they exist, with the same output – consumption functions, but with different mortalities. They may belong to different countries and periods, but this does not matter.

Over the 'critical' age mentioned above, any drop in mortality increases the burden on society, even if it takes place in the active period, since it gives society new debts. Similarly, below the 'critical' age, any drop in mortality is useful to society because it spares men whom society has trained and who are debtors towards it. A drop in mortality above the critical age would make it necessary to adapt consumptions and outputs to restore the balance, unless it were compensated by a drop in mortality below the critical age. Thus a general drop in mortality produces two contrary effects which partly cancel out. If such a drop were to destroy the final balance in the accounts of one generation, this balance could be restored by changes in output or consumption.

In fact the lengthening of life over the last two centuries would not have had much effect on the age distribution had it not been accompanied by a drop in fertility. But the 'critical' age varies with mortality. When the variations of mortality below and above this age are such that there is balance over the total life-spread (without the output-consumption functions changing), the critical age varies in the same direction as mortality. The lower the mortality the lower the critical age.

[1] See J. Bourgeois-Pichat in *Journal de la Société de Statistique de Paris*, March–April 1950.

This can be shown in various ways: for instance by considering the straight section on the graph, which represents life above the critical age. A drop in mortality at any point, for instance at age forty-eight, amounts to the addition of one to society's creditors; since it is too late for the extra man to balance his own account, this will have to be done on a general basis by adding younger men to the group between the critical age and 100, in other words by making this period start at a lower age. In the general accounts from zero to the critical age this slide creates a deficit, which can be compensated by a drop in mortality below the critical age, in other words by the addition of debtors.

With the more simple assumptions that activity starts at twenty and ends at sixty, we see that the critical age would have dropped over the last two centuries, especially if the output-consumption functions had stayed the same.

Mortality	Critical age
Eighteenth century	44 years
1898–1903	$41\frac{1}{2}$ years
1946–48	$37\frac{1}{2}$ years
nil up to age 60 dropping linearly from 60 to 100	36 years

Difficulty of making general accounts

These considerations show how complex the problem is. It cannot be totally studied here but useful research could be carried out: 1. In the *theoretical field*, by building a model taking all the factors mentioned into account, together with others inherent to the system considered.[1] The model would have to be built with an eye to probable and possible situations. 2. In the *practical field*, by setting accounts for each generation side by side with the national accounts made every year. This would entail assessing the output and consumption in each year at various ages. Such calculations would not be insurmountably difficult: they would demand more patience than knowledge. No effort has been made in this direction, mainly because in liberal economies there was no such worry. But social security and the national accounts implied by economic planning have changed the situation enormously.

Forecasts would be even more useful than past accounts: paradoxically society determines very carefully the benefits a boy of twenty will have forty-five years hence and does not worry about what they will cost, even ten years ahead.

[1] This model would rest on three main functions:
P(a,t) or population of age a at time t.
c(a,t) surplus consumption of an individual of age a at time t.
i(a,t) production of investment per age at time t.

26

THE COST OF THE STRUGGLE AGAINST MORTALITY

'If life consisted in thinking about life, it would not be worth living.'

ANON

Every society struggles more or less vigorously and successfully against mortality: individuals and authorities both spend great efforts on this in advanced countries. They meet, however, two difficulties. On the one hand technological and scientific means of fighting mortality are often insufficient; on the other, this aim has to compete with economic activity for the use of technology, because of the shortage of material resources.

Leaving aside the first difficulty, what we mean when we say that technology is put to insufficient use is: *either* that men have to devote their energy to even more vital aims than sanitary ones (e.g. food supplies), *or* that they consider the lengthening of life less important than other objectives – however valuable life may be, this is sometimes the case.

Whatever the case, men's activity is divided in a certain way between economic and medical aims owing to a double phenomenon linked with the eternal, ever-present law of 'harrying by Nature'. When a population with a given amount of resources attempts to struggle against mortality, the lower it is the more difficult it is to reduce any more (yet another instance of decreasing returns); besides, the greater the efforts, the less certain the expected results. Success is both smaller and more problematic.

1. *The rising resistance of death:* Take a population of a given age (either of men or of animals) where for instance 100,000 individuals die every year. First aid, rapid and cheap, will save 10,000 of them. Another 10,000 (or the same proportion again = 9000) can be saved by slightly greater efforts. At the limit, the last few thousands would demand considerable and even infinite efforts. There is an enormous difference between the cost of the few pounds of chlorin needed to make the water of a town drinkable and that of heart surgery.

This increase in cost is a rigorous natural law; though one may change the shape of the curve of growth. On some sections for instance growth may be very weak.

2. *Growing uncertainty over results:* Some policies or treatments may be

applied which make prevention or recovery, not certain, but at least strongly possible, and ensure at any rate the postponement of death: for example, avoiding certain unhealthy conditions will lessen contamination. In a sufficiently large group one may predict the result very precisely. But in other cases this is not so: the scale of results is uncertain and may be assessed very differently. For an individual the uncertainty can be so strong that one may discuss, not only the efficiency, but the advisability of treatment: surgery may well speed up a death instead of postponing it.

Even with an equal probability of success, medical care would be greater if this probability could be measured. Instead of asking himself 'What is the use?' Man would have a clear responsibility that he could not shirk. If he knew for certain that a given costly remedy would ensure one chance in ten of survival, it would be difficult for him to abandon this chance, whether for himself or for somebody else. Longevity acts similarly on men's minds: a young and healthy person never has a precise notion of his expectation of life.

The position of equilibrium

Three kinds of activity compete in society: 1. *Those aimed at covering vital economic needs*, i.e. those directly related to mortality (vital nourishment, protection against the cold etc.). 2. *Those involving prevention, or the distribution of medical care*, or manufacture of medicines or of medical equipment. 3. *Pleasurable activities*.

Leaving aside for the moment the question of the social system, imagine a hermit, with some medical knowledge, and a concern for his life and health. He lives at the hunting and gathering stage: if he should also want to look for rare medicinal plants and roots, this care will compete with his vital economic efforts. It would not be realistic for him to go without food for eight days while he searches for rare leaves, or constructs some medical device. A balance has to be struck between the two vital aims: supplies and health.

Now suppose that his subsistence is assured and he has leisure in which to look to his health. If he is sure that a plant would prolong his life he will make great efforts to find it. But if he only has a favourable but uncertain opinion of this plant he will make the usual arrangements with his conscience and spend his leisure on some more pleasant occupation.

Graphic representation

We will first of all disregard the third form of activity. Total resources are limited and measured in working hours OR, which gives us a vertical line RR'. The segment OR represents the total activity. This can be divided in various ways (OM, MR) into economic and sanitary productions. When M moves to the right, medical care diminishes and economic output increases. The ordinates represent the result, or expectation of life.

Curve 1 is the expectation 'of life with purely economic activity: it increases constantly from left to right but at a rate decreasing as the vital needs are covered. To this expectation of life is added that ensured by medical care, figured by curve 2, which is at zero when M is at R (since this means there is no medical care) or at O (since without food the expectation of life is negligible even with intensive care). There is a maximum somewhere at IJ. Curve 3 is obtained by adding the ordinates of the first two. It has a maximum at KL, to

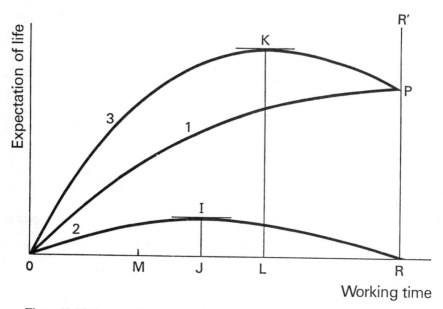

Figure 65. Vital economic activity and sanitary efforts.

the right of IJ, only if the subsistence level is ensured: here, since the slope of curve 1 would be very small towards the right, there would have to be a maximum. *Point L* divides the activities in a way that *minimises mortality*. Nothing suggests that at this point the resources of therapeutic knowledge need be fully used.

Now introduce the third, purely pleasurable activity. It adds nothing to the expectation of life, and therefore reduces it, by reducing the resources OR. This gives us a series of 'curve 3's' representing the total expectation of life, as on figure 66. The total activity OR is divided into 3, for example RR_1 (pleasurable activity), R_1L_1 (medical activity), OL_1 (economic activity).

The maxima K_1, K_2, K_3 etc. drop with the resources OR_1, OR_2, OR_3. However where resources OR are very high, there can be a zone where the vital needs

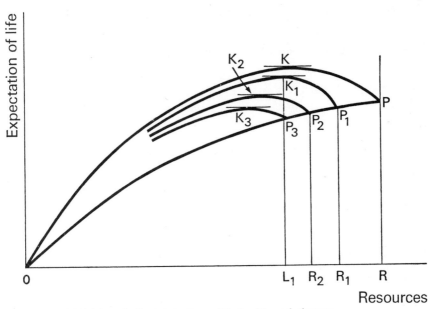

Figure 66. Division of efforts into three: life, health, and pleasure.

and the health needs being more or less covered, the pleasurable activity can develop without affecting the expectation of life noticeably. Here the curves have a very flattened zone and points K are in this zone and almost on the same horizontal line.

The cost of mortality to society

Now drop the hermit and consider a social body – to start with, a family, strongly united and mindful of the life of each of its members. The same phenomena will occur. Sanitary needs, in the shape of money or extra work, can compete with vital economic needs. But with small incomes the latter have priority, though parents often deprive themselves enormously, to the point of endangering their own lives, to save that of their child. But a time comes when the cost is so high that the scales must be tipped the other way: this is where *uncertainty over the efficiency of treatment* comes in. The lengthy and expensive journey to consult a famous specialist would be made, no doubt, if it were to bring certain recovery; but this is not the case; consciences are appeased by the conviction that an effort surpassing one's economic capacity must be necessarily useless. Uncertainty also applies to the continued existence of the deprived parents: fortunately no doubt, their own expectation of life which is competing with that of their children can only be very vaguely measured. *These doubts create a fairly wide area where decisions can be made without much*

257

remorse. Child kidnappers are careful to place the ransom demanded below the parents' resources so as not to discourage them from paying up.

Family resources are not the only pretext: there is the case of the very old grandfather whose expectation of life is in any case fairly small. The uncertain region then varies, again thanks to the happy uncertainty which prevents the bitter thought that one has killed a parent or neglected a way of saving him.

In a society, the competition between vital economic activity and sanitary activity is obvious in various ways. Consider a poor population, where the high mortality can be blamed both on poverty and on lack of medical care. Suppose you have a million pounds a year to spend on it. How should this money be used? Some will avoid the difficulty by saying that one should give both medical aid and economic aid. But immediate practical decisions do not occur in this shape. Others will say that medical aid should come first, others still that these measures would be of no avail because of the very low standard of living. The solution ensuring the smallest mortality is between the two. Some very cheap treatments (such as vaccination) are appreciably efficient: they should be combined with economic measures as much as the situation permits, bringing about the solution suggested by figure 66.

In more advanced societies the conflict is between social or preventive medicine and curative medicine. A balance is struck up between the two. But there remains the third, non-vital activity. Solidarity in society may not be as strong as in the family, yet at a certain degree of cohesion a man cannot be allowed to die without official treatment, offered by arbitrary charitable organisations or the more modern forms of social security giving the right to treatment. This right can be very insufficient: certain treatments are so expensive that even higher incomes could not stand them. George V was able to survive for a little while thanks to extremely expensive equipment which conditioned the whole of the atmosphere around him. What was possible on this occasion for the king could not be applied to any case of congestion of the lungs, even if it were serious. The efforts to save President Kennedy's son in 1963 are another example.

The need for social hypocrisy

This is a very unpleasant field, where there is widespread and partly necessary social hypocrisy. Society cannot condemn men to death on the grounds that economic resources are lacking. In the eighteenth century it had to take charge of waifs and strays: they were brought up in such terrible conditions that barely one fifth (one twentieth according to some), reached the age of adults; but at least a small chance was given them, in the same way as certain societies allowed a small chance of salvation to condemned men, by allowing them to draw lots for their lives. *Thus remorse is attenuated and the responsibility shifted to Providence.* Nowadays it is not possible for a government or a parliament to decide openly that mortality will be maintained at a given level, even by arguing that it would cost the survivors too much to try to reduce mortality further. But uncertainty still appeases and soothes our consciences: it would be impossible to say for sure that a person is dead or will die because it was or will be too expensive to take proper care of him.

When the public learns of special cases (an invalid needing a special medicine or blood transfusion, a plane crashed on a mountain-side, etc.) considerable efforts are made. The whole world worries for a few days about the survival of one child. But usually discretion is the rule, and people are condemned to death for economic reasons. These frequent condemnations are hidden in developed countries. No financier, however ferocious, could refuse the money necessary to cut infantile mortality if it were absolutely certain that so much money would save so many children, and even if the rest of society were to achieve a better standard of living through a refusal. If a million pounds a year were guaranteed to save ten thousand children, it would not appear excessive to spend thus £100 on each child, however low the 'cost price' of a child at this age. The same is true – and more so – for old people; they have never been explicitly condemned for the sake of money, and yet this happens under cover every day. The rare or difficult medicines are reserved to the cases considered more interesting.

Without the general uncertainty over possible results, which causes this attitude, life would be totally different, and death would exercise a far more frightening form of blackmail. But even in the present state of knowledge, society wilfully restrains its efforts against mortality in order to leave to the more healthy people sufficient resources for pleasure. This happens for instance in France, where child mortality is still too high (twenty thousand children over a year old die every year) and could be reduced by several thousands by a campaign for sanitary education. Alcohol kills tens of thousands of men without any serious effort being made to stop it. Vital houses are destroyed simply to cut new roads. The economic and the pleasure activities are more important than the sanitary ones.

Take the case of an airline, or any transport company: in the event of an accident it has to pay out a fixed sum based on an arbitrary scale of prices. The salary of the crew also includes, explicitly or not, a calculated amount of 'danger money'. Practically every accident could be avoided if extensive precautions were taken; yet past a certain point these efforts would be too costly or lead to loss in income because of lower speeds or lack of punctuality. Experience and reckonings point to an *optimum mortality*, but these results are best left unclarified and especially unpublished.

Some men are condemned to death because it would cost too much to save them; yet others are saved or maintained without any apparent economic usefulness. This is the case with many old people and even with very young children; we have seen that in developed countries the cost of a man is only increased by less than 1 per cent by child mortality, which therefore represents around 0·15 per cent of the national income. To spend an extra 0·15 per cent of the national income on fighting child mortality would obviously only save some of the children, the others succumbing to endogenous causes.[1] It appears vain to seek in every case direct economic and financial justification for the drive against mortality. Humanity has a nobler purpose, and its main merit and driving force is perhaps in its assuming a burden voluntarily by considering life more valuable than material things. If accountants were to rule, society would soon come round to euthanasia, the killing-off of old men, invalids, ill-formed children, wounded. How low such a society would then fall, even economically!

The competition between the sanitary and pleasurable activities is masked by the third, the vital activity. It is always possible to define an animal subsistence level, but this is only arbitrary with men. Whether he be a soldier, a wage-earner, a professor, or a tradesman, an individual will always defend his right to conditions allowing him maximum output, and he will include psychological conditions.

This defence used by the individual can equally well be adopted by the socio-political system. It is pointed out that higher subsidies would place such a heavy burden upon public finance that the subsequent disorder would affect output and, eventually, people's health. The whole capitalist doctrine rests on the axiom that unequal incomes stimulate output sufficiently to cover these extra expenses: an axiom we will not discuss here but of which one can quote many cases of abuse. Thus the distillation of agricultural products, subsidised by the French state, not only costs money that could serve to reduce mortality, but also gives the population an extra poison that increases this mortality. But politics intervene, and invoke general considerations of public order, the stability of government, etc., to change the logic. The practical difficulties of the subject are due to the cleverness of men in evading their responsibilities by exploiting the insufficiency of data and information. There are no statistics or documents explaining the increase in cost of the drive against mortality; an understandable deficiency if one considers that each society increases its efforts precisely up to the vague zone where the value of life can no longer be estimated.

Mortality according to the economic level[2]

Statistics on mortality according to income show that the expectation of life increases with income. But the answer is not completely clear, because various

---

[1] See Bourgeois-Pichat's work in *Revue de l'Institut National de Statistique* 1950, 1–2; *Population*, Nos. 2 & 3, 1951.

[2] This problem is more fully dealt with in part 2.

factors (such as knowledge of hygiene) are linked with income, and part of the income is devoted to economic pleasure goods.

There has always been inequality before death. In feudal societies the land-lords' income guaranteed them sufficient food and still does so. In developed societies food is no longer so vital a need, but medical care and various privi-leges of wealth (the possibility of not working for instance) preserve an appre-ciable difference in status. The difference in mortality according to social class, mentioned by various authors (Bertillon, Hersch), tends to drop with the increase of the general standard of living and developments in social medicine. It subsists however even in socially advanced countries such as Britain and Sweden.

In France, according to the data available on male child and adult mor-tality,[1] the expectation of life at birth varies from 62 years for labourers to 75 for liberal professions. In fact if one could take into account senile mortality (unknown in its link with occupations), the gap would be noticeably smaller.

In developed countries the differences between social categories are due to cultural reasons rather than to economic inequality. Above a certain threshold the economic level by itself only exercises a slight influence over mortality; but it is often very closely linked to the cultural level. As soon as this comes about the phenomenon appears clearly. Thus in France child mortality was lower in the families of school teachers (2·63 per cent) than in these of owner-tradesmen (3·45 per cent) in 1951, though the first certainly earned less than the second. We shall return to this in greater detail in part 2.

The dissociation between mortality and economic level also appears in time, when there are drops in the standard of living. The industrial countries have left the critical zone where the standard of living is a standard of subsistence and can cause variations in mortality. For instance between the two wars the great crisis in employment did not affect the mortality curve. In Germany, there were six million unemployed in 1932–3, together with many partially unemployed; here is the general mortality for ten thousand people.

1911–13	160	1930	111
1921–25	137	1931	112
1926	117	1932	108
1927	120	1933	112
1928	116	1934	109
1929	126 (Influenza)	1935	118

By an obviously fortuitous coincidence 1932 was the height of the crisis and the lowest point in mortality. Obviously there were more important factors operating than the standard of living. One could say the same about the other countries.

[1] See S. Ledermann's estimates according to occupation in *Population*, 1st quarter 1960, and Calot's and Febvay's studies.

This was confirmed during the war. In spite of severe shortages involving essential needs such as food and heating, mortality in France only increased slightly, from 154 in 1938 to 167 in 1942 and 161 in 1943, all these figures being lower than in the year of peace 1931. Here medical and social progress was essential. Child mortality only increased slightly, from 65 in 1938 to 77 in 1943. It reached a peak of 109 in 1945 after the liberation, but this was due to grave negligence, particularly in the case of milk, which could have been avoided by a careful policy.

Improvement in the standard of living even occasionally acts against longevity: it encourages alcoholism through a surplus of goods, or over-rich food for sedentary adults, etc.[1] These factors possibly explain why mortality has been increasing slightly for the last few years in the extremely developed countries (especially Scandinavia), amongst higher age groups and classes. On the contrary, in underdeveloped countries, with low standards of living, mortality is dropping sharply: the expectation of life in Ceylon was 40–45 before the war and is now over 60. In Spain, in spite of the low standard of living, mortality dropped to 0·86 per cent in 1961, which would have been considered very low in 1938 even for a young population. These results have been achieved without much expense. This is a new and important event: *a small financial effort brings about a sharp drop in mortality, even with low standards of living*. The consequences of this are considerable and still difficult to discern: the relaxation of the previously closed circuit of life and death will inevitably cause profound social changes (see chapter 11 and part 2).

Once the elementary care is provided, efforts must bear on the standard of living. If in fact longevity is the objective, the two forms of progress should be judiciously combined.

Mortality and validity

Sanitary efforts reduce morbidity as well as mortality. The dead become ill, the ill become healthy, so that one should deduct from the cost of the struggle against mortality the increased output achieved.

The general conclusions on these changes are not necessarily positive in purely economic terms. First, many inactive or old people are not affected by them. Secondly it may be that mortality causes a certain qualitative selection. Besides, the continual increase in sanitary care does not seem to reduce morbidity in terms of time lost. When health services are perfected, care becomes more intensive than before. But, again, the special value of man is that he refrains from using on himself calculations that would be valid for an animal.

[1] The Second World War, an incomparable field for experiments, provided clear but unpleasant and difficult-to-publicise information on over-eating. See for instance the remarkable work of A. Fleisch, *Ernährungsprobleme in Mangelzeiten – Die schweizerische Kriegsernährung, 1939–1946*, Basle, 1947.

Scientific progress and the cost of health

One should also reject the idea that medical progress will slowly reduce sanitary expenses. The whole contemporary trend points the other way. There may be certain very limited cases, such as smallpox vaccination, where the economic gains are large. But medicine rarely develops so simply. The elixir of life and universal vaccination are either pipe dreams or unworkable gadgets. The continual progress of science, large scale specialisation, the devising of more and more effective machinery, merely increase the cost of health services. To begin with, penicillin was a rich man's remedy. It was no sooner democratised than others appeared which demanded a considerable number of working hours to produce.

Thus the rising cost of the struggle against mortality is obviously not only due to certain technical conditions, but is in the general direction of medical progress. The proportion of the national income spent on people's health will go on increasing. In France it is 5–6 per cent of the national income; the French spend more than this on drink.[1]

Free care

The increase in the national cost of medical care would increase still more if care became free and accessible. Waiting hours, free secondary expenses (ambulance transport, etc.), more or less attention given to the patient: these factors may have an important influence on the amount of care asked for. A free service, which would imply that curing is much more important than vital economic needs, thus seems advisable only if the needs themselves are provided for by a guaranteed minimum income (salary, pension, family allowance, etc.). It tends to be justified by the capriciousness of illness, which strikes people indifferently and strikes a given person irregularly in time. This argument is unquestionable in the case of important illnesses and serious accidents.

Suppose that vital needs are more or less provided for, either by society or by the individual, and health services are entirely free. The increase of demand will be considerable if no other brake is applied. Portes quotes the case of a working-class family with measles. Before National Health such a family only had recourse to one consultation and one prescription for the first child affected, whereas it now demands four consultations for each child, or twelve for a family of three children, with obviously diminishing efficiency. It would be old-fashioned to consider this time as wasted. Routine, normally useless medical attention may well turn out to be crucial in certain cases and save

[1] See especially, in *Population* April–June 1955, 'Dépenses de santé et revenu national' (G. Malignac) and, in the April–June 1953 issue, 'La répartition des dépenses de la population française en fonction de ses besoins' (J. Bénard). See also the statistics of the CREDOC on consumption, especially in the review *Consommation*.

lives. This is another instance of the increasing cost of the struggle against mortality, but which has no effect on principles, since one can only decide in view of circumstances. In the present state of affairs, for instance, the opinion of the patient himself is essential since the doctor cannot see everything.

Absolutely free services and prescriptions lead, in the countries where they exist, to other brakes being applied: queues at surgery hours, severity of doctors, which may well turn against seriously ill people, widespread extension of health services at the expense of economic activity.

Where health is concerned there is no limit to the energy that can be put to use: kings have their private doctors. A doctor rarely has all the information he could use; what is more, specialisation extends further and further, and psychosomatic medicine appears to have no limits. At the hypothetical limit one would need a doctor for each person, yet whether as an individual or in society man does not take such great care of his health – it is when he does so that he is considered to be ill. After all, priority should be given to vital economic activity: the only conflict should be between economic activity applied to pleasure and sanitary activities. This does not occur either openly or widely, but if it did, the uncertainty of results would still play a large enough part to defend the pleasure activities, so that health services would never be completely free and would be offset by the difficulties met by the patient in search of care.

27

SUMMARY

'Our world carries immortal youth in its innermost heart.'

TAGORE

At the end of this first stage let us look back on the path followed. First of all, there is little difference between the struggle of a primitive population and that of an animal population against its environment.

The study of more developed human societies is furthered by using the idea of 'optimum population'. Even if this optimum is not considered a desirable aim, it is still a valuable indication which helps analysis and interpretation.

Further research into the problem of population uncovers that of social class. In a feudal society the dominating class fulfils (more or less well) the social function of a rationer and in certain conditions may increase, by its very iniquity, the population living on a given land; increase but not improve. The ruling landowner can only lighten the burden he creates by refraining from consuming the same products as the poor subjects he rules.

Middle classes reduce the population and weigh on the working classes rather than on the feudal lord, because they compete with these working classes for vital goods. Malthusian views are usually linked with a strong middle class.

In an industrial society the middle classes and demographic Malthusianism develop together. This is the essential alternative, in the progress of men, to direct passage from the feudal to the communist system.

The ruling class wants the population to increase if its rule is absolute and deadly. It dominates not only by the possession of the tools of production but by directing its income towards progressive investment and consumption, that is towards progress in every way. While the consumption of the rich and capital investment derive from the same source and the second is not given to a collective social fund, the rulers will stay masters of the game.

A rigorous monetary policy and economic liberalism create crises too deep for the system to be permanent. Keynes therefore, in spite of his great mistakes and the obscurity of some of his views, was to have the better of Rueff. Capitalism has undergone a striking renewal since the war. Not only has the active population increased but its increase seems to be an essential factor in expansion.

A technological development can increase or reduce employment according to the circumstances; but, because of the dispersal of consumption, technological progress on the whole increases employment, reducing overpopulation and liberating the workers. Yet public opinion, still only conscious of the immediate and local phenomena, believes that automation reduces employment. Malthusian conceptions of working time and retirement age also persist.

The training of men to exploit and dominate nature is much more important than the accumulation of capital, on which it has a decisive bearing. Overpopulation, underdevelopment, and lack of education are, if not synonymous, at least simultaneous, and the first two derive from the third. This constitutes a heavy menace to the world.

The economic value of man, an idea which had somewhat faded with the abolition of slavery, now reappears fairly strongly in a new shape with social security and the heightened consciousness of the human community. Longevity has to compete with other aims so that men die whom the technology of the time could well have saved. The uncertainty of death abets the natural tendency to social hypocrisy.

Technological progress, a conquering despot, does not consent to stop. Any slowing down would amount to moving backwards: humanity is condemned to perpetual progress. Real progress may well consist one day in knowing how to live without growing. As yet there are no signs of this, and we still have to push back the limits of the infinite, which is only made of our own capacity for growth.

PART TWO

THE LIFE OF POPULATIONS

1

FROM THEORY TO EXPERIENCE

The first part of this book viewed the economic problems of population theoretically, and led on the whole to counsels of moderation, at least in the matter of population growth. We shall now turn from theory to empirical observations.

The cost of growth

The cost of growth itself (including the cost of training a man and of investing in his housing and tools) was estimated in the first part (see pp. 178–83 and chap. 24). We will assume that the country is underpopulated, so that growth is desirable in itself since it will allow higher productivity and standards of living. This improvement, however, brings with it a decrease of the national income by the *demographic* investments necessary merely to equip the newcomers with the standard tools and accommodation. We must therefore distinguish clearly between the possible advantages of a larger population (a static view) and the cost of growth (a dynamic view).

Thus a businessman wanting to expand his factory and relying on achieving lower costs through mass production, must make allowances for the cost of the investments that go with growth.

Assume first that the growth is to be permanent. Suppose that a population of ten million calculates that if it grows to fifteen million it will achieve higher productivity by the sharing of overheads (civil servants, railways etc.) amongst more people. This increase will demand certain permanent investments, which will have to be reckoned against the future annual gain, giving a kind of expected interest rate. In this case demographic growth may turn out to be a profitable investment; yet one would still have to make sure that it was the most profitable – the same amount invested in the improvement of tools might have been more fruitful.

The problem is in fact complicated a little by the accordion-like reactions of the age distribution. Yet the conclusion is the same: it may well prove to be more profitable for the individual to carry out economic rather than demographic investment.

Even in an underpopulated country the answer is thus ambiguous. In a highly populated country the cost of investment must be added to environmental resistance through the law of decreasing returns, so that important

269

sacrifices may be necessary merely to maintain the standard of living. At first sight this logic *seems very black*.

The case of housing is particularly clear (see p. 180): to ensure a given degree of comfort, a population growing by 1 per cent a year has to make an effort twice as large as a stationary population. And if the latter increases its effort by 50 per cent it will be better housed at a lower cost or with less work. A similar logic would apply to capital equipment. A growing population is thus similar to a growing animal: it needs a maintenance allowance and a growth allowance.

All this suggests that growth is very costly, and that a stationary population is richer and better housed than one which spends all its energy on growth. A diminishing population might even avoid any building work: it might live on the heritage accumulated by preceding generations, and compensate by low consumption certain disadvantages of small numbers (the relative increase in overheads for instance). Some populations should therefore benefit materially from a decrease even if their land was not particularly overcrowded.

But do facts support these theories?

The difficulties of experimenting

It is not easy to check these ideas experimentally. No one factor is ever perfectly isolated. Many factors act simultaneously and confusedly, and some are not suited to quantitative measuring. It is thus hopeless to attempt a mathematical analysis of observed correlations. With no mechanical apparatus to unload him of direct responsibility the observer has to set himself instead very rigorous moral constraints, in order not to be influenced by personal interest, which is relatively easy, by personality or class prejudice, which is less easy, or by the hope of finding the confirmation of his already published theories, which is very difficult indeed. This method, whose outlines and aims I have described elsewhere,[1] is extremely arduous. One must take constant precautions to avoid easy solutions or the comfort of rigid ideas.

To achieve 'objectivity', a word which does not do full justice to the ideal, one must have no fear of displeasing, or of risking one's reputation. The observer had better be an ignorant boor than a polite or timid flatterer, and the latter is all too common in France. Economics suffers, and with it those who are dependent on it. Leibnitz wrote: 'If geometry conflicted with our passions and interests as much as do ethics, we would contest it and violate it as much as we do ethics now, in spite of all the demonstrations of Euclid and Archimedes, which would be held to be paralogisms and dreams.'

[1] *Essai sur la conjoncture et la prévision économique*, Paris, 1938; *Conjoncture et prévision économiques*, Presses Universitaires de France, 1965; *Mythologie de notre temps*, Payot, 1965.

However, one arrives finally at a structure that one must call a doctrine. But even this must be kept flexible, since *new facts will continuously join the already acquired corpus, and alter one's provisional conclusions.*

Another difficulty lies in the presentation of one's results: it is impossible to retrace the progress of ideas or reproduce the enormous mass of documents accumulated and analysed over the last twenty-five years. An observer can reproduce only a few chosen results which may, fitted together, give the same (provisional) conclusion as the complete data. His choice may involve the same dangers as before, and he can only ask the reader to trust in his integrity.

Demography is not confined to speculations on birth and death rates. The variations and distribution of numbers have a strong though discreet influence on all social questions. This will be only one brief exploration, and furthermore new paths are constantly being opened towards the unknown.

2

A LITTLE HISTORY

First observations

Until about 1930 a fairly strict correlation was observed in the world between general welfare and demographic growth. Today it is less obvious, and it should not be accepted too hastily even for the former period. It could only be partial, since population growth is only one factor in general welfare. Besides, which is the cause and which the effect? The physiocrats differed from their contemporaries, in thinking that wealth *allowed* growth, that before a man appeared, there had to be a place for him: his field had to be ready to till. To Bodin's dictum 'Men are the only wealth', Quesnay replied, 'There are as many men as there is wealth'. Let us seek a new answer to this old problem.

Wherever technological progress has been achieved, conditions have been ripe for population growth, and usually the opportunity has been taken. But to judge this more usefully we should observe several countries that have followed the same path through the same stages of civilisation, but differed demographically. This is not very easy. This chapter will choose historical examples so as to discourage easy ideas on the cost of growth, to show that economic considerations are insufficient and that one must have regard for motivation.

Spain, and its neighbours in the seventeenth and eighteenth centuries

In the sixteenth century Spain seemed destined to a brilliant future. The Arabs had been expelled and the discovery of the New World had given the Spaniards more space and more wealth. They were in a position to abandon the poorer lands and concentrate on the richer ones and on profitable activities, achieving enormous gains. An economist, or even a not particularly optimistic observer, would not have doubted this. Yet it was in fact the beginning of Spain's decline. Industry and agriculture fell to ruin. By 'exchanging its men against metals'[1] Spain had set out on the road to poverty. From then onwards its fate was to be very different from that of the rest of Europe; in vain does Hugo's Ruy Blas invoke Charles V. In turn, the economic decline eventually affected demographic evolution.

Without attempting a full explanation, we must try to discover which was

[1] See, amongst others, H. Lacombe de Prezel, *Les progrès du commerce . . .*, 1760.

the cause and which the effect. Some authors lay the blame on political factors: excessive taxation causing poverty, and poverty causing depopulation. Yet over-taxation existed everywhere. Though the *financiers* extorted huge sums of money from them, the populations of France and of other countries never stopped growing throughout the eighteenth century. Emigration from Spain was indeed often caused by poverty, but this characterises most forms of voluntary emigration. And whatever its cause, this emigration was *followed* by impoverishment and a decline, whereas at this time the very elementary techniques and the predominantly rural population were such that the selection of land should have improved the conditions for those who remained: this had happened for instance after the Black Death of 1348. The theory seems wrong.

There is of course a difference between depopulation by plague and by emigration or expulsion. The first is massive and accidental, the second progressive. The first resembles a wound, the second an illness. This point will be taken up in the next chapter.

Ireland in the nineteenth century

The population of Ireland fell by half, from over eight million in 1840 to 4,260,000 in 1940. It seemed definitely overpopulated in 1840, and theoretically one could have forecast a considerable increase in wealth for the remainder of the population, particularly since technological progress accompanied the increase in elbow room. Large funds should have been released by the total lack of demographic investment, and devoted to economic investment.

	Eire	N. Ireland	Total (in thousands)
1840	6548	1649	8197
1870	4053	1359	5412
1910	3140	1251	4391
1940	2960	1300	4260

A century later the country should have been in an era of prosperity. But experience did not confirm this theory.[1] Certainly, the average standard of living was higher in 1940 than it had been in 1840, but this was true of all the countries of Europe, and the increase was no higher in Ireland than elsewhere. Was the decrease in population caused then by emigration and emigration by poverty? Emigration is not the only factor, since the Irish birth rate in the nineteenth century was the lowest in the world apart from that of France. But this is not the question. It is obvious that the drop in population was far from bringing to the Irish the wealth that should theoretically have been theirs.

[1] See R. Fennessy, 'L'émigration irlandaise, phénomène démographique et problème social', *Bulletin de l'Institut de Recherches Economiques et Sociales*, November 1951; and 'Economic survey of the population of Ireland', *The Statist*, 3 February 1951.

Compare for instance Ireland to Denmark; Fennessy,[1] in his remarkable study, summarises the conclusions of Irish authors[2] thus:

The area of Denmark is a little less than two thirds of that of Ireland. Yet according to the 1947 census its population was over four million. whereas that of Ireland was under three million. Yet the natural resources of Ireland are larger than those of Denmark, whose soil is poor and less fertile. One eighth of the total area of Denmark is barren and has not been used so far, whereas in Ireland only 2 per cent of the land cannot be used. The Irish climate is regular and temperate, with an abundant rainfall of 25–35 inches a year. Some valleys, protected by mountains, are particularly fertile and grass grows there practically all the year round. Denmark, on the other hand, is flat and windswept, the winter is long and cold, summers are dry and the rainfall is irregular. Yet the output of Danish agriculture is far higher than its Irish equivalent, and has increased continuously over the last forty years, whereas the Irish has not changed.

To show up this fact clearly, let us take what should be the most prosperous sector in a country depleted of its population: that of cattle raising, best suited to a small population. To this end we have made up a composite index for the various animals in both countries in 1900 and 1938. Between those two dates, the total cattle in Ireland increased by 3 per cent and in Denmark by 77 per cent. Making allowances for increase in population, Denmark still has the advantage: 20 per cent per inhabitant as against 13 per cent in Ireland. If we were to introduce the output itself in milk, meat etc., there would be an even larger difference. One can imagine how the 77 per cent increase in Denmark helped towards the general overheads of the nation, and itself contributed to development.

It will be said that Ireland was handicapped by having to bring up many children and send them abroad just when they were ready to produce. Yet in the period considered the birth rate was generally higher in Denmark (23·5 per cent) than in Ireland (21·3 per cent). Demographic investment was heavier for the Danes than for the Irish and the latter were in any case receiving large sums of money from their relations in England or the United States.

Thus *the drop in population was very expensive for Ireland: experience again contradicts theory.*

Brittany and Gascony

In his travels through France just before the Revolution, Arthur Young admired the wealth and population of the Garonne. In 1840 Gascony still seemed

---

[1] Article above, p. 743.

[2] Mainly F. O'Briain, 'Rural depopulation', *Rural Ireland*, 1949, p. 73; H. Kennedy, 'Our agricultural problem', *Public administration in Ireland*, 1949, vol. 2; T. W. Freeman, 'Emigration and rural Ireland', *Journal of the Statistical and Social Inquiry Society of Ireland*, 1945.

destined to a bright future: its land was rich, its climate healthy, its people strong. The reputation of Brittany was very different.[1] Others too had described the difference between the two areas. Since then their demographic patterns have been opposed: growth in Brittany, decreases in Gascony. The economic prophet might conclude from his theory: 'Happy Gascons, since each of them will have more land and will be able to choose the richest part. Poor Bretons, they will have to squeeze up.' He may even have added: 'if there were to be a war and a food shortage around 1940, Gascony would become the granary of Paris because of its surplus production, whereas Brittany would be of no use to the capital.'

Yet facts contradicted these logical forecasts, as J. Chombart de Lauwe showed in his excellent comparison between the figures in 1840 and those immediately before the last war: in 1840, over an area approximately equal, there was three times as much land untilled in Brittany (2,400,000 acres as against 750,000 acres). There were five and a half million acres of tilled land and vineyards in Gascony and four million in Brittany. Though behind to start with, Brittany did better than Gascony in the end, not only in the output produced per acre (906 francs as against 706) which is surprising since the Gascons have the choice of the best land, but probably even in the output per person (but only by the difference between 6600 francs and 6500 francs, which

Département	Output (in percentage of national total)	Active population (in percentage of national total)	Output per active person (basis of 100 for whole country)
1. Brittany			
Côtes-du-Nord	0·98	1·29	76
Ille-et-Vilaine	1·13	1·53	74
Finistère	1·3	1·79	73
Morbihan	0·72	1·27	57
Total	4·13	5·88	69·7
2. Gascony			
Gers	0·48	0·59	81
Lot-et-Garonne	0·54	0·77	70
Lot	0·25	0·46	54
Dordogne	0·71	1·12	63
Total	1·98	2·94	67·3

[1] See J. Chombart de Lauwe, *Bretagne et pays de la Garonne*, Paris, 1946.

may be smaller than the margin of error in the reckonings, and not to be depended upon.

Having thus overcome the handicap of decreasing returns, Brittany reaped the benefits of its high population. The difference would have been even more striking had it not been fettered by alcoholism, viewed all too complacently by the authorities.

The results of an enquiry made by the *Institut National de la Statistique* into the comparative wealth of the French *départements* confirms these trends.[1]

The figures for Brittany and Gascony after the Second World War, are shown on page 275.

Thus even in the least favourable sector, the output per person in 'poor' Brittany is superior that of 'rich' Gascony. The contributions made to society in general are consequently far greater: railways, roads, schools, electricity supplies etc. become less expensive or more productive in the area of higher density. In 1955 Brittany, suffering from underdevelopment, had fallen behind (Brittany: 62·7, Gascony: 72·4). But the difference would have been far greater had economic considerations been the only factor.

The drift away from the countryside

Similar but less clear conclusions can derive from a general study of the move towards towns. Its advantages for a country are undeniable. The development of industry and trade demands a new distribution of people on the national territory, especially where the old one was not due to purely economic motivations: peasants were formerly obliged to take to unproductive mountain land because the plains were unsafe. The exodus gives everyone generally a higher standard of living than before. The ruins of the dry stone walls of the Cévennes, of the Corbières and of Provence show how hard their peasants had to work to achieve very modest outputs.

But even when conditions are improving we must distinguish between the influence of technological progress and that of migration. It is impossible to measure these two influences. But it is at least obvious that the improvement in the peasant's lot in these areas is not as large as one would have expected given the double advantage of technological progress and the drop in population. Standards of living remain largely below those of the rest of the country.

Sometimes the exodus accelerates and ends up by depopulating the area entirely. This proves that the standards of living of the inhabitants had remained too low. In other cases a new equilibrium is achieved with smaller numbers – sometimes an artificial one created by the salaries of civil servants

[1] *L'espace économique français*, 1951, p. 127, and 1955, pp. 18 and 52, publ. by the *Direction de la Conjoncture*.

or pensioners, or by the various channels through which wealth can flow in from more developed and more populated areas.

France and Europe since 1800

After 1800 France entered a period of demographic torpor. We must consider the historical progression, and also relate it to the situation in other countries and to what France could have achieved had technological progress been given a free rein.

The failure to grow reduced the amount of demographic investment. Consider France in 1850 and suppose that at that time it had taken a different path: for instance a birth rate equal to that of England (i.e. a third higher than it really was). We would find France around 1910 with a population of approximately sixty million instead of thirty-nine million: twenty-one million more mouths to feed, bodies to heat and clothe, minds to educate, people to house, keep healthy and equip with agricultural, industrial, and commercial tools. 'What an enormous burden' a theorist of 1850 may have thought, 'and what enormous impoverishment it would cause. How fortunate that France will not have to undergo the same trials as England.' Yet no one today would seriously uphold the view that a France with sixty million inhabitants would have been any the poorer. This would mean a density of only 112 per square kilometre, which is lower than that of Germany, Belgium, Holland, Italy, and England, and little higher than that of Switzerland: France would still have been below the limits imposed by its natural resources, its geographical position, and its colonial empire.

Some people put the blame on the wars. But other countries have had to cope with them. The fact is that in 1914 the French average income per person was no greater than that in other countries at the same level of civilisation, although theoretically the low level of demographic investment should have made it twice as great.

Take the case of Switzerland, of which a quarter consists of glaciers and absolutely barren land, and another quarter of poor pastures, and possessing neither coal nor iron nor potassium nor metals (until the First World War hydraulic energy played a very small part), nor sea port nor colonies. Its layout does not favour international or even internal communications, and contrasts strongly with that of France. It is impossible to reckon precisely, but one can say that the natural advantages of France would justify a density roughly 50 per cent higher. Yet in 1914 it was already 20 per cent lower, and still the sparsely distributed Frenchmen did not seem to be making the most of their opportunities.

The theorist of 1850 may therefore have based his pessimistic reckonings on weighty considerations, and particularly on the high cost of growth, but he would have been absolutely wrong. In 1966 France, with a small population and a great deal of land suitable for cattle raising but not put to proper use, was reduced to having to import meat.

Again according to the theory, a population with good natural resources sufficiently well exploited should enjoy a certain degree of social equality. The have-nots should run less risk of being crushed by the landowners. In particular a weak demographic structure, causing the younger age groups to dwindle but leaving the capital intact, should lighten the burden on the wage earners as did the deadly epidemics of the middle ages. Yet things did not happen in this way. It may be more and more difficult to find servants and even employees in the depopulated rural areas, an obvious sign of greater freedom. But this has happened in other countries too. Wages in France have never been higher than those of the rest of Europe. The forty-hour week, a bitter Malthusian fruit, was a dismal failure. France may have less unemployment than Italy, but there is also a very healthy employment situation in Switzerland, Germany, or Denmark. The underprivileged have not benefited any more than the privileged from the weakened structure: there are still many wage earners living in mediocre conditions, especially over the age of sixty.

Qualitative differences

Slogans such as 'fewer children better cared for' were attractive and often used. With fewer children one may think that the Frenchman was able to feed them, dress them and educate them better. If in a lowly social situation, he should have been able to use the services of a doctor more often, spend money more freely on the remedies prescribed and have more time to see to the cure. France should therefore have had a lower child mortality.

Back to the facts: in the period 1871–80 child mortality in France was fairly low: 17 per cent died in their first year as against 19 per cent in Switzerland, 20 per cent in Holland, 20–25 per cent in Germany. After 1880 French families practised birth control more widely and had on average slightly more than two children. But these two children were no better protected against death than the three or four Swiss, German, or Dutch children. In 1913 child mortality in the first year in Switzerland was 10 per cent, in Holland, 11 per cent, and in France 12–13 per cent. Germany was a little behind but passed France just before the Second World War, at the same time as other countries left France behind.

Are French children physically or intellectually more developed since they have more space to live in? No: France's place in international sport is a modest one. Cycle races in France are often won by Italians or Belgians. The French national football team which distinguished itself in 1957 included five players of foreign origin. In the Olympic games between 1924 and 1964 France never achieved more than moderate status. Conscripts are no more lusty in France than in Holland or Italy. Intellectual comparisons are much more

278

difficult to make, but it is obvious that no advantage has been gained since 1880 over other countries because there are fewer children in France.

The opposite theory, that quality depreciates with lower numbers, would indeed be more justified by the facts.

Overseas

History tells us of all the glorious conquests: Algiers, 1830; Tonkin, 1885; Madagascar, 1896. One might think that such possessions, of which the first two at least were rich in men and poor in capital, could have associated profitably with a country poor in men and therefore rich in capital. By contrast with Britain and Holland, absorbed in the rearing of their children and the building of schools and houses, our theorist may have seen a great colonial future for France. The outcome is far too obvious to need expanding. Between the two wars rubber, tin, and oil did not flow into Europe from Indo-China but from Malaya and India. Here are the figures for 1929 (in thousands of tons), just before the great slump.

	Rubber	Tin	Oil
French colonies (Indo-China)	10	1	—
British colonies (Malaya, Borneo, Burma)	470	65	760
Dutch East Indies	263	36	5238

Similarly cocoa did not come so much from the French Ivory Coast (16,300 tons in 1929) as from the British Gold Coast (241,900 tons). Compare Trinidad to Martinique, Mauritius to Réunion, compare the three Guianas. At this point a Frenchman might drop the subject and recognise that birth control did a disservice to his country in the very areas where it had most assets.

The results were no better at sea, though it may seem easier to find a few sailors than the capital necessary to launch a ship. Around 1860 the French navy was still the third in the world after those of Britain and the United States. It soon fell behind Germany, then Norway, Japan, Italy, and Holland, two of which have not only a smaller population but a smaller length of useful coastline. The incomparable geographical position of France was wasted; the canal linking the Atlantic to the Mediterranean remained a pipe dream.

Housing in France and Holland

Housing is one of the important factors in the cost of growth. Compare France, whose population is practically stationary, with Holland, whose population doubled between 1900 and 1950. Reckonings show that Holland had to spend 4 per cent of its national income on building houses and France 2·5 per cent for the same end. Had both spent 3 per cent, they would have obtained very different results, and the advantage would have lain with France. The theorist could imagine, with closed eyes, the luxurious conditions in which the French were to live compared with the shanty towns that would result in Holland. Yet houses are far better built in Holland than in France.

Since 1950 the number of houses available per thousand French families has increased markedly. Yet this is precisely during a period of high growth of population – another blow in the face of 'logic'.

The United States

Here is the general growth of population since 1860 (in thousands).

| | Total population | | Population aged 15–60 | |
	thousands	Yearly increase (per cent)	thousands	Yearly increase (per cent)
1860	31,510	3·1	17,330	
1880	50,260	2·35	21,450	1·1
1900	76,090	2·1	44,850	3·7
1910	92,410	2·0	56,400	2·3
1920	106,470	1·35	64,400	1·3
1930	123,080	1·4	76,300	1·7
1940	131,970	0·7	85,000	1·1
1950	151,300	1·4	91,940	0·75
1960	180,700	1·8	100,750	0·9
1965	194,700	1·5	108,000	1·4

The population grew quickly until 1910, and slowed down noticeably after the First World War. Not only did the birth rate drop (from 29·5 per thousand in 1913 to 25·1 in 1925 and 21·2 in 1929) but immigration, intentionally, was almost stopped. Nothing before the war led to suppose that there would be such a sudden halt: the restrictions foreseen were of a qualitative kind (racial, educational, political). As Carl Wittke remarks,[1] the legislation which was conceived in 1920 and applied in 1925 would probably never have existed had there been no First World War. There was at any rate a sudden turn: the annual number of immigrants fell from 1,218,000 in 1914 to roughly 300,000 in 1925–9. Racial preoccupations were not the only concern: population control was partly in everyone's mind. Again, theoretically, this should have resulted in a drop in unemployment.

Yet at this very moment unemployment rose. In 1928 there were two million unemployed; the economic crisis which began in 1929, and was probably due to the sudden stop in the traditional current of migration, increased this trend

[1] 'Immigration policy prior to World War I', *The Annals of the American Academy of Political and Social Service*, March 1949.

and the number of unemployed reached twelve million. The general state of mind was as black as the famous 'black Friday' of 1929: there was too much of everything, too much corn, too much cotton and especially too many men. The birth rate dropped still further, to nineteen per thousand in 1939. After a short-lived revival in 1937 the economy plummeted in 1938: steel output dropped by half to twenty-eight million tons, less than the figure for 1913, and unemployment increased. The only new feature was a flower of evil: the morbid theory of stagnation and maturation. A trend towards despair and population control became prevalent.

After the war the situation changed again: the birth rate rose, and the growth of population accelerated at the same time as economic growth. Though the numbers of unemployed are more generously estimated, they are still much smaller than before the war. Around 1959 the experts and public opinion expressed strong fears lest the emergence of larger age groups caused by the higher birth rates in 1942–3 produce a strong increase in the population of an active age from 1961, causing, together with the progress of automation, more unemployment. Such forecasts became commonplace and were much publicised even after they had been proved wrong. For between 1961 and 1965 unemployment dropped by 20 per cent. The number of employed increased by 3·7 million, in other words more than the population aged from 20–60.[1] We will not comment on these figures for the time being.

Germany after Potsdam

After the Potsdam agreements Germany had to cope with an influx of refugees from the former territories now part of Poland and Czechoslovakia. Yet western Germany was already highly populated before the War (159 per square kilometre). It had one precious resource, coal, but its land was not fertile. The arrival of ten million refugees without capital, furniture, cattle, or machines should, it seems, have created considerable impoverishment. Yet by 1950 the national income per inhabitant had reached its level of 1936.[2] Over the same period France, which had suffered less destruction, had only made up the voluntary drop that had taken place before the war through the artificial and unsuccessful cut in working hours. In the 1950s and 1960s, again contrary to all forecasts, not only did Germany integrate the ten million refugees, now become twelve million, but it encouraged the immigration of more Italians, Spaniards, Greeks, and Turks. From 1950 to 1963 the active population increased by 3,926,000.

Now compare the industrial output of France and Germany starting from

[1] See C. Gotchac, 'Emploi, chômage, population active aux Etats-Unis', *Population*, May–June 1965.

[2] See A. Piettre, *L'économie allemande contemporaine. Allemagne occidentale (1945–1952)* Paris, 1952.

the beginning of the economic, monetary, and political fluctuations in 1929. In 1965 French output was 107 per cent higher than in 1929, German output was 299 per cent higher. These are equivalent to increases of 75 per cent and 172 per cent per person. One fails to see the advantage enjoyed by France or the difficulties experienced by Germany; one would even suspect the opposite. It is only after the French birth rate increased again in 1946 that output really began to rise.

Overpopulated countries

As we said, these examples were chosen ones. Even linked with others such as those of Greece, Rome, Venice,[1] they would not prove that population growth always causes increases in wealth and drops in unemployment. Yet the accepted theory obviously fails very often, and there must be something wrong with it.

There are of course overpopulated countries, or countries with a very rapid demographic expansion. We often see nowadays countries labelled 'developing' collapse or explode under the burden of their growth. But their case should be completely separated from the others. A growth of 2·5 or 3 per cent per year would be very difficult to bear even by a developed country; it obviously proves far too much for the meagre resources of Asia, Africa, and Latin America.

General

Poverty, both daughter and mother of excessive growth, does not contradict the disadvantages of demographic depression. Drops in population have never coincided with periods of happiness, where people have felt more free within their narrow environment. We should therefore distinguish carefully between two different cases: poor populations with primitive or retarded technology, who do not manage to dominate their environment; and populations which set off to conquer nature but lose their energy and enter a crisis. It is the apparent accidents in the latter case that we must now explain.

[1] See, for Venice, E. Rodenwaldt, 'Untersuchungen über die Biologie des venezianischen Adels', *Homo*, 1957, no. 8.

3

THE FORGOTTEN FACTOR: MAN

We are faced on the one hand with pessimistic theories on population, reckoning the cost of growth in terms of investment and viewing unemployment in a narrowly arithmetical light; and on the other hand with a series of facts contradicting them in the case of countries past a certain degree of development. There is an economic theory explaining this contradiction by the advantages of growth (see pages 183 and 193–7): rapid technological progress in particular causes a fairly rapid change in the occupational structure of a population, which can only operate smoothly if it coincides with a certain growth in numbers. There are also psychological considerations. Theories only too often overlook the influence of demographic change itself on men's capacity to dominate their environment and force progress. *Technological progress or the use made of it, and density (or growth) of population are not independent variables as we assumed temporarily at the beginning of part I.*

We will not consider the instances of depopulation in Rome and Greece, because there is little information on them. Besides, the problem is different in our era of continuous technological development. The following considerations are mainly inspired by the experience of France.

Human reactions to stress

An increase in numbers sufficient to create distress prompts human reactions. If men are discouraged, their decline accelerates; if not the laws of equilibrium should only allow them to regain part of the ground lost. An increase of the population past a certain point or rhythm taken to be the optimum should therefore in theory create a residual impoverishment. If you take away two rooms from a family occupying four, it will probably find ingenious ways of making up for the loss but the house will still be less comfortable than before.

However, with human beings an initial handicap may cause a reaction sufficiently strong not only to make good the whole loss but even to create a positive improvement. Remember the invalids such as Pasteur, Roosevelt, Braille, Lemarck, Quételet, Beethoven, Toulouse-Lautrec, whose illnesses were the secret of their success. The same is true in economics. The blockade of Europe during the Napoleonic wars led to the cultivation of sugar beet. Taxation on petrol in Europe has, as Schueller points out,[1] caused considerable improvements in petrol engines.

[1] 'The high price of petrol eventually made for a 100 per cent increase in car traffic, by

283

These instances may be numerous but they are not of course grounds for a general law. It would be an ironic exaggeration to advocate suffering and taxation in the interest of progress. The opposite theory could be supported by very tragic examples. Where then should we draw the line between creative and negative suffering?

Adjustments will take place if the necessary efforts increase progressively, or the individual realises that there is no other possible escape. Demand a sudden and violent effort and you may break a man; and when he thinks he can find a loophole he may not react positively. Where both factors combine appropriately, the individual may be channelled towards heroism, ingeniousness, creativity and progress.

Had taxation on petrol suddenly appeared at the present rate inventors would have indignantly abandoned the struggle and turned to other fields. Or imagine President Daladier summoning the Director General of the SNCF in 1939 and saying, 'During the coming war you will have to run your trains with a personnel depleted by 20 per cent of its youngest and fittest men. You will also have to make do with half of your present locomotives and 40 per cent of your rolling stock. Your coal will be dusty and of poor quality, and other supplies will be just as poor. You will have practically no greasing oil, and I may add that your tracks and staff will be bombed occasionally at the points at which traffic is most intense. And, naturally, you will have to carry more goods and passengers than you do now.' The administrator would have shrugged his shoulders and regretted that a prime minister could not talk seriously at such a time. Yet these results were achieved in 1943 under very unfavourable conditions.

A series of progressive efforts, each of which is seen as the last, allow a man to achieve prodigious exploits he would never have believed of himself.

The two conditions, inevitability and progressivity, are fulfilled when moderate growth occurs in a population with a mind to technological improvement. Growth precludes other alternatives and makes progress imperative. In Germany after Potsdam the difficulties were not progressive: it was necessary to integrate ten, then twelve million refugees. *But there was no other way out.* In 1933 there were 140 inhabitants per square kilometre, six million unemployed and moans about living space; in 1966 there are 240 inhabitants per square kilometre, few unemployed, and a higher standard of living. As Dupréel remarked as early as 1913, *reactions to such challenges can cause an actual improvement.*[1]

Conversely, protected, easy conditions and dwindling constraint cause a series of almost unconscious acts of neglect; *men forget that they were*

speeding up industrial and technological progress. If petrol cost us sixpence a gallon we would still be running 20 h.p. cars.' (See *La vraie réforme fiscale. L'impôt sur l'énergie*, Paris, 1952.)

[1] *Population et Progrès*, Brussels, 1928, p. 252 (written in 1913–14).

more efficient before and think they can do no better in the future. They lose the benefit of their rich environment or low numbers.

This reaction process dominates the laws of population to the extent of invalidating the most logical forecasts. Our knowledge of exactly how the classical rules of equilibrium are broken is still imperfect, but there is interesting information in the works of Dumont, Dupréel, Landry, Toynbee, J. Stassart[1] and in the recent experiences of the world. A short provisional explanation could be that equilibrium should not be viewed statically: static equilibrium exists only where technology is stationary. As soon as knowledge develops, society develops too. It begins to seek a lack of equilibrium instead of a constant state. Mobility must derive from some force, whether it appears favourable or not: sailing ships can use head winds but cannot move with no wind at all.

The following series of examples should demonstrate this human reaction process.

The father

A family is a microcosm of the social phenomena that contradict logical forecasts. Children are a heavy burden: 'How,' the parents of one child may ask (especially before the invention of family allowances), 'could we subsist with three or four children? We are already on a very tight budget.' Indeed the theoretical budgets drawn up in every country for the lowest class of wage-earners suggest how difficult it must be even for a person without children to afford the basic necessities. Similar reckonings for middle classes seem to cast doubt on the possibility of educating the children. Yet there are wage-earners with large families and salaried workers with their children at private schools.

Some do indeed fail. Mortality is higher amongst large families. But L. Henry,[2] L. Tabah and J. Sutter[3] show that this is mainly due to external causes of a more complex kind: poor families have more children, children of high birth rank tend to be less resistant, etc. One often sees families apparently doomed to extinction, surviving and prospering. In the face of exceptional difficulties parents can follow two opposite paths: some give up the struggle and let things slide; but the great majority react – the mother works more efficiently and more strenuously, the father is forced to pay more attention to his career and make the most of the chances that anyone in any situation is presented with, but which lack of a spur may leed him to neglect. All this may be a sum of imponderables which only a very careful study of everyday life would show

[1] *Les avantages et les inconvénients d'une population stationnaire*, Liège, 1965.
[2] 'La mortalité infantile dans les familles nombreuses', *Population*, October–December 1948.
[3] 'Influence respective de l'âge maternel et du rang de naissance sur la morti-natalité' *Population*, January–March 1948.

up, but the result is there: individuals, sometimes with apparent ease, manage feats that they would never have thought themselves capable of, and that make nonsense of conventional arithmetic.

Of course this entails sacrifices and loss of wealth: those without children still have a higher standard of living. Bachelors and families with only one child live off the efforts of large or average sized families. Yet their final advantage is far smaller than theory might suggest, and they sometimes lose it completely.

It is perhaps best left to philosophers to decide which group is happier: our kind of observation does not help much; but it is worthwhile noticing that even from the material point of view bachelors often fall behind, either because they have been improvident or because monetary inflation, normal in a society practising birth control, has gutted their savings. We shall have more to say about this particular factor.

The only child

His case is very well-known: he does not have the same spirit of initiative as the child of a large or average sized family. He is brought up amidst multiple precautions, and misses the useful competitive contacts with brothers and sisters. This affects his character. We shall return to this in a chapter on the family, but it is essentially the same as what happens on a national level. The education of the middle class is distorted by the fact that the son of a lawyer or a businessman sees no reason why he should force himself to deserve a position that will automatically be his. Thus, in countries of only children, there appears an ever-growing weakness which absorbs a considerable proportion of the apparent gains made by agriculture and industry. Younger sons built the British Empire. The decline of Gascony was at least partly due to the disappearance of its famous *cadets*.

Disadvantages such as this must have played a considerable part in international competition in Europe. Millions of Frenchmen have been handicapped by poor education compared with that of the Germans or the British. The mere rivalry between brothers and sisters in a family, without society having to lift a finger, can be as valuable as an enormous investment. Genteel fathers who limit their families in order to employ a tutor do not realise that a younger son can give his brother character in a way that no tutor can.

Reclaiming land

Populations deprived of natural resources have had astonishing successes. Venice was the fruit of necessity. The tribes that settled on what is now called Holland, moderately poor soil by European standards, and continuously threatened in its very existence by the sea, were in no way superior; they were the usual product of mixed tribes and races. Yet by the seventeenth century Holland was the talk of economists and demographers. A large population was making a very respectable living out of these formerly precarious lands. Their continual reaction against the environment had more than made good the initial handicap. Today, Holland has the highest density of the world (360 inhabitants per square kilometre) and the lowest death rate, and it continues to reclaim land from the sea. If it had been more sheltered and safe, it would no doubt have been less populated and its people less courageous and less rich.

Around 1960 Mr Khrushchev started a campaign to exploit virgin territory, so as to encourage growth amongst the faltering agricultural population. Had he not had fallow land available, he would probably have given more attention to the advantages of intensive agriculture and fertilisers.

The destruction of natural resources

Few things are more distressing than the frittering away of soils by an agriculture with no heed to the future. Malthusians such as Vogt often quote soil erosion as a decisive reason for cutting or limiting numbers. This is not the place to discuss the various examples and causes, but it seems that wasting land is usually a feature of not very dense populations: Africa, the Mississippi valley, Brazil, Madagascar, etc.

It is suggested that destruction is the cause and depopulation the effect. The instances quoted in support can equally well be due to the sheer ignorance of the populations in question. And the opposite is much more frequent, as with the Europeans in America, with so much land that they did not think of saving it. The need to build up a permanent regenerating circuit will not occur with any urgency to men in a plentiful environment. There is no competition to enforce it; someone investing into natural capital might fail against his less provident neighbours. If no authority intervenes soil is condemned by its very wealth. On the other hand, the Chinese, the Malays etc. have been exploiting similar soils for thousands of years without exhausting them. Even Europeans are careful at home: there have long been terraced plantations on the hillsides in the Cévennes, in Provence and in Piedmont. Recent depopulation there has brought back the risk of soil erosion.

Deforestation is often due to high densities of population, but when it is followed up by agriculture it is much less dangerous than the mere stripping of land. Besides, growth and high densities should not be confused. On this point the reader might refer to the example, mentioned on page 412, of mining in the eighteenth century. A stationary population, perfectly balanced, would have continued to ignore mines that had been known for ages. Action was only provoked by new pressures.

Regional depopulation

Contemporary history offers few examples of national depopulation, but regional depopulation is frequent. It is obviously due to insufficient resources, but why do the theoretical advantages of low density not apply? Basically because depopulation discourages progress. In a village without youth the old people who remain lack the spirit of adventure or even the means to escape from idleness and routine. They can hardly be inventive when the mechanic or the carpenter have just left the village and the bus may no longer call more than twice a week. The pitiful regression, once started, is inevitable. Even the old things are only just kept in repair, and the dwindling numbers make possible a mediocre extensive agriculture which no one thinks of trying to modernise.

The high living standards in the United States and Australia do not contradict this logic. It is not denied that small populations *can* make good use of large spaces, but historical realities must be attended to. If some Columbus from a populated and progressive America were to colonise a newly discovered Europe, the result would be a completely different kind of economy. Central France would be practically deserted and so would the smaller valleys of the Alps and the Pyrenees; wealth might or might not be greater. But this is a purely speculative debate. It is a historical fact that because it allowed its population to age too fast, France fell into a dangerous decline; one may merely ponder on what it would have become had it followed the advice of those who prescribed an optimum population of 20–25 million for it.

In the interests of higher concentration it is of course sometimes advisable to abandon lands, and such districts then enter a period of difficulty.

It is important to stress that density is less important than variations in density. One cannot fix an optimum population for a country without taking into account its past population history.

Not all emigrations cause distress. England and Germany exported huge numbers of men in the last century and lost none of their vitality. Depressions do arise when the emigration is sufficient to cause depopulation and excessive ageing; childless couples at home are a greater danger than mass departures. The young are the active factor in output and progress. A young population in old surroundings is better than the reverse. Only young men can act on the environment.

No renewal without growth

No organic growth can occur without a change in structure, since the new and old elements are not identical. Between two populations with identical mortality rates, the birth rate, or immigration, is the deciding factor. Up to now, the fall in mortality has not caused an ageing of populations, as we shall see in the next chapter. The younger the population, the quicker it grows. Numerical growth causes expansion, and rejuvenation, of various institutions. This factor plays a part not only in occupational structure (see pages 193–7 and 477–9) but in all other fields.

Take universities for example: in France they are dangerously restricted by material resources. Size is not the only consideration: their quality suffers too. If the population had grown more, and with it the national income, universities would have had more funds. Of course, they would also have had more students to teach; but they would have been able to use growth to the best effect by channelling the extra funds to developing sectors such as nuclear physics, chemistry, etc. Social studies too would have appeared at the right time. Apart from this almost mechanical process there would also have been a youth of mind, which we shall return to in the next chapter.

Can universities not be rejuvenated without growth? Theoretically the older departments could be asked to make way for the younger ones in order to use the available funds to the best effect: this is what happens in a young country where everything is created anew. But, in practice, as we have seen, this is impossible: 'less useful' professors cannot be suppressed to make way for sociologists and statisticians. They will defend every inch of their ground and their concessions will always come too late. Population stagnation it is that has caused the Malthusian, defensive status of French universities. This was bearable as long as the population was stationary but is today costly and indefensible. Expansion is the only way to adjust proportions. *A body can only improve through growth.*

In the private field there are similar instances. A growing population feels the need and the energy to create new types of business: in such an atmosphere it is not absurd to found new concerns, even in a crowded sector, and the result is a general rejuvenation. This cannot happen with a stationary population: the newcomer would meet with strong competition and would have few chances of snatching customers from the old concerns with the benefit of old-established capital. Only new outlets would allow him to gain a foothold in the market, taking the senior firms by surprise, and breaking, if not their monopoly, at least their placid show of competitiveness. It is the same in other fields: *with nothing new to lend it a progressive turn, a body vegetates, whether it be a factory, a fleet, a town or a university.*

The economy as a whole suffers in the same way. In a growing society obsolescent sectors can go into relative decline without any pain; in a stationary population there have to be sacrifices. Thus the French vineyard crisis would have been easily solved had France had ten million more inhabitants: no one would have mentioned the possibility of destroying vines or distilling wine.

The great slump

This is more controversial demographically than the other defeats Malthusianism has suffered. Yet the facts show a satisfactory correlation between the periods of economic and demographic prosperity in the United States, and suggest that the population was the first to enter the depressive phase between the two World Wars (see above pages 280–1).

The brutal stop put to immigration was, if not the main cause of the 1929 crisis, at least a very important factor. With a stronger growth, restrictions would have been broken, valves would have burst. No doubt immigration would have had to have been curbed one day, but it was dangerous to suddenly cut off a flow on which so much development was depending. This view is unpleasant, and has not therefore been seriously considered. It has not been accepted in America, though stagnationist theories are less popular than twenty years ago. Reactions to stress are still underrated.

The disappearance of French savings (1880–1914)

From 1880 onwards the French followed the advice of J-B. Say: 'accumulate savings rather than children'. The generations hardly reproduced their own numbers, and the *Zweikinder System* and even the only child became the rule. But what happened to the enormous savings or opportunities for savings that this entailed?

There are some doubts about the volume of savings. Goldenburg[1] estimated them in Britain, France and Germany as follows:

	Population growth (per cent)	National income saved (per cent)
France	10	10
Britain	57	12–15
Germany	57	15–20

If these figures are correct France, contrary to current opinion, saved less than its two great neighbours, in spite of the smaller requirements of its families. The need for demographic investment and for housing would seem therefore, by a process that remains to be explained, to have forced savings in countries with a growing population. They would have recovered part of their handicap.

But this very effort should have meant, for Britain and Germany, even greater restrictions, and smaller consumptions. The 10 per cent of the French national income, almost entirely available for economic investment, should have brought an increase in individual wealth. While German families were

[1] 'Saving in a state with a stationary population', *Quarterly Journal of Economics*, December 1946.

exhausting themselves in building houses for their four children, the French should have been accumulating a useful fortune.

Here again facts contradict Malthusian theory. From 1871 to 1913 France invested barely 50 per cent of its savings at home (and most of these were lost since four-fifths were in government securities) as against 75 per cent for England and 90 per cent for Germany. Investments in France in 1908 were half in government securities, a quarter in railways (the past) and a quarter in industry.[1] Thus out of 100 francs saved in France, only 12, or one-eighth, helped to develop the economy of the country.

This is no coincidence. A population without children does not believe in the future and can hardly be expected to have the pioneering spirit. Only an utter misconception of history and international ethics can have led anyone to think that a nation of investors could continue indefinitely, relying on previous contracts. On the international scene only the rich get their money back.

The fewer children the Frenchman had, the less inclined he was to capital venture. Péguy called the father of several children the adventurer of modern times, and this was no joke. Three per cent securities, though publicised as family investments, were in fact particularly popular around 1910 amongst those who avoided having children. In their old age these people were to regret bitterly the sons they had sacrificed to these bits of paper. Their investments were intended to help the state and towns to build, develop, and modernise, but again the outcome contradicted the logic. Only by delving into the budgets of the time can one conceive of the weakness, avarice, and obscure mistakes that led to utter dissipation. The colonies too were neglected. Ageing populations do not feel any urge to till new lands. With no younger sons to flock to the colonies, the few people who did go found jobs as administrators.

Even if there had been a lack of openings abroad, and capital had had to be invested at home, it would have been restricted by the lack of men. This may surprise the reader who is content with the commonly accepted ideas. He may point out that there was a constant surplus of unemployed workers, unnecessary civil servants, and tradesmen. True enough: new capital might have absorbed part of this unproductive population, *but demographic depression does not necessarily lead to full or better employment*. Initiative is very unequally

[1] See G. Lutfalla, *Rapports au Conseil Economique et Social.* The report on the financial market (12 November 1952) shows that stocks quoted before 1914 were as follows:

Government loans, and other public funds:	29,013 million francs
Railways:	22,954
Industry, mines:	14,843
Total French stocks	66,810
Foreign government loans:	64,894 million francs
Other foreign stock:	16,550
Foreign total	81,444

distributed amongst men; the less gifted are rarely attracted by productive occupations demanding energy if they have the slightest chance of vegetating.

Unemployment, as well as being very damaging materially and socially, impresses public opinion so that it misleads the wisest observers. Capital in search of a use does not necessarily meet the men in search of jobs, because of a series of selective factors.

Gold to lead

Let us now study how the immense treasure that France was thought to be building up by saving on men, was dissipated. There were many mistakes, some giving temporary satisfaction, others not even this.

There was better food, more meat and, especially, more wine. These were for some time real advantages, confirming the economic reckonings. But the next generation inherited the tastes without any creative investment to satisfy them: budgeting became difficult, resentment appeared against other social classes, against the government, against society. Wine, become a national need, changed from an economic luxury into a tyrant, influencing individuals, the press and public opinion, and even the authorities. The multiple, hidden damage it caused is still widely underestimated. France had overthrown three dynasties and thirteen régimes in two centuries, but was now powerless to overthrow this new sovereign, more extravagant than Caligula and more terrible than Ivan. Meat did not cause similar excess, but was also a despot in its small way: people came to believe in its all-powerful nutritive value, and to despise honest milk, with its noble calories. In the end the high living permitted by demographic changes ended, and only its cost remained. France found itself exchanging the forequarters of slaughtered cattle for hindquarters from Germany because of their better meat value, and its whole economic development has been hindered because this 'noble' product has produced a permanent hot-bed of inflation. The Frenchman may eat better than his neighbours but his digestion brings no satisfaction.

Other losses can be uncovered in practically every field: the building trade became atrophied, the navy stagnated, the colonies declined, all because of the lack of stimulating pressure in France. In Valéry's words, France had no access to the 'degrés lumineux où la sève l'exalte.' Pruning off 10 per cent of a population destroys most of its budding and sprouting sectors, precisely those with more vitality. In the end France was merely sending abroad a few civil servants and tradesmen slightly better than the natives at selling the products the natives had grown.

This was not all. Until the First World War, apart from the problem of alcohol, France was only suffering from a failure to improve. Between the two wars there began a destructive phase. Though stagnating, agriculture was still sufficiently productive to provide more than the decimated population needed in certain fields. The Malthusian fallacy then became a menace: in order to 'absorb the surplus output' sugar beet, wine, and apples were distilled and bought by the state, for between 15 and 20,000 million francs, for no purpose at all. There was what appeared to be a pleasurable use, which was to drink the alcohol: but this was the most costly part of all: every litre of alcohol consumed cost the treasury and social security in accidents, hospitals, lower outputs, delinquent children, and diseases, three or four times more than it brought back in taxes. And, however surprising this may seem, this mass destruction of wealth, population, and intelligence, did not end with the difficult food situation after the last war. Though there was a national shortage of sugar, sugar beet was still being distilled.[1] Public opinion remained cold. This is a typical instance of economic Malthusianism, which we shall meet again in chapter 10.

Other countries went through a similar phase during the great slump, but only for a short period of folly. *It lasted longer and is still apparent in France because of the depressing effect of the demographic collapse.*

Things were not altogether dark, of course, during the first half of this century. There was less unemployment than in other countries and less worry over paying the rent. Life was good, but in the same way as a dream, with its rude awakening.

Housing and building

The French often wonder what wicked spell has brought them such bad housing when their very slow increase in population should have given them the edge over other countries. Specialists and many laymen believe that the building pause after the First World War was due to the legislation on rents: taxation and the restrictions on rented property had the effect of destroying initiative. These observations were correct but the conclusion was too simple. The sterile legislation was not the original cause: one should ask rather why it was passed and maintained in the first place. Other countries which had fought the same war as France, protected their tenants for a time, but restored capitalist incentive (freedom of rent) or else invented a new form (through various subsidies) or combined the two. In France this did not occur for various reasons, mainly due to demographic stagnation. The very slow increase in population made building seem less important. It appeared pointless to victimise the enormous majority of contented tenants for the sake of a few people who could not find homes. More important still, atrophy affected the will to create and build.

[1] In 1946 the individual sugar ration was 500 grams a month. Sugar beet, distilled in quantities equivalent to 210,000 tons of sugar a year, gave 150m. litres of useless alcohol – these quantities would have provided the French with an extra 440 grams of sugar each month.

Building lost ground in terms of costs, also because of the demographic decay. In a stagnant country new methods are never popular: they are too much of a surprise and they cannot develop technically in a narrow market.

The housing crisis thus developed from year to year in an atmosphere of complete public indifference. People used to talk of it as if it were an act of God. Any plans for renewal which might lead to large scale building met with indignant objections: something old had to be destroyed to make way for it, whether a pride, a profit, a principle, a point of view, or a preconception; such things are always energetically defended.

From 1948 to 1955 there were 800,000 new homes built. During this period the population increased by 2,378,000, which corresponds to a need of about 700,000 new houses; but the ageing of existing buildings during the period was equivalent to an additional need of one million houses. Other fresh requirements arose from internal migrations and post-war reconstruction. Thus in a calm period France was unable to build the bare minimum to prevent the situation worsening. A much-respected public figure declared that 'the upkeep of existing buildings will suffice to house the greater part of the population'. These words were so in keeping with the sterile Malthusian frame of mind that they caused no outcry. They took no heed of the requirements of young couples, who were considered to have appeared out of turn anyway.

After 1955 building increased rapidly: the number of houses built rose from 210,000 a year to 400,000 in 1965, and will probably reach 470,000 in 1970. *This spurt is mainly due to the pressure of requirements*, which destroyed certain resistances. Success is by no means yet assured, because Malthusianism has created habits very difficult to change. Having lost the will to create as well as the habit of paying rent, the population awaits passively for the state to build homes and distribute the keys. The return to mature living is a very slow process.

Out-of-date architecture

Because they have to balance accounts, financiers have good reason to be unpopular. Builders and architects, on the other hand, are far more to blame for balking at any novelty. The lack of enterprise is particularly strong in this field. People are terrorised by the past and unable to accept anything contradicting an old custom or an accepted aesthetic value. This is a collective rather than an individual illness: even the 'adventurous' father of a large family is prone to it.

The beauty of New York or Sâo Paolo skyscrapers is of course questionable. Living on the thirty-eighth floor may not be economically necessary. But this kind of growth is the sign of a vital renewal and expresses the flowering of the spirit.

In France the objection to novel, large scale building at the beginning of this century was a new fact. Cathedrals had been built without hesitation in the Middle Ages, the seventeenth century had seen the appearance of Versailles and the eighteenth had built the Place de la Concorde. But already when in 1889 Eiffel put up the highest construction in the world, this individual action was suspected by the Malthusian nation – there was talk of destroying it. In 1952 Zehrfuss's project for the UNESCO headquarters caused a tempest of argument, based on the fear of the new and the large. People were prepared to lose UNESCO to another country rather than accept hideous novelty: it is so comfortable to go on sleeping, with no new buildings to shock you out of it. The Faculty of Medicine and the *Maison de la Radio* in Paris were also amputated so as not to be too novel. The phrase 'on a human scale' was used but this is one of those relative concepts.

Indeed, it is only by accident that France 'produced' the greatest architect of this century. Until 1951 Le Corbusier had built in practically every other country except France. He was admitted there because of the 'perturbation' after the end of the war, and aroused such passions that his builders were dragged into courts of law. He was accused of designing 'a type of building morally pernicious and contrary to French style and aesthetics'. Had such ideas prevailed earlier, the French would still be living in the mud huts of Lutetia. But such reactions would have been unthinkable before our times, being the direct result of conservative Malthusianism.

Fortunately a renewal has taken place over the last fifteen years, a proof of vitality closely related to the growth of the younger generations.

Schools

The building of schools is another striking example. It was obvious as early as 1947 that the higher birth rate, the move to the towns and the extended school leaving age would create new requirements. But the country was loath to make the necessary effort, in spite of the warnings of specialised planners.[1] Only in October 1951 was a commission formed to estimate the requirements. The resulting expenditure was resented by part of the population which was trying to destroy family ideals in order to live more comfortably in the present and avoid undesirable children asking for their due. As with building, there was an obscure, unexpressed but influential desire to adapt the population to its environment rather than the reverse.

There are curious twists to this affair. The overpopulation of schools, at least in towns, was noticed as early as 1949. Public opinion blamed the birth rate, and yet at that time the age groups at school were very small: the number

[1] P. Vincent, 'L'accroissement futur des effectifs scolaires', *Population*, April–June 1948; 'Aperçu démographique sur l'évolution des effectifs scolaires', *Population*, October–December 1949; 'Perspectives sur l'évolution des effectifs scolaires', *Population*, July–September 1952.

of children aged four to seventeen was 7,930,000 as against 9,390,000 in 1938. There should therefore have been 1,400,000 free places – but where were they? The extended school leaving age did not account for the difference, or for the sudden emergence of the problem in 1949. Neither were the internal migrations fully responsible.

The real reason was a relaxation of efforts: it was felt that there was no need to build during the 'easy years'. The expenditure that should have been directed each year to this end was dissipated on sterile projects, such as the distillation of sugar beet. And when the funds were needed, they had of course disappeared; the country panicked at the prospect of a school population smaller than that of 1851, when the educational budget was fifteen times smaller. The country, having lost the sense of youth, was at a loss in front of this emergence of young generations that it had brought about half-consciously in 1939 in an act of sublime reaction to the impending disasters.

In 1965 public opinion still believes that secondary schools and technical colleges are overloaded because of the 'bulge'. This can be easily checked by referring to the situation before the war and the slump restricted the size of the age groups. Let us compare 1939 to 1965. In 1939 there were 612,000 school children in the various types of secondary schools and in 1965 3,100,000. Adjustments to the 1939 attendance and birth rates would make the former figure 710,000. The increase due to the birth rate is therefore 98,000 children. The difference, 2,390,000, is due to the democratisation of schooling, whose effect has been twenty-four times as large. Even if we group the *Cours Complémentaires* and the *Ecoles Primaires Supérieures* (technical colleges) with secondary schools, in order to make a more exact comparison, more democratic schooling is still fifteen times as influential as the birth rate.

History re-written

Imagine what would have happened if France had decided, around 1850, to limit its births more reasonably, at a scale similar to that of Sweden. Its current population would be over 65 million, or approximately 120 to the square kilometre. It would probably be in a brilliant situation. Both wars would have been conducted with more success, but we will not develop this imperialist line of thought. Economically, we would not have the pleasure of reading the admirable *Paris et le désert français* by F. Gravier, but our economic regions would be much closer to the ambitions of this eminent geographer. Paris might not be more highly populated but in place of its sinister, straggling suburbs there would be new buildings and green spaces, as one sees in Amsterdam, Berlin, or Warsaw. The 'desert' would be full of life and turned towards the future. Agriculture would be better equipped, would use more fertilisers and would provide for the higher consumptions. Better outputs and returns would make exports possible. Our mountain dwellers might have learned, like the Swiss, to run hotels and make watches. The canal from the Mediterranean to the Atlantic would give France incomparable wealth, and the Rhône would be harnessed to serve power plants, ships, and the neighbouring plains. With a higher demand and costs only slightly higher the film industry would be more prosperous and would export more; publishing would not be in a chronic state of crisis. Broadcasting would be expandanding providing better programmes. Many industries in the electronic and chemical field, as well as the aircraft industry, would be more profitable and more developed. France would use its own steel and aluminium instead of providing it for others. The railways might be less of a public burden. Generally the standard of living would be higher, and the budget provided by a large and richer population would furnish more funds for scientific research, universities, technical education etc. One imagines a Frenchman with fewer frustration and fear complexes, living a happier life.

Increase in private property

Various social reforms suggest that France (like other countries) has started on the road towards collectivism. This is a hasty conclusion. *The nationalisation of a few sectors of public interest has been largely balanced by a strong conservative increase in private property.* The owners of apartment houses lost many of their rights but this did not lead towards collectivism: more and more people became part owners of their flats and commercial premises.

At the same time industry became less competitive. In a competitive system, customers and markets belong to whoever can appropriate them. They are everyone's and no-one's. It is precisely the wish to conquer them that spurs on to progress. Demographic decay, on the contrary, led to a general crystallisation in France. Individuals and groups surrounded themselves with legal fortresses to impede any change. The economic conqueror, who lowers his prices to attract the customers of others, began to be considered as a sort of Don Quixote, a warrior from another age. Property was the granite on which this rested. In order to rebuild a district or a block, or to pull down a few crumbling houses to clean it up, the common practice in South America, it is said, is to employ one night and one bulldozer. In France, there is such resistance on the part of proprietors or occupiers that the procedure lasts for years and the results are small and costly. In such a régime no one could ever have built either roads or railways. As long as this attitude remains, national planning will be but a series of figures and charts and dreams. As movement creates movement, so stagnation tends to spread.

Examples of this attitude are widespread in France; because of it France, after both wars, spent more than any country on compensating war victims, that is to say on trying to return to the past; as a result fewer houses were built. Property prevailed over creativity.

297

To take another example, the migration from the country to the towns should have left available land but here again the sense of property had a Malthusian effect. The number of holdings completely abandoned is relatively small; but each holding included peripheral or isolated fields that could not be exploited without the use of the central buildings. As a result a very large number of lands were partially abandoned, or given to an extensive and mediocre form of agriculture with returns just large enough to avoid accusations of total neglect.

This does not mean that any recognition of the right of property is Malthusian. Requisitions on housing in peace time compromise the future with very little immediate result. The important thing is that in every circumstance economic facts should be viewed in a dynamic and progressive way.

Among the most sought after forms of appropriation is monopoly. A factory may belong to an owner, but the various firms in one trade do not possess this trade. Yet they tend to believe this more and more. Of course cartels do not only appear in countries in a state of demographic decay: any concentration leads to monopoly. But in France and in various other European countries the process is aimed more at defending acquired positions than at making real progress. Rather than try to increase profits, firms wish to change them into fixed dividends. Import quotas, a French invention, create over a period of time as many purchasable commissions as products. And some were not even sold but given away.

Some objections

This theory that pressure is creative can be attacked from many sides. Why, it may be asked, can Italy not integrate all its unemployed workers into the economic circuit as Germany did for its refugees? And what of countries such as India, overpopulated though rich in natural resources? The answer is that one should also take into account the climate and various human elements that act either for or against progress. These situations of stress are only creative within certain limits and in certain circumstances.

Secondly, it is said that scarcity of labour leads to progress in mechanisation. This law too is only valid in certain circumstacnes. France, with its low fertility, did not seek salvation in productivity. The cause and the effect are really the reverse: it is because the United States is mechanised and developed that practically the whole of the population is in employment, which non-mechanised countries do not achieve. Overpopulation appears rather as the result of underdevelopment. It is clear, anyway, that the economic explanation is too superficial.

One point is certain: other factors cannot suppress the creative effect of demographic pressure nor, especially, the depressive influence of demographic decay.

The French case is particularly significant, because though other countries evolved similarly, the demographic factor was here almost isolated. Demographic decline took effect gradually on the national energies, and hence on economic development.

There could have been another explanation. Demographic decline and the depression that followed could be independent and both derive from some former, underlying cause. Some virus could have penetrated into the French system in the eighteenth or even the seventeenth century, and caused first demographic decline, then economic depression. But there is no foundation for such a theory. What would be the nature of this secret virus? True, demographic decay itself has a cause, which we will be investigating further on, but the fact remains that it preceded the drop in vitality. Its effects on economic behaviour are too plain to be questioned.

This brings us to the question of measures and proportions. To what extent does a need determine an effort sufficient to fulfil it? Italy did not manage to achieve the same standard of living as the other countries of western Europe (apart from Spain, Portugal, and Ireland) because its handicap was too great. Its natural resources were mediocre, its climate soporific especially in the south. Making allowances for this, the Italian standard of living is relatively higher than that of the French.

If the effort required is too great, it can discourage population instead of stimulating it. Encourage an athlete to jump higher and higher by moving a bar up a matter of inches each time, and he will improve his performance. If the bar is moved up too fast he loses his motivation and jumps below it. On the other hand population growth would obviously not be sufficient to ensure progress. In some countries of the Third World it is even an important obstacle to development. Some populations are stifled by their own vitality, like an overdeveloped tree.

This brings us to define more precisely the idea of *optimum rhythm of growth*, already mentioned in part I: it is a reasonable area from which it would be dangerous to stray in one direction or the other. Taking now into account the link between growth itself and the will to progress we may also add that the *optimum growth is always quicker than purely economic factors may suggest*. This is especially true of developed countries, and even in the Third World the national income of various countries has increased faster than the experts who were calculating only from the economic point of view had forecast.[1]

Conversely, *demographic stagnation brings a country to a moral and material crisis that is never foreseen in economic analysis.*

One could also object that the European countries who have almost as many old people as France do not suffer from the same depressive symptoms. Why

[1] See F. Benko, 'Les investissements en capitaux et le progrès économique dans les pays du Tiers Monde', *Population*, July–September 1965.

do even the United States remain infatuated with productivity and economic conquests? First, maturation takes time: the French have been getting older for two centuries now and have only slowly felt the effects, whilst the others were still living intensely. Later, when the ageing phenomenon spread, the affairs of Europe and America were at their least prosperous. The slump in fertility after the First World War had a depressing effect and contributed to the gravity of the 1929 crisis, which was a crisis of faith and intelligence at least as much as one of wealth. After the last World War the West benefited from a revived demographic and economic vitality. But Europe, and particularly Britain, is still affected by ageing. A certain dose of inflation is necessary to compensate the weaknesses of age. A new drop in fertility would bring depressive effects, of a novel kind no doubt, but no less harmful.

The causes of progress

What we have just said is mainly true of countries in the van of progress, having entered the cycle of scientific and material development more or less at the same time. But why did European countries enter this phase first and why are they unevenly followed in this direction? Here the population factor is no longer involved. Demographic pressure has long been particularly intense in various regions of Asia. It caused persistent poverty, or in some cases progress aiming, not at higher outputs, but at extreme economy of resources. The methods of the Chinese peasants in the deltas, planting rice grain by grain and clearing their fields weed by weed were the result of longstanding pressure of hunger and worry about mouths to feed. The life of a peasant in a tight economy of this kind is organised with a minute cleverness which amazes us. It involves such an ingenious combination of economy in materials and movement, adapted to the seasons and the hour, that the technological expert not trained at this severe school would be incapable of adapting himself to it.

This is due to a classical phenomenon in physical or social mechanisms. Movement in a certain direction must come from pressure on one side and opportunity on the other. For society to enter the path of progress this path has to be open, and in certain populations, though they are in a bad state, technology remains desperately stable. Some choose or are given forms of government which do not encourage progress: this is the case where two classes co-exist, the one too rich and idle to make any effort, the other too poor to conceive of any innovation.

There are of course aims that may be placed higher than economic progress: equity, social stability, security etc. We shall return to this question on the subject of the Third World.

Back to France

In France discontent is very widespread; all social classes feel frustrated and so they appear to be if one compares, for each one, requirements and income. Discontent is one of the essential conditions of progress, so this would seem to suggest a powerful motivating force if the way were not blocked by Malthusian attitudes. The interesting question is what the demographic renewal, now in its twentieth year, will produce.

The effects of depopulation and stagnation on ageing are well known, but those of repopulation and of demographic renewal are much less so. The historical examples we have are either of populations decimated by some famine or epidemic, or of countries benefiting from large scale immigration, usually after a conquest. *No example comparable to present-day France, where a renewal is intended or half-intended by favourable legislation, has occurred.* (The precedent of Hitler's Germany from 1933 to 1939 is not applicable, because there the economic renewal was spurred on by very special factors as well as by more births.) In this novel situation it is adventurous to make forecasts. Let us, however, attempt an incursion into the future, always supposing of course that there are no serious perturbations such as a war or a change over to communism.

The rising age groups (those that appeared after 1946) were felt only as an additional burden to start with, in the family as well as on the national scene. The nation pays for part of their consumption (family allowances), and equipment (housing, schools, hospitals etc.) by way of its budget, and another part through private enterprise (development of factories etc.). So far these requirements have had an appreciable but insufficient stimulating effect. The pressure of needs has caused considerable efforts in various fields (housing, schools). It has no doubt contributed to breaking down protectionism, which seemed the ideal until the early 1950s. Sterile isolation was no longer compatible with the growth of the population, and the ensuing large scale conversion brought about the creation of the Common Market. The renewal of agriculture, particularly the urge for progress amongst young farmers, is also accountable to this pressure. The causal links here are of course very tenuous, and it is very difficult to give scientific proof. But there are too many signs for all this to be dismissed as a coincidence.

France is more conscious of the future. However mediocre the official pamphlet published in 1965 on 'France in 1985', the mere fact of having attempted it is significant. The word 'prospective' has become popular. And yet Malthusianism has not given up the fight. A million extra mouths to feed have not yet prevented the distillation of agricultural produce, now become a kind of second nature. Eight million more people to house have not yet significantly changed the sterile and antisocial rent legislation. The urge for improvement and expansion has met so many obstacles and bottlenecks that it has contributed largely to the inflationary pressure, which is stronger in France than in any other western country.

Observations are difficult in such matters essentially because phenomena and their causes are out of step, and are not apparently associated in time. We may however conclude thus: *France has achieved the rejuvenation of its population, but is finding it difficult to rejuvenate its institutions in the same ratio.* More is needed than financial sacrifices; inertia has to be overcome, legislation prompted by the desire for security or for Malthusian appropriation has to be made more flexible and turned towards the future. The struggle is still on between the requirements and the strength of the youth on the one hand and the conservative resistance of the old on the other, between the forces of the past and those of the future.[1] If the former were to persuade the country to return to legislation directed against families and children there would be a danger of a grave failure. For the time being we may hope that inflation will be avoided as too obvious and dangerous a way out, and that the resulting stress will be our salvation.

[1] The phrases 'the young' and 'the old' refer to a frame of mind; they do not imply here a real debate between generations, although there has been one, cleverly avoided in public, but underlying and tenacious, throughout the last thirty years, as we shall see in the next chapter.

4

DEMOGRAPHIC AGEING[1]

Of all contemporary phenomena this is the least doubted, the best measured, the most regular in its effects and the easiest to forecast well ahead, as well as the most influential. Yet it is probably the least known of all. From time to time newspapers enquire into the opinions of various people on which the most important issues of our time are. The answers are varied: broadcasting, sport, holidays, atomic energy, communism, space travel, sexual freedom, town planning, etc. No one ever mentions the ageing of the population. It does not see itself ageing. *The easiest of social facts to measure and observe is the one that escapes notice.*

Definition

The age distribution of a population changes in time. An elementary measure is that of the average age of the whole; but this is not very sensitive and only has a limited significance – a new born baby and a sixty-year old do not add up to the same as two thirty-year olds. Usually, one introduces the idea of an 'active' or 'productive' age, hence a distinction between three groups: young, adult, and old.

The age limits of each group vary from one author to another, and depend anyway on physiological and legal and social factors (for instance the social security age limits). The first limit is usually placed at fifteen or twenty, the second at sixty to sixty-five – these are of course averages. Whatever the ages chosen, the three groups can be seen in various combinations: 1. Ratio of the 'old' to the total population: we shall normally refer to an increase in this ratio as 'demographic ageing'. One can also reckon the ratio of adults to young and old, or ratio of producers to non-producers. 2. Ratio of old to adult: this is mainly used for arrangements concerning old-age pensions. 3. Ratio of old to young: this is the most sensitive of the three but is rarely used because of the place given to economic considerations.

Generally, the phenomena produced by the age distribution can be studied

[1] Apart from the sources quoted in this chapter, see also, J. Daric, *Vieillissement de la population et prolongation de la vie active*, Paris, 1948; *Politique de la vieillesse*, Rapport de la commission d'étude des problèmes de la vieillesse, Paris, 1962; 'Les personnes âgées et l'opinion en France', *La documentation française*, 1962; *The ageing of populations and its economic and social implications*, United Nations Population Study no. 26, 1956.

by the method of 'potential demography' invented by L. Hersch. Here an individual is equal to as many units as he has years to live. Instead of considering his past age one considers his future age.

Before modern demographic patterns

The ratio of old people probably varied very little for many centuries. A population with no efficient medicine and stationary technology has a high mortality rate, and a survival table in which expectation of life at birth is less than thirty years.[1] If such populations were 'stationary' in the demographic sense, their age distribution would be identical to the survival table, with a ratio of old to others of about 8 per cent.

But such populations are not static. They alternately grow (good crops, peace) and shrink (famines, epidemics, wars) around a position of equilibrium which may rise very slowly. We will call them 'permanent' populations. Since the various factors that decimated them affected all age groups almost indiscriminately, the age distribution was that of a population growing slowly, with a pyramid slightly larger at its base than the survival table.[2] Such populations retained approximately the same age distribution, with periods of slow rise and sudden drop, as indicated in figure 67.

From the first to the third pyramid here the population is growing as if it were stable. In the fourth mortality suddenly rises, bringing the population back to its initial state. This is of course a very simplified sketch. In this

[1] It may be worth remembering at this point the United Nations survival tables for $e_0 = 27.5$ and $e_0 = 30$, and Duvillard's table:

Age	Duvillard	U.N. $e_0 = 27.5$	U.N. $e_0 = 30$
0	1000	1000	1000
1	767	738	755
5	583	601	630
10	551	564	594
15	529	540	568
20	502	511	545
30	438	435	470
40	369	352	390
50	297	263	301
60	214	171	204
70	118	82	104
80	35	19	26
90	4	—	1
100	—	—	—

[2] J. Bourgeois-Pichat qualified as *quasi stables* populations with a variable mortality but a constant age distribution. See in particular 'Utilisation de la notion de population stable pour mesurer la mortalité et la fécondité des pays sous-développés', *Bulletin de l'Institut International de Statistique*, vol. 36.

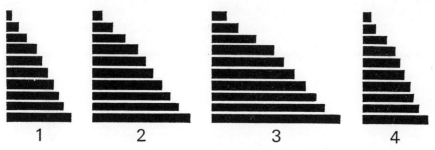

Figure 67. Stages in development of a permanent population.

case the proportion of people aged over sixty is smaller than in a stationary population. Here are some ratios for populations relatively retarded demographically.

	(per cent)		(per cent)
Duvillard's table	8·8	Greece, 1910	6·3
Iceland, 1703	7·5	Rumania, 1930	7·4
France, around 1775	7·3	USSR, 1939	6·6
Austria, 1850	5·7	Egypt, 1950	6·6
Bulgaria, 1880	6·7	Mexico, 1950	5·6
Poland, 1900	6·2	Ecuador, 1962	5·5

Abnormal proportions can be due to recent migrations, as in the United States in 1850 (4·3 per cent), or Ireland in 1880 (10·6 per cent). There may also be abnormal conditions arising from war; but in none of these cases, amongst young (i.e. underdeveloped) populations, are men aware of their own age, for lack of efficient registers.

The ageing of populations first appeared in France in the late eighteenth century and spread slowly to the other developed countries. It is more apparent with the feminine population, which is less subject to wars and migrations.

France	Out of 100 people		Out of 100 women	
	over 60	over 65	over 60	over 65
1776	7·3	4·4	7·3	4·5
1801	8·7	5·5	8·8	5·6
1851	10·1	6·6	11·1	7·2
1911	12·6	8·4	13·6	9·1
1921	13·7	9·1	14·5	9·8
1936	14·7	9·9	16·0	10·9
1946	15·9	10·9	17·9	12·4
1956	16·9	12·0	20·0	14·4
1966	17·7	12·3	20·6	15·0

Since the beginning of demographic evolution the ratio of over-60s has more than doubled, that of over-65s has increased by a factor of 2·5, that of over-80s by a factor of 5·5. For an idea of the number of old people in a pre-industrial population, imagine a present-day population with only two out of five of its over-60s, and two out of twelve of its over-80s.

Amongst other European countries, Sweden, and then Britain and Germany, were a long way behind France. Take for instance the over-60s.

Over 60s	France	Sweden	Britain	Germany
8 per cent of total in	1788	1860	1910	1911
10	1850	1882	1925	1925
12	1870	1912	1931	1937
14	1931	1948	1938	1950
15	1939	1950	1940	1954
16	1947	1956	1952	1960
17	1961	1959	1961	1962

The old have multiplied at the expense of the young rather than of the adult population, in *a long-term movement pivoting around a central age group.*

France	Numbers (thousands)			Percentages		
	under 20	20–64	65 and over	under 20	20–64	65 and over
1776	11,160	13,800	1,150	42·7	52·9	4·4
1801	12,090	15,130	1,600	41·9	52·5	5·6
1851	14,100	20,060	2,430	38·5	54·9	6·6
1881	14,300	22,120	3,130	36·2	55·9	7·9
1911	13,910	23,830	3,440	33·8	57·9	8·3
1921	12,270	33,013	3,514	31·6	59·3	9·1
1931	12,518	24,856	3,854	30·3	60·3	9·4
1936	12,446	24,676	4,058	30·2	59·9	9·9
1946	11,899	23,590	4,359	29·8	59·2	11·0
1956	13,349	25,054	5,244	30·6	57·4	12·0
1966	16,487	26,054	5,981	34·0	53·7	12·3

This movement was associated everywhere, except in Ireland, with a growth in absolute figures. Everywhere (except Ireland), even in France, the adult population increased when there was no war on. But from 1866 to 1946 the proportions of young dropped constantly: in all by about a third from 1776 to 1946.

Ageing continues everywhere, even though in developed countries each generation is slightly larger than the last. In a stationary population with Bourgeois-Pichat's biological mortality there would be 24 per cent over-60s; there are 17·7 per cent in France today. If populations continue to ensure no more than the replacement of each generation by the next, *this proportion will tend towards the* 24 *per cent norm.*[1] Here are some forecasts for various countries in 1980:

	1950	**1980**
West Germany	13·8	18·9
Belgium	16·0	18·6
France	16·2	17·2
Italy	12·0	16·7
Holland	11·6	14·4
England and Wales	15·7	21·0
Spain	10·3	13·6

Causes of ageing

It was long believed, and is still believed by some, that ageing was a result of a higher life expectancy. This, however, is a confusion between two factors. The figures quoted above show that reality is more complex. The French population, practically the only one to age during the nineteenth century, differed from the others, not by its low mortality but by its low fertility: Bourgeois-Pichat has shown that this is a general rule so far, except if there are migrations.[2] Take for instance the German population: in 1881–90 its birth rate was still 34·2 per thousand or approximately the same as at the beginning of the century. Its death rate on the other hand had dropped from about 30 to 22 per thousand, or by almost a third. But there were still only 7·8 per cent of over-60s, as at the beginning of the century.

A little thought will account for this apparent paradox. The drop in mortality has influenced the very young at least as much as the adults. From the point of view of age distribution it is the same to save a very young child and to produce another one. Only a drop in the mortality of the over-30s increases ageing. Up to now lower mortalities amongst the very young and very old have more or less balanced out, and even produced on the whole a slight tendency to rejuvenation, especially at the beginning of the trend. This is not of course a general law but a law of our times. Remedies for cancer or other illnesses of old age will increase the ageing factor, as they will have no effect on child mortality. Ageing coincided with lower mortality in many countries because the latter contributed in various ways to the drop in fertility, as we shall see when studying the social factors of fertility. This narrow link is of great sociological significance. Whether or not it is justified, the reluctance to create new life may reduce the vitality of populations.

---

[1] J. Bourgeois-Pichat: 'Essai sur la mortalité biologique de l'homme', *Population*, July–September 1952.

[2] See especially *Journal de la Société de Statistique de Paris*, March–April 1950.

Material consequences

Some are direct and some not. We shall study the first, leaving the others until we have studied 'moral' repercussions, an imperfect label for the attitudes of individuals and groups.

The old produce less than they consume and must therefore be balanced in society by sufficient numbers of producers consuming less than their total output. Every society must face this problem. The strength of human societies lies in the care they give to the weak. A population which sacrificed the weak to material gains would be on the way to decline. Ageing will therefore create problems in how to provide these surplus outputs. Some authorities (Mortara) believe that the lower burden represented by youth would make up for the increasing numbers of old to be supported. We shall discuss this opinion below. For the time being, we may, without being over-arbitrary, distinguish three historical phases in attitudes towards the old.

1. *The family system:* in an agricultural and patriarchal society each family organises its own compensations, and keeps no accounts. Here ageing could, theoretically at least, happen without serious trouble. (But this is a hypothetical situation: it seems that ageing is necessarily accompanied by social change.)

The two conditions of such a system are that the family should live together and have a common occupation; otherwise it begins to keep accounts, and these are liable to disrupt its solidarity. It requires less effort to feed someone at table if he is accepted in the house, than to send him regularly the cost of this food. The old system will only work in populations of the traditional type: the growth of towns causes splits between the generations.

In Europe this phase lasted until the nineteenth century. It survives, with varying degrees of change, in various country districts, and will continue for some time. But at the first cracks it gives way to the second phase.

2. *The capitalist system:* the disruption of families and the exodus from the country takes individuals out of their protective environment, and they begin to have to think *well beforehand* of their old age, and invest in their own future. At the beginning of the capitalist system this was a matter of saving up during one's active life, and spending the interest, and sometimes the capital, during retirement. The apparent infallibility of this procedure led certain authors such as Mortara and Naville to think that ageing would not create any economic difficulties: the old were merely putting off the consumption that their work had warranted. Numbers would not affect the issue, and in any case the debt owed to the individual did not vary. This was a simple view, confirmed neither by right nor by fact. Let us look at some precise instances very carefully.

Suppose wage-earners or self-employed workers invest part of their earnings personally to provide for their old age; the optimistic theories are confirmed for certain goods – thus a worker may build himself a house, stock it with furniture, linen and other lasting objects – but self-sufficiency is only possible for a few types of goods. It is not practicable to stockpile potatoes or electricity for the end of one's life. Social relationships are necessary: a person saving up accumulates credit on the future output of his country. This brings various individual and social disadvantages. On the one hand there are always spendthrifts and wastrels; the latter can hardly be left to die of hunger. On the other hand, although socially still a proletarian, the retired worker has become economically a capitalist, in possession of shares, land, or securities, and he thus, we now know, runs the risk of inflation.

3. *The socialist stage* makes saving compulsory. It links the various age groups at each moment in time, rather than the different ages of one man: those who are at work pay money directly to those who are no longer at work. It is very tempting to change to this system, since, by making the whole of the capital saved up beforehand unnecessary, it puts large funds into circulation. It is as if an insurance society were to realise all its reserves, planning to pay out future claims with future policies. But how does this system work from the point of view of distribution?

Here too there are risks: while being accumulated capital can easily be diverted from its social aim or devalued by a monetary crisis. This happened to the national insurance system in France after 1930. The old retain the right to a pension but this can only be raised by an increased levy on the adult age groups. Another disadvantage is that pensions never catch up with wages. Finally, it does not solve the difficulties created by ageing but rather emphasises them: when the number of pensioners increases, with those who are financing them remaining stable or even diminishing, financial balance is broken. It does, however, at least have the advantage of clarity: *instead of relying on the delusions of financial confidence, it allows the difficulties of ageing to be foreseen.*

Consider two populations A and B, identical to start with, where the adults save up and make productive investments, resulting in higher outputs. In population A the birth rate does not change and there is no ageing; in population B it drops and after a few years there is a decrease in the number of active adults. With more capital per worker will population B enjoy higher productivity, resulting in the same standard of living as that of population A? In theory a very small improvement would be sufficient for this.[1] But in fact all

[1] If P is the number of pensioners in both populations, p the pension they must have, a_A and r_A the number of adults and the productivity of population A; with a similar notation for population B; the incomes of workers will remain the same if

$$\frac{r_A a_A - Pp}{a_A} = \frac{r_B a_B - Pp}{a_B}$$

from which

$$r_B - r_A = Pp \frac{a_A - a_B}{a_A \cdot a_B}.$$

Suppose the pension p is equal to half the income of an adult, the number of adults in B these reasons are different versions of the superficial optimism about drops in population. Against them there are three kinds of objections.

1. *Economic:* productivity does not only depend upon capital accumulated per worker. One must take into account national overheads, the advantages of mass production and of division of labour and especially, in a period of technological progress, the need to change the occupational structure, which can only be properly done, as we have seen, during an increase in the active population.

2. *Sociological:* gains of this kind are dissipated before they have even been distributed. Relaxation causes loss of ground, as we saw in the previous chapters.

3. *Psychological:* in a capitalist and even in a collectivist society, if accounts are made for each firm it is very difficult to increase a proportional levy. An individual dislikes producing 12 and paying 3 even more than producing 10 and paying 1. He always tends to consider more or less consciously the 12 as his property, especially if the levy takes the form of taxation. In the example found in the footnote the income will drop from 15 to 13 without ageing and from 16 to 13 if there is ageing. The apparent levy will thus have increased by half. Whether legitimately or not, like any capitalist levy, it will be resented by the workers. They owe a debt to the pensioners, but in our times debts are rarely a factor of goodwill.

Up to now ageing has only been the result of lower fertility and the reckonings above are based on this. It is possible that in the future a new form of ageing might appear, with progress in the struggle against old people's illnesses. A remedy for cancer would extend our expectation of life by about four years which would be on the whole idle years, or an additional cost to society.

Will the lower cost of children make up for this loss?

The ostrich mentality has led many people to question the very existence of losses caused by ageing. So far, they say, the proportion of adults has not dropped. Therefore what you lose on the old you regain on the young. This is apparently true in theory. Here are the number of children per hundred inhabitants in France at various periods.

	1776	1851	1901	1951	1966
Below 18	42·7	38·4	34·3	29·9	30·5
Below 15	33·2	29·8	25·8	22·5	25·2
Below 10	23·4	20·5	17·5	16·0	16·9

one-fifth smaller than that in A, and the number of pensioners, P one-third of the number of adults in A. For equality to be satisfied the productivity of B need only be one-thirtieth more than that of A.

310

However the proposition is not fully confirmed, because:

1. The requirements of a child are smaller than those of an old person. The French *Commission Supérieure des Conventions Collectives* reckoned in 1950 the basic requirements of each age group. These are, converted into 1966 currency:

Below 3 years	8,600 francs
3–5	13,000
6–14	17,300
15–17	25,200
18–65 (single)	32,600
Over 65	22,500

So the average requirements of an under-eighteen are 16,400 francs, 27 per cent lower than those of an old man. A proper reckoning would have to take investment into account; but it is small compared with the cost of consumption.

2. The cost of a child is still borne largely within the family framework. Family allowances are a recent invention and in no country do they come anywhere near the size of a pension.

3. The extension of the school leaving age increases the cost of children. Their active life begins later and later: it began on average at fourteen and a half in 1901 and starts at seventeen and a half today.

Recourse to technological progress

The first impulse in this unbalanced situation is to turn to the universal remedy, technological progress, or rather the economic progress resulting from it. If the productivity of a worker rises by 15–20 per cent, one is tempted to think that it would easily make up a deficit of 10 per cent caused during the same period by the ageing factor. The choice of remedy is blameless, but it can hardly be expected to act at the same time on the various ills it is supposed to cure.

There is also a psychological block working against it: if productivity rises, together with incomes, it becomes more difficult in a collectivist than in a capitalist system to avoid raising pensions at the same rate. If a poor worker is able to afford running hot water it would be cruel to deprive him of the means for it after he is sixty-five. The unbalance exists as before, merely at a higher standard of living. Whatever the extent of technological progress, the factors retain their relative values.

The advantages of dynamic situations should, however, bend this logic. Sufficiently persistent technological development does in fact contribute to solving the problem of pensions by producing various time lags between the figures which obstinately refuse to come to a stable equilibrium. On the other hand any pause in progress stresses the ageing factor still more.

311

But appealing to technological progress for help is one thing and accelerating it is another.

The fundamental factor

The wish to elucidate this embarrassing problem without appearing antisocial by quoting unpleasant facts has led certain authors to write in terms of active life and average inactive life; as a result they begin to doubt that any problem exists. This is obviously sophistry. It merely shows that in another kind of system it might have been possible to solve the problems of ageing, without helping in any way to solve present-day deficits. No logic can get around the fact that the social security funds have to meet bills at fixed terms. In a distributive system the numbers of contributors and beneficiaries are the important fact.

In any case, in any system, the inactive live off the active. Only the form of the debt and its moral and legal justifications vary. When the ratio of old inactive people to active adults increases, the levy on adult output must be increased to the benefit of the former group. The question then is *who should pay for this and how the levy should be transferred*. The employers and the state try to remain in their present positions and pass on the responsibility to the wage-earners: either by reducing their pensions; or by increasing the worker's contributions, that is to say decreasing his wages; or else by moving back the retirement age, which changes the ratios. Wage-earners of course disagree, but there is an important difference between the attitude of individuals and that of the unions.

1. *Individuals*. Ask a worker to agree to a cut in his pension or wages, and he will obviously refuse. Ask him whether he prefers to retire at sixty or sixty-five, and he will often choose sixty: he takes his wages and pension for granted, assuming unconsciously that the extra five years should be paid for by his employers or the state.

But we might just as well have asked someone to choose between a house, and a house with a garden, without saying how much they both cost. Ask a worker to choose between retirement at sixty with a pension of £25 a week, or at sixty-five with £30 a week, and the answer is no longer obvious, for here he would be the one to lose by stopping work earlier. He would probably choose the second course, because he would be afraid of not finding work after retirement.

Individuals who can choose, such as peasants or artisans, stop work when they think fit, weighing up rest against income. If the question were put in this way, individuals would usually agree to make up for demographic ageing by prolonging their active life, exactly as they often agree to work overtime to increase their weekly wage.

2. *Unions*. The assumptions of the unions lead them to a different conclu-

sion. The lengthening of the working life is equivalent to an increase in the working population. This, they think, will favour the employers and give them an excuse to keep wages low. The collective interest of workers may be different from their individual interest. The unions thus object to putting back the retirement age, even when its implications are made clear, which is seldom enough. They are better placed in this matter than on the subject of the working week. No positive bargaining is necessary: they merely hold their position and refuse any wage or pension cuts, or change in the retirement age, and leave the employers and the state to find the necessary funds.

Their pressure is one of the main spurs to progress, especially where there is competition between firms; one is therefore tempted to justify it. Yet it is only partly correct to assume that the problems of pensionable age and of working week are similar. In the second case there is no transfer. If shorter hours were to raise productivity in such a way as to maintain output the only difference would be that work had been changed to rest. In the case of pensions, a levy has to be made on output, which is more difficult even if the output has increased.

Even if the union attitude is justified on principle, it does not in fact always produce the desired result. It does not invariably lead to a cut in profits, or to useful technological progress, or to a revolutionary breakthrough. The employers can retaliate, for instance by price increases: the correlation between ageing and the declining value of money in France is clear. The adult generation refuses to support the old and uses (unwittingly) the value of money as a weapon. The decrease in the real value of pensions has been tragic for the old. On the other hand an acceleration of technological progress as a result of union pressure can only, as we have seen, be partly effective. Remember also that the extension of school attendance, obviously necessary, implies an equivalent postponement of retirement.

There is no doubt that later retirement is beneficial to the leading classes and the government. But as things stand now it is not in the interest of wage-earners, especially if they are reformist, to oppose any such step. Or else they should also make precise proposals for the transformation of profit into pension funds: e.g. socialisation of retained profits or of town property values.

The Scandinavian socialists have given more thought to this matter than English or French socialists or union officials. They choose sixty-seven for the lowest pensionable age.

The lengthening of active life

It is perhaps vain to want to solve a partial problem by a general transformation of society. If a population, or a professional or autonomous body wants to equilibrate its system, endangered by ageing, there are three possible solutions: a cut in salaries, a cut in pensions, or a lengthening of active life. The third is by far the best. But it gives rise to strong objections, even from non-revolutionaries and neutrals, because it appears to be socially regressive. Men are so used to seeing the pensionable age brought forward that they do not understand how progress can seem to take a painful step backwards.

Yet ageing derives, we have seen, from the drop in fertility. Social security funds in France are unbalanced because there are insufficient numbers of adult workers. It is the failure of these creative forces that causes social regression. Still, five objections are commonly formulated.

The right to rest: it is inhuman to make old people work. *The principle is unquestionable, but its application is difficult.* We have seen the financial side; we have also seen that ageing, directly caused by the drop in fertility, coincided with a lengthening of life. There are four answers to this objection: 1. The laws of biological ageing have not of course been changed by science; the thirty-year old woman may well be still blossoming nowadays, but her menopause will not be a month later for it. But it is true that men have to work less strenuously than before. Far less muscular work is demanded of them. At sixty they are no longer physically wrecked by years without holidays and meals of less than 2000 calories, as was the case a century ago. If Jean Borotra, a tennis champion at nearly seventy years, had been employed in certain professions, he would by now have been retired, considered incapable of pushing a pen, whereas he can still drive a ball with great success. 2. Women do not generally benefit from the right to rest. They continue to do housework until their strength abandons them. The French pension laws, as most social laws, only apply to paid workers, in other words mainly to men. 3. Does the individual want to rest? It all depends how the question is asked. We have seen how peasants and artisans often choose to stop work later. 4. From the medical point of view, total idleness is often inadvisable.

Decreased ability with age: this is a point made by employers.

Unemployment amongst the young (a point made by the workers): it is indeed an unpleasant surprise to find an old man still active while a young man is out of work. Financially this is not at all advantageous in manual work, where unemployment pay and pensions are more or less the same. In intellectual occupations, it is often profitable, but not always.

Few fields cause more misguided passions than unemployment. Reason boggles at the horrible scourge. There are many sophistries based on an assumed limit to the number of jobs available, and on total interchangeability of workers. Easy formulas such as 'not one immigrant, not one hour of overtime as long as there is one man unemployed' have often ended up by increasing unemployment. For a pensioner this logic may appear more valid, since the old do not form a bottleneck, but have difficulty in finding work.

314

But let us proceed with care: we are once again faced with the tenacious preconception of the times by which society often makes surprising efforts to rehabilitate at any cost an invalid who may be unlikely to live long, but does not pay the same attention to the old, and even tries to eliminate them. Though the outcome is the same, society prefers to write someone off elegantly as 'pensioned' rather than as 'unemployed'.

It is also true that pensioners in search of work may find it if they accept lower wages. Early retirement is then a false solution, a Malthusian remedy which affects only the symptom and not the cause. Old workers are ill at ease in a new occupation. Any restrictions, such as work rationing, would be vain and inhuman: we have no right to exclude somebody from the social system. We should, in any case, remember that an old man at work consumes more and thus creates more employment.

The threat to promotion (in the case of white-collared workers): this is a powerful but superficial observation. Life is lengthening and with it active life, and also each part of active life. Compared with our fathers each of these has increased for us by a good third. We can hardly be expected to regret it and hope that life will pass more quickly, thinking, as do the soldiers in certain armies, that rapid wastage will bring rapid promotion.

Gerontocracy and its problems: it has often been pointed out that if gerontocracy is avoided, managerial staff find it particularly difficult to get new employment. A lower retirement age is suggested. However: 1. It is costly: idleness has to be paid for by someone. 2. The situation is partly due to an earlier drop in fertility, causing a cylindrical or an overhanging age pyramid. It is not the surplus of old people that should be blamed, but the lack of young. 3. Almost automatic promotion is not always related to individual output. Promotion by age may appear socially desirable, but in fact it puts the young at a disadvantage. The difficulty of re-employing an old person lies in his requiring a higher salary than a young person, without necessarily being more capable.

Towards a solution

With time the ratio of old people must continue to increase, and society must adapt itself to, and even forestall this phenomenon. One can form an idea of its extent by merely considering that in 1966 to give to every Frenchman over sixty the subsistence requirements estimated fairly narrowly at 500 francs (£40) a month by the unions, would demand a levy of £4,000 million a year, or approximately one-fifth of the total of family consumption, as well as causing a cut in the national output.

Legislation on pensions is too preoccupied with the erroneous, Malthusian, selfish desire to free the labour market. Retirement is an easy way in which society can get rid of a cumbersome member; but there is no valid reason for rejecting from the economic circuit anyone able and willing to work.

The sudden switch from full activity to total inactivity is physiologically bad. Geriatrics recommend progressive adaptation making allowance for individual features. Social biology returns to the attitude of peasants, who continue work in proportion to their strength.

Ideally, here as elsewhere, an individual should be able to choose freely between various solutions, equal from the point of view of society. This would involve taking real age as little as possible into account, and stressing the biological age and individual preference. Retirement would be progressive, and would conciliate economic, biological, and individual requirements. Practically it would be very difficult to achieve; but occupational advice from forty-five to fifty onwards would help enormously.

In intellectual sectors, and particularly with office work, one should avoid responsible positions all being held down by men who are still useful but are old-fashioned in their views. Careers should be differently geared so that they reach their peak before the end of active life. Former managers could be given special assignments and studies, leaving others to direct the business. Such a novel policy would of course injure many prides, but in fact private initiative has already brought it into being. Institutions should follow this spontaneous tendency.

Pensions should also increase with age, and be higher from about seventy to seventy-five, an age at which a man can no longer tend to his garden, keep his house properly, etc.

The rivalry between the generations

This is a more discreet, hidden version of the struggle between classes. However his subsistence may be assured, an old person lives in fact off the work of the adults. As long as these are multiplying at the right rhythm they can support him without much difficulty. But ageing disrupts this situation, and the lengthening of life also impoverishes the adult population. The average age of heirs to estates has risen from thirty-five to fifty over the last hundred years. Beyond a certain point this burden is no longer accepted. Demographic stagnation and its depressing effects has helped to make the necessary effort seem impossible. This is why France tasted the delicious poisonous fruits of chronic devaluation and rent control.

The French worker did not appear to realise that any weak solutions of this kind were mortgages on the value of money and that devaluation would be fatal to the old. No one, at any rate, said this in so many words. But it is *exactly as if the adults had decided to stop paying for the old*, while not helping the young either. Households headed by fifty year olds, with a good income, were only taxed at 4 or 5 per cent, whereas young households paid 25 to 30 per cent.

This age struggle did not appear openly, because personal positions are in fact more complex than social situations: a worker of forty may well have an invalid wife, bring up children and come to the help of his old mother. Besides, wage-earners need to stay united. Articles or speeches often refer to the old being shaken off the palm-tree, but usually as a plea for the old rather than a criticism of the following generation.

There is, however, a risk that the growing needs of the old may deprive the children rather than the adults. Funds needed to build homes and hospitals could well be directed to the building of schools. Numbers are sensitive to these facts: a man whose income is diminished by taxes or by pension con-tributions, whose house is reduced in size, may well decide regretfully not to have a third or even a second child. Society would thus slide towards inevit-able decadence, like a tree with too much foliage for there to be any young growth. This was the case with France for a long time and there is no certainty that it has been permanently avoided.

Segregation is inhuman

Every society tends to eliminate the undesirables more or less consciously (see chapter 6). This is the case with the old and their monetary pension. There are also efforts, often deriving from excellent intentions, to withdraw the old from social life into special towns, districts, estates. This causes suffering, for the old enjoy seeing youth and life around them.

Informed choice

The diverging views on the right policy for the old are essentially due to the lack of information and particularly to the neglect of demographic factors. It is vain to decide on any retirement age on principle. Choice depends on facts and possibilities, and one can then still have differences of opinion. Anyone is free to prefer the retirement age to be fifty or sixty as long as he is fully conscious of the restrictions that will ensue.

Moral consequences

The repercussions of ageing on the attitudes of a population are less clear than the material results. Theory does not help very much here; it is ill-informed, will answer as we like. Ageing has so far coincided with lower fertility, given a certain time lag, as we were saying in the previous chapter.

There remains to ask what the results would be of ageing purely due to pro-gress in the struggle against mortality. No social experiment exists to guide us.

We should be observing facts, yet at this point one has to stretch beyond them even at the risk of losing touch with them. Gerontological studies have not been directed towards this delicate matter very much. It will at least not be too much of a risk to assume that the attitudes of a population are related somehow to changes in the age distribution. Compare the make-up of the French adult population at various periods:

	1776 (men)	1901 (men)	1952 (men and women)	1966 (men and women)
21–30 years	27·0	22·8	20·5	16·7
30–40	24·1	22·6	17·4	20·9
40–50	20·7	18·4	21·0	17·4
50–60	15·1	16·6	17·6	17·6
60–70	9·0	12·3	13·0	15·3
70–80	3·5	5·9	8·2	8·7
80 and over	0·6	1·4	2·3	3·4
	100	100	100	100
Percentage of under 45s	62·0	55·0	48·4	48·1
over 60s	13·1	19·6	23·5	27·4
Mean age	38	42	45	46

These figures are based on electoral registers. If in 1966 the voting age were to drop from 21 to 18, the proportion of under-30s would rise from 16·7 to 22·3 per cent.

Certain national bodies have aged more, mainly because of their failure to grow. This is the case with political parties. Within each one there has been such an ageing of men and ideas that, *in spite of an almost uninterrupted series of 'left wing' victories over the last half century, France has almost continually, even before the reaction of 1958, been governed by a conservative majority.*[1] This is why political parties are afraid of the young: none has campaigned to lower the voting age to eighteen.

The same has happened on the individual level. The old are not all conservatives nor the young all revolutionary. But the young, being a minority, are condemned to suffer from the ageing of society and cannot contribute all their vitality, or shake the burden of idleness from above them. Only children, still numerous, are not, we have seen, in favour of large-scale changes. Those not

[1] Swings to the left in 1914, 1924, 1932, 1936, 1946, 1956; to the right in 1919, 1928, 1951, 1962. The moves to the right were not as strong as those to the left.

affected by the general apathy thus naturally incline to relatively extreme doctrines, or rather attitudes.

It is also worthwhile pointing out that as long as expectation of life fell short of thirty, technology, and with it institutions, did not vary. Now that men live to seventy, and the proportion of old people is larger, technology is moving, and causing, whether immediately or in the long term, important changes in institutions. Thus, *with history unrolling both faster and in a longer perspective than before, men see their life doubly increased. Their past is further and further removed from their present. They are inclined to be more and more behind their times.* In addition, capricious Nature has given men a particularly good memory for their youth and great difficulty in remembering the immediate past. This is one of the reasons why there is such a widely noticed contrast between material progress and what one might call, for lack of a better phrase, moral progress. The gap can only be narrowed by collective realisation of the evil there is in being seduced by the past.

Western societies must become conscious of this trend, which will only be evil if it is ignored. If a cure for cancer is found in the near future, there might be a quick change, demanding quick adaptation. There is an obvious antidote: not to let fertility weaken, and to look resolutely towards the future even if this means discarding the past.

Society may well one day find a way of coping with the ageing, or even with the diminishing of the population. This will only be made possible by an exceptional degree of self-awareness.

5

SOCIAL FACTORS OF MORTALITY

This chapter will only deal with mortality, though it would be better to study more generally the social factors influencing health, and to take account of morbidity. Unfortunately there is a shortage of statistics, so that we may only judge the state of health of a population by its most obvious result: death. Usually, morbidity and mortality vary together; but they are not rigorously in step, so that we shall have to qualify some of our conclusions.

The drop in mortality

This has been greater than anyone could have imagined over the last 150 years. Men's expectation of life has more than doubled, from thirty to seventy-two years in developed countries. New ways of preventing death are discovered every day. But this only applies to the external enemies of man: germs, viruses etc. The biological illnesses, heart diseases, cancer etc. have so far been more difficult to cope with. Most of the successes against cancer are achieved through surgery, which is not exactly a cure. In other words *the lengthening of life is the grandest result of our progress in the art of destruction.*

Leaving aside individuals, let us consider only sufficiently large and homogeneous groups to give some consistency to the concept of mortality.

There are two non-social factors involved: the physical characteristics of the group, and the climate.

1. *Races and the genetic heritage.* We have already referred to Bourgeois-Pichat's 'biological mortality', the mortality of a group of men assumed to possess all the possible resources of science and technology. With no other enemy than himself Man would live, in such conditions, for about seventy-eight years. This figure is not achieved in any country because preventive and curative care is never perfect. But it is worthwhile asking whether this biological mortality is the same for all races.

There is nothing to prove the contrary. The negro races are particularly prone to sleeping sickness, but the whites suffer more from other diseases. In any case, these are infectious illnesses, therefore curable. We must admit for the time being that seventy-eight applies to Bushmen or Indians as well as to Swedes or Australians. In the United States and in South Africa negro mortality is higher than white but this is for social reasons. On the strength of separate Japanese and American statistics, some authors thought that the

320

whites were more prone than the yellow races to cardiovascular illnesses. But the statistics on Japanese living in the United States are very similar to those on their white American neighbours.

Only in identical social conditions and culture (in the widest sense of the word) will it be possible to decide whether different races are unequally prone to death. Even these counts will show up a relatively recent genetic past rather than a fundamental characteristic of a racial group. The work of Dr J. Sutter and others has shown the close relationship between mortality and inbreeding.[1]

2. *Climate*. This is very difficult to measure statistically because it is a factor that cannot be isolated while the others remain constant. Generally when there are sharp contrasts or when special precautions have to be taken it is possible to speak, even without statistics in support, of unhealthy, lethal climates.

Their influence was preponderant for a long time, but it grows less every day, becoming negligible if sufficient precautions are taken. The great epidemics (yellow fever, cholera, malaria) are slowly disappearing. Mortality in Australia is one of the lowest in the world. In Ceylon it has dropped enormously in spite of the low living standards of the workers. Tropical lands formerly considered as insalubrious can now be inhabited by white families, even with young children. Climate is still important, but there is nothing to prove that the average age of seventy-eight could not be achieved in every country, given sufficient care.

It thus appears that nowadays variations in mortality are essentially due to social factors. Men of a certain group die faster than others because they are less well fed and heated, or cared for in the case of illness. In difficult climates mortality is still more sensitive to social factors: child mortality in a rich and educated population is very small even in the tropics, but it is large in an ignorant and poor population without medical care.

In any case a '*social*' *death is a premature death*. We must study the influence of social factors carefully.

Measuring social mortality

Soviet authors[2] often accuse bourgeois statistics of hiding social inequality by refusing to reckon mortality according to class. One smiles, at the thought of the total lack of Soviet Union statistics on deaths over the last forty years. If Soviet technicians have tried to measure the mortality of peasants, industrial and office workers, engineers, etc. they must be aware of the technical difficulties of this project, which seems simple. Mortality is a fraction: the number of deaths over the number of people liable to die. To measure this one needs:

[1] See the numerous articles on this subject in *Population*.

[2] See especially A. Y. Boyarsky and P.-P. Shusherin: *Demographic statistics*, Moscow, 1951, and the statements of the Soviet representatives to the United Nations Commission on Population.

1. The distribution of deaths by age, occupation or social position, which is not easy to come by. 2. Census figures by age, occupation, or social status, drawn up according to common criteria, which is very rarely the case since census operations and occupational analysis are administratively very different. A person questioned in 1962 on his occupation by a census agent may not give at all the same answer when he is questioned again in 1965 or 1970 by someone engaged in occupational analysis for the government. Certain occupations such as 'doctor' or 'lawyer' are well defined but this is not true of 'carpenter' or 'agricultural worker': the first may be a builder or furnisher, an employee or an employer; the latter may be an absentee owner, or a seasonal worker, or a permanent worker.

The margins of error in both terms of the fraction can accumulate and add up to enormous mistakes, and yet very slight differences are being analysed. Mistakes in direction are quite possible. However, a method has been perfected recently which consists in following a sample, and also avoiding cumulative errors. We shall see an application of it further on.

As well as these difficulties of identification there is the fact that mortality depends partly on a past situation. At the age of forty or forty-five many workers set up their own businesses. If they then die, even through occupational illnesses associated with their previous occupation, they swell the figures of employer mortality. Death is an integral, writes Bourgeois-Pichat. Also, in certain occupations, because they are less healthy than others, there is a medical or spontaneous physical selection at the outset, causing lower mortalities. Statistics might lead one to believe that mining is good for the constitution. These are not the only causes of errors.

When the geographical distribution of people is narrowly related to their social conditions, it may give us clues as to the influence of the latter. Thus, there are administrative districts with a majority of smallholders. But here too we must step carefully: a mountain district such as Haute-Savoie should not be accused of high mortality without the reservation that many deaths occur in sanatoriums or amongst weak people who come in search of the pure mountain air, and go on practising their trade. Such migrations can seriously perturbate statistics for certain age groups.

Comparing the mortality rates of the districts of a town classified according to relative wealth is more reliable. Yet there are still risks:

1. Deaths do not always occur at home, and if hospitals and nursing homes are grouped in one district they will give it higher figures. This can only be eliminated where deaths are registered at the place of domicile, a difficult administrative procedure which has only spread recently in France and is still not generally practised. But mistakes can be avoided by considering various districts together. Also, the margin of error stays more or less the same at any time, so that one can still make comparisons.

2. The populations of various districts do not have the same age distribu-

tion. This factor can be eliminated by careful reckonings based on the fact that the population is generally younger in poor districts.

3. There is no rigid barrier between rich and poor districts.

All these causes tend to reduce the differences between ratios: any differences that may still appear are therefore significant and probably larger than they look.

First observations: from Moheau to Quételet

Moheau, as early as 1778, first compared the mortality of the total population to that of people of independent means; and the mortality of Paris to that of a monastic order. In both cases he found appreciable differences. But these still tentative statistics were soon forgotten, and the dominant class often managed to challenge or minimise the existence of differences, saying for instance that adaptation was possible. However, in 1828 Dr Villermé[1] published his *Mémoire sur la mortalité dans la classe aisée et la classe dirigeante*, followed by his famous *Tableau de l'état physique et moral des ouvriers* (1840). In 1829 Chateauneuf wrote *La durée de la vie chez les riches et chez les pauvres*. The results were striking but not rigorously worked out.

In 1865 Quételet and Heuschling[2] compared the tables made up by Duvillard for the whole of the population and by Deparcieux for *tontiniers*, obviously more wealthy than the average; but no conclusions were drawn from these comparisons. The two tables, though not strictly comparable, show an appreciable difference in expectation of life: almost six years at birth (28 years and 9 months for Duvillard and 34–35 years for Deparcieux). These were already old documents, relating to a premedical era. Interest was obviously increasing in whether medicine had affected the class differences. But such counts were very risky.

Districts of one town

This is the type of count that gave the most interesting results at the end of the nineteenth century and until 1950. In 1897 Bertillon compared the districts of various large towns, classified by living standards reckoned according to taxation brackets. L. Hersch[3] repeated the count in greater detail in 1920, dividing the various administrative districts of Paris into four groups, and observing very great differences. The following tables reproduce the figures for Paris from 1891 to 1946, eliminating the age factor.

[1] See J. Daric, 'Mortalité, profession et situation sociale', *Population*, October–December 1950; E. Védrenne-Villeneuve: 'L'inégalité sociale devant la mort dans la première moitié du XIXᵉ siècle', *Population*, October–December 1961.

[2] 'Statistique internationale', *Population*, Brussels, 1865.

[3] 'L'inégalité devant la mort', *Revue d'économie politique*, 3–4, 1920.

Arrondissements (districts)	Crude mortality rates (per thousand)			Corrected rates (per thousand)		
	1891	1936	1946	1891	1936	1946
Wealthy (6ᵉ, 7ᵉ, 8ᵉ, 9ᵉ, 16ᵉ)	15·8	10·3	10·4	16·8	9·6	9·5
Average (1ᵉʳ, 2ᵉ, 3ᵉ, 4ᵉ, 5ᵉ, 10ᵉ, 14ᵉ, 15ᵉ, 17ᵉ, 18ᵉ)	21·9	12·9	11·3	22·6	12·5	11·3
Poor (11ᵉ, 12ᵉ, 13ᵉ, 19ᵉ, 20ᵉ)	25·3	13·4	11·5	23·9	13·7	12·0
Paris	22·5	12·2	11·2	22·5	12·2	11·2
$\frac{\text{Poor}}{\text{Wealthy}}$ mortality	1·60	1·30	1·10	1·42	1·43	1·26

Although the reckonings probably understress the difference, it is still noticeable. Already in 1936 the gap seemed to be closing, but this was without the correction for the age factor; only in 1946 did the gap really decrease, probably because of social security. It would be very useful to reckon separately for each sex but here there are not sufficient statistics to reveal differences clearly enough.

A similar analysis for child mortality gives the following deaths per thousand births.

Arrondissements	1891	1936	1951	1956
Wealthy	91·9	47·2	24·1	20·2
Average	135·3	61·7	36·5	28·2
Poor	157·2	72·2	33·2	23·9
Paris	136·3	63·5	34·4	25·3
$\frac{\text{Poor}}{\text{Wealthy}}$ mortality	1·71	1·53	1·54	1·18

The gap between rich and poor districts has narrowed noticeably here. Mortality in the poor districts is even lower in 1956 than in the middle districts, though this is probably accidental and unimportant. In spite of the improvement there is still strong social inequality. We shall see however that child mortality is not *directly* dependent on economic resources. It is rather their indirect consequences (housing, education, mother at work) that still affect strongly the life expectancy of the young. There is even greater inequality here for them than for adults.

The social inequality in death is stronger for exogenous illnesses (tuberculosis, alcoholism, etc.) than for endogenous ones (cancer, etc.), as we shall see further on.[1]

Direct surveys

These have been carried out in various countries recently to gauge the influence of social condition.[2]

In France mortality according to socio-occupational group was studied with sufficient standards of comparison, on men aged twenty-five and fifty-five in 1955.[3] The INSEE has been following for the last few years a sample of 460,000 men taken from the 1954 census, and has published the main figures for the period 1955–60.[4]

Occupations	Survivors of 70 from 1000 men aged 35	Corresponding life expectancy at birth, according to United Nations tables
Schoolteachers (state)	732	75
Professionals and directors	719	74·5
Engineers (industry)	700	73
Catholic clergy	692	73
Management		
—Public	664	71
—Private	661	71
Farmers	653	70
Foremen and skilled workers		
—Public	653	70
—Private	685	62·5
Office workers		
—Public	633	68
—Private	623	67
Employers in industry and trade	631	68
Semi-skilled workers		
—Public	590	63
—Private	576	61
Agricultural employees	565	60
Labourers	498	53
	—	—
Total for France	586	63

Mortality from 35 to 70 is relatively high for men in France because of the

[1] See L. Hersch, *Pauvreté et mortalité selon les principales causes de décès à Paris*.

[2] See J. Daric, article quoted above, pp. 680–91.

[3] Febvay and Aubenque, *La mortalité par catégorie socio-professionnelle*, Etudes statistiques, I.N.S.E.E., 1957.

[4] G. Calot and M. Febvay, *La mortalité différentielle suivant le milieu social*, 1965.

influence of alcohol, so the standard United Nations table probably gives relatively low and more widely spread figures. It would be more instructive from our point of view to have the corresponding figures for women.

Such as it is, the range of expectations of life for labourers runs from really backward countries in Latin America and the Far East to the advanced western countries at the top. *But the economic level is less important than the cultural level.*

The difference between the public and private sectors for a given occupation is due to higher entrance selectivity in the public sector, whether spontaneous or intentional, and to better welfare and the different way of life.

Here are the mortality quotients for 1000 people aged 36 to 45 for certain causes of death, in two occupations with low mortality and two with high mortality.

	All causes	Tuber- culosis	Alcoholism and cirrhosis	Heart and arteries	Cancer and other malignant tumours
Engineers (private)	23·8	1·9	1·1	3·4	4·7
Management (public)	22·8	1·0	1·7	2·7	5·1
Labourers	56·8	4·2	7·4	3·4	4·4
Agricultural employees	42·6	2·8	5·5	2·6	3·5

The differences appear clearly: for exogenous causes, they reach a factor of between 3 and 7; with endogenous illnesses the difference is non-existent or even reversed.

In Britain after each census the Registrar-General publishes mortality rates by occupation, standardised to eliminate the spurious age factor.[1] Here are the figures for men aged 20–64 from 1921 to 1950 for England and Wales, reckoned from a mean of 100.

	1921–23	1930–32	1950
1. Professionals, directors	82	90	97
2. Farmers, tradesmen, management	94	94	86
3. Craftsmen, skilled workers, office workers	95	97	102
4. Semi-skilled workers	101	102	94
5. Unskilled workers	125	111	118
Mean	100	100	100

[1] L. Tabah, 'La mortalité sociale: Nouvelle enquête en Angleterre', *Population*, January–March 1955. *The Registrar-General's decennial supplement. England and Wales* (1951). *Occupational mortality*, 1957.

The gap was large in 1921–3 but decreased markedly in 1930–32. In 1950 labourers were still victimised, but the first category was no longer ahead of the middle categories as a whole. For the higher age groups there is now almost total equality.

Reckonings have been made in the United States for five social categories,[1] similar though not identical to the British ones, separating agricultural workers completely. The spread is much larger than in Britain, especially for 'non-whites'. The Welfare State seems to make a big difference.[2]

Child mortality

This is strongly influenced by the social conditions. R. Debré quotes the frequent case of a child sent out to nurse and dying in the country from digestive troubles. One could blame this either on the ignorance of the nurse, or on the social situation of the mother who had to send the child away, or to unwillingness to keep it at home and feed it oneself, or to the lack of medical and hospital care.

For the first time in France and probably in the world, an exhaustive enquiry

Socio-occupational category of father	Total	Endogenous	Exogenous
Businessmen	15·6	10·1	5·5
Intellectuals	16·1	11·9	4·2
Management and senior civil servants	16·1	10·9	5·2
Professionals	16·6	11·9	4·7
Wholesale dealers	17·7	12·3	5·4
Intermediate non-manual	18·1	12·3	5·8
Schoolteachers, medical and social workers	18·5	13·0	5·5
Office and shop workers	22·3	14·1	8·2
Shopkeepers	23·4	15·2	8·2
Skilled manual (self employed)	24·1	15·1	9·0
Skilled workers and foremen (employees)	25·4	14·8	10·6
Sailors and fishermen	27·4	16·8	10·6
Farmers	27·5	16·9	10·6
Semi-skilled workers	29·4	15·8	13·6
Agricultural workers	31·7	17·2	14·5
Labourers	40·5	18·4	22·1
Miners	40·6	16·0	24·6
Total	26·5	15·2	11·3

[1] M. Moriyama and L. Guralnick, 'Occupational and social class differences in mortality. Trends and differentials in mortality'. *Milbank memorial fund*, 1956.

[2] See also E. M. Kitagawa and P. M. Hauser, 'Social and economic differentials in mortality in the U.S., 1960'. *Congrès international de la population d'Ottawa en 1963*, Liège, 1964.

was begun in 1951 into the nature of child mortality. The death and birth certificates of young children were compared, in order to achieve the greatest possible accuracy of result. The survey was repeated a few years later for the generations born in 1959 and 1960. The results for legitimate children in these generations are given above in rates per thousand.[1]

The differences are much larger for exogenous (ratio of 6 to 1) than for endogenous mortality (ratio of 1·6 to 1). We also notice, here and in other figures, that cultural level has a predominant influence. Thus within a given income bracket, schoolteachers and medico-social employees have a lower mortality than shopkeepers, or intellectuals than wholesale dealers.

Generally, income as such is not an important factor. Nursing a child costs almost nothing, and in a developed country good milk is not much more expensive than bad milk. But mothers only too often encounter difficulties when they have to work away from the home; hence high mortalities amongst illegitimate children.

In the United States the social condition of coloured people has a strong influence on child mortality. Here are the figures for 1000 live births in 1963.[2]

	White	Non-white
Mortality amongst newborn	16·7	26·1
Mortality up to 1 year	22·2	41·5

The figures for Britain are similar to those for France. The influence of social class is less marked for endogenous mortality but is still there. Here are the results of a survey, made in 1958, of perinatal mortality (stillbirths and deaths in the first four weeks).[3]

Professions	69
Other non-manual occupations	80
Skilled workers	96
Semi-skilled workers	108
Unskilled workers	128
No husband	140
Average	100

All these figures confirm that child mortality varies inversely with education. Ignorance is more deadly than poverty. Second to this comes the lack of organised welfare: the mortality of aristocratic children two centuries ago was far higher than that of the children of Dutch workers nowadays. Even if the latter

[1] See the article following Croze's paper at the International Congress in Ottawa, in *Population*, August–September 1964.
[2] *Statistical abstract of the United States*, Washington, 1965.
[3] E. and S. Livingstone, *Perinatal mortality*, London, 1963.

were deprived of welfare there would still be an appreciable difference because they are more educated. But in any one period knowledge is often hitched to wealth, though there are frequent mistakes on this point.

Suppose that a group of highly informed European intellectuals were forced by circumstances to emigrate to South America and to live there in poor houses with low wages. Mortality amongst their children would be far lower than for those of the workers in their new country, and only a little higher than that of the intellectuals back in Europe.

Rapid improvement in medical and social services

This has occurred in many countries since the war without the other factors, notably the economic conditions, having undergone any appreciable change. Here is the mortality in three countries at different stages of development, compared with their situation before the war (rates per thousand).

	1938–39	1950–51	1963–64	Drop over 25 years (per cent)
Ceylon	21·4	12·7	8·2	62
Formosa	20·0	11·4	7·6	62
Portugal	15·4	12·3	7·9	49

Developed countries would have needed far longer to achieve a similar drop. Twenty years ago, or even more recently, the experts would have thought it unbelievable that a poor population could lower its mortality rate so much: the life expectancy of Puerto Ricans, Ceylonese etc. is today higher than sixty, or longer than that of the Belgian or the Frenchman in 1938 although they had a far higher standard of living. These figures show how important medical and social services are.

Similar medical and social services with different standards of living

Consider again the old survival tables of Duvillard and Deparcieux: in the eighteenth century medical and social services were no better for the rich than for the poor; the doctors used to kill as many people as they saved. But undernourishment was a large factor amongst the workers: their living conditions and mainly their diet were the main cause of the difference in life expectancy between the greater part of these populations and the moneyed classes. Amongst the higher age groups overnutrition, common amongst the rich, must have caused a large number of deaths. We may expect a minimum gap of six years in expectation of life as a result of poverty.[1]

[1] According to Moheau expectation of life at 20 was 33·5 years in the Paris region for the population as a whole, and 39·9 years for a monastic order.

329

Nowadays, as we have seen, the economic level only plays a small part. There may however be large differences in underdeveloped countries.

Sudden drops in the standard of living

At certain times (war, economic crises) the standard of living (or economic power) drops markedly without any particular damage to the medical and social services or, especially, to the fund of knowledge. Figure 68 shows the progress of general mortality from 1906 to 1943 in France, Germany, and Britain, with the periods of large falls in the standard of living shown in thick lines.

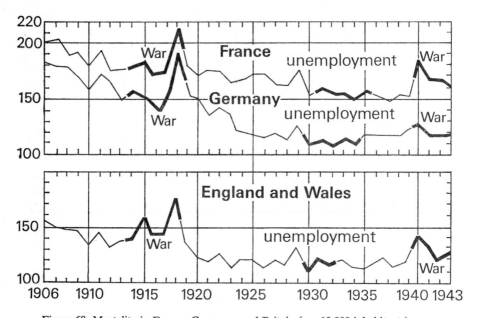

Figure 68. Mortality in France, Germany, and Britain (per 10,000 inhabitants).

It is often believed that the great unemployment crises are deadly, but their influence is now negligible. In Germany for instance the number of totally unemployed was over six million in 1932–3 and there was also a high percentage of partially unemployed – yet mortality went on dropping at the same rate as before. This may be due to the food consumption holding up through unemployment crises, at least through the ones of the 1930s. The lower demand influenced industry and investment, and the overall consumption in vital products did not suffer much from the crisis. The distribution however did change. Office workers, civil servants, employed workers increased their purchasing power at the expense of the totally or partially unemployed. Generally, in spite

330

of the economic distress of a great part of the population, mortality dropped: medical and social services were intact, indeed must have been improving.

Conversely, in 1936–7 the purchasing power of the working class increased strongly for a time; again mortality was not affected.

During the two World Wars there was a noticeable drop in the standard of living, even in food and fuel. But mortality only increased slightly, probably mainly through violent deaths caused by bombing. The high point of the mortality caused by the pandemic 'flu was situated in 1918. But some neutral countries were as strongly affected as those at war. There was no similar outbreak during the Second World War. The high level of 1940 was due to the exceptionally cold winter. We are a long way from the enormous increases in mortality which used to stem from bad harvests and wars. At the time of the inflation, and the occupation of the Ruhr (1923), the Germans were saying that their younger generations had been so affected by years of war and misery that their teeth were in an alarming state. The same generations, however, survived throughout the years of unemployment and, without any apparent weakness, made up the core of the storm troopers of the Second World War.

In 1940–41 French sociologists, doctors, and dieticians were alarmed, and expected a high mortality and an increase amongst illnesses of malnutrition, because of the low food supplies. Persistent undernourishment did indeed bring higher mortality, mainly through tuberculosis. But it was lower than they had thought. The doctors noticed that most people achieved a new balance after losing weight for a period. Sport was never interrupted because of undernourishment. The same occurred in other western European countries at this time: the return of prisoners in ill health, the shortage of drugs, and accidental factors played as large a part as undernourishment. In the wine producing areas in the south of France the inhabitants tried to replace food by wine, and mortality rose more sharply than elsewhere. But really serious increases of mortality were only noted in far more serious situations such as that of Holland in 1945, Leningrad in 1941–5, Malta in 1942–3.[1]

The Second World War showed that to reach the threshold where mortality increases strongly, the various European standards of living would have to drop considerably. The higher mortality amongst the less favoured classes was generally balanced by the drop in over-feeding and alcoholism. The most interesting experience was that of Switzerland, which conducted continuous scientific observations of a population with a limited food supply properly rationed.[2] The daily food consumption (rationed goods and others) oscillated around 2000–2200 calories, 60–62 grams of proteins, 45–7 grams of fats.

[1] See H. Bergues, 'Répercussion des calamités de guerre sur la première enfance', *Population*, July–September 1948.

[2] The figures are given in an exceptionally interesting work, P. A. Fleisch's *Ernährungs probleme in Mangelzeiten. Die schweizerische Kriegsernährung 1939–1946*, Berne, 1946.

Statistics on the frequency of illnesses are usually incomplete and strongly influenced by fortuitous epidemics. The conclusions one can draw on the question of public health or of the physiological value of foods are thus uncertain. In Switzerland the annual frequency of infectious diseases that had to be declared (not including 'flu) increased slightly, mainly because of a diptheria epidemic. During the six war years the frequency of illness amongst school children in Lausanne was 10 per cent lower than during the five years immediately before the war. Absenteeism at school, recorded from 1935 to 1946, diminished during the war years. Illness amongst the 60,000 workers, which had risen regularly before the war, suddenly dropped sharply until 1943.

Probably the wartime diet actually improved public health, in spite of the lack of albumen and fats, at least until 1943. Mortality from infectious diseases other than diphtheria dropped, which points to increased resistance. Though war food was very starchy, deaths from digestive illnesses and appendicitis diminished.

Death by tuberculosis, which was dropping constantly before, stayed practically the same throughout the war; but the illness itself spread fairly widely. Specialists attribute this to increased physical and mental stress, more frequent social contacts, better diagnosing through radio photography, and lastly the minor influence of wartime food.

The surveys and statistics of A. Roos on the pattern of dental illness during the war suggest that it had a particularly good influence: the number of fillings per 100 school children dropped by half, the number of extractions by five-sixths. All the school dental clinics announced a regression of caries. This improvement is attributed to the favourable effect of wartime food because of the restrictions on sugar and sweets and the substitution of brown for white bread.

After the war, with the arrival of eight million refugees in western Germany, and the large scale destruction of housing, many Germans lived for a long time in cellars or overpopulated dwellings. Here are the mortality rates per 1000 compared to those of Switzerland.

Year	W. Germany	Switzerland	Year	W. Germany	Switzerland
1938	11·4	11·6	1947	11·6	11·4
1939	11·9	11·8	1948	10·3	10·8
1946	12·3	11·3	1949	10·2	10·7

After a small maximum in 1946, western Germany mortality dropped below that of Switzerland, which had been spared the war. And yet the post-war figures were swollen in Germany by the deaths of war casualties, by retrospective war-time entries, and by the absence of three and a half million young men who would have brought down the average. This is because the standard of living and of food did not fall below the critical threshold, and the medical and social services were maintained if not improved. The refugees were poorer, but under better supervision, and had a lower mortality than the rest of the population.

An observer only able to judge the historical progress of men through their mortality would for a long time have spotted the incidence of famines and rigorous weather conditions. Today he would spot some hard winters but miss economic and social crises and even perhaps the odd war too.

Mortality by country

The various countries of the world have different economic and cultural levels and different kinds of medical and social services. The richer ones are also better educated, more health-conscious, and better equipped socially. It is therefore no surprise that the average life-span is far shorter in India than in Sweden. But by comparing countries with certain characteristics in common we may be able to bring out the influential factors, amongst developed as well as underdeveloped countries.

Here are the positions of fifteen developed countries classified first according to national income per inhabitant and then by expectation of life, in 1965.

Position	National income per inhabitant ($'s)	Country	Life expectation at birth	Position
1	2710	USA	70	12–15
2	2350	Sweden	75	1–4
3	1900	Switzerland	73	7–8
4	1760	Canada	72	9
5	1570	New Zealand	75	1–4
6	1520	Australia	74	5–6
7	1410	W. Germany	71	10–11
8	1410	Denmark	74	5–6
9	1400	France	71	10–11
10	1285	G. Britain	73	7–8
11	1270	Belgium	70	12–15
12	1250	Norway	75	1–4
13	1060	Netherlands	75	1–4
14	930	Austria	70	12–15
15	740	Italy	70	12–15

These are fairly rough comparisons and classifications. A complete analysis should properly be based on the level of wages and the income of small farmers. But despite the narrower spread of expectations of life which form the second classification, the latter is notably different from that of incomes: although wages are generally higher in Belgium, mortality is lower in Holland than in Belgium. In the United States the expectation of life at birth is lower than in many poorer countries with a better social security system and no doubt also a higher average cultural level.

In underdeveloped countries the differences in mortality are more closely related to the standard of living, though not necessarily. Thus the smaller mortality rates in the Far East, especially with child mortality, contrast with the high rates in many African and even Latin American countries. Here again the cultural factor is important, not merely as a sign of literacy but as a pointer on the way of life.

Town and country[1]

The country was for a long time, and quite rightly, considered more healthy than towns. It has generous supplies of sun and oxygen which are rare in the town. Thus physically inferior, the town also has its classical social ills: drink, prostitution, slums, etc. But this habitual opinion is now outdated. The older districts of towns are still dark and stuffy, but the modern estates are far better placed. Density is the important factor: shanty towns, inhabited by so many social wrecks, have lower mortalities than apartment slums. Spacious modern towns also have many sanitary advantages: there is a better chance of finding good milk or meat in an industrial suburb than on a farm. Medical and social services thrive amongst high densities. A multimillionaire living in the country might well die before the doctor can get to him or because the right equipment is not at hand.

This new situation also exists in countries less developed from the sanitary point of view. Urban mortality is lower than rural mortality in Brazil, though the age distributions would suggest the opposite.

The difference in general mortality between central Paris (9·1 per thousand) and the rest of France (11) in 1964 is probably due to the age distribution. But this cannot apply to child mortality: from 1934–8 to 1950 the exogenous infant mortality in France dropped by 36 per cent; in Paris it dropped by 49 per cent. Meanwhile endogenous mortality, more subject to curative care (midwifery, surgery, etc.), dropped from 14 to 13 per thousand for the whole of the country and from 15 to 10·5 per thousand (by 30 per cent) in Paris. In 1964 overall infant mortality was 19·7 in Paris and 23·8 per thousand in the rest of the land.

To try to eliminate the influence of social levels, partly linked to regional differences, here are the child mortality figures in 1959–60 for the whole of France and for central Paris, for various occupational categories.[2]

The particularly large differences for unskilled labour stress the usefulness of social and medical services.

[1] See below pages 437 to 443.
[2] Again, from *Population*, July–September 1964, p. 745.

Socio-occupational position of father	Seine département	France
Liberal professions, intellectuals, managers and intermediate	14·4	17·3
Employees	20·0	22·3
Employers (trade and industry)	18·1	23·0
Skilled workers	20·8	25·4
Semi-skilled workers	23·1	29·4
Unskilled workers	30·0	40·5
	19·3	26·5

A reservation must still be made: a comparison between the general sanitary conditions might favour the town less than the comparison of mortalities. Because there is less medical care in the country, the same illnesses are liable to be more dangerous there.

Notice also that alcoholism, a widespread factor of mortality, is by no means a privilege of the town. It has spread in the French countryside, with the connivance of the authorities, and contributes in various indirect ways to the higher mortality.

Mortality according to sex

The difference between the mortality of the sexes at a given age is determined both by physiological and by social factors.

More boys die than girls, for physiological reasons. Where the opposite is recorded it is due either to a statistical error or to a peculiar social circumstance: it can occur in retarded populations that girls do not receive medical treatment.

At relatively high ages, again more men die, but it is difficult to separate the effects of physiological from those of social differences largely due to eating, drinking, smoking, working habits.

Overnourishment and alcohol

Overnourishment certainly has an effect on mortality, but statistics on it are as yet very imperfect. The older the patient the more rigorous the diet prescribed by doctors, but this is largely a result of individual opinions. We do not know the extent to which a diet of more than 2800 to 3000 calories, or a certain quantity of fats, really encourages mortality.

Social differences in mortality do indeed decrease with age and even change direction in certain developed countries after sixty. Also Italian mortality, for instance, is higher than English mortality in the low age groups, but lower in

335

the high age groups. But it is very difficult to isolate the influence of moderation in food. Research in the United States, mainly carried out by insurance companies, has strongly denounced obesity as a cause of death, but has not come out firmly against excessive food. Physical activity of course has a corrective influence.

Remember the useful influence of rationing in Switzerland during the war, analysed by Fleisch. It seems that similar observations were made in Sweden during rationing.

Alcohol indirectly causes many deaths in some countries, but they are classified under the name of the actual illness. It is largely responsible for the higher mortality amongst males aged 30–60 in France, as the remarkable work of S. Ledermann shows.[1] Wealth would be an aggravating factor here if it were not usually linked with the cultural level. Poverty is all too often associated with ignorance, or with a great difficulty in finding any other alternative or escape.

Other toxic bodies, such as drugs, obviously have an even worse effect on the body. But they are much less widely consumed.

The minimum subsistence

These comparisons underline the essential influence of medical and social care and of the cultural level past a certain economic level. The latter, which determines in a way a vital minimum, is lower than one usually thinks. The figure of 2800 to 3000 calories, often quoted as a minimum, is excessive from the point of view of mortality. But dietetic experiments can give no precise indication here, so it is perhaps better to retain these high figures than to err in the other direction.

In any case, confusion should be avoided between the optimum and the minimum. There is an optimum diet, both from the point of view of quantity and of distribution, which should be achieved and not passed. It is hard to estimate precisely, since it obviously varies with age, sex, size, work, and perhaps even temperament; 2400 to 3000 calories seems to be a plausible margin for men. Below this comes an undernourishment threshold, beyond which mortality increases through a lower resistance to illnesses such as tuberculosis. This may be due to partial malnutrition, in proteins for instance, so that it is very difficult to state a level in calories. But the Swiss experience showed that if rations are well balanced they can fall without danger well below 2400 calories. Lower still there is a famine threshold, below which mortality increases noticeably. This was passed several times during the war as Miss Bergues showed in the article quoted above (p. 331).

[1] S. Ledermann, *Alcool, alcoolisme, alcoolisation*, I.N.E.D., 1956 and 1964; See also G. Malignac, *L'alcoolisme*, P.U.F., Paris.

In our ignorance on these matters it is easier to resist malnutrition by merely eating more. Here, ignorance itself can increase mortality. Undernourishment no doubt causes fewer deaths than ill-balanced diets.[1]

These remarks on mortality are not, however, applicable directly to sanitary conditions. Where medical and social care is speedy and well organised, a state of imperfect health will appear far less in the mortality statistics.

General remarks on social mortality

For a long time Man's only recourse against death was to tend as far as possible to the demands of his body, by precautions against cold, undernourishment, etc. Curative medicine was of no practical use against mortality. The social factor was only appreciable amongst undernourished populations, where the rich or the powerful could protect themselves against famines or chronic shortages. But the upper classes were more prone to accidental death, especially where they consisted of a military aristocracy.

The era of fast continuous technological progress brought two changes: 1. Economic: an increase in the resources available (starting between 1650 and 1800 in developed countries). 2. Sanitary: more effective hygiene and medicine (starting, in most countries, with the spread of smallpox inoculation around 1750).

These two factors have cut general mortality but increased social differences in mortality. For some time the rich were practically alone in enjoying medical care, because of both cultural and economic levels. For a tragic period in the early nineteenth century this advantage was combined with their traditional economic supremacy.

In a second phase towards 1840–50 in France and Britain, the resources available clearly increased faster than the population, lifting the standard of living of the poor above the vital threshold and reducing their mortality. Then came the Pasteur revolution, which also favoured the wealthy classes to start with, and at last the extension of medical care through the general increase in incomes, social work, and social security. But because of the very development of knowledge, the influence of the cultural level has become predominant.

Figure 69 shows this pattern very approximately. No scale has been included,

---

[1] Compare the nutrition offered by 1 franc's worth of milk and meat in Paris in 1965.

	Milk	Steak
Amount	1·4 litres	71 grams
Protein	40·8 grams	12·6
Fats	46·6	7·6
Glucides	58·3	0·6
Total calories	818	106

This difference is not widely known, even amongst educated people

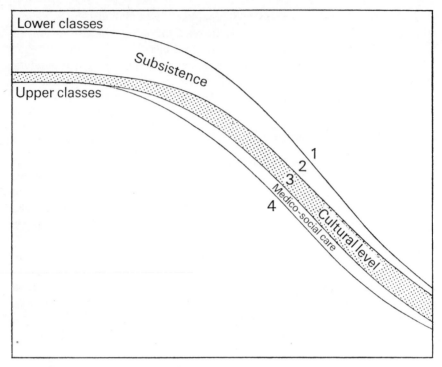

Figure 69. Social inequality in the face of death.

on purpose, since it is impossible to reckon, even roughly, the relative importance of each factor during each period. Besides, the trend may have varied according to countries, with different intervals between the various developments. The area called 'socio-medical care' is a function of economic level and of various factors, of which the main one is rural isolation. The total influence of the economic factor is a sum of its two side effects, the one on subsistence and the other on socio-medical care. Both have largely diminished, the second later than the first, with the advent of social security.

Generalisations[1]

For a national group mortality is a function of: 1. The climate. 2. The genetic factor in the wider sense. 3. The scope and the human and technological level of medical and social services. 4. The general economic level, *especially* that of the poorer classes. 5. Medical and social aid given by the community. 6. The will to use these various means, reflected in customs, habits, the way of living.

[1] See also the remarks in part I pages 220ff. on the division of activity between sanitary, economic and pleasurable pursuits.

Legislation against alcoholism and individual reactions to it are an instance.

These factors are not independent: thus where the third rises, the influence of the first drops.

Before defining the mortality of a social group, let us analyse the factors affecting the attitude and the behaviour of *the individual*: 1. *Power*: mainly the economic power, called rather too vaguely standard of living, or rather too precisely purchasing power. It leads to the satisfaction of vital needs (food, heat) and gives access to medical and social care where these are commercialised. In a socialist system, political or administrative power can also play a part. 2. *Knowledge*: in hygiene, dietetics, child rearing, etc. 3. *Will*: apparent in the way of life, and very precisely in the carrying out of doctor's prescriptions.

We now turn to *social groups*. We may neglect the first three factors, above, since they are usually the same for the whole country. Here mortality is a function of: 1. The material aid given by the community in the form of medical and social care, and sometimes also housing or material benefits. 2. Power (economic especially). 3. Knowledge, or cultural level. 4. Will-power.

Certain factors may be difficult to classify. For instance, mortality amongst the relatively old in upper classes is high, because of excessive activity, worry, and stress. It may be countered by a strong will to live but even then there are occupational, therefore economic, imperatives. In the same way, alcoholism is connected with both the cultural level and the will to live.

The lowest possible mortality

What conditions would a social group have to satisfy, in the present state of knowledge, to obtain the lowest possible mortality? We leave aside for the time being all genetic factors including genetic planning, to consider only the influence of the environment.

One would ideally need a rational diet, with no excess, and perfectly regular habits, and this would mean such sacrificing of other objectives that one would end up with a servile population submitting entirely to controlling authorities, and in a closed environment, completely sterile and no longer allowing any social life. In other words, it is an uninteresting theoretical extreme; anyway, such ideal physical conditions would not necessarily lengthen life, because they might cause mental disorders. In practice, low mortality can be achieved given a sufficient economic level, a high cultural level, medical and social services, assuming naturally that longer life is thought desirable.

In the near future, since medicine is still more effective against exogenous than against endogenous mortality, it seems that various developed populations will approach Bourgeois-Pichat's 'biological' age of seventy-eight. There is already a certain amount of levelling off amongst countries and social classes. Accidents will still take place, of course, but they are essentially exogenous.

Their relative importance increases and becomes considerable for certain age groups (thus 10–20 years). One can place in this category any death which could have been avoided and is due merely to a total disregard for hygiene: for instance a child left carelessly near an open window in winter.

However, the efficiency of medicine against endogenous deaths (especially cancer and diseases of circulation) is no longer negligible; continuous progress, even a revolution, in this field could lead to an expected life span of eighty years.

To go beyond this would involve finding ways of avoiding physical senility, by treatment at or before puberty. Any forecast here can only be subjective, and even affective. Nothing is impossible but nothing is yet done. One point is certain: in spite of the great store of social hypocrisy it will become more and more difficult to refuse an individual positive care on the grounds of his social status. Social mortality will not disappear but it will become less and less intentional or taken for granted.

6

GETTING RID OF THE UNWANTED

Physical organisms eliminate unwanted toxins and dangerous or useless bodies in order to preserve their life or their good working order. Human society too tends to eliminate unwanted members, either useless or dangerous, more or less discreetly, more or less unintentionally. The useless ones are those who cannot contribute to economic and social life: the old, the ill, the invalids, the unwanted new born, etc.; the dangerous ones are the criminals, the degenerate, the antisocial, the madmen, or even sometimes the political enemies, the members of other races or other religions. They can be eliminated directly, by murder, expulsion, exclusion; or with hypocrisy, through bad treatment, refusal of care, even abandonment.

They can be eliminated by individuals: a girl strangling a new born baby, a murder committed for theft or in a fit of passion. But such acts are not being considered unless they can be ascribed as a group to a collective wish in society. We also exclude wars, which will be dealt with later, in chapter 22.

In primitive societies the positive method could be used fairly systematically; the famous custom of shaking the old people off the branches of palm trees seems to be a legend, but other fairly rigorous tests are known to have been used. The respect owed to old people is a reaction against this instinctive tendency, on the part of the social body, or of the old themselves, who persuade the younger generations of their great wisdom or even of their supernatural powers.

Child exposure

This was practised in classical times, and also in a rather different form in modern societies. The probability is that the exposed children will die and population growth will be avoided; and yet no child has actually been killed, each can chance its hand so to speak, and the gods will decide on its fate. Society thus eliminates human beings without having to lift a finger against them, and feels that it has not killed while at the same time it has not had to keep its children. Responsibility is transferred on to the gods. The system was reinforced by the spread of legends telling of exposed children later reaching high positions in society.

The early industrial societies were more dishonest: they simply abandoned children. The practice was to all intents and purposes perpetrated systematically to limit the population without officially allowing infanticide. In Paris before the Revolution more than six thousand children were abandoned every year; amongst these were particularly shocking cases of groups of infants brought there for the purpose. They were given only summary care and suffered a very high mortality. Some sources suggest that the survival rate was 1 in 10 to the age of twenty years; other authors say 1 in 50. Though proclaiming officially that growth was desirable, society took no steps to remedy this situation, and of course no one, unless perhaps the king or God, was responsible for the deaths: the parents left their child in the care of a hospital or some conveyor; the hospital authorities lacked the means to bring the children up properly, and so forth.

Even the Church tolerated the practice in certain circumstances. Lecoq, the superior of the Eudist order, wrote:[1] 'Several theologians, among whom Grandin (in *De Religione*), share the feeling, and argue that parents may do this without sinning, *ob extremam aut vere gravem necessitatem*'. He quotes the case of a woman fearing the return of her angry husband, become a father in his absence. Father Sémelier did not object, in certain circumstances, to children being abandoned and exposed at church doors:[2] 'If the council of Mâcon suffers and allows children born of criminal mothers to be exposed at church doors . . . it is to prevent them actually killing the children'. This is a classical case of a concession made by authorities threatened by the graver offence, which exercises a more or less conscious blackmail.

If such a massacre of innocent children can have occurred at a time when officially population growth was desired, imagine what it must have been in societies where growth was feared.

Prisoners, invalids, madmen

Throughout the centuries the art of spiriting away the unwanted has been perfected. Until very recently prisoners, invalids, and madmen were hidden away and subjected to extremely difficult conditions to produce high mortality: this was not consciously wanted or measured, and was not seen as a massacre, but merely as a series of natural deaths leaving room for newcomers. No one felt individually responsible; society, to preserve its peace of mind, merely had to avoid publicising certain excesses and any kind of statistics on mortality. In 'normal' times orders from above prescribe humane and protective measures for the prisoners; but the orders weaken as they descend the hierarchy, until they are only a pious intention. Inversely, reports of a more and more selective nature are passed back from the prisoners up to the authorities. Public opinion is never very curious on such points; it has no wish to be informed of practices which it might be held responsible for. Occasionally a veil

---

[1] *Traité de l'état des personnes pour le for de la conscience*, Rouen, 1777.

[2] Abbé Boucher, *Conférences ecclésiastiques de Paris, sur le mariage*, 1761.

is lifted. Between the wars Albert Londres' famous report on prison colonies, called *Dante n'a rien vu*, made a sufficient stir for transportation to be abolished.

Very recently, from 1940 to 1945 in France and other countries, mental invalids (and probably prisoners too) were decimated in their institutions, with no premeditation or evil intention. It was merely decided to give priority rations to schools and canteens, and let the other institutions drop below the minimum subsistence level. During the siege of Leningrad the soldiers protecting the town continued to draw normal rations at a time when the civilians were in great distress. The soldiers themselves wanted to share but the authorities had their plan: their object was to avoid at any cost the town being taken by the Germans. In the light of this civilians were not exactly unwanted, but in the hierarchy of utilities and requirements in this society, their lives ranked low; incidentally they would have ranked even lower had the town been taken.[1]

These recent examples explain, without excusing it, society's behaviour towards abandoned children, prisoners, and madmen. It is a modern idea, occurring in an opulent society, to care for them or at least respect them. Formerly, humane treatment would have been a drain on national resources, even supposing wastage had been cut down in other sectors, because not only would the unwanted have multiplied through lower mortality, but each would have required more funds. Brutal treatment was doubly 'economical' at a time when the value of men was, fairly 'logically', held to be rather low.

Outcasts and maladjusted

Another way of eliminating people consisted of two stages: men maladjusted for various reasons to social life and especially to work, became beggars, vagabonds, 'marginals' as we would say to-day.[2] They left the social framework because of unjust taxation, a levy or a minor crime. In a second stage, this led them indirectly either into prison, and the category already described, or into physical decay causing high mortality.

Good people, of course, protested against beggary and suggested bringing these strays back to work, in other words to the soil. But again goodwill was not enough; large sums would have had to have been spent and no doubt exact and impartial reckonings, in terms of human lives, would have shown that such an operation would not have been profitable.

[1] A. Woerth, *La Russie en Guerre*, vol. I, 1965.
[2] See especially A. Vexliard, *Introduction à la sociologie du vagabondage*, Paris, 1956.

'Innocent' genocide[1]

The mass elimination of unwanted men has not yet disappeared. The American Indians, the Australian Aboriginees, and others were recently exterminated in all innocence. There was no plan for a massacre, no executions, no gas chambers; the rulers merely organised their own life comfortably in accordance with their interests. If these populations had avoided being unwanted, by agreeing to work for the rulers, they would have survived and perhaps even multiplied as did the Negroes in the United States or in South Africa. Their quiet, unconscious exterminators have not been blamed at all by world opinion, whereas those who allowed conquered populations to live and even helped them to multiply (the French in Algeria and the Europeans in South Africa) let themselves in for a rough time; in Algeria they even brought about their own expulsion. International ethics are such that while colonisation is frowned upon, murder is allowed, providing it is discreet and not publicly announced.

The word *genocide* was only coined when this very old practice became so to speak officially recognised, therefore unacceptable. In the Soviet Union the period 1918–38 was marked by a very high increase in mortality that cannot be accounted for by the famines. Probably more than a million died in concentration camps, but not by execution; fortune was hard on all the prisoners, but only chance decided between them.

The Nazis used both methods: as well as consciously exterminating Jews in the gas chambers, they also applied the Russian policy in many camps, where intensive mortality was necessary to make place for the new arrivals, but executions were not needed.

There was also a high mortality amongst slaves, but it varied according to the situation. The value of a slave depended essentially on the cost of replacing him. When this was very low (because there was a war or the slave trade was easy) the masters were not encouraged to preserve their goods or take care of them as they would have done for domestic animals. In both cases of course, their attitudes were not rationalised; those responsible merely knew that they were not taking anyone's life.

The secret button

Opinion in the West is now conscious of the fast demographic growth in the Third World. Large scale publicity is given to the 'rise of the coloured peoples' or to the swarming of the hungry; Westerners feel rather like masters or servants in a castle, watching great masses of ragged people multiplying in the countryside around, obviously to no good intent. If a public opinion poll were to ask whether a few hundred millions should be exterminated with

[1] See also below, chapter 20.

napalm or atomic bombs, only a minute number would answer yes. It would however be very different if one asked, with full guarantees of secrecy, the following question:

'If, by merely pressing a button, you could cause the death of a hundred million Indians and two hundred million Chinese, with no suffering, and in entire families so that there would be no human distress, what would you do? I leave you before this box and you are free to put a white or a black ball into it.'

The question could be put to other races, probably with similarly disastrous effects.

Social hypocrisy is such that in certain circumstances indirect solutions of a similarly invisible kind may exist. It has been suggested, with all due euphemism, that one could reduce medical aid to countries that already experience great difficulty in keeping their healthy inhabitants alive. Even in rich, developed countries, funds devoted purely to health are very limited; only the anonymity of the many premature and avoidable deaths saves the situation.

Selection of the strong[1]

It has been suggested that mortality was, physically, a necessary selective factor, and that where it drops the quality of the population will diminish. Were not the 50 per cent who survived to twenty in demographically primitive populations better equipped for life? Various authors adopted this easy opinion (Hooton, Carrel), only to be refuted by Sand and Cépède, more from humane principle than by logic. It is still impossible to answer formally, but it seems that if there is such a thing as selection, it is far less important than might appear at first. Many perfectly constituted children are carried away by some infectious disease that others resist who may grow into sickly adults.

European stock has produced a more athletic population in America, as is shown in sporting events where other conditions (selection techniques and training) are equal. This may be the result of self-selection at the outset, or of a favourable climate in the more general sense, or of the elimination of the weak during the pioneering period. The sporting achievements of Negroes in the United States and other parts of America seem to point to the third explanation, since there was ruthless selection, not exactly at the outset but during the period of slavery.

This is a really unpleasant theory, since it seems to argue for abolishing medicine. But a proper consciousness should not prevent one from acting humanely. 'Inverse selection' did not exist as long as medical progress mainly affected exogenous mortality. Now that endogenous deaths are prevented, the situation is different: diabetics and haemophiliacs can now very often reach puberty and transmit their illness.

[1] J. Sutter and J.–M. Goux are the recognised authorities on this problem.

345

The phenomenon probably also applies today to higher age groups, and contributes to the slight increase in mortality noted amongst old people in very developed countries; but in this case there are no genetic results.

The elimination of degenerates

Direct action can make them physiologically or socially unable to reproduce: only their descendants are eliminated. But sterilisation can be very harsh on a human being.

Certain hereditary faults eliminate themselves: those which cause physiological sterility or death before puberty. The visible ones, with dominant characteristics, disappear more or less spontaneously since the victims do not find a partner. This is not true of recessive forms, which leads some people to advocate sterilisation in order to suppress the faulty gene. Like most eugenic policies, such racial purism is less attractive than it may seem at first. Cases such as that of Martin Kellikak, whose children from his first wife, who was weak in the head, were as degenerate as those from his second wife were brilliant, are dangerous to argue because they isolate and concentrate to the extreme a normally diluted phenomenon.

But sterilisation seemed, at the beginning of eugenics, to be in the line of progress. Some even saw in it a perfect Malthusian method for reducing the poor population and the burden it represented for the rich. McBride in 1936 advocated the compulsory sterilisation of parents who could not bring up their children without the help of public funds. Such theories are based mainly on two reasons, both altruistic and egoistic: 1. One should prevent people being born unhappy. 2. Society has a right to protect itself against those who might bring into the world men capable of harming it, and who will in any case be a burden.

The first is the kind of reason that cannot be proved or disproved. There is no way of knowing whether simpletons or cripples regret having been born. No evidence exists that more of them commit suicide. The other reason is more sincere and far-reaching, but could be dangerous if applied too generally. In some countries even the worst criminals no longer risk the death penalty, and this is the general tendency. If one reverses it, there is very little to stop the disregard of life from spreading. Of course, taking away life and preventing it from appearing are two very different things, but it is obvious that mankind must be extremely careful with the idea of racial purity.

In fact, as with many problems insoluble on the ideal level, this one can be clarified by descending to the particular cases, and trying for each one to weigh up the disadvantages and advantages of the method. First, sterilisation can really only be carried out on homozygotes, a small minority. Secondly, arithmetic will show that in a group where marriages are made at random sterilisation is only useful in the case of frequently occurring malformations.

Over 150 years, or about five generations, sterilisation would reduce the frequency of a character by 60 per cent if it were carried by 1 per cent of the population initially, and only by 10 per cent if it were initially carried by one in ten thousand; and it never totally disappears. As with many social and physical ills it can only be repressed within certain limits, beyond which further efforts have no appreciable result. It only needs a gene to enter the group from outside for everything to be put into question. It is as difficult as trying to keep weeds out of a garden exposed to the wind. In a population divided into isolates or semi-isolates, where marriages are not made at random, sterilisation would be more efficient because the heterozygotes would cross more frequently.

Sterilisation is in any case most inconvenient; it involves violating the private lives of individuals, setting up a complicated procedure, demanding difficult sacrifices. Its disadvantages are such that it can only really be justified in the case of frequent malformations in small populations. The disappearance of isolates, the laws against consanguine marriages, the general mixture of populations, constitute, in most cases, grounds for avoiding this radical remedy.

But the multiplication of hereditary illnesses, for whatever reason, may change the situation one day. There are two possible causes: 1. Medical progress may allow carriers to live longer and procreate more: as with diabetes since the discovery of insulin; or with haemophilia. 2. Radiation affecting genital cells: a disjointed hip condition, for instance, which may have been caused by a mutation due to radium in the soil, has spread widely.

Considerations of public health may make sterilisation seem more attractive; but it is a slippery slope.

Social elimination

The physical elimination of certain categories of undesirables is often, as we have seen, a two-stage process. First comes social elimination, the milder of the two, widely practised in our days of strong temptation. People are left with the means to subsist but their living conditions are forgotten and they are to all intents rejected. This is the case with old people: though great efforts are deployed to cure the victims of accidents or of certain handicaps, this is no longer acceptable where old people are involved (see chapter 4). Everyone thinks that the general intention is to provide them with a comfortable retirement and avoid their having to make tiresome efforts, but social hypocrisy is strong here, and everyone blames everyone else for the poor results.

This exclusion causes excessive mortality due to both material poverty and moral distress; but society, unable to measure exactly, is therefore able to appease its conscience.

7

SOCIAL FACTORS OF FERTILITY

The concept of fertility is more complex than it seems. First of all, a fundamental distinction should be made between fertility and fecundity, *Fecundity* is the reproductive potential of a species: it is a biological concept. *Fertility* is the result observed in a given group over a period of time: it is a statistical concept with social relevance.[1]

Definitions and measurements[2]

Let us attempt a more precise definition. Assume for the time being that the various races or human groups are equally fecund and that this fecundity is constant in time; we may then be able to define and measure human fecundity by the number of children that one thousand women in the most favourable conditions would have during their fecund life (i.e. from puberty to menopause). This is the most convenient and easy definition; there are others involving the interval of time between generations. The fertility of a generation (i.e. one thousand women of the same age) can be measured by the number of children the generation has produced.

It is more difficult to define and measure the fertility of a whole population, since it consists of several generations which may follow different patterns. However, in order to study the social factors of fertility, it is not absolutely essential to agree on a rigorous definition: the laws influencing these factors are far from being sufficiently precise to be measured. Even the qualitative causes are often controversial.

Human fecundity

The natural or physiological fecundity of mankind is imperfectly known and has only recently been examined. This may appear surprising, but biologists cannot measure it because it is largely a question of chance, and of considerable disproportion between causes and effects, defying the most precise measurements.

[1] Note that French demographers use these two words with reversed meanings, thus betraying etymology.

[2] We only give the absolutely essential concepts here. For more information on definitions and counts the reader may turn to specialised works, mainly R. Pressat's *Traité d'analyse démographique*, 1961, and his *Travaux pratiques*, 1966.

Where laboratories can provide no answer, statistical observations are better placed.

Before these began, people were content to quote extreme examples such as that of the woman with twenty-two children, of which none were twins. This may have defined an upper limit, but did not give any clue as to averages or dispersal around the mean. Until recently only the vaguest notions existed of the minimum and mean intervals between two births, with no contraception.[1]

The problem has been approached in very varied ways: by observing either populations reputed to have practised no contraception, or small contemporary groups who for one reason or another refuse these practices, at least for a period of time (large families aiming at the Cognacq award, voluntary samples studied medically, etc.).

Before describing the main results of this research here are some thoughts on the social conditions in which human fecundity can be most efficient. To reduce the concept to its biological, animal level, one would need establishments part stud and part clinic, where women would live in the most favourable conditions, and the authorities would if necessary vary the progenitor or try artificial insemination. As with the search for the lowest mortality, this would produce a servile population. The eighteenth-century utopians (Campanella) and the misguided progressists of the nineteenth century (Binet-Sangle, Vacher de Lapouge) who advocated such systems were mainly inspired by qualitative racialist aims (see page 510n). If such experiments were made on a fairly large scale we would of course have much clearer ideas on human fecundity; though that should not make such a system any the less reprehensible.

The main figures

If a couple comes together at puberty, stays together until the woman's menopause, and has no recourse to contraception, its average number of children will be about ten. In a population living in the best possible conditions this would probably increase to twelve. The dispersal around this mean would be large: some couples are sterile, others can have twenty to twenty-five children.

Fecundity varies from one woman to another, as P. Vincent showed, but it is difficult to measure dispersal around mean fecundity. It is even more difficult to determine the fecundity of a given woman or a given couple. If two couples in similar conditions and not practising contraception have had in their lives respectively three and twelve children, this merely shows that the

---

[1] Here, the first research was published by Pearl just before the war (*Natural History of the Population*, O.U.P. New York, 1939). Then in 1941 C. V. Kiser and P. K. Whelpton made a large-scale enquiry on fertility in Indianapolis and published the results in a series of volumes. Research has spread since the war in France (P. Vincent, L. Henry, J. Sutter, J. Bourgeois-Pichat), and in the United States (Westoff, R. G. Potter, C. Tietze, Freedman, F. Notestein, R. K. Stix etc.). In Canada there is also the research of M.-J. Henripin.

second is probably more fecund: an opinion that can only be formed after the event.

It is possible, indeed probable, that ethnic or national groups are unequally fecund. But the differences are probably very small and certainly smaller than the degree of precision of present-day measurements. It is safer for the time being to assume uniformity.

The number of ten or even twelve is very much lower than the number given by dividing the period of fecundity (thirty-five years, i.e. 420 months, or say 360 months) by the gestation period, even extended to ten months: this gives us forty-two or thirty-six children: a number never observed, except with instances of twins, even for exceptionally fertile women. This is because conception is a chance phenomenon. A woman's probable fecundity during any one cycle, is always well below unity. Also, it drops with age, from twenty onwards, because of three physiological factors: 1. The proportion of definitively

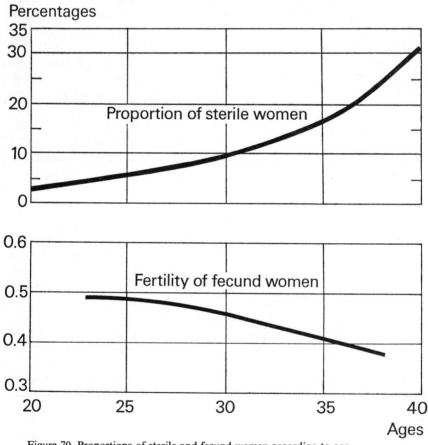

Figure 70. Proportions of sterile and fecund women according to age.

sterile women, small at first, increases. 2. The temporary break in fecundity during and immediately after gestation, lengthens. 3. The fecundity of still fecund women decreases.

Proportion of completely sterile women

Even gynaecologists have little information on this important factor. Figure 70, using the results of Henry and Vincent, gives the sterility curve; it must be noticed that it is approximative and provisional and only intended as an illustration.[1]

Thus at the age of thirty, one woman out of ten is definitively sterile. Unless this is caused by a physiological peculiarity, which can generally be noticed at puberty, a doctor cannot judge the sterility or the fecundity of a woman. One can only talk of a probability.

Fecundity of still fecund women

The temporary lack of fecundity consisting of gestation plus a few extra months varies with certain factors, especially but not invariably lactation. This period has not been well studied; it generally increases with age and causes the chances of conception to diminish.[2] According to Mrs K. Dandekar,[3] this period is of fourteen months, probably a high figure.

For a woman who has become fecund again, the probability of conceiving in any one cycle drops. For young women it is of approximately 30 per cent; one finds higher figures quoted, but usually because authors have observed more or less selected batches. This probability, which naturally varies with the amount of intercourse during the fecund period, drops slowly at first and then faster, again helped by the lesser frequency of intercourse. Here it is obviously difficult to separate social from physiological factors and eliminate the first.

[1] It was obtained by observations of married women, and is therefore a measure of the sterility of couples, though in most cases this boils down to a study of the woman. Since these results are only used for cases involving couples, they remain valid; but in certain cases a sterile woman might be more fecund if artificial insemination were practised from a donor other than the husband.

[2] See L. Henry, 'Mesure du temps mort en fécondité naturelle', *Population*, April–June 1964; 'Variations du temps mort avec l'âge de la femme', *Population*, January–March 1966; R. G. Potter and collaborators, 'A case study of interval dynamics', *Population Studies*, July 1965.

[3] *Demographic survey of six rural communities;* see also *Population*, 1960, pp. 144–7, and 1965, p. 405.

Towards fecundity tables

Bourgeois-Pichat has begun research on these lines.[1] When sufficient experiments have been made it will be possible to draw up fecundity tables, which will be more complex than survival tables, or at any rate than biological survival tables, which also refer to optimum conditions; they should give, assuming that couples are constantly together and do not practise contraception, the pattern for a group of 100,000 women in each month after puberty, following the criteria as shown below.

Number of children	Sterile	Temporarily sterile		Fecund	Total
		Pregnant	After pregnancy		
0					
1					
2					
3					
etc.					
Total					100,000

If this table were established for each month, there would be 400 versions of it, but one could of course use longer intervals (every three or every six months). One could also take into account mortality.

For the time being let us merely give the fertility of an average couple in two populations.

Age of woman at marriage	Canada (eighteenth century)	Crulai (Normandy)[2]
15	12·0	9·28
20	10·8	8·28
25	8·0	6·13
30	5·3	4·05
35	2·8	2·15
40	1·0	0·75
45	very low	very low

If one knows the fecundity in each month of a given period one can already, by a simple reckoning of composite probability, deduce the chances of any woman of becoming pregnant during the whole of the period. Thus if we take a short period, during which fecundity during one cycle is fairly constant, the following table gives the probability of a pregnancy during a given period.

[1] 'Les facteurs de la fécondité non dirigée', *Population*, July–September 1956, pp. 401, 407, 416.

[2] See L. Henry and E. Gautier, *La population de Crulai, paroisse normande*, I.N.E.D., Paris, 1958.

Period	10 per cent	15 per cent	20 per cent	30 per cent
1 month	10	15	20	30
2	19	27·5	36	51
3	27·1	38·6	48·8	65·7
4	34·4	47·8	59·0	76·0
5	41·1	55·6	67·2	83·2
6	46·9	62·3	73·8	88·2
1 year	71·8	85·8	93·3	98·6
Mean delay in conceiving	10 months	6 months	5 months	3 months

For instance, if the probability of her conceiving during one cycle is of 20 per cent, a woman has 59 chances out of 100 of conceiving over an interval of four months. This elementary arithmetic should be more in the minds of the family planning specialists. Imperfectly known, it leads to many mistakes, as we shall see in the next chapter.

Sanitary factors

Ill health can influence fertility either through mortality, or by temporarily reducing the ability to conceive. Some venereal diseases can bring about temporary or permanent sterility by preventing intercourse. Other fairly mild illnesses can make it difficult. The birth rate always drops momentarily nine months after a 'flu epidemic. Yet over-work, food shortages, etc. do not seem to have an appreciable effect on fecundity: they act directly on birth, increasing the incidence of abortion and still-birth.

J. de Castro said, and he has been much quoted, that too much food, and particularly meat, reduced physiological fecundity. His theory had occurred often before in history. Charles Fourier first put it forward as part of his *gastrosophie*, and Doubleday took it up in *The True Law of Population*. He was imitated by Spencer. But no experiment backs them up, and all existing statistics contradict them. None of these theorists were able to distinguish between properly physiological and social factors. It is fairly obvious that well-fed populations usually have fewer children, but this fact needs to be properly interpreted. It is because they are developed and have large enough incomes that they are both well-fed and provident; physiology has nothing to do with it. Besides, many populations have been very fertile as well as eating a great deal: all the expansionist groups, and also the French-Canadians in the eighteenth and nineteenth centuries, the Hutterites, etc. Experiments made on rats by Slonaker, Karlson, Hoelzel, cannot invalidate these human instances.

353

The marriage system

We have seen that human fecundity can only be used to its full effect in socially unacceptable conditions. Various marriage systems can be placed differently in relation to the theoretical maximum (always assuming that there is no contraception).

Marriage may at first sight appear to be a check on fertility, as is any institution limiting or regulating sexual intercourse. But in practice it works the other way by diminishing the fear of, or increasing the desire for children, and creating physiologically favourable conditions. Amongst the various systems that have existed in the world, monogamy is the most fertile. Polygamy is less prolific, in spite of prevalent opinion, which neglects for instance the fact that the men with the most wives tend to be very old. Promiscuity and free pairing usually occur in bad sanitary conditions. The most fertile groups are the strictly monogamous ones, providing their chief material needs are well met and they marry fairly early.

Influence of mortality

We will therefore now assume a monogamous system, and study the fertility of a couple. Even if remarriage followed any death instantaneously, adult mortality would still reduce statistical fertility, since it is as if entire couples were to disappear before finishing their procreative period. But the actual birth rate might not suffer. In an extreme example, if all human beings were to die at forty-five, the drop in births would be smaller than that of the whole population. In fact a reduced mortality generally causes a higher birth rate.

Let us apply two different mortalities to a fecundity of the Crulai type: a high mortality (with no medical care but no famines) typified by Duvillard's survival table, and a low mortality, that of women in France in 1950–51. We assume that remarriage occurs instantly after a death:

Age of the woman at marriage	High mortality			Low mortality		
	Children	Gross reproduction rate	Net reproduction rate	Children	Gross reproduction rate	Net reproduction rate
15	7·85	3·81	2·02	9·13	4·43	4·20
20	7·25	3·51	1·76	8·17	3·96	3·73
25	5·48	2·66	1·25	6·05	2·93	2·75
30	3·69	1·79	0·78	3·99	1·94	1·80

Thus even with no medical care, if everyone married by twenty-eight the net reproduction ratio would be higher than 1. A population fulfilling all three conditions: full marriage, full fertility, and biological mortality of the Bourgeois-Pichat type, would double every thirteen years. Of course, this has never occurred in practice. The nearest case amongst those studied appears to be that of Quebec province around 1850:[1]

Age period	Fertility in period	Total fertility from beginning of period to age 49
15–19 years	0·041	7·96
20–24	0·273	7·76
25–29	0·420	6·40
30–34	0·386	4·30
35–39	0·308	3·11
40–44	0·145	1·67
45–49	0·019	0·95
Total (15–49)	7·96	

The gross reproduction ratio of this population was 3·86. This real fertility was not of course the maximum fertility, since girls did not all marry at fifteen and, though economic conditions were not exactly poor, they were not perfect.

This example shows that *a population with sufficient food and a healthy life should increase fairly quickly even without proper medical care.* If we apply Duvillard's mortality table to the Canadian fertility just quoted, the net reproduction ratio becomes 1·67, i.e. a population doubling in a little over forty years. At this rate our numbers would have been multiplied by 10^{12} in the last two thousand years.

High mortality has not been the only check. A population with natural fertility, similar to that of nineteenth-century Quebec, should have a birth rate of approximately 60 per thousand.[2] In fact 50 per thousand is rare, even taking into account the failure to record children dying a few days after birth. This discrepancy is due to social factors, either direct (celibacy, late marriage, contraception, induced abortion), or indirect (miscarriage caused by fatigue or undernourishment, sterility caused by difficult childbirth or venereal disease, etc.).

We are thus led to study the various factors of infertility preventing this maximum social fertility.

[1] See P. Vincent and L. Henry, 'Rythme maximum d'accroissement d'une population stable', *Population*, October–December 1947. Since this article, mortality has dropped considerably.

[2] Quebec province did reach 60·1⁰/₀₀ in 1834–40. But in 1850–60, though there was still no contraception, it was only 45·1⁰/₀₀. The average for the period 1830–75 was 50·6⁰/₀₀. Earlier, in 1760–70 the rate of 65·3⁰/₀₀ had been achieved, but at this time the population was abnormally young.

Celibacy

We are concerned here with total celibacy – the influence of the marriage age is studied further on.

We know very little of the frequency of celibacy before the age of statistics. In the first centuries of our era, the Church prized celibacy and continence but this does not provide one with any quantitative conclusions. In a population where age at marriage for women follows the pattern of nineteenth-century Quebec, if one half of the population were celibate population growth would cease. This can only have happened in exceptional circumstances. But we are so unsure of very early history that there is not even matter for controversy. It is not so for the seventeenth and especially the eighteenth centuries in Europe.

It has long been thought that in this already developed society celibacy was a strong check to population growth. Many contemporary authors (Landry, Gemaelhing and Duplessis) believed especially that ecclesiastic celibacy was a check to fertility. But the first complete vital statistics for France since 1775, published by Bourgeois-Pichat indicated rather different conclusions. The influence of ecclesiastic celibacy had been overestimated: there were never more than 3 per cent of clergy in the total adult male population, and some had taken to it out of physical or moral unsuitability to marriage. Celibacy was especially widespread in the aristocracy, or at least the landowner class. It must have been unusual in the agricultural proletariat, that is in the majority of the population. We cannot be precise, but one can assume that about 15 per cent of French people were celibate, including the ecclesiastics; that is a little more than today (10 per cent). (See figure 71 below.)

The losses caused by complete celibacy are never wholly a social phenomenon; many celibates suffer from illnesses or infirmities which would make them physiologically useless for procreation. Making allowances for this, the drop in fertility through celibacy is rarely less than 9 per cent or more than 20 per cent for national groups, but it can reach higher levels for certain classes or social groups or in certain historical circumstances.

The study of the factors determining celibacy is sociologically very complex. There are multiple forms, from rigorous asceticism to a life of absolute dissipation. In isolates it can for various reasons be involuntary (physical inaptitude, extremely reduced choice in possible partners), and it is never entirely voluntary. Enquiries into the attitudes of various types of people show that even for males the number of chances (i.e. possible partners) that occurred during their life was usually very small: many conditions have to be fulfilled and if every individual wanted to make a reasonable and fully considered choice there would be even fewer marriages. Fortunately a variety of feelings, of which love is not necessarily the most important, are liable to win over reason.

356

The marriage age

In a population not practising birth control, this is an important factor. Any delay (except for very young age groups) truncates the period of fecundity of its most active part. Figure 71 shows that this factor is even more important for a population with a low mortality (see overleaf).

Let us approach the problem from a different angle and consider a typical stationary female group, to whose age groups we will apply the ratio of married people in Egypt (high) and in Sweden (low) in 1945. This gives us two groups of married women; we now apply the same fertility rates to the same age group in the two populations, with the following result:

Age	Typical female population	Married female population with the marrige ratio of		Births with the marriage ratio of	
		1. Egypt	2. Sweden	1. Egypt	2. Sweden
15–19	1240	291	34	111	13
20–24	1190 ⎱	1930	⎰ 400 ⎱	377	⎰ 75
25–29	1140 ⎰		⎱ 951 ⎰		⎱ 189
30–34	1090 ⎱	1867	⎰ 827 ⎱	238	⎰ 119
35–39	1030 ⎰		⎱ 790 ⎰		⎱ 71
40–44	970 ⎱	1383	⎰ 711 ⎱	30	⎰ 26
45–49	900 ⎰		⎱ 629 ⎰		⎱ 3
Totals:	7560	5471	4352	756	496

Though there are in the two cases about the same number of married women at fifty, there are over 50 per cent more births in the group where women marry young.

When the marriage age varies in a group it has two effects, the first temporary, the second permanent. This can be seen in an extreme case: suppose that in a group where all girls marry at twenty-four, because of a sudden change in customs, this age suddenly drops to twenty-three: 1. In the first year there will be twice as many marriages, and even a few more, because of mortality between twenty-three and twenty-four. Births will increase in proportion during the following years, but this temporary rise will disappear by the second year for marriages and a little later for births. 2. Because in the future marriage will occur earlier the average fertility of marriages will be slightly higher.

At the other extreme, there might be no marriage at all for a whole year. In fact variations are never as abrupt as this, but for this very reason observations are hard to interpret and the distinction between definitive and temporary gains or losses is sometimes forgotten.

357

The marriage age varies according to country, district, and occupation. Agricultural workers often stay single very late, until they can afford to set up house. Air hostesses are usually single, either by contract or because their occupation is difficult to reconcile with marriage. On the other hand a shop-keeper will benefit in his trade by being married. Here, for example, are the proportions of single people in various occupations and socio-occupational categories in Canada between ages fifty-five and sixty-four.

Directors	3·6 per cent	Professions and	
Salesmen	5·8	engineers	7·7 per cent
Transport		Office workers	8·4
workers	5·9	Public services and	
Workers and		entertainment	11
craftsmen	6·6	Labourers	12·8
		Farmers	13·8
		Farm	
		labourers	41·0

Divorce and separation

Broken unions usually cause fertility to drop. Of course they may have been caused by the sterility of couples, which does not mean absolute sterility of either or both members; but usually, since a separation is not immediately followed by another marriage the result is, for the woman, a period of lost fertility, which, in a population not practising birth control, means a drop in total fertility. Any temporary separation (seasonal work, long journeys, illness etc.) has the same effect. These factors are still little known to demographers and represent a very wide field for research.

Living standards

We have already mentioned sanitary and dietary factors. If minimal sanitary conditions are fulfilled and people do not separate, the main influence of living standards on fertility in a population not practising birth control operates through mortality, which affects the classes unequally. Remember too that physiological sterility after a difficult childbirth is often due to social, economic, or cultural conditions. Lactation, which prolongs sterility, can also depend on social position, though this can encourage or discourage it according to fashion.

Figure 71 is intended to show the respective importance of the various social factors on fertility, by comparing the fecundity and the fertility of three types of population: 1. High mortality and high fertility (France, eighteenth century). 2. Low mortality and low fertility (western Europe, at present). 3. Medium mortality and high fertility (Third World, at present).

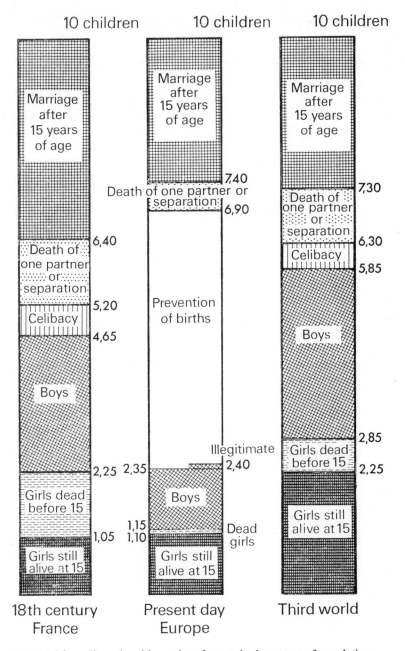

Figure 71. Total fecundity reduced by various factors, in three types of population.

Because of the individual differences amongst populations, especially of the third type, these comparisons are mainly meant to show how by various paths final reproduction figures of a very similar kind can be achieved; they also show the contemporary importance of birth control, dealt with in the next chapter.

The order of factors illustrated is fairly arbitrary, and this may mislead you on the absolute importance of each one expressed in number of children. For example, starting from the top in the middle column and working downwards: because all marriages do not take place at fifteen, the number of children drops to 7·4. Separation by death or divorce brings it down to 6·9; contraception reduces it further to 2·35 but we raise it to 2·4 again to take illegitimate children into account. These 2·4 children per mother consist of 1·20 boys and 1·15 girls; the latter are reduced to 1·1 by mortality up to age fifteen, and this figure is the net reproduction ratio of each generation. Illegitimate children were not included in the other two columns because of their relatively small importance.

8

THE PREVENTION OF BIRTHS[1]

This phrase is intended to refer to any action preventing sexual union from producing its natural fruits. Such action can vary between total or periodical continence and abortion, but it excludes infanticide and exposure.

Currently, the prevention of births is, in developed countries, not only the most important, but also the most variable and the most mysterious factor of fertility. It is the one that makes for the greatest differences between populations, it is subject to the wildest forecasts, and it can be a corrective either to a low or to a high reproduction ratio. Its main rival, mortality, is a kind of one-way factor: one can only foresee its decreasing, barring large-scale catastrophes. It cannot be encouraged or hoped for. Even the variations in the marriage age do not stray beyond fairly narrow limits. In the West, the East, and the Third World, the variation in the prevention of births is the big unknown, influencing all destinies.

To study it properly one needs to distinguish (though historians and public opinion mostly forget this) between: 1. The motivation leading men to limit their offspring (attitudes). 2. The techniques they use (behaviour). 3. The efficiency of the latter (result). 4. The various consequences.

History

Since the most ancient times, couples have tried to prevent births. Generally the methods were of little use, short of abortion, and were not often employed in marriage. Religions and traditions were opposed to practises 'against nature', which were sometimes condemned more severely than exposure or even infanticide.

Abortion, which had always been known, was sufficiently widespread in the sixteenth century for an edict of Henri II to make a declaration of pregnancy

[1] The many passions, illusions, and confusions we try to dispel in this chapter are for a large part fostered or entertained by improper terminology used consciously or not for its ambiguity. With such a delicate subject the debate should be as clear as possible.

Thus the phrase *birth control* is bad for two reasons: 1. It suggests command, mastery; a false sense of security in the present state of knowledge. 2. Most authors and advocates usually take it to exclude abortion, in Europe at any rate, because of the pretence that 'birth control will cause abortion to disappear', whereas in fact abortion too is by definition a way of preventing a birth.

Family planning is more fortunate, at least in English. But its pedantic air in French also carries a false suggestion of rigour and power.

compulsory. Abortion was mainly used to prevent illegitimate births; but, as a factor of sterility, it perhaps reduced the fertility of marriages.

The use of contraceptive methods in marriage is a modern phenomenon of exceptional importance. Landry calls it *The demographic revolution*. It first became widespread in France in the middle of the eighteenth century.[1] Remarkably enough, for a long time no book referred to this great silent revolution.[2] On this delicate and intimate matter eighteenth-century authors, even the erotics, were very discreet. (The same applies to contemporary erotic literature. Contraceptive devices suggest a constraint, a discipline, which it is not easy to glorify at the same time as absolute freedom and relaxation.) The contrast is striking between these delicate libertines, and the medieval or sixteenth-century Church, which did not mince its words in defining a sin. Yet it was they who caused this demographic revolution which spread from France, together with the Revolution, over the whole world. That brilliant and corrupt aristocracy introduced forbidden practices (originally *douches*, the *condom*, and *coïtus interruptus*) from the world of prostitution into that of irregular unions and adultery, and from there to the marriage chamber.

Some people had long been conscious of the need to limit their families. The advice of Mme de Sévigné in her famous letters to her daughter shows that the seventeenth century knew of it. But this and the actual practice were, in the words of P. Ariès, 'two phenomena which were foreign to one another; no one realised that one could remedy the other'. Probably through the influence of the Church, and because of the age-old social fear of sterility, contraceptive practices were assimilated with vices such as sodomy. Even the atheists of the eighteenth century condemned them as a violation of 'Natural Law', the new divinity.

Strangely enough, families with the means to raise children were the first to reduce their number. The children were competing against luxury goods, which were being increasingly marketed in a highly competitive society. The women's wish to avoid painful pregnancies and to keep their figure, also played a part. One can tell that maternity was out of favour, by the widespread use of wet nurses, condemned by Rousseau and other moralists. Contraception spread fast amongst middle class families wishing to preserve or improve their economic level, and even amongst peasant families wanting to avoid divisions of land (especially in Gascony).

Remarkably, in spite of Place and Carlisle, Britain was a century behind

[1] Norman E. Himes' *Medical history of contraception*, Baltimore, 1936, is well documented, but sometimes with legends, and it hardly mentions France. See also: P. Ariès, *Histoire des populations françaises*, Paris, 1948; A. Landry, *La révolution démographique*, Recueil Sirey, 1934, and *Traité de démographie*, Paris, 1945; H. Bergues and others, *La prévention des naissances dans la famille. Ses origines dans les temps modernes*, 1960.

[2] Modern historical studies include L. Henry, *Anciennes familles genevoises*, I.N.E.D., 1959; C. Lévy and L. Henry, 'Ducs et pairs sous l'ancien régime. Caractéristiques démographiques d'une caste', *Population*, October–December 1960.

France in this, although it was so progressive in other fields[1]; it only adopted contraception after passionate debates and famous trials. The movement which had by then started in Sweden and Geneva and elsewhere, spread to all developed countries.

Causes of this decrease in births

Various causes are often quoted: 1. The *abolition of work for children*, and *compulsory education:* instead of earning for the family the child has become someone his parents have to support. 2. *Modern child rearing:* the child used to bring himself up, but is now the centre of much attention. He has acquired more value and more importance and his birth has become a kind of event, about which people think twice. 3. The *drop in mortality:* real fertility is increased by the drop in mortality for low age-groups. With fewer births, one is still left with the same number of children as before. 4. The *loss of the father's authority:* not only has the responsibility to the child increased, but the adolescent no longer contributes materially to the home. 5. The *emancipation of women:* other interests than maternity have appeared, at the same time as the influence of women has increased, not on their children, but on their husbands and society in general. 6. Opportunities for *social advance* (Dumont calls this 'capillarity'). Had serfs been able to hope that their children might become lords, or at least stewards, had they been fewer in number, they would perhaps have acted upon this. Fatherly love has not diminished, but it can be concentrated on one or two children. 7. The *development of general education:* this has provided couples with alternative interests and pleasures. It provokes or makes more easy a kind of reflection that Valéry calls 'presence of mind'. 8. The *increase in the standard of living:* only the rich can afford to be miserly. Standard of living goes together with cultural development, and contributes to the widening of horizons. 9. Widening of *consumption possibilities:* this has increased requirements, especially in the middle classes. 10. The *growth of towns:* this is difficult to separate from the preceding factors; however the lack of space and the higher density of children at home may have helped to change the behaviour of the parents.

This list does not include the lessening in religious feeling, because this is not a positive factor, but rather a diminishing obstacle which has allowed the other possible factors to appear.

The first four factors help to increase the cost of bringing up children, either reckoned in care or in loss of salary. The next two consist in a decrease in parental domination: we saw in part I that absolute rulers are populationist, whereas partial rulers are always more or less in favour of limitation. Loss of power and increased responsibility have had the same influence on fathers as

[1] See especially M. Chachuat, *Le mouvement du 'birth control' dans les pays anglo-saxons*, Paris, 1934.

the poor laws on the moneyed classes in England at the time of Townsend and Malthus. Factors 4, 6, 7, 9, and 10 have caused new ambitions and new cares.

The link between lower mortality and lower fertility (factor 3) needs to be better explained. Take for instance P. Ariès's lucid analysis: once it was made possible and desirable to prevent death and struggle against natural fatalism, the way was logically open to this other kind of resistance against Nature. The prevention of births is part of the same freedom.

The idea of checking death by natural methods has not always been in the minds of men. For it to take precedence the human body had to be considered as a tool that one could repair . . . the forces of death and those of life then became docile to the will and the forecasts of men. It is not by chance that the death rate varied together with the birth rate. They both dropped when men shed their irrational attitude and adopted an objective view of Nature.[1]

The modern Prometheus has stolen the divine fire.

Still, this link is far from watertight. There is still a delay between the two phenomena, to be explained. Let us return to the economic factor. If it were the only one, individual reckonings (though wrong, as we saw in chapter 3) would have led to an almost complete avoidance of children. But various factors contributed to maintaining births at a certain level: the paternal instinct, the need for affection (especially in the case of the first child), an instinctive awareness of the psycho-social balance of the family (see Debré's description below, page 401), the continuation of moral or religious traditions in certain families, and last but not least, insufficient knowledge of contraceptive methods or insufficient expediency in applying them.

The prevention of births has thus been linked to the concept of domination/ freedom, and secondarily with that of property. An important question subsists: why was France a century ahead of other developed countries, especially Britain? There are extremely diverging explanations, and we will merely give the result of personal thought. The answer may be found in the religious atmosphere. France was too advanced and too far from the Tiber to remain in absolute obedience to Roman discipline, but she still observed its canons. Having failed to choose at the right time a religion more convenient to their ambitions, the French were left in a false position. The end of the absolute monarchy in the early eighteenth century allowed the new forces to appear. The drop in fertility in France is, briefly, the result of a 'suppressed reformation'.

Opinions in 1939

The most current opinions were then: 1. The prevention of births satisfies a profound desire arising mainly from the decrease in the mortality of the

---

[1] *Histoire des populations françaises.*

young. 2. In the family circle it is due to and helped by wealth and cultural development. 3. Although it is already excessive in certain countries it has not finished spreading, because the lower social classes are still behind and town life is still increasing. 4. Therefore the future of western populations is dark. Their net reproduction ratio, already lower than 1 in several cases, will drop dangerously.[1]

Some authors even talked of the final downfall of the white race;[2] but because the national populations were still increasing in total numbers, though ageing, general opinion did not worry very much.

The recovery of the birth rate

But in the event this trend was reversed; ironically the birth rate rose in several countries even during the war, though it had dropped during the First World War. Afterwards, its growth was confirmed in all the western countries. Only Germany and Italy, for political reasons, followed a slightly different path. Here are a few simple figures (births per thousand inhabitants).

	1938	1950	Increase (per cent)
US	17·6	23·5	33
Britain	15·5	16·1	4
Sweden	14·9	16·4	10
Switzerland	15·2	18·1	19
Belgium	16·0	16·9	6
France	14·9	20·5	38
Australia	17·5	23·3	33

No doubt the birth rate is a fairly rough instrument of measure; but the differences are too large not to be significant. For some time it was thought that the abnormal births, postponed because of rationing or the war, were swelling the post-war figures. As a result the methods of analysis were changed, but they still confirmed that fertility was increasing. This continued (in spite of many forecasts) during the 1950s, increasing even in countries such as Britain, Belgium, France, and especially in the national or social groups where it was weakest before. In other words the 'vanguard' has stepped back into line twenty years after the end of the war and thirty years after the slump, the birth

---

[1] One recalls especially the demographic forecasts published under the aegis of the Society of Nations by F. Notestein and his collaborators, *The future population of Europe and the Soviet Union: demographic perspectives, 1940–70*, Geneva, 1944.

[2] Mainly H. Decugis, *Le déclin des races blanches*, Paris, 1935; G. F. MacCleary, *Race suicide*, London; and it is worth recalling Gini's fascist theory of the biological decline amongst western democratic populations.

rate and fertility are fairly high, and ensure the replacement of generations. We will thus have to revise the concepts prevalent in 1939.

In communist eastern Europe, on the other hand, fertility continued the drop started at the beginning of the century; thanks to official support for abortion, it occasionally fell below the figures for western Europe.

Classical contraceptive techniques

Many books have dealt with this question,[1] and we shall merely list a few ideas of interest to our theory.

Only two methods are absolutely certain: surgical sterilisation either of the man or the woman, and abortion, if provoked by a doctor or a specialised midwife by insertion of a foreign body. All the other methods are imperfect and all, especially, include an element of constraint which impairs total efficiency: *Periodical continence* requires, even for regular women, abstinence far beyond the ovulation period. Taking one's temperature daily is in any case a regular nuisance. *Coïtus interruptus* reduces sexual pleasure, especially for the woman. The same applies to the *condom*, which in any case can fail. *Jellies, spermicides, douches* are often very efficient but may not suit certain organs or adhere perfectly if there is inflammation. We shall return to two new methods, oral contraceptives, and intra-uterine devices, whose effects are not entirely known.

If applied very carefully with a strong will to succeed, and with medical advice and help, each of the above methods is very safe; hence many errors and confusions. Practitioners often claim an efficiency of 95–98 per cent on samples of women they have studied with care. But this kind of sample is made up of particularly willing and well-advised women, and is not at all representative. It would be a grave mistake to generalise from such results. If every car on the road were to be followed by a police car there would be practically no accidents. We shall return to the subject of undesired pregnancies, and how prescriptions or decisions can fail to be followed.

All our experience, especially from Japan, points to the efficiency of abortion. In a word: 'it is easier to say yes one day than to say no every day'.

The chances of failure naturally increase with the time during which any method is used. Take simple examples, where a cycle is exactly a month long, the average chance of conception is 25 per cent, and contraception reduces fertility by nine-tenths, or nineteen-twentieths, or 99 per cent; arithmetic gives the chances of avoiding a pregnancy:

---

[1] They are numerous, but only too often biased if not distorted by passion, and usually badly documented. The best are: Dr A. Ladret, *Libre maternité*, Lyon, 1961; Dr R. Géraud, *La limitation des naissances*, Paris, 1963. See also A. Sauvy, *La prévention des naissances*, Paris, 1962 and 1965.

Efficiency	5 years	10 years	15 years
90 per cent	0·23	0·05	0·04
95 per cent	0·47	0·22	0·10
99 per cent	0·86	0·74	0·64

The 99 per cent reduction implies the simultaneous use of two methods with exceptional care, and yet it still involves a 26 per cent risk of an unwanted pregnancy over ten years.

Causes of the latest rise in fertility

There are no statistics or counts permitting firm scientific conclusions on this, but generally there are two kinds of factors. Both are fundamentally aspects of the same trend towards a greater optimism, and greater incentives to live. But it is worthwhile studying them separately.

Aid to families: Before the war many people still refused to believe that legislation could cause a rise in the birth rate. They pointed out previous failures (Augustus's laws especially) and claimed that material action could not settle ethical or moral problems, though they still invoked the material cost of the children as a cause, if not in support, of the prevention of births. The clock, they said, could not be turned back.

The war caused a reappraisal, and led authorities to adopt a more benevolent attitude towards families. Beveridge campaigned for this in Britain, and obtained the setting up of the Royal Commission on Population. In France where excessive prevention of births had already caused great damage, the government waited till the very brink of war, to reconsider its policy and encourage renewal (see pages 384–5). Since the war many countries have introduced material aid to families under various forms: relief, housing, schooling, medical insurance, tax allowances. This has reduced the cost of families in proportion to their size.

However they were obtained, these policies produced results. The most sceptic had to change their point of view, and they now tend to overestimate the efficiency of the measures they used to underestimate. They now claim that families tend to have more children than they should, merely in order to get the family benefits. In fact the planning of families is far from being so crude; there is no calculating with pencil and paper. Besides, despite various kinds of aid, the arrival of an extra child is still an economic burden. *The renewal of the birth rate stems not so much from real decisions to have more children, as from the diminishing fear of them.* The new policy has merely lessened the anxieties over new responsibilities, cramped living conditions, or interruptions of work.

Remember here that the inefficiency of contraceptive methods so far, and the subsequent need to resist the sexual impulse, cause great tension in the mind and demand firm and continual willpower. A young couple very rarely knows precisely how many children it intends to have. Asked about this just after marriage people often answer 'two or three'. The final result, which was two given a very strong will, now becomes three allowing for an occasional lapse. This is the real key to the situation.

It is also true that *general fertility is a collective rather than an individual phenomenon*. Social fashion and rivalry are involved. Material aid under its various shapes gives people *a more or less conscious feeling that henceforth children are welcomed by society*, or at least not disliked as much. No woman can actually have decided to have an extra child merely to enjoy the priority passes on the French transport system. Yet this advantage, together with others, has had a collective psychological effect. Mothers of large families, who used to be laughed at, are now highly considered by public opinion. Until the Second World War individualism condemned children. Institutions ignored these useless, unproductive creatures for whom neither houses, taxation, nor working habits were devised. One used to see notices such as 'No children or dogs admitted'. Immediate interests prevailed in this society which cared little emotionally about even ensuring replacement of its numbers.

Nowhere have family allowances caused very large families to increase still further. They did not practice contraception, for various reasons, before, and no new law can therefore make them stop it. In France the new policy was especially effective in producing the second or the third child. If at length families of four or five children also spread, this was mainly due to imperfections in the contraceptive methods used.

Spontaneous movement towards children: This collective phenomenon is very subtle and difficult to analyse. The elements making for it are controversial, but the results are not: the higher fertility also exists in the social groups not benefiting from much material aid, precisely those where the birth rate had been lowest before.

For instance, few occupations are less compatible with motherhood than that of actresses. Before the war they rarely had children, and in their circles children were not welcome. Often it was considered proper that they should keep any marriage secret. Yet only one generation later, actresses are very willing to appear with their children on magazine covers, and to give interviews between two films on their methods of education. Whether or not they actually carry these out, the attitude is there.

Pregnancy generally is no longer such a shameful condition. 'Ante-natal', a revealing word, seems to have appeared during the war amongst the higher or middle classes. It could of course be argued that the birth rate had dropped at about this time below a position of equilibrium, and was bound to rise again; it could also be said that this generation was merely reacting against its predecessor. But it is certainly true that society collectively welcomes children, even in social classes that receive no material aid directly.

Conditions are not the same in the United States, where state aid to families has remained very low and there are only the beginnings of social security.

Unemployment and the idea of the uselessness of men

Unemployment has always existed under one form or another and is still a reality for many underdeveloped populations, particularly where peasants do not have enough land. In this case it does not cause fertility to drop: such populations have not yet reached the stage where a couple both wishes and is able to limit its progeny.

Unemployment has a very different effect in industrial countries. Here the factory gates close before a worker, while an aid fund opens, image of the helplessness of society and indicative of a collective frame of mind: there arises a more or less conscious feeling that men are useless, and that society does not welcome them – a feeling helped by the constant publication in the press of statistics on these 'surplus men'. In the 1930s, marriages only decreased amongst the sections of society directly affected by this insecure situation, but fertility dropped even in groups not involved, such as civil servants. It was so obvious, that the fertility curve in the United States even reflects the economic recovery of 1937 and the crisis of 1938. The feeling that men were unwanted was ill-defined and diffuse, but apparent in the phrase, often heard at the time, 'Why bring more unemployed into the world?' In the United States the new pessimistic theories of maturation and stagnation only served to increase the impression: technological progress was supposed to have come to an end after three fortunate centuries, and the world was entering a static phase.

The crises of the 1930s did not accelerate the drop in fertility in the West as much as some people believed; indeed the curve had sloped away steeply as early as the 1920s, when unemployment was already appreciable and present in the public mind, helped by the after-effects of the war. This may be due, we suggested above, to a position of equilibrium having been passed as early as 1929. The impression of saturation was of course especially strong in the United States because of the restrictions on immigration, at once cause and effect. With the creation of the last of the forty-eight states, Colorado, the feeling was that the world was finally complete, and that the age of the pioneers and the ever-mobile frontier, expressive of the infinite and the unlimited, was over.

With the Second World War and the end of extensive unemployment, the many technological developments and extra requirements, and the international tension destroyed these feelings and theories. A new force began to bend the will to avoid children. The reappearance of political life and the end of isolation in France, both acted indirectly on people's minds and gave them renewed confidence in life.

Painless childbirth and social security

The least well explained of the rises in fertility is the one occurring in several countries around 1955–6, well after the effects of the welfare measures of 1946 had been recorded: this was true particularly of Britain and France. No doubt it was due to economic prosperity (not to be confused with the static notion of a high standard of living), together with the improved natal care and the methods of natural childbirth. Flanagan,[1] studying the families of American officers in America during the war, found that couples avoiding children did so in 10 per cent of cases because of a fear of childbirth; 29 per cent of the officers said that they would have had more children if their wives had been assured of better medical care, and a safe and painless delivery.

Present-day problems

With the usual exception made for societies that have not reached the demographic revolution, let us review the problems in the public eye and see what chance science has of answering them.

First, the debate needs ridding of the superfluous quarrels that clutter it up. Had France kept its 1780 fertility and reduced its mortality as it has, its present population would be 450 million (820 square kilometre) and increasing fast; had mortality remained constant and fertility dropped as it has, there would be only four to five million Frenchmen left and they would be dwindling fast. With present-day mortality a population exploiting natural fecundity could double every fourteen years. However rich, industrious, and heroic, it would soon crumble under the weight of its own exuberance.

The question is not whether births should be limited or not. On this point most people agree; but they diverge as soon as they come to the means to use and the proper laws to pass. The questions are: 1. *Should one oppose contraceptive practices, or some of them, or allow them indifferently to flourish, or even encourage them?* 2. *Should one act indirectly on the prevention of births by appropriate family, housing, and taxation policies, and if so in which direction?* 3. *What means can be used to achieve these ends?*

The attitude to contraception

Science does not answer the first question clearly. A religious doctrine may

[1] 'A Study of factors determining family size in a selected professional group', *Genetic psychology monographs*, 1942.

reflect a dogmatic and determined attitude, but science cannot either approve or oppose. If, to take the most classical example, a social group or a government intends, for religious, traditional or purely political reasons, to prevent any publicity for contraceptive devices, no scientist or technician is competent to oppose politics, which transcend his field. But he must deduce and make public the probable consequences, good or bad, of the policy: he must forecast the incidence of law-breaking, the use of methods escaping the law, the economic difficulties that may result from excessive population growth, or inversely the economic consequences of a recovery in the birth rate.

More generally, he may also denounce the possible contradiction between a prohibitive or repressive attitude in this field, and the general spirit of freedom and tolerance that permeates other institutions. A dictatorship or an oligarchic society are more logically at home in a régime of prohibition than a democratic government, which by definition allows any action that does no one any harm.

Yet two people, equally free from dogmatic views, and perfectly well informed through careful study, can still hold divergent opinions on certain points, which are thus revealed as non-scientific. A good example is that of abortion.

Abortion

Until the end of the sixteenth century the Church still hesitated to consider abortion in the first months as homicide. It debated as to whether embryos had souls. We now know that from the moment of fertilisation there exists a living body, distinct from that of the mother, and already fully determined in its heredity. Victor Margueritte's slogan 'Your body is yours' should be adapted to 'its body is yours'. Yet on what rational grounds can one condemn abortion? Can one assimilate the destruction of such an imperfectly formed being with murder? Is it healthy to excite mothers' sensitivities for such a subhuman cause?

Here, as with any interference into the affairs of the individual, such as eugenics and euthanasia (see below page 514), social imperatives are inspired by society's fear of being carried away. It needs a barrier, a break in continuity somewhere, and only two exist here: conception and birth. In fact birth is, for man, a less decisive event than conception. It does not change his genotype, and has no effect on his constitution. One could perfectly well imagine sophisticated incubating equipment taking charge of the embryo. The real break in continuity occurs at conception.

Many countries (Japan, the socialist republics and even Sweden) cut this knot, but most western countries, India and the Arab world (except Tunisia) are unable to.

Without coming out for or against official abortion, a demographer can and must speak of the consequences it may have on the birth rate, and thus give the authorities and public opinion information of a scientific nature to help decisions without guiding them.

Contraceptive devices

The classical contraceptives (not including intra-uterine devices and sterilisers) do not involve the same difficulties since they have no biological effects. They have not been found to do any harm, so there is no scientific reason for abolishing them. Doubts can however be expressed on their use: 1. In the short term there are psychological effects on the life of the couple. Too many specialists are concerned only with the body. Dr R. Géraud[1] writes 'the gynaecologist's table is a breeding ground for psychological traumas'. 2. In the longer term the woman and the couple should be well advised on planning a family, a point that deserves to be developed separately.

Magic and probabilities

Propaganda for the prevention of births tends to be based more on emotional mistakes than on logic. Its zealots, often ill-informed, have said or led people to believe that there were two eras, one before and one after the invention of birth control. They use (see page 361 n.) suggestive and imperfect vocabulary. French opinion, always ready to believe, if not exactly in the supernatural, at least in the miracles of science, was misled when a proper phrase such as 'family planning' was avoided because it was too precise and down to earth and unevocative. Both the prevention of births and having a child are hard to plan: there has been a misguided impression of certainty, whereas in fact fertility is an extremely unpredictable factor.

Unwanted pregnancies: if women overestimate the efficiency of the methods used and find themselves pregnant 'because of' the system which is presented them with a kind of official assurance, they may, in reaction, decide to be aborted though they would not have done so otherwise. In various countries people's ignorance of arithmetic and of the facts of contraception has led them to consider it the sovereign and necessary antidote to abortion. It is said that births will diminish little or not at all, but that abortion will disappear; yet nothing points this way at the moment. With great efficiency in contraception the number of births will inevitably drop; if it is not efficient there will be abortions. There may be a middle way with both abortions and births diminishing, but the examples of countries where all kinds of contraception are allowed (Britain, parts of the United States, certain Swiss cantons etc.), let

[1] R. Géraud, *La limitation des naissances*, Paris, 1963.

alone Japan and Hungary where they are encouraged, point to extreme reservations on this point.

Failure to conceive: very few gynaecologists know exactly how the proportion of definitively sterile women increases with their age. Some appear not to suspect it at all. As a result they give contraceptive advice to say a woman of twenty-seven, without telling her that she has one chance out of ten of becoming definitively sterile over the next three years. For her a child merely put off may become an impossible child. If such really is the woman's wish there is no harm done, but this is a very difficult point to decide on, since attitudes can change surprisingly with age. It is therefore essential to warn women not only of the physiological risks but of the changes that can occur in them and the dangerous psychoses that can result from avoided maternity. The number of people who wish to adopt children, the high price of babies on the 'black market' in the United States, the dramatic conflicts between the natural mother who reverses her original decision and the adoptive mother who has found an outlet for her emotions, the unexplained suicides around thirty-five, are all proofs of these inherent changes in human nature which confident youth, and often its instructors, ignore.

The opening of contraceptive clinics and the free sale of products should not therefore be an end in itself. It is a dangerous stage to stop at. Action should be taken to make women, as well as men, completely aware of the facts, especially those that natural carelessness may lead them to neglect. In this education the question of the psycho-physiological equilibrium of families should have an important place (see below page 401).

Conditions of family planning

For the time being, the methods available only allow us to act on one of the imponderables, the probability of conceiving. Even if these methods were perfect one could still not talk of family *planning* in the currently accepted sense, except in a very small number of cases. A very young couple wanting only two children would most probably achieve its ends, but only if it set about them immediately.

The danger of unwanted pregnancies will probably be avoided more and more in the coming years. But the danger of sterility will not decrease until new developments in biology reach fruition.

An important misunderstanding still remains to be cleared up. The number of children wanted and the very concept of the freedom to conceive should be in harmony with social conditions. Take the usual example of a family with two children and very little living space having recourse to abortion to prevent the birth of a third: if a third child were to give the couple the means to acquire a third room, then it might be effectively wanted and not unwanted. Then one could really speak of the total freedom of families to develop. Full liberty to conceive is not ensured by the mere availability of contraceptive products and advice – this is a conditioned freedom. In the present-day circumstances this is widely misunderstood: once again we have a case of social hypocrisy. As usual, careful study shows how different the reasons for current attitudes are from those ascribed to them.

Influence of standards of living on the prevention of births

In the previous chapter we studied the social factors of fertility assuming there was no prevention of births. We also saw that the ideas prevailing until the war needed to be carefully revised. The whole question must be approached from a new angle.

In a very developed population people's economic level is no longer as important as it used to be. First it is essential, as in so many other situations, to distinguish it from the cultural level. This is difficult since between twenty-five and thirty capital wealth counts far less nowadays than current income, which is very closely connected with cultural level. Very few statistics make this distinction and allow a double classification.

Even in the United States, where income is very influential, it is less so than cultural level. Here is, out of a sample of six thousand white women interviewed in 1961 during a pregnancy, the proportion of those using no contraceptive method.[1]

Education	Lower than $6000 (per cent)	$6000–8000 (per cent)	$8000 and over (per cent)
Primary	46·3	34·4	28·7
Secondary	34·3	26·8	28·6
Higher	20·6	20·5	16·8

Income is an important factor primarily where women have only primary education. Cultural level is important even for incomes above 8000 dollars.

Even if one confuses the two factors, an important change must be noted: *the difference, long apparent, between upper and lower classes, was due to a time-lag rather than a clash of attitudes.* This is still the case in the Third World. If the general development stops or pauses, differences are made up or appear to be due to other factors. Thus in many countries the lowest fertility is found in the middle classes, amongst salaried workers sufficiently advanced culturally to have recourse to contraception and without sufficient economic means to bring up several children.

[1] Communication number 147 on point B 13 by J. Yerushalmy at the *World conference on population in Belgrade*, 1965.

Housing provides an example of attitudes changing in time: in a first phase, where the working classes have a very low economic level, slums are, if not the main cause of prolificness, at least an obstacle to the prevention of births; and together with the lack of space and comfort there is a general atmosphere of discouragement. During this phase, fertility can be inversely proportionate to the economic level of the family. In a second phase, if housing is improved, the lack of resources causes children to be avoided in order to pay the higher rent. Housing policy might combat this factor; but it does not, even in the Soviet Union, sufficiently to ensure that a family is provided with an extra room soon enough after the birth.

Karl Schwarz, a west German statistician, gives the following numbers of children per thousand marriages in Germany in 1962, classified according to income and to the size of the town they live in.[1] The number of children increases with income in towns over a certain size.

Income	Under 3000 inhabitants	3000–50,000 inhabitants	50,000 and over
Up to 600 marks	1955	1701	1385
600–800 marks	1961	1771	1494
800–1200 marks	1858	1798	1550
1200 marks and over	1944	1882	1630

Influence of religion

Religions are usually recognised as 'populationist' in spirit, or at least as opposed to contraception. Since they are always rooted in some distant past, usually a period of high mortality, they are necessarily conservative demographically. None, however, appear to be strong enough to prevent completely the consequences of technological progress, just as no political authority is able to check progress itself, either from within or without.

Though Catholicism is (despite certain French anti-Catholic authors) the most clearly committed internationally against contraceptive practices, it only retarded, and did not prevent them in Italy, Spain, Canada. Until very recently it carried severity to the point of only admitting periodical continence and certain forms of restricted love-making. It is in the process of trying to conciliate its traditional attitude with the new demands brought about by the progress of thought and the drop in mortality (see below, p. 414).

The Protestant churches have held a more liberal position since the declaration following the Lambeth Conference in 1930.

[1] 'Nombre d'enfants suivant le milieu physique et social en Allemagne occidentale', *Population*, January–March 1965.

Neither the Moslem nor the Hindu religions are formally opposed to certain practices restricting fertility, although they do object to abortion. The governments of India, Tunisia, Egypt, etc., have even taken the initiative in encouraging contraceptive experiments. Their sacred texts are too old, too vague, or too contradictory to forbid a liberal interpretation. High Moslem authorities have disagreed on their meaning, while they cannot question the trend of thought.

The policy of the Jewish Church is still very strict but only partly obeyed.

The difference in fertility between two religious groups in the same country can either be due to the attitude of the respective religions, or to the cultural and social level of the faithful in both cults. These two factors sometimes act in the same direction (Catholics in Canada and the United States, or amongst the Irish in England), sometimes in opposite directions (Moslems and Catholics in the East): this can lead to mistaken interpretations.

But differential fertility, whatever its origin, always leads to the growth of the more fertile group. A crucial political example of this was Algeria. If the fertilities of the Christian population (sometimes very free-thinking) and the Moslem population had been the reverse, the political issue would have been very different. In Canada, the Catholic minority was only saved by its fertility. Here are some figures for other countries (those for Ireland are affected by emigration):

	Ireland[1]		Switzerland[2]			Holland[3]		
	1871	1946	1860	1950	1960	1899	1947	1960
Catholics	89·2%	94·3%	40·7%	42·1%	46%	35·1%	38·5%	40·4%
Protestants	10·3%	5·3%	58·9%	56·3%	52·7%	55·5%	40·1%	39·4%

If there were no conversion from Catholicism to other religions, and especially no loss of religious spirit from one generation to another, this trend would be even stronger. The benefits brought to the Catholic Church by this high fertility have led people to suspect its motive – wrongly, since Rome approves impartially and sometimes vigorously, especially in international organisations, of all societies who fall in with its universalist and much questioned doctrine. The prolificness of its faithful is only one useful result of a position adopted for spiritual reasons, which it is not our place to criticise.

New perspectives

What does the future hold in store? Let us assume that the present state of

[1] *Census*, 1946. Vol. 3, p. 1.
[2] *Annuaire statistique de la Suisse.*
[3] *Annuaire statistique des Pays Bas.*

legislation in each country does not change, and that the economic conditions remain fairly good, without any great unemployment crisis or international accident. We must, however, suppose that there will be progress in contraceptive methods. *Will the renewal of fertility in our generation be permanent, and the new-found balance remain, or will it prove to be a temporary recovery followed by another drop?*

To attribute the renewal to material aid to families, points to the first answer, providing of course that the aid is maintained. If it is an ill-defined reaction, partly due to fashion, there is a constant risk of another sudden drop in fertility. Whatever the reason for the recovery, it may be jeopardised by discoveries in contraception, or legal recognition of abortion, or the sponsoring of contraception on the part of public authorities, all plausible in the near future.

The number of unwanted pregnancies

Surveys have been made, especially in France, amongst pregnant women on whether they wanted their child. The question was best phrased at Tenon and St Antoine: 'They say that there will soon be pills, to be taken orally twice a month, which will absolutely guarantee avoidance of pregnancy with no danger. Would you have taken such pills to avoid this pregnancy?'[1] The answers were:

Yes	..	..	303	i.e.	29·7 per cent
No	..	..	479	i.e.	46·9 per cent
Don't know	..	238	i.e.	23·4 per cent
			1020		100

Assuming that the don't knows could break up in the same proportion into yeses and noes, we have the enormous proportion of 39 per cent unwanted pregnancies. In the same group 613 (i.e. 60·1 per cent) women said they were pleased with the pregnancy, 393 (i.e. 38·5 per cent) said they were not and 14 (1·4 per cent) were not quite sure.

In a survey in Grenoble in 1962,[2] there were even more surprising results. The question, not so clear, was 'Did you want this pregnancy?' 60·8 per cent answered no, 36·7 per cent yes and the rest did not know. A survey at Lyon confirmed the first two.[3]

[1] J. Sutter and F. Morin, 'Attitudes devant la maternité. Une enquête en service hospitalier', *Population*, April–June 1960.

[2] S. Siebert and J. Sutter, 'Attitudes devant la maternité. Une enquête à Grenoble', *Population*, October–December 1963.

[3] H. Pigeaud, J. Sutter, Mme H. Bergues, 'Attitudes devant la maternité. Une enquête à Lyon', *Population*, April–June 1966.

These pregnancies which may shock the mother and disorganise her life to start with, become more acceptable as time goes on. The mind gets accustomed to them, new plans are shaped. It would be to say the least unhealthy to raise the alarm about these reluctant mothers. Youngest children are usually the most loved, and yet they are statistically the ones desired least.

How do unwanted pregnancies occur? Women have the means to avoid them and intend to use them, but life is a tissue of 'accidents', forgetfulness, holidays, disturbed habits, relaxation, moments of optimism, of carelessness, of euphoria.[1] The fact is that if the perfect contraceptive were found the number of conceptions would decrease markedly. Not only these unwanted pregnancies but also all those interrupted on purpose would be avoided or postponed. From the point of view of the birth rate, only the first count, but they are numerous enough. This raises the very interesting question: *by how much would the birth rate drop in developed countries if the perfect contraceptive were found or even if better efficiency was achieved, either by a better use of existing techniques (specialised clinics, widespread medical advice), or with the appearance of new techniques?*

In search of the perfect contraceptive

It would be surprising to see contraceptive practices not following the general movement of progress, particularly since efforts are being made in this field in India (Sanyal) and especially in the United States. Here fifteen years or so ago research was undertaken in new techniques that could be used in the Third World. The Americans were particularly well placed for this; as the wealthiest nation, they have more funds for research, and are also more nervous about the rise of the Third World; another asset is the initiatives of their powerful private foundations. From 1952 to 1964 the Population Council was given twenty-two million dollars mainly from the Ford foundation and the various Rockefeller foundations.

The perfect contraceptive should be: 1. Absolutely reliable. 2. Easy to use. 3. Quite innocuous. 4. Should not diminish sexual pleasure. 5. Should be cheap with relation to family budgets.

It should also require the least possible effort of couples using it. This condition would even apply to developed countries: continuous constraint inevitably causes mishaps and ill-effects.

---

[1] An American doctor tells the following story: A farmer with four children came to see him and described his difficult economic situation and his wish to avoid having any more children. The doctor advised him as follows: 'When making love you must think very hard of the number of children you can support. This will make you careful.' Two months later the man came back with his now pregnant wife. 'Didn't you follow my advice?' asked the doctor. 'Yes doctor, but at the last minute I felt as if I could support fifty children.'

Preventing ovulation: Research was first directed along biological lines, towards the temporary sterilisation of men or women. After various trials and successful experiments in California and Puerto Rico, hormone-based pills preventing ovulation (such as norethynodrel) were produced, mainly thanks to Pincus, Nelson, and Segal. They arrest fecundity for only as long as the oral treatment continues. This method complies with our first condition, above, and apparently also with the fourth, though some authors have reservations on this point. Its cost has dropped considerably and now appears fairly reasonable for developed countries, even without subsidy. Its freedom from long-term effects, however, is still controversial, since we do not have enough experience of it. There might also be an habituation reaction.

Even if long-term effects were scientifically disproved, the novelty of this method would still cause suspicion and discussion and be an obstacle to its spread, even in developed countries. The memory of thalidomide and the fear of similar experiences might act as a restraint.

From the point of view of convenience, this method is better than the classical ones, but it is still difficult to apply to underdeveloped populations, as we shall see in the chapter on the Third World.

Inhibiting implantation: For these reasons the Population Council switched its research from 1961 to the implantation stage. This implies mechanical rather than biological devices, and, as often occurs, they are liable to suffer from the reputation of an unfortunate predecessor, Gräffenberg's ring. Devices such as coils, however, do not produce similar infections and seem to be perfectly acceptable after a period of adaptation.

Their action leads to the expulsion of the fertilised egg, and this strictly speaking could be called abortion; but the objection is moral or religious and not medical. It is very cheap, but there must be antiseptic precautions; a small number of failures by expulsion or infection might prevent its spread for a long time.

However, since no active co-operation is demanded from the couple once the inhibiting agent has been inserted, a new situation appears. The woman can now remain sterile for several months without having to take any precaution. The period of efficiency is even greater than that of abortion, since the device can be tolerated for several months or even a year, whereas abortion only produces a sterile period of a few weeks.

Results

The impact of these discoveries and those to come is considerable, even in developed countries. We have seen that the present equilibrium in France and other western countries in fertility and reproduction is precarious, and only due to the imperfect and imperfectly publicised contraceptive methods. This is obvious from the high incidence of abortion: even in Sweden and Denmark, where sexual education is extremely efficient and methods of contraception are widely known, official abortion has had to be introduced in the hope, perhaps vain, of preventing back-street abortion.

In the survey of six thousand white women in the United States in 1961, it was noticed that there were more unwanted pregnancies amongst Protestants than amongst Catholics. This was partly because the Catholics wanted more children, but it also shows how inefficient the contraceptives used by the Protestants were.

There still remains to define the future influence of the perfect contraceptive on the birth rate. It will have various effects: 1. It may push back the marriage age, which is now often brought forward by pre-marital conception. 2. It may reduce illegitimate births. 3. It may space out the births in any one family without necessarily decreasing their number. 4. It may space them out *and* decrease their number. 5. It may cause people to avoid having so many children.

Not all these effects would produce a lower birth rate. A drop in illegitimate births could even contribute in some circumstances to the number of marriages. Besides, if few children are wanted anyway and the device merely allows them to be spaced out, their number will not necessarily change.

However, on the whole the result will be a decrease. To be able to give a precise figure one would need to have at one's disposal fecundity tables as described above, p. 352, and to be able to survey the attitudes and intentions of married couples in various countries. One would still lack several factors, such as the marriage age, but reckonings would at least be possible. Their importance needs no stressing: it is startling that modern nations should make such considerable efforts in various directions and yet neglect issues concerning the very life of their population.

The end of the equilibrium

Lacking figures, we are confined here to impressions, mainly of a subjective kind. The surveys on pregnancies at Tenon, St Antoine, Grenoble, Lyon, show that more than 40 per cent were unwanted. This does not mean that the perfect contraceptive would reduce the birth rate by 40 per cent, since in certain cases a pregnancy would only be put off for a time. It would, however, make an appreciable difference, by suppressing the unwanted births or because putting off a birth might make it impossible because of the accidents of fertility and the onset of involuntary sterility.

There are indications that over the last few years the birth rate has been dropping in the United States. The spread of the pill and of intra-uterine inhibitors has caused it to drop from 25·3 to 19·7 per thousand between 1960 and 1965.

Another disturbing and unquestionable fact is that official abortion – an absolute weapon – has brought the birth rate down to 15·4 in Rumania and to 13 in Hungary, which is well below the level necessary to ensure the replacement of one generation by the next. A similar result would have been achieved in Czechoslovakia if the government had not begun to discourage abortion in 1964.[1]

These facts seem to suggest that *the natural emotional desire for children is not always sufficient to ensure the survival of a population.* The doubts expressed before the war about the final decline of the white peoples, now forgotten, might well return in another form. The West might well find itself once more in the pre-war situation, where because of the successful battles against mortality, it had to choose between growth and ageing.

There are means to combat this decay: there may be biological discoveries permitting a positive influence on fertility; there is also the rather neglected resource of offering aid to families, in the form of educational facilities, or improved housing, or income to reward a new birth.

The most logical forecasts on the prevention of births have been so often proved wrong in the past that we must be careful here; this should not, however, prevent us from making reckonings about the future, as long as we base them on proper scientific surveys. Fundamental research needs developing, so that unfavourable trends as far as possible be reversed, or at least reduced in time. The very importance of the facts of demography should justify an exceptional state of awareness.

[1] The low birth rate caused the Czech government (decree of 21 December 1962) to impose stricter regulations and introduce a charge for abortion. Births rose again from 217,000 to 236,000 the following year. This was reported to the World Population Conference in Belgrade in 1965 by Professor A. Cernoch.

9

COLLECTIVE WILL AND INDIVIDUAL ATTITUDES

Every population runs the double risk of increasing too fast or of ageing and disappearing. The rhythm of growth in any population has a ceiling imposed by the insufficiency of natural resources, the size of investments for growth, or the speed of technological progress. Demographic growth can of course influence these factors in its turn, but only in a limited way. Until the nineteenth century, at any rate, technological progress was always too slow to allow natural population growth to operate in the face of decreasing returns and the resistance of the environment. Chronic overpopulation was the general rule, in the interests of public safety. And yet some populations diminished and disappeared. Tribes and races were affected and sometimes blotted out by demographic decay: often they were only massacred by an enemy when all hope of survival on their own had been lost.

All societies have feared and had to struggle in various circumstances against their excessive or insufficient numbers. The risk of decline, the only obviously mortal one and also the one that dominant classes or castes had most reason to fear, was the most frequently denounced. This is why most countries have tended to be over rather than under populated. A population with no medical care but enough land can double in forty years. The struggle has usually quickly appeared between men and their environment, and this is in any case the only logical course. A man wavering on a narrow path between a mountain and a precipice does better to lean towards the mountainside. One understands why countries such as China associated the cult of the family and the strong desire for children, with the practice of exposure and infanticide. The massacred children were an insurance into the future, because they could always be allowed to live if necessary.

We should not perhaps always consider only the individual or the state. In many societies the family is the basic unit. In Japan, in imitation of the imperial family which has its roots amongst the gods, the traditional family was one large living organism. Its various members were as closely linked in time as animal cells are in space; an attitude reflected by the meaning of 'house' in feudal terminology. In societies such as this, the head of a family, anxious to have at least one heir surviving up to the age at which he can procreate in turn, realises, even without any technical knowledge of probabilities, that he must have many children if his house is to stand a chance of surviving. If he marries at twenty-five he has no wish to limit his family, since even after the third son he must still think of the risk of high mortality through epidemics. Hierarchy thus favours population growth. A vertical society cannot advocate birth control.

There is probably also a kind of natural selection amongst the populations themselves. Of the many peoples that have existed, according to Notestein, those who ventured nearest to the precipice probably disappeared, in circumstances in which the others merely suffered a famine and shed their excess numbers. The less prolific populations did not need to extinguish themselves completely: their neighbours could be trusted to carry this out as soon as their superiority was confirmed. This theory, however, does not suffice to explain the large variations there are between the various regions of the world. Certainly the African populations, which are less fertile, owe their survival to the wide deserts separating them from the prolific Asiatics. But it is strange that in Africa no prolific population should have appeared and gained the upper hand.

Private interests and the public good

How can societies act to guard against a loss of equilibrium? This could perhaps be achieved in one of three ways: 1. *Individual initiatives*, conscious and well-pondered: One can readily imagine an overpopulated country where the demands of food and education for children are such that parents resort to abortion, exposure, infanticide, etc. as we have seen above. Individual and collective interests would be in agreement. But in reality overpopulation does not discourage parenthood, or, especially, lead to such cruelty. Couples just do not forgo children purely in the interest of society. A population is only regulated by excessive mortality, famines, or epidemics, unless emigration offers a way out. 2. *The calculated influence of the ruling class* over individuals. This second alternative might seem more likely: religions especially have condemned sterility and praised fertility. But they might well have been merely reflecting in this the common fear of emptiness. There are very few examples of a ruling group politically and openly opposing a popular wish to multiply. In ancient Japan there were permanent laws against abortion, which were merely set aside, without being repealed, during periods of famine. Situations are often quite confused: official populationist policies and hymns to fertility coincide with individual initiatives to avoid too many children, which are tolerated or even discreetly encouraged by the political and even the religious authorities. 3. *A collective instinct of self preservation*: According to J. C. Flugel[1] all societies implicitly recognise the conflict between their two main requirements, hunger and love. Unable to attack the populationist taboo directly, they prefer to intervene by setting various occult obstacles in the way

[1] *Population, Psychology and Peace*, London, 1948.

of marriage and sexual intercourse, or legalising or tolerating abortion and infanticide.

The decrease in fertility in France

When contraceptive practices began to spread in France around 1750 the ruling groups were not thinking in terms of a surplus population. Everyone, on the contrary, believed that the kingdom was becoming depopulated. Individual practices which thus appeared to go against the general interest, were generally censured, no doubt even by those who were themselves discreetly using them. Under Napoleon's empire there were signs of a certain permissiveness, but as an absolute ruler Napoleon could not avoid being a hardened populationist.

Later, except on very rare occasions in the nineteenth century, governmental circles never made any mention of a surplus population. In speeches, growth was a firm dogma of civic morality. Yet this was a purely formal attitude; individuals refused more and more to carry out this 'civic duty', and for a long time no legislation attempted to make it any easier to obey. Official policies supported both fertility and a narrow individualism, not perceiving the contradiction between them. The virtues of the home and family were preached and taught, but taxation on housing hit larger families hard. The military disaster of 1870, the first sign of demographic decay, did not cause any significant change in the national consciousness. The family was still an ideal honoured in speeches and crushed in acts. Millions of individual decisions, no doubt wise and in agreement with individual interests, combined to produce the most obvious of collective follies.

In 1914 France just avoided a new disaster, and during the vital struggle which began to surpass its strength, it exhausted itself, losing blood and nervous energy. After the war, bewildered, it still failed to react except by voting in 1920 repressive measures against the prevention of births.

National remorse

1939 seemed an even less favourable moment to begin encouraging births and families: not only was the budget overstrained by the armament drive, but, however useful the laws encouraging births, they could hardly have any effect on the war that was just round the corner. At best, if it had held off for two or three years, the nation would have had an extra burden in the shape of very young children. Yet it was in these unfavourable conditions that the *Code de la Famille*, a real revolution in French institutions, was adopted. *The most aged population on earth took, at the most unlikely moment, steps towards a renewal which no other country in the world had yet had the courage to imagine.*

Indeed, in the middle of the great retreat of June 1940, France created a

'Ministry for Families', quite unable to lend any help to the families fleeing along the roads, but of far-reaching symbolic value. This example confirms the apparent irrationality of behaviour in questions of national vitality. In a latter-day fit of remorse the Third Republic thus, in a sublime and desperate gesture, imitated the insects that die in the act of love, and repaired upon its deathbed half a century of fatal carelessness. On the edge of the chasm that was opening, deserving statesmen such as Daladier and Reynaud sowed the seeds of happier days to come.

Yet very few Frenchmen were ever conscious of this event, the most important turn in the history of their country. Reynaud and Daladier were blamed for the general catastrophes that occurred under their government but were in fact the results of an accumulation of mistakes by others. Perhaps one day a more rational and just France will pay homage to their clearsightedness.

Is there a collective will?

The new rise in births in France and less markedly in Malthusian Europe is, as we have seen, different from the one that has occurred in the new English speaking countries. Though impulsive in appearance, the French decision was more mature, more intentional: it was the result of lengthy debates in public opinion, lasting over more than half a century; it was only brought about by the combination of a long maturing period and exceptional events.

It is a matter for speculation whether and to what extent those who took the decisions were only the instruments of history. It would be difficult to assert that others than Daladier and Reynaud would have taken the same decisions for public survival. Landry believes firmly in the existence of a collective will transcending individuals, and thinks that there was bound to be some instinctive reaction to the danger, even if this was only obscurely sensed. The revived fertility of the United States since the war has been in part attributed to such a reaction. Yet to ascribe something to an instinct of self-preservation is really only to say that one is unable to explain it. Often, as in France, it only appears through the medium of public-spirited and highly perspicacious men. In fact, few could deserve this praise more than Landry himself, who spent the greater part of his life trying to provoke this reaction which in the end only occurred in such tragic circumstances.

Later there was a striking continuity: from 1939 to 1946, through unparallelled trials, governments as different as those of Pétain, De Gaulle, and the Communists, all pursued the work of reconstruction.

The notion of a duty to procreate

One may still ask whether this reputedly impossible task was made easier by a general feeling that procreation was a moral duty. Several authors assume that it is so. P. Vincent writes: 'The people are conscious of the need to ensure society's survival'.[1] This idea, with its reverse, the remorse at having failed to procreate, is difficult to challenge; what is questionable is its efficiency. For half a century it was powerless to stop the slow decay; the parents of only children or those without children at all were never collectively censured. Besides, the complex phenomenon of demographic reproduction is much too imperfectly known for the sense of moral duty to ensure the equilibrium of the population. A poll conducted on a representative sample has shown that French opinion believes fertility is too high. Yet at the same time people said that three was the most desirable number for a family. What they had judged to be too high a fertility was only one of two-and-a-half children per family.

In the last chapter we mentioned several times that, though it seemed to be the result of individual planning, fertility was the result of a general state of mind. *But this collective attitude is not necessarily prompted by the idea of the public good.* There was collective scorn of children in the period of intense individualism; but with the revival of fertility the feeling spread that children were more welcome: this shows the difference between the social attitudes and the public good.

No providential equilibrium

Without the spontaneous remorse and sense of duty shown by the French population in 1939, the revolutionary action taken could hardly have entered so easily into people's habits. When a collective frame of mind exists, as it did here, its supporters show their enthusiasm, those who are unsure submit to it, and its opponents keep quiet – we call it a change of opinion.

The theory of a natural equilibrium produced by the collective desire for survival, can thus only be true within certain limits. Reactions of this kind have been observed, in the United States, for instance, with no change in legislation, yet their failure to occur for so long in France is also significant. Had Hitler succeeded in September 1940, with a few extra planes against England, or in November 1941 in the attack on Moscow, with the weather conditions a little warmer, the destiny of France might well have been decided in a way that made this theory meaningless.

Britain too went through a period of self-analysis during the war. Beveridge wrote at this time: 'An old people can at least try not to think old'. A consciousness of ageing is already a sign of renewal; but it has never been sufficient so far. Fatalism and passive confidence in natural reactions or equilibrium is the most perfidious poison that can afflict a people. The memories of the battle of the Marne and the idea that a national reaction 'must' occur and save the country in the nick of time played their part in the preparations for the disaster of June 1940. *Caveant consules*, certainly, but let others beware too.

[1] 'La famille normale', *Population*, April–June 1950.

It is widely accepted today that because of the drop in mortality, there is a greater risk of overpopulation than of underpopulation in the world. This should not lead us to forget the risk of decadence in an ageing western Europe. An equilibrium of a providential kind may appear to exist over a long span, but only if the many individuals appointed as its instruments do not betray their mission, and especially since only the survivors can write history.

10

THE MALTHUSIAN SPIRIT

The word Malthusian does not refer directly here to the doctrine of the Reverend Malthus. This chapter is intended to define it and limit its field of application.

In the family

The wish to limit the number of one's children to a particular number can either be a product of altruism or of egoism.

Altruism inspires the fear of bringing into the world unhappy, unhealthy, ill-equipped children, or of making the lives of those who are already there more miserable. Children never really curse their parents for having brought them into the world, but elder brothers or sisters could well regret the existence of the younger children, though this is rare enough. Parental altruism is usually based on a personal conception of happiness.

When the arrival of numerous children could be a threat to their very lives, the attitude could be very different, but it is precisely in this case that the limitation of families very rarely occurs. Many parents wish to have children who will achieve more than they have, and this is not unrelated to a certain kind of egoism, though it is at least more socially worthwhile than the major kind of egoism, which consists in being reluctant to forego one's own material comfort or to face the physical difficulties of maternity.

Egoism and altruism rarely exist independently. The proportions in which they occur vary with individuals and with the number of children. The first and second children bring the greatest perturbations into the life of the parents. The first changes their habits while often bringing, as well as the joys of affection, a certain satisfaction of now being able to live as a real family; to refuse a first child is obviously pure egoism – the couple, like Ugolin, is sacrificing children to preserve a father for them. The second child usually makes it necessary for the woman to abandon her occupation and thus brings financial loss; to refuse the second child can thus mean that one wishes not to diminish the chances of the first in life, but it is still partly due in most cases to the parents' fear of losing their own comforts. Here again the need for affection often wins the day. Below a certain social rank, the drop in the standard of living it brings, even without family allowances, is not very large: the older children are required to help in the life of the family, though as a result they are the ones whose education or career suffers. Thus egoism diminishes and altruism increases with the rank of the child.

The prevention of births, or family Malthusianism, is not necessarily a proof of a failure in the ideal of the family, or of a lack of affection for children. Family ties are looser than they used to be a century ago, but not because there are fewer children. A Malthusian couple with only one or two children often has a more closely knit family life, and an only child can be loved as much, if not more, than others.

Whether egoistic or altruistic this Malthusian attitude is provident and, as we have seen, more frequent in well-to-do and educated families. Claudel's famous line 'We had five children; this will make seven . . . woman, go and bring them in' is more likely coming from a poor fisherman than from a businessman.

On the national level

Malthusianism can spread through advice. When a woman persuades her friend or her neighbour to limit her children, she is usually disinterested, or at least her personal interests are not directly involved. She genuinely wishes to help the couple ánd the children they already have. But this is not the case with the militant supporters of birth control, whose feelings may be more complex, and connected with class attitudes, which are far removed from altruism.

It is always difficult of course to sound the bottom of people's minds; there have been many debates on the real intentions of Malthus himself. The rich classes of Britain who agreed with his ideas were prompted by selfish motives: the poor laws were already costing them enough, and if the working classes were to go on multiplying it seemed that reforms more drastic than mere assistance would have to be introduced. The relative stabilisation of the number of poor thus appeared all the more conservative since in referring to continence it did not break with any ethical law.

But Malthusianism has not only occurred amongst the wealthy classes; in some countries, indeed, these classes have taken the opposite attitude, advocating the increase of the labour force in the national interest. The balance between these opposite aims can be broken either one way or the other, and class attitudes are often very confused.

In the world

Only very recently has the debate appeared on the world scene. Famines in India and China used to be too distant to really affect the white nations. Until the last war the 'yellow peril' was more a quip than a reality. Various people did of course see the danger of excessive fertility, and Malthusian propaganda was spread by private initiatives, but the question only assumed its present shape during and after the last war. Both types of Malthusianism are found here, roughly as follows:

1. *Unselfish*: 'These poor people will never rise out of their misery as long as they go on procreating so freely; if we were to follow their example we would soon find ourselves penniless and at the bottom of the economic ladder. Our duty is to teach them the ways of avoiding such bestial fertility. It is the best way of lifting them up to our level and it is all in *their* interest.'

2. *Selfish*: 'We could of course leave these poor folk to their misery and their careless prolificness, but they will sooner or later come knocking at our door. International solidarity is growing, either because distances are diminishing or because we are really progressing morally. So we shall soon have to do something for them; we might not if they remained a distant problem, but one cannot avoid helping people one is hearing of every day. Besides, some international body with an idea of egalitarian justice might one day redistribute men more rationally over the planet. *Our* interest lies in persuading these populations to reduce their fertility.'

The United States have become a dominant power without ever having sought or even suggested an absolute type of domination, of the sort that benefits from the proliferation of subjects. Even for the absolute rulers, and some still exist in the world, the question of population has been profoundly modified by medical developments causing mortality to decrease. The United States, a responsible power with a mind to its possible duties and limitations, rather than a domineering power, is very much afraid of the population growth of Asia, Africa, or even South America. Its own low density of population encourages the feeling. American demographers never fail to point out the seriousness of this problem in university courses, popular magazines, digests, etc. The relative shortage of raw materials in the United States and the need to exploit oil, copper and iron in other parts of the world also contributes to this strong fear.

Since Malthusianism is an emotional state of mind at least as much as a rational argument, it cannot adapt itself to the diversity of cases which would demand different or even opposite solutions. Thus the depopulation of France, obvious until 1946, was unable to disturb world Malthusianism (see also chapter 12).

The disappearance of classes

This attitude is also that of rulers of any sort. Because of it, the question of social class fades away in a country. The prize is very different: any American with even a mediocre position is now at least as anxious to preserve it as to achieve a better one. He knows or feels obscurely that a general redistribution of wealth amongst the three thousand million people in the world would leave him very much the poorer; phrases such as 'proletarians of all countries unite' can have no effect on him whatever. All those famine stricken Indians and Chinese are further removed from the American worker than is the manager of General Motors. A worker may not give up bargaining for better wages, of course, but this is no longer his fundamental interest.

Without thinking at the same economic level, the British (and no doubt the Scandinavian) wage-earner has the same feelings at heart. The dividends of the Anglo-Iranian consortium pour into the treasury, and at least they will help to restore the balance of payments, on which the whole of English life depends.

French workers are at once less informed and more generous, and are not affected so strongly by such arguments: they look abroad less, but do not feel privileged in any way, and are mistaken over their rank in the world hierarchy. They tend to suffer less from racialism than Anglo-Saxons, dream of an insular 'abundance', and fear much less than others the prolificness of distant populations. Whether Catholic or Communist, French workers retain high hopes in the resources of the earth and the justice of men.

The Malthusian sense of economy

The idea of Malthusianism should not be confined to people's attitude to fatherhood. It is a state of mind, appearing in many circumstances, characterised by the fear of excess – faced with two quantities that need adjusting, it tends to lower the highest instead of boosting the lowest.

It is the opposite of courage and generosity. It is illustrated by the old story told about the English tourist at the *table d'hôte* with seven or eight other guests, exclaiming, when the hostess brought in a paltry-looking chicken: 'What a lot of people'. A non-Malthusian would have said: 'The bird is too small, bring another one'. Not that Malthusianism is the same as avarice, but rather the contrary; we have seen that it is not always identified with selfishness. It is a view of life, a type of fear, hope or choice, right or wrong. It is a predisposition, which influences attitudes though not in a necessary way: the situation or the view of the situation also plays its part. The modern American, who is less Malthusian than the Frenchman in domestic economics, is much more so on the problem of the world population.

Economic Malthusianism

This includes any attitude discouraging the increase in wealth, and the feelings behind it. One need not, of course, choose wealth as one's aim; if one has other, non-economic ambitions instead, they are not necessarily Malthusian. It is not Malthusian to reduce the output of textiles or cars in order to produce more armaments. But it is typically Malthusian to limit output so that prices shall not drop.

Malthusianism at its most virulent leads to the destruction of wealth. This occurred especially during the great slump, although it was less widespread than is thought. It can hardly be in the producers' interests to spend money and time on boosting production, only to destroy the goods; they would be better employed doing nothing. Absurd policies such as the systematic distillation of agricultural products only appear with the intervention of public authorities.

Monopolization is not, properly speaking, Malthusian. It is a ferocious act of speculation but need not reduce output.

The most classical instance of Malthusianism lies in agreements between industrial or agricultural concerns to limit their output and maintain the level of prices. Sometimes there is no need for them to impose quotas on each member: as a result of high prices, global consumption remains at the level corresponding to the optimum output. Various circumstances then determine the output of each individual member. Perfect competition being a very rare achievement, this Malthusian attitude is always more or less present in business. Trade, in particular, is more or less Malthusian in all countries and at any time: it always places prices slightly above the level at which offer and demand would be balanced, thus discouraging the regular trade flows.

It is not in the interest of an industrial concern to achieve at all times the highest possible output. In favourable periods of full employment a firm carefully phases out the orders in hand, for fear of being suddenly out of work later on (and this prudent fear is Malthusian); but also at any given moment there is an optimum rhythm of production depending on material equipment, personnel, the overtime rates, etc. Past it, costs rise in spite of the increase in bulk output. It is not solely Malthusian to aim at this optimum rate, but if one does the production in other sectors may slow down: the general activity is dependent on over-activity in the bottleneck sectors. And since the optimum output is not determined with any great precision, Malthusian cautiousness keeps a producer on the safe side if he lacks an adventurous spirit.

Between the blatant destruction of wealth and the more humble fear of cheapening output, there is thus a whole range of attitudes all including some degree of Malthusianism. Thus, even in an ideal market system the rhythm of output is not determined with the precision on which classical theories depend. There is an area, sometimes quite wide, in which the rhythm can depend on individual preferences, differences in sector, country, or period.

J. Duboin, a distant and utopian disciple of Sismondi, and followers of his, interested in the theory of abundance, carried this criticism a great deal further, claiming that technological progress necessarily brings with it a nostalgia for the old scarcity; this view, similar in a way to Marxist theory, is arguable in principle, but the actual extent of the loss suffered is questionable. Different opinions appear the moment one tries to spot the régime with the smallest losses that still fulfils certain non-economic ideals. Those who believe in abundance hold that progress is already so far advanced that a distributive economic system is conceivable, where output would be determined not by market fluctuation, which is more or less vitiated, but by consumption demands. Soviet economists are more cautious than these Utopians. Notice that the upholders of progress often act, as do pure Marxists, like a restraint on output and ideas: after Léon Blum's devaluation in 1936, there was a rapid and extraordinary revival of the French economy, under the double influence of classical speculation and of the alignment of prices on the foreign level. Increased purchasing power naturally began to digest the unused margins of output capacity. However, inspired by social democratic ideals in their most Malthusian form, and terrified at the idea of unemployment, Blum spoilt his revival by excessively and clumsily reducing the working week; this narrow Malthusian gesture changed a political victory into political defeat. Having unlocked the door, in a fit of bravura he turned round and bolted it. No anti-Malthusian abundance theory has recorded this contradictory policy. A valid criticism of Malthusianism should not only blame others for their sterility, but also set examples. Pre-war France was so riddled with negative attitudes that even anti-Malthusians shared some of them.

Alignment against the lowest norm

In military strategy, when riflemen or armoured troops are called on to attack across a large front, they are told to keep a fairly rigorous alignment. Whoever advances in front of the line might pierce the enemy front but exposes himself to an attack from the flank that could lead to death or capture. Thus, where there is little patriotism or aggressiveness, alignment generally consists in staying a little behind the others. But if everybody were to reason in this way the line would not progress at all.

When an economy advances, its different sectors must move, not necessarily at the same speed, but so that the various sectors compensate each other's gains or losses. Here too a key sector might tend to hold back to avoid running the risk of idleness; yet if every sector were to adopt this attitude progress would be impossible. It may be that for accidental reasons one sector is in any case more advanced than another: the output of nuts may be higher than of bolts, the output of corks higher than that of bottles. Here, the two outputs can be aligned either on the lower or on the higher. It is a Malthusian reflex to align them on the lower.

In a planned economy it is always possible, at least in theory, to ensure full employment, even if this involves indemnifying at the full rate workers who are asked to change their branch or who may lack work because of a mistake in the plan. In a market system, however, the distortions have to be borne, and a certain degree of suffering accepted, since *it is one of the basic assumptions of the system that this very suffering constitutes the spur to progress and provokes the right adjustments.* Thus anyone trying to achieve perfect adjustment is Malthusian, for one should always, on the contrary, be a little ahead in time and take a calculated risk. Output should not be aligned on consumption but should always advance faster, and cause consumption. The dangers are the same as for the rifleman who acts out of line, and this occurred more often in the pioneering days of capitalism. Today it is much more difficult to dismiss surplus personnel. But this may lead Malthusian prudence to gain the upper hand and vitiate expansion and employment.

This is why capitalist economies must have recourse to artificial stimulation of demand of an inflationist kind, and also try to foresee if not to plan.

Global views

Global views are generally Malthusian: by presenting all the different sectors or all the workers as interchangeable, they suggest that any irregularity is an excess. Such mistakes usually occur where working hours are concerned.

It is also Malthusian to decide or to require that 'as long as there is still one unemployed person in the country, no immigrant, and no extension of working hours be allowed'. This would be reasonable only in a completely fluid economy where men were totally interchangeable.

The most instructive and conclusive episode of the whole economic history of France between the two world wars was the end of 1938. There was both total and partial unemployment, yet the government decided to allow firms with a long order book to lengthen their working hours: against all forecasts, this policy caused unemployment to drop as follows:

	November 1938	*July 1939*
Percentage of men working for over forty hours a week	3·3	34·8
Percentage of men working for forty hours a week	76·3	55·8
Percentage of men working for less than forty hours a week	20·4	9·4

But the lesson was not understood. It should have led to the prediction of the so-called German miracle and many other analogous developments. But it was too different from accepted ideas to be even recognised.

If you put on gloves that are too small, you will find that your fingers cannot reach the end of them. A Malthusian attitude will whisper to you that they are too large and you may order an even smaller pair. But if you are a non-Malthusian you will order a larger pair and may then get your fingers into the ends (see chapter 16). In a period of crisis a Malthusian worries over the unemployed sectors, and one can hardly blame him; but he believes that they are the key sectors and in this he is quite wrong. The non-Malthusian tries to stimulate the sectors already working at full time, in order to ease the unemployed sectors or bottlenecks, by providing them with extra consumers. In the same way, in a traffic jam, an intelligent policeman will encourage the cars that do have a little space in front of them to move faster. These are the firms with orders: if encouraged to move faster they will leave space behind them for others to move into.

A survey of Malthusian behaviour

We have already said that one should not call Malthusian all actions opposed to an economic development, or preventing an increase in the national income. Often it should first be asked what caused them – strikes are not Malthusian unless their object is to reduce output and ensure better conditions for one sector and its personnel, which may cause the rest of the economy to suffer.

– Any destruction of goods or limitation of output is Malthusian, as is any distillation or spoiling which would not be profitable in a free market.

– Prices fixed above the natural market level are almost always Malthusian. There are however reservations here on how to define 'the market price'.

– Protection, especially through customs barriers, is more often Malthusian than stimulating.

– The suppression of a discovery or a useful invention is a typical form of Malthusianism.

– A cut in working hours is not necessarily Malthusian. It can improve the distribution of the national income and lead a firm to improve productivity. We saw in part I the effect of such a cut. The introduction of the 8-hour day in 1920 was not Malthusian; but that of 1936 was, in fact if not in intention, since its aim was to 'share out the available work', a typical Malthusian phrase based on resignation.

– A move for an earlier retirement age is Malthusian. It is justified if leisure time is deliberately preferred to output, but not if its real intention is to eliminate men from active life in order to reduce unemployment.

– Policies discouraging double employment, or employment for pensioners are Malthusian in most cases.

– The same applies to restrictions or prohibitions on work for married women, if they are made in order to reduce unemployment.

– Confining rents (or any prices) below a certain level is narrowly and doubly Malthusian, if it is not accompanied by a vigorously progressive policy. Not only does it discourage building, but it reduces the national income, by an imperfect distribution of existing housing.

– Commercial property and increases in land prices based on siting and not productivity is a Malthusian kind of appropriation. Property is Malthusian when it does not safeguard the output of wealth.

– Publicity has Malthusian effects when it strays from its etymological purpose and persuades instead of instructing.

– Support for old-fashioned activities which are no longer justifiable commercially is almost always Malthusian.

– Any creation or retention of a post not justified by output (in the wider sense of the word) is Malthusian.

– Direct taxation is Malthusian, especially when it penalises productivity.[1] Direct taxation of unearned income is not, as long as guarantees are offered to savings.[2]

– Unpaid work is often Malthusian, in spite of appearances, because of the illusion it gives that a sector is operative when it is really wasteful.

Sterile protectionism

Many of the above practices stem from a wish to protect the economy without at the same time renewing it.

Pure protection of rents puts poor tenants out into the street, mere protection of immigrants without the necessary investments suppresses immigration, pure protection of wages without any recognition of marginal workers can turn a poorly paid worker onto the dole, etc. Many of the policies of socialist capitalism have uneconomic and antisocial results, because the legislators refuse to recognise the iregularities of a situation, and want to iron it out, only forcing those they intended to protect into an even crueller situation, or out of existence.

There are many examples of this misguided sense of responsibility. After the liberation of France in 1944 the various governing bodies, struck with idealism, rivalled each other in insisting on quality. They demanded far higher standards of building than were current at the time rather than greater numbers of houses. As a result children deprived of air and heat died, couples without a common roof were forced apart. But at least responsibility was avoided: had houses been jerry-built the government would have been blamed for forgetting that we live in the twentieth century and not in the Middle Ages. As long as housing develops on a small scale but to exacting standards the rulers can show scale models off proudly in their offices and propaganda, and blame the narrow-minded financiers for refusing to subsidise a nation-wide drive for buildings of this quality. The Malthusian protector is right in the mind of the time, but almost certainly wrong when the results are judged later.

---

[1] See A. Sauvy, 'La rémunération progressive', *Revue Economique*, December 1953.

[2] Economic Malthusianism can be found completely described, under its various headings, together with experience gathered from continuous observations, in A. Sauvy, *Mythologie de notre temps*, 1965, pp. 162–4.

In 1966 the shanty towns in the Paris region are a standing indictment of the post-war legislators.

A similar attitude appears, we have already seen, when the retirement age is discussed. The age is automatically placed too low by the unions, to encourage promotion and increase leisure, and the financiers try to make up for this by reducing salaries and pensions. In the end promotion occurs on too small a scale and pensions are so low that retired people have to find work, in very bad conditions. The objectives have not been achieved but the unions are absolved from responsibility for the situation in the eyes of their subscribers. No doubt their duty is to press the ruling class to reforms, but when this pressure is too strong or in the wrong direction, when no account is taken of the 'breaking point', the only result achieved is the vain satisfaction of having done one's duty.

The pure intentions of qualitative Malthusianism appear everywhere and generally agree with the classical image of the middle classes. All these apparently protective measures leave part of the population out in the cold without houses or jobs; they create an illusion of overpopulation, a mass of unadapted families which do not fit the standard laid down and are unemployed and practically excluded from society.

Before He made the world, the Creator, according to the snake in Valéry's poem, was content with the 'purity of non-being'. One day He grew tired of this Malthusian attitude.

The failure of social democracy in many countries, France especially, can be explained by its mere application of brakes, with no driving motor. The failure of the creative spirit is naturally expressed, on the level of the family, by a dislike for children. In 1936, when the French Popular Front came to power, there could have been massive nationalisation, widespread planning. and vigorous aid to families. It was content with decreeing such misguided improvements in wages and reductions in working hours that it was doomed to fail. Malthusianism can be all-embracing. Slowly, property regained its privileges. The workers' parties are no doubt pleased to be able to point at the reluctance of capitalism in agreeing on a minimum of social justice. But it is hardly necessary to continue proving the fact, which is accepted. Because of the Malthusian spirit a chance was lost to advance towards social justice.

Active communism cannot be Malthusian, since it places itself on a collectivist and national level. It often opposes economically progressive policies even when it is in power, for political reasons considered to be above economics and which economists are not allowed to discuss. But in capitalist countries the Communist party often proposes Malthusian measures. Also, by provoking strong social-democratic reactions, it brings about even more firmly Malthusian ideas.

Economic Malthusianism and institutions

Monopoly is fundamentally Malthusian. Concentration and cartelisation need not be total or even totally explicit, to favour Malthusianism. Any drop in the number of producers, any forming of more or less personal links between them, creates a feeling of solidarity which may not actually encourage them to lower production, but lessens the will to produce.

Property too can be so, for a variety of reasons: the satisfaction of ownership may prevent creative investments (see the *latifundia* in Latin America); or there may be no stimulating land taxation; or there may be little competition. In many circumstances, we have seen, a concern would not gain by a higher output, and its policy can vary with individuals' attitudes.

This is more or less the opposite of what happens in procreation, a natural act that one can only prevent by a wilful attempt. The output of wealth on the other hand is an unnatural act which needs a will to come into being. If the will fails, output is affected even though no obvious factor may have appeared to reduce it.

Trade unionism is anti-Malthusian when its claims are well directed and stimulate technological progress, but it often falls into the mistakes described above and lowers the output of wealth by preventing better productivity. Britain is perhaps the country where this is most apparent, because its attitudes are so profoundly rooted in the past. They were excusable, if not legitimate, in the nineteenth century, when progress was recessive, but have no meaning in the twentieth century, especially now that the government has trade-union support. The unions are acting against their own interests as well as against the public interest.

Relationship between economic and demographic Malthusianism

Where the limitation of families is too strong, and the population only increases through ageing, economic Malthusianism becomes virulent. Malthusian policies have been applied several times to growing populations. They can be caused either by monopolies, or by abnormally acute crises (as with the destruction of coffee in Brazil in the 1930s). But a population undermined by demographic Malthusianism is fatally tempted by stagnation, as the remarkable example of France shows (see chapter 3 above).

Let us recall a few facts about that century-long hesitation in front of progress, and those utopian backward-looking dreams. In 1842 A. Mimerel, a founder of the *Confédération du patronat français* (Employers' Federation) wrote a programme of six points of which the last three are accurately summed up by R. Priouret as follows: 1. French industry must not normally worry about exports. 2. The frontiers must be closed to all foreign goods. 3. Investment must be limited: if necessary the state must intervene to stop it.

After 1880 demographic Malthusianism appeared still more acutely in various sterile attitudes. The Méline tariffs of 1892 pushed agriculture along the downward path; at the same time subsidies were given to sailing boats in the face of competition from steam, and for the culture of madder, suffering from the invention of synthetic dyes. The need was constantly proclaimed of a 'return to the land'. In the 1930s J. Caillaux, President of the Senate Finance Commission, was still to assert that France was over-industrialised. Immediately after the last world war foodstuffs were destroyed during a period of rationing; the representatives of agriculture tried to prevent the diminishing of the agricultural population; the owners of the larger chemical industries refused to accept the usefulness of building new factories, and so on. The renewal begun in 1939 was not yet fully conscious, and economic Malthusianism had only retreated slightly; *it is only receding with inflation and it may still cause a new demographic fall.*

There is another lesser-known form of this evil: linguistic Malthusianism, again characterised by the fear of creating.[1]

Europe and the Common Market

Western Europe in turn has been marked by Malthusianism. It only ensures economic progress by encouraging continuous inflation, a kind of double game that falsifies values, expedient in making unexpected achievements possible, but leading to equally important chances being missed. This is the case with the Common Market. In principle it is anti-Malthusian and creative of wealth, through better division of work and higher productivity. When the Europe of the Six was envisaged in 1950, at a time when it was planned to extend it further, this was clearly stated. But industry, in France at least, was reluctant to shed its age-old protections.

Now, fifteen years after those cradle songs, we can see the extent to which the forces of stagnation have stifled the creative spirit. Reduced tariffs have of course had a good stimulating effect. *But no positive creative action has yet been taken*: neither the electronic nor the aviation industry, nor any other, has put to use the much desired existence of a market of 180 million people, and the export openings it should bring. France, Germany, Italy, Belgium, and Holland still continue to buy long range aeroplanes, amongst many other things, from the United States. If the latter had had customs barriers between the fifty states they would never have developed an aircraft industry at all.

Neither has the closely-knit cultural community, which could have led to better understanding, been developed. Debates have mainly centred on the transfer of a few agricultural products, a very interesting question no doubt,

[1] This topic has been described by me in: 'Une forme de Malthusianisme: langage et population', *Population*, July–September 1952; 'Rénovation du français', *Revue de Paris*, March 1963; 'Menaces sur la langue française', *Revue de Paris*, November 1963.

but only relevant to a minute part of the income of the community and involving no creation of wealth except in a few specialised areas. The thorny conflicts which threaten periodically to put an end to the Community, could have been easily solved had new sources of wealth been created first.

The E.E.C. is entering a crisis because it has shied away from creativity.

11

THE FAMILY

Though there have been many studies on the family and one is tempted merely to refer the reader to them, it can hardly be left out of a work such as this. Two aspects are especially interesting: the optimum number of children (in view of a given objective), and the curious reversal of age-old values which we have been witnessing for the last half-century.[1]

Family equilibrium

This would be achieved given the ideal number of children. This optimum, like the population optimum, depends on various ends. If purely economic satisfactions are sought, then the optimum is zero in certain kinds of modern families, whereas it was equal to the maximum in traditional peasant communities. But the psycho-social balance of the family itself is a more important aim.

Robert Debré,[2] an eminent specialist, has studied this question with care. He claims that a family with only one child is especially unbalanced.

There is no doubt that the only child is a special kind of being; not only does he feel at every moment of his life that all the gestures, care, and worry of the father and mother are converging on him, but he knows with certainty, more or less consciously, that the future is absolutely his. He cannot fail to believe himself the centre of the world. He is destined to be treated too long as a baby, and then too long as a child: if only he could not grow up at all! If only the lost youth of his parents could be permanently re-enacted in him! He will become demanding, like any 'spoilt' being, and he is destined to the disappointments and sufferings of any being ill-prepared for life, as well as to the measly pleasures of an understandable egoism.

In a family of two children these troubles are lesser but they still exist: 'Our experience shows that the difference between an only child and two children is, as a general rule, considerable. But it also points to the fact that two are not enough.'

The family optimum, which is also a social optimum, is usually supposed to be either three, four, or five children. Indeed, a family of three is the smallest one that will ensure the renewal of the population. Below this figure quantity

[1] See R. Prigent and others, *Renouveau des idées sur la famille*, Paris, 1953, and especially J. Stoetzel's article on 'Les fonctions familiales'.
[2] In 'La famille heureuse ou l'optimum familial', *Population*, October–December 1950.

and quality thus decay together: life avenges the insult directed at it. In a country where mortality is low the optimum of three, four, or five is sufficiently above the renewal level to permit a fairly large increase. But this is reduced if the number of children in question is merely the initial objective in marriage, and is based on a plan to space the children out. So in this case, the family optimum is very close to the social optimum.

Decline of the family as an institution

The part played by the family unit in the life of societies (life in the strictest sense) needs no stressing. It represents a living community needing no strict legal basis: a balance of forces, so difficult to find anywhere, based on absolute authority tempered by sexual or paternal weaknesses. The family in the widest sense also has an economic and social function. It is a small society.

Like all instutions, it was able to last indefinitely as long as technology was stationary; but when progress began, even the firmest of social structures were questioned. The discoveries of the compass, of America and of gunpowder had determined the crisis of the family or perhaps an evolution, of which no one could see the end.

Molière's Chrysale in *Les Femmes Savantes*, already had great difficulty in defending the domestic virtues. Like the moral and political authorities, he could feel science shaking the delicate balance he had inherited and wanted to pass on to his children.

From the eighteenth century the history of the family is one of slow decay. From a conservative point of view, any change is a move in the wrong direction. With the doubts cast on the absolute sovereignty of kings came similar doubts within the family unit. At the same time various works asserted the equality of women and men, without causing scandal This was not feminism, as we would define it today, but it was a step towards it. The mere fact that paternal authority was so often stressed showed that it was being doubted. People even spoke out for divorce and whispered about ways of limiting families. Contraception spread around 1750 into progressive sections of society (i.e. part of the aristocracy and of the upper middle class).

In the nineteenth century children over twenty-one began to marry of their own free will and set up house often a long way away from their parents. The exodus into the growing towns and the appearance of industry contributed widely to this dislocation. Economic progress and geographical dispersion led relations to live completely separate lives; men had to rely on their savings to subsist in old age. Even in its reduced state the family unit lost its solidarity: the emancipation of women and the relative emancipation of children encroached little by little on the father's authority. It was not, as is often thought, the movement for work for women that caused the change. Even after the First World War women at work were still largely a novelty in the middle class.[1] But it took place more and more outside the home. Business became more and more separate from the family unit.

After education became compulsory in France, but before the appearance of family allowances and free education, children gradually disappeared. Marriage was preserved because of the advantages of a community needing no absolute authority and no constitution: between married people, first physical unity, then force of habit, was enough to maintain life in common, which could hardly be disrupted without causing some pain. Children might reinforce these links but were no longer considered as absolutely necessary.

In middle class families the progressive disappearance of servants led to the emancipation of children and especially of girls. As with all long-term trends, this one was partly spontaneous and partly caused by an active vanguard, which merely had to be of its time to be ahead of the inert masses. At this time playwrights and novelists clearly took the part of marriages for love against marriages for convenience; the feminist movement appeared with all the more self-assurance since it felt it was struggling against primitive practices. Free love became a kind of social platform, comparable to having more rest days or union rights. If causes such as this are wagers, then feminism was a safe banker.

The early twentieth century, proud of its new title, dared to look even further forward. Yet, Léon Blum in his book *Du Mariage* (1900), still only advocated trial marriages: 'It took some courage to surmount the attraction I felt for free love.' However new, and from a certain standpoint logical, his idea, he was well behind others, such as Binet-Sangle, who in his *Le Haras Humain*, described almost scientifically the sharing of women, dreamt of by Campanella and the utopians. Eugenics seemed to lie in the expected path of progress.

For the time being, abortion, openly advocated by some authors, became a normal part of life. In all European civilisations, the birth rate dropped, without causing any alarm since the population was still growing. Anarchism and other advanced theories advocated fewer births, to reduce the flow of cannon fodder and work slaves. They laughed at mothers with large broods, and scorned the animality of reproduction. The family, in short, defended especially by conservatives and reactionaries, began to appear an out-of-date survival, which society merely tolerated.

The First World War precipitated certain trends. Women gained a foothold in factories, where they sometimes held posts of responsibility. Girls continued their emancipation in the frantic post-war parties and it became fashionable to get engaged without telling one's parents. It was at this time that Victor Margueritte's *La garçonne* told women that 'their body was theirs'. In the eyes of many the disintegration of the family was still in its early stages. Soviet

[1] See J. Daric, *L'activité professionnelle des femmes en France*, Paris, 1947; 'Quelques vues sur le travail féminin non agricole, en divers pays', *Population*, January–March 1948: F. Léridon, *Le travail des femmes en France*, Paris, 1964.

403

policy continued to attack it. Lenin proclaimed complete freedom for women, if not for children, and legalised abortion. Even before Huxley, various authors imagined a new kind of reproduction without the help of women. Those who foresaw the human incubator were not considered more revolutionary than those who had advocated votes for women around 1830.

Curiously enough, only the retarded supporters of the family had any demographic sense of the future. An enlightened intellectual might remain of his time and live in a 'bourgeois' way, but he could foresee profound changes for the coming generations. In 1920 the prophets were blithely announcing that the century would see the end of this survival from another age. Indeed, there could well seem to be no doubt about the future from their viewpoint. For the last four centuries prophets had forecast the gradual break-up of the traditional family and had always been right. Was it not tempting to suppose that this trend would continue? The Soviet Union seemed to be setting the pace.

A renewal after the war

Now, however, in the middle of the century, a very new situation exists. The family has not recovered its former cohesion, but is very much in favour as one sees by: 1. *Family allowances* for children and sometimes even for a wife who stays at home. These appeared in France between the two wars and spread thanks to the war to most countries. 2. The *rights of families*: until the Second World War very few national constitutions mentioned these. Out of the 39 national constitutions written after the last world war J. Daric found that 33 had included clauses on families and their rights and 4 mentioned the rights of individual members of families. 32 mentioned the right of protection by the state. These countries were dispersed, with as many in the western and the Communist blocks as in the underdeveloped countries. 3. The *Universal Declaration of Human Rights* of 1948, which contrasted with the individualistic *Déclaration des Droits de l'Homme et du Citoyen* by asserting that 'the family is the natural and fundamental element in society and the state.' 4. The return of *parental authority*, the *restraints imposed on divorce*, and the *prohibition of abortion* in the Soviet Union. 5. The *retreat from polygamy* to monogamy, especially in Moslem countries. Similarly, the Chinese Popular Republic has prohibited concubines under the family roof. 6. The *rise of the birth rate* in the West.

It seems therefore that a centuries-old trend has been reversed, judging by the variety of civilisations and political systems where these things have occurred. There are two possible ways of accounting for this, apart from the fact of the official Soviet reversal.

The fear of decay: Between the two wars the drop in the birth rate accelerated in the West. At the same time the new demographic techniques showed that a population could have a positive balance of births over deaths, even though it might already have been for some time in a period of demographic decay. The discovery of the net reproduction rate, then called the 'Kuczynski' rate, helped to single out and publicise this fact.

The 1929 slump stressed or seemed to stress the drop in the birth rate. In some capital cities (Oslo, Vienna) the reproduction ratio had fallen to about 0·4, a figure that seemed to point to rapid decay. This was brought to the public consciousness, in France especially, and after an underground penetration during the war, ideas came to fruition.

At the same time some countries returned to a more extroverted policy: France experienced the shame of an invasion directly attributable to its sterility, the United States saw their Soviet rival rise against them, Australia in 1941 felt the breath of the yellow world on its deserted lands.

Lack of a substitute for the family: This much more important factor was first discovered by the Soviet Union. Communist authorities and writers assert that their doctrine has not changed, yet only after having been in power were they able to realise the true cost of training a man. The progressive revolutionaries, in their enthusiastic criticism of the old system, had not appreciated the extent of this responsibility. The family, a kind of refuge between laws and economic relationships, can accomplish tasks of which society appears, for the time being, incapable.

The cost of children has now been estimated much more precisely by Lotka, Henderson, Malignac (see above, pp. 233–47). In many countries the war made necessary experiments of a far more instructive kind than the classical orphanages. It is obvious that to replace all the care of the mother by paid labour, including Sunday and night work and overtime, would demand far too large a fraction of the national income.

The question of quality also arises. Mothers are widely thought to be less successful than specialised nurses, yet experience has contradicted this (see the work of Spitz and Heuyer). Whether or not it brings germs to her child, a mother's kiss is an indispensable part of its affectionate environment. Children brought up 'rationally' and separated from their mothers are affected by what Heuyer called 'hospitalitis'. They are like people who feed on prepared fruit for the sake of hygiene, but thus deprive themselves of various vitamins. Affection is a requirement as vital as an obscure vitamin. The kibbutzes are far from fulfilling the hopes they inspired, and one wonders what their fate would be in a country less united and tense because of the national danger.

Biology has failed to answer this question posed by progressive opinion. Men are still produced in the same way as they were three thousand years ago. There are better anaesthetic techniques in childbirth but there have been no basic changes. This 'technique' is backward and forces other aspects of social life to conform to it.

Neither has equality of the sexes been achieved. The principle of work for women is being posed anew with the spread of part-time work, because the long-awaited emancipation of the housewife has really only ended in imposing on her a double task: her professional one and her home one.[1] Couples with the same professional qualifications have had to have recourse to that old and simple process, division of labour within the family.

In emancipating children, the decay of the family has been a factor of juvenile delinquency. Most delinquents come from unsettled family backgrounds. Society has thus come to realise that the family has a necessary function and, unable to create a new organ, has decided to restore the old one. Progressive opinion has been abandoned, because it had forgotten an essential factor.

On the other hand the increased expenditure imposed on families by the longer years of schooling and the decreased parental authority, has caused them to begin to fail in their essential function, which is to train sufficient numbers of men. The family has had to be helped, or at least recognised. Until recently, families only had legal rights in the person of their head: as a result their earnings were taxed as one income, at the higher rates; through taxation on housing, families were made to pay for their needs rather than for their resources. Children were thus considered as the result of the eccentricity of parents, who would have been better advised to raise dogs or collect pictures. A compromise had to be reached between the families, who had decided to go on strike, and the authorities, who found they could not do without them. Aid was introduced and families, now more certain of their strength, are trying to prevent their protectors from interfering with them. At the same time, though less consciously, another benefit was given to families who, able to evade taxation, have tended to form minor self-governing groups, usually contrary to general economic interests: consumption and production circuits within a family, bartering between relations and so on. Hence the idea that certain businesses are only workable 'on a family basis', thanks to its various compensations or advantages, explicit or no.

Free unions exist but are no longer defended so ardently. Society has freed itself from free love, whose adepts had tended to elevate it into a system. The Greenwich Village artists no longer have to conceal their marriages. Actors and acresses team up, whether legally or not, without the former ritual. The *demi monde* has disappeared or rather has mingled with the real world, making the situation clearer.

Modern drama and novels still often criticise the family unit, with new

[1] See J. Stoetzel and A. Girard, 'Budget temps de la femme dans les agglomérations urbaines', *Population*, January–March 1948; A. Girard, 'Budget temps de la femme mariée dans les agglomérations urbaines', *Population*, October–December 1958; A. Girard and H. Bastide, 'Budget temps de la femme mariée à la campagne', *Population*, April–June 1959.

weapons borrowed from psycho-analysis, but it resists and appears to have become immune. Whole families often visit the theatre to see plays exposing the most violent Freudian complexes, and return home without showing the slightest disquiet.

The wish to leave one's children something more than one's name, either a fortune, a social situation or a frame of mind, is still a powerful motive for action in many countries, even the Soviet Union. This gives the family considerable power. By the education received at home and the material and cultural advantages it brings, the families of the governing classes can transmit in part their intellectual level and hence their income. Whether in the Soviet Union or in France, total equality of education appears unattainable, as long as the family continues to exist (see below, pp. 491–4).

All this does not mean that the situation is final; far from it. In a dynamic technology, where in fact many fields are still behind the stage they would reach even if progress were to cease abruptly, nothing can be final. The assumptions are continually changing. By a strange process, family allowances, originally an article of social justice, have been integrated quite naturally into the general system of social security which itself was at the start intended to replace the old family solidarity.

The past cannot be recovered. The stark *Maternities* of Picasso move us more than the sweet family scenes depicted by Greuze, and show the extent of the changes that have occurred.

The so-called reformers who had to back out when they saw the resistence opposed by the situation, are reforming their ranks. It will not always be necessary to combine in one institution the satisfaction of sexual needs, the convenience of living units and the rearing of children. But even without the resistance of religions and materialist moral systems directly based on them, no important change can take place without important biological or economic developments.

12

THE POPULATION OF THE WORLD

For a long time this phrase merely referred to a sum, an idle addition. It merely indicated the relative importance of each country in the world, and even such comparisons were of limited interest, since one knew very little about the most populated countries in the Far East. In the last few years the 'problem of the population of the world' has been posed, usually meaning the 'overpopulation of the world'. Those who mention it usually wish to point out the excessive growth of the human species and the risks this entails.

In fact there is so little solidarity between countries that this problem has never really been put properly. Not only does the Communist world pursue its own isolated line, one might even say its double line, but even in the capitalist world migrations are slowed down by frontiers, power is broken up into geographical units and it is only really inside each individual country that real problems of population exist. Timid mentions are made of a western European population, because there are the beginnings of solidarity between the various countries here.

For the time being, there is no more a problem of world population than there is a world budget. This topic is therefore an anticipatory one. It could be formulated thus: if men were strongly linked together, for instance by a world government, there would be problems of food, space, and employment, due to the surplus of the population for the resources available. The wish for, and perhaps even more the fear of, solidarity brings about the idea of the world population. It is fatally a Malthusian view, since half the people in the world are hungry. The well-fed inhabitant of a developed country feels no emotion at all at the thought that part of the planet is uninhabited; he is more struck by the other, overpopulated part. One is thus led to anticipate on the future and define the problems likely to arise from the pooling of resources, or even from mere collaboration; but the Malthusian view easily urges very complex solutions. Some countries would find themselves accused of overpopulation, others would be asked to make room for the less fortunate men. Such a view even lacks any internal logic to commend it. As long as the national units subsist as they do now, everyone's life is necessary to society in general. Centres of decay would be dangerous for all. There is therefore a 'false problem of the world population'. A problem is not in fact true or false in itself but it can be badly defined, and this is the case here.

More particularly, no book is less liable to help solve the problem than

Vogt's *Road to Survival*; and many other books in the same line are little better. Their emotional and feverish Malthusianism has rather the reverse effect.

A badly defined problem

Let us assume, however, that one day the nations achieve a sufficiently high degree of solidarity to be able to ask themselves clearly whether the world is overpopulated. Remember that one must always distinguish between temporary overpopulation or underdevelopment, and real overpopulation.

Bleeker and Van der Maden used unemployment to measure the surplus population: 'We will consider as a surplus the part of the population which, in spite of appropriate action to remedy employment, and demand being normal on the internal and external markets, has not achieved and may not be able to achieve regular employment of a kind that would ensure an income compatible with an acceptable standard of living.' This definition may be correct for an industrial country but it is absurd to apply it to the scale of the world. In talking of the world population one should be thinking mainly from the point of view of supplies.

Is there an exact method of comparing the growth of the world population to that of the production of supplies? Scientists find this question very embarrassing, but emotions do not feel the same reluctance, and forge ahead into unchartered fields where any antics are allowed. In fact comparing an enormous population, which we can only conceive with great difficulty, with enormous amounts of supplies, is at the very best an attempt to measure the immeasurable.

Many of the theories that appear scientific are in fact emotional. A Malthusian of today who has not read Vogt is thus heard to say: 'A layer of fertile earth only about thirty inches thick is supposed to provide food for three thousand million men.' How could one establish a ratio between these two figures without any mention of the area involved? This is merely a piece of bravura based on the enormous lack of proportion between the two figures, an attempt to frighten the listener out of his critical wits.

The opposite theory is backed up by similar arguments. The theorists of abundance use evocative phrases: 'the generosity of nature', 'the gifts of science': 'Everything will light up as if by enchantment, the sap will be renewed to an inconceivable extent. Inventions will occur at an unparalleled speed.'[1] These people quote the odd example of the lake of Constance: if the whole of humanity were plunged into it, its level would only rise by about nine inches; by using the fact that it is only a dot on a map of the world, one contrives to give the impression that humanity has plenty of space and can multiply rapidly without risk. None of these arguments are at all rigorous.

[1] J. Duboin, *Libération*, Paris, 1936.

Geometrical progression of the population

Malthus' well-known theory that supplies progress arithmetically has no foundation, but his idea that the population progresses geometrically is worth preserving. We have already seen (chapter 7) that a population not practising contraception and benefiting from present-day medical science could in an extreme case double in thirteen years, whereas Malthus thought he was being generous in forecasting that this would take twenty-five years. But the exact speed is not all that important: whether it doubled in thirteen or twenty-five years humanity would, in very few centuries, not only burst through the economic ceilings, and the limits of available space (people have to be able to move around), but even the absolute ceiling in terms of supplies, determined by the terrestrial mass. Doubling in twenty-five years, a population of 1 would reach a million in five centuries: after that time, each descendant of the 2500 million present-day men would be left with an area fifteen inches square. After thirteen centuries the weight of mankind would be larger than the weight of the earth including its atmosphere.

These reckonings are not really meaningful; an error of two or three decimals is only of secondary importance. However, discounting the possibility of interstellar migration, which would solve the problem completely, one conclusion is certain: humanity cannot grow indefinitely at this rate. Its progress will sooner or later be checked, either by a rise in mortality or by a drop in fertility. Here a Malthusian will conclude: 'Well, if you want to prevent death's counter-attack, you must take the initiative in another field, and cut fertility.'

Let us not go quite so fast, and merely say that *assuming high mortality is undesirable, humanity will sooner or later have to reduce its fertility.* Time is not a negligible factor, and by that 'sooner or later', the two schools are so clearly split that they launch into passionate arguments. But let us first examine the other term of the equation.

The increase of supplies

How can one base forecasts of the production of supplies? The usual method is to extrapolate from some present or past trend. This can be done in various ways, of which two are obvious: 1. Supposing that techniques now known will spread universally. This leads to the conclusion that 'in the present state of science, when its fruits have been fully distributed, the earth will support comfortably 5, 10, or 15,000 million men and no more. Beyond this the situation would be difficult and the time left to us to diminish fertility is therefore very limited. We must act at once though it is already a little late to avoid any risk of over-mortality.' 2. Others consider the first method over-cautious in assuming that the progress of knowledge will stop. 'Where would humanity be,' they ask, 'if it had only banked on what was already acquired and had refrained from relying on the future? In the bronze age no doubt. It is as logical and more scientific to assume that developments will keep occurring at the same rate as they have in the past. Even if one is reluctant to rely on the acceleration of progress, it is unreasonable to suppose that it is suddenly going to stop in 1969 after continuous development over two centuries.' In other words prudence in this matter is very imprudent.

The extrapolation is, however, very difficult: there will certainly be nuclear, chemical, or biological breakthroughs, but no specialist can say precisely of what kind, at what time or with what results. A source of energy may be about to disappear when suddenly new reserves are discovered, or new sources developed. The distillation of sea water for instance is technically fairly easy; it is merely a question of when it will become economically viable.

Time is the great unknown here. To meet already explicit requirements it is in any case necessary to rely on discoveries yet to be made but possible, such as the synthesis of chlorophyll which may be achieved in five or fifty years; or on others not yet conceivable, which are a favourite ground for speculation amongst progressive and optimistic intellectuals. Without saying that discovery is the opposite of science, let us stress the fact that discovery is of its very nature unforeseeable. Science has not always developed in the expected direction. Imaginative prophecies have sometimes come true, but some still await the scientists' attention.

Even if the rather vague concept of scientific progress were to be sufficiently clarified to provide a means for measuring it, this would still not solve the problem of its direction. We are less interested here in abstract scientific progress than in the supplies it will provide. If it continues at the present rate, will supplies necessarily increase at the same rate too? Will the resistance of the environment allow agricultural outputs to rise at the same speed as before?

There is also the social question of the diffusion of practical knowledge. The human problem of spreading over the whole world methods developed and proved in certain countries is an immense task, which opens up enormous possibilities. If the whole world were cultivated as Holland is, its present population would be very well-fed. But this point is overstressed by Colin Clark who, in his optimism, hastens to multiply the total area of dry land by Dutch outputs. The whole problem of development will be examined again in the chapter on underdeveloped countries.

For the time being progress is following a very different path. Hundreds of millions of televiewers may watch the Olympic Games or a football match beamed via an artificial satellite, but there are still shortages of food calories.[1]

---

[1] See the instructive list of papers read at the *United Nations Conference on the application of science and technology to the interests of underdeveloped areas*, held in Geneva in February 1963.

Past predictions

This problem of scientific foresight is to some extent clarified by the various prophecies made in the past about men and their resources. Strangely enough, Malthus came at the dawn of unprecedented economic progress, and he gave his counsels of moderation at the precise moment when for the first time in the history of humanity they were becoming less necessary.

There had been predictions in narrower fields: in the eighteenth century there were widespread fears of an imminent shortage of wood. The population growth caused by the abatement of famines had led to higher consumption of forests either for housing or for developing new land. The needs would have justified the plantation of forests, on a scale related to the demographic growth. One understands the apprehensions of the time, but this very rarely led to Malthusian ideas, which are dictated by temperament rather than by necessity. As it happened, the fears were unfounded since considerable progress occurred in coal mining. This was by no means a coincidence. It is precisely the pressure of needs for heating and industry that led age-old prejudices and reluctances to be overcome and resources already known to be developed properly.

This example might easily suggest some providential intervention, but it should not lead to a passive optimism. Difficulties do not disappear on their own; they are overcome only by a population that believes in the need for lively human reactions.

An interesting geographical prophecy was made just before the Revolution by the progressive Abbé Raynal:[1] 'It would be foolhardy to determine the future population of the United States . . . but it will be surprising if as many as ten million men are ever able to find subsistence on these lands. The country will be more or less able to support itself only provided its inhabitants can learn to be content with parsimony and mediocrity.' No comment is necessary here.

Conversely, many optimists have denied the possibility of overpopulation, or have generously pushed back the limits of such an occurrence. The Marquis d'Argenson, who was farsighted enough to prophecy, in the reign of Louis XV, the invention of air-borne armies, also thought that France was capable of feeding fifty times its population of the time; i.e. twice the present population of China.

Scientific studies

Studies of the possible increase of supplies have been carried out, for food by the United Nations Food and Agriculture Organisation, and for raw materials by a commission of American experts presided by Paley;[2] there are also various other reports.

[1] *Révolution de l'Amérique*, 1781.
[2] *Resources for freedom*, Washington, 1952; 'La population mondiale et les besoins en

Where they try to estimate the productive capacity of the earth these authors are the victims of their prejudices. The optimists often quote the reassuring figures of 10–15,000 million men. 100,000 million has already been mentioned, though not very seriously. On the other hand Fritz Baade, after detailed research, arrives at the figure of 30–38,000 million.[1] Many pessimists do not even quote figures at all. R. Dumont though a resolute progressist, conscious of all the resources of scientific agriculture, is not confident that there will be sufficient supplies of food in 1980.[2]

What is certain is that insufficient efforts are being made, even in developed countries, to use natural resources properly. Not only are there fewer positive steps in this direction than the needs warrant, especially in Europe, but there is still regrettable wastage, such as soil erosion, or the socially useless consumption of large forests every day to provide newsprint for publicity. Malthusianism of course thrives on such waste. But efforts to prevent it are inconvenient to powerful private or even national interests. There is also a case, forlorn for the time being, but worth stating, against the squandering of resources by countries and even individual firms. Because of international competition, no country is able, when reckoning costs, to consider its wealth as a long-term investment or something to be preserved. Because of this, the number of men that the earth can support is diminishing.

In short, this is less a technological than a social and political problem. We have the knowledge to increase the output of food and wealth, and the main question is not whether it will be sufficient, but how we can apply it. If all countries were linked under an international authority this would be done fairly quickly. This is why the problem of the world population is, as we said, badly posed. It is narrowed for the time being by the attitude of developed countries towards large-scale demographic growth, and their reluctance to make the sacrifices they may be asked for.

The various attitudes[3]

It is not surprising, therefore, that answers to the 'problem of the world population' are more often inspired by private interests or sentimental prejudice than by proper study. Leaving aside evasions of the question, such as the interest in space research, judgments are affected by three important factors often acting together.

Social position (on the world scale): Here we find again the attitude of the

matières premières', F. Tabah, *Population*, October–December 1953. There have been many works on the problem since, but of insufficient depth.

[1] *La course à l'an 2000*, Paris, 1963.
[2] *La Chine surpeuplée. Tiers Monde affamé*, Paris, 1965.
[3] See also chapter 10 above.

ruler varies: populationist when absolute, Malthusian when his power is offset by duties (see part I).

Religion: Catholicism has taken a clear position. Curiously, the desire to discourage sin has led it into an optimistic and materialistic view of world resources, quite apart from confidence in the generosity of Providence. Yet why are Catholics worried by the prevention of births being made official in India or Turkey? How can pagans sin by intercourse not in view of procreation? And is this sin more alarming than others? The Catholic Church is not, as has often been suggested, merely encouraging its faithful to multiply – self-interest would rather be opposed to the proliferation of others. The real reason is probably the fear of seeing these practices spread amongst the Christian populations in Asia, and the subsequent international legalisation of contraception, and recognition by doctors. Hence its lively protests in the World Health Organisation and the United Nations.

Individual optimism or pessimism: Independently of class or religion, there are always optimists who are passionately interested in any new inventions and never worry about the failures and disappointments they often lead to, and pessimists who filter their information in the other way and mourn the coming disappearance of iron or oil resources. Both have plenty of room for speculation.

Thus a Protestant American with a pessimistic turn of mind has three reasons to be afraid of trends in world population, whereas the Polish or French Catholic of a fairly poor background but who is an optimist at heart, is in the reverse position. We are very far from objective truth. Yet, whether the situation develops clearly towards progress or towards overpopulation, the upholders of the opposite theory will be held to be criminal. Either they will have tried out of social or national egoism to sterilise populations that wanted to live, or they will have led humanity into a fatal proliferation.

There is at present a curious emotional contradiction in the attitude of western Europe and the United States. The apprehension in these areas about the world overpopulation should lead people to be Malthusian at home; logically they ought to reduce their own numbers to make room for the Chinese or Indians. But their feelings are not at all logical.

We shall describe the Communist point of view further on: it could be considered either as a variant of the religious position, taking religion in the widest sense, or as systematic opposition to the present rule without any clear reasons of its own. Their attitude might change radically if the Communist countries achieved the domination of the world and inherited the responsibilities this entails.

The attitude of the Third World is rather disconcerting: it does not consider the interests of the world as a whole. According to their political colour, the various countries avoid a proper study of the issue or carry out emotional campaigns of an unrealistic kind. They may be right, morally, in criticising the profits of international industrial concerns. But they are not so considerable if one considers that their transfers of wealth have been more than offset so far by the aid they have been given. The raw material market, which is often criticised not only by the Third World but by many westerners, is usually misinterpreted, as we have already seen (above pp 216–17): in fact the Third World is not criticising the wasting of natural resources, the real mistake, for if this were to increase, it is thought, markets would be strengthened. The whole problem is approached from the wrong angle.

Neither has the Third World understood the part it could play in disarmament. The over-armament of the great powers means that their external aid will certainly be insufficient, and might even cause a grave food crisis. It has not yet occurred to the two thousand million undernourished to unite and demand a block transfer of funds from the financing of death to a care for life. It would be worth trying at any rate, and one might then at least be able to talk meaningfully of a world population.

13

OVERPOPULATION IN A DEVELOPED COUNTRY

Whoever travels through the swarming communities of Asia, the hunger areas of the world, may either rest on his first impression that there is a surplus population, or conclude that the technology is hopelessly out of date and the social régime inappropriate. It is not the same in other parts of the world. One can hardly talk of real overpopulation in a country producing (or able to produce) the quantities of goods and services needed to enable its population to survive. There are two viewpoints here: 1. *A static view*: everyone has or could have enough to live on, but if the population were smaller the living standards would be higher. 2. *A dynamic view*: there is no overpopulation but the population growth is too fast and the relative standard of living is suffering.

The first view rests on the concept of optimum population, the second on that of optimum growth. From the static point of view let us study the things men might lack: natural resources (food, water, air, raw materials), work, or merely space to live in.

Natural resources

Either for historical reasons (exhaustion of mines) or because of a high density of population or because of the very demands of their industrial growth, the developed countries in Europe, including the Communist countries, import an appreciable part of the raw materials and the energy (especially oil) needed for industry and agriculture. The United States, which was for a long time a supplier, is now an importer.

In some of these countries (Britain, Switzerland, Germany), agriculture does not suffice to feed the population, even with the help of fishing. One is tempted to say that these countries possess more men than their soil can feed, which is the classical criterion of overpopulation. But the case of agricultural foodstuffs should be considered apart from that of industrial materials. Over the last few years the number of people it was considered possible to support on home-grown food has been increased considerably. France could produce 50 per cent more than it does. In Holland the polders are no longer such an essential factor of agriculture: the developments in glasshouse culture are changing the whole problem of the area needed for food production.

But in the International debates where each of the partners tries to sell its produce to the others, shortages of a peculiar kind appear: consumption is moving away from food that can be produced industrially (corn) towards products of a labour-intensive kind (meat). Cattle breeding is a threatened, archaic activity, only surviving for the time being because of tradition. The new intensity of agricultural production requires, in any case, a greater consumption of raw materials and these have to come from abroad. For the time being this problem is not acute, simply because in the rest of the world many countries suffer the opposite shortage. Iraq and Kuwait, for instance, would be hard put to consume all the mineral resources they possess. Others have to sell foodstuffs, even vital ones, to afford the industrial products they need, or to pay for their transport.

But if what is called underdevelopment were to disappear, if all countries reached the same technological level, the requirements in raw materials and energy would be much larger. We have referred to the question of a world-wide balance (see previous chapter). The question remains whether the natural resources of the world are sufficient to cover the increasing needs of all countries.

There are various ways in which the industrial countries may survive without one having to talk of overpopulation: 1. Their technology can remain constantly above that of the other countries – in other words underdevelopment can continue. 2. Some countries, even after development, may still, because of their large resources, find it profitable to export raw materials. 3. With the progress of synthetic materials (not only rubber and jute but also cellulose, proteins, etc.) and of new sources of energy (solar cells) materials at present considered useless may be so changed in status that the whole problem of natural resources may fade away. 4. The countries with few natural resources could also provide services, open themselves to tourism, operate international shipping, following the examples of Switzerland, Norway in the nineteenth century, and, more recently, Britain.

But such a distant possibility is hardly worth discussing, though this is no reason for condoning the wastage of oil, paper, metals, etc. that is allowed by a false sense of security. By abolishing publicity for pets in New York newspapers for one year, one could provide an African country such as the Cameroons with all the school books it requires.

The problem of petrol deserves specially close study, for it is practically the only example of a massive consumption for non-vital individual purposes. It wastes natural resources on an enormous scale, and can increase still more.

Water

This is the one natural product that need neither be synthesised nor exchanged because of its very abundance. 100,000 cubic miles of it fall on the Earth every day, and evaporate again. Because of infiltration and evaporation only about

10,000 cubic miles can be used; supposing that 50 per cent could be used again repeatedly after wastage, this gives an available stock of 20,000 cubic miles. Given present-day consumption, requirements are estimated at 250 cubic miles; but in the year 2000 if every inhabitant requires 55,000 cubic feet, and the world population is six thousand million, 4000 cubic miles will be required. At this rate of progression, resources and requirements will be equal in the year 2050.

But even then, overall equilibrium would mean serious local shortages. Crises occur already, not merely in arid areas, but in highly populated temperate countries. There are many reports of falls in the level of reserves. At the same time, rivers and oceans are increasingly polluted. However, desalination could be an interesting prospect in some areas.

Water, the type of the product suffering from decreasing returns, is thus a factor of overpopulation; its effect could be diminished if technology were better applied, but the fruits of progress would be quickly absorbed.

Work

Between the two wars the age-old phenomenon of unemployment was suddenly revealed to all. In the developed countries popular opinion blamed it on technological progress. The machines were slowly encroaching on the workers, and the shortage of work would spread. If it were so, there could indeed be relative overpopulation in terms of employment. One would have to 'ration' work by limiting working hours, or else reduce the population.

This easy view does not stand up to proper analysis, as we have already seen (Part I, chapters 15–17).

There is far less chronic unemployment in industrial than in agricultural societies. In the latter, underemployment is the rule. There is much more real unemployment in Egypt or in Pakistan than in England or the United States or even in the France of 1780. But nowadays industrial unemployment is registered, aided, and counted. Technological progress has slowly reduced overpopulation, but has brought it to light where it still exists.

There is no reason why it should be impossible to give everyone work, since the task of producing is unlimited. A collectivist society can no doubt practise this more easily than a capitalist society, but the latter is equipped in its own way. Over the last few years unemployment in the capitalist countries has dropped to a very low level, far below that found in various forms in technologically retarded areas. This is true even of the United States, where unemployment figures are reckoned generously. The general rise in prices is in part responsible; but the unemployment it prevents would in any case be due to defective occupational patterns (see below, chapter 18) and not to any real lack of work.

In other words, organisation may be distorted or faulty, but work is always plentiful except in the case of extreme overpopulation (for instance in the Far Eastern river deltas).

Space

Men's need for vital space is a more subtle, difficult requirement to define than the previous two. To discover whether it could determine a form of overpopulation in developed countries, one would as usual have to define the word *vital*. If this is taken in its narrowest sense, space is overabundant. Even Dutchmen have over half an acre each, and could thus live over fifty yards from their nearest neighbours without having to build on different levels. They should not lack oxygen or space to move around in. But taking *vital* in a wider sense, social requirements are a different proposition. They lead men to group together, not only because large spaces have to be given to agriculture, but so that labour can be divided profitably.

Crowding is regrettably intense in towns, even in vast countries with small populations. J-F. Gravier, justly but unsuccessfully, exposed the contrast between Paris and the 'French desert'. We have already mentioned the idea of optimum density, and the problem of country planning, expanded upon below, p. 446. Notice here that the worst slum conditions are not proofs of overpopulation, merely of bad social organisation. We have also mentioned in part I (p. 228) the form of overpopulation found in seasonal holiday resorts.

Dynamic population

The traditional concept of static overpopulation is constantly proving less realistic than that of over-abundant growth: once again, it is better to think in terms of *optimum growth*. Beyond a given rhythm of growth, the economy suffers: the standard of living does not necessarily drop but it is not as high as it could or should be.

The overpopulation of schools and hospitals, the shortage of housing, are not a proof of over-rapid growth. They merely show that for one reason or another the building drive has been insufficient. In the 1930s there was an acute housing crisis in France, where the population was stationary or even diminishing. It only disappeared for a time because of the economic crisis. It is worthwhile pointing out that the shortage of schools and hospitals in the 1960s is higher in France than in Holland, the USA, or the Soviet Union, although the growth and birth rates are higher in the latter.

The real signs of this state of over-fast growth are very difficult to spot. Only subtle research can determine the optimum growth, especially since so-called human factors, non-measurable, are involved. It may be that, although useful in the present, growth has painful aftermaths, whichever way it develops. A vehicle turning into a siding or into a poor track can very well keep up its speed, but is better advised to slow down and make the transition less abrupt. Conversely, slow, apparently euphoric growth may be an early forerunner of dangerous and costly ageing.

Any reckonings should thus be farsighted, but at a risk of greater uncertainty. Marginal studies of development normally lead to counsels of prudence, but it is dangerous to follow these too closely, for the benefits of growth are less obvious than its cost or than the discomfort of eventually uprooting oneself from the past.

14

OVERPOPULATION IN THE THIRD WORLD

Present overpopulation can merely be (see Part I, p. 220 and following) one aspect and a consequence of underdevelopment. In a country such as Switzerland, the 375 inhabitants to the square mile, if deprived of equipment or education, would be extremely poor and would suffer cruelly from hunger and cold. Conversely the inhabitants of Brazil, Congo, or Iran owe their food shortage not to excessive numbers but to underdevelopment. From the point of view of potential, most of the countries of the Third World are not over-populated, and all could improve their conditions substantially by putting their agricultural land to better use, prospecting their mineral resources better, creating industries, and so on, the fundamental condition of all this being the proper training of men.

Technology travels at various speeds

The result of the contact between the civilisations of the Third World and the western or socialist countries was the importation of the latter's acquired techniques, but at varying speeds. There are indeed three types of techniques: 1. Techniques against death. 2. Techniques against births. 3. Economic techniques increasing the output of wealth.

Of these three only the first travels quickly: it requires little capital, few technicians, and, especially, *does not require the active collaboration of the population as a whole*. With a book of instructions, an unqualified person can add chlorine or permanganate to a town's water supply at little expense. Vaccination itself is extremely cheap. An uneducated but well trained assistant can vaccinate with a high ratio of safety, not high enough for western countries, but sufficient to save a large number of human lives. Scared populations might conceivably refuse to be treated, and in this case these techniques would penetrate much more slowly. But normally consent is easily obtained. Vaccination does not require much follow-up care of the patient, and it demands passive agreement rather than active collaboration. And though it may seem elementary, it has a far greater effect on mortality than does curative medicine.

The classical contraceptive techniques, on the other hand, require active collaboration, with the exception of intra-uterine devices, which are difficult to insert. *Coïtus interruptus*, the proper use of a condom, a douche, or a calendar, something of a penance even in developed countries, are problematic amongst populations who have not crossed the economic and cultural threshold that we call critical though we cannot define it precisely.

Economic techniques also require active collaboration, often impossible in underdeveloped populations. It is very easy to buy an American car if enough financial aid is given; fairly easy to learn to drive it; far more difficult to repair or even maintain it. Modern machines can usually only be paid for by highly efficient use. Simple tools, spades, saws, hammers, axes, could help populations not far past the stone age but this form of aid is very seldom used (see Part I, p. 225) and its scope is limited. Everywhere real development is checked by the inability of populations to make efficient use of advanced techniques. As a result there is great difficulty in maintaining productivity, especially of food.

The disparity between the penetration of techniques preventing deaths and those preventing births causes a more rapid population growth than that of Europe in the nineteenth century. At that time, with a birth rate of 35–40 per thousand and a death rate of 25–30 per thousand the European population normally grew by less than 1 per cent a year. Nowadays many countries grow by more than 2 per cent, and 3 per cent is far from unusual, as in Mexico, Venezuela, Turkey, Malaysia, etc. It took the western countries two centuries to increase their average life span from thirty to sixty; this has been achieved in some countries (Ceylon, Formosa) in twenty years. *The lengthening of life has thus been ten times faster, whereas improvements in the standard of living are still problematic.*

With a relatively high average life-span and an exceptionally young age distribution, the populations of the Third World sometimes achieve astonishingly low mortality rates, such as western populations have never known. Thus:

Hong Kong	4·9 per thousand	United Kingdom	11·3 per thousand
Puerto Rico	7·1	United States	9·4
Formosa	5·7	France	10·7
Singapore	5·7	Sweden	10·0

These countries with very low mortalities all have a high density of population, which helps the spread of medical care; high mortalities are mainly to be found in Africa, in sparsely populated areas.

The penetration of knowledge about the prevention of death is far from complete, even in the most progressive countries of the Third World, but its effect on mortality rates will henceforth be smaller: if in Ceylon the average life span were suddenly to increase from 60 to 75, mortality would drop from 9 to 4 per thousand, a relatively low gain in human lives compared with the drop from 30 or 35 to 9 per thousand.

One may hope that on the other hand the penetration of contraceptive or economic knowledge will accelerate and catch up thus putting an end to the present dramatic distortion.

The two solutions

Emigration on a large scale must be excluded, and so the acceleration of these two forms of technology suggests the two possible solutions to the problem: the one economic and the other demographic.

Economic: The answer here does not, as people have long thought and still think, lie in the importation of capital, but in the training of men. Highly qualified men can pay for machines in a very short time, especially if they accept, during the transitional period, wages lower than those of the western countries. But the most sophisticated machines will be only a disappointment if left in untrained hands. The principles of development are contained in the old Chinese proverb: give a man a fish and he will eat for one day, teach him to fish and he will eat every day.

There are figures to show that too large a part has been attributed to capital in economic expansion. Thus in 1951 the United Nations experts reckoned that the 1527 million people in the underdeveloped world would need 19,000 million dollars a year to pay for a demographic growth of 1·25 per cent per year and achieve a progress of 2 per cent per year in the income per inhabitant. These 19,000 million dollars were only investments into agriculture and industry, and excluded social investments such as education, health, etc. Actual investment was always much lower than this, and demographic growth was always faster, yet the income per person still went up although according to reckonings it should have gone down.[1]

Appreciable progress can be achieved against non-economic factors such as superstitions. Thus if the attitude of Indians with regard to animals and especially sacred cows were to change one day, there would be appreciable economic improvements with no capital needed. Neither Japan nor the Soviet Union needed external investments to develop, because they achieved the necessary cultural revolution.

Demographic: Many works have been devoted to economic development but only a small number have dealt with the obstacles to the penetration of contraceptive techniques. All too often it is because of an emotional assumption that the problem is already solved, or at least that the difficulties are fewer than they are. Since we are dealing with social biology the problem must be examined at some length.

---

[1] See F. Benko, 'Les investissements en capitaux et le progrès économique dans les pays du Tiers Monde', *Population*, April–June 1965.

423

Obstacles to the prevention of births

In a traditional society devoted to the cult of fertility there are essentially two kinds.

From governments, ruling classes, and religious authorities: They may oppose revolutionary measures either out of a wish for power or prestige, or because they consider them immoral or subversive, or because, ill-informed on the new economic problems, they think that the existence of a large labour force still serves the interests of the country or its rulers. The latter are habitually shocked by any 'unnatural' check to fertility. They can also be particularly sensitive to the value placed on male descendants, stemming from traditionally high mortalities. According to another Chinese proverb: 'To have a son is to have no son; to have two sons is still to have no son; and only three sons can be counted as one son.'

Again, countries under a colonialist régime could only turn away from any policy of population control. The only defence of a subjected and weak species lies in multiplication. Any efforts of the governing powers in the other direction would have provoked a lively instinctive opposition. Freedom has not automatically changed this attitude. The new countries all pass through a phase of nationalism answering Jean Bodin's dictum: 'The only strength and wealth lies in men'. The old idea that the power of the ruler and the greatness of the country is measured by the number of subjects or citizens still retains remarkable credit.

The population ensuring the highest possible power is, we saw in Part I, always larger than that giving the highest possible standard of living (economic optimum): thus any government that is dictatorial or undemocratic (in the western sense of the word) is attracted by population growth.

The countries that have long been politically independent (Latin America, Iran, Ethiopia) were even more attached than some others to tradition, or religion, or the principles of domination described.

Thus around 1950 the Third World was almost unanimously against the prevention of births, or ignored it, with the same result. But slowly ideas progressed, and at the General Assembly of 1962 approximately a third of these countries voted in favour of contraception. The following table, adding up to an almost complete map, shows the various inter-penetrating and interfering currents.

The Catholic countries and all those influenced by Catholicism are against birth control; none of the Protestant countries are. There is a profound difference between Asia and America, all the more so if one only considers Latin America and if one extends Asia to Arab Africa. The figures then become 15, 9, and 3 for enlarged Asia, and 2, 4, and 11 for Latin America. This may be due to religion, or to cultural differences caused by ancient or present-day

For birth control (32)	Abstentions (35)	Against birth control (30)
Africa (10)	Africa (12)	Africa (6)
Algeria	Mauritania	Liberia
Tunisia	Senegal	Togo
Morocco	Sierra Leone	Dahomey
United Arab Republic	Ivory Coast	Cameroon
Guinea	Niger	Gabon
Mali	Tchad	Madagascar
Ghana	Central African Republic	
Nigeria	Ruanda	America (11)
Burundi	Tanganyika	Argentina
Uganda	Sudan	Uruguay
	Ethiopia	Brazil
America (2)	Libya	Bolivia
Chile		Peru
Costa Rica	America (6)	Columbia
	Canada	Venezuela
Asia (11)	United States	Honduras
Turkey	Panama	Salvadore
Cyprus	Cuba	Guatemala
Syria	Jamaica	Mexico
Iraq	Haiti	
Pakistan		Asia (3)
India	Asia (8)	Lebanon
Nepal	Israel	Iran
Ceylon	Saudi Arabia	Philippines
Thailand	Afghanistan	
Malaysia	Burma	Europe (10)
Japan	Cambodia	Ireland
	Indonesia	Holland
Europe (7)	Nationalist China	Belgium
Iceland	Mongolia	Luxembourg
Norway		Austria
Sweden	Europe (9)	Czechoslovakia
Denmark	United Kingdom	France
Finland	Poland	Italy
Yugoslavia	Hungary	Spain
Greece	Albania	Portugal
	Bulgaria	
Australasia (2)	Rumania	
Australia	USSR	
New Zealand	Ukraine	
	Byelo Russia	

religions, but it may also be related to the ways in which the two areas are populated. Latin America still has vast untilled lands, whereas in certain regions of Asia overpopulation is a traditional fact. These explanations do not make the difference any the less remarkable, since in matters of birth control, logic is rarely respected.

In Africa the countries in favour of birth control are usually those furthest from European rule. The Marxist orthodoxy does not influence them so much as hesitation in front of this new problem.

Since the 1962 vote, the trend has increased and the majority is now in favour of the prevention of births. The fundamental reason for this change is to be found in the economic field. One of the first gestures of any government in the Third World is to establish a national plan. For some time this may only be a façade, or merely a list of desirable objects. But after a few years experts begin trying to cost the investments required for the desired growth, using in particular H. B. Chenery's formulae. They are then so impressed by the enormous capital needed (and would still be so even if Chenery's method did not lead to a somewhat high estimate, as we saw above p. 423), that they begin to ask themselves by how much the cost of education, for instance, would be reduced if there were fewer births. The experts usually experience some difficulty in persuading their government, their dictator or their one party. But the obvious truth has progressed, especially in Arab countries.

Approached in their turn, the religious authorities find new interpretations of the old texts, usually without difficulty. As for the traditional ruling and owning classes, though they may not have a clear idea of a power optimum, they have often (though not always) appreciated that excessive numbers could act against their interests by increasing public expenses considerably. Absolute rule has given way to relative rule, a basically Malthusian structure.

The countries that have not followed this trend have usually had space to spare, and are thus less open to the argument for demographic investment. Scientifically they could well claim to have an even greater need for a rapid increase in population, in order to benefit from the advantages that density brings to transport and public services, and that numbers bring in the form of division of labour, and wider distribution of national overheads. Their reckoning, if it were conscious, would not, however, be valid for a population growth of over 2–2·5 per cent a year.

But generally governments have stopped preventing birth control, and have begun to support it with varying degrees of enthusiasm.

From families: The old pattern of society led fathers (especially peasants) to wish for as many children as possible, for material or emotional reasons. Once they come to realise the burden this implies, they may still object to antagonising Providence, Nature, Destiny, or the like. Even if they pass this barrier and are fully informed on how to prevent births, they may still fail.

There have been important changes over the last few years. Public opinion polls in many countries have shown that many women do not really want a large number of children. This is not surprising. Even La Fontaine's poor woodcutter, however 'primary' a worker, rightly considered his children as a burden, on a par with his feudal services,

Surveys of various kinds have been made to discover the number of children wanted. The mean numbers they lead to vary from 2·7 to 4 children per family; none give anything near the real figures (around 6), or the mean number a couple could have if it lived together during the whole of the woman's fecund life.

Thus a survey in Turkey in 1963, covering 5100 couples who had had on average six children, was based on the question: 'If you were just married and could have exactly the number of children you chose, how many would you want?' The answers were as follows:

Children wanted	by men	by women
0	2	3
1	2	2
2	17	24
3	27	25
4	15	16
5	14	8
6 or more	16	7
'As God wills'	6	12
'Don't know'	1	3
	100	100
Mean number	3·8	3·5

In Chile the mean number wanted in 1959 was four children. The question 'How many children would you like if you were just setting up family?' was put to 2500 women in various cities, and their answers gave the following mean numbers:[1]

Panama City	3·54
Rio de Janeiro	2·66
San José (Costa Rica)	3·98

Surveys in the Far East showed that the ideal number there was 4·3 in Formosa (3·8 in towns); 4·1 in South Korea; less than 4 in India; and 2·5 in Japan. The probability is that new surveys in these regions today would give smaller numbers.

A sample of one hundred married women in Thailand gave the following figures:

[1] The figures here are probably on the whole a little too low, since they are based only on the answers in the form of definite numbers. They excluded answers like 'As God wills'.

Real number of children	Women wanting more	Women not wanting more	Total
0	87·7	12·3	
1	70·1	29·9	
2	51·9	48·1	
3	29·3	70·7	
4	14·5	85·5	100
5	6·5	93·5	
6 or more	2·8	97·2	
In all	29·8	70·2	

However, the general validity of these results is not absolutely certain since surveys are mostly made in highly populated countries where the need to limit births is more strongly felt. The results might be very different in Africa. Also, as in any survey of this sort, the samples must have been unconsciously selected – but these reservations have no bearing on the sense of the movement. *There has definitely been a change in awareness, and large groups of people are now reluctant to have too large a family.*

Encouraging the prevention of births

Before the Second World War no national policy had encouraged the limitation of births. The USSR after the Revolution left the door open to abortion, but less for demographic than for political reasons. The first systematic attempt to reduce numbers was in Japan just after the last war; then came Puerto Rico and India; then widespread national movements or approvals of the policy of the Population Council or of the International Family Planning Federation.

Eugenics in Japan: The 'Eugenic Protection Law' of 28 June 1948 cast a pudic veil of qualitative ideas over an essentially quantitative aim: to reduce the number of births. It authorised the sale of contraceptive devices, and this led to a flurry of publicity. Paragraph 14 also allowed doctors and surgeons to have recourse to abortion and sterilisation under various conditions.

The effects were rapid: the birth rate fell from 27 per thousand before the war and 34 per thousand in 1948 to 17·5 per thousand in 1957, and it has stayed more or less the same since then. No similar drop had ever been observed in any country. The reproduction rate is now in the region of 0·9, so that the country is in a state of possible depopulation.

For some time the number of abortions was almost equal to the number of births; though of course there could be more than one abortion per woman per year, this shows that contraception was generally inefficient, especially to

428

start with, even though this was a relatively developed population. Another fact is that *in spite of this fast drop in the birth rate and the state of possible depopulation, the Japanese population is still increasing as quickly as before the war*. This is because mortality has dropped sharply from 17 to 7 per thousand. The Japanese are growing faster than the French although the latter have a reproduction rate greater by about a third[4].

Of course, the youth of this population is only a temporary fact. Japan has entered a period of intense ageing. At this rate, in 2015 one person in four will be over sixty. Japan is thus an interesting prototype.

Intensive aid in Puerto Rico: This country, burdened by more than 600 persons to the square mile after the war, received two kinds of aid from the United States: an open door to emigration into the states, and large-scale material and technological aid. Its education budget increased fifteen-fold over twenty years; the proportion of illiterate aged over ten dropped from 70 to 12 per cent. Births dropped from 42 per thousand after the war to less than 30 per thousand in 1965. The aid given in the public sector alone amounted to 15 per cent of the national income.

This proved that a drop in the birth rate could follow economic and cultural development; but the figures make it a difficult example to prescribe. On this scale, the whole of the income of the United States would not suffice to subsidise the Third World generally. This experiment does not really give us enough useful information on the economic and cultural threshold below which it is possible to obtain a drop in the birth rate through classical methods.

China and its mystery: The Chinese government had some difficulty in reconciling Marxist orthodoxy and the imperious need to slow down population growth. It first switched in 1956-7 to a policy favouring the prevention of births (intending to cut the birth rate by half over ten years), but returned to orthodoxy in 1958 after the publication of optimistic estimates of crops, subsequently recognised to be gravely wrong. After this, propaganda and policy returned to their former direction, but less aggressively. The Chinese government is undoubtedly the one able to achieve the best results in this field. Unfortunately it publishes no demographic figures, even on mortality. The silence is not so much a matter of policy; the statistics and registers are poorly organised. One may, however, assume that the death rate in China is close to 10 per thousand and the birth rate slightly below 30 per thousand.

India: Contraception became a national objective with the first quinquennial plan of 1951-6. The second plan made further provisions for publicity and research, and the third plan stressed particularly the educational problems involved. The 1964 budget for family planning was of 5 million dollars, i.e. one cent per person.

From 1956 to May 1965, 10,986 family planning centres were opened; this figure includes clinics and hospitals, and about 6000 distributing centres. 54,000 people were taught to pass on knowledge of contraception, 6271 in regular courses and the others in crash courses. 1700 advisory camps were organised for about 60,000 people; 90,000 lectures were given to 20 million people; 2000 films were projected to 11 million people.

In addition, some 884,972 people (569,500 men) were sterilised. For 1964 alone the number was 264,109. The operation is free but only practised in some states. It is only authorised if the person has at least two children and the partner's consent. Given a rate of 7 sterilisations for 1000 inhabitants, it has been estimated that the birth rate would drop by 50 per cent over ten years. But the Calcutta Bureau of Statistics is less optimistic. The result will depend largely on the age of the woman in the couples practising sterilisation, and this factor is never included in statistics.

Other countries: Some countries have a national family planning programme, and in others the governments have merely given support to private or local initiative. In late 1964, there were only five of the former: India (1950), Pakistan (1960), South Korea and Tunisia (1964), and Turkey. Abortion was officially recognised in Tunisia in 1965. In that year the International Family Planning Federation had agencies in forty-one countries: the five above, and other developed countries.

A large-scale campaign was conducted in Formosa, at first limited to the town of Taichung, but extended at the end of 1964 to the whole of the island. Ceylon is technically assisted by the Swedish government; clinics have been opened in Egypt, Thailand, and Singapore. The movement has been largely limited to Asia but is beginning to spread to Moslem Africa, Central Africa, and more recently, but intensively, to Latin America.

Resistance

An extremely primitive population with an animal-like existence is quite incapable of applying any method whatsoever. A very poor family, uneducated and badly housed, lacks the forethought, the material resources, and the singleness of purpose to submit to the constraints of the various classical methods. Since even a developed population has many mishaps, it is not surprising to learn of the unforeseen difficulties even when it is only a matter of following a calendar.

With these techniques, there seems to be an economic and cultural threshold below which one can hardly expect any result. Where can this threshold be? Can it be defined in either economic or cultural terms (income or education)? This is difficult to decide because various other factors may be involved. This is so with the 'European precedent': the standard of living of the French around 1760 when birth control began in France was far below that of Britain in 1875 when the birth rate began to drop there. With Britain in mind, the threshold may seem very distant in retarded countries; but this would be wrong, because techniques have progressed a great deal and government policies now encourage them.

In any case, since there is a threshold in each country, development needs to be studied as an important factor of birth control. It was particularly relevant, for instance, in Puerto Rico.

The cultural level is also influential, in its wider sense: it can include the emancipation of women and of older children, contacts with other populations, etc.

Results

Given all these difficulties, it is not surprising that efforts to cut births by classical methods have mostly failed. The most comprehensive and striking proof is found by comparing the demographic forecasts made by the United Nations after the censuses of 1950–51 and those of 1960–61. Fertility has so far coincided with the highest probabilities envisaged.

Another way is to observe the variations in birth rates in countries with decent statistics. Here are some figures for 1963–4:

Ecuador	4·7 per cent	South Africa (Indians)	4·68 per cent	Jordan	4·64 per cent
Salvadore	4·68	South Africa	4·63	Iran	4·6
Mexico	4·54	(half castes)		Tunisia	4·51
Venezuela	4·3	Gambia	4·49		
		Madagascar (minimum)	4·24		

These figures might seem to point to an almost total failure, but on closer examination there are rather less pessimistic conclusions: 1. In many countries the birth rate has begun to drop in certain sections of the population. 2. In a few countries the overall birth rate has begun to drop. 3. Developments in contraceptive techniques will entirely change the factors of the problem over the next few years.

The invisible drop

In underdeveloped countries statistics are very imperfect. It is even rare to find an efficient register of births. There is no knowledge of differences according to social classes. A few hints are given by surveys, which have shown that in several countries the more educated or the richer classes have started to reduce their families. We will quote two examples: a Moslem and a Latin American one.

In the United Arab Republic fertility is higher amongst Moslems than amongst Christians but clearly decreases where the level of education rises.

Here is the mean number of children per woman married for thirty years or more, given by the 1960 census.

Level of education	Rural areas	Urban areas	Whole country
Illiterate	7·2	7·9	7·3
Elementary	6·5	6·1	6·4
Primary	5·9	5·3	5·6
Secondary	3·7	3·3	3·7
University	2·7	2·6	2·6

The difference is remarkable in that these are relatively old women, influenced by fairly longstanding factors.

In Santiago a survey made in 1959 related the mean number of live births per married woman to the degree of education:

Illiterate or a little primary education	4·4
6 years at primary school	3·3
6 years at secondary or commercial school	2·8
4 years or less at university	2·1
More than 4 years at university	2·6

Here because the sample was small (it seems that there were fewer than a thousand women) we should disregard the minor differences between the last three categories and stress the obvious difference between the average of the last three, and the first two groups.

Similar results have been reached in several countries; but if this change of attitude only affects for instance 5 per cent of the population and only brings in this 5 per cent a drop of 20 per cent in fertility, the effect on the general birthrate is only of 1 per cent. Such a slight drop can be masked by the rise in fertility normally resulting from a drop in adult mortality giving couples a

Birth rates	Singapore	Malaysia	Formosa	Hong Kong
1955	44·3	44·0	45·3	38·7
6	44·4	46·7	44·8	39·7
7	43·4	46·2	41·4	37·9
8	42·0	43·3	41·7	38·8
9	40·3	42·2	41·2	36·6
60	38·7	40·9	39·5	36·0
1	36·5	41·9	38·3	34·2
2	35·1	40·3	37·4	32·8
3	34·7	39·4	36·3	32·1
4	32·1	—	34·5	29·4
5	29·9	—	33·3	28·5

longer active life. The particularly strong decrease in perinatal mortality has contributed to raising the birth rate.

But if the birth rate drop spreads from the élite to larger sections of the population, the effects can be more striking. This has occurred in recent years in at least four countries (leaving aside the special case of Puerto Rico): the figures in the table at the foot of page 432 are per thousand total population.

The drop has ranged from 25 to 33 per cent over ten years. Britain achieved this only over thirty-five years and Sweden over eighty years. These four countries are in the same part of the world and are partly or wholly populated by Chinese. This is not a sufficient explanation, since the drop can hardly be due to a racial difference. Besides the birth rate has also begun to drop in certain districts of Ceylon. But there is another common characteristic, obviously demographic: in all four countries *child mortality is very low*, well below that of France before the war or of Portugal today and similar to that of developed countries:

		(per cent)			(per cent)
Malaysia	(1963)	5·7	Portugal	(1963)	7·3
Hong Kong	(1963)	3·3	Hungary	(1964)	4·0
Singapore	(1964)	3·0	France	(1938)	6·5
Formosa	(1963)	2·6	France	(1964)	2·5

Of course the reckoning of child mortality in the Far East is imperfect. Probably some of the early deaths are counted amongst stillbirths. Still, this comparison is useful, and suggests the following conclusion.

The care and value of children

If a woman is capable of submitting to the regular demands and care necessary to preserve the life of a young child she should be equally able to impose the same discipline to herself, and apply contraceptive methods. Besides, a woman who takes great care of her young child becomes conscious of its importance and its value. Where only primitive care is taken and mortality is high, women are truly sorry at the death of children, yet they consider it with a certain fatalism because they valued them less.

One of the reasons for the drop in the birth rate in France around 1760 was precisely the important place given by society to children, who had been practically neglected up to then. There was a proliferation of books either on childbirth or on child care and general education.

The present situation in the Far East shows clearly the path to follow. *The teaching of child care is the way to prepare the ground for contraceptive practices.* Instead of urging people, as has all too often been done, especially in western countries, to dislike children, better results are achieved through the more humane and less sombre teaching of how to love children. This largely explains a point about child allowances which the public so often misunderstands;

they were first introduced for reasons of social justice, but they can very well contribute to *reducing* the birth rate in careless populations by encouraging the sense of economy and foresight. Similarly, it is since the governments of the Third World have been planning their economy and have started to keep accounts that they have begun to look favourably on the prevention of births.

Appearance of new techniques

We have already seen how the rise of the Third World has prompted research into new and more practicable methods of birth control for retarded populations (see above, chapter 8). Here, even the 'pill' is an imperfect method: taking medicine regularly in accordance with a calendar is easy in the West but not elsewhere. In Ceylon one husband decided to take the pills himself because he claimed to be more reliable than his wife.[1] There is also the well-known story of the mistaken, superstitious use of the abacus calendar.[2] Besides, though the cost has fallen sharply in the last five years and is sometimes subsidised, the expenditure demanded of the family can still prevent contraception in a poor country. It is much more difficult to distribute a product free than to provide a free service. To sum up: however convenient, the birth control pill still demands of couples, women particularly, active participation which leaves the way open to mistakes, forgetfulness, failures. This is why the Population Council has directed its research towards intra-uterine devices.

These, whatever their imperfections, certainly do not suffer from inefficiency, even of a practical kind. Couples may be passive, for the only initiative needed is their consent, as in the case of surgical sterilisation or abortion. When properly inserted and checked regularly, 'IUD's' can be effective for approximately one year. There is no danger of frequent lapses, as with other methods. Also, when they do remain in position for a year their efficiency is higher than that of abortion, whilst the operation necessary to insert them is minor, and less dangerous than abortion.

However, intra-uterine devices must be inserted and checked by experts. Scientific authorities think that it will be possible to educate mere midwives to the required level and dispense with a doctor's control. But even then, retarded countries will lack the necessary personnel. One reaches odd conclusions: *the considerable efforts of the white races, or 'developed' peoples, to reduce the prolificness of the others, may have their first effects on the birth rate of the less prolific, and thus increase rather than reduce the lack of balance in the world.*

[1] *International Planned Parenthood News*, December 1965.
[2] See A. Sauvy, *Malthus et les deux Marx*, Paris, 1963, p. 202.

The certainty of growth

In any case, even if the birth rate is to drop sharply, the population will still grow fast. Compare the forecasts made by the United Nations in 1963 for growth at current rates and at the lowest probable rate:

	1960	1980 current rates	1980 slow growth	2000 current rates	2000 slow growth
Eastern Asia	793	1139	963	1803	1114
Southern Asia	858	1418	1316	2598	1855
Africa	273	458	434	860	684
Latin America	212	387	352	756	514
Total	2136	3402	3065	6017	4167

The 'low hypothesis' depends an an important drop in fertility, since the difference between the two figures for 1980 is mainly based on the population under twenty, or about half of the total population. Yet the population will still almost double in forty years. A mean forecast gives the following falls in the birth rate per thousand:

	1960–65	1975–80	1995–2000
Eastern Asia	32·5	27·2	19·9
Southern Asia	42·3	35·6	26·6
Africa	45·5	44·6	40·0
Latin America	39·3	36·2	30·2

To avoid any population growth the birth rate would have to decrease by:

42 per cent in the Far East
56   in southern Asia
50   in Africa
63   in Latin America

Also, however sharp the drop in the birth rate it can only be effective on the population in search of employment in sixteen years from now. By then the latter will have increased by more than half. *Therefore quite exceptional efforts towards economic development are needed in any case.*

Ageing and various distortions

Unless the improbable happens and mortality rises again but only amongst the adult age groups, the population of the Third World must now go through a phase of ageing; in certain countries it will be faster than it was in Europe. Taking the mean United Nations forecast, between 1960 and 2000 the ratio of over 65s should rise by 70 per cent in Formosa (3 to 5·1 per cent), by 65 per cent in southern Asia, by more than this perhaps in China, by 81 per cent in the temperate part of southern America. These ratios could be even higher if the mean forecast is insufficient, and they are only the beginning of an important trend. *The world is left with an alternative: large-scale ageing or prolificness.*

Even if the more optimistic figures prove correct, and barring a sharp return of mortality or a large-scale accident, mankind will still need a long time to return to a fairly stable age pyramid. In the extreme case where from the present onwards mortality were to remain constant and the fertility rates were to settle at a level giving integral replacement of generations, more than a century would be needed to iron out the most important distortions. Because mortality is still not affected by the whole range of known techniques, and is therefore destined to drop further, it is probable that there will be no kind of stability achieved over the next two or three centuries. And if new discoveries prolong the life of men beyond today's limits, this demographic adventure will have an outcome still more difficult to foresee.

15

GEOGRAPHICAL DISTRIBUTION OF MAN

The way in which men should be distributed over a given land (i.e. politically united and continuous, or in which there are at least no major obstacles to travelling) has never been a great problem, either because the distribution was chiefly the result of a series of individual decisions or because rational organisation would have involved few embarrassing choices: in an agricultural society men must disperse so that everyone finds enough land to feed himself. The only factor that might interfere was the search for safety, and there was usually a compromise between the two aims. But with urbanisation and industrialisation the question of distribution has become more arbitrary and problematic.

Three questions are involved: 1. What should the geographical distribution aim at? 2. If the real distribution is different from the best one possible, is it desirable to change it to achieve or approach the ideal? 3. If one decides to change it, how can this be achieved?

The essential objectives men can be seeking are economic wealth, social justice, demographic and medical health, military defence, or a pleasurable or clement climate. We shall examine them in turn. Other less important factors may also intervene: thus morality, religion, mixture of populations, interior police efficiency, conservatism. These objectives may be mutually contradictory: the army would prefer industry to be dispersed in an uneconomic way, the economist or the financier will shock the socialist or the regionalist by distributing men to serve productivity; also, within each objective there may be inner contradictions. There must therefore be a compromise between all these diverging trends.

Economic objective

Here, in a given land, one wants to ensure the highest possible output, given the technology and trade openings available, through a careful geographical distribution. The productivity of a man or a tool being more or less the same everywhere, the first preoccupation will be to reduce transport of all kinds as much as possible. The distribution of men exploiting primary resources is in the main imposed by the lie of the land: farmers must live near their farm, fishermen in ports near to the fishing areas, miners, quarrymen, etc. near to their work. The range of choice is only local in scale, and even here, natural factors such as the existence of water supplies very often dictate an answer. Geographers have made good studies of this problem.

The distribution of secondary workers, those transforming primary products, is more a matter of speculation. Should they be near to their primary resources or to their market? In the second case, they usually choose to live in towns, together with most of the tertiary workers. This solution is the obvious one for certain occupations such as maintenance workers and builders. For real industrial workers the general economic interest points to the first answer. The heavier and the more raw the material they work with, the more desirable it is to process it on the spot. Ore must obviously be purified on the site of the mine, whereas the jeweller or metal-worker who eventually makes use of it can very easily be located in the town.

With the development of transport and the new intensive treatments of raw materials, the influence of the materials themselves has diminished, and new factories are located in a more arbitrary way. But another factor must be taken into account: the existence of a population capable of industrial work. This is not only a question of qualification; it includes what one might call the industrial state of mind. It is always difficult to create an industry in a purely agricultural or artisan area. On the other hand an existing industrial area will grow shoots almost spontaneously.

Tertiary workers, using relatively few materials, are more mobile and can be distributed from this point of view in a more arbitrary way. They are, however, more dependent on the location of customers. Schoolteachers, postmen, certain kinds of tradesmen, doctors, etc. must live in a community of some size.

However, if one wanted to create, out of a vacuum, a new fully independent town, one would have a wide choice of location. A new country founding a capital usually pays more attention to political than to economic reasons: Washington or Ottawa were placed on the limits of two political zones, and the siting of Brasilia was also made to satisfy political conditions.

Old towns are not always sited at the spot that would nowadays be judged best. The two islands of the Cité and of St Louis no longer seem to play an essential rôle in the life of Paris and the city would have been better placed, a modern observer may think, at the junction of the Seine and the Oise, or somewhere else in France. If Marseille had to be rebuilt it would be resited on the estuary of the Rhône; Berlin or Madrid could equally well be moved.

Nowadays new purely tertiary towns can be sited mainly in order to minimise transport costs. Every man consumes roughly two pounds of food a day, which is costly to bring to him. For this reason, A. Allais advocated simply creating new towns in the country. In fact the organisation of markets is a more important factor than the actual distances.

Even if all the basic data were perfectly known, it would still be a very complex problem to determine the best distribution of men from a purely economic point of view. Besides, the data would change constantly. If the relative cost of transport were to drop suddenly, all the previous reckonings would be wrong; choices would then have to be made not only in view of the present situation but in view of the most likely technological and demographic evolution.

The size of towns

How does this appear from a purely economic viewpoint? Generally, technological progress causes the tertiary sector to grow and stresses the division of labour while making transport easier; it thus encourages urbanisation. But here, still more than with the general distribution of men, one must separate clearly the solution best adapted to private interests and that most suited to the general interest. All other things being equal, the administrative expenses per inhabitant drop as the town first grows, but rise again beyond a certain point. Hence an optimum size, which is very difficult to measure, is in fact usually smaller than the real size, for two reasons.

1. When the optimum size is achieved the marginal cost of an additional inhabitant is higher than the average cost. A gallon of water consumed by the newcomer will cost more than the gallon supplied to those already there, even if the old plant is not yet paid for, because water has to be sought further afield. But the new inhabitant will not pay more for water; like the others, he pays the average price and will therefore tend to be identified with the mass even though his arrival is in fact costly. Similarly, the new car owner pays the same parking or road duties as the old, although his existence is more of a nuisance than theirs. A community can hardly proceed otherwise. Yet it would have to do so for private and public interests to be the same.[1] Because of this the economic limit is usually largely passed; the additional inhabitant will only think twice about coming when conditions have become very difficult (very expensive water supply, extremely congested streets, high taxation). In practice this ceiling is never achieved so that the size of giant conglomerations goes on increasing beyond reasonable porportions.

This kind of marginal cost is the reverse of the one described in part I in the case of national immigration. There the new immigrant took part in the national duties, notably in social security, while costing less, but was not personally rewarded for this; for reasons of efficiency, firms could be led to reject him as submarginal even though for the community his output was larger than his consumption.

2. The second reason is of a socio-political kind: a town defends its rights politically and today this creates false values. Thus Paris constantly developed its advantages thanks to its central position and even to the fear the other

---

[1] If the town's debt is very high there may be financial reasons for raising the population over the optimum level, but this would have no effect on the economic disadvantage.

439

districts have of it. The cost of delivering a letter, for instance, is much lower in Paris than in a backward area of France; but the reverse is true with many other things: the loss made by the railways in the Parisian region is borne partly by the provinces.

In every country and at all times, critics have denounced excessive, gigantic cities. The history of towns is accompanied by constant laments over their growth. In fact the sizes condemned one or two centuries ago have been largely passed in a way that seems to prove that the critics of the past were merely reactionaries, and that those of today might well be too. This logic is not, however, valid here, because, as we have seen, private interests lead the town to grow far beyond its optimum size without this being realised. Besides, the progress in individual travelling has reduced the optimum size of towns in terms of inhabitants, and yet they still continue to grow.

Urban property

Liberal theory could impose a ceiling on the growth of a town, determined by the enormous tribute to be paid to the owners of land. Yet this corrective factor is counterbalanced by the ever greater advantages found by tradesmen, businessmen, and even individuals, in living near the centre. In any case the ceiling would be far higher than the optimum size. But over the last few years the cost of land has become a public issue, and spurred legislators to a few insufficient but significant restrictions. Even from the economic point of view, and especially from the social point of view, the correct solution would be to tap the increase in land values so that it benefited the community.

Depopulated areas

There is also the reverse problem: that of insufficient numbers. One should distinguish carefully (see part I, chapter 3) between the concept of optimum population and that of the minimum density necessary to ensure economic livelihood. Of course, some new countries have managed very well with low densities or rather with very uneven densities. But even their experience has shown that the sparsely populated areas were very unstable; areas had frequently to be totally evacuated. In Europe this would no doubt occur too if populations were not now firmly rooted. If one were not considering any extra-economic factors, the solution most suited to a depopulated area would usually be the most brutal one: either to give it life by creating new sources of wealth able to populate it more fully, or to bring about an evacuation, and either abandon the land for reafforestation, or introduce a seasonal tourist population. The concept of optimum population is more valid for a limited area than for a whole country.

Technological progress has relieved overpopulation (see part I) and at the

440

same time modified the optimum distribution over any given land. It is more and more worthwhile concentrating the population into a reduced space. The French population seems to inhabit a country several sizes too large for it. Yet even very highly populated countries include large expanses with hardly any inhabitants at all.

As soon as the productive value of land is no longer the main issue, the question of human relationships becomes predominant. The education of children is a more and more important factor, and so are the medical and social services. The need of couples to find two sources of employment can hardly be met in a sparsely populated district. All this points to a concept of *optimum density*, which is still largely unexplored. It used to be a question of land, but now it is more a question of space.

Social objective

A society may be said to want a just distribution of income and full employment. This brings one back very quickly to the ground covered above when speaking of land values in towns.

Another desire would be a healthy communal life. This approach, often considered in the past, stresses the difficulties of urban life and the social evils resulting from it, the most recent being juvenile delinquency. Poverty in the country is always more presentable and less apparent than in towns, even if from a strictly economic point of view it is the same. A poor peasant can easily be considered to have a certain bucolic charm. For a long time prostitution, alcoholism, and slums were considered a privilege of towns, a sign of corruption; hence the many sermons preached over the last two centuries for a return to the land and its virtues.

But once the first miserable period of the proletariat was passed, a new trend appeared in industrial countries. Though unable to eliminate prostitution some countries have restricted it and lessened its threat. Alcoholism has become even more widespread in certain country areas than in large towns. The traditional disadvantages of living together, we have already said, have largely disappeared in the more modern districts of towns. The better openings for education, either technical or general, amount to a great advantage over the country.

Over the past few years the traditional dislike for large towns has been narrowed down to flat life, and towns made up of dispersed individual houses have become more acceptable in France. Flats, it is said, lack spirit, humanity, and create neurotic or psychotic townsmen. Observations do not confirm these prejudices, all economic considerations apart. Statistics quoted in support of the new movement are usually biased, if not made up wholesale. Research carried out by the INED in 1965 showed that the general feeling is one of satisfaction, though satisfaction is perhaps the wrong word in that it

Suggests fulfilment and plenty. Large-scale suburban flat developments do at least have the advantage of creating either entirely new requirements such as playing field, libraries, etc., or of satisfying old ones that were repressed in the old populous districts. This is one of the most interesting instances of requirements multiplying much faster than the output of wealth.

Demographic and sanitary objectives

These are: the lowest possible mortality and illness rates, and adequate fertility rates, which may be more or less consciously planned.

There is at least no doubt that *mortality* must be reduced as much as possible. Towns were long believed to be centres of high mortality. The legendary healthiness of the countryside was always contrasted with Baudelaire's 'mortality on misty suburbs'. Popular legends suggest that people live to a century only in the pure air of the mountains: such stories are still very much to the fore in Soviet newspapers. No doubt this was true for a long time. But it is being reversed. The country still has its air but has not improved it, and men can take better care of themselves when they are within easy reach of each other. A social worker or a doctor can visit an industrial worker's house much more easily than an isolated cottage. Modern town planning ensures that large conglomerations have plenty of air and light. There may be more illness in town but there are fewer deaths.

The genetic factor must also be mentioned. The breaking up of isolates over the last two centuries has had good effects everywhere by reducing the number of homozygotic defects.

The problem of *fertility* is more complex: we have seen that it is always higher in the country, but the difference is becoming very small in some cases. Here one should distinguish between geographical dispersion as such and other factors that go with it: occupation, religion, way of life, tradition, etc. The arrival of peasants in towns seems to sterilise them, but this does not prove that the systematic dispersion of workers' families of Malthusian culture would increase their birth rate. The advantages of space and gardens are quoted, but it has not yet been proved that families living in these conditions have more children than real urban dwellers.

In short, dispersal does not have decisive advantages from the demographic and sanitary point of view. Conditions of life are more important than lesser or greater density. Population or distribution policies will not long have to give such high priority to the sanitary question, providing certain essential aids to families and medical and social services are preserved.

Military objective

Unfortunately military security is not and never has been a negligible factor

442

in the distribution of men. Fertile but unguarded plains were deserted and people lived on towering unproductive mounds. Once national unity and internal safety was ensured the trend was reversed, the mounds abandoned and towns began to burst their walls. It proved difficult and costly to build industry a long way from its raw materials, and at this time military considerations had little influence on the civilian population.

The development of aircraft caused new headaches. In the age of bombs, the ideal situation for industries was dispersed, far from the threatened frontiers. Between the two world wars France, Germany, and Russia all had to reckon with this new requirement. But the lessons of the last war show that nobody could really be protected from the fighting. Mountainous, poor, non-industrialised regions suffered cruel guerilla warfare. A quiet part of Normandy, devoted to the holiday industry, was subjected to an invasion that no pre-war strategist could have foreseen. Since then the progress of atomic weapons has been so fast that almost total uncertainty reigns in the field. The present-day concentration of economic resources in a few small areas creates obviously attractive targets, whereas, with the weapons currently stronger than the armour, the best tactics would seem to lie in dispersal.

Climate

This factor has only recently become important. Even unhealthy districts used to be highly populated as long as life was possible there. Then came the seasonal migrations of rich Englishmen to the French Riviera or the Swiss valleys. Between the two world wars climatic migrations became customary: people without any firm roots, and of independent means, such as authors, chose to live on the Mediterranean or the Californian coasts and brought with them their tradesmen and their tradesmen's tradesmen. If general welfare increases the classical drop in the utility of goods can give rise to a stronger wish to live under pleasant skies. This change has been helped by the switch towards tertiary occupations (the further removed one is from one's environment the easier it is to choose the environment) and by the increasing tendency to fear the cold since the spread of central heating.

There has also been such important progress in improving unhealthy conditions that a new situation exists in certain areas. Practically none are now considered as fatal to whites as long as they take proper precautions and condition their immediate environment.

Combining the various aims

The economic objectives appear to prevail today. If a new area is colonised somewhere in the world, as soon as some sanitary and social precautions have been taken, the main aim is to increase output and employment and pay for the cost of the equipment. But within a new society, thanks to the developments in technology and economics, the physical location of men is becoming less imperative, and this will allow other factors, such as climate, to play an increasing part.

Factors of imperfect distribution

If a country has arrived at a sufficiently precise conception of the ideal distribution of its population, and it is realised that the situation inherited from the past does not conform to the ideal, this may be due to various reasons: 1. Climatic change. This very rarely happens quickly. 2. Technological and social change: discovery and use of coal, mechanisation of agriculture, development of education, all make population movements desirable if not necessary, and they never occur without delay. 3. Change of objective: the need for safety may be replaced by economic ambitions, making population in certain mountainous regions an anachronism. 4. Irrational migration: individual migration can lead to abnormal situations in which a return is advisable – this is particularly true of certain congested areas. 5. Differences in fertility or mortality: fertility especially can vary widely between two areas, and it is generally higher amongst poor and retarded rural populations: for instance in southern Italy, Andalusia, etc. Between two rural districts of unequal fertility there can appear important differences in density with no geographical justification; natural migration never totally makes up for this – thus there has only been slow migration from the high fertility areas of western France towards low fertility Gascony, in spite of the efforts made to encourage it.

Attitude towards imperfect distribution

The question is whether, in a liberal society, one should encourage a corrective trend, and, in a planned economy, whether one should intervene to help it, and to what degree. From the specifically economic angle, the problem is mainly one of transport and can be simply formulated: *Should men or goods be transported?* Should the men be moved permanently or for a long period to the points where their productivity would be highest, such as the sources of raw materials, or should they be left where they are and provided with raw materials and sources of activity? There can be two kinds of obstacles to correction.

Economic: During the destruction of Berlin by bombs in 1943–4, the Nazi party, whether out of desperation or bureaucratic inertia, laid down plans to reconstruct the city. The first impulse was to create an entirely new Berlin on a better chosen site and leave the ruins as they stood. Such a step had much to commend it. Yet reckonings would quickly have shown that the requisitions to be made, the rebuilding of the entire rail and road network on a new basis, the underground supplies of gas, electricity, and telephone cables, added up to figures dictating a new Berlin on the same site, although there was so little of it left. Of course, in such a situation reckonings depend mainly on the prices one places on land. It would also be true to say that land prices only rise up to the limit beyond which they would cause the old site to be abandoned.

Now consider the siting of Marseille, chosen more than twenty centuries ago because of its small natural harbour, which now has no economic interest at all. If the city were to be resited, it would be placed further west near to the Rhône. But the enormous expense and general reconstruction necessary would undoubtedly be prohibitive, even if there were no human resistance. The expenses incurred would of course increase the national income and would have a positive interest rate on the national scale but amongst the mass of investments possible in France, many others would bring higher returns; the moving of Marseille would shock even the least sensitive accountants.

In other circumstances memories from the past can be a source of income from tourists (Venice, Toledo, etc.) and thus tie a city to its original site. One might say that in modifying their environment men have changed the ideal site by crystallising a past situation.[1]

This crystallisation is, however, precarious in certain cases: often an industry set up near to the sources of raw materials remains there after the materials have been exhausted because of the importance of the buildings and the qualified personnel. The Belgian zinc industry now imports its raw materials from Mexico; Mazamet in the south of France is still one of the centres of the world wool trade; Marseille continues to specialise in oils. But this is all transitory wealth. If one day Mexico contrives to set up a zinc industry and protects it for a time, it will inevitably replace the Belgian one; Mazamet may at any time be short-circuited by Australia; the blast furnaces along the Loire estuary are direly threatened by the rational system of railway charges and the prospect of a free market in iron. It may be, of course, that national planning leads to preserving the anachronism to avoid having to displace at great cost men deprived of work; it may be cheaper to offer them temporary employment on the same spot than to build factories and houses elsewhere. The problem then becomes one of time, and of deciding whether to maintain and reconstruct existing plant or to let it dwindle away.

Human: Men may have roots in their native area even though their presence has become archaic. In the days of free enterprise human resistance was not

---

[1] This is a general feature in civilisation. It is extremely costly to change the most illogical remnants of the past, such as the linguistic irregularities consecrated by usage, or the duodecimal system. As time passes it inevitably becomes more expensive for Britain, for instance, to adopt the metric system.

taken into account. Men had to follow industry willy-nilly and pile into large towns and industrial regions. Whatever the complaints of the regionalists in France, the human drainage towards Paris went on for over a century without very much being done about it. The conservative instincts of men were dominated by the pitiless reckonings of costs. Even the most idealistic of local politicians was only too willing to arrange jobs in town for his electors as railwaymen or postmen. In the United States, whole areas were literally drained off. Ever since the initial agricultural colonisation of New England, which was not very suitable for agriculture, the drift to the west has continued relentlessly. Had the land been colonised first by Asiatics from the west, the converse would have happened, with the movements following at any given moment very close behind the optimum of the time.

But in Europe today resistance is much stronger and until there is a highly complex planning system, it will usually be necessary to resort to stop-gap measures, and give people work where they are, even if they are in the wrong place. Occasionally governments act early: thus in order to avoid excessive urban growth, which might lead to political and social unrest, the Swiss conservatives cleverly contrive to maintain country dwellers on poor land by enforcing artificial prices. Usually, however, the opposite occurs: people bring pressure onto the government to protect their old activity or at least its location. The closing of a worked-out mine is always bound to cause a national drama. The concentration of rural property has long caused lively resistance, first from idealists and then from workers' groups, though the economic factor usually wins in the end. The natural result is that a peasant is either ejected or attracted elsewhere by economic pressure, or is encouraged to move in an organised group to another richer area well provided with energy and raw materials.

Only a politician can choose between the economic interests that advise migration and the social or electoral interests that lead to conservatism, because there is no common factor to these two objectives. There may be some compromise, but not of a sort that can be determined by arithmetic; here human choices are more important than figures.

Regional planning

Attempts at rational population are not new. The Dutch aimed at it for centuries with their polders; there was the colonisation of the New World; the kings of Prussia had it in mind[1]; here and there, marshy lands have been drained and dry lands irrigated.

In western Europe where there is a high density of population, it is a matter of general policy, though each country has its particular brand, either to cor-

[1] See C. Lévy, 'Un plan d'aménagement du territoire au XVIIᵉ siècle: "La Métropolitée" d'Alexandre Le Maître', *Population*, January–March 1957.

rect recognised defects in the distribution of population by causing appropriate migrations, or slow down natural movements considered as undesirable by raising living standards in the areas that are being deserted. These policies affect various fields and come under various ministries, and are correspondingly difficult to co-ordinate and apply. One can use either direct authority (especially in the case of planned economies) or prohibitions (building permits), exhortations, and subsidies.

The stronger the intervention of authorities, the more people object and bargain, even in the face of an offer. Great mistakes have been made, especially in housing policy, because governments have attempted to be too paternalistic. Men prefer their own mistakes to those of others, sometimes even to their own better judgment. As in any political matter, the result is achieved when the majority toes the line while still feeling it has chosen freely.

A frequently quoted example of successful direct intervention is the big reduction in post-war unemployment in the 'devastated areas' by the British Labour government; local government policy in Britain is often quoted too. In France regional planning or *aménagement du territoire* has become, with the appearance of a ministry of national planning, an essential instrument of economic policy. Decentralisation and regionalism have become an important issue, though of course actions are still not on a par with intentions.

The rather mythical idea of a return to the land that has haunted so many minds seems to have more or less disappeared in most countries, at least in its old reactionary form. The excursions into nature that long holidays with pay permit probably have something to do with this more reasonable attitude; though the most important factor is the industrialisation of agriculture.

On the question of the distribution of population there is still a great deal of work to be done, both politically and scientifically. Perhaps even the mention of 'science' in this field is whimsical.

16

INTERNATIONAL MIGRATIONS

A 'migration' is a move of a certain scale made by a number of people (excluding soldiers). It can consist equally well of daily trips of workers into a large city (commuting, alternating movements or *Pendel-Wanderung*) and of permanent removal from one continent to another. It will not, however, apply here to tourist travel, even of a permanent kind, or to seasonal migration, even that of workers; we will only deal with real changes of residence involving permanent settlement in new surroundings. Also, we will be more concerned with international migrations, having dealt with internal ones in the preceding chapter. We shall then turn (chapter 17) to the question of the assimilation of migrants; the economic aspects of migrations have already been studied (part I, chapter 22).

Causes

The following distinctions should specify the problem: 1. Which person or organisation, whether social or political, decides on the move? 2. Why was this decision taken?

First, there can be either voluntary or forced migrations. They are in a sense 'forced' if the elements make a move necessary: this can be the case with drought, floods, famine, changes in climate, volcanic eruptions, etc. But here the migrants retain to some degree the choice of the time at which they move and the destination they make for. The term 'forced migration' is better reserved for cases where this is not possible: deportation or expulsion, as during the last war and its aftermath. The chiefs of a tribe can also bring about a forced migration of all its members.

Between wholly voluntary migration and pure deportation there is obviously a series of intermediate cases: in an area where a factory constituting the only source of work closes down, it is difficult to talk of voluntary migration. If, immediately it closes, the workers are all attracted to another area, their move is to all intents a forced one. Or it can happen that by changing their residence the wealthy bring about a necessary migration of the poor living off their expenditure. When the aristocracy flocked into London or Paris after the Renaissance they were followed by a flood of country dwellers. But in these cases the migrant has a frame of mind different from that of the refugee, since he at least believes that he has chosen his new life. The same applies when migration is encouraged by a superior authority but the result of an individual decision; the reasons that prompt the authority and those that compel the individual can be economic, social, sanitary, political, religious, etc.

Where the migration is voluntary, individuals can be prompted by reasons of the following kinds:

Economic: Life may have become too difficult, either because they have too low an income or because work is short. Sometimes without actually being *rejected* migrants are *attracted* by prospective gains elsewhere. This applied to the migration of the British into their dominions, to that of Chinese tradesmen into various parts of the Far East up to the last war, to that of Algerian Moslems into France, etc. The economic impulse can range from the precise comparison of the wages or incomes in the two countries, to the 'dreams of brutality and heroism' that Hérédia attributes to the conquerors of the New World. The question is not whether the migrant will find better conditions in the new country, but whether he thinks he will.

Social: When people are ill-adapted to their environment they may learn to live with it, as we shall see in the next chapter, or decide to leave, either for political, racial, or religious reasons. Though the environment is usually responsible for this unhappiness, the actual decision to leave may come from the individual, sometimes in the face of intolerant authorities: take the case of the East Germans migrating over the border into West Germany in the 1950s. Similarly, the first emigrants to the United States were mostly religious sects who were not actually persecuted but who felt they would be able to flower better on the new territory. The racial migration into Israel also falls into this category. Other cases occurred in areas often pillaged by troops.

Geographical: An unhealthy environment does not cause as many migrations as one might think. There was no exodus during the great epidemics, though the instinct for self-preservation might have prompted it. People have tended in modern times to go and live in pleasant climates (French Riviera, California) but this is usually a case of internal migration.

The authorities usually organise or encourage migrations for either political or economic reasons; racial or religious motives are subsumed into political attitudes in such cases. There are few purely religious decisions, such as the expulsion of Jews and Arabs from Spain; the herding of Red Indians into reservations was, at least in part, prompted by economic reasons. The same applies to the population of colonies or recently conquered territories. The slave trade, especially the importation of Negroes into America was more of an economic phenomenon, and so was the transportation of workers from various countries into Germany during the Second World War.

A proper study of a migration would also have to show the causes of non-migration, the reasons why the prospective migrant does not go to certain destinations, or, more frequently, does not move at all: unhealthy conditions, plain inertia, tradition, ignorance of possibilities abroad, etc. Without necessarily thinking of nomadic peoples, one must pay attention to the existence of unstable groups, ready to move at the slightest difficulty or at the slightest hint that things are better elsewhere.

Economic and demographic migrations

Emigration always has demographic consequences, even if it is temporary, since it separates couples and reduces the birth rate. But there is a useful distinction to be drawn between 'economic migrations', of workers (usually males), either single or separated from their families and intending to return to their country at the first opportunity; and 'demographic migrations' of entire families, or at least people of both sexes. The second group are a permanent asset to a country, providing they are stable. But the first type has no very permanent effect even if the male workers stay and perhaps marry in the new country: they have still broken the balance between the sexes.

There is one exception to this: when a country has suffered great losses in men. This was the case, for instance, when Spanish and Italian workers immigrated into France after the First World War.

Social problems posed by international migration

These are many. Here the 'attitude of countries' refers of course first to the authorities, and then by extension to public opinion. But the attitudes of various social groups, trade unions especially, and of people coming into contact with the immigrants are also very interesting.

Attitude of the country the migrants leave: This conforms to the general attitude of rulers, described at length in part I. The ruler dislikes any decrease in the number of his subjects. Many pre-industrial authors criticised colonies for taking the life blood out of the mother country, which, in losing subjects, was being drained of power. La Morandière, a typical champion of domination, advocated sending mainly foreigners to the colonies.[1] Parliamentary democracies long took the opposite view. Not only did they not wish to retain individuals against their will, but they did not see in these departures any certain cause of loss. Only military considerations, arising from the concept of absolute rule, could occasionally cause some worry. Thus the German Imperial Government, closer than the others to absolute rule, insisted on keeping in touch with emigrés and helping them to return by a law on dual nationality.

With the fascist dictatorships between the two world wars, the absolute rule complex became predominant again; the Italian government made great efforts to retain its nationals or bring them back. But after the return of

[1] *Appel des étrangers dans nos colonies*, 1763.

450

democracy to Italy after the war, the official attitude was again reversed: the individual had become in a way a burden, because of the unemployment in a régime of relative rule, and emigration was encouraged again. The other western European countries took a similar line: the fear of unemployment and of overpopulation caused several of them, Holland in particular, to encourage emigration.

The Indian government also chose to act as does the relative ruler, and would doubtless not object to part of its surplus population leaving for Africa or America, if such a move were possible.

During the period of union between Syria and Egypt, President Nasser planned to encourage emigration into Syria; of course he saw this more as an internal migration.

The Soviet government is actively opposed to emigration, not exactly for economic reasons, but on a question of austere political principle: an individual belongs to society and therefore to the state. The Soviets are also afraid lest émigrés turn against Communism (see below chapter 23).

In new countries the wish to keep nationals at home is usually very strong. We shall return to the question of high quality emigration further on.

Public opinion is not usually concerned at all with emigration. An arrival is more readily noticed than a departure.

Attitude of the receiving country: Here it is important to distinguish between the positions of authorities, of political parties, of public opinion, of professional organisations, and of individuals. Generally any immigration into a relatively stable country causes troubles and some opposition. As soon as the 'frontier' of the United States had receded as far as the western seaboard, the idea of restricting immigration appeared. This kind of opposition can be expressed in economic, social, political, racial, or religious forms, or appear as blatant xenophobia. The most general rule is that unions always object to immigration in their own trade. This is as true with doctors and farmers as with manual workers. The latter fear not only unemployment but also the greater evil of competition from foreigners less demanding about working conditions, more amenable to the employers and therefore liable to cancel out several years of arduous union gains. This places the unions in a rather delicate situation when one of their principles is international solidarity and fraternity. In fact, whenever unions obtain conditions better than those defined by the brutal law of offer and demand, there results a sense of property, and property naturally generates a Malthusian attitude.

This is strong even in underpopulated countries: 'We will admit immigrants but only insofar as the need is felt for them, in other words in the sectors where there is no home candidate for a job.' These are the famous 'vacancies' that Tucker denounced as nonexistent. A market economy is a dynamic organisation, therefore perpetually off balance. The various occupations are complementary and not competitive and a superficial observer will therefore never see any real vacancies, but only surpluses. In fact, it is by increasing numbers in the sectors not suffering from a surplus that one can eventually increase the employment offered all round.

Thus, far from being a source of unemployment, a reasonably select immigration is, given sufficient investment, a remedy against the most dangerous because the most covert form of Malthusianism. A protective policy ignoring this rule sets off the classical Malthusian mechanism: a negative attitude in the occupations threatened, and indifference in those that might gain, exactly as in the discussions on customs barriers.

This very human desire to protect one's work leads to ferociously inhuman attitudes. Remember the arrival of the masses fleeing the fascist tyranny in Spain in 1938–9. It was not decent to send them back, so the French authorities merely parked them in camps, allowing them to subsist but not to create wealth.

With full employment and the desertion of certain trades by home workers, this Malthusian attitude to immigration has relaxed in France. But even in a full parliamentary democracy political decisions are never quite in conformity with public opinion. The authorities submit to certain necessities but only discreetly and often in hiding.

Generally, racial, political, and religious considerations are more important in determining national attitudes than economic ones. In the United States quotas and prejudice prevent the immigration of races considered undesirable. In Canada the growth of the more fertile French Catholic minority has caused enough apprehension amongst the Anglo-Saxon majority to provoke a policy of immigration in the western states. In Australia the fear of an Asiatic invasion of their half-empty continent had caused the authorities to change their very Malthusian attitude on immigration; but the return to peaceful conditions caused, if not a return to pre-war attitudes, at least a paring of the initial plans.

Racial discrimination, though sometimes resting on economic ratiocination (sharp competition from less demanding workers), is more frequently due to some idea of racial superiority or to the fear of being unable to assimilate the newcomers and of being burdened with a minority causing political unrest (this is the case with Britain in the 1960s).

Attitude and behaviour of the migrant: Migration is unsettling in the individual's life. The migrant, used to a certain geographical and social environment, suddenly lands in another one, of which he usually has little knowledge. Not only his economic and financial conditions must change, but also every aspect of his life: weather, food, clothing, etc. The new environment usually appears somewhat hostile and sets off classical defensive or offensive mechanisms. Of course, the migrant himself first took the offensive, but he is usually a very

452

poor conqueror. The general effect is that he becomes more sensitive and more emotionally developed. The shy man becomes even more shy in this troublesome situation, the complainer finds plenty of scope for his mania.

The migrant can of course encounter a variety of conditions: total isolation, as with the marginal tramp portrayed by Charlie Chaplin, or a specially prepared environment calculated to attach him to the new country. The differences are great and they justify a distinction between push and pull types of migration. In the former the individual is ejected by unfavourable circumstances; in the latter attracted by the opportunities of a new land.

Free and organised migration

It is relatively rare these days to see individuals moving spontaneously towards a new area which is not prepared for them. Even refugees, such as those leaving Germany after Potsdam, either have some idea of where they are going (usually to join some relative or friend) or are taken charge of by a welcoming organisation more or less suited to its purpose.

These fall into two types, though most situations include features from both.

Individual or family welcome: Etcheberry, a Basque shepherd, leaves France to be a shepherd in Arizona. He was invited by his uncle, who emigrated thirty years ago and who wrote that he would find many fellow Basques there, friends and relatives. He has been offered a tempting work contract, or at least moral guarantees that he will get good work. On his arrival at La Guardia he is met by a fellow Basque who transfers him to another plane, and when this lands another Basque takes him to his new house. He is slowly initiated to the work and the environment. Traditional Basque food and decorations await him. Later if he makes a small fortune he may return to his native land.

The same is true of the Italian who leaves to be a cook in New York or the Algerian who comes to France. They find friends, housing, employment all ready for them. In certain extreme cases there is hardly any change at all: a Genoese coming to Nice, a Spanish Catalan coming to Perpignan meet no hostility except from the authorities who place administrative or police conditions on their stay: they may find that the need for a work permit restricts them, but this will not affect them much unless other emotional grievances are added.

The attitude of the migrant will vary according to the sense of responsibility he brings to the change in his condition. When he has made his own choice between various possible courses, he will be able to adapt more easily. Pride may help him surmount difficulties, either accidental or purely geographical.

Collective welcome (by public or private organisations): Differences of attitude are even sharper in the case of migration organised by authorities. What

453

occurs most frequently is that an employer's organisation, disguised as a national body, recruits foreign labour and undertakes to bring it to a welcoming environment, providing housing and even sometimes food and social welfare. Here individuals become more particular, usually encouraged by outsiders. As a general rule one only puts up with bad living conditions at home. People living happily in the most uncomfortable houses will find hard beds or badly lit corners insufferable in hotel rooms. Really shabby accommodation which would not have been objected to had the immigrant chosen it himself, may appear scandalous if it is offered him by an organisation. If he is a bargainer he will be content to complain in a situation he could easily have remedied for himself were he not expecting someone else to do it for him. The disappointments he inevitably suffers in the new life will be blamed on the organising body, whether or not it is responsible.

Thus organised migration must be very well organised. Unless it guarantees the migrant conditions far better than those he had before, it must endeavour to make him feel he has made the choice himself and owes it to himself to succeed in his new position. Precautions are even more necessary in an agricultural colonisation of new territory than with an industrial migration. The agricultural migrant has to face a capricious natural environment he is not used to, and a first unsuccessful harvest may leave him with no resources or courage; besides, any return home of the adventurers can imperil the movement in general, because it causes doubts and fears amongst prospective followers.

Establishing a regular flow

All this shows clearly how a regular flow can be created and kept up in a new country. The first migrants need a very well organised reception, including physical, moral, and occupational selection, with special efforts towards the creation of roots. Once the first wave is permanently settled they can spontaneously attract fellow countrymen, relatives and friends, either to help them or to recruit their help in enlarging a business. Individual welcome thus slowly replaces collective welcome.

The total expenditure is high for the pioneers but it drops sharply afterwards; and since the proportion paid for by the community also drops, the general cost of migration is a descending function. Also, as the population increases, individual productivity improves in the classical way, through division of labour, spreading of overheads over a larger number, etc. Public funds benefit after a certain point. Thus the economic point of view as well as the psychological one lead to the same conclusion: the initial efforts should not be spared. But these are often so expensive that authorities often hesitate to make them.

Emigration is selective

Migrants do not appear at random in a population; they are self-selective according to certain characteristics, not necessarily qualities. Selection was stringent at the time of the pioneers, but today there are attenuating factors. It still applies largely to organised immigration of industrial workers, though not into the United States, where the immigration policy has other objectives.

More men than women migrate as a rule, when the movement is economically based; but this old law is changing today. Consider for instance the number of migrants in and out of the following countries in a year around 1961.[1]

	Males	Females	% of men to women
Immigrants to			
France	39,926	8,975	445
Federal Germany	487,002	245,682	199
Canada	32,106	39,583	81
USA	123,196	151,376	81
Australia	65,920	61,666	107
Emigrants from			
British Guiana	18,116	10,971	165
Holland	19,812	18,200	109
Greece	36,209	22,628	160
Portugal	19,590	13,936	141

Canada, the United States, and Australia clearly attract a different kind of migrant. Where there is a proportionately large number of male emigrants, men are leaving ahead of their families, under the pressure of needs.

Selection by age is stronger than selection by sex. Usually young adults

Age	Total	per cent	Population of Bulgaria (%)	Population of Holland (%)
0–9	107,000	11·1	16·8	19·6
10–19	127,200	13·2	16·6	18·4
20–29	369,400	38·5	15·4	13·7
30–39	195,500	20·4	16·6	18·1
40–49	81,800	8·5	11·6	11·6
50–59	45,000	4·7	11·3	10·3
60 and over	34,900	3·6	11·7	13·3
Total	960,800	100	100	100

[1] *U.N. Year book*, 1962. Figures on migration are unfortunately very irregularly published. In 1965 the most popular country was Australia.

455

emigrate. Compare the distribution by age of a large sample of immigrants into Germany, Australia, Canada, and the United States in 1961, with that of two European countries not badly affected demographically by the wars, Bulgaria and Holland.

There are far fewer children and old people amongst the immigrants, fewer old even than in a demographically primitive population (where approximately 6 per cent of people are over sixty).

Thus emigration causes ageing, whilst immigration makes a population younger. The age selection is partly spontaneous and partly dictated by regulations on immigration. As we saw in part I, the social value of a man drops to nil between forty and forty-five. Public reckonings are not quite as brutal as this, but many countries only accept immigrants younger than forty.

There is also a selection by health. This used to be spontaneous, like the other two (cripples, consumptives, and madmen did not emigrate) but it is increasingly enforced very rigorously by medical checks. Thanks to this initial selection, together with the subsequent struggle for survival, the populations of the new countries are more lusty – given equal training, they can usually beat Europeans in sporting competitions. One should add that there is probably also genetic superiority resulting from the mixture of populations in the new countries.

Selection by occupation has varied in history. An immigrant may of course change his line: there were no trappers, lumberjacks, or gold-diggers in Europe. Many countries operate a fairly rigorous occupational selection at entry by checking work permits or contracts. However overpopulated they may be, underdeveloped countries never stop asking for skilled workers who may precisely be able to combat the overpopulation, but they are the ones who are reluctant to leave: they are rarely unemployed and usually fairly well established in society. Labourers are more liable to migrate; even at home they are less stable, and move from one job to another, with the variable economic situation.

Intellectuals often emigrate for political reasons; the chosen victims of revolutions and coups, they usually find it difficult to integrate at the desired level into the hierarchy of a new country unless their qualifications are rare and liable to be recognised anywhere. White Russians had to learn to drive taxis in Paris. No country is short of lawyers, solicitors, civil servants, tradesmen, or even shorthand typists.

One could also show, rather more controversially, that people with a particular type of intelligence or an enterprising personality tend to emigrate more. But it is difficult to pin down these traits, and since appropriate tests have only been devised recently, they cannot apply to emigration before the twentieth century. Tests made on immigrants to the United States confirm that there may be some degree of selection, but research has not yet reached the stage of precise definitions.

High quality migrations

These are especially interesting and they are not new. Descartes worked for a long time in Holland, Lagrange came to live in France, generals have often commanded foreign armies and artists frequently migrate. But traditionally such moves were made at random and cancelled each other out; today they are systematically directed towards certain countries.

In the three years between 1962 and 1964, 16,200 foreign scientists took up residence in the United States. Arrivals had increased from 1200 a year in 1947, to more than 6000 a year. Of the 631 members of the American Academy of Science in 1961, 151 were born abroad and 116 had had their basic training abroad. Of 51 Nobel prizes awarded to Americans, 15 were to scientists of foreign extraction. This is partly due to liberal home policies of the United States, which attract scientists away from the Malthusian rigidness of European and particularly French regulations. But it also has a great deal to do with the sheer size of the country, and its powerful resources. Almost inevitably, any brilliant Canadian will be lost to his country, even if he does not migrate for better money. Because of the common language, Great Britain and Australia are also particular victims of this 'brain drain'.

It is extremely expensive for a country thus to lose part of its élite. It often occurs with underdeveloped countries, especially if they are fairly small.

Moral selection

This is much more difficult to measure and even to define. Spontaneous migration is connected with character, and demands qualities of enterprise, but only amongst a group of people (surplus workers for instance) already defined by other criteria. In a sense those who leave are the most enterprising amongst a group with very low standards of initiative, since they have not been able to find a job in their own country. Moral selection will therefore vary considerably from one migration to another, and it is often a negative factor of choice.

Consequences and social role of migration

Opinions vary a great deal. Some consider it an evil, others a lesser evil or even a remedy to certain social ills such as poverty and unemployment. The distress of migrants uprooted and deprived of their gods is often rather upsetting. But where does the responsibility lie? In the social régime of the country he has left, where an efficient policy against unemployment and poverty would be a more humane remedy? This would imply that there is no such thing as lasting overpopulation, only insufficient development. Indeed, in many cases, by putting the environment to better use it would have been possible to give both work and food to the people who were ejected. But this is a narrow view based on a rather stuffy nationalism: if demographic investment is less expensive in another country, if its soil is richer and space is more abundant, then migration will be profitable to the two countries as a whole. There must be an optimum solution for both, as there is for the individual migrant. But there remains to ask whether the overall gain makes up for the individual distress.

The latter is sometimes very strong. But if the choice was freely made, could one not say that the migrant preferred a material gain to his own comfort? This is a very debatable point.

We saw, when talking of internal migration, that there is a tendency to create work for men on the spot, or in other words to place social traditions and habits before economic reasons. Curiously enough, this is not true with international migrations, where there is no overall collaboration. Thus the French community may make great efforts to maintain inhabitants in Alpine valleys, but it will not think twice about depopulating Castille or Aragon, as a joint political body might do. If there were not many other factors discouraging them from this, one might conclude that men are more inclined to cross frontiers than to migrate within their own land.

Emigration is more actively encouraged when it is customary in the district, and especially when it is a normal thing to hope to return. It then becomes an accepted part of life; having always witnessed it since childhood, a young man is not at all surprised when his turn comes, and when he does move part of his environment will be awaiting him.

The selective character of emigration can have an important influence on the country. We mentioned in chapter 2 the depressing effect a drop in population could have, on Spain in the seventeenth century, or on Ireland or Gascony in the nineteenth century. But this has not been true of all emigrations: Germany and Britain kept on sending their younger generations abroad throughout the nineteenth century without any apparent loss. This is because it only took away a real surplus population, which would have had great difficulty in finding work at home; but this creaming-off by emigration may well have been one of the causes of the Europe's decline.

The selection by sex can have various effects. Some think that it is because the first immigrants into the United States were mainly men that women play such a large part in the country's values. In other American countries this factor led to racially mixed marriages or unions, and hence to far-reaching social and racial changes.

New tendencies since the war

The reversal of the current of migration: This was already suspected between the wars and has been confirmed. People now generally move towards developed countries, even if they are already highly populated. There are two reasons for this: first, the workers in the developed countries have abandoned certain arduous or ill-paid occupations (precisely as a result of development and education); secondly there is unemployment or underemployment in the less developed countries, and in addition, a wish of the young to escape from tribal or family influence. This new form of migration causes various problems of a social and political kind. Sometimes the immigrants are unwelcome, in spite of the advantages the country will derive from them as servants. In 1963 and 1964 the British government was forced to restrict immigration from Commonwealth countries.[1]

The Swiss government found itself in an even more delicate position, for 700,000 foreigners were working under contract in Switzerland in 1963, and there were various other categories of foreigners, amounting in all to about one-seventh of the total poulation. Laws had to be passed to restrict these numbers, in spite of economic necessities.[2]

The increase of temporary migrations: The possibility of returning home for an annual holiday, and of transferring social benefits, especially pensions, narrows the gap between the two countries; workers increasingly return home when circumstances permit.

For the future the most important question, but also the one that will have to receive the least publicity, will be that of high-quality migrations. If nothing is done to prevent them they will represent a considerable gain for certain areas, and especially the United States.

[1] See C. Moindrot, 'Réduction de l'immigration de couleur en Grande Bretagne', *Population*, January–March 1964; C. Moindrot, 'Les vagues d'immigration en Grande Bretagne', *Population*, July–September 1965; R. Delerm, 'La population noire en France', *Population*, April–June 1964.

[2] See *Rapport de la Commission chargée de l'étude du problème de la main d'œuvre étrangère*, Berne, 1964, reported in *Population*, January–March 1965.

17

ADAPTATION AND ASSIMILATION
OF IMMIGRANTS

This is a complex problem both for the individual and for society. The aim of a receiving country is to prevent any possible kind of tension: not that it wants to make the immigrants identical to the average or to the mass of its nationals, but in order to mingle them so that they will not stand out too much, or remain conscious of their separateness. In other words the receiving population wants to 'hear no more' of foreign minorities. But we should first view the problem from the individual's point of view.

The immigrant's progress

If he ever becomes assimilated, and this is usually one generation later, a migrant will have passed through three main stages:

Settlement: On crossing the frontier the first change he encounters is currency; it is easy to become familar with it, but more difficult to appreciate its value. If a place has not been found him by acquaintances or by an organisation, he will have to find food and lodging. His first choice will not be the best, and will probably prove expensive or badly located. This first phase lasts from his anxious arrival to the time when he has more or less built up a regular life, and no longer has to live off the small capital he brought with him and which drained away faster than it should, for reasons that any traveller knows. He will have somewhere suitable to live, though perhaps not very comfortable, he will eat regularly, whether well nor not, and have means of subsistence. He will also have established regular postal communications and will be able to plan beyond the next day. He may not have permanent employment or a guaranteed wage but this was probably true before he left home too. He is now no longer an alien, but an immigrant.

Adaptation: This first vital phase, which is mainly a matter of ensuring survival, is the one immigration organisations try to shorten as much as possible. Next comes adaptation, which can take two almost opposite forms: a man can adapt himself to his new environment, or build an environment similar to the one he knew before. He must in any case adapt himself to the climate, learn what to wear and how to keep warm, and perhaps become accustomed to various difficulties the nationals do not seem to notice. Italian migrants have been known to return to their poor but sunny village in Italy, merely because of their bad impression on arriving in Lorraine in winter time when there was snow on the ground.

Adapting oneself to the social environment is first a linguistic process: it takes several months to make oneself understood. This inevitably has some kind of effect on the immigrant's personality, makes him more timid or more proud, under the injuries inflicted by smiles or rebuffs. A tourist, with plenty of cash, may find foreigners surprisingly willing to make efforts to understand him, but a worker in a similar situation is liable to encounter involuntary reactions, which may discourage him. At this stage it is not usually necessary for him to change his religion, but he must get used either to the total absence of ritual or to a slightly different one from that of his own country, and this can also add to his difficulties.

Adaptation to food can be very difficult; it is inevitable at first, since immigrants usually eat in restaurants, canteens, or with a local family, but it is not definitive since they have a chance to return to their former habits.

There are many other aspects of social life requiring adaptation: entertainment (sports, cinema, concerts, etc.), friendly and sexual relationships, clubs (cultural, sporting, trade unions), all need to be grasped before the feeling of possession and the new mental balance they provide can be acquired.

But all this does not ensure assimilation; it leaves the immigrant with the feeling of being a foreigner, and does not always make him want to stop being one. His accent or his pronunciation, his way of dressing, and, in a small community, his reputed origin, may lead the locals to maintain him at a distance, often through a derogatory nick-name, 'Polak', 'Froggie', 'Spade'. He is accepted but no more.

There may be an effort to rebuild the old environment, providing there is a certain geographical concentration of immigrants, either in a common occupation, or in family life or through networks of acquaintance: the old clothes, houses, and cooking may reappear. In extreme cases such as that of the Japanese in Sâo Paulo, there may be very little contact between the immigrant and the indigenous group, and individuals may never reach the frontier of their group if they are not involved in any trade. Here a massive migration may lead to the coexistence of two populations.

Total assimilation: This is not a further stage in the same process, for in the cases just mentioned *adaptation can prevent assimilation*. It can solve immediate social problems by merely generalising them to the group. The overall pattern can be represented as follows.

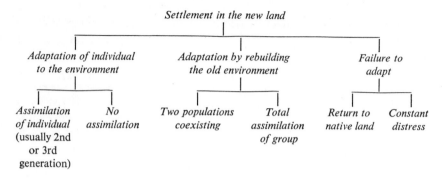

Types of immigration

The contrast between individual adaptation and assimilation is illustrated in the various types of immigration.

Family immigration: This is often called demographic immigration. It makes for greater stability, but does not always lead to assimilation, for a family can retain its national characteristics much more easily. If a number of families come to the same area, then mixed unions may become very rare, and in the limiting case an immigrant group may maintain itself within the native population.

But on the other hand individual immigration of workers is usually male. Either the immigrants do not intend to settle, or they make a mixed marriage and thus break the balance of sexes in the native population. So, demographically, families are always more welcome, though a policy of adaptation or of short-term social appeasement will in fact take precedence over the desire for rapid assimilation.

Agricultural or industrial immigration: A similar contrast exists between urban and rural immigrants. The first are in closer touch with the new environment providing they do not arrive in a large group; they react more to the attraction of the new country, and are liable to adapt more easily unless there is specific resentment against them.

Farmers, on the other hand, are more self-sufficient, and need have no contact with the new society. They learn more about the earth and the natural conditions than about the men. Yet these natural roots, though preventing quick cultural assimilation, probably help to deepen it in the long run. Feeling for the earth can become strong enough to silence the call that may come one day from the native land. Of course, the rural immigrant can, like anyone else, emigrate to the town. But his stay next to the earth will probably have had a sufficient influence to retain him. By and large, rural immigration is more conducive to assimilation.

Factors of assimilation

Total assimilation is easier at the second or third generation. Research on Mexican immigrants into Midwest City in 1960 gave the following figures:[1]

	Language spoken at home	Language spoken by the children
Spanish	46	5
Mostly Spanish	9	4
Half Spanish half English	17	26
Mostly English	7	31
English	7	32
Difficult to determine	14	2
Total	100	100

The difference is quite striking. The three essential factors are geographical dispersion, and mixed education, and marriages, which go together. We have already described how geographical dispersion of immigrants favours adaptation and mixed marriages. Schools also have a very important role; the success of the American melting-pot is directly due to the strictly compulsory English education in the United States. There is much more than education involved: school friends, in the playground and later in the streets, help form a child's personality, whereas that of his parents can at best be distorted. After schooling the immigrant child is so close to total assimilation that he sometimes resents his parents' attachment to customs he no longer sees the reason for. Conversely, education in the original language makes assimilation considerably longer.

Mixed marriages are the logical conclusion of mixed schooling. As soon as there is no real repulsion between the nationalities (and the factor of repulsion is usually religious or racial) it is statistically probable that the minority will disappear rapidly. Unions between two foreigners of different nationalities produce children who assimilate extremely quickly.

Where the immigrant population is largely in an inferior social position (as with immigration of labourers) a mixed marriage is usually dominated by the native partner because assimilation is seen as a real social promotion. Social contacts are made mainly with the relatives and acquaintances of the native partner. The immigrant partner, spurred to modesty if not to shame, tries to forget his origin and usually does so unless some aggressive remark is let slip.

All civic activity helps towards assimilation: national service, civil service,

[1] T J. Schaff. 'Changes in public and private language among Spanish speaking migrants to an industrial city', *Migrations Internationales*, vol. 3, nos. 1–2, 1965.

and nationalised services all lead individuals to mix and the remaining groups to disperse, even if they are not consciously applied to this purpose.

Political aims

Assimilation in the strict sense supposes that the national population is already homogeneous; yet it is never so. One may therefore ask whether the immigrants integrate more to any particular fraction of the population: an extremely important problem when there is already in the country a question of coexistence. At one time the Anglo-Saxon population of Canada, afraid of the fertility of the French population, had recourse to immigration, knowing that the Dutch and German, and of course the English immigrants, would assimilate rather to the Anglo-Saxon group.

Social and political assimilation is a more delicate matter: a worker can integrate either into a highly advanced trade union movement, or into a traditionalist group, less hostile to the ruling class. This problem has a distinct influence on immigration policy. In France in 1946–7 the Communist Ministry of Labour discouraged individual immigration, where the worker might be 'on good terms with his boss'. Conservative governments, on the other hand, avoid the immigration of industrial labour and prefer peasants in families and possibly in religious groups. They may argue that the assimilation of the latter is more complete and deeper, once again only to hide their real motives, which lie in class consciousness.

France between the two wars

This is a good example of the various factors of assimilation. Italians came in a rather dispersed way, as peasants, rural workers, building labourers. Without their own schools, they became acclimatised in spite of the efforts of the Italian clergy and fascist government. In 1940–44 France found itself with 800,000 inhabitants hailing from a country now in the position of victor, or at least occupant, without any real trouble ensuing.

The Poles came in compact groups, especially into the mines and metal industries. Because of the great distance from their home country, and the wide difference of language, immigration had to be organised, and it was thought advisable to reconstitute part of the Polish environment through schools, clergy, sporting or musical clubs, etc. Twenty years later many Poles responded to the call of their country although they went home to a poor and devastated land.

Naturalisation

The implications of this purely legal act are often exaggerated. Naturalisation certainly hardens the break that was appearing between the immigrant and his home country. It may lead to new military obligations, and he may even be considered a deserter at home, though this can also free him from an inferiority complex, and give him confidence. But the request for naturalisation is not a proof or even a suggestion that he wishes to be assimilated; it may be prompted by the material and moral advantages of nationality: a naturalised citizen can work freely, exercise political rights and put an end to police supervision or unpleasantness from neighbours. The latter can in fact encourage quick naturalisation, while at the same time discouraging real assimilation.

If naturalisation is an individual right, an individual who has never been conscious that he had the status of a foreigner need not try to maintain the differences that still separate him from the population amongst which he lives.

Naturalisation should be completed by a change of name; but, in France at any rate, ill-founded nationalism and rigid bureaucracy prevent this kind of assimilation.

Attitude of the native population

Assimilation is only too often considered solely from the immigrant's point of view, implying that it is up to him to disappear and not be heard of again. Yet assimilation can be reciprocal: the conquest of Britain by the Normans finally led, after a period of coexistence, to the absorption of the rulers, though in the process much of the culture of the subjects, their language for instance, was modified. And in any case the adaptation of the immigrant depends largely on the welcome given him. The native population only too often encourages segregation and an artificial reconstitution of the old environment, which prevent assimilation.

There is always some prejudice against foreigners: at best they are possible competitors. If they are poorer they are only allowed to take up the jobs and live in the houses the natives do not want, and because these inferior conditions are imposed on them, they are then accused of hereditary ignorance, dirtiness, illness, or even dishonesty. Children easily follow the example of their elders, and become aggressive and bullying, whereas if left to themselves they do not practise either racial or social segregation, they know no frontiers and they are even able to overcome the difference in languages with surprising agility.

Even with xenophobic adults, the principle may not always be applied to the particular case: Homais, Flaubert's village atheist, hated all priests except the local one, whom he knew personally; a rabid antisemite may have very good Jewish friends; but these personal relationships do not prevent collective wariness from developing and surging up at the slightest opportunity.

The ruling class in the native population is led by nationalism to two strongly contradictory attitudes: on the one hand it tends to fear the appearance of any minority and the changes it might bring to the national character, or even the loss of purity of the 'national blood'; but on the other hand it would like to have more citizens to rule.

Many countries practise forced assimilation, forbidding foreign language newspapers or clubs for instance. Nowadays the tendency is to liberalism, after strict selection on arrival. The development of communications, the spread of annual holidays, the appearance of social security, have, as we have said, changed the character of migrations and tended to make them more temporary than before. Assimilation is thus no longer such an important problem.

Alterations in the national character

When a nation assimilates immigrants, we have said that they may do some of the assimilating themselves, and this might cause the national character to change too. This depends essentially on numbers and social and cultural level of immigrants. The case of the Normans in England is an extreme one. Yet, without fusion or simplification, the mere fact of British rule in India was sufficient to make English the official language there, used for all education past a certain level. This has also been the case in many African countries with European languages used by the colonisers. But it will only occur nowadays if there is no real national language, and it is thus not really a change of character.

In the general case (e.g. France, United States, South America) immigrants are either of low social status or lacking it completely. They are then assimilated so fully that their origins are very hard to spot, especially if they have adapted their names. Whether the national character has changed is a moot point, for it is the sum of many complex factors. The difference between Americans and British is due partly to the mottled ancestry of the former, but also partly to the different lives they have led over the last three centuries.

Can the descendants of immigrants possess sufficient patriotism? Very often those who enquire are themselves of fairly recent immigrant stock. New converts are always more fervent than old believers and new nationals are probably more fervently patriotic. If not, it is precisely because they are not properly assimilated.

The influence of the original immigrants on a community is very difficult to assess. Traditions and ambitions, passed on subconsciously, may well surface suddenly. But it is surprising how often enlightened people indulge in the woolly catalogues of Celtic, Saracen, or Visigothic attributes of this or that group. In such a totally unscientific field, the imagination runs wild.

18

OCCUPATIONAL MIGRATIONS

This problem has already been referred to in Part I, but its increasing importance justifies another, more detailed, analysis. It is one of the problems
generally neglected by modern economics, whether pure or applied. There
was some excuse for this in the day of liberalism, when men's hopes had to
bend before the requirements of the economic machine, but it is a different
matter now, especially since an imperfect occupational structure and the resulting difficulties are often misinterpreted demographically and wrongly
dealt with.

Occupational migration is taken to mean not only changes of occupation
during adult life but changes modifying the pattern of the active population: arrival of young people or immigrants, or departure through deaths,
retirement, emigration. The central question here is that of the optimum
occupational distribution for a given aim.

Real and required population

Every active person has two aims: to obtain the highest possible income in
relation to his occupation and ability and to find an occupation fulfilling
certain conditions, such as a light work load or pleasant surroundings.

The total population, however, has a different aim: the satisfaction of
public and private requirements.

Ill-effects of distortions

Any population is distributed at any given moment into various occupations,
but this distribution may not be the one best suited to the requirements of the
time. Some occupations may be oversubscribed, others undersubscribed,
Carrying the situation to an absurd extreme, one could say that, if a whole
population were producing nothing but soap, and there was no international
trade, the occupational distribution would not be suited to the requirements.

More generally, a particular occupational population[1] is able to turn out a
certain group of products in accordance with its ability and current technology.
If all individuals were to work full time in their occupation, they would

---

[1] This phrase is used in preference to 'active population', to show that it is a question of
structure and not merely of total numbers.

produce a certain number of tons of coal and corn, lengths of material, Spanish lessons, etc. For a given price scale, this has a certain global value. But is the structure of this total output suited to the ideal pattern of consumption?

Now look at the problem from the point of view of the consumers, ready to spend their income. A family earning say £1500 a year, given a certain price scale, will make up its budget in a certain way determined both by its wishes and by the prices obtaining. (It matters little whether products, services, or equipment are consumed.) *In other words to establish a budget is really to 'order' a certain number of working hours in various sectors.* The total of all these individual orders gives a number of working hours for each occupation, and, if working time is fixed, and productivity constant, it determines a certain occupational population that we may call the *required population*.

If each family's income is very low, the total required population is very low too. As the national income increases the required population increases also, but irregularly according to the occupation considered. Now suppose that our consuming population has exactly the income it is capable of producing. It may be that the total required population and the real population are the same. *But this equilibrium is of little value if it is not also achieved in structure, that is to say for each individual occupation.* The required population will include for instance more plumbers and charwomen but usually fewer film stars and lawyers than the real population.

Thus the population contradicts itself: if it can be said to have a collective will, it wants to consume certain products but it intends to produce others. The question is, what causes these distortions and how can one correct them?

Causes

The causes of distortion are six in number:

Technological progress: This is the most frequent cause but it can take several forms. 1. It may bring about an improvement in quality, or a drop in price for a given product, thus reducing the demand for other products, and changing the shape of the 'required population'. The depressed product is not necessarily in the same range of goods as the rising one. Thus the drop in the price of cars and their improvement over the last forty years have reduced the demand for certain types of clothing and building, and for other stagnant industries or services. 2. It may cause production to be maintained or even increased with a lower number of workers: this is the classical case of technological unemployment. Here the employed population in the sector must fall, temporarily at least. 3. It may cause savings in raw or semi-processed materials. This is so definitely a processive development that the ensuing occupational distortion is hidden by the growth of employment. For example the device by which one cable was made to carry hundreds of telephone links was as good as the discovery of a new Copper Belt. But it so contributed to general progress that the demand for copper remained as high and no miners or copper workers lost their jobs. No doubt the occupational pattern was changed but it is very difficult to see exactly how. 4. It may substitute one raw semi-processed material for another: as when synthetic dyes brought an end to the culture of madder.

Generally, we have already seen in Part I that in a developed society technological progress increases the amount of employment, or, if it remains constant, increases the wages earned; for, contrary to common opinion, the majority of these developments are processive, and tend to lessen the privileges of property and monopoly. But there are very few kinds of development that do not cause some change in the occupational structure, and none can fail to affect the 'required population'.

Changes in fashions: The tastes of consumers can vary. Between the two wars and for no apparent reason many men stopped wearing hats. This caused redundancies in the hat industry and its suppliers. But the savings on hats caused other purchases making for higher employment in other sectors. These kinds of changes are very difficult to foresee. Long-term producers have an influence that should not be over-estimated; but publicity can have considerable importance.

External changes: Every country is liable to suffer from them as long as it is not in a completely closed system. They can affect prices, imports, or exports, and trade openings including all kinds of invisible 'trading'. Thus the building of roads in Yugoslavia, Greece, or Rumania has succeeded in attracting western tourists and prevented them from spending as much in their own countries; the latter will have to make up by exporting more, and their working population will thus have to vary in two distinct ways. External changes can be lasting if due to far-reaching causes such as the discovery of oil in the East; or they can be caused by temporary variations in competition.

Differential fertility: This has less to do with occupations than with social mobility, since occupation is not transmitted from one generation to another as strongly as social level. It does, however, have important effects in one sector, that of agriculture. Here occupation is transmitted, and also the birth rate is usually higher. Partly because of this, the United States always has a surplus of farmers: the average number of children per complete family is about four in agriculture and two-and-a-half in urban occupations. As a result the rural population would increase by a half at each generation without migrations, whereas the urban population would stay more or less stationary.

Mistaken orientation of the young: Two important social factors are often insufficiently co-ordinated. On the one hand the economy develops according to its own laws, under the influence of technology, social progress, and economic and financial policy. In doing this it requires each year a certain amount of builders, engineers, doctors, electricians, etc. On the other hand, universities and schools form the minds in a certain way which, without promising them a desirable occupation, predisposes them to certain vocations rather than others. The two factors can be well out of step. This can of course be blamed on technological progress, which has failed to provide enough coercion. But there definitely are distortions directly due to bad training.

Education was not originally conceived as a preparation for an occupation. The national desire for full employment, or the adaptation of the labour force to requirements was a secondary preoccupation. This can still be felt in the way our secondary education creates not only aptitudes but inabilities to suit certain occupations, particularly unqualified tertiary ones. It leads to consider manual labour as a kind of disgrace. In France the Langevin Commission and many educationalists who advised the teaching of manual skills in secondary schools were not enthusiastically followed. The young man of seventeen, or even the young boy or girl of fifteen leaving school are doomed to a tertiary life; only very few are ever found seated at tractors or machines. The enormous number of imperfectly qualified tertiaries which pours out every year into an economy not geared to it, has to be content with almost any form of employment. Each has to display vigorous efforts in order to create a place for himself. As a result and according to the economic situation, there is always a surplus either of tradesmen or of civil servants; this also explains various pressures to increase numbers of clerks, to reduce the effective number of working hours, and to increase all the professions. Here real unemployment is much less frequent than underemployment: tradesmen are often only active for about two or three hours a day; journalists, artists and others may spend much more time looking for work than carrying it out.

However this surplus population manages to live, it weighs on the economy and slows down the progress of the national income by reducing financial surpluses, which are a capitalist society's only channel of investment. This situation exists in all European countries because of the economic depression resulting from the two wars and the progressive economic and political liberation of their overseas possessions. But it is very reluctantly recognised, because tertiaries are the only ones to express opinions on the point and because the view is felt to have an unfortunate reactionary colour. Tradesmen criticise civil servants for being too numerous and they return the compliment, but the two categories, as a group, do not make any common confession. Causes are often mistaken for effects: since large numbers of tertiaries can be a sign of wealth it is too easily assumed that their large numbers will bring wealth. It is as if someone were to buy a fur coat or a jewel in order to become rich.

470

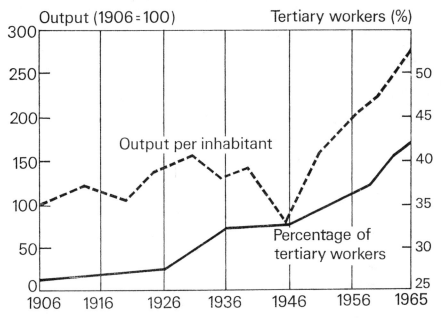

Figure 72. Output per inhabitant and ratio of tertiary workers in France.

In the Soviet Union the educational reform of 1958 and many other later measures were intended precisely to counteract this effect, which leads fatally to bureaucracy.

Recognising this surplus does not, of course, amount to arguing against the spread of education as such. The degradation of diplomas is not a bad sign as long as it is accompanied by general development. Many youngsters work as shorthand typists after completing a secondary education, and this is no longer a surprising or even alarming situation.

Some also argue that the distribution at every given moment is ahead of its time and that it never pays to alter it. But it is worth remembering that too much advance on ignition can do permanent damage to an engine. Certainly, in the general development of any society, certain phenomena are ahead of the others and lead them on – they are a desirable feature. But here the advance is too great and has the opposite effect of slowing down progress. Unfortunately to denounce it can easily appear a reactionary gesture, especially since the historical precedents are ambiguous: Thomas More complained of the surplus of courtiers and parasites, and at about the same time Fromenteau pointed out that there were too many men of law. Many conservatives of the eighteenth century opposed the education of peasants on the grounds that it would make them 'good for nothing'. To remedy the drift away from the country some, like La Morandière, even suggested sending all the useless members of society back to work on the land: 'They will work and we will enjoy'. This 'return to the land', so often advocated later, is a typical form of social reaction.

But these considerations should not modify our previous remarks about unqualified tertiary workers: indeed they show how, because of the bad memories of past attitudes, obvious facts can be ignored. No doubt, permanent unemployment is unavoidable in certain occupations. Solicitors without briefs are not new, and neither are artists without fame or writers with no publishers. But to this traditional surplus there is nowadays added an extra surplus which threatens to increase regularly.

Occupational Malthusianism: Any private occupation with sufficient organisation to think of itself as a group tends to be Malthusian, in trying to retain all its members and restrict the access to it. In this way venal positions discreetly appear in various sectors. This attitude is easily explained, but it sometimes misfires. If generalised, it can lead to impoverishment affecting all other groups – and the group itself would, in certain cases, benefit from an increase in numbers. If a hotel is built in a new resort, its owner will be well advised to encourage others to follow suit, since this will increase the reputation of the place and give him publicity.

Public employment is not affected in the same way: civil servants do not try to decrease their numbers or to prevent their increase, although their real interest would lie in this direction. Whereas private occupations start from the assumption that their markets are limited and have to be shared, the public sector behaves as if numbers and the salary of each member were independent initial data.

In the United States occupational Malthusianism is even stronger in certain occupations than in Europe. A corporation that has been able to achieve a monopoly is able to preserve it for a very long while.

As with the imperfect orientation of the young, occupational Malthusianism can be blamed on insufficient flexibility in the face of technological change. It is however very often an active cause of distortion.

Unfortunate effects of distortions

Whatever their causes the distortions we are considering should appear in two shapes: on the one hand men without employment, and on the other hand jobs vacant with no one to fill them. But reality is very different: *any distortion leads to underemployment or unemployment of part of the population, but the vacancies are not as obvious*. And the structure of occupations can be more conveniently adjusted by declaring redundancies than by attempts to recruit new workers when the requirements are not clear. As a result employment falls, the national income lies below its maximum, and the 'required' population is brought into line with the employed population. There is unemploy-ment in the oversubscribed occupations, and because of this widespread optical illusion one diagnosis becomes obvious: there are too many men, the population is too large.

Figure 73 shows how in a population divided into four sectors, the required occupational structure is obtained by a reduction of employment. The sector with 600 workers forces the others to reduce to its own proportions, in this case by 25 per cent at least. The shadowed areas are the unemployed popula-tion. In fact the mechanics are a little more complex, reductions are not rigorously proportional, there is always a certain flexibility.

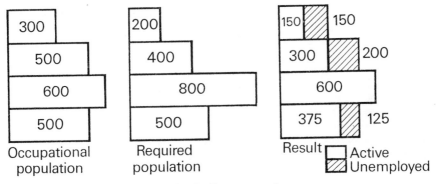

Figure 73. Occupational distortion leading to unemployment.

Thus there can be surpluses but no vacancies, because as far as men can see, society is a kind of grand production line where all occupations are comple-mentary. These illusions lead to the well-known complaints such as 'too many tradesmen' or 'too many farmers', or 'too many lawyers'; but one rarely hears phrases such as 'not enough builders', 'not enough furniture makers', 'not enough television engineers or doctors'. The balance is achieved by substrac-tion, once the possibilities of immigration and of longer working hours have been exhausted. *Public opinion hardly ever sees the situation in terms of an insufficiency of population,* for this only appears clearly in accidental circumstances (e.g. the shortage of miners after a war).

These phenomena are easy to observe in a balanced economy without in-flation. The systematic stimulation of demand reduces them and changes the approach. In a sense the inflation in the capitalist countries since the war has been a way of avoiding Malthusian paralysis.

If the complementary character of various occupations were simpler and easier to grasp, Malthusianism would be less prevalent. When there are only two groups involved (as in the case of men and women at a dance) one can just as easily say that there are too many men as that there are too few women. The same can occur in a simple economic situation, as in an office employing shorthand typists: if they are too few the rest of the staff may be unable to produce; but if one of the latter runs dry, a typist will have to take up her knitting. Here the remedy is obvious: to add whichever is lacking, or adapt the ratio. But in a complex economy with very many occupations, the effort of imagination needed to reach such a solution is too great. *The surplus workers are not inclined to say that what they lack is 'a whole economic circuit' made up of workers of other occupations.* This is too subtle for men desperate to return into an existing circuit, which they can in fact only do by causing others to be unemployed. *The illusion is strengthened by the duplication of this situation within each sector where a clever observer might discover vacancies: the resulting appearance is of saturation, if not of real unemployment* (see above, chapter 10). Public opinion always tends to notice competition but not complementary situations.

Tucker's description and rejection of this law of outlets has long been known but neglected. Classical economists, confident in the fluidity of men and things, ignore him. Keynes unfortunately passed him by, and so did the oversimplified theories of purchasing power. Schacht alone, between the two wars, seems to have understood this mechanism.

As a result capitalist societies past a certain level of organisation always tend to a Malthusian approach. Of course, even before the post-war corrective of inflation, no one actually suggested killing off the surplus population, but the unemployed workers were rejected from the economic circuit, by bringing forward the retirement age, or by urging them to emigrate, or by persuading women to stay at home, etc. A logical conclusion of this attitude is that the birth rate ought to drop. Attention is focussed on the depressed sectors, when in fact *the key of renewal lies in the fully employed sectors, which are not in the news.*

Remedies to the distortions

Some are only pain-killers, others are real remedies.

Automatic regulators: Theoretically freedom easily solves all problems of equilibrating and optimising, particularly in the field of occupational distribution. If there is a distortion and the 'required population' contains for instance more carpenters and fewer glaziers than the real population the equilibrium may be restored in one of two ways: 1. The prices of woodwork can rise through demand and those of glass drop through competition amongst glaziers. This will affect the attitude of the consumer, who will increase the demand for glass and decrease that for furniture, so that the required population approaches the real population. 2. The reverse can also occur: since carpentry is now more profitable, it will attract more workers, either by transfers from other occupations or by recruitment amongst the young, and the opposite will take place in glass work.

The equilibrium will be restored by this double trend, or at any rate the oscillations will become fewer, and unless there is a sudden and considerable change there will never be any large cleavage between required population and real population, always provided of course that productivity and working hours remain the same.

This is the classical liberal mechanism; but in fact things do not always follow the theory. Nothing guarantees, even in a very fluid and liberal market economy, that adaptation will be fast enough. Besides, the two factors of regulation have a very different elasticity: except with certain products, demand is sufficiently elastic for there to be a wide area of adjustment in prices; but wages are more rigid. Occupation too is rigid: it is rather difficult to change, and the decision usually only comes after a lengthy and cruel period of unemployment. When occupational readjustments do eventually occur, they may be too numerous, tipping the scales in the other direction. Indeed, if all men were equal, the same idea might perhaps occur to them all at the same time. Since, fortunately, they are not, the process can only be very slow.

Automatic regulators are thus imperfect, even in an absolutely free economy.

Unequal working hours: This is one of the pain-killers rather than the cures. It solves certain difficulties in the short term but in fact makes real adjustment less likely. The post-war French economy is a case in point.

International trade: This, viewed demographically, subtracts from the working population those who are working for exports and adds to it those who are working abroad on products that will eventually be imported. As a result many kinds of distortion can be corrected. International tourism, for instance, may provide openings, in an imperfectly developed country, for a largely uneducated and probably unemployed population, as hotel servants, cleaners, drivers, guides, etc., and permit the country to acquire industrial goods that could not be produced at home because the population is not sufficiently trained. But trade is not a universal cure. Imperfections may be common to several countries (for instance the lack of skilled workers, the surplus of tradesmen) or not lend themselves to correction by exchanges of goods (this is the case with the building trade, primary education, medical services, etc.).

International migrations (see above, chapter 16): They could theoretically correct any distortion but there are many obstacles. As has just been pointed out, distortions may be common in neighbouring countries (in western Europe for instance). There are a few contemporary examples of success in this:
– The immigration into France of Polish miners and Italian and Spanish farmers and building workers between the two wars.
– The immigration into industrialised western Europe of unqualified workers from Algeria, Greece, Portugal, Turkey, etc. after the last war.

– The migration of Negroes from the West Indies to their former metropolis, France or Britain.

– The temporary immigration of teachers and technicians to various African countries.

Conversions and retraining: This is an occupational migration in the proper sense of the phrase since it occurs during the active life. It is usually painful, because it attempts to change a longstanding habit. This is shown by the importance lent to people's occupation in the description of their identity – as if it was an essential part of personality. Labourers, of course, do not change their occupation: they merely switch to jobs varying in distance, pay, and fatigue. Some changes, however, are seen as promotions, and are accordingly prized.

As we saw in Part I migration can be caused by attraction or rejection:

1. *Attraction* occurs when an individual spontaneously changes to another job or position because it is more pleasant or better paid. It can even happen that expanding industries needing specialised labour attract skilled workers from laggard sectors by offering better wages. Switches to the tertiary sector are highly desired: e.g. the uncle calling on his nephew to help him run a business, the football club offering a sports shop to its prized centre-half, the offer, part friendly, part shrewd, of a partnership to an old war comrade. These migrations amount to social 'promotion' (studied in the next chapter).

2. *Rejection* occurs when an occupation can no longer employ enough people: a factory switching over to automation or stagnating, a stagecoach company changing into a railway, with no more jobs for postilions, a farmer no longer able to renew his equipment or without enough land to make it a going concern, a solicitor or actor left behind by better or luckier colleagues, and trying to find some other way of life. Such migrations are painful but there is a distinction to make between a wage-earner and a capitalist. A manual worker can more easily learn a new occupation than used to be thought, as long as the training is organised and free. A training course, a covering wage, and the prospect of more stable if not better paid employment, overcome many resistances under the age of forty. It is only for older workers or those who also have to change their domicile that the step is painful. But the owner of tools or equipment, even on a small scale, runs the risk of losing all or part of his capital in this conversion; and the change of direction at this level requires a fairly agile mind, which is not very common. Since the migration of wage-earners is rarely organised satisfactorily (people are never prepared to make for peace-time switches the efforts they willingly provide during wars) owners and wage-earners often unite to defend their interests and their habitual occupation.

3. There are many *intermediate situations* between attraction and rejection. An artisan without much capital, an independent operator whose customers are

dwindling away or who can no longer compete against a large industry but who sees other openings, may well in the end be 'forced to quit willingly'. The drift towards the towns and the neglect of agriculture follows this pattern. Since in our continuously progressing technology, such a switch is necessary, in a market economy the god of liberalism and equilibrium *must* grant higher wages or better working conditions to the developing occupations. The same god manages to reject a few surplus men by reducing the level of wages, and thus condemns agricultural workers, or at least part of them, to a standard of living constantly lower than that of the industrial workers. In a planned economy it would theoretically be possible to do otherwise since in theory authority can do anything. In fact it is much more convenient to leave or to create a sufficiently wide difference in conditions to encourage the move to take place spontaneously. Thus the town worker will have better living conditions than the kolkhoz worker. It is the same, in the Soviet Union, with geographical migrations: they are not achieved by deportation but by exhortation accompanied by some material stimulant.

4. *Trying to prevent occupational migrations*: Where change is painful, resistance is now more organised than before. When Boucicaut effected his trading revolution in France, a series of Malthusian measures were taken to favour orthodox trading methods, and since the First World War the authorities have more and more tended to intervene. Workers no longer break machines as they did in the early industrial times, but they clamour through their unions. Afraid of unemployment, governments subsidise or favour out-of-date and uneconomic sectors of industry. Capital has even better methods of defence, and approaches the authorities directly. Thus in France the surplus wine and beetroot growers managed to promote various public policies, centring on the destruction of their products through distillation, making for a price freeze and a static situation. Taxes are imposed on electric motors to subsidise wheel-barrows, for is not the possessor of a wheel-barrow socially more worthy of pity than the large, well-equipped, anonymous company? Thus instead of being adapted to the requirements of the moment, the occupational population tends to be considered as a given factor and to be preserved in various ways all boiling down to reductions in the national income. In this context *corporate attitudes are inevitably conservative and Malthusian.* Under cover of defending their occupations many organisations defend any existing situation, and try to preserve obsolete techniques. It is quite normal in Europe, and especially in France, to see the anachronism people are attached to either denied or under-estimated: society falls behind progress, out of an attachment to middle class and artisan values, such as individual houses and a 'human scale' in everything.

Directing the rising generations: We saw in Part I (pp. 194–8) that a growing population is able to adapt itself more easily than a stationary one. Its elasticity allows it to adjust its occupational structure to known requirements. But even in a growing population and even if all the young are directed towards the sectors lacking workers, the equilibrium will only return gradually. If, for instance, the ratio of tertiary workers is 35 per cent when it should be 30 per cent, and a new age group represents 3 per cent of the active population, the desired equilibrium of thirty to seventy might be achieved after five years. But since such rigorous orientation is not possible or desirable for various reasons, the adjustment can only be made over an even longer period unless other factors come into play. Thus a retarded agricultural population, with surplus numbers, needs far more than five years to be brought down from 35 to 30 per cent of the total population without occupational migration. In the interval technological progress will again have changed the required population. The lack of equilibrium will probably remain permanently.

A stationary or declining population takes far longer to correct any distortion than a growing population. Not only are the younger age groups smaller but a much larger proportion of them follow their father's vocation. Younger sons are by far the more flexible to adaptation, and this advantage should not be underestimated.

To direct the young one should pay great attention to individual aptitudes. It is not sufficient merely to try to distribute them according to the requirements of the population. A system of graded rewards is insufficient to correct occupational distortion, especially as these grades are not always very well calculated. In a surplus occupation, the only one that is in evidence, wages resist any attempt at decrease; and in any case many social considerations other than wages are brought into the choice of an occupation.

Whatever the growth of the population this problem exists in any country. Even if there is no distortion at present, it may still come about in the future. Studies of this kind were unknown before the war but are developing in our decade. If one knows the distribution of active population wanted after n years, and (an easier task) the occupational distribution of those leaving the working sphere by death or retirement, one can calculate the number of arrivals needed and thus the number of young to train in each sector. This model is complicated by various factors, notably occupational migrations proper, which, we have already said, are far from negligible.

But there still remains a largely unknown factor: forecasts on the active population can hardly go beyond the next fifteen years, and some are unable even to contemplate such a long period; yet a young man starting life will have to remain in an occupation for forty-five years, and the more specialised he is the more he may be bewildered by any technological change. To avoid, or at least, diminish this obstacle, education should take care to develop in people's minds the faculty of adaptation.

Adapting the old: The old are often, if not ill-adapted, at least affected by decreasing returns in their own occupation. We have already said (sections on demographic ageing, and on the elimination of undesirables) that modern society often tends to prescribe earlier retirement in order to get rid of cumbersome people; this is a wrong and inhuman policy and it should be replaced by a progressive adaptation to new duties, which would amount to a real reorientation of occupation, starting in certain cases from the age of 45–50. Such a policy would have to overcome many obstacles such as occupational statutes. As in the problem of housing, many rights would stand in the way of any kind of mobility. The key difficulty lies in people's attachment to things and ways of life, from which society as a whole suffers.

Directing technological progress: This is an important problem which has been so far neglected or often envisaged merely from the point of view of capitalist returns, which we would call partial returns.

There is first an essential distinction between processive developments, which widen the environment and create more room for more men, and recessive developments, which make it harder to accommodate men in the environment by reducing the available space. As processive developments are more numerous than recessive ones in developed countries, thanks to the changes in consumption patterns, this problem is especially alive in underdeveloped countries, where perhaps not the direction of technological progress but the use of imported techniques need to be carefully studied.

The situation is different though not unrelated in developed countries. If it appears that occupational migration is very difficult or lengthy because men are attached to their various occupations, it may be useful to reduce the scale of these migrations by switching technological progress in the right way. This does not mean trying to preserve desperate anachronisms, as for instance to speed up stage-coaches to avoid having to build railways. Econometric reckonings can show to what extent the national income will benefit by any such policy. In an absurd extreme one could imagine a population perpetually migrating and never getting down to any work. The same reasoning can be made here as with the question of renewal of equipment.

Such precautions are all the more legitimate since often in a capitalist society the partial viability of any sector is the only one that is valued. The perturbations following a technological development do not usually affect the people benefiting from it, even if they are a nationalised industry. The head of a firm does not consider his responsibility to extend beyond it.

Generally (we thus find this hard principle at every turn) any organised occupation brings pressure on the authorities to avoid, perhaps not technological progress, but its effects, and wheelbarrows get subsidised by electric engines.

Should the victims of progress receive compensation? This would only be fair to workers. But compensating capitalists is one of the many contradictions of modern economics: if those riding with progress are to receive profits from it and the victims compensated, the game is easy to play for both and it is not clear where the money is to come from. The state cannot provide comprehensive insurance without requiring high premiums in the form of taxes.

There is at least no doubt about the desirability of a national system of accounts to provide clear information on what is costly and what is profitable for the nation. The better the accounts the more difficult it will be for politicians and private interests to promote dangerous policies in the name of the general good. Sooner or later the European capitalist countries will realise that investments of a certain scale must be rationally planned, and that occupational migrations constitute the key of development and the answer to many so-called surplus populations.

As for influencing the course of technological progress by direct intervention, many groups argue more or less explicitly that discovery, like fate, is blind and turns in the most unexpected directions, sometimes the least necessary. Indeed, we are able to sit in our armchairs and watch a sporting event beamed at great expense off a satellite, a luxury for which Louis XIV or Aurengzeb would have readily paid millions of pounds. Yet we can enjoy it in slums and shanty towns, such is the strange contrast between requirements and achievements. But does this not show how desirable it would be to direct research towards vital or semi-vital requirements? And could one not, in particular, try to preserve natural resources, instead of spreading chemical waste, or consuming forests that cannot be replaced at the same speed?

Here again local economic viability, rather than long-term national interest is often wrongly given priority. In addition, there is a fundamental difficulty in international competition. If a country, in a fit or wisdom, were to switch its technological research towards vital requirements and towards the long-term future, it would find itself in an inferior position in the short term. This is especially, but not only, true of capitalist countries. For the Soviet Union under the relentless pressure of international competition, gave satellites higher priority than housing and other individual requirements. Public opinion too is excited by the magnificent sight of the conquest of space, and would be disappointed if progress were to slacken in this field.

In the Third World the pressure of demand for tertiary occupations is no lesser, even though it often emphasises the food shortage. Any 'intellectual' technique is more popular than physical techniques.

It seems today that any real reassessment of the direction of technological research is a forlorn hope. Yet we are wasting and misusing resources, and will stand condemned, after the event, by generations to come.

Adapting consumption to the active population: This method consists in changing not the occupational population but the required population. The dictum: 'When you don't have what you like you had better learn to like what you have' becomes 'If you don't want to produce what you want then you must consume what you produce'.

We have already called attention to the forces of inertia that prevent adaptation, often with the connivance of active policies. There is also a tendency to direct consumption towards the pattern acquired by the active population through education and private ambitions. Both encourage it to shun technological effort and especially manual labour. Every year the population in search of work increases in certain oversubscribed sectors. The overdevelopment of certain forms of minor trade is one of the results. Legislation and taxation tends to favour them, not only for political reasons but because the personnel in this sector is incapable of any kind of reconversion. The married woman who sells handbags on a stall underneath an archway is very difficult to re-educate.

Yet by appearing to make these truly marginal activities worthwhile, authorities have only a minor effect on consumption. Of course, as long as a shop exists, some customers will come in, but underemployment will persist and there will in the end be a slow adaptation. It is a different matter in sectors showing no immediate profits, which subsist in the so-called public interest, a partly arbitrary label. Ours is not the first century to suffer from a surplus of civil servants, indeed there are fewer now that civil servants are not the only group to have pensions. But reckoning the salary of a civil servant demands ten or twelve arithmetical operations, and several minutes of careful checking. This and other formalities lead to the employment of administrative and financial personnel. The 'Parkinson factor' is not devoid of use: it helps to satisfy a sense of justice. But it would not have appeared or developed to this extent had our education left us with a shortage of accountants.

The same can be said of social security and insurance in general: if clerks, accountants, underwriters, managers were less plentiful, insurance would concentrate into more selected areas where the risks are on a larger scale, more easy to administer and socially more worthwhile. As it is, it has proliferated with ease into scattered areas. This should not be taken as a criticism of the situation; the point is merely that it has been partly dictated by the make-up of the active population.

Neither is it legitimate to prefer absolutely and without exception the requirements of the consuming population to that of the active population which is largely the same, once vital requirements are satisfied. A self-sufficient individual may well shirk certain kinds of work, even at the expense of important needs: this is up to him to decide, as long as he is perfectly conscious of his actions and their consequences. A population too is free to choose more pleasant types of activity, but it should not be surprised if shortages occur due to imperfect orientation of its energies, and it should be willing to offer larger rewards to the people who have to undertake the less prized form of work.

481

Migration in the three sectors

Let us now return to the sectors of activity defined by Clark and Fourastié on the basis of increasing or decreasing returns, this time from a more social viewpoint: each sector has different factors of attraction for an individual or a family.

A *primary* worker (farmer, fisherman, miner, etc.) is in direct contact with nature and its variations, hardships and furies. He suffers from weather, has to work in wind or mud. Not only is his occupation physically difficult, but it also carries with it a social stigma ('bumpkin', 'clodhopper') and in addition it is often insufficiently rewarded. The primary worker, usually a country worker, has fewer comforts, belated social legislation, and particularly out-of-date sanitary care and education. It is not surprising that he aspires to better conditions, by promotion to the secondary or the tertiary sector.

The *secondary* worker, or manual industrial worker, is still in contact with raw materials and accomplishes strenuous and dirty work, which often leaves its mark on his body. But he works in a more conditioned environment, protected from the weather; his tools are placed at a convenient height for him and he does not have to lower himself to them.

The *tertiary* worker is no longer at all in contact with nature or raw materials. Not only is his environment conditioned, but the work is neither dirty nor strenuous. He can enjoy wearing a white collar and drawing a monthly salary. Contrary to what is usually said (but usually by tertiary workers), the qualified manual worker is only rarely better paid than the intellectual worker in an inferior position. Comparisons are only valid if working hours are equal. Yet any absence of a manual worker is deducted from his wages. The material handicap this strict rule brings him is also a humiliation. His productivity is more easily measured and controlled, another form of submission that the tertiary worker does not usually suffer. Also, the tertiary sector includes all the prized and recognised positions. Social promotion is so difficult for the manual worker in France that apart from a few sporting careers trade union promotion is practically his only opening. By directing his children towards the tertiary sector he gives them a better chance of rising, buys them a ticket in the great social lottery.

Thus there is progressive liberation as one moves from the primary towards the tertiary sector: liberation from nature, then from matter, then to a large extent from men. Its advantages are accompanied by higher rewards and greater possibilities of promotion. One understands the general desire to graduate to a higher sector.

The three sectors largely correspond to a social stratification. A young farmer will often want to replace his horses by a tractor quite apart from economic considerations. It is not merely that 'the soil is lowly', but that tending to a horse is a 'low' occupation whereas repairing a tractor motor places him amongst the aristocracy of metal workers. To lead his horse through the village is often to risk taunts from the village girls. But on his tractor he becomes the Roman on his chariot. He has won his stripes.

Migrations and technological progress

Generally therefore, as productive activity and consumption increase, technological progress causes occupational migration from the primary to the tertiary sector. As the most immediate requirements, those closer to nature, are satisfied (food, heat), consumption switches towards services or products further and further removed from the natural environment. More and more secondary and tertiary workers and fewer and fewer primary ones are required to produce a given object such as 100 calories of meat. There is thus a happy agreement between social necessity and individual ambition. According to Clark there is a direct correlation between the ratio of tertiary workers and the national income per person. But this is difficult to check, since one needs comparable figures, whereas the definition of a tertiary worker varies from one author to another. For a given national income, there seems to be a higher proportion of tertiary workers in Europe than in Anglo-Saxon countries.

If the rhythm of migration follows the increase in national income, and differential fertility, there should be no fundamental distortion. But total harmony is never achieved: either there are laggard sectors, such as the agricultural population of the United States; or others develop too fast as when an increase of income which had up to then been constant, slows down or stops – migration maintains its own impetus, less by changes of occupation amongst mature workers than by the choice of jobs made by the young on entering the workforce. Figure 73 gave, for France, the rise of output per person on the basis of 100 for 1906, together with the number of tertiary workers for 100 active people. Until 1929 the two curves progressed together, but from the 1929 crisis to 1946 output dropped, while the increase of tertiary workers only slowed down. From 1946 output began to rise the faster.

General

It seems that men's desire to choose their occupation freely will increase in the decades to come. This may well shock a visitor from another planet, or the theorists of abundance, who may see in the spread of unproductive employment a kind of refuge against unemployment. They would be wrong, for there is no lack of employment in the deserted occupations. But they might still say: 'Why such obstinate efforts to find a particular activity? Economics are not designed to produce work, but to enable you to consume. If you were to stop trying to control each other, you would release such a large number of workers that you could easily cover your needs by a distributive system and reach the desired abundance'.

Such a view rightly stresses the social uselessness of certain activities, but it fails to appreciate the real meaning of 'requirement'. It is not new, and does not stem from the great slump, since it is to be found in Thomas More, and in most of the utopian thinkers. It was equally valid, if not more so, in the pre-industrial society, where recognised requirements were strictly limited in number, and where the expenditure of kings or great merchants could quite rightly be considered as sumptuary.

In Marx's time, when the disappearance of the state was contemplated, the horizon of requirements was not very wide: housing, food, clothing, heat and culture were sufficient. But the reckonings of his time are now vitiated by the growth of requirements, which is outpacing production. It is no longer considered extravagant for any couple to want its private conveyance.

The Soviets have only partly understood how the increase of requirements, both public and private, compromises the accomplishment of distributive justice. Narrow horizons are the general rule: either men refuse to believe there is anything beyond what they can see, and thus fear a future shortage of employment; or they drift off into some dream.

As long as general abundance, in other words over-abundance, does not exist, there will always be a need for multiple controls; this leads both to a vicious circle, and to the disagreeable prospect of a society where half the men would be employed in controlling the activity of the other half.

A sudden cut in working hours is a sword thrust that could only be successful if backed up by far more penetrating reforms than are at present contemplated.

19

SOCIAL MIGRATIONS

Social migrations are often bracketed into 'social mobility', but we prefer the more general phrase. Social migrations could be studied without reference to their direction, but this is usually the most interesting question.

Social level is not always easy to define. Formerly it was a question of status and condition rather than occupation. One was an aristocrat, a landowner, a manual worker, a vagabond. Nowadays people's occupation as well as their level in the occupation plays an essential part: they are managers, foremen, farmers, employees, etc. If it was only a question of income the situation would be clear, but it is not. An occupation can attract men because of its pleasantness, or the type of work, or the status lent to it by society. A small-time clerk may think himself superior to a domestic servant even though his income is lower. Social hierarchy, largely a convention, is the result of all these individual preferences. It is vain to criticise some of its peculiarities, and we must be content to observe.

The various possible changes

It would be possible merely to study how the social structure of a population develops. For instance, censuses show that over the last fifty or even hundred years there has been a large drop in the number of agricultural workers, who have a very low position in the hierarchy, and a rise in the number of civil servants, clerks, skilled workers, etc. But it is usually preferred to follow the fortunes of an individual or a family.

Social migration occurs: 1. When a person rises during his active life – this is often called social promotion. This happens when a schoolteacher, while at work, sits further examinations and obtains a better post, or when a clerk becomes promoted into management, or a shop assistant buys a shop and becomes an employer at the end of his life. 2. When a young person reaches a social status higher than that of his parents: e.g. the son of an NCO going to Sandhurst, the daughter of a working class family becoming a schoolteacher, etc.

Social level is transmitted from one generation to another more faithfully than occupation: the son of a dairyman can work for a grocer or a butcher without changing his social level. The notion of social class depends on this. If at each generation the higher posts were distributed at random or according to merit, there might be unequal conditions but one could not talk of class feeling or class struggle.

There is no social mobility if all children retain their parents' status, as when society is divided into castes. Total stability is achieved if all the following conditions are satisfied: 1. Constant technology and stationary population. 2. Children retaining their parents' status. 3. Equal fertility, or rather reproduction ratio, for the various social classes or categories.

Otherwise the balance will be broken and mobility will appear. Thus: 1. *Technological progress* changes the distribution of work and even its nature, suppresses certain occupations and creates others, usually at a higher level. 2. *Population growth* usually causes perturbations. There have been very few cases of lands with such a small population that it could retain its structure while increasing noticeably (Canada in the eighteenth and nineteenth centuries is one example). 3. The *socio-political system* can change, and lead to greater or lesser promotion on merit, a factor that competes with birth status. 4. *Differential fertility* amongst classes causes mobility. If the upper class is less fertile capillarity appears; if on the contrary it is more fertile or its death rate is lower, downward movement may occur.

Gross and net migrations

A stable social structure can hide various compensatory trends, and we must thus distinguish, as we have done with other types of migrations, between gross and net migrations. Only the first deserve to be labelled 'social mobility'. Even if they cancel out, exchanges between social groups present considerable sociological interest. In a limiting case, all individuals in one generation could change their condition in a gigantic permutation, while the total situation remained the same.

Measuring devices

Here are the most often used or the most fruitful.

Comparison between successive censuses of social categories: This gives an idea of general trends but only in the form of net migrations; it does not measure social mobility.

Research into the ascendants of a representative sample: Each individual of a given social category is asked to which category his parents and grandparents belonged. The INED made a survey of this kind in France in 1950.[1] Here are some of the figures given:

[1] M. Brésard, 'Mobilité sociale et dimension de la famille', *Population*, July–September, 1950.

Social group ↓ ——→ of fathers of sample	Total	Businessmen, professionals	Civil servants, technicians, administrators	Tradesmen	Farmers	Minor civil servants, clerks	Industrial workers and labourers	Agricultural workers and labourers
—Businessmen, professionals	100	**32·2**	11·0	22·9	6·8	16·9	10·2	—
—Civil servants, technicians, administrators	100	12·1	**17·1**	21·4	8·6	27·2	10·0	3·6
—Tradesmen	100	3·7	2·4	**53·8**	14·3	8·4	13·2	4·2
—Farmers	100	1·0	1·7	5·7	**82·9**	1·5	2·6	4·6
—Minor civil servants, clerks	100	1·7	4·3	18·2	14·5	**31·2**	25·6	4·5
—Industrial workers and labourers	100	0·7	1·5	12·3	15·1	13·6	**47·8**	9·0
—Agricultural workers and labourers	100	—	0·3	3·7	39·3	4·7	15·2	**36·8**
—Total ⎰ Percentage	100	3·1	3·1	17·9	34·1	12·6	20·7	8·5
⎱ Size of sample	3023	94	95	540	1033	380	625	256

Assuming that social rank diminishes from left to right and from top to bottom we see in the triangle to the right of the diagonal in bold type the cases of social ascent and in the triangle on the left the cases of social descent. There are more of the first than of the second because the structure of the population was changing. There was probably even more social climbing than the table shows because the survey only enquired into the ultimate occupation of the parents, who may have progressed during their lifetime. Some answers may also have been distorted by reluctance to speak of one's modest origins.

This sort of survey can also enquire into the number of children, or, more usefully, the number of brothers or sisters of each person: this would measure the influence of the size of families.

Research into the ancestry of a homogeneous sample: For example university teachers, railway engineers, grocers, etc. Because of the general move upward in society, results are more interesting if one works on a group of high status. In 1958 the INED made a large-scale survey of the factors of success, interviewing 2018 people, all with some degree of celebrity.[1] Here is a summary of the more interesting figures:

[1] A. Girard, *La réussite sociale en France*, Paris, 1961 (Cahiers de l'INED).

487

	1 Occupation of fathers of the sample of celebrities	2 Socio-occupational distribution of the population in 1896	Ratio of 1 to 2
Farmers	5	46	0·11
Industrial workers	3	30	0·10
Tradesmen	11	9	1·22
White collar workers	13	10	1·30
Higher civil servants	68	5	13·60
	100	100	

The occupational distribution in 1896 corresponds roughly to that of celebrities' fathers. The disproportion is striking.

Research into the descendants of a representative sample: This is often also a homogeneous one. The most interesting sample would be one of people aged 40–50 whose children have already found their vocation.

Research into the social status of the parents of a sample of students at various levels of education: This would gauge the degree of democracy in education, a sign or factor of social mobility. Research of this kind could be modelled on that undertaken by the INED under A. Girard, the results of which are analysed below.[1] Here conclusions can be drawn not only on numerical results but also on motivation, and one can thus track down the essential factor of social mobility.

Longitudinal research, following a cohort in time: This is long and costly but it yields very significant results.

In all such surveys various factors can be studied: the number of children per family, the age of the parents at the time of birth or at marriage, the regional origin, etc. But it is not always easy to isolate any one factor. Many mistakes have been due to failure to take into account the correlation (at any rate, at certain periods) between social status and children per family. One may want to gauge the influence of the number of children for each social category. Here, for instance, is the length of schooling in years (a factor of social ascent) tabled against the number of children and their social origin:

[1] The material was mainly analysed by myself and A. Girard and published as 'Les diverses classes sociales devant l'enseignement. Mise au point générale des résultats', *Population*, April–June 1965.

	1 child	2 children	3	4	5	Average
Businessmen and professionals	13·6	12·8	11·9	14·6	13·4	13·0
Civil servants and management	13·4	13·7	12·9	12·0	13·5	13·1
Farmers	8·3	7·9	7·3	7·4	7·1	7·5
Tradesmen and artisans	10·2	9·7	9·5	8·9	8·1	9·1
White collar workers	11·0	10·5	10·3	9·2	9·7	10·4
Industrial workers and labourers	9·2	8·4	7·8	7·3	7·3	8·0
Agricultural workers and labourers	7·4	7·5	6·8	6·8	6·8	7·0
Average	9·6	9·1	8·6	8·0	7·7	8·6

The larger the family the shorter the schooling. There are a few exceptions, but probably because of the smallness of the sample, and there is certainly no doubt about the middle social categories, even though the difference is not large at the top, and is non-existent at the bottom (because of the minimum school-leaving age). Schooling does not vary very much after the fourth child. But the children of families of more than four children are particularly handicapped. If the family is both large and poor they have very little chance of rising through education.

Differential fertility can be measured through classical statistics (censuses, registers of families) as well as by enquiries into special samples. The statistics have to be completed by certain facts such as legislation, customs, opinions, technological change, etc.

The pre-industrial world

When birth had an important legal role, social mobility could only be very small. Various perturbations, however, occurred during the eighteenth century. The middle class rose through business and, education, whilst in France the aristocracy was reluctant, at the crucial time, to indulge in economic activity.[1] The effort of the middle class, having made its money, to achieve aristocratic rank through marriage or honours is only a secondary phenomenon.

The drop in mortality amongst the aristocracy (fewer wars, fewer duels, better hygiene) was hard on large families impoverished by the subsequent division of their wealth as well as by new social requirements. Others only maintained their rank by recourse to celibacy, ecclesiastic or not. Contraception followed.

The rise of the middle class is measured less by the wealth it acquired than

[1] See J. Hecht, 'Un problème de population active au XVIIIe siècle en France: la querelle de la noblesse commerçante', *Population*, April–June 1964. See also above, Part I, p. 198.

489

by its proliferation. The social pyramid gained a midriff, which meant a large increase in requirements in addition to that resulting normally from the increase in population. In England this was absorbed by progress in the production of wealth, but in France it gained explosive force and is the fundamental cause of the Revolution: the misery of the people and the greed of the rich were not new factors in 1789.

Like any great change, the French Revolution permitted a great deal of social climbing: the abolition of privilege, the emigration of the aristocrats, the sale of the *biens nationaux*, the changes in institutions, the long wars all favoured the rise of talent that had formerly been contained by the social shell. The whole period shows how rich any society is in very talented men who cannot break through the barriers of institutions, customs, prejudices.

Industrial society

During the whole of the ninteenth and the beginning of the twentieth centuries there was very little social mobility, and the equality of men proclaimed by French law did not go beyond the legal field. The transmission of wealth by inheritance, the high cost of education, the low number of marriages between classes all had a conservative influence in France, whereas in the United States in the bubbling, disorderly discovery of new wealth some famous social promotions were possible. In spite of appearances, the low rate of growth of the population was itself an adverse factor of mobility. No doubt a family with only one child could educate it more easily, but on the national scene the economic stagnation had a conservative influence: there was very little new business, and hence no new openings for the young. Malthusianism favoured anything belonging to the past.

In spite of this great social inertia some mobility was provided by the change in the social structure through progress and differential fertility: the middle class was generally less fertile than the working or peasant classes. Thus the number of agricultural workers in France dropped from $3\frac{1}{2}$ million in 1890 to $2\frac{1}{2}$ million in 1914 and to 1,850,000 in 1939. Of course, this was in a sense counterbalanced by the proletarisation of artisans and peasants become wage-earners, but such a change is not always a degradation.

There are a series of surveys sufficiently comparable to suggest the extent of the change between 1896 and 1936. In this period the active agricultural population dropped from 5,674,000 to 4,222,000. The difference was largely made up of workers and very small, underemployed, farmers. Where did they go? The number of industrial workers stayed more or less the same, but the number of white collar workers increased by 650,000 between 1901 and 1936 and probably by $\frac{3}{4}$ million from 1896 to 1936, whilst the number of civil servants rose by 310,000 over the same period. Within each group the structure changed in a comparable way, to the benefit of the higher categories.

The two wars caused important changes in France: social ascent through trade and industry; decline in the fortunes of the rich, through inflation rather than war damages; a relative drop in higher civil servants' salaries and a relative increase for the middle and lower categories; immigration only affecting the base of the social hierarchy. But just before the Second World War social ascent was still an exception judging by the population of secondary schools tabled by social class. Ascent from the proletariat to the higher strata was rarely achieved in one generation.

Present situation in France

There has been, as in the other western countries, greater social mobility since the war. Promotion can be caused either by personal success, marriage, or education. The first depends on various factors such as good fortune or unscrupulousness, but they cannot be collectively appreciated. The second, marriage, only plays a small part, even for women. Research made by the INED into the choice of partners[1] shows that people usually marry into their own classes.

Education according to social level in France

The influence of education is constantly increasing, with the progress of technological knowledge and the rise of public employment.

The fact that different social classes were educated differently long appeared quite natural. Secondary education was a privilege of the middle class, and the lower class could only get primary education. Little by little, this began to be considered, not exactly unjust, but undemocratic: the nation was perhaps depriving itself of talent by not cultivating it. During the first half of the nineteenth century the transmission of social status through education was commonly denounced as one of the privileges of wealth. Free education at all levels was considered, especially in France, as a specific remedy to ensure equality. It has not, however, had this effect; indeed, the middle class has had most of the benefit.

The supporters of equality through education have been too impressed by the importance of income levels and wealth after they have lost their dominance. They lacked statistical knowledge and did not make up for this with much thought. In 1953 the INED made a systematic survey of the orientation and selection of children of school age. For the first time the process was examined stage by stage. The results showed up the situation in a very different light, though prejudices have not been changed by them. In 1962 and 1963

[1] See A. Girard, *Le choix du conjoint. Une enquête psycho-sociologique en France*, Paris 1964. (Cahiers de l'INED.)

there was another enquiry into the conditions of entry into secondary education, a fundamental stage.[1]

Social inequality is diminishing slowly from year to year, though it is still very large in France. It is obvious amongst university students. Figure 74 compares the structure of the active population in 1954 with that of the students in 1963.

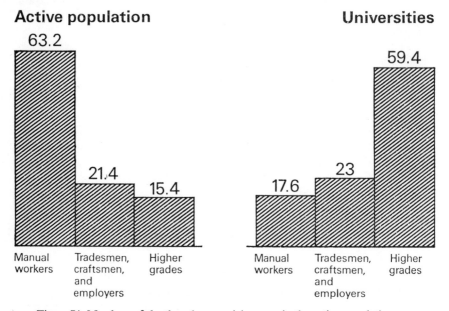

Figure 74. Members of the three large social groups in the active population and at university.

There is a progressive selection from the age of 10 onwards in the shape of the various leaving and entrance examinations in a student's career. The approximate percentage of working class children at each stage in French education is given opposite for the generation which began its secondary school education in 1957.

1. The first obstacle, success at school *up to the eleventh year,* is less well negotiated by the poorer children. Yet wealth can have played no part at this point. The parents of children below eleven are usually aged between thirty-five and forty-five, and have not yet inherited their own parents' wealth. Income is more important, whether earned or unearned. It is fairly narrowly but not absolutely linked with cultural level. The fact is that whenever they

[1] The first figures and the detailed bibliography can be found in *Population,* April–June 1965.

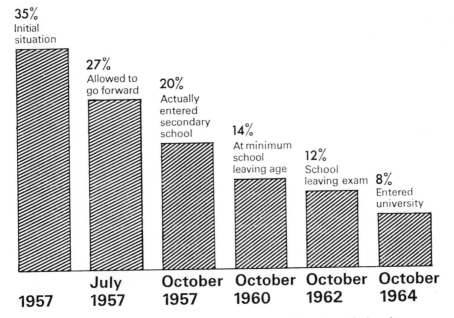

Figure 75. Proportion of workers' children at the various stages of education for the generation entering secondary (grammar) schools in 1957.

can be separated, the cultural level obviously has an influence while the income has practically none. Thus the children of school teachers obtain better marks at school than the children of tradesmen. Whether this is due to help from parents, or indirectly to the family environment, or to genetic factors (fairly important as we shall see in the relevant chapter), parents thus to a large extent bequeath their cultural level to their children.

2. Even given equal merit at this stage, the proportion of children who actually enter into *secondary schools* varies according to social class. For very intelligent children there is a small difference, with a percentage of 91 per cent for working class children and 100 per cent for children of the upper middle class (with an exception for rich landowners who may be a long way away from the schools). For less intelligent children, the difference is considerable: of these, 3 per cent of working class children and 50 per cent of upper middle class children enter secondary schools. 70–75 per cent of the latter go to grammar schools (*lycées*) whereas only 33 per cent of the former do so. The rest go to secondary moderns (*Collèges d'Enseignement Général*).

This second selection can be explained by the higher ambitions of the upper middle class parents, and their fear of social descent. A working class parent will accept the fact that his children leave school at the same age as he did, but a teacher, an engineer, a businessman, will try very hard to get them up this

493

indispensable step. They are in any case better placed to do so. Teachers are on the spot, engineers and lawyers will be better able to obtain an interview with a headmaster and get their child in. They will be talking to a man of their class, to institutions created by their class.

3. As the child grows, wealth becomes more important. It is irrelevant at the beginning but looms large around the age of fourteen (the minimum school-leaving age in France). Until then the cost of studies is not important and in any case it cannot be avoided. But from the fifteenth year onwards a poor family will suffer from the failure of a child to earn money or help in the household. Cultural level still has a part to play: an elementary schoolteacher will leave his children at secondary school even if he is poor. But if both factors combine against the child he will be sacrificed. The hardest situation is to be the eldest of a family of four or more. The boy in this situation will be put to work or into apprenticeship; the girl will have to help her mother at home. In both cases a great deal is lost if the child was even moderately promising.

The influence of the economic level remains strong as long as there are not sufficient provisions for educational grants.

A general view of social promotion

In developed European countries social inequality is now rather a question of income and still more one of cultural level than of wealth. Because of this equal rights to education and free education are no longer sufficient to ensure the equality of children. The cultural level inherited from the parents ensures the preservation of social status, and justifies the term 'class'. It is, however, only partially transmitted; and in any case the distribution of occupations is constantly changing to the benefit of the higher ones. The lower classes, industrial workers especially, are far more conscious than they used to be of the need to educate their children; also the lower occupations are more and more filled by immigrant labour.

As a result of these various movements there is more social mobility and less division between classes. The mere fact that children from various social backgrounds are together in the same school for several years contributes perhaps not to a fusion but at least to an effacing of frontiers. This is the essential fact, as we shall see in the following chapter.

Total social mobility and absolute equality of education are inconceivable as long as the family is preserved; but large-scale changes are afoot.

20

COEXISTENCE OF POPULATIONS

There have been many partial studies of this, mainly on a historical basis, but there have not yet been bridges between the work of historians, geneticists, ethnologists, geographers, sociologists, and demographers. We will merely attempt an outline of a field still largely unexplored.

Let us start by defining the terms. By *coexistence* we mean that the groups live close together under the same political authority or without a definite frontier in a politically unified territory. Notice the difference between political coexistence of two neighbouring states and social coexistence within one state. By *population* we mean a group of people with physical, racial, or cultural characteristics that can be transmitted or are sufficiently apparent to be recognised fairly clearly, either because there are few mixed marriages or because there is strong repulsion between the two groups. This point will be clarified further on.

The two populations can differ either by a hereditary physical trait (Negroes and whites) or by acquired but transmissive characteristics (language, religion) or simply by birth or group consciousness (as with castes), or clothing, or appearance. But for there to be division and coexistence, these differences must be sufficiently apparent and they must bring together individuals with the same characteristic and give rise to a group consciousness liable to cause social tension. There are for example problems of coexistence at the moment in the United States (Negroes and whites), in Switzerland (three linguistic groups), in Belgium (Flemish and Walloons), in South Africa (whites, Indians, Negroes, and half castes), in India (Moslems and Hindus), in Lebanon (Arabs and Christians), in Israel (Jews and Arabs), in the Far East (Chinese and Malays), in various negro countries, in Bolivia (Indians and whites), etc. But the conflict between Israel and the Arab countries is not a problem of co-existence as we have defined it; the same applies to the division of Germany, Korea or Vietnam into two parts. Social classes pose a different problem.

Origin of the division

There are various possible causes: 1. Lengthy union under one political authority of two areas with different populations: e.g. Switzerland, or the old Austro-Hungary. This can be originally due to political domination. 2. Peaceful or violent immigration: the Normans into England in the eleventh century,

495

the British into Ireland, the British, Dutch, and Indians into South Africa; or the importation of slaves (the Negroes into the United States). The migrants must constitute sufficiently compact or self-conscious groups. 3. Sudden or slow division into two groups of a population that had up to then been united: e.g. Catholics and Protestants in various countries after the Reformation.

These various causes, especially the first two, can combine, or date back so far that they are difficult to distinguish.

The various possible developments

Apart from a status quo, there can be various developments which can of course combine: extermination can accompany an emigration or fusion. Thus, in the case of Ireland, there was partly extinction (the famines were a result of misery), partly emigration towards the United States, and partly fusion through mixed marriages, and finally a sufficiently clear partitioning for problems of coexistence to be considerably reduced both in the Republic and in Northern Ireland.

Demographic extinction through high mortality: Statistically this can be described as a constant excess of deaths over births until disappearance ensues. In fact there is always a certain amount of fusion with the ruling population. This kind of phenomenon is very difficult to follow, because populations under such stress are unable to keep anything resembling a register. The process can be due to one of two factors:

1. *Extermination*, wished for or at least caused by the ruling population. History tells us both of systematic massacres and of less premeditated but equally cruel methods. Where there is no obvious killing one can argue as to whether the population has disappeared through excess mortality or lack of fertility. There are similar considerations on whether animal species are disappearing because they are being hunted or because they are not reproducing normally. The answer can vary, but it is usually that mortality is too high. The occasional disturbances in fertility are always rather obscure.

The most significant example of extermination is that of the Jews in Germany and Poland, in which the Nazis practically succeeded. Others have been less systematic but equally effective: when the British occupied Australia they did not have any avowed intention of killing the natives, but they were reluctant to live with them. There was such a wide gap between the two civilisations that coexistence was unthinkable. The British slowly colonised the country driving natives ahead of them and away from their haunts, causing enormous decreases in numbers by mortality or sterility. Those who kept in touch with the invaders were swallowed up by alcohol or various diseases.

The same is true of the Americans in the seventeenth century. They did not intend to kill all the Indians but they invaded their territory pitilessly, and

496

used their material superiority to drive them out and harrass them. There were two factors of incompatibility: the distaste felt by the British for mixed unions, and the resistance of the Indians to slavery or domestication, which made them undesirable parasites in the new civilisation. Not accustomed to an agricultural life, they did not know how to live in a restricted territory. They were already of rather low fertility before the invasion because of the high incidence of abortions and various marriage customs (higher fertility could only have been achieved together with better soil husbandry), and difficult conditions inevitably caused them to disappear rapidly. They were ill-adapted both to the new invaders and to their environment, and they were biologically doomed. Neither the British in Australia nor the American pioneers were at all disappointed when the useless species disappeared, for at this time there was no general wish to preserve natural species of either animals or men.

In the early colonial days in Algeria people talked of 'driving the natives back' or of wiping them out,[1] or even of sending them to colonise the desert. The first policy would have led to an apparently unintentional massacre.

There are practically no cases of a ruling population trying to eliminate an undesirable group through sterility. The murder of new-born males in Egypt in Moses' day had another object too, and can only be interpreted as a compromise between the use of mortality and that of sterility. The Nazis may conceivably have tried, in various countries, to separate men from women in order to cut the birth rate. They certainly allowed Germans privileges in this respect.[2]

At the end of the colonial era the only non-European ethnic groups surviving were those with strong demographic vitality (Asia, Arab countries) or those occupying a land considered unfit for whites (Africa). This fact illustrates a particularly distressing side of international immorality. The ruling populations which have exterminated the others, even at a recent date, enjoy not only peace at home but general consideration abroad. World opinion has no blame for the Australians or the Americans for having murdered the natives. Those who do suffer or have suffered from internal problems (e.g. the French in Algeria) are those who have been either too humane or too lax to apply drastic methods, and later have to cope with coexistence. This is not applause for the present policy of the Europeans in South Africa, merely regret at the readiness with which international opinion forgives past crimes but condemns unhappy legacies.

2. *Differential fertility*: This can cause a population under pressure from another to become extinct, particularly if there are no contacts (mixed unions, 'conversions') between the fertile and the sterile sections. Pearson reckoned that since in Denmark 25 per cent of the families have 50 per cent of the

[1] See the reasons given for the *Loi du 24 février 1833*.

[2] See S. Ledermann and A. Sauvy, 'La guerre biologique', *Population*, July–September 1946.

children, at the second generation 78 per cent of the population and at the third 98 per cent would descend from them. A population become a small minority generally loses its cohesion and its distinctive traits, and either blends into the growing majority or retreats into isolates too small to survive, where the young experience more and more difficulty in choosing a partner and have to resign themselves to celibacy or to mixed unions.[1] If the biological progress of such a demographic invasion could be followed step by step one would observe the less fertile group slowly breaking up and retreating into strongholds which in turn would fritter away, until the final summation: surrender or die.

Expulsion and emigration: Emigration can follow a risk of extermination. In the fifth century the Anglo-Saxons eliminated the Britons from England by a combination of the two. Short of this, one can impose such hardships on a minority that it is to all intents and purposes expelled, though it may officially be emigrating voluntarily. In the sixteenth century the Moors were expelled from Spain – a radical solution, providing there are no reprisals.

Very recently the Czechs, who for the past few centuries had been living in ambiguous partnership with the Germans in the Sudetan states, decided that after the years of Nazi rule life in common was no longer possible, and expelled the minority into Germany; between the two wars, Greece and Turkey exchanged parts of their populations to end the coexistence in both countries.

In the Baltic states conquered by the Soviet Union, the fraction that surrendered to the invaders will sooner or later blend with the Russians; the rest were deported. Similarly, during the Second World War the Tartars disappeared from Crimea as an ethnic group. The Karchis, the Balkars, the Kalmuks, the Tchetchens, were deported in 1943–4, though survivors were allowed to return after Stalin's death. The Israelis too ejected some Arab groups or prevented them from returning.

Division of the territory into two sufficiently homogeneous parts, governed independently. If the territory is a recently conquered one it is not so much coexistence as a division of spoils or the limits of a conquest. Partition is always very difficult to achieve peacefully. It occurred when Sweden and Norway split in 1905, but these two peoples were not in sufficiently close contact for the common political authority to have to envisage social, as opposed to political coexistence.

The most frequent case is the liberation of a group that has long been dominated and is sufficiently concentrated geographically: thus the well-known explosion of Austro-Hungary after the First World War. But here minorities subsist in the new territories, so that coexistence has merely taken

---

[1] The problem of isolates and the minimum population is dealt with above (Part 1, Chap. 9) and in J. Sutter's articles in *Population*, and his book *L'eugénique*, Paris, 1950.

another form. It is the same with India and Pakistan, where massacres and migrations have not managed to achieve total separation, and Kashmir remains a disputed territory.

Other examples of partition are Holland and Belgium in 1830, Turkey after 1918, Ireland in 1921, Korea in 1952, Vietnam in 1954 (the last two cases are political divisions rather than a separation of populations). This is a radical surgical solution, always strongly opposed within the two populations, especially if the geographical frontier is hazy – but it can give lasting results.

Blending of populations into a group without cleavage. This is the most interesting case for the demographer, though statistical observations of it are more complex. It is achieved when the characteristics of at least one group become indistinguishable, or when there is no longer a clear enough demarcation line to be a pretext for division and friction. It can be either a physical (or, more rarely, a cultural) blending, leading to what is in fact a new population; or else, by a conversion usually of a cultural kind, one group can identify itself with the other.

There are, no doubt, hereditary characteristics not of a physical kind; however, not only do we have very little information about racial differences in intelligence, artistic ability, etc., but even if they exist they always overlap so widely (see Haldane) that the division is vague, and can be no basis for segregation. There are thus only three kinds of differences.

PHYSICAL CHARACTERISTICS: When two populations differ by a physical characteristic, only a small fraction of unions need be mixed for the proportion of half-castes to increase constantly. The physical characteristics which separate populations (size, colour of skin, etc.) are easily recognisable ones, determined by multiple genes, so that mixed unions produce a continuous spectrum. It would be a different matter if for instance men could recognise each other's blood group by sight, and make it the basis of a caste system.

In Brazil and Mexico there have been so many mixed unions that the problem of coexistence has faded away. Some really black and really white men still exist, but there is no visible cleavage between them, and hence no racial feeling. On the whole the whites hold the highest social positions, but the division is not clear, because there are many poor whites too.

If a ruling population wishes to preserve its 'purity' it must take extremely rigorous measures of a very arbitrary kind (see below, p. 504). It must not only forbid mixed unions, and thus risk acts of violence, but also practise systematic segregation, kindle racial repulsion and assert its own superiority in the face of all scientific evidence. Such 'pure' populations soon come to attribute to heredity defects (such as ignorance, uncleanliness, unhealthiness), due to the environment of their rivals, descending thus into the ever-recurrent popular prejudice. The 'pure' must also be very strict on their racial frontier, and relegate half-castes into the inferior population. This attitude is also found where racial characteristics carry legal or social advantages, which might be frittered away by any inroad into the racial frontier. This explains the vehemence, even of non-racialists, against any mixed union in South Africa.

In fact, since individual race prejudice never completely disappears, two physically different populations take a very long time to blend; even if the United States were to abolish all segregation and to campaign against it in homes and at work, many centuries would pass before men of 'pure' white skin were to disappear. For a long time unions would not be made at random, and even if they were the Negroes would disappear much faster than the 'pure' whites.

When the racial characteristic does not provoke any systematic choice of partner (as with blond and brown hair) it takes a very long time to disappear (especially if it is caused by different genes, in which case it can never do so), but one can talk of total fusion as soon as coexistence no longer presents any problems.

It is obvious that the concept of division needs clarifying: it is an essentially social phenomenon, since no physical incompatibility between two human species has ever been recorded. The scientifically proven cases of incompatibility between two individuals (as with the Rhesus factor) are rare and are not perceptible by the individuals themselves. Failure to interpenetrate must therefore be due to religious or racial distinctions. And since mixed unions can never be totally avoided, in studying the persistence of division between groups it is important to find out what becomes of the children of such unions.

CULTURAL CHARACTERISTICS: Here too cultural 'half-castes' can appear, and there can also be 'conversions', not only in the religious sense. Men can voluntarily or involuntarily pass from one group into the other.

1. *Language*: There are many known cases of an eventual blend between populations separated for a time by language. It is the case with most present-day nations. Usually one dominant language wins over the others: the one used by the ruling class or the majority, or else the one first set down in writing. If there are several dialects in a territory this does not necessarily imply a case of coexistence, though it can lead to it if two dialects are sufficiently used in literature to create cultural consciousness (Catalan and Castilian in Spain).

The case of Britain is significant: here English slowly eliminated the Celtic languages; in the same way, in the United States, Germans and Italians lost their mother tongue even while remaining in compact groups; in North Africa and Lebanon Berbers, Jews, and Christians all speak Arabic. The pattern is the same everywhere: the language of the ruling group dominates in trade, in public affairs, in the army, in literature, in newspapers. The subjected population, not necessarily a minority, has to learn it to obtain work, and it is then natural to use it in any mixed group of several people. To speak a language during the greater part of the day means that one is inclined to continue at home in the evening, and the dominant language will thus penetrate into mixed, or even homogeneous families that originally used the other. Schooling and playmates complete the process for the children, and indeed can be sufficient in themselves: a minority group of children is, by simple probability, bound to split up, unless segregation is particularly virulent, and so to lose its mother tongue. The dominant language is often considered superior, noble, and this accelerates the process though complete unity can take a long time. We shall return to the violent and sudden reactions that can occur.

Linguistic unity does not necessarily bring about the blending of populations: the Copts in Egypt, the Jews in North Africa, speak Arabic but are still demographically autonomous; the same is true of the Negroes in the United States.

The language that wins in the end can have come under the influence of the others – as with English, permeated during the Middle Ages by the language of the Normans and the French dynasties.

2. *Religion*: Religions are less amenable to integration than languages: for one thing one cannot switch them during the day, so that even if reciprocal friction is not too strong the duality may remain. One can be absorbed after a conquest, though this is practically impossible when the cults are stable and codified. But even without fusion two religions can move closer, not only by mutual tolerance but by accepting practices and customs they had condemned before, and even changing their own views; thanks to the obscurity of ancient texts, such alterations are always possible providing they do not appear to have been imposed from the outside by a human agency.

Sometimes the ruling population persecutes the other until it adopts its religion, and in this case there is invariably some extermination or emigration. The most famous example is the repeal of the Edict of Nantes. Religious persecution may convince some of the weaker people, but it exasperates, and strengthens the faith of, the others.

One can say that unification has been achieved as soon as a spectrum of attitudes is established between the two fervent extremes, with atheists and agnostics in the middle. If this buffer group is sufficiently large there can be a kind of integration without homogeneity, merely because the causes of friction have become very small. The lack of a clear line of division makes a break impossible.

Migrations and differential fertility can lead one group practically to disappear. Thus the town of Ratisbon became Catholic through the immigration of rurals who were more fertile than the Protestant townsfolk.

Mixed marriages cause very difficult conflicts, but usually lead to a decrease of faith in the next generation, which contributes to the buffer group and towards unification. However if tension is sharp, children can be snatched by one cult or the other, making integration impossible. The more united the family at large, as opposed to the couple, the more difficult the compromise, since in a family the cooler members are dominated by the more fervent ones. Besides, mixed marriages are usually less fertile than marriages of a single cult.

When the two populations only differ in their religion, unification can best be produced by other preoccupations. Economic difficulties and class struggles have helped to lessen the rivalry between Catholics and Protestants and form the necessary sandwich group.

The clergy, of course, always fights against compromise: this is the case with the French Canadians. Or again, here is what the Abbé Mévellec has to say about the behaviour of the Bretons in Aquitaine:

> For us missionaries [the words] 'developed', 'assimilated', are derogatory and synonymous of decay of personality, loss of traditions and of the natural virtues of the race. Why? Because the first to submit to the customs of a country, when they are of mediocre value and especially if they have no value at all, are the least liable to strive and to struggle, the least convinced, those with the least personal dignity, the weak and the wavering, the rejects, who constitute the human scum. They take on the faults of the country they come to and lose the qualities of the one they have left. This is a universal phenomenon.[1]

LEGAL DISTINCTIONS: They can take various forms, from slavery to degrees of citizenship. But nowadays they rarely persist from one generation to another unless they are also founded on physical or cultural characteristics. Many present-day populations stem from a mixture of a slave population with a ruling population. Often the first dominated by pressure of numbers, and contributed most of the eventual physical characteristics, while adopting not the whole culture but the idea of their masters' culture. Such groups usually believe that they descend from the masters, though there are exceptions: the Mexicans are proud of their double origin.

COMBINATION OF VARIOUS DIFFERENCES: Integration is far more difficult if more than one characteristic, for instance religion and language together, separate the two groups. This occurred in Canada: without the difference of religion the English language of the rulers would have slowly won over French, and both groups would have thought of themselves as British. But the clergy very cleverly used the language to maintain the religious distinction.

This is even more true when there are racial or nationalistic distinctions on top of the other two, as in Algeria. The racial differences were just obvious enough for it to be possible to tell an Arab from a European; in addition the Moslem religion identifies itself with the state, source of right and justice.

Integration is all the more difficult if one of the populations feels an affinity with a neighbouring state. Austro-Hungary might eventually have formed a stable confederation if the Rumanians, Poles, Serbo-Croates and Italians had not been conscious of their 'brothers' close by. The existence of Arab national-

---

[1] 'Le paysan breton dans le mélange cosmopolite rural de l'Aquitaine', *Études sociales*, March 1953.

ism in the Middle East made first difficult, then impossible any kind of integration between French and Algerians in Algeria.

The clergy is usually against integration, but the situation can be more complex: Canada remained faithful to the British Crown mainly because of the Voltairianism of France. Geneva avoided the obvious attraction towards France, geographical as well as cultural, solely because of the strength of Protestantism.

In a colonial territory physical distinctions often coincide with a very clear social and cultural difference, even without a religious or a linguistic problem. Mixed unions have difficulty in providing an intermediate population because there are so few and the half-castes experience difficulties in achieving social and mental balance. They are rejected by the ruling population, which does not distinguish them clearly from the natives, but they do not want to 'fall back' into an inferior condition; they are in a false position. Hence the widespread prejudice against half-castes, based on an identification of environmental factors with hereditary ones. Their only crime lies in not being sufficiently numerous to impose their law, or at least to make their presence felt.

Historical evolution

Is integration easier than it used to be? Is there a trend towards worse tensions or towards easier reciprocal penetration by the emergence of other sources of worry?

The formation of modern states was largely influenced by the hazards of treaties and royal marriages. These fragile, heterogeneous political units, were then subjected to strong centralising influences because of technological progress, ease of communications, the spread of education, the radio, the growing civil service, etc. Victor Hugo writes:

> Et dans l'informe bloc des multitudes sombres,
> La pensée en rêvant sculpte les nations.

But thought is not enough, and needs to be somewhat helped by the kind of forces that have helped to blend or unite such ethnically different groups as the Scots, the Welsh, and the English. The latter are not totally united, but form a coherent state where the collective spirit is stronger than the causes of internal strain. Similarly, the arbitrary frontiers drawn up in 1815 effectively changed the French of Chimay into Belgians and those of Sarrelouis into Germans. The national spirit is largely a convention, which can be artificially developed.

But fusion can be made more difficult by a regional spirit arising naturally at the wrong moment. In Catalonia or Georgia it was too late to cause a permanent cleavage, for the forces of reciprocal penetration were already stronger than the centrifugal ones. But elsewhere a group consciousness has been brought about, sometimes by accident, by a poet or a political mistake, and has caused ever-growing tension. Today the inroads into national consciousness due to the division of the world into communist and non-communist blocks are further encouraged by economic unity; but our frontiers, at first purely political and personal, and later national and imperialistic, have had time to harden and crystallise into barriers protecting not only powerful interests but sometimes a whole social order. Inner splits are increasingly unlikely.

In the new African states very different groups coexist: the fear of falling into arbitary rule is such that colonial frontiers have been almost everywhere strictly respected, and preferred to ethnical frontiers.

Slow conversions and violent reactions

In the face of a slow conversion that he fears and is conscious of, a human being usually reacts violently. The body, when the alarm is given, develops a fever; the mind, which realises it is being infiltrated, suddenly changes its view. Valéry's *Pythie* feels herself, in a cold sweat, invaded by a new spirit:

> J'ai perdu mon propre mystère
> Une intelligence adultère
> Exerce un corps qu'elle a compris.

And reacts in pained fear. Similarly, a group slowly being conquered and assimilated by a ruling population can react violently; this occurred with Flemish Belgium when it realised it was in danger of slowly but surely losing its culture.

A majority group that believes its racial purity is at stake also reacts violently. The only way of avoiding the mixture of races in the United States was by an extravagant ideology: the whites 'had to' depict the Negro as a sexual maniac, or at least be seen to repress with the utmost rigour his acts of violence, real or imaginary, sometimes his violent looks, in order to create a feeling of repulsion against him. The Negro problem thus assumes an essentially sexual tone. But to explain is not to excuse. The general mixture of races would have been a very lengthy process, and such a distant prospect is not particularly alarming. Chile lives without segregation and is not degenerate.

The Nazi reaction against the demographic, economic and moral dangers threatening Germany after 1918, and against the slow mixture with the Jewish elements, was even more violent. Perhaps the politicians merely used the racial weapon to promote other aims; but many were genuinely overcome by the ancient prejudice against 'bad blood', which is still very widespread and can reappear in favourable circumstances. The increasing number of mixed unions in high circles could only be prevented by frantic and violent propaganda, for otherwise it would have been difficult to deal with marginal cases. But they were only stopped because integration had not progressed quite far enough.

Long-term coexistence, or modus vivendi

When none of the preceding cases occur, a *modus vivendi* inevitably appears, for acute tension cannot be maintained indefinitely. The groups then retain their personality from one generation to another and live in amiable disagreement. This does not always mean that either or both definitely accept the situation: it is an unusual and always precarious state, liable to flare up in appropriate circumstances. It can be most successful where there is a common fear of external forces. It can take several possible shapes.

Ruling population in a minority: This often occurred in the days of slavery, and applies today to the Anglo-Dutch in South Africa. The ruling population maintains itself by force and forbids mixed marriages, which would tend to make segregation more difficult. Coexistence is precarious, because of the risk of revolt.

Ruling population in a majority: This applies to the whites in the United States. This situation can last a long time, since the subjected population is at the mercy of the other, as were the Jews in many countries in the past. The minority is more often distinguished by racial and religious characteristics than by its language. But there can be a stratification by occupation: the minority can acquire the monopoly of some trade or industry and retain it from one generation to another with marriages inside the group. The situation can be interrupted by crises, either revolts of the minority or violence by the majority (pogroms, lynching, etc.).

Equal rights: If two different religious groups are separated, or united, by an intermediate range of tepid believers or atheists, we have said that this is to all intents an integration. It is the case, in present-day France, with the Protestants and Catholics. The Jewish question, however, has at best reached a *modus vivendi*, since here religion is not the only factor of difference: racial characteristics, and peculiarities of names which make identification easy, make for hostility. Tightly-knit groups of Protestants may still survive in France, but the same can be said of Corsicans and yet they are not really an enclosed population. One can only speak of duality and agreement to differ where tension is still apparent.

Whether ruling, dominated or with equal rights, the minority is always in danger of being absorbed, either by conversions or through differential fertility. We have already mentioned how strong an influence the dominant

505

language can have, and pointed out that there are minimum numbers for a population. There is also minimum density. An isolate of four or five hundred can manage to perpetuate itself if it is closely grouped on an island, in a valley, or in a ghetto. But with dispersal, contacts become insufficient. When the average number of annual marriages is no higher than five or six, chance may cause only eight boys and four girls to meet in any given year, which makes marriage very unlikely unless extremely strong cohesive forces prevent one of these boys from preferring one of the forty or fifty girls he has met outside the group. Larger populations can survive for a long time if there is no mishap. Ilse Schwidetzky quotes the example of Saxon groups of Siebernburg, and Germans in the Volga, retaining their characteristics over as long as twenty-five generations.[1] The Samaritans in Palestine are an even more curious instance; and there are many closed populations in the United States.

Though a minority has great difficulties of number, it can benefit from its smallness. Whether obliged to group together or spontaneously isolated by the disappearance of the more dispersed members, it may achieve a solidarity that the majority does not possess, and detach itself from the amorphous mass; though this can often in itself be a cause of tension, as in the case of the Jews in various countries.

Belgium is a classical example of a *modus vivendi*; the Flemish and the Walloons are equal under one king, and have the same laws, but retain their linguistic difference in more or less dormant rivalry. In Switzerland coexistence is the nation's only *raison d'être*. During the Second World War the German-Swiss were even more anti-Nazi than the French-Swiss because they were more exposed to the attraction of Germany. Had they been alone, they would have had great difficulty in avoiding an *anschluss*. Plurality is so essential that the German-Swiss were somewhat concerned by the progressive disappearance of the *romanche* language and made several unsuccessful attempts to revive it. Switzerland presents another curious example of coexistence in the *canton* of Appenzell, which is split into a Catholic nucleus (*Rhodes intérieures*) surrounded by Protestants (*Rhodes extérieures*), who have been living together thus for several centuries. But the strong immigration of Italians, it is feared, may break the traditional religious equilibrium.

Differential fertility can jeopardise a *modus vivendi*: some Dutch Protestants are afraid of the growth of the Catholics, and the situation is similar in Canada. In Belgium the Walloons are trying to improve their fertility and have followed the French example in opening the door to Italian workers.

Franco-Algerian relationships between 1830 and 1962

The vagaries of politics first brought the French and the Algerians together.

[1] *Grundzüge der Völkerbiologie*, Stuttgart, 1950.

Coexistence initially consisted of pure domination, then slowly evolved. It took two different forms in France and in Algeria.

In Algeria the French were in a minority and had to rule to avoid being ruled over or slowly eliminated by violence or loss of rights. Real coexistence could only have been achieved by abolishing or weakening the ethnic frontiers. But the conditions were unfavourable to this, because the cleavage of languages practically coincided with religious and racial differences, and was connected with the social stratification. Integration would have been in sight had an intermediate population existed: for instance an Arab-speaking group detached from the Moslem religion, or a Moslem group speaking only French. With these four populations, plus the Jews with French nationality but retaining their individuality, and if sufficient efforts had been made to ensure social and cultural promotion of the subjected elements, violent clashes would have been less likely. The tensions would have cancelled each other out. Even if the Berbers had been essentially different from the Arabs, in language and cultural or religious characteristics, the resulting triangle would have been more complex and less explosive than duality. *Paradoxically, multiplicity makes for integration.* But the number of mixed unions was in fact very low, and their children were rejected by both groups. Efforts to encourage unity were half-hearted, and always a generation late.

The attempts at achieving cultural unity were also too weak and wrongly directed. Literary and legal studies were developed, but this was a reckless frontal attack of the problem, and it gave the subjected population weapons with which to condemn the rulers. Cultural understanding is a delicate flower, which needs firm roots, preferably in science and technology, based on common experience and observation.

Political necessity led to granting citizenship to all Moslem Algerians. This act of liberalism had little impact in Algeria itself, for most of the Moslems chose to retain the Islamic statutes, but it made migration to France more easy, and put a new face on the situation. Until 1939 the immigrants into France were almost exclusively workers, who came temporarily, to earn wages higher than their requirements and thus assemble a small capital to ensure a living for their family. Although strictly male, this immigration had important effects, not so much through mixed marriages, which usually became French, as by the contacts with a different life, free from the Islamic constraints. But although these workers encountered difficulties in France, in such a different environment, there was never a real problem of coexistence.

The more recent immigration of negroes to France has produced similar problems, even in the absence of legal, linguistic or religious differences. It is difficult to speak of coexistence as long as very few women immigrate; but there can be racial tension, as in Britain.

Political parties

We have said that the coexistence of social groups is a different sort of problem. Political parties do not usually form 'populations' because they are linked by very large numbers of indifferent or tepid thinkers; in any one family there can be people of various political tendencies. There are however some marginal cases: Communism is so concerned with unity and afraid of cleavage that it tends to maintain a gulf between the party and other people. But this trait is not sufficiently well transmitted for it to qualify as a real case of coexistence.

21

QUALITY[1]

Demography is everywhere and nowhere. It has no natural frontiers and it can grow or be reduced by conventions. Theoretical demography, limited to the observation of three narrowly defined characteristics, age, sex, and matrimony, is only a branch of mathematics (self-perpetuating sets); and applied demography is a statistical technique.

Any human statistics consist in bracketing unequal unities. Censuses attempt to lessen this arithmetical heresy by taking into account age, sex, and matrimony, but the groups thus isolated are still not homogeneous. Why are any further subdivisions labelled qualitative? Merely because they resist precise measurement. Thus, the age factor, quantitative in a population with efficient data collecting on births, becomes qualitative in a tribe which has no registers.

Physical and mental characteristics are called qualitative because the definition of factors such as intelligence is not rigorous, or because observations are only partial, as with blood groups. The fragmentary, often suspect, data that result, cannot be of use to quantitative demography as such. Further distinctions will appear when it is remembered that one can influence these characteristics. Sex and age cannot be changed by man; matrimony has sociological implications, but is mainly a legal concept. But the others, if this is deemed desirable, can be changed by appropriate action, the science of which is called eugenics.

Eugenics[2]

This has been in men's minds since before Plato, and has been given various names (such as Quillet's *Callipédie*). Most Utopians considered it in some form. But, apart from elementary hygienic precautions, eugenics had even fewer chances than medicine of getting anywhere before the age of science and systematic observation. Once the general desire for progress appeared, it is not surprising that man thought of applying it to himself, or at any rate to his body.

[1] Only a few aspects of qualitative demography are dealt with here. Because of its great importance, there was no room for the problem of consanguineous unions. Useful studies of this are to be found in *Population*, particularly by J. Sutter, F. Tabah and J.–M. Goux.

[2] See J. Sutter, *L'eugénique*, Paris, 1950; also V. Audit and M. Tisserand-Perrier, *L'eugénique et l'euthénique*.

Such was the intention of Galton, who coined the word eugenics (long after the name Eugénie), but people had already worked a great deal towards improving animal species. With the move away from the family ideal, the idea of crossing and selecting men rationally, already stressed by Campanella, gained impetus.[1] Apart from some Nazi experiments (see W. Darré) the movement was not followed, and even Galton's ideas have had less impact than his contemporaries may have believed. The fear of releasing uncontrollable forces, or of violating the sanctity of private lives has exercised a semi-conscious restraint.[2]

Acceptable or not, plans to improve the human race have opened the way to qualitative demography.

Number and quality

In various countries, and especially France, the supporters of high birth rates have often come up against qualitative slogans such as: 'Fewer children but better shaped, fewer miserably brought up degenerates'. We saw in chapter 11 that the contrast between quality and quantity has its limits: France did not in any way improve its offspring during the four generations when it reduced their numbers drastically.

When a country has passed certain sanitary and economic standards, a cut in the birth rate has no influence on weight, height, or achievements in sport or intelligence. It even leads to a certain inverse selection, since mentally deficient families go on proliferating. Character also suffers past a certain critical threshold: we have already described the 'family optimum'.

Transmission of intelligence

There are two obstacles to the scientific study of hereditary intelligence: the difficulty of experiments, and the range of the conclusions drawn from them. The latter can serve political or social theories on the lookout for scientific justification, and it is thus particularly difficult to preserve independence of judgment in the matter.

Here is Galton's theory, as amended later by various authors: 'Intelligent' people have on the average fewer children than 'unintelligent' ones. Since intelligence is partly hereditary, the intelligence of a population must diminish

[1] See Binet-Sangle, *Le haras humain*, and Vacher de Lapouge, *Les sélections sociales*, 1884. Here is a quotation from the latter: In certain conditions, a very small number of absolutely perfect males would be able to fertilise all the women deserving to propagate the race . . . One healthy producer could ensure 200,000 births annually . . . zootechnical and scientific reproduction would thus have replaced bestial and spontaneous methods. This key to the future is lying in a closed-off field. Who will dare to pick it up and use it?'

[2] Though the ideas were developed recently by M. Rondot, in *Trois erreurs de notre temps*, Vichy, 1964.

over the centuries, as the carriers of intelligence genes move upwards in society, reach the upper classes, and become sterile. The progressive decay of humanity which would follow can only be avoided by an organised breeding with specially intelligent stock, or by social stability achieved by a system of castes which would prevent selection by intelligence.

As an alternative to stability one might also suggest promotion by chance or 'even better' by an inverse selection. But here, what society would gain in the possession, it would lose in the application, for intelligence and power would be kept carefully separate.

One sees how mistaken the human mind can be. The Nazis actually had recourse to selected genitors (for slightly different reasons), such is the strength and attractiveness of this kind of prejudice. We must examine this falsehood point by point.

Differential fertility: The prevention of births, we have seen, develops, in various countries, with social status. Various criteria of social rank have shown it: income, cultural level, place of residence, occupation, and it is obvious in populations now beginning to apply birth control. But this does not prove that it has always been so or that it always will be so. Birth control is only a few generations old. The levelling-out of fertility rates now occurring in the developed countries suggests that it may only be a transitory phase. Indeed in some cases fertility is higher in the upper classes.

Intelligence and social level: Are these two related? For the parents' generation, cultural level is, we have seen, one of the main conditions of high status; but it cannot be equated with intelligence.

It is not so for their children. Measuring intelligence by tests whose results, taking age into account, give the 'intelligence quotient', various experiments on children show quite conclusively a correlation with social level. Here are the figures given by a survey in France in 1944 on 95,237 pupils of primary schools[5] (points obtained, tabled against father's occupation).

				Ages			
Occupation	$6-6\frac{1}{2}$	7	8	9	10	11	12
Farmers	42·1	55·3	74·8	91·3	107·3	120·6	128·6
Workers	47·7	61·3	81·2	98·7	112·2	125·3	131·1
White-collar workers	54·1	70·6	87·6	106·4	121·2	132·9	140·6
Tradesmen and managers	62·3	75·9	97·4	115·0	128·6	139·6	144·0
Professions	72·1	89·1	111·3	128·6	141·4	146·2	152·7

[5] *Le niveau intellectuel des enfants d'âge scolaire*, Paris, 1950–54. Another, wider survey was begun in 1965.

The difference is appreciable at all ages: children aged nine in professional families are at the same level as children aged twelve in farmers' families. This is confirmed by surveys in other countries.

Heredity and environment: The actual interpretation of these figures is much more controversial as it involves the respective parts played by heredity and environment. The first experiments, between the two World Wars, concluded hastily that the so-called superior classes and races were intrinsically superior. Later the influence of the environment was stressed. The child of a lawyer or a teacher is more forward than that of an agricultural worker, we have seen, because he hears conversations that spur him to development, or is intellectually encouraged, and often better fed and housed.

There are various ways of observing the respective influence of the two factors: for instance, the case of 'real' twins led by chance to grow up in different surroundings.

The controversy is settling nowadays, in that neither influence is denied. Recent research suggests, according to J. Sutter,[1] that hereditary factors have the edge. Galton's fears could therefore have some foundation, providing the higher categories had fewer children than the others. But we have seen that this is not so in a developed population. Besides, what we call intelligence, without strictly defining it, probably depends on a great number of genes. As a result, even if degradation by inverse selection were to occur, it would probably be much slower than pessimists like Cattell thought (he envisaged a relapse into stupidity in three centuries). So that if differential fertility is only a transitory feature, the danger disappears.

Besides, the probability reckoning is more complex than it seems, and factors such as age of the mother (which varies inversely with the degree of intelligence) can act in the other direction: and the simultaneous lowering of child mortality and of the birth rate leads to a noticeable drop in the average age of the mother.

The matter is still important and undecided and calls for more research.

Racial differences

The Nazis did permanent injury to science by introducing despicable foreign considerations into an already difficult question. Not only has ethnology as a whole been highly suspect in Germany since the war, but the fear of being called a racialist has paralysed judgment elsewhere, and the word 'race' is avoided even where it is perfectly justified. We are widely informed on physical characteristics, but observations have still not been orderly and methodical enough. The chance of using military recruitment as a testing point is unfortunately disregarded. Rigorous sampling is not widespread, and many obser-

[1] In *L'Eugénique*, p. 197

vations are partial, and liable to be misleading. Given proper methods however, it may soon be possible to draw up the complete distribution of a given characteristic (mean number and dispersal around the mean) in a given group.

The distinctions between certain physical characteristics are so sharp that the zones of dispersal do not override at any point. The whitest of a tribe of Negroes is probably much darker than the darkest Norwegian. But this is not true of mental characteristics if one takes a large enough group. We do not know whether the whites are more intelligent than the Negroes but we are certain that the most intelligent Negro is far more intelligent than the least intelligent white, and this fact is sufficient to invalidate any kind of segregation for the purposes of rational selection. But there is much confusion in this field because of the more pervasive influence of environment. Many characteristics commonly attributed to race are no more hereditary than language or religion. But experiments on a group conveniently defined by a physical characteristic are difficult, for its very existence may eliminate the environment factor completely. A negro child brought up in a white family may acquire complexes that a white child brought up in the same family would not, because the latter is at home. Racial prejudice itself suffices to create differences that will later be wrongly attributed to heredity.

The question of probability remains. Even if a fault in a given population is wholly attributable to environment (for instance a tendency to steal) it is logical to suspect an individual in this population, because he has a higher chance of possessing the characteristic.

Prejudice against half-castes is, we have seen, without foundation. The faults attributed to them are all due to environment. What little genetics do tell us even suggests that cross-breeding is favourable to heredity. The best way to avoid racial quarrels in a country is thus, genetically as well as socially, to encourage mixed marriages: they may not integrate the population but will at least produce a large buffer group.

Genetic incompatibilities

These can cause either sterility between two partners, or various malformations, sometimes lethal, in their descendants. Other partnerships, on the other hand, favour their descendants. This might lead one to want to harmonise couples systematically, but it is not to be recommended, for it would be, to say the least, premature. Even the strictest incompatibility we know, that of the Rhesus blood factor, is very rare. It may be that more conclusive cases of incompatibility will be discovered, which could lead to a more extensive application of the pre-marriage certificate demanded in France. But it would seem that such incompatibilities would occur far less frequently than hereditary or transmissive illness, or malformation of one of the prospective parents. This brings us back to the problem of compulsory sterilisation, already discussed above.

Euthanasia

This does not exactly involve quality, but it must be mentioned here because it illustrates how apparently humane policies can turn against humanity. In individual cases it is hard to condemn people who claim to have put someone out of his pain. No reader of Martin du Gard's *Les Thibault* can censure Antoine, the doctor who ends his father's agony. Yet the slightest move towards official or legal approval could encourage society in a very dangerous direction.

We should distinguish, as with Malthusianism, between altruistic and egoistic euthanasia. Suffering is such a painful sight that often egoism can be disguised as unselfishness. Euthanasia is inextricably involved with social hypocrisy. With so many impatient heirs waiting for deaths (shall we ever know exactly how many deaths are provoked or accelerated because of this in the country?) euthanasia is only too widely practised already, by individuals. Society is not blameless either: the old are rarely 'finished off', but they are often given far less care than they deserve. The reasons are basically material, but are disguised as humanitarianism ('It will be a relief for him') or as convenient doubt ('If I was sure of saving him I would try, but why prolong his misery?').

Social hypocrisy is in a sense necessary here. Society cannot recognise as legitimate actions for which individuals may take full responsibility.

Heredity of acquired characteristics

This famous controversy is dominated, as many other burning questions, by prejudice and passion. If all the efforts of oratory deployed on either side of the Iron Curtain over the Lysenko affair had been expended on observations and comparisons we would be nearer, perhaps not to the elusive truth, but to a plausible explanation accepted by both groups.

Popular prejudice is strongly in favour of this idea. The myth of the degeneration of a race because of its environment always finds supporters in any circumstances. The laws of Mendel and Morgan have weakened the age-old prejudice, but science only consists of provisional truths, convenient explanations. No one can announce scientifically that something judged to be impossible today will always be so. There was therefore no reason for so much passion over Lysenko's theories, except that a general conception of society was at stake.

The Soviet régime, strives after emancipation of a certain type, and objects to any logic tending to justify the existence of classes. For reasons we shall consider later, it does not favour eugenics in the literal sense though in attempting to change the environment it is willing to ignore the impressions of the moment. But by reaction Mendelian biologists have gone too far in the opposite direction, without valid grounds. Experience should be the only consideration.

Research is intense in this field and there are continuous discoveries, but it seems that for the time being at least there is no way of applying them.

General

A distinction should be made between eugenics and euthenics, both of which study and aim at the improvement of Man, the first by genetics, the second by environmental change, including private and social hygiene, dietetics, studies of working conditions, and housing, etc. The second meets with little opposition of principle, but this is not true of eugenics.

The people and groups who strongly object to sterilisation, artificial insemination, compulsory marriage partners, are often those who oppose contraception. The opposite party is usually against the mixture of races. In other words, the attitude that gives rise to these distinctions is the same that divides the purists and the liberals. Some go even further, tend towards anarchism, and oppose compulsory vaccination, the declaration of contagious illness, pre-marriage certificates, etc. At the other extreme is the Nazi belief, which aims at a hierarchy similar to Huxley's *Brave New World*, topped by the supremely pure Aryans. No one refuses the possibility of creating, by selection, a human race with certain physical characteristics deemed superior, such as height, weight, speed, etc. But there are reservations to be made on the health of such a species: pure animal breeds are often more delicate. And above all, more important than physical or even intellectual qualities, there are considerations of personality. Humanity would hardly derive much benefit from physical or intellectual selection if it brought with it a moral decay.

It has even been suggested that the sperm of great men could be collected and preserved, to be administered later by artificial insemination. Such suggestions provoke curiosity rather than real passion. For the time being eugenics is not a real enough possibility to cause proper debate. A society can do without it in any form (even pre-marriage certificates) and not incur any appreciable damage, providing there is some awareness of hygiene. The family unit has resisted such trends of thought, as we have seen. But notable changes could occur one day given certain biological discoveries. Man can endure the worst trials as long as he knows of no way of avoiding them. But as soon as solutions appear he is very reluctant to listen to those who argue that he should not use them.

515

22

WAR AND POPULATION

The relationship between war and population is far from clear. Eminent sociologists have showed how complex it is, and there is still room for surprise. To consider the problem in its entirety would demand a whole book: we shall merely correct certain oversimplifications, attack an all too prevalent unilateral thesis, and suggest certain corrections.

The 'demographic relaxation' theory

The theory that overpopulation causes war is attractive at first sight:[1] when men lack room they are held to feel the need to spread out and take the land and wealth of others. Even if they do not succeed, the losses incurred would reduce the population, bringing everything back to 'normal', and a new cycle would begin. There are variants and additions to this theory: some suggest that youth needs to fight to use up its energy; others that the old men send the young to their death, with the sublime sadistic indifference of Corneille's elder Horace. War, it is said, thus has a real social function, that of 'demographic relaxation'. This makes it in a sense inevitable, like other 'necessary evils' in the life cycle. The specific remedy would be depopulation.

Other works on war do not mention population at all, an obvious failing.

Various types of wars and of problems

Some of the problems will appear if we first classify wars as follows, according to their relationship with overpopulation: 1. Premeditated war to improve standards of living (and other objectives) by conquering territories or markets, invoking the demographic argument of *Lebensraum*. This is typified by Hitler's war, for which overpopulation was the excuse rather than the cause. 2. Premeditated war to ensure the subsistence of the population. Here 'living space' is a real cause. 3. Unpremeditated war for survival. Pressing needs lead to an exodus without any fixed aim, and war inevitably follows, without explicit intention. 4. Spontaneous war, not with demographic or even economic aims, but as a fatal result of demographic pressure unbeknown to the populations or their leaders.

[1] See especially Devaldès, *Croître et multiplier, c'est la guerre*, Paris, 1933, and the works of G. Bouthoul. Both these authors are unfortunately marred in their judgment by passionate Malthusian prejudice, and this is fatal in such a delicate matter.

There may of course be separate categories of wars not linked with population. But would not the very existence of its effects justify us in saying that war has fulfilled a function? With the authority of Bergson ('A constant effect can be considered as a function'), Claude Bernard and, more loosely, Durkheim, Bouthoul writes: 'We may proceed like the biologist who invokes Nature's intentions every time he attributes a function to an organ; what he means is merely that the organ is adequate for this function'.[1] Yet if it were so, every social phenomenon, good or bad, would have a function, and the reasoning could then apply to death in any shape. It may be plausible to say that death fulfils a social function, but this does not get us very far.

An historical approach would consist in classifying all the wars we know enough about according to the links they may have had with overpopulation. This would be an immense task, full of traps, but it would no doubt reveal how varied the situations are.

Effects of wars on population

Before approaching the delicate subject of intentions, motives and degrees of awareness, we must first simply define the effects of war. We may only consider it quantitatively here: qualitative effects are complex and very controversial.

Is 'demographic relaxation' a fact? P. Vincent has doubts, and remarks that until recently wars were not very lethal.[2] Very often more goods (crops, buildings, tools, etc.) were destroyed than men, in which case war would have increased rather than decreased overpopulation. Obviously, it is dangerous to generalise without studying various periods and various degrees of civilisation.

These reasons do not seem sufficient to destroy the relaxation theory – but they show that proportions and rhythm and the respective speeds of economic and demographic renewal after a war must be taken into account.

First, leaving aside for the time being the weapons of the future, which obviously present immense dangers, it is easy to observe that men can more easily destroy each other than nature or accumulated capital wealth. It is not sufficient to reckon military losses alone. The destruction caused by an army on the march and the epidemics it brought reduced the population much more than the fighting itself. Even when wealth was destroyed but lives were spared, this inevitably caused famines. The question is whether output per inhabitant then grew faster than the population. It seems that it usually did. Cereals grow in a year, but man only becomes 'productive' after several years. Without of course supporting the legend that battlefields were 'fertilised by blood', we may note that not until 1914–18 did wars begin to render them useless to

---

[1] 'Guerres et population', *Revue de Défense Nationale*, October 1946.

[2] 'Guerre et population', *Population*, January–March 1947. The average mortality rates by armed action over quite lengthy periods, studied by various authors, turn out to be lower than the natural surplus of births in a population not practising birth control.

agriculture. Besides, how, in a systematically overpopulated or fully populated land, could the population have regained its former numbers without some economic improvement?

Consider, as a very simple model, a population with practically static technology, which was the general case until very recently. Assume that a third of the wealth and a third of the population are destroyed by war. The population was formerly higher than the economic optimum, and so the two thirds surviving are able to use 50 per cent more land than they did before. Even if the tools of production have been destroyed, and this never happens completely, they can choose the best lands, or increase their pasturelands.

The younger men are usually the ones killed in wars, and the birth rate therefore drops. Until recently losses through fighting were small and probably had very little influence, but the number of deaths through illness was high, and many soldiers did not return to their native country. In certain cases, if the adult population had been particularly taxed, immigration was necessary: here relaxation was obviously a fact. Condé's famous remark: 'One night in Paris will make up for all that' (wrongly attributed to Napoleon) was very optimistic.

But just because war was one of the 'necessary evils' that restored the natural equilibrium, it does not follow that it had a function, for other evils, especially food shortages, were more 'efficient'. We saw in Part I that when two species are competing, the victims save the predators from famine; the question of which fate was more desirable for the victim was not answered, and the choice is not of course a real one, but it would seem that man would prefer to fall a victim to nature than to be murdered.

The above model only applies of course to demographically primitive populations, where fertility is very close to the natural level. It is a very different matter with developed populations, where not only does technological progress reduce the surplus numbers (by increasing the optimum population as we defined it), but it is itself influenced by war. Warmongering has good and bad effects (we owe motor cars and aeroplanes to it), but it is in any case more costly than the material destruction of warfare, for the latter leaves the way open to renovation whereas the armament budget competes directly with investment, on which any modernisation depends.

Domination and democracy

The fact that war causes depopulation does not prove that men fight (or prepare for war) with this aim in mind, or that overpopulation leads them inevitably to seek abroad the resources lacking at home. To understand the causes of a war, we must first know who could profit by it and who could have some hand in provoking it. We are thus led to consider the influence of the political régime.

A totally dominant ruling class, we have seen, tries to increase the number of its subjects to give itself greater power. In fact very few sovereigns or aristocracies had any idea of an optimum number. From Bodin to La Morandière, they all advised indefinite proliferation, thus creating a taboo that is still with us. It is therefore difficult to see how a ruling class can have intended a war to reduce an overpopulation, when not only was it not conscious of the fact, but it believed the opposite to be desirable. The concept of overpopulation spread as the phenomenon itself diminished, and this is no coincidence or paradox. Vertical societies have no fear of overpopulation.

Besides, all those feudal or royal wars did not lead to the conquest of empty territories, but to the subjection of the losers. Provinces and towns were annexed with their inhabitants. The latter were never expelled, since they could go on tilling their land but contribute the profits to the conquerors.

The conquest of America led to near-systematic extermination; but here again, the war was provoked not by overpopulation but by the resistance of the Indians to slavery. Had they accepted it, they would never have been parked away in reservations to die off. They would have suffered the fate of the Negroes, who had to be imported. No doubt the pioneers on the frontier often fought with a tribe for its territory, but this is no longer a war of the feudal type.

In a democracy it may well occur that free citizens, conscious of being too numerous, wish to occupy territories emptied of their inhabitants, in order to give themselves optimum space, labelled 'vital space' for this purpose. The wars from 1815 to 1945 could thus be held to be rather closer to the concept outlined above. Conquering a market or natural resources does not remedy overpopulation, but it is equivalent to annexing a new territory. *But these wars have occurred precisely since the disappearance of absolute overpopulation.* Fascist governments represent from this point of view only a more aggressive form of democratic imperialism. The 'party' does not rule as a class, which wants its subjects to multiply, but as a relative ruler, who can only remain in power by ensuring that his subjects have acceptable living standards and sufficient cause for pride.

Yet even here the desire to conquer not only land but people has never quite disappeared. When Mangin and the extreme right in France campaigned for the 'return' of the left bank of the Rhine they were not asking for empty land, but for an increase in the national power. They contrived to believe that the Rhenans had pleasant memories of Napoleon's occupation and could be 'assimilated', or at least subjected to the French. The Germans would probably have taken a different view and expelled a large part of the population of Champagne and Lorraine if they had won either of the two World Wars. This would have been the result of French underpopulation rather than of German overpopulation. Demographic depression can also be a cause of war.

Italy, after its victory in 1940, no doubt wished to expel the inhabitants of

Savoy, Corsica, and Nice and redistribute land and employment. But how many people, of whatever nationality, would be prepared to risk their lives or those of their children in such a dangerous enterprise, merely for the sake of higher living standards? Obviously strong mystical reasons, seductive appeals to die for one's fatherland, are needed to prepare a nation for war.

Strangely enough, the only example of the total evacuation of a territory resulted from the Potsdam agreements of 1945, though the Czechs, Poles, and Soviets are precisely the nations whose ideology refuses to accept the very concept of optimum population and overpopulation.

A survey of all the wars since Charlemagne, or even further back, would thus include very few waged in order to check overpopulation. But can it have been an unconscious cause? Again, only by studying a whole range of examples can one realise how few confirm such a naive generalisation. The polemicist Bouthoul, in spite of his strong malthusian views, admits that overpopulated China lived in peace for a long time, whereas the sparse Red Indian tribes were always at war. But there is a difference between demographic density and demographic pressure. The Indians might, because of their primitive technology, lack resources in spite of their small numbers.

Consider again the feudal system at the beginning of the modern age. After an exhausting war some respite was obviously necessary, in order to repair material rather than human losses. The king had emptied his chests, and his subjects had to be given time to fill them up again. A return of the crops to their former level was not enough; the prospect of another war demanded a whole system of taxation and saving. It may be that rulers were conscious of the parallel need to build up the population again, but this is no proof of cause. A more convincing demonstration would be provided if it were shown that sparsely distributed peoples did not fight. But this could only occur in an extremely retarded state of technology. Men have fought and invaded one another ever since prehistoric times.

Putting resources to the best use

We have said that the optimum for power is always higher than the economic optimum. It is only reasonable to expect the attitude of a population to vary with its numbers. If they are equal to the economic optimum, the best policy lies in the improvement of its living standards. If they equal the power optimum warlike expansion may be the course chosen: this is the critical point – relative overpopulation is more dangerous than acute overpopulation.

Consider the three fascist powers that started the Second World War: Germany, Italy, and Japan attacked Poland, Ethiopia, and China. Germany was less populated than Poland, or, more precisely, demographic pressure was smaller there. Polish miners came to work in the Ruhr, and not the reverse. Neither was Italy more overpopulated than Ethiopia: its birth rate was lower.

It probably hoped to find there badly exploited natural resources, that it could use to help reduce its own unemployment; but such an expedition must be financed out of the national income, with money that could be used to feed and employ more people at home. *Overpopulation thus had to be moderate for war to be possible.* The case of Japan is even more significant: this was both the most progressive and the least prolific country in Asia. It was the one suffering least from overpopulation, since its development enabled it to use part of its income for unproductive ends.

Now consider India and Pakistan. When their separation in 1947 more or less hardened the religious cleavage, some authorities held that war was imminent. Indeed, there have been occasional bouts of fighting with limited means, and it is no doubt regrettable that both countries still spend too much on armament, but neither has enough surplus strength and vitality to be tempted by the adventure of war; the Kashmir conflict consisted, even in 1965, mainly in skirmishes in the committee rooms and corridors of the United Nations.

Intense overpopulation is thus less dangerous than relative overpopulation. A totalitarian power often gives the army high priority and presses its subjects towards military strength while attenuating overpopulation by high mortality amongst the weak. But, with or without homicidal intentions, this meets with varying degrees of success.

Every country, as it develops, is liable to go through a critical phase where the conquest of territories or markets becomes tempting, precisely when it has passed through the period of acute overpopulation and absolute rule.

Demographic depression

Storms are not caused by high atmospheric pressure as such but by differences in pressure between two neighbouring zones. Similarly, wars are not due to the unrest of compressed populations, but to differences of pressure.

The Roman conquests can probably be ascribed, to some extent, to overpopulation in a particularly ordered community; but the barbarian invasions were certainly the result of a depression. Though density was lower in the forests of Germany, there was room for more men in the empire. Whatever the political and social decadence of Rome, it would have been easy to ward off the invading tribes had pressure been as strong there as in Germany, and density therefore much higher.

With the native populations of America and Africa, insufficient density rather than depression caused the invasion. France too has suffered from demographic depression: its enemies found both their confidence and the necessary moral excuse in the apparent social justice of taking from a decadent people an area it could not cover itself. Such a motive would appeal even to the most austere legality and morality if there were too flagrant a disproportion; and since there is no criterion defining the moment at which the right of invasion begins, this excuse is a firm favourite. Italian fascism used it to feed its propaganda and pseudo-scientific theories.

The half deserted continent of Australia may well come to tempt the populations of the Far East, particularly when they begin to organise their own land better and be more at ease in it. The Australians have sensed the danger and are resigned to accepting immigrants.

Generations and classes responsible

The aristocratic or patrician class is most often blamed for wars; but we have seen that they have no strong desire to avoid overpopulation. The subjected class is neither aware of its state nor able to improve it. The destitute proletarian is no more disposed to conquest than to the prevention of births. It is the small-time owners who are most inconvenienced by the lack of elbow room; and from the political point of view the relative rulers are the ones who may press for expansion, to satisfy their own requirements or those of the subjects without modifying their own lives. Thus it tends to be the middle classes in a broad sense who are responsible for invoking overpopulation and its relief. It is they who constituted the framework of the fascist régimes. The unemployed labourers are not as turbulent as Bouthoul suggests. They are often undernourished and usually demoralised and are of less service to revolutions and *coups* than ardent or ambitious intellectuals.

The responsibility of generations is more difficult to establish. Generalisations about bubbling and exuberant youth were disproved by the last war, which broke out precisely at a time when the five hollow generations of the years 1915–19 had reached military age (20–24). History, as usual obliging, can always provide, out of its varied armoury, some example to satisfy those who consult its oracle.

Conclusion

This rapid summary, which would need completing by a consideration of the many non-demographic and even non-economic causes of war, points especially to the complexity of the question and the dangers of overstressing what may turn out to be secondary factors. This is a timely conclusion, in that the conflicts that have arisen since the last world war (Korea, Vietnam), and the threat of a third World War are not justified by demographic considerations. The United States is no more overpopulated or in danger of overpopulation than the USSR, though the attitude of China may be based on the certainty of surviving even the most devastating conflict. Indonesia is arming against Malaysia but only for political reasons and not because of the overpopulation of Java (it is itself unable to populate Sumatra). The Israeli question is slightly different: overpopulated Egypt would no doubt be pleased to acquire a new territory. But Egypt does not dream of attacking Lebanon or Jordan for the same reason: the racial factor is obviously the more important here.

Amongst the bones of discontent of the present day, the desire to reduce real or supposed overpopulation takes second place to ideological and political tensions.

23

THE MARXIST POINT OF VIEW:
THE SOVIETS AND THE CHINESE

We have already mentioned Marxist attitudes on population at various points, and this is a general survey.

The Marxist doctrine

To understand the attitude of orthodox Communists and especially of the USSR one needs to consider the historical origins and the subsequent development of Marxism. Malthus had asserted that the misery of the people stemmed from its numbers, and Marx, like all the socialists of his period, reacted violently against this class selfishness that reversed the real responsibility: he considered apparent overpopulation merely as a consequence of private property. In a socialist régime there could be no population problem, and especially no overpopulation. Later the Marxists stuck to this point of view, which was more a criticism than a real theory, but did not lend much importance to the problems of population.

At the end of the century, however, both social democrats and anarchists came out in favour of birth control. In opposition to their régimes, they campaigned for a fertility strike, to avoid creating cannon and machine fodder. But the Communists, especially Rosa Luxembourg and Klara Zetkin, took the opposite stand, on the grounds that for the working classes numbers are an essential factor in the struggle for liberty. Devaldès[1] suggests two reasons for their attitude: a belief in the providential generosity of Nature, and the need to maintain misery in order to foment the revolution. This is rather too summary an explanation: an orthodox Marxist, at that time, would consider the prevention of births as a capitulation to Communism, a reformist gesture. For him both overpopulation and the low birth rates were consequences of bourgeois property.

This divergence appeared clearly on the international scene after the Second World War.

Official statements at the United Nations

During the first session of the Population Commission at Lake Success, Mr

[1] *Croître et multiplier, c'est la guerre*, Paris, 1933.

Rabichko, the delegate of the Republic of Ukraine, said: 'I would consider as barbarous any suggestion, in this commission, of encouraging the limitation of marriages or the limitation of births in marriage. An adequate social system should be able to cope with any increase in population. Unemployment due to overpopulatian is a result of capitalist property. The economy should be adapted to the population and not the reverse.' This attitude was confirmed at various times both in the Economic and Social Council and at the Technological Council.[1] Many official Soviet speeches and books have stressed the rational organisation of their territory, and particularly the colonisation of frozen or torrid wastes.

The already developed and populated Communist countries such as Hungary shared this orthodox view at first. Communist China also upheld it for several years.

The Communist attitude on migration at the United Nations has been just as firm: capitalism is attempting to remedy the evils it has brought on to itself, and emigration, like malthusianism, is reprehensible. If everyone was given work and acceptable standards of living no worker would have to leave his home country.

Interpretation

Here are the two reasons suggested by Devaldès: 1. The Soviet Union, where Communist doctrine was being shaped and hardened, has enormous wealth. Its confidence in nature and science is strengthened by its reaction against bourgeois pessimism. 2. This same reaction, together with the disapproval of all compromise, leads the USSR to reject any policy liable to save capitalism. Attention nowadays is focused far less on the working classes than on the underdeveloped countries: here, an efficient attempt to restrict births would attenuate the demographic pressure on capitalism. The Soviet policy was quite logical as long as population growth did not loom too large in the Soviet Union or the popular republics.

Some years ago, this official attitude already seemed extremely precarious. Though Marx and his disciples had been noncommittal on the question, their views were still officially subscribed to. But if you talk of population policy with a Western Communist who is not informed of the party view on this point, he may well take a more Malthusian line. In fact the Soviets are rather poorly informed on the matter, because they do not consider it important.

---

[1] In 1949 in Geneva a demographic dictionary was envisaged, and a list of words to define and translate was drawn up. Some members of the commission thought that as well as pure demographic terms such as 'birth rate', 'expectation of life', etc., there should be doctrinal terms, such as Malthusianism, birth control, etc., but the Soviet delegate Riabouchkin objected to these two words, on the grounds that 'such mistaken concepts should not find a place in an official dictionary'.

The same applies to their views on migrations, and there is an additional reason here: the Soviet Union has always been extremely strict in claiming all its citizens and accepting no foreigners. For a long time Soviets were even forbidden to marry foreigners. This is still a political rather than an economic question for them.

In the book by Boiarsky and Shushurin already mentioned, *La statistique démographique*,[1] there are many correct views on the demographic development of capitalist countries and especially on the dropping birth rates. The opinions expressed are often similar to western ones, though with important omissions. But some sections reveal insufficient knowledge and a very simplified view of social relationships. Demographic measurement techniques are obviously still imperfect, and the experts, like the UN spokesmen, are silent on many important points or rest on surprising falsehoods.[2]

Policy

The policy in the early days of the régime was that of the socio-anarchical left: abortion and contraception were allowed, divorce was easy, the sexes were totally equal, women should work, etc.; all these policies were liable to reduce the birth rate, in fact if not in intention, which is what happened.

There was a reversal of policy in 1936: abortion and contraception were forbidden. Another step was taken in 1944: free unions were no longer recognised, divorce became much more difficult and substantial family allowances were introduced. A whole set of medals and rewards was instituted for mothers of large families (up to twelve children). Paternity summonses were forbidden lest they point to a married father and cause a family to break up.

Later, however, family allowances were cut; the law was changed to state that wages would be sufficient to live off, and children would no longer require

[1] A handbook for higher education, published by the Moscow Institute of Economics and Statistics (1951).

[2] Here are two examples. In *News* (December 1951) Boiársky states that mortality has risen in the poorer classes of the capitalist countries. To prove this in the case of Britain, he compares a maximum with a minimum. Mortality in Britain has varied as follows:

1925	12·2	1936	12·1
1926	11·6	1937	12·4
1927	12·3	1938	11·6

Boiársky chooses the figures for 1926 and 1937 to suit his conclusion, forgetting to point out that the general mortality rates are increased by the ageing of population. In fact in 1925–7 and 1936–8 general mortality was stable but in the meantime the expectation of life had increased by approximately three years. It would be surprising if a valid demographic theory could be built on such shaky foundations.

In 1965 at the World Congress on Population in Belgrade, P. M. Rabinovich declared that the economic crises of capitalism caused marked rises in mortality. But the figures he quotes, and interprets wrongly, relate to the nineteenth century, which clearly illustrates how out of date their science is.

so much help. At the same time, official abortion was reintroduced. Since 1955, policy has been liberalised but strongly favouring individualism; and large families have a very low standard of living. On many points traditional morality has been restored and reinforced. There are rigorous standards of modesty, and virtue is honoured. Sexual freedom is considered a form of bourgeois decadence.

As we have seen, external migrations are forbidden. But large scale movements are organised within the Soviet territory, especially towards Asia, though they are partly cancelled out by individuals returning West.

In the republics of eastern Europe, the scale of demographic investments needed, and the unsufficient scale of production, have led to the organisation of contraception and abortion, and there has been a sharp drop in the birth rate.

The opponents of the régime ascribe the revival of populationism between 1936 and 1944 to disastrous failure of the classical anti-family policies of the extreme left, and a return to a reinforced version of traditional morality. The supporters of the régime answer that it was all intended: in 1920 it was necessary to have recourse to abortion to destroy the bourgeois family, but the family was restored as soon as social and economic conditions allowed. The second version is, probably largely true. The law of 1920 allowing abortion said: '. . . since the remnants of the past and the difficult economic circumstances force many women to it'.

And yet when Lenin inaugurated Communism he, like many contemporaries, was optimistic over economic prospects. Only later did he change his attitude, with the famous remark: 'Communism is the Soviets . . . plus electrification'. His optimism, natural and necessary in any revolution, and his distaste for the indissolubility of marriage, hardly prompted him to consolidate or honour the family. No democrat or socialist, he said around 1920, can fail to demand freedom of divorce. But experience revealed the high costs and the poor results of collective child rearing. And the desire to achieve power and create a great country rapidly and inevitably brought populationism to the fore. From the static point of view they are no doubt right: only great catastrophies justify retaining the economic view; but, amongst the difficulties of rapid growth, Boiarsky does not mention the cost of demographic investment.

From 1941 to 1945 there were enormous losses, the birth rate was low, and infantile mortality was high.[1] Fertility needed to rise. Obviously, family allow-

---

[1] According to Dr Biraben, Soviet mortality was probably as follows:

1939	23·2	1945	33·0	1951	9·6
1940	18·4	1946	22·7	1952	9·3
1941	36·3	1947	21·6	1953	9·0
1942	53·4	1948	15·8	1954	8·9
1943	50·2	1949	13·7	1955	8·2
1944	45·6	1950	9·6	1956	7·7

These figures include war losses, reported on in *Population*, 1958 (special issue on the USSR) and October–December 1960.

ances had, as in other countries, a double effect: on fertility and on the social structure. But their reduction in 1947 is difficult to explain. A family of eight children has three times as many requirements as a childless couple, and allowances must be socially necessary. However, by this time, the birth rate was again fairly high: 25–27 per thousand. The fairly rapid growth demanded important demographic investment, and there was a particularly acute housing crisis. The birth rate had to suffer. *The family allowances seem thus to have been directed more at fertility than at social justice.* It is difficult to explain how a régime so keen on replacing the concept of profit or output by that of requirement should be so reluctant to recognise the requirements of children.

On the question of migration, it should be remembered that a journey from the Ukraine to the Turkestan is as much a migration as a move from Spain or Italy to France. Since Russia is larger than the whole of western Europe its official objections to international migration are largely a matter of opportunism.

Reasons for the statistical silence

This has been broken but the data given are still very summary. Why publish the tonnage of steel or the numbers of cattle but not the numbers of men? Some believe that the known figures are not sufficiently precise or complete. But there are very good techniques for correcting basic errors and filling up blanks, which have developed a great deal since the war, because of the need to know more about the population in the underdeveloped countries.

The reason is probably that the use of statistics such as these is still largely arbitrary. As soon as the results are not in conformity with expectations, tension can arise, and statisticians are understandably reluctant to take the political risks. The destiny that awaited the authors of the Soviet census of 1937 is significant, perhaps even more so for the Chinese than for the Soviets.

Also, before the war, the first refusals to publish anything concerning population were due to the fear of revealing the results of famine and deportations. In 1940 the veil was about to be lifted, as the 1939 census shows. But the war caused large-scale losses and plunged the statistics back into darkness. This attitude throws an interesting light on the concept of population in a collectivist society: there have to be *global reckonings inhuman lives.*

During the German invasion civilian losses were large and not all were due to enemy action. In order not to provide material for foreign propaganda, the Soviets have always tried to hide this, and place full responsibility on the Germans, yet it is not surprising or even to the discredit of the régime that some mistakes occurred. In a country with large resources miscalculations will only affect the standards of living; when the resources are very small and the need to win a battle is absolutely vital, they take the shape of human lives. The outcome of the war, and with it the fate of a great part of the population, depended on the battles of Leningrad, Moscow, and Stalingrad: it was therefore worthwhile sacrificing a minority of civilians to save the others, and the soldiers on the Leningrad front were given three or four times more rations than the civilian population.[1]

The expectation of life at birth (seventy) is now practically the same in the Soviet Union and in western countries, and this is a remarkable achievement considering the state of the country after the revolution. There is therefore no more reason why statistics should be kept secret.

Recent trends

The classical Marxist doctrine, on demographic points as on others, was a reaction against situations and attitudes of the mid-nineteenth century. It was therefore inevitable that it should change, with time and experience. The most significant gesture so far is the attitude of the Soviet delegates at the UN General Assembly in December 1962. Faced with a Swedish proposal for technical assistance in the prevention of births, the Soviets were not as indignant as usual, and abstained from voting. Since then, though still anti-Malthusian on the whole, they have been less adamant. Today they give priority to economic development in the Third World, and the prevention of births is still only one possible factor of this.

In the popular republics the change has been more noticeable. In Poland and Yugoslavia, demographic investment proved to be too expensive, and began to jeopardise economic development. The oversimplified Soviet concept of overpopulation was shown up. In a country that is not overpopulated the population may still be growing too fast. In all the republics, except Albania, the prevention of births, and abortion, caused such a sharp drop in the birth rate that in some cases (Hungary, Rumania) the replacement of generations is not assured: one can hardly believe now that low birth rates are bourgeois. Some progress has also been made on the subject of migrations. In 1962, though in a complementary position, Czechoslovakia and Poland were still reluctant to envisage any immigration of Poles into Czechoslovakia; later they became less adamant and in 1965 Yugoslavia even signed an emigration treaty with France.

Dogma is dwindling away and empirical attitudes are becoming prevalent, but we have still to see a Marxist doctrine of population: it will require careful demographic studies and some detachment from the old situations that gave rise to the initial dogma. The origins need not be denied, but it should be quite clearly a second generation theory.

[1] See A. Woerth, *La Russie en guerre*, Paris, 1965, vol. 1.

The case of China

When it first came to power, Mao Tse Tung's government followed Marxist orthodoxy strictly. Then in 1953 a movement towards the limitation of births appeared, which led to the legislation of 1957 allowing contraception. In 1958 belief in the 'great leap forward' in agriculture caused a return to orthodoxy, with the assertion that in a socialist régime overpopulation was impossible. Later, contraception propaganda began again, but more discreetly. The only motive invoked now is the health of the woman and her need to work. Thus the Chinese are cleverly combining orthodoxy with the voluntary limitation of births. But they too still have a great deal to learn about demography. Not only are no statistics published, but no reference is made to population in propaganda pamphlets.

Perhaps there is still disagreement on the matter. But the figures are certainly not all known to the chiefs. Registers are still imperfect; there are techniques for making up such deficiencies, but, as we have said, they cannot be used in such a régime. The users must be granted independence of views, which might turn out to be very dangerous.

China's attitude towards nuclear war combines the ancient ruler's search for power and safety in numbers: there is a certain disdain for engines of war that would at worst thin the Chinese ranks. But this relative indifference may also be due to the fact that they do not count men enough.

Eugenics

Marxist doctrine stresses environment at the expense of heredity. It reacts against atavism, and the old ideas of upper classes on the passing down of inequality. Heredity and human genetics have long been excluded from the syllabuses of Soviet universities. The environment must allow the human species to flower. Indeed it would be very useful if acquired characteristics could be transmitted, and this wish has occasionally been mistaken for reality. But the freedom of the individual should not be interfered with on genetic grounds, whether in marriage or otherwise.

This liberalism, which contrasts with many other attitudes, is liable to very different interpretations. Officially it is due to a deep-seated care for humanity, and confidence in the environment. But one may wonder whether, in its difficult ideological struggle with capitalism, socialist society is not merely trying to avoid any possible risks. The dangerous paths of applied eugenics would not fail to inspire revulsion, and if the régime had such enormous power at its disposal it would cause even greater disquiet.

The attitude of the Chinese government on this matter is unknown to us, but it is probably not very different. Here, as in western societies, biological discoveries could one day bring about a radical change. The Soviets respect the individual as far as procreation goes, but they have broken with many western prejudices. Soviet hospitals do not hesitate to transfuse blood from dead people at the rate of four precious litres per cadaver; in the West, it is difficult enough to squeeze it from living people.

Here again the points of view may well come closer together in time. When the Soviets really step out they open up paths that become tempting, if not imperative; when dogma and passion lead them into dead ends, their basic desire for progress and their confidence in humanity bring them sooner or later to choose a more salutary direction.

24

POPULATION POLICY[1]

In 1948 the United Nations surveyed the population policy of various countries. When verbal questions were put to people the answers were usually naively negative: 'Our government does not consider this matter' or 'Our laws and our politics disregard demographic problems'. Yet all these countries had a fiscal policy, customs, an agricultural policy, regulations on immigration, a marriage code and other laws that may influence the numbers and conditions of men.

Population policy is even more difficult to define than demography itself: as there is a pure, strictly quantitative variety of demography, so policy can be merely concerned with numbers, or act on purely demographic structures. But such a policy implies knowledge of various other factors such as unemployment, taxation, land ownership, education, etc., and it could itself achieve much wider objectives, in fields apparently very distant.

Even a policy confined to the quantitative aim, or merely to action on the birth rate, would still be affected in one way or another by various other factors, consciously or not.

For or against intervention

All our observations point to the fact that intervention exists anyway. A man may say that he has no policy regarding his liver, and ignore its existence, but he still has eating habits. The question is merely whether there should be intentional, fully conscious laws regulating population development. When Adam Smith and the early liberal thinkers thought that the birth rate would regulate itself on wages, with fluctuations around the natural equilibrium, not only were they professing a strange confidence in man's psychological resources and his long-term wisdom, but they were making all sorts of assumptions on what could be called non-intervention.

In fact no society, even one in love with natural equilibrium, could make do

---

[1] See J. Doublet, 'Des lois dans leurs rapports avec la population', *Population*, January–March 1949; H. E. Eldridge, *Population policies. A survey of recent developments*, Washington, 1954; J. Doublet, 'Réflexions sur 10 années de législation', *Bulletin C.A.F.*, 1958; T. Vignal, *Bibliographie analytique de la politique démographique de la France depuis 1948*, Conservatoire National des Arts et Métiers, 1960; P. de Bie, 'Politique familiale et politique démographique', *Cahiers du Centre d'Etudes de la Population et de la Famille*, no. 2, 1963; and United Nations Population Opinion Survey, *Population Bulletin*, October 1964.

without laws influencing population development. The early liberal theories on selection and on the economic optimum are open to grave criticism, even theoretically; moreover, even in the purest physiocratic theory taxation was not unambiguously determined by natural laws. This is the essential point. Any society with a certain degree of development has a taxation system and a code of laws; like all laws, these have as a by-product, if not as an objective, certain demographic phenomena.

Objectives of population policy

These can be, quantitatively: 1. To reduce mortality and morbidity as much as possible: no objection has ever been formulated to this point, though it poses problems of interpretation. 2. To regulate fertility, avoiding extremes. 3. To organise migrations in the general interest.

There are also indirect, qualitative aims: 1. To provide satisfactory development and living conditions to the least fortunate classes: this includes by implication the whole of economic, social, and cultural policy, increase in the national income, just distribution, full employment, geographical and occupational distribution, development of education, etc. 2. To ensure selection on merit.

These various aims are not all directly pursued. Authorities have various channels of action, sometimes called 'levers', designed for more immediate purposes; but the various ministerial and administrative sectors that work for these particular objectives often forget that they are not ends in themselves. Their efforts should be bound together by the constant thought that behind taxations, prohibitions, subsidies, etc., there lie men.

Longevity

No one is likely to demand an increase of mortality, so the question appears straightforward. Yet developed countries would have to change their policies quite noticeably if they were to really try to achieve greater longevity.

Where mortality is still fairly high little effort is needed to reduce it quickly. But all societies are clever at avoiding difficult dilemmas. The leading classes will contrive not to reckon how many human lives might be saved by a given tax, for instance on large landed property. Besides, mortality only depends partly on medical and social services. A policy of food production and distribution and progress in education, are needed for complete results.

Let us assume that a competent and disinterested government really wishes to achieve the greatest possible longevity. The issue is still not clear. Some will want all efforts to be concentrated on economic development, because sacrificing a human life today may mean gaining ten tomorrow, or, to put it otherwise, a life saved by a financial sacrifice now, means twenty condemned later. There is indeed a conflict between the present and the future: it is the classical economic conflict between investment and consumption, transposed in terms of human lives. The Soviets have tended, and more or less consciously, to reason thus (see above, p. 528). *Pushed to extremes such logic could lead to a ferocious policy, even to a massacre.*

In the developed countries, the problem is rather different. Mortality depends much more on care and on the way of life than on income. Promoting longevity here would lead to inacceptable austerity measures. As it is, the proportion of the national income spent on health increases every year and theoretically has no limit; but in fact there are always other imperatives to prevent all energies from being directed towards prolonging lives. Otherwise society would tend towards an 'iatrocracy', or government by doctors, with the economy disposed accordingly.

Individuals disregard their own chances of longevity in order to lead a more pleasant life, and it is not therefore surprising if authorities do the same. An economist could indeed justify many social weaknesses by 'stimulating and necessary profit', but we will disregard this perhaps inevitable hypocrisy, and concentrate on the more poignant conflict between longevity and freedom: exemplified in the use of toxic materials, and mainly alcohol.

Alcohol[1]

This has already been mentioned in various chapters. The problem is not a very different one for France and western countries from that of opium for certain Far Eastern countries. The evil it does is very widespread and still underestimated, but whether authorities should intervene is controversial and their effectiveness is problematic.

Let us disregard the economic and occupational aspect, however important. The fact that two to three million people make a living from something does not justify it if its results are wrong. There is certainly a problem of political balance here, but theoretically the only controversial point can be the extent to which those who have built up lethal businesses under complacent authority should be indemnified.

A more delicate question arises when one considers action on the consumer. Is it legitimate to prevent him consuming his income as he pleases? Should he not be sole judge of his own health? Why should he not be able to distil and consume home-produced alcohol? The first consideration is that of the family. An individual's right to dispose of his own life is only complete if he lives alone. It is limited by the possible distress or the sordid destiny of his wife and

[1] See G. Malignac, *L'alcoolisme*, Paris, 1962 (3rd edition); S. Ledermann, *Alcool, alcoolisme, alcoolisation, données scientifiques de caractère physiologique, et social*, Cahiers de l'INED, no. 29, 1956, and *Alcool, alcoolisme, alcoolisation, mortalité, morbidité, accidents du travail*, Cahiers de l'INED, no. 41, 1964.

children. Further, the ever increasing complexity of social bonds is making the problem clearer. *The existence of social security places personal health in a new perspective.* For most people in France social security is compulsory, and normal people thus suffer indirectly from the existence of alcoholics and have the right to redress, exactly as people with fire insurance policies have rights against other policy holders who do not take any precautions against fire. But ignorance on these matters and wrong conceptions of the state and of society lead to widespread indifference to wilful intoxication.

The right to suicide is a misapprehension: when a climber or a bather ventures forth in dangerous conditions, against the advice of guides or life-guards, claiming that he will not ask for any help, he knows very well that help will be forthcoming anyway, and that men will risk their lives to save his. The same applies to anyone who claims the right to distil the products of his own land. He is no hermit, and is constantly involved with society: in illness he benefits from the accumulated scientific research, and in an emergency he will not refuse the compensation offered by society.

The individual freedom invoked by alcoholics is at cross purposes, for instance, with military obligations. Everyone's help is required for the defence of the nation; yet alcohol is a greater threat to armies than deserters or conscientious objectors. And when he becomes a potential danger on the roads, an individual should accept the minor imposition of a drop of blood or a sample of his breath. Policies should be as firm and imaginative in reacting against this silent, pervasive evil, as they should be cautious in matters of real eugenics. Every country already allows many restrictions on individual freedom that are far less justified than this.

Numbers or wealth

Assuming that an answer has been found and implemented in the matter of mortality, how should one influence numbers, which can also vary through migrations and births? If greater numbers will increase wealth, then the answer is obvious, though the optimum rhythm of growth, the division between the present and the future, has still to be defined. But in the opposite case, should one prefer large numbers of poor men or small numbers of rich men? Despotic rule and nationalism will prompt a search for the power optimum, whereas the western individual will opt for higher living standards, if the choice has to be so brutal.

One cannot prescribe a generally valid and precise rhythm of demographic growth, but it is possible in certain cases to see that growth is too fast, too slow, or is having a bad effect. Thus the situations of Japan and France in 1945 demanded diametrically opposed policies.[1] We must first distinguish between a policy directed against overpopulation and one directed against depopulation.

[1] Though the outcome in both was the founding of an Institute for Population Studies.

Policy on births

Malthusian: History includes various examples of anti-natal policies: societies have allowed or tolerated abortion or infanticide. The most striking modern instance is that of Japan (see above, pp. 428–9). We pointed out in the relevant chapter that there could be a conflict between such a policy and social considerations. By helping families to raise their children one may be encouraging them to proliferate even more, but in abandoning them one would run the risk of a decay in quality. In fact, this problem is not as important as it might seem to be. Fears were expressed when family allowances were first introduced in Algeria; but when a population ignores contraception and is not conscious of children as a burden, the risk of a rise in the birth rate is slight. The effect allowances might have would be to check a tendency to voluntary sterility. But even here it does not always occur thus: allowances are small anyway in countries where they matter, and they encourage families to lend a greater value to the child. If assistance is properly directed to include social welfare work, lessons on child-rearing, including some discreet advice on contraception, *it can, by revaluing the mother's duties, help to reduce births*, Stopping allowances after the fourth child, the policy adopted in Tunisia, is not only unjust, but useless.

Encouraging births: There are very few examples of policies directly intended for this, but many institutions have this effect: fertility cults, respect for fathers, family unity, etc. Until very recently it was fashionable to express scepticism about such policies, and quote the failure of Augustus's or Colbert's attempts. But in the last twenty-five years events and research have developed, and the means of action are now well known. They fall into three categories: 1. *Repressive means*: Police repression of abortion. This brought about a revival in the German and Austrian birth-rates. But it is only compatible with a police state. As with most crimes prevention is the only really efficient action. Repression, as usual, is useful but only to contain the crime within limits. 2. *Pure stimulants* present the families with the prospect of a fairly high immediate gain such as a large maternity allowance. But this may encourage them to let children appear, without making sufficient provision for bringing them up. From the strictly financial point of view these stimulants provide better returns for a given expenditure: a lump sum in the near future is more attractive than a monthly allowance, even though the latter be higher in global value. But the quality of the results is poor. 3. *Social means*: They consist in encouraging family life, granting special privileges linked with children. Here the moral atmosphere is as important as the material advantrage: the parents are given the impression that society welcomes their child and has a place for it.

A general rise in living standards (through wages, for instance), will not usually increase the birth rate – the real answer lies in a differential policy favouring the families with children. Similarly a general housing policy does not help: there are no more children in large modern flats than in hovels; it would be a different matter if a family were given *larger accommodation a· it grew*.

Family allowances

After Boulainvilliers first thought of a social security system based on deductions from wages[1] several authors suggested monthly allowances to families according to their number of children.[2] But it took until the twentieth century for the practice to appear.

The principle has often come under attack, and still has a small number of critics, although it is the logical complement to compulsory education and technological development. A family with four children, now that schooling is compulsory and the birth rate has dropped, has greate· difficulties and fulfils a more important social function. If this function is not rewarded it will only be carried out if there are other stimulants, such as the need for affection or fatherhood. Objections to subsidies for 'other people's children' are thus only a belated form of old-fashioned individualism. Allowances are as justified as old age pensions – they are a form of pre-salary given to an apprentice to society.

This introduces the qualitative angle. A large family cannot bring its children up properly and in good health on a single wage (one cannot count on a wage for the mother). The matter was controversial formerly, but cannot be so now that ignorance has been dispelled by dietetic studies of the food necessary to health and growth. Socially the allowance must cover these needs, and must therefore be the same for all, unless it is only granted to poor families. But this is not sufficient: vital requirements cannot only be reckoned in calories and vitamins. In countries where wages are mostly high other subjective needs and unavoidable social requirements appear. The less fortunate families will not be able to cover physiological needs even if theoretically they have enough money. Thus *there is a case for allowances both when the birth rate is too low and when wages are not high*. No country should refuse to give allowances to really large families: even in the United States the wages of an agricultural worker would not provide for the subsistence of eight children.

In poor families the socially or physiologically vital needs of a child are about half those of an adult. Yet no country has yet granted such large allowances.

[1] In *Mémoires présentés à Monseigneur le duc d'Orléans*, The Hague and Amsterdam, 1727.

[2] 'Far from passive taxation per head, I would suggest remunerating them actively. Each function would be rewarded by a salary to encourage applicants. Each child born would receive a small allowance until the age of ten.' Marquis de Bessar, *Recueils, fragmants académiques, téologiques, juridiques, moraux, politiques, tragi-comiques*, 1767.

Not that the enormous transfer of funds this would mean is deemed impossible for a task such as that of ensuring the continuation of society: but society prefers the less expensive way of relying on the natural desire for children. The first child fulfils this role and does not need to be paid for – the saving this represents permits greater help for the children who will only appear if encouraged. There are also other forms of encouragement, less expensive than allowances. Finally, society benefits from the many children who were not intended; this lowers the expenditure still further below the level given by arithmetical spreading of the cost of children over society.

A pure populationist policy might go further still, and ensure that children would not place any family in an inferior economic position given its social status. Here the allowance would be proportionate to income, or to salary, up to a certain level. This policy, which could be attacked on other grounds, has never been applied. Some of the objections come from financial circles, which claim that it costs the state less to subsidise the children of the poor than those of the rich. For a given total expenditure, allowances to the bottom of the scale, or equal allowances for all, would be more efficient. Another advantage is that of social mobility: promotion is easier than descent, and room at the top is more easily filled than gaps at the bottom.

The various kinds of allowances place sterile families or bachelors at a disadvantage, whether their status is intentional or not. A sterile family thus suffers doubly, in its lack of emotional outlet and in its purse. Until a just distinction can be made between refusal and impossibility (a tall order) this is a national injustice that cannot be remedied.

Allowances in money or in kind

Any lender or donor naturally wishes to be assured that the sacrifice he has made is being put to good use. He has no legal right to this. A reward for a given action is not a favour, to be offset by strict attention to one's wishes. Yet there is undoubtedly some justification for giving families free housing or holidays rather than cash. The excesses and ignorance of some families suggest that the state could look after them better: proper accommodation and medical and social care would be better for them than lavishing expensive toys on the children or disregarding them completely. Unfortunately this paternalistic view could be made to justify any intervention by the state, from unemployment benefits and pensions to interest rates and even wages. It could easily lead further than was intended. Such action can only be justified in cases of disorganised families, and then *not in the name of society but for the sake of the children.*

For a given expenditure, a cash allowance is better than a benefit in kind, for it brings further advantages. This is true even if the cash is spent on buying what would have been purchased anyway: *the family has experienced the psychological satisfaction of the nominal sum, and the fleeting glimpse of many other purchases.* But public opinion is more ready to criticise cash allowances. It is very quick to condemn any misuse of them, though this attitude is not extended to unemployment or old age benefits.

Taxation

Its essential aim is to provide funds for the treasury, but it also has other objectives, one of which is social justice, and various side-effects, one of which is an influence on the birth rate. Taxation can be just in two ways, by reflecting accurately existing inequalities of wealth, or by seeking to reduce them by redistribution. It is not always easy to tell which is being pursued. However, given certain principles, it is obvious how the family should be justly treated in taxation. If for instance income tax is progressive at a given rate, this means that *for a given standard of living, tax should be the same*: thus the first pair of shoes bought in a year should be free of tax, the second slightly, and the third more heavily taxed. To be just taxation should use a family quotient; and since the ratio of the child's requirements to those of the adult diminishes as income increases, the quotient should be appropriately reduced for the higher brackets.

Housing too should be taxed with an eye to family requirements. Children's rooms have long been charged for at luxury rates, as if they contained a collection of rare butterflies. Rates still make too few allowances for children in many countries, and especially in France. They are reckoned on requirements rather than on resources.

Taxation, in thus ignoring children, condemns them. Its intentions are just, but it lowers fertility. Public opinion always assumes that any allowance made for the number of children is an instrument of social justice, when taxation of families is not as a whole even just in itself.

We have not mentioned the many other kinds of taxation that could be criticised on this score: indirect taxes, death duties, etc.

Attitude towards contraception

A government may forbid it, tolerate it or encourage it. Its motives may be demographic (birth rate too high), or social (freedom for women and couples, difficult conditions for mothers, psychological problems, etc.). Freedom fits in with demographic interests when the latter demand a lower fertility. But the two considerations may be opposed and should be thought of as separate, to avoid the usual mixture of ignorance and hypocrisy.

If efficient contraceptive methods were more widespread, the birth rate would be even lower than it is. *When they do spread, or their dissemination is allowed, aid to families should therefore be intensified.* The introduction of contraception should be accompanied by stimulants to the birth rate, in order to conciliate individual welfare and the future of the community. Take the case of the woman about to conceive a third child in an insufficiently large dwelling: society can avoid the abortion either by providing her with contraception or by giving her a larger home; unfortunately it will probably prefer the first policy, which is much cheaper. Governments, and nations generally, still refuse to reckon generously in these matters, and prefer to rely on the many half-wanted children to keep the community alive – this reliance may one day be proved tragically wrong.

Abortion

Many more countries now allow abortion on wider grounds than the mother's safety: Sweden, Japan, Tunisia, the Soviet Union, the eastern European Republics and China. Their objectives are in some cases demographic (Japan, Tunisia), in others social (Sweden). It is not for us to deliver moral or even medical judgments on the matter; but we must insist on the political efficiency of such a policy.

Not only does official abortion reduce fertility when it is too high, not only does it allow the number of births to be adjusted fairly precisely to the level required (as in the case of Czechoslovakia, already described), but it is consistent with a differential policy. It is difficult to restrict the sale of contraceptives once they are allowed, even if a prescription is required – but abortion can be limited to a given category of people, or even to given individuals. It is a powerful instrument, with all the dangers and advantages of power. Intra-uterine devices also can have a far-reaching influence in a country where medical services are nationalised and obedient: half-way between abortion and contraceptives, they have the same political advantage as the former, and are not exposed to the same criticism.

Migrations

Marginal inhabitants, we have seen, have opposite effects on towns and on whole countries. In the former they do not pay they way, and in the latter they deserve a better welcome. The expenses they cause in terms of housing and social investment are well known, but the support they give to overheads is completely disregarded. Because of this, even if occupational groups were not actively opposed to any migration into their sector, immigration would not be sufficiently intense in a country like France that needs it. A lucid politician is placed here in a situation where he has to force public opinion slightly. Immigration policy must rely on the growth of employment that immigration itself will bring. Refugees should all be allowed to work, and no foreigners should be made into second-class citizens by police regulations.

540

A similar problem exists with emigration. The European governments all energetically encouraged emigration towards the New World around 1950, but they lacked the forethought to regulate the departure of highly qualified people, which does a great deal of damage, both here and in the Third World. Here again the non-evident situation is not acted upon.

Assimilation policy should be based on two principles: tolerance and schooling; where necessary, dispersal can be encouraged in various ways (military recruitment, labour exchanges, transfer of civil servants).

Geographical distribution

Here, as in the quantitative field, it is pointless to argue over the desirability of intervention, which is a fact. Consider for instance a valley that has been in a state of depopulation for a hundred years or so because things appear to be following their natural course: 1. There is an educational problem. The minimum number of children per schoolteacher employed influences population; so do longer schooling, and school bus services. 2. There is a power issue. Private enterprise is a very secondary factor where electrification is proposed. 3. There are communications questions. A railway or a new road in this or another valley changes the existing situation. 4. There is the matter of costs of public services: postal union favours the lesser-populated areas; the opposite applies to medical and social services.

One could quote many other sources of influence: water and forestry administration, agricultural engineering, technical education, military recruitment, tourism, building. They are often unco-ordinated, sometimes at cross purposes. Though no official decision may have been taken on the 'lost' valley, its fate has been constantly debated and twisted by vaster or narrower interests whose influence is not always apparent.

Policies since the last World War have taken more notice of problems of distribution. In Britain there was a drive to help the areas devastated by unemployment and build up medium-sized towns. The problem is also looming larger in the minds of the French authorities.

Occupational training and unemployment

This is one of the least explored problems. State intervention has had, as one might have guessed, a quicker effect on wages than on the orientation of training. As a result there are grave distortions leading to the appearance of surplus populations in some sectors. But it is very difficult to condemn an individual to descend the social hierarchy or to lose a privilege he was not aware of. Here again, considerations of responsibility lead to governments preferring the greater evil that appears natural to the lesser inconvenience resulting from intervention.

541

In all the countries where, for whatever reason, the automatic regulators do not function well enough, the authorities should deal directly with the problem of permanent full employment. For this it is necessary that the employed and the required population should coincide, and it can thus only be achieved if occupational orientation can shape the ambitions of the active population accordingly. The whole educational policy should take this essential objective into account.

In a country that is overpopulated or in danger of overpopulation economic policy should check recessive developments, which bring permanent unemployment and distress for non-owners. Employment must be increased by *expanding the 'environment'*, which can be achieved by processive and creative investment.

Women at work

Like all powerful movements, the emancipation of women was blind, or at least narrowly blinkered: the object was to deliver women of household chores and give them access to work. The campaigns fortunately opened a (still insufficient) number of masculine reservations to women, but have not yet fully achieved their aim.

Work for women was not new amongst the lower classes. The change was only felt in the middle class. But in any case, women have not been freed from household responsibilities merely through acquiring a new burden. Until very recently social reforms only applied to occupational duties, and thus to men only: the five or six day week, holidays with pay, pensions, etc., all very desirable reforms, *did not affect household work and thereby increased it in proportion*. A few improvements have been achieved: children's holiday camps, family allowances, health services, one-income allowances. But ideologies are far ahead of reality as far as nurseries, mothers' helps, etc. are concerned. Women, after their so-called emancipation, now have a combined demographic and economic burden.

It may seem uneconomic to confine an educated woman, perhaps a qualified teacher, at home by paying her an allowance as a non-working mother: this can happen in France if the wage she could earn is lower than the wage of the maid she would employ, plus the above allowance. But the qualitative approach should not be left out of these bare reckonings: a mother's care for her own children is irreplaceable without great expense. A conflict thus arises between convenient conservatism and erratic progressivism. The best step in the near future would be for husbands to take on part of the household work. Here education is the only channel of influence open to politics.

Generally, the benefits of greater productivity should be passed on to women, for instance by allowing them to work part-time during their most strenuous years.

Biology

Governmental intervention in this field is quite liable to seem frightening. Even apparently profitable policies such as the sterilisation of the handicapped present equally obvious dangers. But there is no reason why new biological and other discoveries should not make intervention imperative. For the time being the most desirable of the immediate objectives is the breaking down of isolates and the extension of exogamy.

Administrative chart

It may be of interest to sketch out the main lines and means of action of a population policy, divided into existing ministries.

Agriculture: Soil preservation. Distribution of property. Tenure. Regrouping of property. Size of enterprises. Marginal lands. Intensive or extensive methods. Depopulated areas. General regard for food balance (calcium, etc.). Production of alcohol.

Board of Trade: Social utility of goods. Concentration of firms. Decentralisation.

Defence: Recruitment. Service families. Dispersal of foreign recruits.

Economic affairs: Preservation of natural resources. Full employment. Appropriate investment. Development. Regional planning.

Education: School-leaving age. Technical education. General education. School health services. Children's holiday camps. Education for foreigners. Scientific research.

Home policy: Censuses. Registers. Restrictions of various kinds (alcohol, drugs, etc., abortion).

Housing and Town Planning: Building of family units. Distribution of accommodation. Rent legislation. Urban amenities.

Justice: Legislation on marriage and divorce. Juvenile delinquency.

Labour: Full employment. Family allowances. Social security. Work for women. Occupational training and migrations. Pensions. Immigration.

Population and Health: Sanitary policy and everything connected (social services etc.). Immigration. Naturalisation. Consanguineous marriage. Sterilisation. Abortion. Contraception. Co-ordination of population policy. Physically and mentally handicapped. Invalids.

Post Office and Communications: Rail and postal rates, and their influence on geographical distribution.

Treasury: Taxation in general, and family allowances in particular. Land taxation. Indirect taxation. Rates on dwelling houses. Excise on alcohol. Individual's debt.

All departments: Democratisation of recruitment. Dispersal of immigrant personnel.

25

CONCLUSION

A society is made of men, and in the study of population we meet them all. But the field is so vast that it is easy to be content with one's own perspectives and horizons. In the early nineteenth century the science of population was shattered by the explosion of knowledge and the multiplication of anxieties and points of view. The bits that survived have been carefully developed by scientific research, but they no longer fit together and they tend to become ends in themselves.

Politics are even more fragmentary. A parliamentary assembly is presented every year with a long series of problems, large and small, and is asked for its laconic judgements in the shape of sums voted. The only synthesis comes from the entrepreneur, who gambles on the whole affair as inspiration, or the whim of his friends, or at best his private interest, moves him.

However lengthy it may have appeared to the reader, this volume is no more than a modest attempt to sketch out the life of a population. My successors will no doubt improve, concentrate, synthesise it still more to present the science in its best and most complete light. The laws of population are changing and elusive: man progresses, and his self-awareness often follows behind.

The provisional conclusions reached in the first part, where the economic point of view was predominant, were only partly valid once we had given back to man the wide initiatives that this convention had denied him. In the second part it became obvious that the most important problems, those most closely affecting men's welfare and livelihood, are practically unknown in influential circles, where they are turned into distant abstractions (such as ageing) or surveyed superficially, in ignorance of hard facts (such as the population of the world). As a result, wishful thinking is left free to build its fanciful castles in the air.

The division of the world into political blocks stresses the drama of the eternal march into the unknown that began with the first man; some periods thought they saw their way, but others did not spare it any thought at all. We have the frightening privilege of knowing of at least two catastrophes, war and hunger, into which a large part of the world's 3,500,000,000 and their accumulated achievements are in danger of falling. Fortunately, both evils can be exorcised by the same remedy. If the study of population and its risks could create some preoccupation common to both camps, and divert their attention from other preoccupations, a new path would be opened that could not fail to be successful, at least in the sense that life is above all a matter of survival.

544

INDEX

545